The Handbook of Business Discourse

THE HANDBOOK OF BUSINESS DISCOURSE

Edited by Francesca Bargiela-Chiappini

EDINBURGH UNIVERSITY PRESS

© editorial matter and organisation Francesca Bargiela-Chiappini, 2009
© the chapters and their several authors, 2009

Edinburgh University Press Ltd
22 George Square, Edinburgh

www.euppublishing.com

Typeset in 10/12 Ehrhardt MT and Gill Sans
by Servis Filmsetting Ltd, Stockport, Cheshire, and
printed and bound in Great Britain by
CPI Antony Rowe, Chippenham and Eastbourne

A CIP record for this book is available from the British Library

ISBN 978 0 7486 2801 8 (hardback)

Contents

Foreword

Finally we have *The Handbook of Business Discourse*, a gift to the diverse lot of us who study discourse in organisational and professional contexts. Similar areas of research, such as organisational studies, have benefited from handbooks for some time. I've bemoaned the fact we have had none for business discourse and, at one point, even toyed with the idea of editing one myself.

Through the years, many a colleague or student has asked for materials to guide their research or teaching of business discourse. As is customary, I've provided sample syllabi, academic articles and discussion time. But I've always wished there were a more 'official' overview to recommend as well.

With tenacity and commitment, Francesca Bargiela-Chiappini has managed to enlist some of our most seasoned researchers to originate one. Not only does this *Handbook* suggest the scope of business discourse as a field of study, but it also codifies some of the approaches and methodologies used.

Academics researching and teaching business discourse share a curiosity about the operations of texts in organisational and professional contexts (and vice versa). But we come at it in different ways, thereby complicating attempts to characterise our collective output. I think Bargiela-Chiappini's edited *Handbook* helps us celebrate, validate and advance this endeavour.

Priscilla S. Rogers
Ross School of Business
University of Michigan

Acknowledgements

I would like to thank the people who made this volume possible.

I am very grateful to Sarah Edwards, senior editor at Edinburgh University Press, for encouraging me to take on this project. I also want to thank Máiréad McElligott, assistant commissioning editor, for her unfailing administrative support over the many months of preparation of the typescript.

Special thanks are due to the advisory board, the independent reviewer and the many scholars and researchers who undertook the painstaking task of reviewing the work of their peers.

Finally, I would like to dedicate the *Handbook* to the contributors, without whom this volume would not exist.

Editorial advisory board

Notes on contributors

Deborah C. Andrews, professor of English, University of Delaware, USA, has published several texts, including *Technical Communication in the Global Community* and *Management Communication: A Guide*. A researcher and speaker on many aspects of professional communication, especially in an international context, she is the former editor of *Business Communication Quarterly* and author of articles in major journals and anthologies.

Leila Barbara is professor of linguistics at the Pontifical Catholic University of São Paulo and research fellow A1 at CNPq (National Council for Science and Technology), Brazil. She is attached to the Graduate School, applied linguistics programme, where she advises MAs and PhDs and lectures mainly in the area of systemic functional grammar, description of Portuguese and English, discourse analysis, and research methods in applied linguistics. Her recent research involves the analysis of Portuguese in use and its relation to other languages, mainly English and Spanish. She coordinates an inter-institutional project, DIRECT, partly sponsored by CNPq, on language at work and about work and on the discourse of business communication in Portuguese, Spanish and English.

Tony Berber Sardinha received a PhD from the English Department of the University of Liverpool. He is an adjunct professor with both the Linguistics Department and the graduate programme in applied linguistics, Pontifical Catholic University of São Paulo, Brazil. His main research interests include corpus linguistics, applied linguistics, business discourse, metaphor and computer programming.

Boris H. J. M. Brummans (PhD, Texas A&M University) is an assistant professor in the Département de Communication at the Université de Montréal, Canada. Currently, he is researching (organisational) communication from a Buddhist point of view, living for part of the year in Ladakh, India.

Anne Marie Bülow is a professor in the Department of International Culture and Communication Studies at the Copenhagen Business School, Denmark. She is primarily interested in strategic communication, both the interpersonal and organisational varieties, and in negotiation studies. Her most recent publications concern crisis communication and corporate apologia.

Gulmira G. Burkitbayeva is professor in the Department of Professional Languages at the Kazakh University of World Languages, Almaty, Kazakhstan. Her research interests are text and discourse, business discourse, and genres in their written forms. Her publications include *Text and Discourse*, *Types of Discourse*, *Business Discourse: Ontology and Genres*, *Business Letters* (with A. Aldash).

Mathieu Chaput is a doctoral candidate in the department of communication at the Université de Montréal, Canada. He holds an MSc and is currently writing his dissertation on the communicative constitution of a new political party in the province of Québec.

Mirja Liisa Charles is professor of English business communication at the Helsinki School of Economics, Finland, where she is head of the doctoral programme in international business communication. Her main research interests include English lingua franca communication in multinational corporations, particularly English business negotiations. She has published widely and is a frequent speaker at international conferences.

Winnie Cheng is a professor and director in the Research Centre for Professional Communication in English, Department of English of the Hong Kong Polytechnic University. Her research interests are corpus linguistics, conversational analysis, critical discourse analysis, pragmatics, discourse intonation, and intercultural communication in business and professional contexts.

Chye Lay Grace Chew is an independent corporate communications consultant, whose interest lies in intercultural communications, an interest developed from her personal experiences while studying and working in Japan and Vietnam. She sees the learning and understanding of cultures and languages as imperative for an understanding of business globalisation in today's context. To this end, her works have revolved around communication issues.

François Cooren is a professor and chair of the Départment de Communication at the Université de Montréal, Canada. His research interests lie in the areas of organisational communication, language and social interaction, and communication theory. He is currently conducting a research project with Médecins sans Frontières (Doctors Without Borders).

Stanley Deetz is professor of communication and director of peace and conflict studies at the University of Colorado at Boulder, USA. His several books focus on corporate relations to society, organisational communication and stakeholder collaborations. He was a senior Fulbright scholar and is a National Communication Association distinguished scholar and an International Communication Association past president and fellow. His current work investigates native theories of communication and democracy and their consequences for mutual decision-making, and promotes alternative conceptions and practices.

Ronald E. Dulek is Miller Professor of Management at the University of Alabama, USA. He recently received the Kitty Locker Outstanding Researcher Award and the National Alumni Association's Outstanding Teacher Award. Last April, seniors at the University of Alabama selected him as inaugural recipient and speaker for the University's Last Lecture Award.

Gail T. Fairhurst is a professor of communication at the University of Cincinnati, USA. Her research interests include organisational communication, leadership and organisational discourse. She has published over fifty articles in communication and management journals as well as book chapters, including contributions to *The Sage Handbook* *of Organizational Discourse* and *The New Handbook of Organizational Communication*. She is the author of *Discursive Leadership: In Conversation with Leadership Psychology* and co-author of *The Art of Framing: Managing the Language of Leadership* (with Robert Sarr). Her work has been the recipient of numerous awards including the 2005 International Communication Association Award for Outstanding Article for the communication discipline (with Linda Putnam), the 2007 and 1997 Best Book Award from the National Communication Association, Organizational Communication Division. She also serves on several editorial boards and is currently serving as an associate editor for *Human Relations*.

Laurent Filliettaz is assistant professor at the University of Geneva, Switzerland, in the field of adult education. He received his PhD in linguistics in 2000 and is the author of several books and articles analysing verbal interactions in professional settings from the perspectives of discourse analysis, pragmatics and various theories of action. His current research programme consists in promoting applied linguistic methods in the field of vocational education and training.

Giuliana Garzone is professor of English at the University of Milan, Italy. She has published extensively on translation and interpreting, on English for specific purposes and in particular on legal discourse, as well as on the use of new technologies in language teaching and learning, with special regard to phonetics and phonology. Her current research interests concern mainly the application of text linguistics and genre analysis to research on translation and interpreting and the intercultural aspects of communication in management.

Marinel Gerritsen holds the Christine Mohrmann chair in the Department of Business Communication Studies at Radboud University, the Netherlands. Her research interests include the differences between cultures in communication and the impact that this has on intercultural communication, the use of English as a lingua franca in business contexts, and the interface between English as an international language and the local languages in use.

Julio Gimenez is senior lecturer at Middlesex University in London, UK. He has researched and published in the fields of business discourse, writing pedagogy and communication in the workplace.

Margaret Baker Graham is professor of English in the rhetoric and professional communication programme at Iowa State University, USA. She is also editor of the *Journal of Business Communication*. Her research interests include narrative studies and how academic disciplines are culturally situated.

Diane S. Grimes holds a PhD from Purdue University and is associate professor of communication at Syracuse University in Syracuse, New York, USA. Research and teaching interests include critical organisational communication, diversity issues (focusing on race, whiteness and gender) and visual culture. Publication outlets include *Management Communication Quarterly*, *Journal of Organizational Change Management*, and the *Electronic Journal of Radical Organization Theory*.

Rick Iedema is research professor in organisational communication and director of the Centre for Health Communication in the Faculty of Humanities and Social Sciences, University of Technology, Sydney, Australia. His research interests lie in the way communication in hospitals contributes to the organisation of clinical work. He has (co-) published three edited volumes: *Hospital Communication*, *Identity Trouble* (with Carmen

Caldas Coulthard) and *Managing Clinical Work* (with Ros Sorensen). He has published a single-authored book, *Discourses of Post-Bureaucratic Organization*, and is currently working on a monograph with Carl Rhodes, David Grant and Hermine Scheeres.

Guowei Jian is an assistant professor of communication in the School of Communication at Cleveland State University, USA. His main research interests include organisational communication and discourse, organisational change, information and communication technologies at work, and intercultural communication. His research appears in *Discourse & Communication*, *Communication Research*, *Communication Monographs*, *Management Communication Quarterly*, *Communication Studies* and the *Journal of Broadcasting and Electronic Media*.

Yeonkwon Jung is a lecturer in the School of Journalism & Mass Communication, Korea University. He holds a PhD from the University of Edinburgh and an MA from the University of Hawaii. He has held teaching and research appointments at various universities, including the University of Michigan, the Helsinki School of Economics, and Chuo University. His research has appeared in *Genre Variation in Business Letter Writing* and *Asian Business Discourse(s)*.

Kenneth C. C. Kong is an associate professor of linguistics in the Department of English of Hong Kong Baptist University. His academic interests include discourse analysis, intercultural pragmatics, English for specific purposes and language education. He has published extensively in these areas.

Lan Li is an assistant professor of the Department of English, Hong Kong Polytechnic University. She holds an MPhil and a PhD in applied linguistics from the University of Exeter. She is a fellow of the Chartered Institute of Linguists, and her publications cover business communication, lexicology, lexicography, corpus linguistics and sociolinguistics.

Leena Louhiala-Salminen is senior lecturer and researcher in business communication at the Helsinki School of Economics (HSE), Finland. She is also programme director of the new HSE Master's programme in international business communication. Her main research interests include the various genres of business communication and the role of English as the business lingua franca.

Rosina Márquez Reiter is senior lecturer at the University of Surrey. Her research focuses on (Spanish) sociopragmatics, intercultural communication and institutional discourse. She is author of *Linguistic Politeness in Britain and Uruguay* and *Spanish Pragmatics* (with M. E. Placencia). She has published scholarly papers on indirectness, face, politeness, pragmatic variation, speech acts and conversational structure.

John G. McClellan is a doctoral candidate in communication at the University of Colorado at Boulder, USA. His research focuses on the discursive quality of organising. As a former organisational change strategy consultant he has a special interest in issues of collaboration, innovation and change.

Estrella Montolío is a lecturer in Spanish linguistics at the University of Barcelona, Spain. Her work focuses on combining theoretical and methodological aspects of grammar, pragmatics and discourse analysis, and its application to the study of academic and professional discourses. She has been a guest lecturer at numerous Spanish, European, and North and South American universities. She also acts as advisor on matters of communication for several institutions and large corporations.

Louise Mullany is associate professor of applied linguistics in sociolinguistics at the

University of Nottingham, UK. Her research primarily focuses on language and gender in business, media and medical settings. Her work has appeared in a range of international journals and edited collections, and she has recently published the monograph *Gendered Discourse in the Professional Workplace*.

Shanta Nair-Venugopal was formerly professor in sociolinguistics and intercultural communication with the School of Language Studies and Linguistics, Universiti Kebangsaan Malaysia, and is currently a principal fellow at the Institute of Occidental Studies, National University of Malaysia. Her publications include books, chapters in books and anthologies, and articles in *International Journal of the Sociology of Language*, *Language and Intercultural Communication*, *Journal of Intercultural Communication*, *Journal of Asian Pacific Communication*, in *World Englishes*, *Asian Englishes*, *Discourse & Communication* and *ESP Across Cultures*. She sits on the executive editorial board of the *Journal of Asian Pacific Communication* and *ESP Across Cultures* and has been featured as an interculturalist from the Asian Pacific region in *Business Discourse*.

Catherine Nickerson is visiting faculty in the Communication Unit at the Indian Institute of Management Bangalore and an associate editor for the *Journal of Business Communication*. She has lived in India, the United States, the Netherlands and the United Kingdom, and she has been teaching and researching in business communication and the use of English as an international business language for the past fifteen years. Her most recent book, *Business Discourse*, received the Association for Business Communication's Outstanding Publication Award.

Lúcia Pacheco de Oliveira is professor of English and applied linguistics at the Catholic University, Rio de Janeiro, Brazil. She is interested in contrastive studies, including cross-cultural and disciplinary genre variation in academic and professional discourse. Her current research includes the compilation of a representative corpus of Brazilian Portuguese (CORPOBRAS PUC-Rio).

Patricia S. Parker is associate professor of communication studies at the University of North Carolina at Chapel Hill, USA. Her research, teaching, and community activism focus on discourses of race, gender, class and power in organisation processes, especially as they influence girls' and women's leadership development and empowerment. Her publications include a book on African American women's executive leadership, as well as several articles and book chapters appearing in edited volumes and journals. Her current work, supported by a Kauffman Faculty Fellowship for social entrepreneurship, engages African American young women in low-income neighbourhoods to become advocates for positive change and social justice in their communities.

Rebecca Piekkari is professor of international business at the Helsinki School of Economics, Finland. Her area of expertise is international management, with a specific focus on language issues in multinational corporations. She has also written about the use of qualitative research methods in international business. Her articles have appeared in the *Journal of Management Studies*, *European Management Journal*, *International Journal of Cross-Cultural Management*, *International Business Review*, *Management International Review*, *Corporate Communications* and *Business Communication Quarterly*. Her most recent book is the *Handbook of Qualitative Research Methods for International Business* (with Catherine Welch).

Ingrid Piller is professor of applied linguistics and director of the Adult Migrant English Program Research Centre (http://www.ameprc.mq.edu.au) at Macquarie

University in Sydney, Australia. She is an applied sociolinguist with research interests in intercultural communication, language learning, multilingualism and language aspects of globalisation.

Brigitte Planken is an assistant professor in the department of Business Communication Studies at Radboud University Nijmegen, the Netherlands, where she teaches courses in English for Special Business Purposes and business communication research. As a researcher she is affiliated with the Center for Language Studies at the same university, and her research interests include the use and impact of English as a lingua franca, corporate social responsibility reporting and stakeholder perceptions, and rapport management in intercultural negotiations.

Fernando Ramallo is a lecturer in linguistics at the University of Vigo, Spain. His work focuses on sociolinguistics, discourse analysis, minority languages and language diversity. He is the co-editor of the journal *Sociolinguistic Studies* (with Xoán Paulo Rodríguez-Yáñez) and of *Discourse and Enterprise* (with Anxo M. Lorenzo and Xoán Paulo Rodríguez-Yáñez).

N. Lamar Reinsch, Jr, is a professor of management at the McDonough School of Business, Georgetown University, USA. He is a fellow of the Association for Business Communication and a former editor of the *Journal of Business Communication*. His research interests include both message variables and communication technologies.

Ingrid de Saint-Georges is lecturer and researcher in the Faculty of Psychology and Educational Sciences at the University of Geneva, Switzerland. She earned her doctoral degree in sociolinguistics in 2003. Her published work includes articles concerned with crisis management, organisational discourse, learning and apprenticeship, time and multimodal semiotics, and discourse analysis. She currently works in the field of adult education on a project focusing on communicative processes in vocational education and training.

Dalvir Samra-Fredericks is reader in organisational behaviour at Nottingham Business School, UK. She previously worked at Aston Business School and Derby University. Earlier, in a different 'life', she worked in private- and public-sector companies. Her research pivots upon a talk-based ethnographic approach – extended to include audio/video-recordings – of managerial élites and strategists doing their everyday work over time and space. This research has been published in a number of journals.

Hermine Scheeres is associate professor at the University of Technology, Sydney, Australia. Her research and publications are cross-disciplinary, spanning organisational studies, language and discourse, and adult learning She has managed and worked on research and consultancy projects for government departments and organisations, and she has been a member of expert and assessment panels for curriculum and professional development in higher and further education. Her current research includes projects investigating organisational change, learning and communication related to health-care practices.

Amy M. Schmisseur is an assistant professor in the Department of Communication at the University of Kansas, USA. Her primary research interests include the communication of emotion in the workplace and planned change communication. Her most recent work can be found in The *Journal of Business Communication* and *Discourse and Communication*.

Mary Simpson is a lecturer in the Management Communication Department,

Waikato Management School, University of Waikato, Aotearoa/New Zealand. Her doctorate explored how market, medical and retirement discourses infuse everyday communication among corporate management, employees and residents within retirement community organisations. Her research interests concern organisational participation and she combines critical-rhetorical and discursive analysis in her work. She has recently published in *Discourse and Communication*.

Eleonora D. Suleimenova is professor in the Department of General Linguistics at the Kazakh National University, Almaty, Kazakhstan. Her research interests are text, general and cognitive semantics, and sociolinguistics. Her publications include *Meaning and Sense, Language Identity, Language Situation and Language Planning, Revival of Language*.

Hiromasa (Hiro) Tanaka is a professor in the Department of International Studies at Meisei University in Tokyo, Japan, where he teaches intercultural communication, and a graduate course on language curriculum development. He spent eleven years as a consultant with several multinational business corporations in Japan and the United States.

Christina Wasson is associate professor in the Department of Anthropology, University of North Texas, USA. She is a linguistic anthropologist whose work explores the intersections of communication, organisations and technology. She has published articles and book chapters in the fields of anthropology, organisation studies and discourse studies on topics such as language use in organisations, team decision-making and virtual groupwork.

Tony J. Watson is professor of organisational behaviour at Nottingham University Business School, UK. His interests cover industrial sociology, organisations, managerial and entrepreneurial work and ethnography. Current work is the role of 'identity work' and narratives in the shaping of the work activities of managers and entrepreneurs in the context of their 'whole lives'.

Mark Zachry is associate professor of technical communication at the University of Washington, USA, where he teaches classes in the theoretical foundations of communication, user-centred design and design research. He is editor of *Technical Communication Quarterly* and co-editor (with Charlotte Thralls) of *Communicative Practices in Workplaces and the Professions: Cultural Perspectives on the Regulation of Discourse and Organizations*.

Yunxia Zhu teaches at the University of Queensland Business School, Australia. Her research interests include discourse and communication, written communication, cross-cultural management and business negotiation. She has published extensively in international journals such as *Text, Discourse Studies, Discourse and Communication, International Journal of Cross-Cultural Management, Business Communication Quarterly, Journal of Business Communication* and *Language and Intercultural Communication*. She won the Distinguished Publication Award of the Association for Business Communication in 2006 for her book *Written Communication across Cultures*.

Theodore E. Zorn is professor of management communication, University of Waikato, Hamilton, New Zealand. He teaches and conducts research in organisational communication, particularly focusing on organisational change, influence processes and new technologies. He has published more than seventy books, articles and chapters.

Reviewers

Gerald J. Alred, University of Wisconsin-Milwaukee, USA
Benjamin Bailey, University of Massachusetts-Amherst, USA
Valérie Carayol, Université Bordeaux 3, France
Paulo Cortes Gago, Universidade Federal de Juiz de Fora and Universidade do Estado
    do Rio de Janeiro, Brazil
Christine Coupland, University of Nottingham, UK
William Donohue, Michigan State University, USA
Stephen Fox, Lancaster University Management School, UK
Pervez Ghauri, Manchester Business School, UK
Michael B. Goodman, City University of New York, USA
David Grant, University of Sydney, Australia
Bill Harley, University of Melbourne, Australia
Robert L. Heath, University of Houston, USA
Nigel J. Holden, Lancashire Business School, UK
Shona Hunter, University of Leeds, UK
Maria Isaksson, Norwegian School of Management BI, Norway
Daphne Jameson, Cornell University, USA
Naoki Kameda, Doshisha University, Japan
Anne Kankaanranta, Helsinki School of Economics, Finland
William J. Kinsella, North Carolina State University, USA
Veronika Koller, Lancaster University, UK
Charlotte Linde, NASA Ames Research Center, USA
Miriam Locher, University of Berne, Switzerland
Jane Lockwood, Hong Kong Institute of Education, China
Meredith Marra, Victoria University of Wellington, New Zealand
Laura Miller, Loyola University Chicago, USA
Colleen Mills, University of Canterbury, New Zealand
Sara Mills, Sheffield Hallam University, UK
Roslyn Petelin, University of Queensland, Australia

Robert Phillipson, Copenhagen Business School, Denmark
Gitte Rasmussen Hougaard, University of Southern Denmark
John A. Sillince, University of Strathclyde Business School, UK
Elaine Swan, Lancaster University Management School, UK
James R. Taylor, Université de Montréal, Canada
Susanne Tietze, Nottingham Business School, UK
Quang Truong, Maastricht School of Management, the Netherlands
Bonnie Urciuoli, Hamilton College, USA
Andreu van Hooft, Radboud University, the Netherlands
Stanley Van Horn, University of Illinois, USA
Iris Varner, Illinois State University, USA
Anne Warfield Rawls, Bently College, USA
Hilkka Yli-Jokipii, University of Helsinki, Finland
Lindsay Yotsukura, University of Maryland, USA
Gu Yueguo, Chinese Academy of Social Sciences, PR China

Transcription conventions

((text))	Comment
(.)	Micro-pause
(???)	Unintelligible text
(00.0)	Length of pause in seconds, e.g. (20.0) = 20-second pause
(text)	Action
[. . .]	Untranscribed text
[	Interruption or overlap
[text]	Sensitive text, e.g. references to names of people, financial figures, products etc.
{text}	Speaker description
\<talk\>	Talk that is slower or more 'stretched' than surrounding talk.
=	Immediate latching on
e::	Elongated sound
italic	Emphasis
<u>underlining</u>	Rising intonation

Introduction: Business discourse

Francesca Bargiela-Chiappini

On words and labels

A question that I was asked by some contributors and reviewers during the preparation of this *Handbook* was how *I* defined 'business discourse'. It is pertinent question, to which I think I have more than one answer to offer. The answers may or may not resonate with all the contributors to the *Handbook*, even though they have generously agreed to write for it. In so doing they have trusted in a project that is likely to keep the original question 'What is business discourse?' alive, while their collective work stands as a token of the vibrancy of this relatively new field of studies.

Defining 'business discourse' in a short and exhaustive answer is, I think, next to impossible. A bird's-eye view of the contents of the *Handbook* explains why. This volume seeks to chart a new territory of multidisciplinary scholarship where linguistics, communication studies, organisation studies, ethnomethodology, critical studies, sociology, international management etc. would come together under one banner, each to offer its distinct perspective on what *it* understood 'business discourse' to be. For many chapters, the editorial brief stopped at the contributors' guidelines, in an attempt to give the contributors enough room to present their material in such a way as to accommodate the priorities and distinctive character of the specific discipline or approach. This flexibility has been especially important for the essays in Part Four: Localised Perspectives, where varying degrees of development of the field, historical and geographical peculiarities and the status of the contributors – often writing as representatives of a relatively small academic cohort of researchers – have resulted in a mosaic of unique insights.

The impracticality – worse, the futility – of attempting to impose an a priori understanding of business discourse on such a rich and eclectic collection could have resulted, I believe, in stifling individual creativities in the name of a standard or norm that in fact does not exist even for the editor of the *Handbook*. If this sounds like an apology for scholarly anarchy, I should hasten to say that there have been attempts to engage with notions of business discourse, in which the editor was also implicated; I will rehearse some of the arguments in the next section. I suspect such endeavours are often motivated by the need to belong to an existing, recognised entity, or to make sure that an entity is created that provides the security of self-identification through self-labelling. There is also a sense of achievement in 'naming into existence' something that was not there before or elevating an obscure phrase to the status of a field of study. Either way, one is making a position statement by unfurling a banner on a patch of previously unoccupied, or unclaimed, territory.

This could be seen as a rhetorical move; Zachry (Chapter 5 in this volume) describes rhetorical analysis as a flourishing methodology with an illustrious pedigree. I doubt whether the invocation of, and argumentation for, business discourse would pass the triple test of the 'rhetorical appeals', the Aristotelian means of persuasion – ethos, pathos and logos (Zachry, this volume; see also Samra-Fredericks 2004). Perhaps what follows might just be analysed as a piece of (self-reflexive) demonstrative rhetoric in that 'it is focused on establishing the merit of something for the public . . . [and] is concerned with the present and that which is at hand' (Zachry, this volume, p. 71).

'Discourse' as a metaphor for dialogue

It is with a self-reflexive posture that we first approached British and Italian management meeting discourse over ten year ago (Bargiela-Chiappini and Harris 1997), at one level seeking to show how pragmatic features were deployed in sense-making by social actors in the respective countries, but at a more ambitious level also setting the premises for the long-term, four-fold project of bridging the gap between:

- disciplines (linguistics–management studies);
- methodologies (pragmatics–organisational ethnography);
- academia and management practice (partnership research);
- systems of thought (challenging a western ethnocentric understanding of 'culture').

Meeting discourse was therefore a first platform from which to engage with management and organisation studies at a time when both were in the throes of the 'linguistic turn' (or discursive turn, for some). Linguistics, pragmatics and discourse analysis provided the approaches and analytical tools that would enable the qualitative interpreter to get as close as possible to the processes of meaning-making in organisational interaction. As 'discourses' and their definitions proliferated in organisation and management studies, the opportunities for cross-disciplinary dialogue became more numerous, at least on the European scene.

The 1990s proved to be a fruitful decade for explorations of discourses in work and professional settings (e.g. Drew and Heritage 1992; Sarangi and Roberts 1999; Gunnarsson et al. 1997). The first definition of 'business discourse' that we proposed dates back to that period (Bargiela-Chiappini and Nickerson 1999). It was a contribution to the growing number of studies that used 'discourse' in their titles (e.g. institutional discourse, professional discourse) and as such it could be seen as an unconscious way of carving out a niche in a territory that was becoming quite crowded and contested. Our understanding of business discourse at the time was that it is a process of 'talk and writing between individuals whose main work activities and interests are in the domain of business and who come together for the purpose of doing business' (Bargiela-Chiappini and Nickerson 1999: 2). Writing in and for business was conceived as social action, an activity through which organisational actors create understanding, meaning and knowledge. Leanings towards a moderate social constructionism laid the foundations for the next move, an exploration of what has become known as 'organisational discourse'.

My foray into organisational discourse (Bargiela-Chiappini 2004a) was an exercise in disciplinary dialogue, made possible by the interest in 'discourse' that I shared with colleagues in other disciplines. The contributions to the special journal issue that emerged from this encounter illustrate a range of understandings of 'discourse', partly influenced by the disciplinary background of the authors, but also highlight some important similarities, especially in relation to the effects of discursive practices on organisations and their members. The sociohistorical discourses of gendered identities are laid bare in a critical communicology approach to the study of airline pilot representations in the USA (Ashcraft and Mumby 2004). By focusing on the dialectics of materiality and discourse, communicology posits a notion of discourse which 'enacts and makes possible material changes in the world' (p. 26). Citing the example of an organisational meeting, Ashcraft and Mumby go on to argue that the event 'has substance only insofar as there is a discourse that enables us to enact, engage in, and make sense of such an event *as* meaningful' (ibid., original emphasis).

The tangible effects of the interplay between discourse and materiality are also examined through the rhetorical analysis of (dis)organising tales from two very different European cities, Rome and Stockholm. In a comparative analysis of the theatrical web of metaphorical meanings generated by the media (and the conniving citizens) in Rome, and the relatively 'flat discourse' of the Swedish media (reflexive no doubt of the much calmer temperament of its citizens), Czarniawska (2004: 62) concludes that metaphors are not only ornamental tropes, '[t]hey are part of organising processes, and not necessarily a positive one: metaphors can disorganise a city while organising the understanding of its citizens'.

Metaphorical language is also a tool of the 'discourse of managism' (Watson 2004: 75), the latter being a collaborative production of management consultants and managers. A distinctive component of such discourse is what Watson calls 'managerial pseudojargon' (ibid.), which in both its weak and strong expressions draws amply on metaphors. It is mainly in its 'strongly discursive usages' that managerial pseudojargon is 'implicated in attempts to mystify and neutralize the political and value dimensions of managerial work', to the extent that, Watson concludes, 'its mystification of just what managers are accountable for may lead to their ultimately being held accountable for very little' (p. 80).

A discourse analytical appreciation of the pragmatics of subordinate–superior decision-making unveils some of the features of organisational control that may be missed by a superficial reading of what is presented by management studies as participative decision-making (Yeung 2004). Metadiscoursal markers, rhetorical questions and pronominal shifts are among the linguistic devices that managers strategically deploy to exercise unobtrusive coercion. Here, again, 'discourse' constructs and maintains relationships (of power and control) with real consequences for people's lives as well as, presumably, for the economic performance of the organisation.

By the early years of the new millennium, business discourse as a mainly European endeavour had become an opportunity to revisit organisation studies through organisational discourse. Around the same time, business discourse was also meeting business communication and trying to learn lessons from the history and developments of this field in the USA. Reflecting on the lamented lack of a coherent disciplinary identity in business communication (Graham and Thralls 1998) and heeding the invitation to 'convergence' and 'commonality of purpose' (Rogers 2001), we proposed a 'partnership research' approach (Bargiela-Chiappini and Nickerson 2001), which consists of collaborative research between scholars in cognate disciplines but also between scholars belonging to traditionally distant disciplines, e.g. linguistics and management.

To that effect, and to offer a distinctive, though not necessarily incompatible, perspective from that of business communication, business discourse was defined as 'contextual and intertextual, self-reflexive and self-critical, although not necessarily political, [and] founded on the twin notions of discourse as situated action and of language as work' (Bargiela-Chiappini and Nickerson 2002: 277). 'Discourse' was seen as a symbolic point of convergence of an epistemological and methodological sharing between disciplines in the social sciences and humanities, which had already embraced the 'discursive turn' and might contribute in the long term to shaping business discourse as a new interdiscipline. From its inception, emphasis on qualitative research and scholarship has informed substantive developments in the field of business discourse (Bargiela-Chiappini et al. 2007), underlining a preference for close examination of aspects of business practice in a variety of settings and, as some of the chapters in this volume illustrate, also looking at modalities other than text. In this sense, it may not be so fruitful to incorporate business discourse research into business communication (see Louhiala-Salminen, Chapter 23 in this volume), although this volume will no doubt stimulate reflection on the relationship between the two fields which will enrich both.

Interestingly, three contributors to this volume (Guowei Jian, Amy Schmisseur and Gail Fairhurst) have undertaken elsewhere the unenviable task of dispelling some of the confusion generated by the uses of 'discourse' and 'communication' in the domain of organisation studies. Their conclusion will appeal to some, probably many, of the contributors to this volume: '[w]hile there is an inextricably close relationship between discourse and communication, our view of the mix is that organisational actors operate *in* communication and *through* discourse. By this we mean that in communication actors co-create their subjectivities in the form of personal and professional identities, relationships, communities, and cultures through linguistic performances' (Jian et al. 2008: 314). I hope they will bear with me if, in my response, I chose to add to confusion instead, by treading the path of terminological ambiguity and forestalling closure (Bargiela-Chiappini 2008). There is at least one other notorious precedent I/we should own up to: entertaining parallel conversations with intercultural business *communication* (Bargiela-Chiappini and Nickerson 2003) *and* with intercultural business *discourse* (Bargiela-Chiappini 2004b).

The essentially dialogic nature of the 'discourse' of business discourse has thus far emphasised the catholic constitution of the field, its openness to dialogue with other fields, approaches and disciplines, but also its commitment to sustained engagement with important scholarly debates bubbling all around its permeable boundaries. Perhaps the most productive of challenges for business discourse in recent years has been raised by the concept of 'culture' and disputes on its interpretations.

The meeting with 'culture'

When looking for suitable labels for the parts of this *Handbook*, the most difficult to pin down was the one for the localised perspectives; the current label was suggested by Shanta Nair-Venugopal (personal communication) as 'evoking both place and space as well as grounded context'. It will become clear from reading the 'localised perspectives' why 'culture' alone cannot unlock local practices. Socioeconomic change, language planning, language policies, rhetorical and philosophical traditions, the colonial legacy and western management ideologies, to name a few, all concur in a complex characterisation of the interplay of discourse, business and human interaction in specific geohistorical *locales*. The 'East Asian scene' (Vietnam, China, Korea and Japan), while perhaps drawing on Confucianism, is also varied in many other respects. For example, we are reminded that Chinese business discourse has its origins in an ancient rhetorical tradition that continues to inform current forms of expression (Zhu and Li, Chapter 26 in this volume). Not only that, but the authors also bring to our attention recent efforts to compare ancient eastern and western rhetorical traditions and map their separate evolutions, a diachronic perspective that affords a deeper appreciation of some of the cause of the localised distinctiveness of today's business discourse.

History also looms large in the evolution of the multilingual workplace scenarios in Malaysia (Nair-Venugopal, Chapter 29 in this volume) and in Hong Kong (Cheng, Chapter 36), where the colonial legacy has led to very different linguistic configurations to those present in their neighbouring countries. In Malaysia, the struggles continue between supporters of 'standard' English, and those who argue for the proven effectiveness of the 'localised' version, Malay English, in workplace interaction (Nair-Venugopal, Chapter 29). If 'culture' is political (Wasson, Chapter 15), language planning is even more so, and it cannot be disentangled from the socioeconomic contingencies. Reprofiling a whole country as trilingual after decades of domination by a foreign tongue is central language planning on a grand scale. Sulemeinova and Burkitbayeva's account (Chapter 33) of the early stages in the formation of Kazakhstan's new trilingual identity touches on the issue of the difficult balance to be achieved in the new forms of business communication between the revival of the rhetorical tradition of Kazakh, the persistence of Russian as a dominant language and the increased influence of English. Research in business discourse in Kazakhstan offers the analyst the unique opportunity of charting the evolution of discursive practices as they emerge from the flux of language planning objectives and individual linguistic competences, corporate demands and resistance from persisting local practices and preferences.

In his challenge to ethnocentric stereotyping, Tanaka (Chapter 25) bursts open the myth of the predictability of Japanese behaviour in intercultural business communication. For example, silent behaviour in meetings is often remarked upon in the literature as a cause of misunderstanding; the Japanese are not alone in being singled out as inexplicably 'silent'. The Finns apparently keep them company (Piller, Chapter 24), but as the author points out, one only needs to dig a little deeper into the interaction (rather than generalising through essentialist categories) to find that some Finns come across as 'quiet' because they feel they are linguistically less competent than their counterparts.

Engagement with 'intercultural business communication'[1] forced us to problematise the locus of culture and to critique the use of 'national' culture as an ineffective and western ethnocentric analytical category. A more self-reflexive posture by qualitative researchers analysing intercultural communication in business settings means also more sensitivity to emic research and indigenous categories, which in turn requires dipping into anthropology and cultural psychology (Bargiela-Chiappini and Nickerson 2003). Re-examination of taken-for-granted conceptual vocabulary and dissatisfaction with the alternatives offered by intercultural communication prompted a redefinition of culture as process: hence, *interculturality*, which is 'the process and the condition of cultures-in-contact' (Bargiela-Chiappini 2004b: 29). The dynamic character of culture(s) is an essential consequence of contact between individuals and groups and the source of change of their practices over time through mutual influence.

Interculturality is a heuristic that seeks to capture 'culture in the making' in intercultural encounters; at an abstract level, it marks a conceptual shift from the (self-)imposition, on data and scholars alike, of western ethnocentric categories and dichotomies such as 'national culture' and individualism/collectivism (Bargiela-Chiappini 2005). It is a sign of healthy scholarly debate that 'culture' should continue to engage researchers and thinkers across disciplines; a recent volume enlists over 300 definitions of 'culture' (Baldwin et al. 2006) – 300 and growing . . .

Culture may be a fiendishly elusive word to define but its complexity does not lie in the word itself. On this point, Raymond Williams writes:

> Between languages as within a language, the range and complexity of sense and reference indicate both difference of intellectual position and some blurring or overlapping. These variations, of whatever kind, necessarily involve alternative views of the activities, relationships and processes which this complex word indicates. The complexity, that is to say, is not finally in the word but in the problems which its variations of use significantly indicate. (Williams 1983: 92)

Postmodern critique in anthropology warns that the construction of 'difference' between communities and identities rests on relations of power and inequality, which define what can be understood in relation to what (Gupta and Ferguson 1997: 17). Culture, in the singular, has worked as a means of 'ordering and defining the world' (Mitchell 1995: 111), by 'bringing the "strange" into the ordinary' (ibid.) through ethnographic processes of localisation, exoticisation and integration, which have been seen to furnish the capitalist project. Furthermore, culture has been subjected to politicisation by constitutencies within and outside academia: for example, the 'cultural turn' in organisation studies has led to the manipulation of culture as an instrument of managerial control: 'managers are deploying both old and new ideas of "culture" in order to gain workers' active participation in new ways of organising production, profit and power' (Wright 1998: 12). The contestation of the ideology of culture(s) has led some anthropologists to the radical move of dropping the concept as the subject matter of their discipline (Street 1993; Yeongoyan 1986). In so doing, they might have anticipated Charles (this volume, p. 458) who muses: 'Clearly, culture as a concept needs to be revisited. Or should it be ditched? Is the new global business discourse cultureless?'

The shift from culture as a bounded object to culture as a process of co-constructed meaning creation has brought to the attention of anthropology (and organisation and management studies; see Samra-Fredericks 2005; Nicolini et al. 2003; Whittington 2006;

Balogun 2007) the concept of *practice*. *Cultural practices* have replaced individuals alleg-edly representing and enacting bounded cultures. Interculturality is therefore expressed in the indexical patterning of cultural practices which fine-grained analyses can capture in the instant of their realisation. Instead of looking at, for example, intercultural business negotiations through predictive behavioural categories or dichotomies (Bülow, Chapter 11 in this volume) based on generic cultural attributions, we could perhaps start anew and focus on how interactants 'do negotiating' and what categories they bring to bear on their collaborative work.

Cultural differences may then be seen to emerge from interaction and suggest themselves to the analyst and interpreter. Incidentally, it is naive to think that analysts could approach the 'data' without preconceptions or prejudgements; their background, disciplinary expertise, and prior experience of, and exposure to, cultural practices as active members of one or more communities will have 'primed' them. Self-awareness and self-reflexivity are therefore important attributes of the interpretative research process. They are particularly valuable when working in a 'multicultural' analytical team, to realise how behaviours which are similar on the surface are interpreted differently by different participants: for example, silence in Japanese business meetings may be a sign of attentiveness or simply the behaviour of junior interactants whose voices are not supposed to be heard; instead it is often mistaken for an expression of consensus by some western counterparts, with potentially disastrous outcomes for the meeting (Tanaka 2006; Yamada 1992; Fujio 2004). Here mention should be made of the import in cultural practices of management ideologies; western (Anglo-Saxon) ideologies which prescribe, among other things, what happens in meetings and negotiations are probably the most highly codified, elaborated, and widely taught, used and translated (Baum 2007; Czarniawska 2007; Tietze 2004, 2008). Alongside nonverbal behaviour (Hall 1973), they are the other 'silent language' of intercultural business prac-tices whose deafening noise we in the west do not seem to be able to hear.

The significance of interpreting emerging 'cultural difference' as an interactional realisation rather than imposing off-the-shelf categories that obfuscate and prejudge the nature and significance of difference cannot be overemphasised (exemplary is the case of 'politeness'; Márquez Reiter, Chapter 13 in this volume). A prerequisite to intercultural analysis is self-knowledge, which also includes knowledge of the business practices in the analyst's own community. Second, when granted privileged access to intercultural busi-ness encounters, the analyst enters a relationship with the participants that seeks out simi-larities in the awareness of difference(s). In order to develop this attitude, time, empathy and willingness to learn from the other are the foundations on which to establish long-term relationships, whenever possible and practical, thus building into the research a longitudi-nal perspective that is often sacrificed in the name of quick feedback to the practitioners. In this perspective, the participants are valued as agents who can interpret their situation reflexively and take a stand; interpretation in this sense is 'constituted as a dialogue in which I try to understand how the other sees what I take to be at issue; it thus shows itself to be grounded in understanding the self-understanding of another about something we both relate to' (Kögler 2005: 264). The ethical advantage of such interpreting is that it avoids the reification of the other by the analyst but at the same time does not elevate the other above the self; this is a delicate balance to achieve and maintain in the 'analyst-analysed' relationship; the critique of hegemonic cultural categories also demands that we should be aware of powerful positionings as western interpreters of intercultural discourse.

Critical?

Reflecting on the target and the nature of the critique in critical management studies, two positions can be identified, namely the militant and the humanist: the first premised on commitment to the victims of corporate power, the second on the personal benefits (for management students) of developing as more self-reflexive managers. On this latter point, Samra-Fredericks's (2005) ethnomethodological approach illuminates power-as-done as well as advocating ethnomethodology (EM) as a form of research we can and should take into the classroom (Samra-Fredericks 2003a) . In this way, we converse across communities and bring to life our research as well as expose 'students' to modes of questioning the taken-for-granted.

Some of the chapters in this volume call for political engagement in campaigns of words and deeds (Alvesson and Willmott 1992, 1996). For example, Parker and Grimes advance a compelling argument for researchers and practitioners to attend to the in/visibility of race in organisations. They also propose a programme of decolonisation of management communication theory construction, research and organisational practice. Deetz and McClellan articulate their critical project in terms of 'understanding, distanciation and critique, and generative transformation' (p. 126), which aims to engender alternative discourses 'by directing attention to power relationships emergent through discourse, replacing consciousness with language as the focus of analysis, intervening in the discursive systems that marginalise alternative values and engaging in research as a communal process' (p. 129). The political aim of gender equality guides the feminist perspectives examined by Mullany, who recommends diversification of research focus to include non-white, non-western women, women in less well-paid, low or part-time positions, while various forms of 'gendered violation' (Hearn and Parkin 2006: 111, cited in Mullany, p. 222) call for a much more intense scrutiny of interpersonal relationships in all levels of the organisation.

One of the less apparent ways of 'doing' critical research is proposed by Iedema and Scheeres (Chapter 6). It seems to me that their advocacy of the all-pervasive, and yet usually ignored, human phenomenon of affect has potentially huge implications for what business discourse analysts 'see' when they observe human interaction. We are reminded how the political process of 'seeing' what has always been there, but has thus far been ignored or dismissed or silenced, should pierce the veneer of normalised discourses (Parker and Grimes, Chapter 22). One such discourse, in fact the dominant one, is the rationalist discourse of knowledge, underpinned by distance and objectivity (Sturdy 2003). In spite of convincing arguments elaborated in a range of disciplines which underscore the essential emotional component of rationality (e.g. Turner and Stets 2005; Kopytko 2004), business discourse research has not yet engaged productively with it.

For sociologists, the role of emotions in human societies is far from marginal: 'experience, behavior, interaction, and organisation are connected to the mobilization and expression of emotions. Indeed, one of the unique features of humans is their reliance on emotions to form social bonds and build complex sociocultural structures' (Turner and Stets 2005: 1). Why otherwise fine-grained analyses of organisational members at work should have ignored this defining character of human behaviour until recently is, then, a moot point; one of the few researchers who has sought to capture emotions in the making has used 'an ethnographic approach which places centre-stage recording *lived experience happening* across time/space' (Samra-Fredericks 2004: 12; original emphasis; see also Samra-Fredericks 1996a, 1996b, 2003b).

'Seeing' lived experience presupposes sustained involvement with the moment-by-moment detail of the realisation of local practices, right into the slippery depths of emotional discourses where participants' humanity is perhaps at its most vulnerable. This 'entanglement' of the researcher with the sensitivities and problems of the practitioners (Iedema and Scheeres, Chapter 6), be they managerial élites (Samra-Fredericks 2005, Chapter 7) or marginalised workers (Parker and Grimes, Chapter 22), requires an affective engagement which 'shifts our attention to the unusual and the unexpected, whether that manifests as creativity, innovation, surprise, excitement or intensity' (Iedema and Scheeres, p. 87).

In pragmatics, the role of affect has been recognised as one of the most important contributions by non-Cartesian approaches to cognition such as discursive psychology, social constructionism and distributed cognition. Methodologically, 'the integration of affect/emotion and pragmatics is the first and most important step towards a holistic framework or theory for analyzing linguistic data in context' (Kopytko 2004: 522). According to relational pragmatics, interactants monitor their own emotions, other's emotions and the perceptions of their own emotions by others (p. 536). Affect is ubiquitous, socially constructed and distributed, and influences linguistic choices at all levels, from phonetic/phonological through to pragmatic/stylistic; in turn, emotions in human interaction are modulated by social and cultural norms, power relations, gender, age, etc. (Kopytko, p. 539; see also Samra-Fredericks 2004, 2005).

This is not the place to discuss whether emotions subsume affect, sentiments, feelings, etc. (cfr. Turner and Stets 2005: 2); regardless of the terminological debate and the semantics of individual labels, the phenomena they denote seem to me to require a significant epistemological shift in the positioning of the researcher in the act of 'doing research'. No longer is she using a methodology to capture something outside of herself, while watching emotion-making as a detached and 'objective' spectator; instead, in order to share the emotionality of the people she is present to, she must be willing to be implicated sympathetically in the participants' lives. This commitment requires the mobilisation of the researcher's own emotional resources into sympathetic sense-making, thus bridging the gap between rationality and emotionality both ontologically and methodologically. The risks of such personal involvement are real but the insights afforded by co-participation are far greater, and illuminate thus far invisible (in business discourse research) yet pervasive aspects of interpersonal experience.

According to Iedema and Scheeres (personal communication), affect animates discourse analysis with an interventionist, or as the authors put it, 'entrepreneurial', spirit whereby it 'becomes a means of articulating how we enact our relationships, what we can learn from each other, and how together we can intervene in business realities and write about these activities for others elsewhere'. The political edge of discourse research that 'seeks out tension and difference' (Iedema and Scheeres, p. 81) chimes with the activism of 'seeing' race in Parker and Grimes (Chapter 22), the transformative agenda of Deetz and McClellan (Chapter 9) and the feminist advocacy of Mullany (Chapter 16). There is enough here to infuse business discourse research with the critical breath which reconnects it with human practices (Samra-Fredericks, 2005: Chapter 7; Samra-Fredericks and Bargiela-Chiappini 2008).

Business discourse as a verb . . .

The etymology of the word 'discourse' offers an opportunity to take these reflections one step farther. The *Oxford English Dictionary* (*OED*) lists several meanings for both the noun and the verb. Starting with the noun, 'discourse' literally means 'running to and fro, conversation'. More enthusing are the obsolete or archaic meanings, e.g. 'narration, tale, account, the faculty of conversing, conversational power'. The meanings for the verb are no less suggestive: to run, move, or travel over a space, region, etc.; or, even better, in the obs. /arch. category we find 'to speak or converse with (a person), to talk to; to discuss a matter with, confer with; to speak to, address, harangue'. We can begin to expand the meaningfulness of business discourse and extend its epistemological horizons by conceptualising it as travelling across disciplines, methods and 'cultures', conversing and discussing with the scholars, researchers and practitioners, running to and fro challenging established notions and positions; subverting rather than settling, provoking rather than reassuring, and being stimulated by difference rather than aggrieved by it.

Speaking about the positive challenge of interdisciplinarity in business communication, Priscilla Rogers issues a healthy warning: 'Let's guard the language we use to define our role, lest we become victims of our own discourse. If we explain ourselves as outcasts in search of an academic home, lacking respect from peers and administrators, then we may eventually succumb to our own self-fulfiling prophecy' (Rogers 2001: 246). This volume shows that there are a few of us who believe, if not in the ambitious (impossible?) prospect of business discourse as an interdiscipline, at least in the attainable objective of a dialogue *across* disciplines.

. . . and the researcher as a composer

Most of the chapters in this volume contain implicit or explicit reference to the role of the researcher or analyst, while some highlight the disparity between the privileged positions of certain researchers (and their research) and the invisibility of others. Pacheco (Chapter 30) observes how research published in certain areas of the world never receives visibility outside of its linguistic boundaries. English as the language of international publishing is blamed for the 'invisibility' of much research that is published in other languages, but there is no easy, practical answer to this very important limitation, which, incidentally, affects many other multidisciplinary areas of research originating in the Anglophone area (e.g. politeness studies). Many international conferences which would be attended by researchers interested in business discourse, business communication or management and organisation studies tend to be in English, not to mention international conferences in pragmatics and sociolinguistics. What makes such events possible and popular among researchers, who generally benefit from their multinational character, is, paradoxically, the use of English as a *lingua franca*. English is not a panacea (see in this volume Gerritsen and Nickerson, Chapter 14; Piekkari, Chapter 20; Tanaka, Chapter 25) and may always give native speakers an advantage over non-native speakers, especially, but not only, in terms of the ideological baggage that educated native speakers can afford to take for granted; in practice, other languages can and are used in informal interaction at conferences and other international research meetings when multilingual speakers, given the opportunity, will code-switch to a language other than English with colleagues from the same geographic area. At times, however, the explanation of invisibility is to be searched for elsewhere; for example, Montolío and Ramallo (Chapter 31) remark on the poor participation of Spanish researchers in an international conference on business discourse organised on their home ground.

Language restrictions (limited competence in English?), or, more likely, funding or travel restrictions, force many researchers to operate from the periphery of international networks; the role of the researchers who occupy privileged zones in such networks is to act as catalysts and bridges between the periphery and the centre and between institutional, geographic and disciplinary areas. The researcher then becomes a 'composer', an individual who puts together, makes up, forms, fashions, frames and constructs together with other researchers, wherever they may be located. This spirit of creative openness, curiosity and generosity has made this *Handbook* possible; indeed, collaborative ventures such as this volume are not only good for the growth of the field but also practical bridge-building activities. English has enabled participation by non-native speakers in this international project: in turn, I hope they will continue to be interpreters of business discourse (however they may choose to define it) in their communities, and in their respective languages.

The researcher as 'visible composer' also *outside* of the academic community is the model that many authors in this volume would perhaps consider as the ideal (Cheng, Kong, Pacheco, Zhu and Li, Montolío and Ramallo, Wasson, Mullany, Nair-Venugopal, Tanaka, Samra-Fredericks, Watson, Jung, etc.). Different levels of involvement are represented, or are advocated, in the *Handbook*, each depending on the author's circumstances: the range includes independent consultants (e.g. Chew), consultant-academics who regularly switch between fields and personae (e.g. Tanaka), academics who have spent extensive periods in the field and have also acted as consultants (e.g. Watson, Iedema, Scheeres, Piekkari, Cheng), others who have worked in organisations/business for a time and who have entered academia but whose research has led them back into companies (e.g, Samra-Fredericks) and academics who have carried out fieldwork in companies (e.g. Nickerson, Wasson, Gimenez, Mullany, Filliettaz, de Saint-Georges, Piekkari, Nair-Venugopal, Jung).

Consultancy positions (e.g. Piekkari, Chew, Tanaka, Watson) or 'shadowing agreements' (see Samra-Fredericks, Chapter 7 in this volume) almost always afford privileged access to sensitive data, which the researcher may or may not be able to use for research or teaching purposes. Even less intensive and extensive patterns of presence in the field give rise to practical and ethical implications with regard to the establishment of trust-based relationship, relationship maintenance while in the field and beyond, feedback on the findings and research integrity. Those of us who have done fieldwork in companies, and perhaps have not always had the benefit of personal contacts, will know how hard it can be to obtain that first meeting with a gatekeeper. The question 'What's in it for us?' will usually have been raised long before a meeting is granted, and in some important ways it will inform the whole dynamics of establishing one's credentials, assessing degrees of openness and availability, establishing who is likely to be or become a mentor, presenting suitable suggestions or ideas for discussion, etc.

Through these processes, the researcher becomes ever more implicated in a complex network of interpersonal relationships, to which real people with real lives and everyday problems bring their own unique understandings of the situation. Issues and identities are negotiated as the researcher is drawn ever deeper into a dimension where self-reflexivity is required in order to make space and time for a critical (self-)appraisal of the demands advanced by the business collaborators, as well as by the research activity itself. At times, (ignorance of) research findings may turn out to be potentially very damaging for the company's business; for example, the researcher-consultant may have the uncomfortable task of pointing out that certain practices are alienating sections of the staff or the foreign partner in a joint venture. Not reporting this information would be unethical of the researcher but reporting it may damage his relationship with senior management (Tanaka, personal communication).

The urgent need for applied research highlighted by some of the contributors (e.g. Cheng, Dulek and Graham, Charles, Pacheco, Montolío and Ramallo, Reinsch) needs to be balanced by concerns for the integrity of the research per se, as a source of knowledge to be disseminated to and through the academic community. Once again, the researcher as a composer needs to strike a balance between the expectations of the business partners and her responsibility to further knowledge beyond what may at times be business concern for quite specific, practical outcomes. In fact, there need not be a polarisation between the two dimensions of research, the practical and the academic. Where fusion seems to have been realised, to the benefit of both the companies and academia, is in the field of design anthropology (Wasson, Chapter 15). Here the researchers are practitioners, they are based in the companies for which they work and they publish state-of-the-art research in academic journals.

This introduction would have to continue for many more pages to do justice to the issues raised by the contributors to this volume. It is time to let the chapters speak for themselves, and to finish by mentioning three further important points. The first is the need for multimodal and multidisciplinary analysis in business discourse. Watson (this volume, p. 235) reminds us that 'language is everywhere but it is not everything', with those drawing on ethnomethodology and multimodal research agreeing on this point too (in this volume, Samra-Fredericks, Brummans et al., Garzone, Gimenez, Filliettaz and de Saint-Georges). Let us not forget about materialities, media, affect and nonverbal communication, among others. The second is the need for the business researcher-composer to concentrate her efforts on bringing 'east' and 'west' together, thus heeding calls for the dismantlement of what is one of the most persistent and divisive conceptual dichotomies (Hendry and Wong 2006). The third and final point, eloquently discussed by Parker and Grimes (Chapter 22), is the long overdue critical engagement with the invisibility of race (and the unquestioning attitude towards 'whiteness' and its effects on the practice of research), but also with the silence that surrounds the exploitation of too many workers in too many countries and sectors, whose voices are very rarely heard in the field of business discourse research. At the end of a presentation I gave in the early 1990s on the discourse of management meetings I was challenged by a linguist in the audience with a question that stays with me to this day: 'Why empower the powerful?' It is something for us all to think about, as we take self-reflexivity one step further and take seriously our commitment to a transformative agenda (cf. Deetz and McClellan, Chapter 9).

Note

1. I use 'intercultural' to refer to comparisons of cultures in contact, 'cross-cultural' to refer to comparisons of different cultures in situations of non-contact, and 'intracultural' to describe behaviour within a culture (Gudykunst 2002).

Acknowledgement

I wish to thank Dalvir Samra-Fredericks and Sandra Harris for their insightful comments and suggestions on an earlier draft of this introduction.

References

Alvesson, M. and H. Willmott (eds) (1992) *Critical Management Studies*. London: Sage.

Alvesson, M. and H. Willmott (1996) *Making Sense of Management: A Critical Introduction*. London: Sage.

Ashcraft, K. L. and D. K. Mumby (2004) Organizing a critical communicology of gender and work. *International Journal of the Sociology of Language*, 166: 19–43.

Baldwin, J. R., S. L. Faulkner, M. L. Hecht and S. L. Lindsley (2006) *Redefining Culture: Perspective across Disciplines*. London: Routledge

Balogun, J. (2007) The practice of organizational restructuring: From design to reality. *European Management Journal*, 25: 81–91.

Bargiela-Chiappini, F. (2004a) Introduction: Reflections on a new research paradigm. *International Journal of the Sociology of Language*, 166: 1–18.

Bargiela-Chiappini, F. (2004b) Intercultural business discourse. In C. N. Candlin and M. Gotti (eds), *Intercultural Aspects of Specialized Communication*. Bern: Peter Lang, pp. 29–52.

Bargiela-Chiappini, F. (2005) Asian business discourse(s): An introduction. *Journal of Asian Pacific Communication*, 15(2): 207–28.

Bargiela-Chiappini, F. (2008) Discourse or communication? Living with ambiguity. *Discourse & Communication*, 2(3): 327–32.

Bargiela-Chiappini, F. and S. Harris (1997) *Managing Language: The Discourse of Corporate Meetings*. Amsterdam: John Benjamins.

Bargiela-Chiappini, F. and C. Nickerson (1999) Business writing as social action. In F. Bargiela-Chiappini and C. Nickerson (eds), *Writing Business: Genres, Media and Discourses*. Harlow: Longman, pp. 1–32.

Bargiela-Chiappini, F. and C. Nickerson (2001) Partnership research: A response to Priscilla Rogers. *Journal of Business Communication*, 38(3): 248–51.

Bargiela-Chiappini, F. and C. Nickerson (2002) Business discourse: Old debates, new horizons. *International Review of Applied Linguistics*, XL(4): 273–381.

Bargiela-Chiappini, F. and C. Nickerson (2003) Intercultural business communication: A rich field of studies. *Journal of Intercultural Studies*, 24(1): 3–15.

Bargiela-Chiappini, F., C. Nickerson and B. Planken (2007) *Business Discourse*. Basingstoke: Palgrave Macmillan.

Baum, J. A. C. (2007) Cultural group selection in organization studies. *Organization Studies*, 28: 37–47.

Czarniawska, B. (2004) Metaphors as enemies of organizing, or the advantage of a flat discourse. *International Journal of the Sociology of Language*, 166: 45–65.

Czarniawska, B. (2007) Has organization theory a tomorrow? *Organization Studies*, 28: 27–9.

Drew, P. and J. Heritage (eds) (1992) *Talk at Work*. Cambridge: Cambridge University Press.

Fujio, M. (2004). Silence during intercultural communication: A case study. *Corporate Communications*, 9(4): 331–9.

Graham, M. B. and C. Thralls (1998) Connections and fissures: Discipline formation in business communication. *Journal of Business Communication*, 43: 268–77.

Gudykunst, W. B. (2002) Issues in cross-cultural communication research. In W. B. Gudykunst and B. Mody (eds), *Handbook of International and Intercultural Communication*, 2nd edn. Thousand Oaks, CA: Sage.

Gupta, A. and J. Ferguson (1997) Culture. Power. Place: Ethnography at the end of an era. In A. Gupta and J. Ferguson (eds), *Culture. Power. Place*. Thousand Oaks, CA: Sage, pp. 1–32.

Gunnarsson, B.-L., P. Linell and B. Nordberg (eds) (1997) *The Construction of Professional Discourse*. London: Longman.

Hall, E. T (1973) *The Silent Language*. New York: Anchor.

Hendry, J. and H. W. Wong (eds) (2006) *Dismantling the East-West Dichotomy: Essays in Honour of Jan van Bremen*. London: Routledge.

Jian, G., A. M. Schmisseur and G. T. Fairhurst (2008) Organizational discourse and communication: The progeny of Proteus. *Discourse & Communication*, 2(3): 299–320.

Kögler, H.-H. (2005) Recognition and difference: The power of perspectives in interpretative dialogue. *Social Identities*, 11(3): 247–69.

Kopytko, R. (2004) The affective context in non-Cartesian pragmatics: A theoretical grounding. *Journal of Pragmatics*, 36: 521–48.

Mitchell, D. (1995) There's no such thing as culture: Towards a reconceptualization of the idea of culture in geography. *Transactions of the Institute of British Geographers*, 20: 102–16.

Nicolini, D., S. Gherardi and D. Yanow (eds) (2003) *Knowing in Organizations: A Practice-Based Approach*. Armonk, NY: M. E. Sharpe.

Oxford English Dictionary (*OED*) Online, accessed 1 March 2008.

Rogers, P. (2001) 'Challenge' is a positive word: Embracing the interdisciplinary nature of business communication. *Journal of Business Communication*, 38(3): 242–7.

Samra-Fredericks, D. (1996a) The interpersonal management of competing rationalities: A critical ethnography of board-level competence for 'doing' strategy as spoken in the face of change. PhD thesis, Brunel University.

Samra-Fredericks, D. (1996b) Talking of emotion for the development of strategy in the boardroom. In C. Combes, D. Grant, T. Keenoy and C. Oswick (eds), *Organizational Discourse: Talk, Text and Tropes*. London: KCM Press, pp. 197–202.

Samra-Fredericks, D. (2003a) Strategizing as lived experience and strategists' efforts to shape strategic direction. *Journal of Management Studies* (special issue), 40: 141–74.

Samra-Fredericks, D. (2003b) A proposal for developing a critical pedagogy in management from researching organizational members' everyday practice. *Management Learning*, 34(3): 291–312.

Samra-Fredericks, D. (2004) Managerial élites making rhetorical and linguistic 'moves' for a moving (emotional) display. *Human Relations*, 57: 1103–43.

Samra-Fredericks, D. (2005) Strategic practice, 'discourse' and the *everyday* interactional constitution of 'power effects'. *Organization*, 12(6): 803–41.

Samra-Fredericks, D. and F. Bargiela-Chiappini (2008) Introduction to the Symposium on the Foundations of Organizing: The contribution from Garfinkel, Goffman and Sacks. *Organization Studies*, 29(5): 1–24.

Sarangi, S. and C. Roberts (eds) (1999) *Talk, Work and Institutional Order: Discourse in Medical, Mediation, and Management Settings*. Berlin: Mouton de Gruyter.

Street, B. V. (1993) Culture is a verb: Anthropological aspects of language and cultural process. In D. Graddol, L. Thompson and M. Bryman (eds), *Language and Culture*. Clevedon: BAAL and Multilingual Matters, pp. 23–43.

Sturdy, A. (2003) Knowing the unknowable? A discussion of methodological and theoretical issues in emotion research and organizational studies. *Organization*, 10(1): 81–105.

Tanaka, H. (2006) Emerging English-speaking business discourses in Japan. *Journal of Asian Pacific Communication*, 16(1): 25–50.

Tietze, S. (2004) Spreading the management gospel in English. *Language and Intercultural Communication*, 4(4): 175–89.

Tietze, S. (2008) *International Management and Language*. London: Routledge.

Turner, J. H. and J. E. Stets (2005) *The Sociology of Emotions*. Cambridge: Cambridge University Press.

Watson, T. J. (2004) Managers, managism, and the tower of babble: Making sense of managerial pseudojargon. *International Journal of the Sociology of Language*, 166: 67–82.

Whittington, R. (2006) Completing the practice turn in strategy research. *Organization Studies*, 27(5): 613–34.

Williams, R. (1983) *The Sociology of Culture*. New York: Pantheon.

Wright, S. (1998) The politicization of 'culture'. *Anthropology Today*, 14(1): 7–15.

Yamada, H. (1992) *American and Japanese Business Discourse A Comparison of International Styles*. Norwood, NJ: Ablex.

Yeongoyan, A. A. (1986) Theory in anthropology: On the demise of the concept of culture. *Comparative Studies in Society and History*, 28(2): 368–74.

Yeung, L. (2004) The paradox of control in participative decision-making: Gatekeeping discourse in banks. *International Journal of the Sociology of Language*, 166: 83–104.

Part One: Foundation and Context

1

Europe: the state of the field

Catherine Nickerson and Brigitte Planken

Introduction

Business discourse research in the European tradition has been characterised in the following five ways (Bargiela-Chiappini et al. 2007):

1 It has generally been the preserve of applied linguists, many – but not all – of whom come out of the English for specific business purposes (ESBP) world.
2 It has usually involved some form of close text analysis – often in the discourse analytic tradition – and has often focused on authentic, i.e. real-life, written texts or spoken events.
3 Although English has been a dominating influence, as in other research traditions around the world, the European tradition has also included the investigation of European languages other than English.
4 It has been contextual in its approach, seeking to find ways to explain the relationship between the macro and the micro in its analysis.
5 It has until recently been largely neutral in its approach to the analysis of business discourse, i.e. it has not sought to identify or redress any existing hegemonies in the European business world as evidenced in its discourse.

In the 'Discussion' section of this chapter we will discuss each of these five characteristics in turn and trace how they have been of influence in shaping the work of European business discourse research. In each case we will refer to the methodologies used and to the most interesting findings, together with what we believe to be the most promising recent developments.

In the 'Future developments' section we will turn our attention to what we believe the future will hold for the European tradition. In this respect, we will look at a number of different approaches. First, we will focus on the work of the British applied linguist Helen Spencer-Oatey, whose work on rapport management in intercultural communication provides a fascinating view of business discourse as an essentially co-operative, relationship-oriented, activity. Second, we will explore the influence of new media and the emergence of multimodality as an important concern for business discourse researchers, as they seek to keep pace with the business world. Third, we will discuss the very recent critical turn in business discourse research in Europe, particularly in the work of those researchers interested in issues of inequality related to gender, such as Julio Gimenez and Louise Mullany, and we will speculate on how this might be of influence in other areas of business discourse. As in the first part of our discussion, in each case we will discuss the approach taken, and illustrate its application with specific reference to the individual researcher's methodology and findings. These three approaches, we believe, will have far-reaching consequences for business discourse research, not only within the boundaries of Europe, but also beyond.

Background

European business discourse research grew out of the applied linguistics tradition. The majority of the researchers working on business discourse within European business trained originally as applied linguists and many – although not all – have at some stage in their careers also been trainers of ESBP. These two factors have undoubtedly left their mark on the development of the field, not only in terms of the methodologies used, but also in many cases in the underlying motivation for the research carried out. In our 2007 publication (co-authored with Francesca Bargiela-Chiappini) on business discourse world-wide, we profiled the work of a number of European scholars whose work has been of influence in the formation of the European field from the beginning of the 1990s onwards. These included, for instance, the Finnish researchers Mirja Liisa Charles and Leena Louhiala-Salminen, the Italian researcher Francesca Bargiela-Chiappini, the American researcher Gina Poncini, who has been based in Switzerland and Italy since the 1970s, and the Belgian researcher Sonja Vandermeeren, who is based in Germany. Of these five, two (Vandermeeren and Bargiela-Chiappini) are sociolinguists or linguists by training, and the other three are applied linguists with long experience as ESBP trainers. Other aspects of the European business discourse tradition are also reflected in the work of these five, as we will discuss in more detail below. First, European research has involved the analysis of many different business genres, and some researchers have completed detailed analyses of several. Charles, for instance, has investigated negotiations and meetings; Louhiala-Salminen, fax communication, email communication and meetings; and Bargiela-Chiappini, meetings, human resources management (HRM) magazines and corporate websites. Although some researchers have specialised in one particular genre or form of (business) communication, the majority have developed an interest in how language is used to get things done in general within business organisations. Second, the work of these five researchers shows an interest not only in English as a dominating business language in the European (and global) business context, but also in other European languages used for business purposes. Vandermeeren's work, for instance, has included English, French, German and Dutch; Bargiela-Chiappini's work has included both spoken and written Italian and English; and Poncini's work has included up to fourteen different national cultures, with almost as many different languages. The influence of applied linguists and of multilingual communication in the European context, and the concern with forms of communication used within the business arena as a whole, are all topics that we will discuss in more detail below.

Discussion

The influence of the applied and sociolinguistics traditions is clear in the analytical methods that have been used by European researchers in the course of the past two decades. Language has been viewed as discourse, i.e. it has been analysed in context rather than in isolation, and the analytical methods applied have largely been existing methods that have been borrowed and adapted, rather than being developed specifically for the analysis of business discourse. In 1999, Louhiala-Salminen commented that the community of business discourse scholars seemed to share 'a general understanding of the identification of the utilitarian goal of developing and disseminating knowledge that increases the effectiveness of efficiency of business operations' (1999: 26), and it is the applied nature of this goal that has driven European business discourse research and determined the choice of analytical approaches that have been selected as being the most appropriate to facilitate its pursuit. European business discourse researchers have used and been influenced by, for instance, the ideas of the Birmingham discourse analytic tradition, e.g. Charles's work on business negotiations and Poncini's work on business meetings; by the work of the genre analyst Vijay Bhatia, e.g. Nickerson's work on email and Louhiala-Salminen's work on fax communication; by Spencer-Oatey's work on intercultural communication, e.g. Planken's work on negotiations; and by Kress and Van Leeuwen's theory of multimodality, e.g. de Groot's work on annual general reports and Bargiela-Chiappini's work on corporate websites. As suggested by Louhiala-Salminen, the goal has been to understand more about 'how people communicate using talk or writing in commercial organisations in order to get their work done' (Bargiela-Chiappini et al. 2007: 1), and not primarily to contribute to the development of theory. As we will discuss below, this is also a reflection of the data-driven nature of the European tradition.

European business discourse research is, and has always been, data-driven. In keeping with the applied nature of the research agenda, European researchers have based their work on empirical data, whether in the form of survey data (e.g. Vandermeeren, Charles, Marschan-Piekkari), close text analysis of different business genres (e.g. Planken, Poncini, Nickerson, Louhiala-Salminen) or experimental investigation (e.g. Gerritsen, de Groot, Van Meurs; see e.g. Gerritsen et al. 2000). Whereas several researchers have relied on a variety of different methodologies in their investigation of business discourse and have looked at many different genres, all have based their investigations on empirical data. It is this hallmark of the European tradition that most differentiates it from the North American one. Furthermore, whereas the North American tradition has largely been about macro-theories, the European tradition has largely centred on micro-analysis.

Three studies can be referred to here to illustrate the data-driven nature of European research, each in turn representing authentic, simulated and manipulated data. The first is the study of Business English as a lingua franca (BELF) in the Scandinavian context, by Louhiala-Salminen et al. (2005). The second is the study of intercultural negotiations by Planken (2005). And the third is the investigation of the effects of cross-cultural differences in the effectiveness of advertising appeals by Hoeken et al. (2003). The data referred to in the BELF study were the following:

1   a set of survey data based on written questionnaires and interviews to investigate issues such as daily communication routines, language choice in a given situation

and the characteristics of what respondents considered to be 'typically Swedish'
and 'typically Finnish';

2 video-recordings of four meetings that took place in BELF;

3 114 emails written in BELF.

Each set of authentic data was used to investigate a similar aim, i.e. how employees
perceived their own and the other's culture and how this was reflected in the discourse
realisations in both the spoken and written genres that were in use within the Swedish and
Finnish corporations studied. This study also includes a variety of different methods of
data collection and analysis, i.e. open and closed questions and statistical analysis related
to the survey, discourse analysis (DA) in the investigation of the meeting discourse, and
genre analysis in the analysis of the email correspondence.

In Planken's case, the data was analysed using Brown and Levinson's (1987) theory
of politeness within the framework of rapport management proposed by Spencer-Oatey
(2000a; see below for further discussion). Finally, in Hoeken et al.'s study, manipulated
data (different versions of the same advertisement) were used in an experimental setting
to investigate the effects of using different types of value appeals that are thought to reflect
various (European national) cultural differences (Hofstede 2001) in advertising texts, i.e.
the research team investigated whether an advertisement designed to appeal to 'security'
would be more or less effective than one designed to appeal to 'adventure' within a given
national culture. As is the case with simulated data, the researchers in experimental studies
like this one aim to control for – or neutralise – the potential effects of certain variables
so that they can test for the particular effect of another variable; in the case of Hoeken et
al.'s study, the effect of referring to a certain value appeal on readers' perception of the
advertisement. In many studies, the experimental phase of the investigation is prefaced
by a corpus investigation (e.g. de Groot et al. 2006), which provides input for the (materials used in) the experiment (e.g. de Groot 2008). Experimental investigations in business
discourse research largely originate in the field of document design. Document design is
essentially concerned with the investigation of what makes a document work, i.e. what
makes it informative, persuasive or instructive, and it has been a hallmark of business
discourse research in the Benelux countries since the late 1980s.

Another important hallmark of European business discourse research has been the
access that researchers have had to languages other than English. Although, of course,
English has been a dominating presence in much European work – as it is elsewhere in the
world – many other European languages have also been investigated. Bargiela-Chiappini
et al. (2007) provide the following information to illustrate this point:

> Despite the dominance of English, an increasing variety of other European lan-
> guages used in business discourse have been investigated, including French (van
> der Wijst 1996; Christian 1998), Dutch (van der Wijst 1996), German (Zilles
> 2004), Spanish (Villemoes 2003; Tebeaux 1999; Candia 2001; Charteris-Black
> and Ennis 2001; Ulijn and Verweij 2000; Conaway and Wardrope 2004), Danish
> (Grindsted 1997), Norwegian (Neumann 1997) and Portuguese (Silvestre 2003;
> 2004; Pereira 2004). (2007: 31)

In general terms, European research – perhaps in keeping with its roots in applied
linguistics – has emphasised language and discourse in its research investigations, and

there has been relatively little emphasis on culture. Exceptions to this include the recent work by Louhiala-Salminen et al. (2005) that has looked specifically at the reflections of Swedish and Finnish culture respectively in BELF interactions, Gerritsen and Vercken's (2006) work on raising students' intercultural awareness to prepare them for intercultural business communication situations, and de Groot's work on cultural differences in the Dutch-English and British-English versions of annual general reports (de Groot 2008). Once again, in this respect, the European tradition has been somewhat different from the more macro-theory-oriented North American tradition.

A further characteristic of European business discourse research has been a concern with how the organisational, i.e. sociocultural, context impacts on the discourse used in business. Contextualised language use is of course a hallmark of the English for specific purposes (ESP) and language for specific purposes (LSP) field in general, and of (ESP) genre analysis in particular, and this influence has been apparent in much of the work carried out. European researchers have frequently investigated the relationship between contextual variables, such as the economic conditions or the corporate language policy in place, and the way in which variations in these factors determine code choice, i.e. which specific language is selected, and the characteristics of the discourse, e.g. which genre, medium or linguistic realisation is selected. Bäck's work on code choice, for instance, discusses three levels at which the choice of code may be determined: a macro-level (e.g. language policies), a meso-level (e.g. the power balance between a seller and a buyer) and an individual or micro-level (e.g. the knowledge of foreign languages of a certain employee; Bäck 2004). Bäck suggests that these three levels will combine together and lead to a choice between (1) adaptation, e.g. the choice of the partner's first language; (2) non-adaptation, e.g. the decision to use the speaker's own first language; and (3) standardisation, e.g. the selection of a business lingua franca. This concept of adaptation, non-adaptation and standardisation in language choice has been an influential idea since the beginning of the 1990s. It underpins Hagen's work on the use of foreign languages in different European corporation in a number of EU-funded survey projects (e.g. Hagen 1993, 1999), and also the study of lingua francas in companies in Germany, France, the Netherlands, Portugal and Hungary by Vandermeeren (1998, 1999).

In other European work, the influence of context – both cultural and organisational – has been investigated through close text analysis. Charles's work on negotiations, for instance, has established how the relationship between a buyer and a seller in a negotiation – e.g. whether it is an old or newly established relationship – influences the discourse strategies that are used (e.g. Charles 1996). Nickerson's work on email in an Anglo-Dutch multinational corporation traces both organisational and cultural influences on the realisation of the discourse (Nickerson 2000). And, as we discussed earlier in this chapter, Louhiala-Salminen et al.'s (2005) work on BELF interactions in two Swedish–Finnish joint ventures looks in detail at how national culture determines the discourse strategies used in both spoken and written business genres.

A final characteristic of European business discourse research has been its largely neutral stance – at least until very recently. With a few exceptions, issues of inequality have not been at the forefront of the European research agenda – as they have been in Australia and New Zealand, for instance – and European researchers have pursued a descriptive, mostly neutral, set of objectives. The intention has been to describe what is happening in the business interaction or document, perhaps to design a better language training course or a more effective document, but not necessarily to empower the users of the text or the participants in a meeting. One exception to this is the work of the Finnish researcher Rebecca Marschan-Piekkari. From the mid-1990s onwards, Marschan-Piekkari has explored the communication practices at Kone Elevators in Finland. She has focused on various aspects of organisational life, including the structure of the organisation, the effectiveness of the communication that takes place, and in particular the (unequal) power relations that come into being when a corporation adopts an official corporate language (e.g. Marschan et al. 1996, 1997; Marschan-Piekkari et al. 1999, 2005). Several other researchers working in the European context, e.g. Louise Mullany, Julio Gimenez and Marlene Miglbauer, have recently also started to explore unequal power relations in the organisational context. We will discuss their work in more detail in the next section.

Future developments

In this section we will look at three developments which we believe will drive the European research agenda in the future. The first of these constitutes an emphasis on intercultural communication not as a problem but as a solution, as exemplified by the work of Helen Spencer-Oatey. The second is the influence of macro-theories of multimodality and hypermodality, as the global community deals with the increasing use of new, computer-mediated media in the business environment. And the third is the gradual emergence of critical approaches and a focus on issues of inequality.

At the very beginning of the twenty-first century, the British linguist Helen Spencer-Oatey published an edited collection which focused on the management of rapport through talk across cultures (Spencer-Oatey 2000b). In this collection, Spencer-Oatey outlines a rapport management framework, which draws on social pragmatics, politeness theory and face theory, and essentially explains the ways in which interactants use language in order to manage relationships. The model offers a way to account for all aspects of an interaction and its management, and as Bargiela-Chiappini et al. comment, 'In this way, it is of potential interest to business discourse researchers interested in accounting for aspects of relational talk in business interactions, ranging from politeness forms and accommodation strategies to contentious and conflictive strategies, as well as the linguistic manifestations of power, and the motivations that might underlie such behaviours' (2007: 42). What sets Spencer-Oatey's work apart from many other (macro-)theories on intercultural communication is that it emphasises not only the potential for communication failure, but also the potential for communication success. Given the fact that countless numbers of intercultural business encounters are being successfully completed every day, particularly in the European context, both perspectives would seem to be necessary in understanding business discourse.

Spencer-Oatey's own work within the rapport management framework has focused on Sino-British encounters (e.g. Spencer-Oatey and Xing 2003). In the European context, the 2005 study by Planken is an application of the rapport management theory to business negotiations. Planken investigated the use of safe talk and personal pronouns within (simulated) negations between experienced and inexperienced negotiators, and found considerable differences between the two, not only in the categories of safe talk selected and their frequency of use, but also in the two groups of negotiators' use of pronouns, most specifically the institutional 'we'. Poncini's 2004 study of multicultural business meetings takes a similar approach. Although Poncini does not refer specifically to the rapport management framework, she deliberately avoids viewing intercultural communication as inherently problematic, and focuses instead – like Planken – on how participants achieve and facilitate task-oriented discourse through the use of personal pronouns, specific lexis and evaluation strategies. Poncini focuses, in particular, on how the group works together to facilitate communication, using English as a common language and drawing on their established business relationships to create what she terms 'groupness'. In this respect, she captures much more of the realities of business life and business discourse involving interactants experienced in dealing with different cultures and speakers of different languages than the traditional 'one-speaker-one-culture' perspective. We believe that this approach will continue to influence the way in which European researchers approach intercultural encounters.

The second area of influence in the future will undoubtedly (continue to) be the advent and introduction of new media and the application of multimodality and hypermodality. In recent years, there has been an increasing interest in the new types of media that are used in business in general, and more specifically the application and influence of multimodality in business communication, e.g. the 2007 collection of papers on multimodality in corporate communication edited by Garzone et al. European business discourse researchers are at the forefront of such research on new media. Louhiala-Salminen's work on fax communication, for instance (1997, 1999), foreshadowed the decline of the business letter, and was continued by researchers such as Gains, Kankaanranta and Nickerson in their investigations of email discourse (Gains 1999; Kankaanranta 2006; Nickerson 2000). Web-based communication has begun to be of particular interest, as exemplified by Askehave and Nielsen's (2005) study of the 'genre' of the homepage, and their subsequent extension of genre analysis from a multimodal perspective, and by Bargiela-Chiappini (2005) in her hypermodal analysis of a banking website drawing on Lemke's (2002) theory of hypermodality, in which 'not only do we have linkages among text units of various scales, but we have linkages among text units, visual elements, and sound units' (Lemke 2002: 301). Likewise, the 2006 study of visual themes in a corpus of Dutch-English and British managerial forewords to annual general reports by de Groot et al. draws on the multimodal discourse approach of Kress and van Leeuwen (2001), and shows a significant difference between the British statements and the Dutch-English statements. We expect that European business discourse researchers will continue to explore the applications of multimodality in relation to new communication media, and that, as in de Groot's work (de Groot 2008) and Askehave and Nielsen's (2005) extension of genre theory, they will reassess and further adapt existing (applied linguistics) approaches to text analysis in the process.

The final area that we believe may be of interest to European business discourse research in the future is that of critical research focusing on uncovering inequalities in the business environment that are realised through discourse. In 1994, Deidre Boden published a landmark study of talk in organisations, and although this did not set out primarily to identify inequalities in the organisations under investigation, it remains an important influence on researchers interested in power relations, particularly as these are expressed through spoken interaction. The very recent work by Louise Mullany (2007) and by the London-based Argentinean researcher Julio Gimenez (2006) looks at gender and discourse in management settings, and explodes the myth of 'masculine' and 'feminine' speech styles as being determined by sex. A similar approach is taken by Marlene Miglbauer in her work in progress on intercultural business communication in the banking context in Austria and Croatia, with a particular focus on gender and power. In addition to these studies of gender and power, as we have discussed above, researchers such as Charles and Marschan-Piekkari (2002) and, most recently, Rogerson-Revell (2007) have also begun to explore power relations within multinational corporations as a result of the fact that such corporations more often than not opt to use English. Marschan-Piekkari has referred to the 'shadow structures' that arise alongside the official communication structures within an organisation as a result of employees building a communication network according to foreign language proficiency in order to survive. Given the commonplace nature of BELF and International Business English (IBE) interaction in the European context, we believe that European business discourse could usefully develop a less neutral agenda in order to understand more fully the situations, or indeed challenges, faced by European businesspeople.

Conclusions and implications for scholarship, research and teaching

European business discourse research will continue to be influenced by its applied linguistic heritage, together with a renewed interest in the design of multimedia documents. To some extent, the field will be defined by conferences such as those organised by the European Association for Business Communication, and Europe-based periodicals such as the *Information Design Journal*, which publishes papers on all aspects of document design, incorporating advances in verbal and visual information design. The interest in the intercultural and the multimodal aspects of business discourse will continue to provide fruitful areas of inquiry, and experimental (quantitative) approaches will become more familiar to the community at large, alongside the established mainstays of survey, corpus-based and more qualitatively oriented research. Furthermore, researchers will increasingly adopt multimethod approaches, incorporating a combination of (qualitative and quantitative) approaches, gleaned from multiple disciplines. European researchers will continue to investigate communication involving other European languages, as well as BELF and IBE interactions, and the role of the native speaker of English in communication with foreign language speakers of English in business settings, and the status of native speaker English as a 'teaching target' in courses of ESBP, will come under scrutiny. European researchers will continue to focus on the micro-analysis of (mostly) real-life data and may become increasingly critical in their approach, by considering issues of power and gender in the shaping of (intercultural) business discourse.

In terms of teaching and training, European business discourse research will continue to inform ESBP in particular, while postgraduate courses in (international) business communication, offered by educational institutions such as the Radboud University Nijmegen in the Netherlands, and the Helsinki School of Economics in Finland, will continue to act as a focal point for innovative research and teaching. It may also be that European researchers will learn a lesson from their North American colleagues as a result of this and begin to author research-based textbooks for use in other European institutions offering ESBP.

In conclusion, it can be said that European business discourse research is thriving and, unlike the North American tradition, it has not felt the need to define its disciplinary boundaries (see Bargiela-Chiappini et al. 2007 for further discussion on this point). In many respects, the European university system has been kind to business discourse researchers, and perhaps because of it roots in the established disciplines of applied linguistics and document design, many of those active in the field are now reaching senior academic positions. As a result, they are in a position to influence EU funding initiatives, e.g. the successful funding application to the Finnish Research Council which will investigate the effectiveness of corporate communication in multinationals across the EU and will involve researchers from four different institutions; and they are also actively involved with the supervision of doctoral-level research, e.g. the European Association for Business Communication hosts a PhD colloquium at its annual convention which is always well attended by senior researchers from around Europe. Such Europe-wide initiatives, together with the presence of doctoral research, has allowed the European tradition to develop a useful network of like-minded researchers, to encourage inter-institutional publication and multidisciplinary initiatives, and to develop depth, detail and variety in the types of analysis carried out.

References

Askehave, I. and A. E. Nielsen (2005) What are the characteristics of digital genres? Genre theory from a multimodal perspective. *Proceedings of the 38th Hawaii International Conference on System Sciences.* http://csdl2.computer.org/comp/proceedings/hicss/2005/2268/04/22680098a.pdf. Accessed 24 April 2006.

Bäck, B. (2004) Code choice im österreichischen Export in die Romania: Ein Modell und drei Fallstudien. PhD thesis, Wirtschaftsuniversität Wien, Vienna.

Bargiela-Chiappini, F. (2005) In memory of the business letter: Multimedia, genres and social action in a banking website. In P. Gillaerts and M. Gotti (eds), *Genre Variation in Business Letters.* Bern: Peter Lang, pp. 99–122.

Bargiela-Chiappini, F., C. Nickerson and B. Planken (2007) *Business Discourse.* Basingstoke: Palgrave-Macmillan.

Boden, D. (1994) *The Business of Talk: Organizations in Action.* Cambridge: Polity.

Brown, P. and S. Levinson (1987) *Politeness.* Cambridge: Cambridge University Press.

Candia, R. (2001) The business letter in Spanish: A cultural perspective. *Global Business Languages,* 6: 134–9.

Charles, M.L. (1996) Business negotiations: Interdependence between discourse and the business relationship. *English for Specific Purposes,* 15(1): 19–36.

Charles, M. L. and R. Marschan-Piekkari (2002) Language training for enhanced horizontal communication: A challenge for MNCs. *Business Communication Quarterly,* 65(2): 9–29.

Charteris-Black, J. and T. Ennis (2001) A comparative study of metaphor in Spanish and English financial reporting. *English for Specific Purposes,* 20(3): 249–66.

Christian, J. P. (1998) French and American business professionals: A discourse analysis study of cultural differences. *Intercultural Communication Studies,* 8(2): 1–18.

Conaway, R. and W. Wardrope (2004) Communication in Latin America: An analysis of Guatemalan business letters. *Business Communication Quarterly,* 67(4): 465–74.

Gains, J. (1999) Electronic mail: A new style of communication or just a new medium? An investigation into the text features of email. *English for Specific Purposes,* 18(1): 81–101.

Garzone, G., P. Catenaccio and G. Poncini (eds) (2007) *Multimodality in Corporate Communication.* Bern: Peter Lang.

Gerritsen, M. and P. J. Verckens (2006) Raising students' intercultural awareness and preparing them for intercultural business (communication) by email. *Business Communication Quarterly*, 69(1): 50–9.

Gerritsen, M., H. Korzilius, F. van Meurs and I. Gijsbers (2000) English in Dutch commercials: Not understood and not appreciated. *Journal of Advertising Research*, 40(3): 17–31.

Gimenez, J. (2006) Language, gender and power in the workplace: Work stories from communities of practice associated with the Other. PhD thesis, Queen Mary, University of London, London.

Grindsted, A. (1997) Joking as a strategy in Spanish and Danish negotiations. In F. Bargiela-Chiappini and S. Harris (eds), *The Languages of Business: An International Perspective*. Edinburgh: Edinburgh University Press, pp. 159–82.

Groot, E. de (2008) *English Annual Reports in Europe: A Study on the Identification and Reception of Genre Characteristics in Multimodal Annual Reports Originating in the Netherlands and in the United Kingdom*. Utrecht: Netherlands Graduate School of Linguistics.

Groot, E. de, H. Korzilius, C. Nickerson and M. Gerritsen (2006) A corpus analysis of text themes and photographic themes in managerial forewords of Dutch-English and British annual general reports. *IEEE Transactions on Professional Communication*, 49(3): 217–35.

Hagen, S. (1993), *Languages in European Business: A Regional Survey of Small and Medium-Sized Companies*. London: Centre for Information on Languages Teaching and Research: City Technology Colleges Trust.

Hagen, S. (ed.) (1999) *Communication across Borders: The ELUCIDATE Study*. London: CILT.

Hoeken, H., Brandt, C. van de Brandt, R. Crijns, N. Dominguez, B. Planken, and M. Starren (2003) International advertising in Western Europe: Should differences in uncertainty avoidance be considered when advertising in Belgium, France, the Netherlands and Spain? *Journal of Business Communication*, 40(3): 195–218.

Hofstede, G. (2001) *Culture's Consequences*, 2nd edn. Thousand Oaks, CA: Sage.

Kankaanranta, A. (2006) Hej Seppo, could you pls comment on this! Internal email communication in lingua franca English in a multinational company. *Business Communication Quarterly*, 69: 216–25.

Kress, G. and T. van Leeuwen (2001) *Multimodal Discourse: The Modes and Media of Contemporary Communication*. London: Arnold.

Lemke, J. (2002) Travels in hypermodality. *Visual Communication*, 1(3): 299–325.

Louhiala-Salminen, L. (1997) Investigating the genre of a business fax: A Finnish case study. *Journal of Business Communication*, 34(3): 316–33.

Louhiala-Salminen, L. (1999) 'Was there life before them?' Fax and email in business communication. *Journal of Language for International Business*, 10(1): 24–42.

Louhiala-Salminen, L., M. Charles and A. Kankaanranta (2005) English as a lingua franca in Nordic corporate mergers: Two case companies. *English for Specific Purposes*, 24(4): 401–21.

Marschan, R., D. Welch and L. Welch (1996) Control in less-hierarchical multinationals: The role of personal networks and informal communication. *International Business Review*, 5: 137–50.

Marschan, R., D. Welch and L. Welch (1997) Language: The forgotten factor in multi-national management? *European Management Journal*, 15: 591–8.

Marschan-Piekkari, R., D. Welch and L. Welch (1999) In the shadow: The impact of language on structure, power and communication in the multinational. *International Business Review*, 8: 421–40.

Marschan-Piekkari, R., E. Vaara, J. Tienari and R. Säntti (2005) Integration or disintegration? Human resource implications of the common corporate language decision in a cross-border merger. *International Journal of Human Resource Management*, 16(3): 333–47.

Mullany, L. (2007) *Gendered Discourse in Professional Communication*. Basingstoke: Palgrave Macmillan.

Neumann, I. (1997) Requests in German–Norwegian business discourse: Differences in directness. In F. Bargiela-Chiappini and S. Harris (eds), *The Languages of Business: An International Perspective*. Edinburgh: Edinburgh University Press, pp. 72–3.

Nickerson, C. (2000) *Playing the Corporate Language Game: An Investigation of the Genres and Discourse Strategies in English used by Dutch Writers Working in Multinational Corporations*. Amsterdam and Atlanta: Rodopi.

Pereira das Graças Dias, M. (2004) Constructing identities and searching for partner-ships in a meeting of Portuguese and Brazilian businessmen. In C. Gouveia, M. C. B. Silvestre and L. Azuga (eds), *Discourse, Communication and the Enterprise*. Lisbon: ULICES, University of Lisbon, pp. 169–94.

Planken, B. (2005) Managing rapport in lingua franca sales negotiations: A comparison of professional and aspiring negotiators. *English for Specific Purposes*, 24(4): 381–400.

Poncini, G. (2004) *Discursive Strategies in Multicultural Business Meetings*. Bern: Peter Lang.

Rogerson-Revell, P. (2007) Using English for international business: A European case study. *English for Specific Purposes*, 26: 103–20.

Silvestre, M. C. B. (2003) Continuities and changes in gender relations in the entrepre-neurial discourse: From representations to leadership practice. A critical discourse analysis. (Permanencias e mudanças nas relações de genero no discurso empresarial: Das representações as praticas de chiefia. Um estudo de analise critica do discurso). PhD thesis, University of Lisbon, Lisbon.

Silvestre, M. C. B. (2004) Top positions in Portuguese entrepreneurial context: A place of male and female asymmetries. In C. Gouveia, M. C. B. Silvestre and L. Azuga (eds), *Discourse, Communication and the Enterprise*. Lisbon: ULICES University of Lisbon, pp. 283–304.

Spencer-Oatey, H. (2000a) Rapport management: A framework for analysis. In H. Spencer-Oatey (ed.), *Culturally Speaking: Managing Rapport through Talk across Cultures*. London: Continuum, pp. 11–46.

Spencer-Oatey, H. (ed.) (2000b) *Culturally Speaking: Managing Rapport through Talk across Cultures*. London: Continuum.

Spencer-Oatey, H. and J. Xing (2003) Managing rapport in intercultural business interac-tions: A comparison of two Chinese–British welcome meetings. *Journal of Intercultural Studies*, 24(1): 33–46.

Tebeaux, E. (1999) Designing written business communication along the shifting cultural continuum: The new face of Mexico. *Journal of Business and Technical Communication*, 13: 49–85.

Ulijn, J. and M. Verweij (2000) Questioning behaviour in monocultural and intercultural technical business negotiations: The Dutch–Spanish connection. *Discourse Studies*, 2(2): 217–48.

Vandermeeren, S. (1998) *Fremdsprachen in Europäischen Unternehmen: Untersuchungen zu Bestand und Bedarf im Geschäftsalltag mit Empfehlungen für Sprachenpolitik und Sprachunterricht*. Waldsteinberg: Heidrun Popp.

Vandermeeren, S. (1999) English as a lingua franca in written corporate communication: Findings from a European survey. In F. Bargiela-Chiappini and C. Nickerson (eds), *Writing Business: Genres, Media and Discourses*. Harlow: Longman, pp. 273–92.

van der Wijst, P. (1996) *Politeness in Requests and Negotiations*. Dordrecht: ICG.

Villemoes, A. (2003) How do southern Spaniards create the conditions necessary to initiate negotiations with strangers? *Hermes, Journal of Linguistics*, 31: 119–34.

Zilles, S. (2004) Offers in German and Irish English business negotiations: A cross-cultural empirical analysis of micropragmatic and macropragmatic aspects. Paper delivered at the ABC European Conference, Milan, 22 May.

2

New Zealand and Australia: the state of the field

Theodore E. Zorn and Mary Simpson

Introduction

Business discourse research is alive and exceptionally well in Australia and New Zealand/ Aotearoa, with a substantial body of work that exhibits an exciting variety of approaches, topics and methods. This chapter provides a concise review of the state of business discourse research 'down under' and extends earlier work by the authors (Simpson and Zorn 2004) reviewing the state of organisational communication in New Zealand and Australia. The chapter includes work by scholars based in Australian and New Zealand universities as well as business discourse research conducted by other scholars in Australia or New Zealand contexts. It includes work from scholars who primarily identify with applied linguistics and sociolinguistics, communication studies, management/organisation studies, public relations and advertising.

Our conceptualisation of business discourse is heavily influenced by our training and research in organisational communication, but is also influenced by developments in discourse studies throughout the social sciences. In order to comment on the state of business discourse research in New Zealand and Australia, we begin by contextualising the field, exploring definitions and disciplines. We then use four 'points of difference' to organise our discussion of the major trends and influences in the literature. These four points of differences are the extent to which: (1) levels of analysis are micro, meso or macro; (2) the research orientation is dissensus or consensus; (3) text is treated as foreground or background; and (4) organising is treated as a context for discourse or discourse is treated as a means of organising. Through discussing these points of difference, we highlight key features of business discourse research in Australia and New Zealand.

Context

The field of business discourse study has emerged from studies of language in business and diversified to become an eclectic disciplinary field (Harris and Bargiela-Chiappini 2003: 155–6). 'Business discourse' has been defined as 'talk and writing between individuals . . . in the domain of business . . . for the purpose of doing business' (Bargiela-Chiappini and Nickerson 1999: 2) and 'founded on the twin notions of discourse as *situated action* and of *language as work*' (Bargiela-Chiappini and Nickerson 2002: 277, original emphasis). That is, discourse is not merely descriptive or referential but, to paraphrase Austin (1962), we *do things* with words and discourse *as action* functions as such in context. Furthermore, business discourse may be understood as contextual and intertextual, concerning the negotiated (inter)actions of social actors in their everyday activities within organisational contexts. With the influence of sociological, organisational communication and critical discourse studies, business discourse as a field of study must be considered broad and the boundaries of the field blurred in its intersection with related fields.

Dimensions of discourse

As a number of authors have pointed out (e.g. Grant et al. 2004), the term *discourse* is polysemous, reflecting numerous conceptualisations and research traditions. Discourse operates, and may be analysed, at multiple levels (e.g. Alvesson and Karreman 2000). First, there are broad, macro-level (societal) discourses – what Fairclough (1992: 5) refers to as '"discourse" with an article ("a discourse", "discourses", "the discourse of biology")'. Discourse is used here in the Foucauldian sense of 'a historically contingent body of regularized practices of language . . . that construct and legitimate the way we see things and talk about them' (DeCock 1998: 2). Second is meso-level (or organisational level) discourses such as a more or less coherent body of texts or set of language practices generated by or within an organisation or institution (e.g. public statements about the organisation's position on sustainability). Such discourses are embodied in organisationally or institutionally sanctioned texts that come in a range of spoken, written and pictorially symbolic forms, and help to constitute organisational reality (Hardy et al. 2005) by producing 'identities, contexts, objects of value, and correct procedures' (Taylor et al. 1996: 38). Third is micro-level discourse as reflected in internal documents and the conversations and meetings of organisational members. Of course, these various levels of discourse are mutually influencing (Alvesson and Karreman 2000). For example, macro-level and meso-level discourses create a context in which micro-level discourses are produced and interpreted. Conversely, micro- and organisational discourse may reinforce, shape or challenge societal level discourses.

Interconnections between micro-level interaction or 'situated activity', generic meso-level discourse in intermediate work and non-work settings, and macro-level or societal and cultural contexts have been noted in social research generally (e.g. Layder 1993), as well as in professional discourse (e.g. Candlin 2002), business discourse (e.g. Bargiela-Chiappini and Nickerson 2002), and critical discourse studies (Fairclough et al. 2004; McKenna 2004; van Dijk 2001). Significantly, Candlin (2002: 1) specifically calls for a research model 'which does not subordinate the macro to the micro or vice versa, and which honours a range of research methodologies'. That is, while foregrounding one, connections are made with the others.

Dimensions of business

The term 'business' may be interpreted as applying to strictly commercial transactions or activities. However, 'business settings' and 'domain of business' can be broadly interpreted to include a range of contexts in which members of various kinds of organisations interact to achieve business, organisational or relationship goals. Thus organisations of all types refer to their 'business plans', the 'business case' for an initiative, and even the 'business of' the organisation. Thus, drawing on our roots in organisational communication and discourse studies, we consider business discourse to refer to communication as talk, text and discursive practice within, between and about organisations.

Therefore, in this chapter we take the view that business discourse is an inherently communicative category belonging to and deriving from the social domain that finds expression in talk written text and practices in situated activities, within business settings (broadly interpreted) which are contextualised further by values, power and ideologies.

Australian and New Zealand Contexts

There have been a number of specific cultural and historical developments in Australia and New Zealand that have influenced the development of business discourse scholarship. First, both countries have relatively small populations, and thus relatively few universities and pools of scholars for studying any subject. This has arguably made disciplinary boundaries more porous than in larger countries and has resulted in business discourse being studied by people from multiple disciplinary affiliations and academic departments (see Jones 2005; McKie and Munshi 2005; More and Irwin 2000; Simpson and Zorn 2004). For example, a recent edited book focused on corporate social responsibility discourse (May et al. 2007) included New Zealand and Australian authors from departments of management, management communication, strategy, accounting and political science. The relative youth of the two countries and their academic institutions has perhaps also facilitated the interdisciplinarity of business discourse research (and research more generally), in that newer institutions are often less constrained by traditional boundaries.

Second, there is a strong qualitative research tradition, so that management/organisation studies scholars have been much more likely to embrace the 'discursive turn' in the social sciences than more quantitatively oriented traditions in, for example, organisation studies and communication studies in the United States. This factor is coupled with the fact that New Zealand and Australia have a handful of internationally prominent, influential scholars, nearly all of whom embrace discourse-oriented research. Examples include Christopher Candlin at Macquarie University, Sydney; Rick Iedema and Stewart Clegg of the University of Technology, Sydney; David Grant at the University of Sydney; Cynthia Hardy at the University of Melbourne; Janet Holmes at Victoria University, Wellington; Shirley Leitch at the University of Wollongong; and David McKie of the University of Waikato. Each of these scholars has influenced numerous doctoral students and colleagues to embrace discourse-sensitive approaches to organisation studies.

Finally, the relative dearth of large corporations in the two countries has led to many studies of small businesses, government agencies, and not-for-profit organisations. This is yet another reason for the importance of defining the 'business' of business discourse research broadly.

Method

To identify relevant articles we took a networking approach. We began with the bibliography developed for an earlier journal article (Simpson and Zorn 2004) and undertook a literature search of known Australian and New Zealand researchers. We also emailed these and other potential business discourse researchers in both countries, requesting each person to confirm our list of his or her publications, to add recent or additional publications, and to give the names of other known business discourse researchers.

We subsequently compiled a list of over 250 journal articles and book chapters from 1999 to 2007, which we categorised using the broad themes of micro-, meso- and macro-levels of business discourse. While this sample of literature was used for the chapter, we do not refer to them all. Given space limitations, the review is necessarily illustrative rather than comprehensive. Thus, we selected works that best illustrated central issues in business discourse scholarship within New Zealand and Australia.

Discussion

There are, no doubt, multiple ways to interpret the research on business discourse in New Zealand and Australia. Our goal here is to illustrate the common themes and the variety of the extant research. To do so, we have identified a number of points of difference that we have discerned from a close reading of the relevant literature. In each case, the points of difference may be seen as continua rather than discrete categories. Few studies represent the extremes on any of these dimensions; rather, most studies tend to emphasise one pole or the other.

First, as indicated in our discussion of discourse above, the literature may be seen to reflect differences in level of analysis or focus: micro, meso or macro. These levels of analysis will constitute our primary means of organising the literature that follows. A second point of difference is what Alvesson and Deetz (2000) identified as dissensus–consensus. Consensus-oriented studies focus on describing dominant, coherent or unified views of discourse practices – for example, identifying typical or common categories of practices. Consensus-oriented research is often labelled interpretive or descriptive. Dissensus-oriented research, on the other hand, focuses on challenging, questioning or identifying tensions and power relations within prevailing discourse practices. In business discourse studies, such research is often labelled critical, poststructural or postmodern.

A third point of difference is the degree to which text is foreground or background in the analysis. Some research – particularly (but not exclusively) micro, consensus approaches – provides extensive excerpts of conversation or other text in its analysis, often accompanied by fine-grained linguistic analysis (e.g. Holmes and Stubbe 2003). Other research uses text sparingly, mostly in support of abstract analysis that is foregrounded. While much business discourse research foregrounds text, a number of studies treat text as secondary to theoretical analysis (e.g. Lowe and Roper 2000; Xavier 1999).

Fourth, an important dimension of difference is the degree to which the research emphasises organising as a context for discourse versus discourse as a means of organising. That is, the primary focus of much business discourse research is on what can be learned about aspects of organising and organisations, such as the change processes or organisational culture (e.g. Davenport and Leitch 2005; Iedema et al. 2006). Other research is

much more focused on the discourse features themselves, viewing the organisation primarily as a context for uncovering qualities of language use (e.g. Language in the Workplace
Project (LWP) studies).

Finally, research may be usefully differentiated in terms of being theory-emergent
versus theory-driven, or what Alvesson and Deetz (2000) call the local/emergent-elite
dimension. Some research sets out to test, extend or apply existing theory whereas other
research primarily attempts to generate theoretical conclusions from examination of the
data.

Certainly there are other dimensions of difference that we could see. For example, the
degree to which discourse features are quantified is another. However, these five points of
difference seemed most useful in identifying commonalities and emphases within the New
Zealand and Australian business discourse literature. It is also important to recognise that
these features are often, but not necessarily, clustered together, as will be seen below. In
what follows, we organise the review by the levels of analysis and discuss other dimensions
within the micro, meso and macro sections.

Micro

Micro-level business discourse research includes studies that focus primarily on describing features of language in use in workplace settings, especially fine-grained analysis of
interaction between two or a small number of people (e.g. Daly et al. 2004; Holmes and
Stubbe 2003) or of written documents such as business letters, emails, meetings minutes
or other organisational documents. Micro-level business discourse research, in its purest
form, is particularly prominent among scholars who primarily identify with the discipline
of sociolinguistics. For example, Holmes (2000b) studied the way women managers
perform social identities through discourse in meetings. This research drew on part of
the extensive corpus of data gathered for the LWP, which was designed to identify characteristics of effective interpersonal interaction in a variety of New Zealand workplaces.
This particular study is interesting methodologically because it is typical of much micro-
oriented business discourse research in quantifying certain features of discourse – in
this case, the amount of talk by participants in meetings – and, even more typically, by
foregrounding fine-grained textual analysis of excerpts of interaction for their linguistic
structure and features – in this case, as a means to identify the strategies women managers used to manage meetings and construct their identities. This example constructs the
organisation as a context for discourse, exploring the ways discourse features work to
construct identities.

Other micro-level research examines the specific roles of language (e.g. small talk,
use of humour, and interactions at meetings) in 'doing' power or 'doing' collegiality
(e.g. Holmes and Stubbe 2003), or in sense-making (Mills 2000, 2002). These issues are
explored by analysing a variety of 'text sites' (e.g. meetings, conversations, interviews) in a
range of different settings including corporations, factories and government departments.
The general goal of such analysis is to explore the ways in which language functions to
enable individuals to negotiate the inherent tensions of work roles and relationships or to
make sense of workplace reality.

As may be seen in these examples, micro-oriented business discourse research tends
to be text-foregrounded, theory-emergent and consensus-oriented, as well as oriented to

treating organising as a context for discourse. However, this cluster of features does not always hold true. For example, some micro-level research reflects a dissensus approach, such as Holmes and Marra's (2004) study of relational practice – the largely unrecognised collaborative and supportive work that goes on in workplaces. These authors challenge the idea of equating relational practice with 'women's work', demonstrating that both men and women use relational practices and questioning the view that relational practices rely solely on feminine styles.

Meso

At the meso-level, the focus is on discourse practices within an organisation, institution, or industry, for example, studies of discourse practices that characterise a particular organisational culture or industry, or discourse practices used systematically in creating organisational change (e.g. Davenport and Leitch 2005; Zorn et al. 2000). The research of Iedema and colleagues is illustrative in focusing on the discursive dimensions of work within organisational change and resulting 'textualisation' of the workplace (Iedema and Scheeres 2003; Iedema et al. 2006).

Business discourse research focusing primarily on the meso-level of analysis is particularly prominent among scholars in communication studies and management/organisation studies. For example, Treleaven et al. (1999) identified discourse patterns in the consultation processes surrounding restructuring at an Australian university. Data included excerpts from official university documents, interviews and emails. As in the Holmes (2000b) study, there is some quantification; in this case, identifying the number of relevant public documents authored by men and women. Unlike micro-oriented studies, in meso-level studies the textual excerpts are not foregrounded or scrutinised for linguistic structure but rather are presented as examples to characterise the broader patterns of discursive practices – in this case, consultation for organisational change. It is important to note that Treleaven et al. link their meso-level discourse patterns to macro-level discourses (also see Doolin 2002; Iedema et al. 2003, 2006; Henderson et al. 2007; Simpson and Cheney 2007). Similarly, Xavier (1999) identified relationship management roles and discursive practices played and followed by financial communicators. In this study, text is very much in the background, serving as occasional evidence to support the abstract categories identified.

Macro

Macro-level business discourse research includes studies that focus primarily on regularised practices of language use that are broader than the organisation or institution – that is, patterns of language practices that are characteristic of an entire society or culture or even an international pattern. References to sustainability discourse, quality discourse or 'managerialist' discourse often refer to internationally understood systems of logic. Macro-oriented business discourse research is not as neatly aligned with particular disciplines as are the other two levels of analysis. Much of the research reflecting a macro-approach is theory-driven, particularly influenced by critical social theorists. For example, Roper and colleagues' work analysing the discourse of business takeover regulations (Gallhofer et al. 2001; Lowe and Roper 2000) draws on Latour and Fairclough to explain the discursive struggles in constructing the terms of debate that affect public opinion and public policy.

Iedema and Scheeres (2003) provide a good example of a study that nicely interweaves meso- and macro-levels of analysis. These authors used two case studies to demonstrate how workers in diverse settings are having to learn new discourse practices or 'immaterial labour' (Iedema et al. 2006) in response to widespread reconstitution of work practices. Their methodology is a combination of ethnography and discourse analysis, with multiple sources of textual data, including interviews, field notes and documents. Discourse as data is used extensively, but often is backgrounded to abstractions about discourse practices.

Other macro-oriented work also focuses on broad social trends but from theoretical perspectives other than those typically aligned with critical approaches. Jackson's work analysing popular management effectiveness programmes serves as a good example. Situating his methodological approach within the tradition of rhetorical analysis, Jackson identifies the discursive features that make popular programmes such as Senge's learning organisation (Jackson 2000) and Covey's *Seven Habits* (Jackson 1999) so appealing to managers around the world. Methodologically, this research involves close readings of texts to identify rhetorical strategies and tactics, such as rhetorical visions, action themes and symbolic cues. Text is background and the analysis is theory-driven, specifically by Bormann's symbolic convergence theory (Bormann et al. 1994).

Trends in New Zealand and Australian business discourse research

The discussion above has identified a number of dimensions that characterise points of similarity and difference in business discourse research in Australia and New Zealand. In this section we briefly note the degree to which the research that we have reviewed is clustered toward one or the other pole of each dimension.

Business discourse research in New Zealand and Australia is far more likely to reflect a dissensus rather than a consensus approach, although consensus-oriented intepretivism is clearly evident in research such as Colleen Mills's (2002) study of how blue-collar workers made sense of communication practices. Other examples include Jackson (1999, 2000), Xavier (1999) and Zorn and Gregory (2005). However, critical approaches that examine the likes of power relations and influences of managerial and market discourses are advocated and evident in research from a range of sociolinguistic (e.g. Candlin 2002; Holmes and Stubbe 2003) and critical discourse studies (e.g. Doolin 2002; Iedema et al. 2003). The prevalence of dissensus-oriented research is likely to be due to the pervasive influence of internationally prominent Australian and New Zealand scholars who draw heavily on critical perspectives (e.g. Clegg 1989; Grant et al. 2004; Iedema and Wodak 1999; Leitch and Neilson 2001).

Perhaps not surprisingly, the research reviewed tended to favour text-foregrounded research. There was certainly variance in terms of the degree to which that text was foregrounded in the analysis, but even most studies that we have labelled as text background featured at least some excerpts of text. Sociolinguistic research such as the LWP studies exemplified the most extreme text-foregrounded research (e.g. Holmes and Marra 2002, 2004; Holmes and Stubbe 2003; Stubbe et al. 2003). However, most of the business discourse research reviewed presented analyses of text as used in workplace conversations, meetings, phone calls, workshops, (e.g. Iedema and Scheeres 2003; Iedema et al. 2003,

2006; Mills 2000, 2002) and/or other organisational texts such as internal documents and advertisements (e.g. Bell 1999; Henderson et al. 2007; Simpson and Cheney 2007). Many also analysed text from interviews as either the primary (e.g. Doolin 2002, 2003; Motion and Doolin 2007) or supplementary data source (LWP studies). There were relatively few extreme cases of text serving purely as background to conceptual analysis, although certainly many examples in which conceptual analysis was more prominent.

Most research we found in the Australian and New Zealand business discourse literature was theory driven. For instance, studies of humour (Holmes 2000a; Holmes and Marra 2002), relational practices (Holmes and Marra 2004), and the use of expletives (Daly et al. 2004) draw on and critically examine politeness theory (Brown and Levinson 1987). Other examples include research that builds on Foucault's (1979) writings on surveillance to develop alternative theories of resistance and compliance by exploring workplace interaction (Clegg et al. 2002; Iedema et al. 2006). However, alongside the substantial theory-driven body of research are multiple examples that emphasise drawing conclusions from close examination of the text, without being primarily theory driven (e.g. Holmes 2000b; Zorn and Gregory 2005).

Beyond the dimensions of difference on which we have focused, three other trends stand out. First, a common theme across much of the research is the focus on negotiated identity in workplace situations; language is critical to this whether in face-to-face situations or mediated communication. For example, research involving team leaders (Iedema et al. 2006; Daly et al. 2004), managers (Holmes 2000b), clinicians as managers (Iedema and Scheeres 2003; Iedema et al. 2006; Doolin 2002, 2003) and factory workers (Daly et al. 2004; Mills 2000, 2002) all illustrate the ways in which language and/or discourses enable and constrain identity construction and enactment.

A second theme is that most research attends to the complexity of language use in business settings by emphasising its nuanced and multifunctional aspects. For example, familiar understandings of resistance and compliance are found to be far more complex when workers' talk is examined in the context of emerging organisational discourses and negotiated identity (Iedema et al. 2003). Also, Daly et al. (2004) show how aggressive forms of humour paradoxically contribute to team culture and thereby challenge conventional ideas on collegiality and humour in the workplace.

Finally, there is an abundance of business discourse research that in one way or another focuses on organisational change. Substantial work has addressed interaction in the process of organisational change (e.g. Mills 2000; Zorn 2002b). Other research has focused on the discourse of popular change programmes (e.g. Jackson 1999, 2000; Zorn et al. 2000). Finally, research has also focused on the ways that discourse practices are changing to reflect societal and labour market changes (e.g. Iedema and Scheeres 2003; Treleaven et al. 1999). Organisational change was one of the topical foci that Jones et al. (2004) identified as an important challenge for organisational communication researchers. Our sense is that business discourse researchers in Australia and New Zealand have taken up that challenge.

Future developments

The state of business discourse in Australia and New Zealand seems to us to be remarkably healthy, with a wide range of topics, methods and theoretical perspectives evident. Still, it is useful to consider potentially fruitful areas of research that are not prominent in the literature reviewed. In this section we briefly review opportunities for development, that is, methods and topics that seem underrepresented in the literature reviewed.

First, we note that rhetorical analysis is a recent and underdeveloped addition to business discourse literature in Australia and New Zealand. While Jones (2005) notes its absence in New Zealand organisational communication research, rhetorical analysis has been used, albeit sparingly, in organisation studies more broadly (e.g. Jackson 1999, 2000; Walker and Olsson 2001). More recently, Henderson et al. (2007) and Simpson and Cheney (2007) demonstrate the value of combining rhetorical and critical discourse analyses of organisational members' talk and organisational representations in publicly available texts. Like sociolinguistic studies of advertising (e.g. Bell 1999; Piller 2003), such research extends language use from being situated within workplace settings to include mediated messages.

Second, we identified a small body of research that directly relates to cultural issues of business discourse (e.g. leadership and ethnicity; cultural styles in meetings; culture and health-care; Chinese business communication). For instance, Munshi's work critiques the Eurocentric bias in public relations practice and research (e.g. Munshi and Kurian 2005; Munshi and McKie 2001). However, given the large immigrant populations in Australia and New Zealand, and the prominence of immigration, diversity and international trade in Australia and New Zealand, that there is not an abundance of research in this area is surprising. Certainly this general area presents a huge opportunity for business discourse research to contribute to national and international debates on an important set of issues.

Third, our review revealed little in the way of business discourse research on communication technologies. Several discourse-oriented studies of technology implementation stand out (e.g. Doolin 2003; Zorn 2002b) but little in the way of computer-mediated discourse. One exception is a study by Ainsworth et al. (2005) which examined online consultation analysing postings on two e-forums. Given the prominence of communication technology in contemporary workplaces, and the significant role of such technologies in changing organisational practice and discourse practices, it seems this is an area that presents a significant opportunity to business discourse researchers.

Conclusion

Within the New Zealand and Australian contexts there are commonalities across business, professional and organisational communication, management/organisation and discourse studies (Jones 2005; McKie and Munshi 2005; Zorn 2002a). Reviewers of this work also note a broad range of research, including interdisciplinary approaches as well as functional, interpretive and critical theoretical approaches (Jones et al. 2004; Simpson and Zorn 2004) and a wide variety of available discourse analysis methods (Stubbe et al. 2003). The review of the literature discussed here would support such views. We consider the state of business discourse research in Australia and New Zealand to 'punch above its weight' on the world stage, due to the prominence in this part of the world of discourse-sensitive approaches in studying communication practice.

References

Ainsworth, S., C. Hardy and B. Harley (2005) Online consultation: E-democracy and resistance in the case of the development gateway. *Management Communication Quarterly*, 19(1): 120–45.

Alvesson, M. and S. Deetz (2000) Critical theory and postmodernism: Approaches to organisational studies. In S. R. Clegg and C. Hardy (eds), *Studying Organisation*. London: Sage, pp. 185–211.

Alvesson, M. and D. Karreman (2000) Varieties of discourse: On the study of organisations through discourse analysis. *Human Relations*, 53(9): 1125–49.

Austin, J. L. (1962) *How to Do Things with Words*. Oxford: Clarendon Press.

Bargiela-Chiappini, F. and C. Nickerson (1999) Business writing as social action. In F. Bargiela-Chiappini and C. Nickerson (eds), *Writing Business: Genres, Medias and Discourses*. London: Longman, pp. 1–32.

Bargiela-Chiappini, F. and C. Nickerson (2002) Business discourse: Old debates, new horizons. *International Review of Applied Linguistics in Language Teaching*, 40(4):273–86.

Bell, A. (1999) Styling the other to define the self: A study in New Zealand identity making. *Journal of Sociolinguistics*, 3(4): 523–41.

Bormann, E. G., J. F. Cragan and D. C. Shields (1994) In defense of symbolic theory: A look at the theory and its criticisms after two decades. *Communication Theory*, 4(4): 259–94.

Brown, P. and S. Levinson (1987) *Politeness: Some Universals in Language Usage*. Cambridge: Cambridge University Press.

Candlin, C. N. (2002) Introduction. In C. N. Candlin (ed.), *Research and Practice in Professional Discourse*. Hong Kong: City University of Hong Kong, pp. 1–36.

Clegg, S. (1989) *Frameworks of Power*. Newbury Park, CA: Sage.

Clegg, S. R., T. S. Pitsis, T. Rura-Polley and M. Marosszeky (2002) Governmentality matters: Designing an alliance culture of inter-organisational collaboration for managing projects. *Organization Studies*, 23(3): 317–37.

Daly, N., J. Holmes, J. Newton and M. Stubbe (2004) Expletives as solidarity signals in FTAs on the factory floor. *Journal of Pragmatics*, 36: 945–64.

Davenport, S. and S. Leitch (2005) Circuits of power in practice: Strategic ambiguity as authority delegation. *Organization Studies*, 26(11): 1603–23.

DeCock, C. (1998) Organisational change and discourse: Hegemony, resistance, and reconstitution. *Management*, 1(1): 1–22.

Doolin, B. (2002) Enterprise discourse, professional identity and the organisational control of hospital clinicians. *Organization Studies*, 23(3): 369–90.

Doolin, B. (2003) Narratives of change: Discourse, technology and organization. *Organisation*, 10(4): 751–70.

Fairclough, N. (1992) *Discourse and Social Change*. Cambridge: Polity.

Fairclough, N., P. Graham, J. Lemke and R. Wodak (2004) Introduction. *Critical Discourse Studies*, 1(1): 1–7.

Foucault, M. (1979) *Discipline and Punish: The Birth of the Prison*. New York: Vintage.

Gallhofer, S., J. Haslam and J. Roper (2001) Applying critical discourse analysis: Struggles over takeovers legislation in New Zealand. *Advances in Accountability*, 8: 121–55.

Grant, D., C. Hardy, C. Oswick and L. L. Putnam (2004) Introduction: Organizational discourse: Exploring the field. In D. Grant, C. Hardy, C. Oswick and L. L. Putnam (eds), *The Sage Handbook of Organizational Discourse*. London: Sage, pp. 1–36.

Hardy, C., T. B. Lawrence and D. Grant (2005) Discourse and collaboration: The role of conversations and collective identity. *Academy of Management Review*, 30(1): 58–79.

Harris, S. and F. Bargiela-Chiappini (2003) Business as a site of language contact. *Annual Review of Applied Linguistics*, 23: 155–69.

Henderson, A., C. K. Weaver and G. Cheney (2007) Talking 'facts': Identity and rationality in industry perspectives on genetic modification. *Discourse Studies*, 9(2): 9–41.

Holmes, J. (2000a) Politeness, power and provocation: How humour functions in the workplace. *Discourse Studies*, 2(2): 159–85.

Holmes, J. (2000b) Women at work: Analysing women's work in New Zealand workplaces. *Australian Review of Applied Linguistics*, 22(2): 1–17.

Holmes, J. and M. Marra (2002) Having a laugh at work: How humour contributes to workplace culture. *Journal of Pragmatics*, 34: 1683–710.

Holmes, J. and M. Marra (2004) Relational practice in the workplace: Women's talk or gendered discourse? *Language in Society*, 33: 377–98.

Holmes, J. and M. Stubbe (2003) *Power and Politeness in the Workplace*. Edinburgh Gate and London: Pearson Education.

Iedema, R. and H. Scheeres (2003) From doing work to talking work: Renegotiating knowing, doing, and identity. *Applied Linguistics*, 24(3): 316–37.

Iedema, R. and R. Wodak (1999) Introduction: Organizational discourses and practices. *Discourse & Society*, 10(1): 5–19.

Iedema, R., P. Degeling, J. Braithwaite and L. White (2003) 'It's an interesting conversation I'm hearing': The doctor as manager. *Organisation Studies*, 25(1): 15–33.

Iedema, R., C. Rhodes and H. Scheeres (2006) Surveillance, resistance, observance: Exploring the teleo-affective volatility of workplace interaction. *Organisation Studies*, 27(8): 1111–30.

Jackson, B. G. (1999) The goose that laid the golden egg? A rhetorical critique of Stephen Covey and the effectiveness movement. *Journal of Management Studies*, 36(3): 353–77.

Jackson, B. G. (2000) A fantasy theme analysis of Peter Senge's learning organization. *Journal of Applied Behavioural Science*, 36(2): 193.

Jones, D. (2005) Spot the difference. *Management Communication Quarterly*, 19(2): 288–98.

Jones, E., B. Watson, J. Gardner and C. Gallois (2004) Organizational communication: Challenges for the new century. *Journal of Communication*, 544: 722–50.

Layder, D. (1993), *New Strategies in Social Research*. Cambridge: Polity.

Leitch, S. and D. Neilson (2001) Bringing publics into public relations: New theoretical frameworks for practice. In R. L. Heath (ed.), *Handbook of Public Relations*. Thousand Oaks, CA: Sage, pp. 127–38.

Lowe, A. and J. Roper (2000) Share-market regulation in New Zealand: The problematisation of takeovers legislation. *Policy Studies*, 21(2): 115–32.

McKenna, B. J. (2004) Critical discourse studies: Where to from here? *Critical Discourse Studies*, 1(1): 9–39.

McKie, D. and D. Munshi (2005) Connecting hemispheres: A comparative review of 21st-century organizational communication in Australia/New Zealand and the United States. *Review of Communication*, 5(1): 49–55.

May, S. K., G. Cheney and J. Roper (eds) (2007) *The Debate over Corporate Social Responsibility*. New York: Oxford University Press.

Mills, C. (2000) The interfaces of communication, sensemaking, and change. *Australian Journal of Communication*, 27(1): 95–110.

Mills, C. (2002) The hidden dimension of blue-collar sensemaking about workplace communication. *Journal of Business Communication*, 39(3): 288–313.

More, E. A. and H. T. Irwin (2000) Management communication for the new millennium: An Australian perspective. *Management Communication Quarterly*, 14(1): 142–51.

Motion, J. and B. Doolin (2007) Outside of the laboratory: Scientists' discursive practices in their encounters with activists. *Discourse Studies*, 9(1): 63–85.

Munshi, D. and P. Kurian (2005) Imperializing spin cycles: A postcolonial look at public relations, greenwashing, and the separation of publics. *Public Relations Review*, 31(4): 513–20.

Munshi, D. and D. McKie (2001) Different bodies of knowledge: Diversity and diversification in public relations. *Australian Journal of Communication*, 28(3): 11–22.

Piller, I. (2003) Advertising a site of language contact. *Annual Review of Applied Linguistics*, 23: 170–83.

Simpson, M. and G. Cheney (2007) Marketization, participation, and communication within New Zealand retirement villages: A critical-rhetorical and discursive analysis. *Discourse & Communication*, 1(2): 191–222.

Simpson, M. and T. Zorn (2004) Locating the frontiers of organisational communication scholarship in New Zealand and Australia. *Australian Journal of Communication*, 31: 13–34.

Stubbe, M., C. Lane, J. Hilder, E. Vine, B. Vine, M. Marra, J. Holmes and A. Weatherall (2003) Multiple discourse analyses of a workplace interaction. *Discourse Studies*, 5(3): 351–88.

Taylor, J. R., F. Cooren, N. Giroux and D. Robichaud (1996) The communicational basis of organization: Between the conversation and the text. *Communication Theory*, 6: 1–39.

Treleaven, L., D. Cecez-Kecmanavic and D. Moodie (1999) Generating a consultative discourse: A decade of communication change? *Australian Journal of Communication*, 26(3): 67–82.

van Dijk, T. A. (2001) Multidisciplinary CDA: A plea for diversity. In R. Wodak and M. Meyer (eds), *Methods of Critical Discourse Analysis*. London, Thousand Oaks and New Delhi: Sage, pp. 95–120.

Walker, R. and S. Olsson (2001) Stakeholder engagement, social responsibility and persuasive appeal of the clipboard. *Journal of Corporate Citizenship*, 3: 85–98.

Xavier, R. (1999) Changing roles for changing times? How listed companies interpret their role as communicator. *Australian Journal of Communication*, 26(3): 49–65.

Zorn, T. E. (2002a) Converging with divergence: Overcoming the disciplinary fragmentation in business communication, organizational communication, and public relations. *Business Communication Quarterly*, 65(2): 44.

Zorn, T. E. (2002b) The emotionality of information and communication technology implementation. *Journal of Communication Management*, 7: 160–71.

Zorn, T. E. and K. W. Gregory (2005) Learning the ropes together: Assimilation and friendship development among first-year male medical students. *Health Communication*, 17(3): 211–31.

Zorn, T. E., D. Page and G. Cheney (2000) Nuts about change: Multiple perspectives on change-oriented communication in a public sector organization. *Management Communication Quarterly*, 13(4): 515–66.

3

North America: the state of the field

Deborah C. Andrews

Introduction

Business discourse as a field and as a concept sits at the crossroads of many definitions and disciplines in the North American context. So this chapter first looks at some of those definitions and disciplines. Within this variety, however, certain common developments and trends in research have emerged. These are reviewed briefly. Next, the chapter characterises, again briefly, the setting for business discourse in the twenty-first century. The remainder of the chapter notes several directions in current research that address this setting and cites specific North American projects to demonstrate those trends.

An interdisciplinary field

'Business discourse' as a term implies a linguistic approach to the topic, an approach that examines the shaping of discourse communities through shared values and codes. That term is used in North America, but other terms are also common, especially in the academy, where most research is centred and students are introduced to the field. These other terms often take the shape of modifiers of 'communication': professional, management, organisational, business, speech, technical, corporate. In MBA programmes, courses are usually labelled 'management communication' and are sometimes differentiated by channel: 'written', 'oral' or 'interpersonal'. At the undergraduate level in the USA, the term 'business' is more likely to be included in course titles: 'written communications in business', 'business communication', 'business writing'. Some leading Canadian universities, however, use 'management communication' to label undergraduate courses. Differences between 'business' and 'technical' communication courses often centre on student enrolment (the first addressing students of business and organisational behaviour and the second those in engineering and the sciences); or on genre (the first focusing on emails, short reports and other organisational documents, and the second on laboratory and research reports and technical articles); or on audience (the first covering documents within organisations or for clients or the public, the second covering works for specialists). But the distinctions blur, an effect noted in another term rivalling all these: 'professional communication' or 'professional writing'. In addition, courses in corporate communication, composition, and rhetoric may include what this *Handbook* calls 'business discourse'. These courses have been taught in English departments; or in communication departments (including speech communication); or in separate programmes in technical or business communication, sometimes housed in colleges of engineering or business. The expansion and differentiation of the field as a site of research beyond the mere teaching of practice, however, is represented by new and sometimes free-standing graduate programmes; by newly formed university departments largely devoted to business and technical discourse; and by new research centres devoted specifically to professional communication, like that at Michigan State University.

In addition to programmes in this field, the professional associations that represent researchers and educators suggest the range of interests. There are many such associations in the USA and Canada – to name a few: the International Communication Association, the National Communication Association, the Association of Teachers of Technical Writing, the National Council of Teachers of English, the Association for Business Communication, the Canadian Association for the Study of Discourse and Writing, the Society for Technical Communication and the National Speech Association. Each of these publishes at least one journal, whose articles suggest current interests and developments. Significant journals in the field include *College Composition and Communication, Technical Communication Quarterly, Journal of Business Communication, Business Communication Quarterly, Technostyle, Technical Communication* and *Management Communication Quarterly*. Many associations also support active listservs, chat rooms and blogs for discussions among members, including mentoring and research advice. That researchers often belong to two or more of these associations suggests the interdisciplinary nature of what we are calling business discourse.

Some associations provide modest support for original research. In addition, government agencies are increasingly recognising this field as a legitimate target for funding. In the USA, this includes the National Science Foundation, the National Institutes of Health and the National Endowment for the Humanities (especially the Digital Humanities Initiative); in Canada, the chief government supporter of research in this field is the Social Sciences and Humanities Research Council of Canada.

This brief overview suggests that the field is richly interdisciplinary, pulling on methodology and theory in rhetoric, literary analysis, cultural studies, anthropology, organisational behaviour, industrial psychology, English studies, composition, design studies and management, to name a few. In Canada, where both French and English are recognised languages, translation studies are also significant, although they are less so in the USA.

Brief history of North American research

Composition studies have a long history in the USA, particularly in the academy. While the study and practice of business writing also date to the early twentieth century, it was during World War II that the field began to receive major research attention. That reflects in part the needs of the military and accompanying industries for extensive documentation, including manuals for operations and training. In the build-up of industry after the war, communications researchers focused particularly on practice, on efficient and effective communications within the hierarchies of large and established corporations. Handbooks and professional as well as company style guides emphasised such qualities of writing products as brevity, clarity and conciseness. This rather narrow view of business writing, however, yielded to more complex analysis later in the twentieth century. Mumby (2007), for example, in reviewing the development of organisational communication as a discipline in the USA, sees a shift in the 1980s from this focus on practice and systems to a new emphasis on corporate culture and interpretative research. A popular study published in the USA, Deal and Kennedy's *Corporate Cultures: The Rites and Rituals of Corporate Life* (1982), gave a framework for such thinking. Not merely reflecting organisational structure, communication has increasingly been seen as shaping an organisation. Insights from anthropology and ethnography help inform investigations into collective sense-making and the relationship between communication, power and organisations.

In addition, researchers have used a linguistics/hermeneutics approach, strongly influenced by European theorists, to analyse organisational communication. Composition-oriented US researchers have applied the tools of rhetorical analysis to an expanded corpus of materials from business and engineering.

Carliner et al. (2006: 3) review another direction of research: studies of information design, 'whether readers can understand a text' and document design, 'whether readers can find information in it'. They note that those definitions, by the way, are reversed by European researchers. As evidence for this trend towards information design they cite the plain language movement in the 1960s in North America and Europe and the turn towards usability in the 1980s, when users were encouraged to participate in the shaping of documents for their use. The creation of the Document Design Center of the American Institutes for Research (founded in 1946), for example, signalled this approach.

Yet another direction of research attention is corporate reporting and reputation. Researchers (e.g. Argenti 2005) investigate the dynamic exchanges between companies and their constituencies, especially as enabled by new technologies. They also analyse the content, timing and media of messages as they reflect corporate strategy, the creation of corporate identities and the enhancement of corporate reputation, as well as the narratives that encapsulate and advance an organisation's culture, orient new members to that culture, and motivate an audience to engage in a chief executive's or other leader's story. Historical studies of corporations are often based on company records as well as such business archives as that at the Hagley Library and Museum in Delaware (e.g. Yates 1993, 2005).

The setting for business discourse in the twenty-first century

As this brief historical review suggests, researchers are engaging in an increasingly fine-grained, more theorised and more thoroughly interdisciplinary approach to communication in business, broadly understood. Texts – online, on paper, spoken, visual, verbal – are examined as artefacts of social as well as business systems, as social acts that shape and are shaped by a variety of forces. This approach addresses the transformed environment of business, and thus of business communication, in the twenty-first century (Scott et al. 2006).

Friedman (2005) provides a useful if perhaps oversimplified explanation of this economic transformation, a process he sees as having occurred in three phases. In the first, Globalisation 1.0, *countries* sought out a global economic stage following Columbus's opening of trade between the old and the new world. Religious or imperialistic (or both) motivations caused exploration; natural and human energies powered it. From 1800 to 2000, a period Friedman calls Globalisation 2.0, *multinational companies* were the key drivers of a global economy. As Henry Adams, the distinguished nineteenth-century American historian, notes in his autobiography, steam and credit changed the world: transportation technology (railways, steam engines), communications technology (telephone, telegraph) and a range of financial instruments and institutions led to extensive international economic growth. Continued development of such technology and institutions expanded economic opportunities while making the world even more interconnected. Around 2000, however, according to Friedman, we entered a new era, Globalisation 3.0. In this, not nations or companies but *individuals* are the main agents of change; ubiquitous, cheap telecommunications have created a level playing field (thus the earth is flat) and opened business competition to 'every color of the human rainbow': 'It is now possible for more people than ever to collaborate and compete in real time with more other people on more different kinds of work from more different corners of the planet on more equal footing than at any previous time in the history of the world. (Friedman 2005: 8)

Lankshear and Knobel (2006: 38) provide a somewhat different but similarly useful framework for looking at how communications technology has changed the setting for business discourse. They use the terms 'Mindset 1' and 'Mindset 2' to denote the two sides of the transformation. Mindset 1 is characterised by physical/material and industrial principles and a manufacturing-oriented workplace. Company structures are hierarchical, with production occurring in a company unit (often in one country) and workers highly supervised. Emphasis is placed on vertical communication and control through traditional bureaucratic structures. Documents and the reality they represent are stable over long periods. Expertise and authority are rooted in individuals and institutions. 'Mindset 2,' the current setting for business discourse, is characterised by postindustrial principles. Organisations are becoming increasingly complex, diverse in their employees, and distributed in response to changing market and labor forces. They are eliminating entrenched bureaucracies. Organisational products are less likely to be commodities and more likely to be enabling services. As Thomas (2007) notes, 80 per cent of American jobs today are service-related. Expertise and authority are distributed and collective; texts are in flux in response to a speeded-up pace of change. Social relations occur in digital media space, not in physical space.

The nature of work, and of communication that fosters and constrains work, has thus been transformed (e.g. Adler 2002). Thomas points to several implications of these changes, including the reduction of layers of management in organisations that has led to the use of 'self-management teams'; the push to make decisions at lower levels; a greater focus on horizontal communication, including virtual work teams that span the globe and cross-functional teams that efficiently focus on specific customer needs; and an emphasis on worker flexibility in adapting to an environment of constant change.

Current directions in research

In characterising this setting in such terms, North American researchers have also seen it as an attractive site for investigation. Mumby (2007) notes four directions in organisational communication research that, with modification, can help frame this chapter's discussion of the broader field of business discourse. The remainder of this chapter presents a highly selective sample of specific North American investigations that illustrate each of these four often intersecting directions: interdisciplinary methods (a direction discussed extensively by Dulek and Graham in Chapter 35 of this *Handbook*); emphasis on individual communication; new concepts of an organisation; and a new rhetoric of digital expression.

Interdisciplinary methods

First, researchers across many disciplines are sharing and adapting methodologies to examine, for example, power relationships; the formation of individual identities and accommodation of differences in gender, abilities and the like; the concept of regulation within organisational and professional settings; and the effects of information technology. In doing so, academics are collaborating with practitioners who can provide on-the-ground insights into problems and solutions. An excellent model of such research is that created by Henry (2000). He and his collaborators, graduate students in a course called Cultures of Professional Writing who were practising professional writers, studied 83 workplace field sites between 1993 and 1999. The students observed the sites (many in government and professional associations and societies, given the location of the study near Washington, DC, but also private businesses), collected documents as artefacts of the culture of the site, and took notes on specific aspects they wanted to assess. Henry used several theoretical perspectives to analyse this large database of participant–observer ethnographic accounts (which he terms, following Lyotard, *petits recits*), including social constructionism, narratology, rhetoric, discourse analysis and economic theory.

A particular concern was the implications for discourse of a shift from the high-volume industrial economy of Mindset 1 to the current high-value economy (Mindset 2); from impersonal, instrumental writing to writing whose authors understand that they 'not only compose but are composed by the discourses of the workplace' (Henry 2000: 6) and thus can contribute to profits through 'continuous discovery of new linkages between solutions and needs' (Henry 2000: 5). As knowledge workers, writers add value in a setting of dispersed decision-making and collaborative enterprises, although their lower status at work may hinder their access to necessary information. Writers may find themselves caught up in document routing processes that are repetitive and thus may be unable to see new possibilities; on the other hand, they might bring their skills at organisational analysis to bear on reshaping the documents that convey organisational procedures. The ethnographies point out areas of dissonance between what may be taught as appropriate business communication practices (clarity and brevity) and what may give power within an organisation (obscurity and information hoarding).

Henry thus examines the complexities of how language and discourse practices shape the identities of writers in the workplace and how a global economy and new media have rendered 'earlier subjectivities required by the workplace archaic and even counterproductive' (p. 165). In moving from analysis to suggestions for activist intervention based on his findings, Henry (2000: 88) argues for an end to the 'erasure of the "I"' in student and workplace writing, a practice in which writers communicate 'predetermined thoughts rather than. . .exploring and instantiating reality'.

Emphasis on individual communication

Second, as Henry suggests, the transformed setting for work places greater emphasis on communication among individuals and thus more attention is being placed on 'in situ, moment-to-moment, everyday communication practices of organisation members' (Mumby 2007: 3297). Such practices, as Friedman (2005) notes, are becoming increasingly significant in Globalisation 3.0. For example, Jackson (2007: 6) looks at the phenomenon of social computing: large numbers of individuals create an ever-increasing number of postings on text-based discussion boards, social networking sites and blogs, many of which support multimedia content and all of which help to create 'readymade data sets on a scale we have never before experienced'. Researchers are developing methods to tag and interpret all this information. Hermann (2007) used both a discursive and a textual method to analyse the process of sense-making as individual investors in Berkshire Hathaway conversed in some twenty online threads posted to the Motley Fool website (TMF.com). Simoff and Sudweeks (2007) developed a methodology, 'complementary explorative data analysis', to examine online communication behaviours. They applied this methodology to data from two different virtual team projects to determine if 'the number, length, and content of messages are sufficient criteria to identify emergent leaders in both synchronous and asynchronous environments' (p. 94). Turner and Reinsch (2007) identified a phenomenon they call 'multicommunicating', in which individuals handle multiple communications at once, allocating their communications presence in an 'attention queue', a conversational hierarchy that reflects the relative status and power of the conversation partners. Their findings call attention to the speeding up of communication and the need for a new understanding of what constitutes communication competence and polite behaviour.

New concepts of an organisation

Third is a 'shift toward viewing organisations as changing, dynamic, permeable sites of discourse' (Mumby 2007: 3298). This new perspective has fostered several interesting research projects directed at a broad range of settings including health-care, start-up companies, non-governmental organisations and other not-for-profit settings.

Zachry and Thralls (2007: vii), for example, take a new look at the concept of regulation, 'what regulation means and the means of regulation', as it plays out in routine or regularised discourse within organisations and professions. The several contributors to their anthology explore through a variety of theoretical and methodological lenses the complex relationships between policies and laws and the discourse that defines and enables communication. They uncover contingencies and interconnections within various settings, the 'recombinant, extensible, and expansive situatedness of communicative practices' (p. x). They also demonstrate various concerns for agency, where people are 'understood to be complex sites of conflicting social, biological, education, and other materially conditioned factors that are not of their own devising' (p. xi).

In other technical communication studies, researchers are also emphasising performance, that is, how individuals can use public discourse to achieve political and environmental goals in a community (Simmons and Grabill 2007) and to mitigate risk in medical procedures and dangerous work environments (Sauer 2006). Thomas (2007) is investigating collaboration among government agencies in the face of terrorism and natural disasters. Her project is one of several funded by the US federal government after the very obvious failure of agencies to work together when Hurricane Katrina devastated New Orleans in 2005. Through an interdisciplinary approach with colleagues in organisational theory and behaviour, she collected stories from senior US homeland security managers in a variety of agencies (police, fire, medical, military); developed a model that identifies 'key factors that enable or thwart an organisation's capacity to collaborate'; and created a diagnostic tool for measuring that capacity in an organisation (Thomas 2007: 292).

Researchers in corporate communication are directing attention to how leaders are communicating in new, more networked organisational structures, how they frame their corporate strategies and communicate their vision and procedures persuasively to those inside and outside their organisation. The quarterly and annual reports of US corporations, once a fairly stable, printed genre, are yielding to more dynamic and interactive electronic forms in which customers and shareholders shape both content and presentation. Thus researchers continue to look at the genre and genre systems of business discourse (Yates et al. 1999; Yates 2002; Miller and Shepherd 2004). As new media enable new reporting approaches, government policies in regulated industries, especially financial ones, will both reflect and shape those approaches.

Another new kind of organisation and new area for research is virtual organisations and virtual teamwork. Virtual collaboration requires the development of mutual knowledge and a hybrid team culture across the many global and organisational cultures represented by individual team members. Researchers examining virtual teams are identifying vulnerabilities in such work (Early and Mosakowski 2000; Yates et al. 1999). Cramton (2002) cites five vulnerabilities. First, team members may 'fail to communicate and remember contextual information' about others at remote locations, including features of the equipment they use and competing responsibilities and pressures, as well as local holidays and customs (p. 358). Second, the team may distribute information unevenly, with some members not on appropriate distribution lists or not capable of receiving messages as easily or swiftly as others. Third, individuals may not see the same information as salient if, for example, subject lines on email messages are not changed when new information is introduced into a threaded discussion or a problem or new issue is not properly highlighted. Fourth, individuals may differ in their relative speed in taking on tasks and responding to messages because of their own work styles, their differing sense of the priority of the project, their differing access to the technology, and the stability of the technology at their site. Fifth, individuals may be uncertain about the meaning of silence. Locally based subgroups may also form and cause divisions in the team as a whole.

A new rhetoric of digital expression

Finally, in this brief and obviously selective discussion of research directions, new technologies and a transformed setting for business require a new rhetoric of digital expression. In *The Economics of Attention*, Lanham (2006) uses a traditional rhetorical approach to build strategies for persuasion in the digital age, where the scarce commodity is not 'stuff'; we are drowning in stuff, in things. Instead, it's attention that's scarce, and allocating attention is a matter of style, what, for purposes of popular discussion, he calls 'fluff'. Lanham proposes that the new figure of speech for this age is *toggling*, a 'rhythm of attention' that alternates between the reality or substance being described and the surface description on the page or the screen. Readers sometimes look 'through' the expressive surface of text and visuals to see transparently to the substance and sometimes look 'at' to see an author's self-conscious, dramatic style and expression. Lanham extends his toggling metaphor to larger issues of substance and style and, in doing so, presents a sweeping and complex rereading of business, political and artistic phenomena.

For universities, traditionally creators and repositories of knowledge, the shift to an attention economy means that the arts and letters, which teach how to 'attend to the world' (Lanham 2006: 14), trade places with engineering and sciences as modes of formal inquiry. 'The design of an object. . .becomes as important as the engineering of the object. The "positioning in the market" of an object, a version of applied drama, will be as important as either one' (Lanham 2006: 14). Visual artists are the new economists, according to Lanham. For them, the 'locus of art' has become not the object but the response, the 'attention it required' (Lanham 2006: 15). 'Design school, perhaps combined with library school, may be a better preparation for the felt realities of current business life than the MBA mills dedicated to the economics of stuff. Or, perhaps even better, a degree in the history of drama' (Lanham 2006: 19).

Lanham, among other researchers, also argues for a new definition of property (including intellectual property) afforded by the internet. Property in the stuff economy can have only one owner and can be used up when shared, a condition Lanham cites Garrett Hardin for memorably noting in his essay 'Tragedy of the Commons'. When villagers use the common ground of a community for grazing their sheep, they use it up. Lanham argues a new theory of the 'comedy of the commons' created by the web. In the digital economy, the commons becomes 'an ever-richer community resource. The more people graze on it for their own purposes, the bigger it becomes. . . .It thus combines the power of a free market, where individual gain leads to collective benefit, with the cooperative ownership of the cultural conversation' (Lanham 2006: 13).

Another leading US public intellectual and researcher, Lawrence Lessig (2004), however, calls attention to the limits that corporations and legislative bodies place on this free exchange for their own proprietary gain. Lessig, like Lanham, emphasises the importance of the social base for creativity. In doing so, both focus on how entrepreneurs, writers, artists and others appropriate and reuse materials to create new products and concepts, a process greatly aided by computer technology. This process has come to be called 'remix', a term originally referring to how audio engineers use technology to rearrange, add to or subtract elements in a musical composition to create adaptations of a song. More broadly, 'remixing' applies to any gathering of items from a variety of sources in a new composition. But the tug of war between individuals who seek to use these items and the corporations that want to limit their use continues to put limits on the freedom of the internet.

At a different, surface level of expression, Lanham analyses type and style as attention structures. He contrasts the possibilities of linear print text with digital expression in which text, images, motion and sound can all be generated by the same digital code. Digital expression greatly enhances the choices one can make about how to express information and fosters heightened stylistic self-consciousness. Like Henry (2000) and other postmodern cultural theorists, Lanham argues that what he calls a CBS (clarity-brevity-sincerity) approach to expression, perhaps appropriate to an industrial economy, will not work in the digital environment. To be persuasive online, individuals need to encourage social relationships and interactivity. That encouragement requires an attitude more common in an oral than in a written approach.

New media are thus leading to new forms of literacy in the academy and in the workplace. Many US researchers are studying and developing those new literacies (e.g. Lankshear and Knobel 2006; Selber 2004; Johnson-Eilola 2005). For example, Johnson-Eilola is looking at the potentials for automated interactivity, a term he uses to suggest how a text can, in effect, read its reader. Through the convergence of manufacturing, identification and location technologies, like global positioning and universal product codes, a text inscribed on an object could track its lifetime and its owner's use.

New media provide tremendous challenges – and hold tremendous promise – for individuals as they communicate in the era of Globalisation 3.0 (Friedman 2005). These media underlie each research direction cited in this brief discussion: interdisciplinary methods, emphasis on individual communication, new concepts of an organisation, and a new rhetoric of digital expression. North American researchers and practitioners will thus continue to pay attention to them as they seek ways to enhance communication in the global workplace.

References

Adler, N. J. (2002) *From Boston to Beijing: Managing with a World View*. Cincinnati: South-Western.

Argenti, P. (2005) *Corporate Communication*, 4th edn. New York: McGraw-Hill Irwin.

Carliner, S., J., P. Verckens and C. de Waele (eds) (2006) *Information and Document Design: Varieties on Recent Research*. Amsterdam and Philadelphia: John Benjamins.

Cramton, C. D. (2002) Finding common ground in dispersed collaboration. *Organizational Dynamics*, 30(4): 356–67.

Deal, T. E. and A. A. Kennedy (1982) *Corporate Cultures: The Rites and Rituals of Corporate Life*. Reading, MA: Addison Wesley.

Early, P. C. and E. Mosakowski (2000) Creating hybrid team cultures: An empirical test of transnational team functioning. *Academy of Management Journal*, 43(1): 26–49.

Friedman, T. (2005) *The World is Flat: A Brief History of the 21st Century*. New York: Farrar, Straus, and Giroux.

Henry, J. (2000) *Writing Workplace Cultures: An Archaeology of Professional Writing*. Carbondale: Southern Illinois University Press.

Herrmann, A. F. (2007) Stockholders in cyberspace: Weick's sensemaking online. *Journal of Business Communication*, 44(1): 13–35.

Jackson, M. (2007) Should emerging technologies change business communication research? *Journal of Business Communication*, 44(1): 3–12.

Johnson-Eilola, J. (2005) *Datacloud: Toward a New Theory of Online Work*. Cresskill, NJ: Hampton Press.

Lanham, R. A. (2006) *The Economics of Attention: Style and Substance in the Age of Information*. Chicago: University of Chicago Press.

Lankshear, C. and M. Knobel (2006) *New Literacies: Everyday Practices and Classroom Learning*, 2nd edn. Maidenhead and New York: Open University Press.

Lessig, L. (2004) *Free Culture*. New York: Penguin.

Miller, C. R. and D. Shepherd (2004) Blogging as social action: A genre analysis of the Weblog. In L. J. Gurak, S. Antonijevic, L. Johnson, C. Ratliff and J. Reyman (eds), *Into the Blogosphere: Rhetoric, Community, and Culture of Weblogs*. http://blog.lib.umn.edu/blogosphere, accessed 28 December 2004.

Mumby, D. K. (2007) Organizational communication. In G. Ritzer (ed.), *The Encyclopaedia of Sociology*. Oxford: Blackwell.

Sauer, B. (2006) Living documents. In J. B. Scott, B. Longo and K. V. Sills (eds), *Critical Power Tools: Technical Communication and Cultural Studies*. Albany, NY: SUNY Press, 171–94.

Scott, J. B., B. Longo and K. V. Sills (2006) *Critical Power Tools: Technical Communication and Cultural Studies*. Albany, NY: SUNY Press.

Selber, S. (2004) *Multiliteracies for a Digital Age*. Carbondale, IL: Southern Illinois University Press.

Simmons, W. M. and J. T. Grabill (2007) Toward a civic rhetoric for technologically and scientifically complex places: Invention, performance, and participation. *College Composition and Communication*, 58(3): 419–48.

Simoff, S. J. and F. Sudweeks (2007) The language of leaders: Identifying emergent leaders in global virtual teams. In K. St.Amant (ed.), *Linguistic and Cultural Online Communication Issues in the Global Age*. Hershey, PA: Information Science Reference, pp. 93–111.

Thomas, G. F. (2007) How can we make our research more relevant? Bridging the gap between workplace changes and business communication research. *Journal of Business Communication*, 44: 283–96.

Turner, J. and N. L. Reinsch, Jr. (2007) The business communicator as presence allocator: Multicommunicating, equivocality, and status at work. *Journal of Business Communication*, 44(1): 36–58.

Yates, J. (1993) *Control through Communication: The Rise of System in American Management*. Baltimore: Johns Hopkins University Press.

Yates, J. (2002) Genre systems: Structuring interaction through communicative norms. *Journal of Business Communication*, 39: 13–35.

Yates, J. (2005) *Structuring the Information Age: Life Insurance and Technology in the Twentieth Century*. Baltimore, MD: Johns Hopkins University Press.

Yates, J., W. J. Orlikowski and K. Okamura (1999) Explicit and implicit structuring of genres in electronic communication: Reinforcement and change of social interaction. *Organization Science*, 10: 83–103.

Zachry, M. and C. Thralls (eds) (2007) *Communicative Practices in Workplaces and the Professions: Cultural Perspectives on the Regulation of Discourse and Organization*. Amityville, NY: Baywood.

4

Discourse, communication and organisational ontology

Boris H. J. M. Brummans, François Cooren and Mathieu Chaput

Introduction

Social theorists have long been preoccupied with the question of what an organisation (or what organising) is. This chapter looks at the way research conducted in business discourse studies and organisational communication studies can inform this question of *organisational ontology*. To start, we briefly look at business discourse research – and organisational discourse research more generally – and foreground some key issues that merit further inquiry. In turn, we develop a theoretical perspective, grounded in recent organisational communication research, which tries to address these issues by offering a lens that allows researchers to analyse how an organisation comes into being and continues to be. To illustrate this perspective empirically, we present an analysis of the way interactions during a large forum enabled the 'birth' of a new political party. We conclude with a discussion on the implications of our perspective for future research.

Business discourse and organisational ontology

Rooted to an important degree in applied linguistics, one of business discourse research's main aims is to understand how social actors 'do business' through talk and text in business presentations, meetings, negotiations and so on (e.g. Bargiela-Chiappini and Harris 1997; Poncini 2004). By comparing these types of interactions across cultural contexts, scholars in this field show the intimate connections between language, culture and organising. Arguably, the force of business discourse research lies in its attention to the detailed ways in which actors use language in everyday settings in various cultures and, in so doing, accomplish particular social orders. In this sense, it shows similarities with organisational research that is ethnomethodological in nature, in particular conversation analysis (e.g. Boden 1994). However, it tends to be broader than 'pure' conversation analysis (e.g. Drew and Heritage 1992), paying attention to the larger contexts in which interactions take place (Sillince 2007), for example by drawing on genre theory (Kankaanranta 2006).

An important starting point for organisational research grounded in conversation analysis is the notion that organisations are 'ultimately and accountably talked into being' (Heritage 1984: 290). This idea formed an important point of departure for Boden's (1994) book *The Business of Talk*, which argued that 'the structuring properties of turn-taking [in conversations] provide the fine, flexible interactional system out of which institutional relations and institutions themselves are conjured, turn by turn' (p. 74). Hence, the book showed how an organisation is really a set of layered, interweaving ('laminated') conversations, structured through 'membership categorizations' ('manager', 'employee', etc.) used by organisational agents to account for the social order they enact.

Boden's work can be critiqued, first of all because it tends to overlook how agents' micro-discursive practices 'scale up'; that is, how communication enables them to act together as an organisation by putting a particular collective discourse into practice through various forms of interaction (see Cooren et al. 2007; Letiche 2004; Sillince 2007; Taylor and Van Every 2000). As some organisational discourse scholars have recently argued, organising happens through talk in micro-interactions, but it is also discursive in a much larger sense, where 'discourse' implies the use of text – in a broad sense – in context (Letiche 2004; Sillince 2007). Others have pointed out that organising implies more than socially constructing and interpreting the symbolic and, more specifically, the linguistic, textual or discursive (Cheney and Ashcraft 2007; Cooren 2004, 2006; Cooren et al. 2007; Letiche 2004). This research forms part of a growing debate in organisation studies about the role of materiality in organising (see special issue 12(3) of *Organization*) and intersects with Gumbrecht's (2004) claim that the social sciences and humanities tend to privilege the construction and interpretation of meaning when it comes to understanding how human beings are in, and experience, the world.

Building particularly on the work of Gumbrecht, Cooren and Letiche, we believe that the privileging of the discursive (the use of text in context) leaves an important part of the spectrum of human organisational experience out of sight and presents a limited view on the way an organisation is constituted. In this chapter, we take the stance that discourse of course plays an important role in the way human beings make sense of, and experience, the (organisational) world (Fairhurst and Putnam 2004), but that this sensemaking and experience are also influenced by other 'things' whose existence is not *only* dependent and defined by discourse. For example, the way employees experience an organisational leader may depend on the use of text in context, but also on his or her looks, the materialities of the organisational environment in which people operate; and so forth.

Based on this idea, we use Cooren and colleagues' earlier research to develop and empirically demonstrate a perspective that may help scholars refine their study of how organisations are enacted through interactions, and how subtle relationships between individual human and nonhuman agents and an organisation as a collective agent come about through the mobilisation of discourse and materialities in specific settings. We hope this perspective will allow scholars to rethink what, and how, an organisation *is*, in the most literal sense. Since our view is influenced by actor-network theory (ANT), we begin our discussion with a brief introduction to this theory (for a more extensive introduction, see Latour 2005).

Organisational ontology through the lens of presentification: actor-network theory as a point of departure

In the 1980s and 1990s, several scholars, among them Latour (1996) and Callon (1986), developed ANT, a social theory that conceives of the world as consisting of various configurations or networks of human agents (CEOs, housewives, factory workers, professors) and nonhuman ones (computers, documents, buildings, trees, mammals, tools). Similar to Tarde's (1895/1999), their goal was to create an approach to the study of social life that would no longer put human beings at the centre of the universe, as so many social theories had done (and do), but would show how the world is enacted through interactions between various agents (see Latour 2002) – an agent being anything that, or anyone who, 'makes a difference' (Cooren 2006: 82) in the ongoing stream of experience.

A good illustration of the view purported by ANT was given by Callon (1986), who studied an actor-network that revolved around the cultivation of scallops in the Saint Brieuc Bay. Callon mentioned that, having discovered an artificial way to cultivate scallops in Japan, French scientists joined with representatives of the Saint Brieuc Bay fishery in France to counter the declining scallop catches in this region. All seemed well, except that the scallops 'refused to "collaborate"' (Cooren and Taylor 1997: 241) by attaching themselves to the installed breeding collectors. As Callon observed, in this situation, the scientists and fishery representatives could be seen as agents, yet so could the scallops. Other human and nonhuman agents also made a difference: the sea, a nonhuman agent subjected to experimentation; the local fishermen and women, human agents; or the breeding collectors, nonhuman ones.

While Callon's example fittingly illustrates the notion that the world is a large arena of interlinking actor-networks, it simultaneously points out ANT's limitations. First of all, ANT's distinction between human and nonhuman agents is problematic, for it defines nonhuman agents in the light of human ones and thereby circumvents the very question of what it means to be human *and* what it means to be an agent. Although we adopt this duality in this chapter to stay faithful to the ANT literature (and for lack of a better alternative), it is important to note that human agents often seem to be defined in the light of *non*human ones. For example, a news reporter stated recently that there is little difference between cops and guns if cops shoot reflexively. In this case, *both* are seen as agents in the sense that they make a difference in the unfolding of social life by acting like machines. Likewise, dictators or psychopaths are often referred to as 'monsters' or 'animals', suggesting that humans can act just like nonhumans. Examples like these indicate that it is often far from clear to what terms like 'human' and 'nonhuman' refer because this opposition, like any, is always already 'in deconstruction' (Derrida 1976). Consequently, how social life is constituted and enacted always depends on (1) the way agency is conceived (What does it mean to be an agent? What does 'making a difference' mean? What does it mean to 'have the capacity to exert power, authority, or influence'?); and (2) the way this agency is conceived in a chain of human and nonhuman agents (Where does the chain begin and end? What or who is included or excluded? Why?; Cooren 2006; Brummans 2006). A second limitation is that, while it has offered an intriguing view on social life as a plethora of intersecting actor-networks, ANT analyses have overlooked the role of communication in processes of organising (see Taylor and Van Every 2000).

We believe that addressing both these issues is necessary to proffer an informed response to the question of what and how an organisation is, and aim to achieve this by framing organisational ontology through the lens of what we call 'organisational presentification'.

Organisational presentification

To understand how an organisation's ontology is (re)constituted in interactions, it is important to consider that not only individual agents play a part in the enactment of social life, but also collective ones. In Callon's example, the French government can be seen as a collective agent because it allowed and encouraged the experimentation by funding the scientists' research project. In addition, these scientists mainly operated as a group, another collective agent. Cooren and Taylor (1997) highlighted exactly this idea, yet pointed out more specifically that organising, acting together in view of specific aims constituted through continuous retrospective sensemaking (Weick 1979), occurs through communication. Communication allows human agents to (1) *mobilise* human and non-human agents into a specific configuration or network of agents (e.g. an organisation like Microsoft, Coca-Cola, or the United Nations); (2) *translate* individual agents' interests into the common interests of the entire network, so that the agents communicate (speak, write, act) *on its behalf* or *in its name*; and, in turn, (3) act as a collective agent vis-à-vis other ones.

As we have already stated, while ANT claims to re-establish a form of symmetry between human and nonhuman agents, it still seems to privilege *humans* as the principal agents who mobilise an actor-network – the same critique holds true for Cooren and Taylor's 1997 article. However, we believe that nonhuman agents are able to do this as well, and that mobilisation really is a matter of *communication* – in the Latin sense, from *communicare*, 'to make common' (see also Letiche 2004) – between human agents and nonhuman ones. For example, one could say that an erupting volcano mobilises a fire brigade (as a collective agent), or that an epidemic mobilises Doctors Without Borders (as a collective agent) in Ethiopia. Perhaps it is only in terms of translation that human agents 'outperform' nonhuman ones. However, even here one could argue that nonhuman agents play an important role, for translation, originating from the Latin *transferre*, 'to bring or carry over', involves communication between human agents, but also between human and nonhuman ones.

In fact, while it seems, at first sight, that translation (and mobilisation) always depends on human intention, it may also occur as an unintentional effect of communication (see Cooren and Taylor 1997). Looking at a group of gorillas, for instance, one could say that representatives of the Dian Fossey Gorilla Fund International translate these animals' interests when they act on the animals' collective behalf and protest against deforestation. Nevertheless, in a way, the gorillas also translate the representatives' interests because *they* give these individual human agents and their organisation as a collective agent a *raison d'être*. Thus, the gorillas can just as well be said to act on behalf of the humans, even if they are, supposedly, unaware of it. Hence, when looking at a social situation, it is important to ask: who or what is able to make a difference in the way a situation is defined and enacted – 'framed' (Goffman 1974)? Perhaps the national government promoting deforestation is able to convince the public that *it* is the principal agent, not the gorillas. However, by simply being in the world, roaming around in the jungle, the gorillas may also 'convince' the public that *they* are the principal agents – the ones that 'count' or make *the* difference. Seen in this way, how a situation is understood is always a matter of communication, which involves the way agents intentionally and unintentionally mobilise other agents (gorillas mobilising the Dian Fossey Gorilla Fund International; President Bush mobilising the US army in Iraq; professors mobilising textbooks to teach courses) and translate their interests, thereby (re)constituting and transforming actor-networks and creating a *certain* sense of who and what they are.

In this chapter, we thus take the idea of mobilisation a step further than Cooren and Taylor (1997) did, arguing that, by mobilising agents and translating their interests, communication allows individual agents to present themselves in everyday life (Goffman 1959), but also, and mostly in tandem, collective ones. We will denote this ongoing process of making something or someone present in time and space by using the term 'presentification' (Cooren 2006). In turn, we argue that what we are or what an organisation *is*, in the most literal sense of the word, depends on how communication between agents allows 'us' or 'it' to be embodied or 'incarnated' in a certain way. That is, if something or someone is indeed made present, it means that it was somehow embodied or incarnated. The incarnation that enables presentification occurs through the interplay between spoken and written language (conversations, speeches, documents, memos, posters) nonverbal language (gestures, symbols), context (circumstances, previous interactions) and materialities (costumes, buildings, desks, computers). For example, the Microsoft Corporation exists, and continues to exist, through a plethora of incarnations that allow it to be presentified (and thus be experienced) in a certain way. Instances of such presentification can be seen when Bill Gates presents the corporation's annual strategic plan to its shareholders (using a computer and software that his corporation manufactured) or when employees react to this presentation and change their ways of doing things (or resist it). Hence, it is through presentification that an organisation *identifies itself*, and *becomes* or *is identified*. It establishes an organisation's '-ness', as in the 'Microsoft-ness' of Microsoft or the 'United Nations-ness' of the United Nations; that is, what it means to be *this particular* organisation, and in what way being this organisation makes a difference in a chain of agents whose boundaries are continuously negotiated and renegotiable.

To illustrate how the perspective we have developed can be used to study the constitution of an organisation's ontology we will provide a brief empirical analysis of a specific moment in time in the history of Québec Solidaire, a new political party in the Canadian province of Québec. This organisation's presentification had been occurring for a while through meetings in which human agents tried to mobilise human (e.g. by trying to persuade each other about certain key characteristics or insinuating liaisons between certain individuals) and nonhuman agents (e.g. using notepads, fancy PowerPoint presentations, computer screens, projectors, meeting halls, tables set up in a specific shape), and tried to translate individual *human* interests, in particular, into the interest of the collective agent they were creating (e.g. by suggesting that Québec needed a party like the one they were about to 'officialise'). Through regular meetings like these, members developed a written document, called 'The Declaration of Principles', which stated the main values of the party and served as a way to identify the organisation vis-à-vis other organisations (other parties such as the Parti Québécois). The declaration stated: 'We are ecologists. We are from the Left. We are democrats. We are feminists. We are alter-globalists. We are from a province with a plurality of origins. We are for a sovereign province based on solidarity', and was regularly projected on screens and shouted out loudly and vigorously in meetings (accompanied by hand-clapping and cheering). This mobilisation of verbal language non-verbal language and materialities all helped to incarnate the party's identifying features vis-à-vis a particular historical setting, to give it a 'form' that could be experienced as being present, debated, loved, hated and so on.

As far as context was concerned, Québec Solidaire's creation involved the fusion of a political party (Union des Forces Progressistes) and a political movement (Option Citoyenne) in an ongoing attempt to unify the left as a collective agent in Québec's political arena vis-à-vis parties that constituted the increasingly powerful right. Those creating the party saw its formation as an important event in the province's political history, turning, maybe for the first time, the forces of the left into an 'unavoidable' contender for the other major parties.

The brief analysis we present focuses on only one aspect of Québec Solidaire's ongoing process of presentification, which became particularly clear during one meeting (as we stated, many meetings we did not analyse preceded this moment): the *naming* of the party. In other words, the analysis demonstrates how naming the collective agent 'Québec Solidaire' enabled *it* to become present as a collective, which, in turn, allowed it to be made present again and again – to be '*re*presentified' – until this day. Although it is only one aspect, we believe that naming is an important facet of organisational presentification, because it allows agents to communicate on behalf of, or in the name of, a collective *nomen* (Cooren and Taylor 1997; see also Argyris and Schön 1978). In line with Austin's (1962/1975) and Searle's (1969) speech act theory, we argue that the act of naming plays a vital role in the way an organisation's birth or incarnation is accomplished. We believe though that the *tour de force* of creating something (like a collective or the US Declaration of Independence; see Derrida 1986) through naming, which then starts to 'haunt' many agents, involves numerous acts of *presentification* rather than only '*speech* acts'. That is, the collective is a communicative effect, which springs forth from the interactions between a plurality of agents acting on each other's behalf – and in each other's name. Hence, by focusing our analysis on this aspect of presentification we do not mean to imply that 'Québec Solidaire' is *just* a name; on the contrary, it is a plethora of incarnations (its main office building, its representatives throughout Québec, the logo that can be seen throughout the streets of Québec prior to elections) that make the organisation present in a certain way. As an actor-network, an organisation is thus a sort of leviathan (Callon and Latour 1981), portrayed by Hobbes as a creation composed of many beings, a monster with many heads, mouths, limbs, and brains; a notion, which suggests that an organisation *is*, literally, many things (Cooren et al. 2005).

To investigate the presentification of Québec Solidaire, key meetings between principal agents over a prolonged period of time were filmed. We realise that our own presence with a camera is likely to have affected how the organisation's presence was *co*produced. However, like many researchers, we took this 'double hermeneutic' (Giddens 1984) as a given of undertaking interpretative research. Nonetheless, while filming, we remained 'passive' observers and did not 'actively' participate in the ongoing interactions. The verbal interactions were transcribed. Whenever we observed nonverbal, material or contextual aspects that we deemed important for these interactions, we included these observations in the transcript. In view of our 'plurified conception of organising' (Cooren et al. 2005), innumerable interactions between agents could be included in our analysis.

In accomplishing this task, a researcher evidently faces practical limits, which brings us to an important point concerning the 'operationalisation' of the concept of presentification: a researcher's decision about where to 'cut' the chain of agencies when studying the organising of a particular actor-network (i.e. who and what to include and exclude as agents involved in the process of organising) has important ethical implications for the way this process is understood (Brummans 2006).

Québec Solidaire's presentation

For the meeting we analysed almost a thousand delegates from the fusing political party and movement gathered to deliberate on, and then vote for, the party's name. Four names had been proposed prior to the meeting: 'Québec Solidaire', 'Union Citoyenne', 'Union Citoyenne du Québec' and 'Union des Forces Citoyennes'. Before the meeting started, there was clearly something 'in the air', a visceral sense of excitement, which expressed itself through people speaking enthusiastically, moving around actively and (some) anxiously, ruffling papers and so forth. It seemed there was a discernible sense of anticipation, which seemed to be amplified by many nonhuman agents (the large old auditorium built in Graeco-Roman style; the squeaking of standing microphones; a large projection screen behind the stage where the chair of the meeting and other delegates were going to sit). This was the meeting in which the party would be named, a name *with* which they would have to live 'for the rest of [their] existence', as one delegate adamantly stated in the first excerpt we will discuss. Through his communicative act, the delegate reacted to the chair's proposition to suspend deliberations and immediately start with voting for the four names that had been proposed (transcripts were originally in French):

Excerpt 1

112	Delegate:	[I do not agree because I think we have arrived at an extremely important anchor point. We are going to have this name for the <u>rest</u> (moving
113		
114		right hand up and down to stress his point; fixing eyes, suggesting
115		focus) of our existence.
116		(Silence and then some people in the audience applaud.)
117	Delegate:	And (.) And we took time to decide on The Declaration of Principles,
118		we took time – we (moves right hand up and down to stress his point)
119		will take time on the statutes, and if it is necessary, we will have one
120		drink less at the party, we (moves right hand up and down to stress
121		his point; eyes fixed; stays in one place as if wanting to keep his posi-
122		tion) can prolong the length of this work session.
123		(Various reactions from the audience: applauding, cheering, and
124		some booing.)
125	Delegate:	Here, this proposition here, I know this is not your intention, Mr.
126		President, but we are going to live with it (moves right hand up and
127		down to stress his point) in the media, among citizens, when we will
128		have power, we will live with this name (moves right hand up and
129		down to stress his point).
130		(Laughing, cheering, and applauding by people in the audience.)

Excerpt 1 suggests that, by stating 'we are going to live with it' (line 126), the delegate implicitly treats the name to be chosen as a (future) agent that will be doing things on behalf of the organisation (i.e. 'express the values of the future party', 'provoke adherence to a new societal project', not shown in transcript), bringing to mind Cooren's (2004) observation that 'textual agents' (documents, memos, names, logos) play an important role in the unfolding of organisational life, yet pushing it further by showing that they incarnate some important aspects of the organisation. The example suggests that the name will act by making the party present (i.e., presentifying it) in a certain way, allowing party members to become identified through their *identification* with '*it*,' and via it with the organisation that is coming into existence. An interesting web of associations is therefore enacted between name (textual agent), party (collective agent) and individual (human) agents, each of whom comes to communicate *for each other*, and allows *each other* to be incarnated, representified, leading to a specific translation of interests.

The excerpt also shows how the delegate accounts for the way organising occurs (the way the meeting is done), as well as for the way the organisation will be through its name. Several nonverbal markers (the tone and volume of his voice; hand gestures; fixedness of eyes and posture) suggest that he is adamant about ensuring that time is set aside for deliberating the future party's name. Through these markers, everything happens as if a certain force and energy were made present or mobilised to support what he is putting forward. It is not only *he* who speaks, but also a certain passion that appears to be expressed through the gestures, posture, gaze and tone. But where does this passion come from? We could speculate, based on the way he acts, that if the speaker seems so adamant about the selection of the name, it is because this name will communicate on *his* behalf (i.e. in *his* own name), making both him *and* the organisation present in a certain way to whomever it will encounter (or whoever will encounter it).

It is moreover interesting to see how the speaker moves from speaking on behalf of 'himself' to speaking on behalf of the collective (the audience) by shifting from 'I' to 'we' (lines 112–13). In so doing, he turns himself into a spokesperson for the collective, something in which he apparently 'succeeds' because most of the audience members respond to his move by applauding and cheering (lines 116, 123, 130) – although some seem to disagree, because they boo. It is in part this form of nonverbal communication that allows a great many individual agents to accept this one speaker as one of *their* spokespersons and to incarnate themselves already as a collective; that is, to align themselves vis-à-vis each other through communication, and experience the collective agency that their communication has brought about. It is therefore through communicative acts like these that the web between name, party and individuals is enacted and stabilised, suggesting that a collective agent is an effect of interactions, but also one that *affects* interactions – in that it has to be dealt with and makes a difference – as soon as it is 'in effect' (again reminding us of Derrida 1986, who made a similar observation regarding the *tour de force* involved in the constitution of the US Declaration of Independence).

After other delegates had intervened, giving their opinions about the importance of a particular name, the deliberations 'saturated', and delegates increasingly seemed ready to vote for a definitive name. The voting was accomplished by mobilising (raising) a red card if someone was in favour of a particular name. Interestingly, the red cards were given only to those who were allowed to vote, and hence acted as agents that differentiated legitimate members of the future party from illegitimate ones (news media representatives, people from a television crew, researchers):

Excerpt 2

426	Chairman:	So I am now asking people to vote if they are in favor of Québec
427		Solidaire, raise your card (the chairman, visibly excited, speaks
428		from the stage behind a table, using a microphone).
429		(20.0)
430		(A visible majority of delegates raise their cards and move it
431		back and forth through the air, joined by euphoric shouts.)
432	Chairman:	Lower your cards.
433		(10.0)
434	Chairman:	Now listen, I think that it is a pretty close call.
435		(People in the audience laugh and mumble excitedly.)
436	Chairman:	I now ask, I now ask to vote <u>for</u> Union Citoyenne.
437		(5.0)
438		(A few delegates raise their card; people laugh and talk.)
439	Chairman:	No, listen. I think that every person here has the right to
440		express their vote, so I ask you to do the entire exercise. (1.0)
441		Thank you.
442		(Laughing and excited mumbling.)
443	Chairman:	Union Citoyenne du Québec.
444		(6.0)
445		(A few delegates raise their card; laughing and excited
446		mumbling.)
447	Chairman:	Thank you. Union Citoyenne des, Union des Forces
448		Citoyennes.
449		(3.0)
450		(Approximately a dozen delegates raise their card.)
451	Chairman:	Thank you. So, um, I proclaim that <u>Québec Solidaire</u>
452		<u>[will be the name of the party.</u>
453		(People in the audience stand up, shout, stamp their feet and
454		applaud; the sound is deafening and has an impressive emo-
455		tional impact.)
456		(3.0)
457	Spokesperson:	<u>Québec Solidaire! Québec Solidaire! Québec Solidaire!</u>
458		(Name repeatedly shouted by many people in the audience,
459		accompanied by rhythmic applause.)
460		(38.0)
461		(Shouts from people in the audience.)
462		(40.0)
463		(Name repeatedly shouted again by many people in the audi-
464		ence, accompanied by rhythmic applause.)
465		(30.0)

466	Spokesperson:	And so (2.0) so with (.) so with our Declaration of Principles
467		and with this name, we now officially have a new political party
468		(.) To us!
469		(Applause and shouts.)

From the entire meeting we analysed, we believe this passage offered the ultimate illustration of the way an organisation is presentified through communication. Note the euphoria that fills the room (shouting the new name, applauding) when people see that almost everyone acts as a collective by raising the red card at the same time in favour of the same name – something which, apparently, comes as somewhat of a surprise because, before voting, the chairperson suggested that it would perhaps be necessary to vote twice in case of a 'close call' between two names. It is thus as if people suddenly realise that the collective/party has come into existence, like Victor Frankenstein realising: 'It's alive!' In addition, the passage illustrates our earlier point that the speech act of *proclaiming* (line 451) or 'calling *out*' really is an act of presentification, accomplished through the mobilisation of spoken and written language and nonverbal signs, as well as material objects (microphones, chairs, an impressive auditorium, physical human bodies). Interesting also is the joint *repeating* of the name (by shouting it) after it has been chosen, creating the impression that all those present want to reinforce (representify) their new organisation's existence again and again.

Finally, after the euphoria has somewhat diminished, one of the two founding organisations' spokespersons makes an important concluding remark: 'And so, so with so with our Declaration of Principles and with this name, we now officially have a new political party. To us!' (lines 466–8). This remark suggests the belief that naming the organisation through various acts of presentification has *officialised* its existence. In addition, it exemplifies how naming plays a vital role in the 'consubstantialization' (Burke 1950/1969) between a newly 'born' collective agent and a great many individual ones ('To *us!*'), allowing all these agents to be identified in space and time by making them present in a particular way.

Implications

In this chapter, we have tried to show that, while language is an important force in the way social life (and organisational life more particularly) unfolds, it is not the only force. To broaden the study of an organisation's constitution, we developed a perspective that will hopefully encourage researchers to study the *experience* of an organisation in terms of its discursive and material aspects. As Laclau and Mouffe (1987) claimed, material objects exist independently of systems of symbolic relations, but their meaning becomes a function of a system of socially constructed rules within which they are integrated (what Laclau and Mouffe referred to as 'a discourse'). Going beyond this idea, we have attempted to illustrate that material objects are not agency-less; they act in that they make a difference just like other agents. Therefore, they are not simply 'at the mercy' of a particular discourse, but also allow 'it' to be made present. Hence, one could say that an organisation identifies itself, and is identified by, *a* discourse constituted through everyday discursive interactions over time (Fairhurst and Putnam 2004), but that an organisation is more than *just* a discourse (a linguistic construction) and that organising involves more than the use of language in context alone.

We hope that our analysis of Québec Solidaire's presentification has offered a convincing, albeit brief, illustration of this point. While this chapter does not allow us to provide a more extensive analysis of the way this organisation's everyday micro-communicative practices unfolded into an organisational ontology over time through various acts of presentification, it is not difficult to envision and conduct such an analysis. In fact, even in the few interactions we analysed, the seeds of Québec Solidaire's ontology could already be seen, for example, in the way speakers put great effort into defining the organisation's identity vis-à-vis other political organisations (other collective agents in the social arena).

Our idea of presentification suggests that individual agents presentify a collective agent, which, in turn, allows *them* to be presentified in a certain way. This does not mean that, in time, a collective agent starts to manage itself *by itself*. As we have argued, an agent is an agent only through communication with other agents. Nevertheless, a collective agent does make a difference in the unfolding of social life and thus, in a way, *manages* other agents – a point well illustrated by *The Corporation*, a recent book (Bakan 2004) and documentary (Achbar and Abbott 2005). Of course, the Enron 'monster', which, in the end, controlled many people's lives, or a Kafkaesque bureaucracy come to mind, but 'lighter' examples are conceivable as well: Apple Macintosh employees experiencing their organisation as being innovative and 'quirky' and hence feeling compelled to act in a quirky way and defend the corporation as such in public; or Disneyworld employees acting in line with the organisation's ontology by not taking off their costumes above ground. Clearly, there are also plenty of examples of individual agents who try to change an organisation's ontology because they feel it marginalises their way of being by (re)presentifying them in a certain way. In this chapter, we have tried to show how this scaling up and down between individual and collective/organisational ontology always occurs through communication, which allows various agents to mobilise and be mobilised, translate interests and have their interests translated.

Although we supported our ideas with only scarce empirical evidence and left much to the reader's imagination, we hope that the presentification lens we have developed will spark new ways of empirically studying how an organisation's ontology is constituted. Seen through this lens, for example, organisational identity/image become concepts that are 'in deconstruction' (Derrida 1976), in line with what Cheney and Christensen (2001) have recently argued. Moreover, our perspective sheds new light on the concept of organisational identification. From our perspective, organisational identification refers not so much to the inculcation of organisational decision premises (Tompkins and Cheney 1983) as to the process through which individual agents come to communicate on behalf of a collective agent (and vice versa) by presentifying it through various incarnations. We believe this conceptualisation approximates Burke's (1950/1969) notion of identification even more closely than the one Tompkins and Cheney (1983) proposed some twenty-five years ago. Finally, our perspective opens up new ground for studying the way an organisation's pervious boundaries are enacted (see special issue 57(1) of *Human Relations*). In the light of ANT, it is obvious that boundaries are experienced as real even if they are 'constructed' and thus continually negotiated, making it difficult to pinpoint what is 'inside' or 'outside' – or what is 'internal' or 'external' communication (see again Cheney and Christensen 2001). From our point of view, what and how an organisation *is* is a matter of 'cutting' the chain of agencies in a particular way, which has very particular consequences for the constitution of the world. In turn, it is by influencing this cutting that agents, whether human or non-human, individual or collective, can affect the way things are, and are organised.

References

Achbar, M. and J. Abbott (dirs.) (2005) *The Corporation* (film). New York: Zeitgeist Films.

Argyris, C. and D. Schön (1978) *Organizational Learning: A Theory of Action Perspective.* Reading, MA: Addison Wesley.

Austin, J. L. (1962/1975) *How to Do Things with Words.* Cambridge, MA: Harvard University Press.

Bakan, J. (2004) *The Corporation: The Pathological Pursuit of Profit and Power.* New York: Free Press.

Bargiela-Chiappini, F. and S. Harris (1997) *Managing Language: The Discourse of Corporate Meetings.* Amsterdam: John Benjamins.

Boden, D. (1994) *The Business of Talk: Organizations in Action.* Cambridge: Polity.

Brummans, B. H. J. M. (2006) The Montréal School and the question of agency. In F. Cooren, J. R. Taylor and E. J. Van Every (eds), *Communication as Organizing: Practical Approaches to Research into the Dynamic of Text and Conversation.* Mahwah, NJ: Lawrence Erlbaum, pp. 197–211.

Burke, K. (1950/1969) *A Rhetoric of Motives*, 2nd edn. Berkeley: University of California Press.

Callon, M. (1986) Some elements of a sociology of translation: The domestication of the scallops and the fishermen of St-Brieuc Bay. In J. Law (ed.), *Power, Action and Belief.* London: Routledge & Kegan Paul, pp. 196–233.

Callon, M. and B. Latour (1981) Unscrewing the big leviathan: How actors macro-structure reality and how sociologists help them do so. In A. V. Cicourel and K. Knorr-Cetina (eds), *Advances in Social Theory and Methodology: Towards an Integration of Micro- and Macro-Sociologies.* Boston, MA: Routledge & Kegan Paul, pp. 277–303.

Cheney, G. and K. L. Ashcraft (2007) Considering 'the professional' in communication studies: Implications for theory and research within and beyond the boundaries of organizational communication. *Communication Theory*, 17: 146–75.

Cheney, G. and L. T. Christensen (2001) Organizational identity: Linkages between internal and external organisational communication. In F. M. Jablin and L. L. Putnam (eds), *The New Handbook of Organizational communication: Advances in Theory, Research, and Methods.* Thousand Oaks, CA: Sage, pp. 231–69.

Cooren, F. (2004) Textual agency: How texts do things in organizational settings. *Organisation*, 11: 373–93.

Cooren, F. (2006) The organizational world as a plenum of agencies. In F. Cooren, J. R. Taylor and E. J. Van Every (eds), *Communication as Organizing: Practical Approaches to Research into the Dynamic of Text and Conversation.* Mahwah, NJ: Lawrence Erlbaum, pp. 81–100.

Cooren, F. and J. R. Taylor (1997) Organization as an effect of mediation: Redefining the link between organization and communication. *Communication Theory*, 7: 219–60.

Cooren, F., S. Fox, D. Robichaud and N. Talih (2005) Arguments for a plurified view of the social world: Spacing and timing as hybrid achievements. *Time and Society*, 14: 263–80.

Cooren, F., F. Matte, J. R. Taylor and C. Vasquez (2007) A humanitarian organization in action: Organizational discourse as an immutable mobile. *Discourse & Communication*, 1: 153–90.

Derrida, J. (1976) *Of Grammatology*, trans. G. C. Spivak. Baltimore, MD: Johns Hopkins University Press.

Derrida, J. (1986) Declarations of independence. *New Political Science*, 15: 7–15.

Drew, P. and J. Heritage (eds) (1992) *Talk at Work: Interaction in Institutional Settings*. Cambridge: Cambridge University Press.

Fairhurst, G. T. and L. L. Putnam (2004) Organizations as discursive constructions. *Communication Theory*, 14: 5–26.

Giddens, A. (1984) *The Constitution of Society: Outline of the Theory of Structuration*. Berkeley: University of California Press.

Goffman, E. (1959) *The Presentation of Self in Everyday Life*. New York: Anchor.

Goffman, E. (1974) *Frame Analysis: An Essay on the Organization of Experience*. Boston, MA: Northeastern University Press.

Gumbrecht, H. U. (2004) *Production of Presence: What Meaning Cannot Convey*. Stanford, CA: Stanford University Press.

Heritage, J. C. (1984) *Garfinkel and Ethnomethodology*. Cambridge: Polity.

Kankaanranta, A. (2006) 'Hej Seppo, could you pls comment on this!' Internal email communication in lingua franca English in a multinational company. *Business Communication Quarterly*, 69: 216–25.

Laclau, E. and C. Mouffe (1987) Post-Marxism without apologies. *New Left Review*, 166: 19–106.

Latour, B. (1996) On interobjectivity. *Mind, Culture, and Activity*, 3: 228–45.

Latour, B. (2002) Gabriel Tarde and the end of the social. In P. Joyce (ed.), *The Social in Question: New Bearings in History and the Social Sciences*. London: Routledge, pp. 117–32.

Latour, B. (2005) *Reassembling the Social: An Introduction to Actor-Network-Theory*. Oxford: Oxford University Press.

Letiche, H. (2004) 'Talk' and Hermès. *Culture and Organisation*, 10: 143–61.

Poncini, G. (2004) *Discursive Strategies in Multicultural Business Meetings*. Bern: Peter Lang.

Searle, J. R. (1969) *Speech Acts: An Essay in the Philosophy of Language*. London: Cambridge University Press.

Sillince, J. A. A. (2007) Organizational context and the discursive construction of organizing. *Management Communication Quarterly*, 20: 363–94.

Tarde, G. (1895/1999) *Monadologie et Sociologie*. Paris: Les Empêcheurs de penser en rond.

Taylor, J. R. and E. J. Van Every (2000) *The Emergent Organization: Communication as its Site and Surface*. Mahwah, NJ: Lawrence Erlbaum.

Tompkins, P. K. and G. Cheney (1983) Account analysis of organizations: Decision making and identification. In L. L. Putnam and M. E. Pacanowsky (eds), *Communication and Organizations: An Interpretive Approach*. Beverly Hills, CA: Sage, pp. 123–46.

Weick, K. E. (1979) *The Social Psychology of Organizing*, 2nd edn. New York: McGraw-Hill.

Part Two: Approaches and Methodologies

5

Rhetorical analysis

Mark Zachry

Introduction

As an approach to understanding discourse, rhetorical analysis is a methodology with a long tradition shared by scholars from various disciplines. The general focus of rhetorical analysis is to arrive methodically at insights into the performance of a communication event (or assemblage of events) through an investigation of select features of the event. In this regard, rhetorical analysis shares some characteristics with other analytical approaches like narrative analysis and content analysis. Rhetorical analysis, however, is specifically grounded in a particular set of ideas and theories drawn from the rhetorical tradition, which itself has a long and complex history. Rhetorical analysis, therefore, offers scholars a principled approach to describing how communication worked in a given instance. Such descriptions are often productively layered with value judgements; in such configurations, rhetorical analysis is often called rhetorical criticism.

Background on rhetorical analysis

Scholarly work in rhetorical analysis has flourished in the last few decades. With the concurrent expansion of mass media and educational training through much of the world during this time period, interest in understanding how people respond to the multiple symbolic forms to which they are exposed has expanded. Many thinkers interested in such issues have turned to rhetorical concepts to make sense of the complicated relationship between people's beliefs and behaviours and the symbolic forms to which these individuals are exposed. The western tradition of rhetorical thought provides one source of ideas that have been particularly influential in such analytical efforts.

Rhetorical analysis is practised by scholars in many fields, but it has been most widely used by those in speech communication, writing studies, literary studies and biblical studies. Recently, scholars working in cultural studies have also found rhetorical analysis to be a productive framework for structuring their inquiries. Scholars from these fields and several others who specialise in rhetorical analysis as a way of creating knowledge about human communication often identify themselves primarily as rhetoric scholars. Rhetoric scholars typically focus their work on one context or another. So, for example, individual researchers may focus their work on the rhetoric of science, the rhetoric of technology or political rhetoric. Such specialisations are often associated with specific disciplinary fields. Scholars in professional communication, for example, who study communicative practices associated with business and industry have found rhetorical analysis to be a productive tool in their work.

Methods of rhetorical analysis

In a fundamental sense, rhetorical analysis relies on rhetorical theory to support the analyst's work. That is, rhetorical analysis depends upon concepts from rhetorical theory to underpin its framework for analysis. This framework, however, is complicated by the fact that rhetorical theory in itself represents a large and varied body of thought that originates in the ancient era and extends to the present day. Across this long history, people have proposed innumerable theoretical concepts and constructs to describe communicative practices. Consequently, rhetorical theory now represents an extensive and internally inconsistent body of ideas. The rhetorical analyst, then, must first select the subset of ideas from rhetorical theory that will be employed to support the analysis. As discussed below, this selection by the analyst holds implications for both the approach and scope of analysis that will be conducted.

In its basic approach, rhetorical analysis shares many characteristics with a range of textual analysis methods. It requires the analyst to consider both the overall communicative purpose of a text and how its constituent parts contribute to (or sometimes detract from) the realisation of that purpose. In so far as the analyst is identifying and labelling characteristics of the text, rhetorical analysis represents an empirical methodology. That is, part of rhetorical analysis requires that the analytical work be accountable to the presence (or absence) of textual elements that anyone trained in this form of analysis should be able to recognise when looking at the textual artefact(s) under consideration.

However, a complete rhetorical analysis requires the researcher to move beyond identifying and labelling in that creating an inventory of the parts of a text represents only the starting point of the analyst's work. From the earliest examples of rhetorical analysis to the present, this analytical work has involved the analyst in interpreting the meaning of these textual components – both in isolation and in combination – for the person (or people) experiencing the text. This highly interpretative aspect of rhetorical analysis requires the analyst to address the effects of the different identified textual elements on the perception of the person experiencing the text. So, for example, the analyst might say that the presence of feature x will condition the reception of the text in a particular way. Most texts, of course, include multiple features, so this analytical work involves addressing the cumulative effects of the selected combination of features in the text.

In the most general sense, rhetorical analysis follows the sequence of activities represented in Figure 5.1. This representation of rhetorical analysis is sufficient for understanding the broad work of the analyst. Representing individual instances of analysis, however, would often complicate this model. For example, it is conceivable that an analyst might be engaged in the activity described in activity (4) of Figure 5.1 and decide that it is productive to include yet another text in the analysis, which then returns a portion of the work to activity (1). So, while it is possible that some instances of rhetorical analysis might be

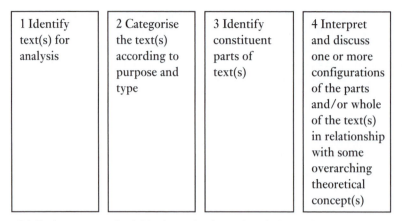

1 Identify text(s) for analysis	2 Categorise the text(s) according to purpose and type	3 Identify constituent parts of text(s)	4 Interpret and discuss one or more configurations of the parts and/or whole of the text(s) in relationship with some overarching theoretical concept(s)

Figure 5.1 Basic sequence of activities in conducting a rhetorical analysis

accurately represented as a linear sequence of activities, progressing from (1) to (4) it is not necessary that all instances conform to this linear sequence.

One of the key variables that shape an analyst's work is the configuration of rhetorical theory upon which the analyst draws. In a profound way, the theoretical perspective the analyst employs affects the nature of the analysis. To understand the implications of theory on the work of rhetorical analysis, it is useful to consider some of the broad theoretical perspectives that have predominantly characterised this work.

As it is practised today, rhetorical analysis typically relies on one of three general theoretical perspectives. So, while a survey of contemporary scholarly work employing rhetorical analysis would initially suggest significant variations from instance to instance, it is helpful to understand that the work most often belongs in one of three general categories:

1 traditional;
2 new rhetorical;
3 critical–postmodern.

An astute observer will readily note that many examples of rhetorical analysis do not fit completely into one or another of these categories. For example, analysts working from a critical–postmodern perspective are often likely to borrow freely from ideas associated with either or both of the traditional or new rhetorical perspectives. However, for the purpose of making sense of the general variations that exist in this area of scholarly work, these categories are useful.

Traditional

The first broad theoretical perspective underpinning rhetorical analysis can be classified as traditional in the sense that it includes ideas that precede the modern era and that have conditioned more recent thinking about the nature of rhetoric. This perspective includes the work of individuals from the classical era to roughly the beginning of the twentieth century. Within this broad timeframe, however, the ideas that have been most resilient and influential in rhetorical analysis are those associated with the classical period and specifically with Greek and Roman thinkers. Most notably, the contributions of Gorgias, Isocrates, Plato, Aristotle, Cicero and Quintilian have profoundly shaped scholarly understanding of rhetoric and its value in analysing communication. For rhetorical scholars, the variations between the ideas associated with these different figures are significant and the subject of a productive, ongoing body of scholarship. In terms of rhetorical analysis, however, the most influential figure here has been Aristotle, who offered a systematic theory of the means of persuasion. For many analysts working from a traditional theoretical perspective, the concepts and terms associated with Aristotle's *Rhetoric* represent the foundation of their work.

Of central importance to the work of rhetorical analysis is the recognition that people are able to persuade others to believe things through communication. How such persuasion occurs has always been a primary concern in rhetorical studies and is an issue productively considered by Aristotle and his contemporaries.

A defining characteristic of traditional rhetorical theory as it developed in ancient Greece is to explore how rhetoric works by identifying and defining its constituent parts. So, for example, Aristotle defined rhetoric by dividing it from dialectic and from other ways that humans can be compelled to believe something (e.g. through torture or physical coercion). Rhetoric in this configuration, then, is the use of artful, language-based means to effect belief. According to Aristotle, individuals persuade others through three means: the character or credibility of the source of communication (ethos), the stirring of emotion in the individual(s) being persuaded (pathos), or proof of truth (or apparent truth) through reasonable argument (logos). These three means of persuasion came to be known as the *rhetorical appeals* and are often a central organising principle for the work of a rhetorical analyst working from a traditional perspective.

In addition to identifying and describing these rhetorical appeals, Aristotle offers a classification system for *categories of rhetorical performances*. Following this scheme, rhetoric is productively understood as being either deliberative, forensic or demonstrative (epideictic). In its deliberative form, rhetoric is focused on the question of what should be done and is thus concerned with issues of expediency. Deliberative rhetorical performances are therefore oriented towards deciding future courses of action. Rhetoric in its forensic form concerns establishing what is just and unjust through judicial deliberations about things that have occurred. Consequently, its concern is assessing past events. Finally, the demonstrative or epideictic form of rhetoric is focused on establishing the merit of something for the public, such as whether a given individual deserves society's praise or censure. Demonstrative rhetoric is thus concerned with the present or that which is at hand. For rhetorical analysts, these categorical descriptions of rhetorical performances are often a productive means for making sense of communicative events and their relationship to the broadly shared experiences of others.

In addition to offering a means of categorising the varied types of rhetorical performances in which humans participate, Aristotle (like several other thinkers from the ancient era) considered the ways in which communication worked to lead people to think differently. Two prominent concepts through which classical rhetorical philosophers considered this issue are *two argumentative forms*: syllogisms and enthymemes. Syllogisms, which can be broadly defined as deductive, premise-based arguments, were considered to represent fully developed logical statements. For example, the following three-part argument represents syllogistic reasoning in which there is a major premise, minor premise, and logical conclusion:

> When interest rates are high, our firm does not borrow money for capital projects.
> Interest rates are at an all-time high now.
> Therefore, now is an unacceptable time to borrow money for a new construction project.

Enthymemes, by contrast, are arguments in which one or another of the premises is omitted. For example, the following two-part statement offers an enthymematic argument:

> Our local university has notified us that they have talented interns looking for workplace experiences next semester; therefore, we should consider if we have anywhere in the organisation where we might use the assistance of a student intern.

Such enthymematic arguments are more common than formal syllogisms in the day-to-day interactions of human communication. As any language observer can discover, enthymemes represent argument-based reasoning as it is most commonly practised; they are the informal, everyday arguments that allow people to reason pragmatically about their beliefs as they conduct their lives. The ability to understand and analyse enthymemes thus is central to the work of rhetorical analysts working from a traditional rhetorical perspective.

Beyond the level of analysing arguments, though, traditional rhetorical theory offers a framework for conceptualising the overall performance of a communicative act. This framework is represented in the idea of *the five rhetorical canons*. These canons, or loosely rule-bound categories of activities, are invention, arrangement, style, memory and delivery. The canons serve the needs of the analyst by organising the multiple points of consideration possible when the analyst is attempting to account for the totality of a rhetorical performance. In this regard, *invention* corresponds to the configuration of activities through which the originator of the communication decided upon what would be done in the instance of communication being analysed. *Arrangement* implies the strategically engineered form of the communication through which it achieves its results. *Style* entails the crafted use of linguistic forms for expression. *Memory* refers to recall of ideas for presentation and thus emphasises the performative nature of communication. *Delivery*, likewise, centres on the performative, but particularly focuses on the action of communicating. In different analytical contexts, one or some portion of these rhetorical canons may receive more attention than the others. All the canons, however, have proven generative in supporting the analytical work of rhetorical scholars working from a traditional perspective.

Finally, for rhetorical analysts working from the traditional perspective, a wealth of other concepts has been explored for providing different perspectives on understanding what is at play in a given communicative event. Extended catalogues of such concepts have been offered by rhetoric scholars over time, which suggests both the volume and robustness of this analytical approach. Among the most influential of these concepts is a group that originated in the ancient era and that continues to resonate in the work of analysts. *Kairos*, an ancient Greek term denoting an opportune time, has long been influential in thinking about rhetoric because it has provided analysts with a powerful concept for considering the timeliness of communicative events. *Topoi*, which also has its origins in ancient Greece, refers to the categories of ideas by which humans organise their thinking. For example, topoi include statements of definition, fact, causality and pledges as well as the testimony of witnesses. The ability to recognise and name the topoi present in a communicative event gives the analyst some measure of the inner operations of a given event. *Stasis* refers to understanding what is at issue in an argument. In analytical terms, it opens judgemental questions (conjectural, definitional, qualitative, translative) about the assumptions underpinning a rhetorical performance. Additional concepts from the ancient Greeks, like *techne*, *praxis* and *phronesis*, have also been deployed productively by rhetorical analysts, particularly as they situate the practice of rhetoric within human activity, investigating such issues as the place of skill, art and ethics in the practices of communication. Such areas of inquiry are strongly implied in the traditional perspective on rhetoric, even as they impinge on other areas of inquiry outside the realm of rhetoric itself. As rhetorical theory came to be developed in the new rhetorical and critical-postmodern forms discussed below, these divisions between areas of inquiry have been challenged in notable ways.

New Rhetorical

In the first half of the twentieth century, rhetorical theory began to be remade by a group of thinkers who recognised that the study of rhetoric had become increasingly impoverished over recent centuries. This impoverishment had developed on two fronts. First, for many, rhetoric had become closely associated with styles of elocution that had emerged in the predominantly oral popular culture that had flourished since the Renaissance. In other words, rhetoric became associated with devices of oral performance designed to delight or sway the minds of a popular audience. Correspondingly, in written communication, rhetoric had come to be associated with embellishment and the use of poetic devices by others to make texts more entertaining or appealing. The potential for rhetoric to be associated with such surface-level matters had been anticipated and thoroughly explored by thinkers in the ancient era; by the end of the nineteenth century, however, this association with what it meant for a text to be *rhetorical* was deeply rooted in the popular imagination.

Second, in juxtaposition with this conceptualisation of rhetoric as ornamentation, the serious communication associated with the work of industry and science had come to be considered arhetorical. That is, such communication was believed by many to be grounded in language that empirically corresponded with reality. As these assumptions were becoming deeply entrenched in popular thought, a handful of rhetorical theorists worked through the early and mid-twentieth century to re-establish rhetoric as a sophisticated framework for analysing and thus making sense of how human beliefs and behaviours are shaped by patterns of communicative practices as well as by discrete communication events.

Several thinkers participated in this revival of rhetorical inquiry and accompanying expansion of rhetorical theory. As prominent individuals such as Kenneth Burke,

Chaim Perelman and Lucy Olbrechts-Tyteca led the way, a host of others participated
in developing rhetorical analysis as the basis for increasing human understanding of the
complicated social movements and events that people faced as the new century unfolded.
For example, Perelman and Olbrechts-Tyteca collaborated on a theory of rhetorical argumentation that challenged the assumptions of logical positivism. They offered instead a
model of argumentation based on ethics and values, productively arguing that reality is
realised socially through rhetorical achievements that broadly structure human thinking.
Kenneth Burke's contributions to the new rhetorical perspective are even more numerous,
covering an extensive array of ideas about the use and misuse of language by humans. For
Burke, the ability to understand and analyse the social uses of rhetoric was powerful in
that it made it possible to understand the nature and reason(s) for human action. Humans'
uses of symbols defined their nature, according to Burke, but he also held the belief that
symbols used humans – affecting their behaviour in ways that required sophisticated tools
of analysis. His unique form of analysis was something he labelled dramatism, an analytical approach that continues to be productively used by scholars. At its most basic level,
dramatistic analysis requires the analyst to view human action as theatrical, discernible
in a pentad of interrelated elements: act, scene, agent, agency and purpose. Beyond this,
Burke contributed to the new rhetorical perspective by proposing a conceptual framework
for understanding the complicated relationship between human understanding and deeply
held beliefs (ideologies). According to Burke, human engagement with rhetoric – in terms
of both its production and its reception – is filtered through terministic screens. Such
screens metaphorically account for the fact that language does not correspond directly to
reality, but instead filters and selects.

   The inquiries of rhetorical analysts working from a new rhetorical perspective tend to
focus less on an exhaustive cataloguing of textual elements (as is sometimes the case in a
traditional approach) and more on understanding communicative events in complicated
social terms. In particular, these analysts do not limit consideration of how rhetoric operates to a consideration of types of text, or to linguistic textual features that prompt certain
responses for those experiencing the text. Instead, these analysts consider such matters
as complicated, historically conditioned relationships between language and reality, uses
of extra-textual symbols, and the interplay of communication events with the relentlessly
changing social conditions of humanity's day-to-day existence. With this integration of
rhetorical and social concerns, the process of rhetorical analysis becomes even less codi-
fiable than it was following a traditional perspective. At the same time, though, it also
becomes a more robust approach for gaining insight into the complicated relationship
between communicative practices and the beliefs and behaviours of people. Another major
perspective, the critical-postmodern, accounts for the final body of work in contemporary
rhetorical analysis.

Critical-Postmodern

In the final decades of the twentieth century, the work of rhetorical analysis was shaped in
complicated ways by work in critical-postmodern theory. Like many prominent thinkers
from the rhetorical tradition, those associated with critical-postmodern theory viewed
human knowledge as existing in the realm of the probable, or as being that around which
most people can be persuaded to believe. In other words, this theoretical perspective

marks a radically different way of thinking about truth and reality from those ideas that had dominated scholarly inquiry throughout much of recorded history. Two key additions that the critical-postmodern perspective has made to rhetorical analysis are a focus on how power is rhetorically constructed and a foregrounding of critique as an inherent component of analytical work.

Starting from the assumption that rhetoric constructs reality, analysts working from a critical-postmodern perspective have productively explored how specific uses of language codify and perpetuate what counts as real or the truth in society. Through strategic and pervasive uses of rhetorical practices, these analysts note, certain ideas and ways of thinking are privileged in society while others come to be perceived as abnormal, heterodox and even illogical. Power, thus, is inherent in such privileged uses of language because it adheres to the perceived order of things in society. Furthermore, for many analysts working from this perspective, the totality of humanity's designed existence is open to rhetorical analysis. That is, all objects shared by people in their lifeworlds are viewed as inherently symbolic and performative in the same sense as the texts that have traditionally defined communicative events for humans. It then follows that rhetoric (and by extension, rhetorical analysis) can be productively extended to read the whole social-symbolic matrix within which humanity exists.

An additional component of rhetorical analysis conducted from a critical-postmodern perspective is the practice of critique. According to analysts working from this perspective, this critique dimension of rhetorical analysis emerges from the recognition that all forms of analysis are built on processes of selection and repression. Such processes are inherently based on a system of beliefs or an ideology (though not one that is always recognised or acknowledged by the analyst) that perpetuates certain ways of seeing the world and suppresses others. For these analysts, foregrounding concerns such as democracy and social justice in analysis gives the analytical work an authentic relationship to humanity rather than to the perpetuation of some other artificial construct that serves an objectionable or at least dubious agenda. In this regard, some current rhetorical analysis has been informed by larger critical enterprises that are influencing the practices of knowledge-making in general.

It is worth noting here, too, that many analysts who employ a critical-postmodern perspective associate their ideas with those of the sophists of the ancient era. In particular, critical-postmodern rhetorical analysts find some correspondence between their ideas and sophistic notions of the relativity of knowledge and knowing as well as the inherent paradoxes in human reasoning. As was the case for the sophists in the ancient era, contemporary critical-postmodern analysts are often positioned in opposition to dominant theories of rhetoric and their value for the work of analysis.

Rhetorical analysis in professional communication scholarship: Two examples

In its varied forms, rhetorical analysis plays an important role in the construction of knowledge about professional discourse. In some instances, rhetorical analysis is combined with other scholarly approaches such as historiography or ethnography, enabling scholars to focus attention on some particular communicative event (or configuration of events) as they construct broader arguments. In other words, rhetorical analysis is often used as an embedded methodology in a larger study. Often, for example, rhetorical analyses are embedded in studies of genres in business and industry. In many instances, such studies combine rhetorical analysis with linguistic analysis to consider the features that character-ise a given genre (e.g. dos Santos 2002; Hyland 1998; Amernic and Craig 2004).

In some cases, though, rhetorical analysis is used as the primary methodological approach for developing insight into particular forms of business discourse. For example, rhetorical analysis has played a key role in studies of corporate strategies (e.g. Skerlep 2001), annual reports (e.g. Yuthas et al. 2002) and marketing materials or strategies (e.g. Ewald and Vann 2003; Martin 2007). It has also been employed often as a method for understand-ing different configurations of texts that define organisational discourse (e.g. Heracleous 2006) or the complex relationship between individual identities and organisations (e.g. Linstead 2005). In the field of public relations, different forms of rhetorical analysis have proven invaluable for understanding and developing corporate strategies (e.g. Moss 2003). Rhetorical analysis has also been explored recently as a means of understanding business and organisational communication in digitally mediated spaces, including email, intranets and business websites.

The power of rhetorical analysis for developing insight into the communicative prac-tices associated with business and industry is evident in two studies focused on notably different communicative events. The first is Sharon M. Livesey's examination of a four-part series of advertorials published by ExxonMobil in the *New York Times*. In this study, through which Livesey ultimately compares rhetorical analysis with discourse analysis, the analysis is based on a new rhetorical perspective. Specifically, she uses concepts drawn from the work of Burke to '[consider] the devices by which texts frame meaning, create understanding, and promote (or fail to promote) identification between rhetor and audi-ence, thus facilitating co-operative action' (Livesey 2002: 117). Her rhetorical analysis of these four advertorials as a complex communicative event begins by productively considering the dramatistic elements of the event. The 'scene,' for example, is presented in its social complexity, presented as an 'environmental crisis constructed by a growing coalition of scientists and world governments' (Livesey 2002: 127). The advertorials play in this scene, according to Livesey, by reshaping the identities of the actors involved. Through strategic uses of language, these texts '[alter] linguistic meanings and relation-ships in ways that reshape ExxonMobil's own and other actors' identities'. Following Burke's theory, the advertorials create 'shifting characterizations [that] promote different identifications and identities, blurring and confusing the capabilities, responsibilities, and effects of agents and acts' (Livesey 2002: 127–8). Through an examination of the moves ExxonMobil makes in different passages of the four advertorials, Livesey shows how the corporation works to realign identities within and assumptions about the whole global warming debate with the net effect of redefining the entire nature of the problem. As she illustrates, the rhetoric of the advertorials works to associate different ideas and values with key terms in the discourse, effectively altering motives in the drama of the global warming debate. Through this analysis, then, Livesey calls attention to how the sequence of advertorials engages in transforming and reversing rhetoric and, by extension, ways of thinking about the debate.

Illustrating yet another perspective on how rhetorical analysis is used in professional communication research, Hanne Nørreklit uses rhetorical theory to examine critically a business management tool, the Balanced Scorecard. Nørreklit employs rhetorical analysis as a means of investigating this popular tool for strategic managerial control of corporate accounting systems. The rhetorical analysis, however, does not focus on the Balanced Scorecard tool itself, but rather on how it was represented in a 'management guru text' entitled *The Balanced Scorecard* (Nørreklit 2003: 611). This analysis, then, is concerned with understanding the popularity of this managerial tool on the basis of its representation in a widely distributed book. To conduct this rhetorical analysis, Nørreklit employs various ideas from rhetorical theory to consider how the argument for using the scorecard is advanced in the book. In particular, the analysis draws from traditional rhetorical theory to consider how the book uses the appeals of ethos, pathos and logos, as well as how it employs specific forms of language or stylistic devices – analogies, metaphors, irony, abstraction and intertextuality – to advance these appeals. As the analyst documents, 'the text makes extensive use of analogies, metaphors and metonymy' for varied effects, which 'draws attention and appeals to both the emotions (*pathos*) and reason (*logos*)' (Nørreklit 2003: 603). As is typical in rhetorical analysis, though, Nørreklit interprets these empirical observations about the content of the text with an analysis of their deployment and effects. According to Nørreklit, the varied uses of these devices 'violates the rules of sound argumentation . . . in that a number of the analogies and metaphors employed are not very good images of the phenomena to which they refer' (Nørreklit 2003: 603). In essence, the rhetorical analysis here points to disingenuous communication that begins to account for the fact that the text could be both popular and flawed.

Nørreklit subsequently layers this analysis with a consideration of the forms of analytical arguments through which the authors of the book advance their argument. Drawing on the work of Stephen Toulmin, a philosopher who had developed a method of analysing how good arguments vary from field of study to field of study, Nørreklit examines the basic argumentative moves made by the authors of the book. This examination leads Nørreklit to conclude that the rhetorical justification for the Balanced Scorecard is not 'based on solid and unbiased reasoning and documentation'. Instead, this analysis suggests, 'the argumentation . . . appeals through *logos* on an untenable basis and appeals extensively through *pathos*. The argumentation is blurred by the stylistic devices used and by the authors' *ethos*' (Nørreklit 2003: 609). This example of rhetorical analysis is ultimately interesting because it illustrates how such analysis can be used to consider both how the authors of a text attempt to persuade, *and* how that analysis can be fashioned to yield a deeper insight about the text than would otherwise be possible if the text were judged only on the basis of its popularity.

The future of rhetorical analysis

As an approach to constructing knowledge about how human beliefs and behaviours are shaped by the symbolic forms with which they interact, rhetorical analysis remains a productive research methodology. Over the many centuries through which it has been practised, rhetorical analysis has proven to be a resilient tool for systematically making sense of how the texts and other designed forms communicate to people.

For researchers in professional communication, the possible applications for rhetorical analysis are seemingly limitless. For example, as digital technologies multiply and otherwise complicate our traditional assumptions about the nature of communication, rhetorical analysis seems to offer the flexibility needed for analysts to continue to develop insights for others. It is instructive to consider, for example, that rhetorical analysis emerged in the ancient world as a way of explaining persuasive oration. As the media through which communication (business and otherwise) became more expansive (including, for example, scribe-produced books, printing presses and duplicating machines), rhetorical analysis maintained its relevance. As communication is increasingly now distributed across networks and generated by algorithms rather than single authors, rhetorical theory continues to be developed.

An additional interesting front along which rhetorical analysis will develop is its incorporation of multiple and competing cultural perspectives. Whereas there are certainly efforts made to standardise the practices of communication in different industries and in multinational corporations, the globalisation of business and society promises to unfold in unpredictable ways that will be evident in our communicative practices. Theories of rhetoric, for example, are likely to have to be elaborated so that they are not dominated by western philosophy to the extent they have been over history.

The work of rhetorical analysis is likely to continue to be paired with other methods of investigation. In such pairing, rhetorical analysis may be embedded in large-scale studies, including those in which genre research, narrative research or even ethnographic methods play a dominant role. In other instances, studies primarily focused on rhetorical analysis will be likely to continue to borrow strategically from other methods, particularly as such methods are useful for enhancing the interpretative and critical needs of researchers.

In any discussion of rhetorical analysis, it is difficult to overstate the importance of the contributions to rhetorical theory made by thinkers from the classical era. However, as studies over the last few decades based on rhetorical analysis demonstrate, this approach to studying and understanding communication is not bound by outmoded ideas from the distant past. Rhetorical analysis is a vibrant and dynamic form of scholarly inquiry that holds promise for researchers in professional communication.

References

Amernic, J. H. and R. J. Craig (2004) 9/11 in the service of corporate rhetoric: Southwest Airlines' 2001 letter to shareholders. *Journal of Communication Inquiry*, 28(4): 325–41.

dos Santos, V. B. M. Pinto (2002) Genre analysis of business letters of negotiation. *English for Specific Purposes*, 21(2): 167–99.

Ewald, H. R. and R. Vann (2003) 'You're a guaranteed winner': Composing 'you' in a consumer culture. *Journal of Business Communication*, 40(2): 98–117.

Heracleous, L. (2006) A tale of three discourses: The dominant, the strategic and the marginalized. *Journal of Management Studies*, 43(5): 1059–87.

Hyland, K. (1998) Exploring corporate rhetoric: Metadiscourse in the CEO's letter. *Journal of Business Communication*, 35(2): 224–44.

Linstead, A. (2005) *Organization and Identity*. New York: Routledge.

Livesey, S. M. (2002) Global warming wars: Rhetorical and discourse analytic approaches to ExxonMobil's corporate public discourse. *Journal of Business Communication*, 39(1): 117–48.

Martin, G. (2007) *The Role of Exigencies in Marketing: A Rhetorical Analysis of Three Online Social Networks*. Saarbrucken: VDM Verlag Dr. Mueller e.K.

Moss, D. (2003) *Perspectives on Public Relations Research*. New York: Routledge.

Nørreklit, H. (2003) The Balanced Scorecard: What is the score? A rhetorical analysis of the Balanced Scorecard. *Accounting, Organizations and Society*, 28: 591–619.

Skerlep, A. (2001) Re-evaluating the role of rhetoric in public relations theory and in strategies of corporate discourse. *Journal of Communication Management*, 6(2): 176–87.

Yuthas, K., R. Rogers and J. F. Dillard (2002) Communicative action and corporate annual reports. *Journal of Business Ethics*, 41(1–2): 141–57.

6

Organisational discourse analysis

Rick Iedema and Hermine Scheeres

Introduction

This chapter provides an overview of the changes and innovations that we see in contemporary business organisations and their implications for employees. These changes and innovations involve new technologies, restructured product lines or services, and new managerial, professional and occupational tasks and responsibilities. What the research that is reviewed in this chapter suggests is that these developments manifest most dramatically in how employees relate to one another, what they say to one another, how much they say to one another, and how frequently they (have to) communicate with each other (Adler 2001; Child and McGrath 2001). For that reason, the focus of the chapter is on how changes within business organisations impact on employees in those organisations – not on the discourses of how people do business with one another across organisations.

To date, changes in business organisations have been discussed in terms of a rise in 'knowledge work' (Drucker 1993), or work that centres on the producing, sharing and applying of data and information. Businesses need 'knowledge workers' because of 'the informationalisation, networking, and globalisation of the economy' (Castells 2004: 218). But besides knowledge work being a domain in itself (like market analysis or stockbroking), knowledge work now increasingly permeates most businesses and all levels within a business, independent of whether their output is goods or services. Since knowledge often begets knowledge, the emphasis on knowledge work produces a positive feedback spiral. Knowledge creation leads to faster rates of organisational restructuring and production redesign, a phenomenon that is further fuelled by new technologies and in turn leads to new knowledge creation. Scholars have coined the term 'fast capitalism' to describe the rapidity with which these dynamics are played out (Armitage and Graham 2001; Gee and Lankshear 1995; Virilio 1986).

Fast capitalism has considerable consequences for who workers can be and what they can do and say. To accommodate increasingly rapid change, their traditional and static conceptions of time, self and work have to give way to ones that are more flexible. Think of the end of the 9-to-5 workday, the advent of flexitime, employment casualisation and the intrusion of work-related technologies into the home sphere. All these elements blur the boundaries between private self and work self. Castells sees these changes as going even further, because of to the way interpersonal styles of being and interacting are gaining increasing significance in the business workplace. It is not only assertiveness, initiative and adaptability that are increasingly valued at work, because emotional and listening skills are now also gaining predominance: 'the new economy increasingly requires the skills that were confined to the private domain of relational work to be brought to the forefront of the management and processing of information and people' (Castells 2004: 228). So, next to knowledge work as explanation for what is happening in the new economy, emotional labour is a notion used to shed light on new ways of feeling and relating in the workplace (Hochschild 1983). As businesses shift into flexible production, ongoing restructuring and improvement, and the search for product uniqueness, the impact on workers is that they spend more effort and time on rethinking work processes and on building relationships: 'even factory workers are said to require interpersonal and decision-making skills previously reserved for managers' (Barley and Kunda 2001: 77).

In the remainder of this chapter, we begin by fleshing out how discourse analysis has approached these developments. In the section that follows we take some time to review the literature that deals with social and organisational change. Following that, we move on to consider empirical evidence to make tangible what that literature talks about, and to pinpoint domains where discourse research has thus far not ventured. Besides illustrating that employees talk about their work in ways that were quite uncommon just a couple of decades ago (Gee et al. 1996), the data also bears out that staff do complex kinds of emotional work to make possible new practices, such as teamwork and project tasks. Against the backdrop of this analysis, we will sketch what a discourse analytical agenda looks like for the future, and how it can benefit the study of twenty-first-century business discourses and practices.

Background: Business discourse in the context of increasingly rapid product and organisational redesign

At the most general level, business and organisational discourse analysis takes two forms. On the one hand, there is the kind whose principal concern is to make generalisations about what characterises business organisational texts. These texts can be spoken, written, visual or in any other semiotic form. This discourse analytic approach seeks 'to outline the typicalities, the patterns and regularities, as well as the constraints and boundaries' that are visible in such texts, and it 'grounds its arguments in empirically derived [linguistic] data to make its claims' (Iedema 2003: 27). Researchers who deploy this kind of discourse analysis tend to postulate what linguistic features of specific texts are typical of business organisational discourse, and what discursive knowledge is needed to be able to reproduce those texts.

On the other hand, there is the kind of discourse research that seeks out tensions and differences in what businesspeople and employees say and mean. This approach is 'oriented towards uncovering possibilities of organisational change and innovation' (Iedema 2003: 27). By highlighting tensions and contrasts in what people do and say, meanings are revealed that might otherwise have gone unnoticed, and that can contribute to opening up new ways of working and doing business (Boje 2001).

One influential proponent of the first kind of discourse analysis is Norman Fairclough. He began to write about social and organisational change in the late 1980s (Fairclough

1992). At the time, his analysis provided a turning point for the analysis of discourse in social and organisational life. He was able to link discursive change to social and organisational change, and articulate dominant trends in business–employee relationships. He linked the analysis of business discourse into his claim that more and more aspects of social and interpersonal life are put to the service of capitalist production and income generation, with business activity increasingly colonising the employee's lifeworld (Habermas 1987). Fairclough's reasoning privileged a critical, dystopian narrative: capital and business developments follow a predictable and singular trajectory, reaching across employees' social and interpersonal lives until these are fully subsumed to the interests of business.

Given the current rate of social and organisational change, it is now time to reassess the principles that Fairclough began articulating over a decade ago. While his analysis provides an important perspective on contemporary discourse, it appears that the ground has begun to shift, and that the central assumption that inspires his work – (workplace) change can be explained as an increasing colonisation of people's personal lifeworld – is increasingly difficult to defend. Recent research suggests that Fairclough's base premise – the zero–sum opposition between employees' and businesses' interests – has begun to unravel because of how employees are and want to be implicated in how modern businesses do business and in what they produce. To be sure, we do not discount capitalism's power to destroy environments and marginalise people (Knights and McCabe 2003), but we can no longer maintain that employment in a business or business entrepreneurship per definition equates with a denial of ethics and self (Spinosa et al. 1997).

More recent depictions of the contemporary business organisation therefore outline rather different trends. And it is here that we encounter our second kind of discourse analysis – a kind that does not concern itself purely with linguistic regularity and discursive predictability, but delves into complexity for traces of new trends (Iedema 2007). In contrast to the former kind, this latter discourse analysis avoids predisposing the researcher to framing their analysis of (business) practice in dystopian (or, for that matter, utopian) terms. That is, this second approach regards (business) practice as harbouring a multitude of tensions and contradictions that are likely to be beneficial in some ways, less so in others. This second approach to discourse analysis defers judgement about what it studies and how it studies it. It is not concerned with privileging 'power and control' as lenses for understanding business discourse, and nor does it centre on identifying 'what works' as the discourse analytical answer to business success. Instead, this approach foregrounds what has thus far remained unnoticed. It does so by 'reading worldwide developments in non-obvious traces' (Iedema et al. 2007). How does this work?

Let us look at how this second approach unpacks one of the characteristics that we noted above was common to contemporary businesses: organisational change. Organisational change tends to be legitimated with reference to continuous improvement, learning and market responsiveness. We change to make things better, to enhance income, or to extend our power – all of which are overly simple explanations (Chia 1999). In reality, change has become 'the name of the game'. Business organisations change because this has become the norm: not changing is no longer a viable business option. This is not just because products become obsolete faster than ever before, or because competitors are able to revise their production streams thanks to more flexible technologies. In effect, change has become a resource in and for itself, a way of identifying the business and its up-to-date-ness. Nigel Thrift goes so far as to claim that 'No necessary progress or evolution is taking place in the field of business; rather the field is periodically restructured into a new configuration of profitability.' This new configuration, however, is itself 'nearly always unstable and can nearly always sustain only a certain amount of learning before events intervene and new patterns of learning become necessary' (Thrift 2004b: 876). On this analysis, business change is about establishing 'new kinds of economic credibility' (Thrift 2004b: 876) whose essence lies in being temporary.

In the modern business organisation, then, we find increasingly 'unstable interaction systems' (Deetz 2003). Employees have constantly to reinvent norms for working, relating, behaving and speaking. Here, it is difficult to locate clear trends and definable discourses as Fairclough could a decade and a half ago. What we can point to are *traces* of increasing frequency and intensity of communication in the contemporary business workplace. But what do such traces look like, discourse analytically speaking? Let us turn to two case studies to exemplify this analysis of 'non-obvious traces'.

Methodology: data collection and analysis

The first case study is based on research done by Hermine Scheeres during 1998 and 1999 (Scheeres 2004). As part of this research, she observed workplace practices in a local gaming machine factory, and this consisted of making regular tours of the factory floor, attending and tape-recording team meetings and training sessions. She also shadowed a team facilitator, building up a record of field notes in the process. The broader project of which this work formed a part sought to describe the communicative and discursive consequences of contemporary work and organisational change for employees (Scheeres 2004). For the purpose of the present discussion, we selected from among these sources transcript data of a problem-solving meeting involving frontline production staff.

Entrepreneurialising oneself

Extract 1 provides a record of a brief exchange during one of the frontline employees' team meetings. The team meeting is led by 'Carol', and it focuses on identifying problems affecting the production of gaming machines. The principle that underpins the meeting is 'problem-solving plus' (PSP), which is a technique enabling employees to address and solve recurring incidents.

Extract 1: Team meeting data; team leader Carol = C; TM1, 3, 5 and 6 = team members

1.1	C	Anyway. Let's just get back to
1.2	TM6	(laughs)
1.3	C	to do you want to go out there and actually talk to the guys doing the job cause
1.4	TM6	No.
1.5	C	The problem is locks missing or incorrect?
1.6	TM5	No I think we haven't finished last week the story.
1.7	C	What story?
1.8	TM5	What we started. Because (???)

1.9	TM1	[And we were we were supposed to bring more information about it
1.10	C	[Yep.
1.11	TM5	Well. er even even if there is a lock missing I will not get a er er er hand-written report of something like this probably let us know yeah we have the, we have some sort of a lock missing but at this stage, er er, I not know of any lock missing. Now what we were talking about last week somebody should come up with an idea of . . .
1.12	TM3	[Something
1.13	TM5	Something with the lock
1.14	TM3	[something changed.
1.15	TM5	Yeah someone from this group. I believe, in my view is we are fitting the locks in the wrong position. Always.
1.16	C	What do you mean?
1.17	TM5	I mean we are fitting the locks in the wrong place.

The extract shows the team leader named Carol trying to guide the meeting to talk about locks that go missing and that are incorrectly fitted (locks are needed because gaming machines collect money). Despite her supervisory rank, Carol's suggestion that team members should talk to the people who fit the locks (turn 1.3) is dismissed by TM6 ('No'; turn 1.4) and TM5 (turn 1.6). In less than fluent English, TM5 goes on to say that the meeting should return to a different PSP issue – 'last week the story' – that was left unresolved: formulating a production target statement.

In all, the exchange moves from Carol (the supervisor) suggesting what to do ('talk to the guys doing the job'), to TM5 and TM3 taking over and co-constructing a narrative around how the locks are fitted 'in the wrong place'. In 'taking the floor' (Edelsky 1981), team members TM3 and TM5 capitalise on the opportunity to speak. At the same time, because PSP provides a new forum requiring thus far little-practised ways of (public) speaking, the employees find themselves enacting new ways of being and relating. That is, asserting their viewpoints as employees is not equivalent to saying what they meant to say all along, but involves saying things they may not have been aware were sayable. What they appear to do here, then, is capture the moment in an entrepreneurial way (Spinosa et al. 1997). That is, they contribute knowledge that is important and specific to them ('something with the lock . . . something changed'), and give it relevance by inserting it into a general discussion about work process.

Extract 1 is emblematic therefore of how staff (are expected to) become mutually responsive and entrepreneurial in their approach to and definition of work. Being entrepreneurial involves articulating knowledge that helps improve their work and identifying new opportunities and solutions, such as fitting locks onto the gaming machines in a way that they know from doing the work is the 'right' place. Being responsive points to the increasing pressure to interpersonalise how employees relate to one another.

The interpersonalisation of business organisational discourse

The second piece of data will enable us to explore further the implications of new ways of working, such as participating in PSP meetings. It appears evident that saying new things carries significant personal consequences. How do I reconcile myself to being or becoming different, or to saying things I was not brought up or trained to say? This question goes to the heart of the interpersonal implications of the increasingly rapid changes and innovations we see taking place in contemporary business organisations. To begin to answer this question, let us consider a stretch of interaction that took place in a large Australian textile manufacturing company, reproduced here from Lesley Farrell's original work (2000).

Like Hermine Scheeres, Lesley Farrell combined ethnographic observations with tape-recorded and transcribed in situ talk to understand the impact of organisational change on employees. She explains how the company's management is acutely aware of its increasingly precarious position in the global marketplace as competition from a number of neighbouring low-wage economies is intensifying. As part of a broader initiative to promote organisational learning, participative management structures and competitive innovation, the meeting brings five supervisors together from different sections of the organisation to talk about how to further these three aims. This initiative, Farrell notes, positions the supervisors as being responsible for successful interactions among 'their' groups of frontline employees. As extract 2 demonstrates, the meeting addresses the issues that this new responsibility creates for the supervisors.

Extract 2: Supervisor meeting

2.1	Ben:	we thought you know maybe maybe I should be the facilitator for Gay's group or something where I'm away from the people a bit and um
2.2	Sally:	yeah
2.3	Ben:	just have a background in what's going on but just sort of keep them on the right track and let them they've got to really then rely on each other instead of relying on the supervisor to do work
2.4	Gay:	well I think kind of in the groups that are gonna come along that's what's gonna have to happen. I mean I know the first one's that start off I think we have to go down this path to try to direct people onto the path and therefore we kind of will be in charge of the meeting but then we have to get people to start their own teams and us sort of just being a facilitator rather than
2.5	Joe:	the team leader
2.6	[. . .]	yeah
2.7	Gay:	I mean it's hard to get started I think that's where people are having trouble and that's why they're kind of looking to you Ben and you know things like that
2.8	Pete:	I'm not the only one I'm having trouble maintaining the thing
2.9	[. . .]	yeah
2.10	Pete:	I just can't maintain it at the moment you know a couple of days you know a couple of days crook there and you know just the amount of work that builds up it just goes back of the queue sort of thing it's shocking
2.11	Joe:	so what you really want is the um you've got a group you start a group and you want one of those people sort of come out and [. . .] facilitate the group

2.12	Pete:	just to maintain the group you know like just to keep it just keep the work flowing
2.13	Ben:	what I'm trying to get across
2.14	Pete:	cause
2.15	Ben:	is I'm too close to the people because I
2.16	[. . .]	yeah
2.17	Ben:	already go outside of the group and then I'm their supervisor outside on the on the floor where maybe if I was facilitating another group where I'm not I'm not above them you know I'm not their supervisor or whatever um I can go back to my job they can go back to theirs and they still um you know it's this their more their team than
2.18	Sally:	yours

In this stretch of talk, the supervisors are beginning to grapple with their growing number of responsibilities. These responsibilities include ones that are conventional, in so far as they have a supervisory role with regard to the procedural work that their teams do. They also include new responsibilities that are relational and that are (therefore) work-intensive. The supervisors' role as 'team leaders' and 'facilitators' centres on 'maintain(ing) the thing [group]' (Pete at turn 2.8). And it encompasses interpersonal tactics like acting as team leaders for someone else's team to create some distance and diminish dependence (Ben at 2.1; also 'I'm too close to the people' at turn 2.15). This ethos of being self-steering and self-reliant is again expressed in Ben's turn at 2.3 ('rely on each other instead of relying on the supervisor'), in Gay's turn at 2.4 ('people to start their own teams and us sort of just being a facilitator'), and again in Joe's turn at 2.11 ('you want one of those people sort of come out and [. . .] facilitate the group'). Then, at turn 2.17, Ben rearticulates his idea to separate his twin responsibilities of being supervisor of the work and facilitator of new relationships and initiatives.

There is an interpersonal intensity coming through in the therapeutic concerns that are articulated: 'away from the people', 'rely on each other', 'hard to get started', 'people are having trouble', 'you want one of those people to . . . come out', 'maintain the group', 'too close to the people', 'I'm not above them', 'they know it's more their team . . . than yours'. These discursive features suggest that the supervisors' focus on facilitative work involves disrupting traditional hierarchies (see turns 2.3, 2.4, 2.17) and ensuring the relational work goes on in the face of production pressures (2.10). As they articulate these sentiments, they are very open and honest with each other, confessing to having problems and concerns ('it's hard to get started' [2.7]; 'I'm having trouble maintaining the thing' [2.8]) and fears ('just can't maintain it at the moment' [2.10]).

Seen from a broader perspective, this meeting as a whole enables the supervisors to support each other through sharing feelings and experiences and offering empathetic comments (e.g. Joe at 2.11: 'so what you really want is . . .'). In that sense, the meeting is not made up of existing scripts, standard procedures and learned genres. Instead, it is a space where the supervisors explore, enact and invent new ways for 'going on' (Wittgenstein 1953). Thus, they meander from troublesome experience ('a couple of days crook there', Pete at turn 2.10) to troublesome experience ('I'm too close to the people', Ben at turn 2.15), as well as trying to express as yet unspoken thoughts (cf. what I'm trying to get across', Ben at turn 2.13). Progressively, Gay, Pete, Joe, Ben and Sally invent possibilities for how to proceed, who to be, how to relate and what to say.

Discussion

As noted above, business and organisational change has been accounted for in two ways. First, researchers have described the growing prominence of knowledge work (Blackler 1995). As the analyses above illustrated, new business practices encourage employees to produce new expertises to capture value. This puts limits on the significance of hierarchy and rank, as well as blurring tasks and pre-existing roles and relationships. It opens up the way for those with ideas and initiative to create new opportunities for themselves, but it also produces uncertainty (Alvesson 1993). Second, much attention has been paid to the importance of emotional skills at work (Goleman 1995). Research has shown that new business practices can yield personal achievement and pride, but also result in stress, frustration and even anxiety (Fineman 1996, 2005) because of to the personal costs associated with producing emotions for the benefit of unknown others (Hochschild 1983).

Despite their apparent differences, these accounts – the rise of knowledge work and the intensification of emotional labour – closely parallel one another. Over and above pleasing clients and impressing managers with new ideas, employees are now also expected to invent new ways of being, doing and saying as part of how they work together. That means, in turn, that employees are co-producers of the current business environment, even though existing types of theorising tend to treat that environment as either external to employees (causing uncertainty) or as acting on them in 'unnatural' ways (by demanding emotional labour).

Seen in that light, concepts such as knowledge work and emotional labour fall short when asked to describe changes and experiences in the contemporary workplace. We would unduly stretch the notion of knowledge work in applying it to how TM3 and TM 5 co-produce their insight into the locks being wrongly fitted (extract 1, turns 1.13–1.15). By the same token, describing what TM3 and TM5 did as knowledge work would erase from view the affective energy that drives them to speak in front of the others (Iedema et al. 2006b). Similarly, the concept 'emotional labour' falls short in so far as it discounts employees' spontaneity and vitality, because it privileges emotional expectations and stresses imposed from elsewhere. We suggest that a different way of understanding employees' experiences is called for.

From this point on, then, we differentiate between emotion and knowledge on the one hand, and affect on the other hand. Knowledge and emotion are notions that position people's conduct as subservient to existing discourse practices – that describe reactive and cumulative behaviours, not innovative and self-motivating ones. Knowledge and emotion are notions that render invisible the extent to which people can act in unpredictable, non-linear and sometimes unexplainable ways. Affect, in contrast, helps broaden our appreciation of human vitality, creativity and interestedness (Massumi 2002; Thrift 2004a). Our adoption of the notion affect, then, serves not merely to confirm our view that employees are constantly confronted with having to negotiate and invent ways for 'how to go on' (Garfinkel 1972; Wittgenstein 1953). Importantly in the context of contemporary business, affect shifts our attention to the unusual and the unexpected, whether that manifests as creativity, innovation, surprise, excitement or intensity.

Our concern with affect serves to mark that, in the contemporary business, *the unexpected is increasingly expected*. '. . . [T]he value of productive activity is . . . found in . . . the play of uncertainty and the direct manipulation of affectivity' (Clough et al. 2007: 74). For Clough and colleagues, affect is at the basis of what produces (business) value. Of particular interest to our inquiry into contemporary business discourse is that affect reorients us from describing what predetermines, regulates or patterns employees' and organisations' actions, to appreciating the *openness* of the present, and the extent to which openness has become the new benchmark for 'being doing a business employee'. The importance of paying attention to the indeterminate nature of the present becomes evident when we think about how employees constantly negotiate and invent scripts and genres for new, attention-grabbing and noteworthy business practices. For us, the analysis of business organisational discourse cannot ignore this 'turn to affect'. This turn has important implications for how we study and characterise the discourses of and in the contemporary business organisation. These implications are explored in the concluding section of this chapter.

Conclusion: implications for discourse research in business

The turn to affect has moved research into areas where on-demand, experience-based conducts are more and more prominent. Examples are conflict resolution, open (honest) disclosure (of mishaps), innovative leadership, moral governance, performance improvement, career/personal development and business coaching. The prominence of these practices is evidence that 'affect is realised to be a very time-efficient way of transmitting a large amount of information' (Thrift 2004b: 878).

For discourse research this means two things. First, the focus of discourse research shifts from an objectification and in-depth dissection of discourse practices to presaging emerging practices and genres. Given that discourse practices are evolving at an increasingly faster rate, articulating generalising claims about specific practices or practice types becomes a tenuous activity: these practices are unlikely to remain stable for long, and it is difficult now to make firm claims about actors' relationships to and roles in these practices. It is more fruitful for research to focus on the emergence of affect-based conducts, driven by new policies and creative initiatives.

For example, in aviation we have seen how crew resource management has for some years now served as a technique for enhancing airplane personnel's attentiveness to colleagues irrespective of their rank and training (Helmreich and Merritt 1998). In public service organisations, we witness governmental approaches to risk management that rely on disclosure and 'being honest' (Lamb 2004). In business, there are moves afoot to render discourse practices more responsive to governance models, ecology impact assessments, and standards of gender equity. In these and related ways, businesses and staff are foregrounding affect, or openness to opportunities and sentiments embedded in the present. Discourse researchers need to pay attention to how these new conducts come about, how they are experienced, how they affect people, and how they evolve.

Second, discourse research needs to shift in terms of its methods. Where discourse analysis has for some time now privileged the analysis of texts obtained from the businesses where this work is done, the present interactive climate demands more and faster feedback between researchers, if not also more feedback between researchers and policy-makers, and between researchers and employees, as 'researchees'. Inevitably, this feedback needs to be as much affect-based as are the conducts that discourse analysis confronts in contemporary businesses. In the past, the researcher–business relationship was premised on the conventional discourse analytical approach that involved collecting textual evidence and devising theory-oriented conclusions 'from a distance'. This approach now risks being too one-sided, not sensitive to local complexities, too linguistically specialised, and therefore insufficiently informative for non-discourse analysts. In this regard, combining discourse analytic methods with ethnography will afford more immediate feedback, exchange and uptake (Engeström 2000). At the same time, ethnography is oriented to creating social and interpersonal relationships, much of which is affect-based. A discourse ethnographic approach is therefore potentially productive of alternative realities, as a result of the relationships it creates and works with (Iedema et al. 2006a).

Applications to teaching and training

Traditionally, our view of business culture was that we needed to align employees to predetermined procedural routines and emotional regimes (Schein 1983). This view is complicated now by businesses expecting employees to embody initiative and innovation. We have moved from considering good business to depend on the alignment and control of potentially unruly personnel, towards regarding good business to be contingent on inspiration, enthusiasm and intensity of participation (Thrift 1999). This shift has substantial implications for educators and trainers engaged in workplaces. How best can the affectualisation of work be taught, or more importantly, how is it learned? And perhaps even more fundamentally, how can educational institutions ensure there is a curriculum that 'covers' new ways of being a contemporary worker?

Conventional models of communication training tended to privilege the individual thinking subject who acts on the basis of cognitive schemas and emotional frames. No attention was given to the productive, creative and co-constructed dimensions of in situ practice (Barnes 2001) and distributed cognition (Hutchins and Klausen 1998). Understanding and engaging with affect-based practice in the twenty-first century organisation necessitates a different approach.

Given the close link between affect and change, teaching change is teaching affect. This means that curricula, in focusing on emerging discourses and practices, need also to address the personal implications for workers of these developments. Clearly, affect-based work is closely linked to the new ideal of 'the flexible worker' (Gee 2000). Education, teaching and learning in the contemporary business are therefore not about enabling employees to settle on new if rather different identities. Instead, what emerging pedagogic methods need to encompass is how employees can be enabled to *distance* themselves from identity per se through recognition that identity cannot be 'natural and necessary'. This, in turn, involves reconfiguring who people consider themselves to be, and accepting that what they do with ease is no longer a legitimation for who to be, how to speak, or how to do their work.

References

Adler, P. S. (2001) Market, hierarchy, and trust: The knowledge economy and the future of capitalism. *Organization Science*, 12(2): 215–34.

Alvesson, M. (1993) Organization as rhetoric: Knowledge-intensive firms and the struggle with ambiguity. *Journal of Management Studies*, 30(6): 997–1016.

Armitage, J. and P. Graham (2001) Dromoeconomics: Towards a political economy of speed. *Parallax*, 7(1): 111–23.

Barley, S. R. and G. Kunda (2001) Bringing work back in. *Organization Science*, 12(1): 76–95.

Barnes, B. (2001) Practice as collective action. In T. Schatzki, K. Knorr-Cetina and E. von Savigny (eds), *The Practice Turn in Contemporary Theory*. London: Routledge, pp. 17–28.

Blackler, F. (1995) Knowledge, knowledge work and organizations: An overview and interpretation. *Organization Studies*, 16(6): 1021–46.

Boje, D. M. (2001) *Narrative Methods for Organizational & Communication Research*. London: Sage.

Castells, M. (2004) *The Power of Identity. The Information Age: Economy, Society and Culture, Volume 2*, 2nd edn. Oxford: Blackwell.

Chia, R. (1999) A 'rhizomic' model of organizational change and transformation: Perspective from a metaphysics of change. *British Journal of Management*, 10: 209–27.

Child, J. and R. G. McGrath (2001) Organizations unfettered: Organizational form in an information-intensive economy. *Academy of Management Journal*, 44(6): 1135–48.

Clough, P., G. Goldberg, R. Schiff, A. Weeks and C. Willse (2007) Notes towards a theory of affect-itself. *ephemera*, 7(1): 60–77.

Deetz, S. (2003) Authoring as a collaborative process through communication. In D. Holman and R. Thorpe (eds), *Management and Language*. London: Sage, pp. 121–38.

Drucker, P. (1993) *Post-Capitalist Society*. New York: Harper.

Edelsky, C. (1981) Who's got the floor? *Language in Society*, 10(6): 383–421.

Engeström, Y. (2000) From individual action to collective activity and back: Developmental work research as an interventionist methodology. In P. Luff, J. Hindmarsh and C. Heath (eds), *Workplace Studies: Recovering Work Practice and Informing System Design*. Cambridge: Cambridge University Press, pp. 150–66.

Fairclough, N. (1992) *Discourse and Social Change*. Cambridge: Polity.

Farrell, L. (2000) Ways of doing, ways of being: Language, education and working identities. *Language and Education*, 14(1): 18–36.

Fineman, S. (1996) Emotion and organizing. In S. Clegg, C. Hardy and W. Nord (eds), *Handbook of Organization Studies*. London: Sage, pp. 543–64.

Fineman, S. (2005) Appreciating emotion at work: Paradigm tensions. *International Journal for Work Organisation and Emotion*, 1(1): 4–19.

Garfinkel, H. (1972) Studies of the routine grounds of everyday activities. In D. Sudnow (ed.), *Studies in Social Interaction*. New York: Free Press, pp. 1–30.

Gee, J. (2000) Communities of practice in the new capitalism. *Journal of the Learning Sciences*, 9(4): 515–23.

Gee, J. and C. Lankshear (1995) The new work order: Critical language awareness and fast capitalism. *Discourse: Studies in the Cultural Politics of Education*, 16(1): 5–19.

Gee, J., G. Hull and C. Lankshear (1996) *The New Work Order: Behind the Language of the New Capitalism*. Sydney: Allen and Unwin.

Goleman, D. (1995) *Emotional Intelligence*. New York: Bantham.

Habermas, J. (1987) *The Theory of Communicative Action 2: Lifeworld and System – A Critique of Functionalist Reason*. Boston, MA: Beacon Press.

Helmreich, R. L. and A. C. Merritt (1998) *Culture at Work in Aviation and Medicine: National, Organizational and Professional Influences*. Aldershot: Ashgate.

Hochschild, A. R. (1983) *The Managed Heart: Commercialisation of Human Feeling*. Berkeley: University of California Press.

Hutchins, E. and T. Klausen (1998) Distributed cognition in an airline cockpit. In Y. Engeström and D. Middleton (eds), *Cognition and Communication at Work*. Cambridge: Cambridge University Press, pp. 15–34.

Iedema, R. (2003) *Discourses of Post-Bureaucratic Organization*. Amsterdam and Philadelphia: John Benjamins.

Iedema, R. (2007) Essai: On the materiality, contingency and multi-modality of organizational discourse. *Organization Studies*, 28(6): 931–46.

Iedema, R., D. Long, R. Forsyth and B. Lee (2006a) Visibilizing clinical work: Video ethnography in the contemporary hospital. *Health Sociology Review*, 15(2): 156–68.

Iedema, R., C. Rhodes and H. Scheeres (2006b) Surveillance, resistance, observance: Exploring the teleo-affective intensity of identity (at) work. *Organization Studies*, 27(8): 1111–30.

Iedema, R., S. Ainsworth and D. Grant (2007) The contemporary 'clinician-manager': Entrepreneurialising middle management? In C. Caldas-Coulthard and R. Iedema (eds), *Identity Trouble: Discursive Constructions*. Basingstoke: Palgrave, pp. 273–91.

Knights, D. and D. McCabe (2003) *Organisation and Innovation: Guru Schemes and American Dreams*. Maidenhead: Open University Press.

Lamb, R. (2004) Open disclosure: The only approach to medical error. *Quality and Safety in Health Care*, 13: 3–5.

Massumi, B. (2002) *Parables for the Virtual: Movement, Affect, Sensation*. Durham, NC: Duke University Press.

Scheeres, H. (2004) *Governing (at) Work: Doing, Talking and Being in the Workplace*. Unpublished PhD thesis, Brisbane: University of Queensland.

Schein, E. H. (1983) The role of the founder in creating organizational culture. *Organizational Dynamics*, Summer: 13–28.

Spinosa, C., F. Flores and H. Dreyfus (1997) *Disclosing New Worlds: Entrepreneurship, Democratic Action and the Cultivation of Solidarity*. Cambridge, MA: MIT Press.

Thrift, N. (1999) Performing new cultures in the new economy. *Annals of the Association of American Geographers*, 90(4): 674–92.

Thrift, N. (2004a) Intensities of feeling: Towards a spatial politics of affect. *Geografiska Annaler*, 86B(1): 57–78.

Thrift, N. (2004b) Thick time. *Organization*, 11(6): 873–80.

Virilio, P. (1986) *Speed and Politics: An Essay on Dromology*. New York: Semiotext(e).

Wittgenstein, L. (1953) *Philosophical Investigations*. Oxford: Blackwell.

7

Ethnomethodology

Dalvir Samra-Fredericks

Introduction

Ethnomethodology (EM) is a sociological endeavour whose founder, Harold Garfinkel, took inspiration from Schutz, Durkheim and Talcott Parsons. In particular, Parsons's work on the Hobbesian problem of social order was recast by Garfinkel as a members' concern accomplished through a complex array of taken-for-granted methods and reasoning procedures. As a non-positivistic study of members' (human beings') everyday and naturally occurring social interactions, EM aims to illuminate 'foundational sociological issues' (Button 1991; Heritage 1984; Samra-Fredericks and Bargiela-Chiappini 2008). From the start Garfinkel's EM was 'directly concerned with questions of organisation and organising' (Rawls 2008: 702) but had a focus on organis*ing* processes that entailed examining the 'temporal and sequential details of organisation' (Boden 1994: 47). Garfinkel also influenced the development of conversation analysis (CA, also termed linguistic ethnomethodology) founded by Harvey Sacks (with Schegloff, Jefferson, Pomerantz and others), whom Garfinkel met in the 1960s. CA undertakes two forms of study, one examining the 'social institution *of* interaction' and the second examining the 'management of social institutions *in* interaction' (Heritage 1997: 222–3; see also Drew and Heritage 1992), and hence the latter deals with 'institutional talk' (for example, between a professional and a lay member, such as a courtroom judge and a defendant). While both EM and CA attend to situated social action, sequential order and orderliness, given space issues, this chapter will specifically focus upon Garfinkel's EM and subsequent developments. Consequently, the diverse EM canon and the debates it has instigated are set aside, with only particular EM programmes of empirical research – embracing 'institutional talk' – being touched upon here.

A need to clarify terminology also arises since this chapter is in a *Handbook of Business Discourse*: 'discourse' evades neat definition, given its varied usage across the humanities and social sciences. It has, for example, been defined in two ways by Alvesson and Karreman (2000) in the organisation studies (OS) field: *d*iscourse with a small 'd' encompasses conversation, talk and language use, and *D*iscourse with a capital 'D' refers to societally or institutionally imbued practices and is often employed within Foucauldian poststructural or postmodern approaches (e.g. 'Discourses of Capitalism', 'Discourses of

Masculinity': see Samra-Fredericks 2005a). In this chapter, then, 'talk' or 'language use' is employed. Moving onto the second term in the little, 'business': ethnomethodological studies tend to refer to 'organisation' and/or 'workplace' studies, with workplaces including offices (e.g. newsrooms), control centres (e.g. traffic control centres), operating theatres, doctor–patient/teacher–pupil interactions, sales work, archaeological field 'digs', legal settings and so on. Such settings span private and public forms of businesses. For the purposes of this chapter, either 'organisation' or 'workplace' will be employed.

In EM and EM influenced studies, then, members' talk-in-interaction – taking talk as a social process – together with embodied practices and technology or tool use are subjected to fine-grained analysis. However, EM studies in management and organisation studies (MOS) remain rare, and this is especially surprising if we note just two long-standing MOS research interests: the question of what constitutes effective practice, and an interest in process and process theorising. EM and allied bodies of scholarship offer an insightful, theoretically informed route for empirical studies of these phenomena, and to demonstrate such possibilities, the chapter will draw on one study of senior managers doing their everyday work in a large UK private-sector organisation (reproduced from Samra-Fredericks 2005b, forthcoming): it forms part of a larger programme of work which has sought to examine the ways such organisational members stabilise the everyday ebb and flow to constitute 'strategy', 'organisation' and, more widely, 'social order' (Samra-Fredericks 1996, 2003, 2004a, 2004b, 2004c, 2005a, 2005b). From research which includes audio- (and in some cases video-) recording of organisational members' naturally occurring interpersonal routines over time and space, just one minute slice of interaction is reproduced here. It was between two senior managers refining for the nth time the strategy document. Drawing upon Goodwin's (1994) ethnomethodological account of 'common discursive' methods, a glimpse is given of the ways these organisational members constitute aspects of 'professional vision' and inherently fashion their key 'object', the market or 'environment' *as if* 'out there'. From this, an indication of the nature and scope of an ethnomethodological 'take' upon talk-based organising processes – which this *Handbook* terms 'business discourse' – is outlined.

The chapter will begin with a summary of EM and the pioneering stance established by Garfinkel, leading onto a very brief outline of sociological research which examines the practical, sequential and interactional accomplishment of 'the workplace'. The reason why it often entails audio- and/or video-recording of everyday practice *happening* (processes) is also touched upon. The next section reproduces one illustrative example from the author's study of senior managers writing the annual strategy plan. Taking just one contributory angle – their use of classifications as one specific 'method' – the excerpt begins to offer a basis from which to consider the claim that EM and EM informed studies enable particular and/or additional understandings of the skilled coordination involved in yielding 'mutual intelligibility' or 'sense' for accomplishing those taken-for-granted objects (in this chapter, 'the market'), tasks (here, writing the annual strategy plan) and that entity known as organisation, as well as yielding an identified actor as this-or-that 'type' (here, the senior manager, and elsewhere, expert or novice: Samra-Fredericks forthcoming). A brief conclusion follows.

Ethnomethodology

Garfinkel (1967) coined the term 'ethnomethodology' in the 1950s to capture the central interest in members' 'folk' or everyday, taken-for-granted methods or reasoning procedures for doing or accomplishing a social order that constitutes sense. Meaning requires order, as Rawls (2008: 703) summarises: the 'empirical elaboration of how this is achieved through sequential devices and reflexive attention' is Garfinkel's 'unique contribution to social theory'. Taken-for-granted activities such as talking to a friend or lining up in a queue or 'reading' a computer screen – the familiar – are made unfamiliar, and are shown to be intricately ordered and made mutually intelligible through highly contingent and situated practical action (see papers in Samra-Fredericks and Bargiela-Chiappini 2008).

It is the ethno- (folk) methods in terms of the everyday, mundane knowledge and reasoning procedures deployed by members to 'make sense of' and 'act on' the situations in which they are involved which are of core analytical interest. Together with scrutiny of situated action and the contexts of accountability as opposed to the individual or the institution(s), two core EM principles – reflexivity and indexicality, both commonplace today – were coined by Garfinkel in the 1950s–1960s, and underpin EM's theoretical base. Further, as Boden (1994: 46) asserts, ethnomethodologists 'recommend for serious study what Garfinkel calls "fact production" in flight', as was incisively undertaken in Garfinkel's (1967) early study of jury deliberations. As Suchman (1987: 57) was later to assert too, the 'outstanding question for social science . . . is not whether social facts are objectively grounded, but how that objective grounding is accomplished'. But what is a challenge is accessing the 'seen-but-unnoticed background features' or practices of social situations. As these are a 'commonsense' or tacit resource available to us all, Garfinkel (1967; see also Rawls 2008) also faced this problem of how to render it available to reflection and research. It was through the breaching demonstrations (experiments) that one route was discerned, and subsequent developments in terms of undertaking audio- and video-recordings also enable researchers to slow down and revisit members' split-second and complex interactional doings, and from this to subject them to fine-grained transcription and description which exposes these seen-but-unnoticed background features.

As a call to study organisational life 'in flight' (Garfinkel 1967) or 'as it happens' (Boden 1990), members' or practitioners' naturally occurring, embodied talk-in-interaction and their inherent use of practical reasoning procedures or ethnomethods, as well as tools, technologies, artefacts and so on, mean that we inevitably go beyond 'some woolly process of social construction' (Boden 1994: 63). Achieving mutual intelligibility in workplaces is deemed to necessitate finely tuned or coordinated forms of constant mutual orientation to those taken-for-granted methods (the situated constitutive expectancies; see Rawls 2008) for order(s) to be produced. Equally, the member is not to be considered as a whole person but only as a situated identity in relation to a particular situation. This gave rise to the term 'identified actor', referring to a member who *is* also a sequential achievement (Garfinkel 2006; Rawls 2008). One route for investigation is the verbal or verbalised element; hence the interest in talk, words, or language use. Another is members' embodied movement; for example, gaze or gesture. A third is the subtle orientations to, and use of, physical objects, artefacts and tools, the study of which remains rare in MOS, but which 'workplace studies' have insightfully illuminated. In this chapter, given space limits, I focus on words and language use, and necessarily set aside members' use of physical objects together with embodied movements such as gaze and/or gesture (available elsewhere; Samra-Fredericks forthcoming).

Management and organisation studies: practice and ethnomethodology

In the MOS field, a handful of studies of situated action drawing upon Garfinkel's stance, and examining the talk, tacit knowledges and sequential order for doing the work in question, includes Suchman (1987) and Orr (1996). Others known to be more broadly influenced by Garfinkel's EM include Weick (1969, 1995: 11), Van Mannen and Barley (1984), Gephardt (1978) and Manning (1979). Still other MOS scholars advocating EM's contribution are summarised in Samra-Fredericks and Bargiela-Chiappini (2008) and include, for example, Clegg et al. (2004), Knights and Willmott (1992), Linstead (2006), Richards (2004) and Willmott (1998). More widely, in the field of social theory and the turn to '*practice*', Schatzki (2005; but see Rawls 2008) also mentioned EM. However, it is still the case that while MOS scholars recognise the value or contribution of EM, empirical studies remain rare.

Beyond MOS, Bittner (1965/1979), Silverman and Jones (1973, 1976) and Boden (1994) stand out as EM/CA researchers who have studied 'organisation' and whose work – while known in *some* quarters of MOS – would contribute to a reconceptualisation of orthodox phenomena such as bureaucracy, meetings, teamwork and detailed explication of various tasks. Indeed, beyond MOS there is a vibrant and growing body of research located in the 'workplace studies', 'technology studies' and/ or 'computer-supported cooperative work' programmes which do subject members' practice to detailed forms of analysis. Through video-recording of work practices *happening* (Luff et al. 2000; Hindmarsh and Heath 2000, 2007; Heath et al. 2000), the situated and interactionally coordinated ways members use language or talk, gesture, tools and various artefacts are seen to contribute to particular long-standing and substantive topics within MOS, such as practice, skills and competencies, expertise and knowledge use, technology use, teamworking and so on. Moreover, these phenomena have been explicated across a range of settings and 'tasks', such as the management of customer behaviour (Brown 2004), solving problems in traffic control centres (Heath and Luff 2000), telesales call centres (Whalen et al. 2002) or the coordinating 'work' for effective selling in auction houses (and others: Heath and Luff 2007; Greatbatch et al. 1993; Goodwin 1994). *How* members orient to and use an artefact or object, for example, in the course of talking and writing about it is one feature that could easily be illustrated in the excerpt below if space were available. While lack of space also forbids detailing Goodwin's (1994) ethnomethodically informed three-fold schema, a brief summary is given next, since it is deployed against the illustrative excerpt to indicate aspects of EM's focus and contribution.

Goodwin's schema

Goodwin's (1994: 626) ethnomethodological study of 'professional vision' undertook detailed analysis of lawyers' and archaeologists' practices for 'seeing' and stabilising their core 'object of knowledge'. Goodwin's (1994: 626) three practices, also termed 'methods' (the term adopted in this chapter), are deemed to 'contribute[s] to efforts by linguistic anthropologists, practice theorists, and conversation analysts to develop anthropologically informed analyses of human action and cognition as socially situated phenomena'. The three methods are *classification schemes* (in terms of *both* everyday forms of language use and specialist forms or jargon, and use of coding devices); *highlighting* (through gesture and tool use but also, in our case, through writing or positioning portions of text in particular places); and the production and use of *material representations* (the charts and tables which they produce and include in the document; equally, the document itself is a material representation of the epiphenomenon 'organisation–environment couplet'). As noted earlier, it is the first method only – words and classifications – which is touched upon here (see Samra-Fredericks 2005b, 2009, for a fuller account of all three methods).

Noting too that particular collaboratively constituted 'objects' animate the discourse of a profession, in this chapter I examine the discourse of strategic management (Samra-Fredericks 2005a) and how organisational members invoke features of this discourse *and* create *both* a tangible 'object' in the form of the strategic plan or document and intangible 'objects' which remain elusive conceptual phenomena – that is, here, the market. It is these objects which animate a spatially distanced and complex networked 'community' of academics, consultants, institutional and financial analysts, and practitioners known in common as senior managers or strategists. In so doing, these objects reproduce a particular world and no other. Further, in contrast to Goodwin's (1994: 626) archaeologist who 'constructs' a map of a field site – a 'built material cognitive artefact' – from engagement with a material entity, the soil, our strategists build a 'material cognitive artefact' (the strategic plan) with no material entity to which it neatly corresponds. The plan remains in the cognitive and conceptual realm, and the fact that there is no material entity to which it neatly corresponds means that their efforts in seemingly making *present* and creating the *illusion* of materiality in terms of 'the market' or more broadly 'environment' 'out there' is perhaps even more spectacular (Samra-Fredericks 2005b).

Professional vision is also acknowledged by Goodwin as unevenly allocated, and this echoes Foucault's (1981) work on 'how the discursive procedures of a society structure what kinds of talk can and cannot be heard, who is qualified to speak the truth, and the conditions that establish the rationality of statements' (Goodwin 1994: 626; Samra-Fredericks 2005a). The uneven allocation of 'who is qualified to speak the truth' means that people must gain the qualification, and in the excerpt below, we do glimpse the complex, subtle and intricate ways a director (Peter, a pseudonym) displays his qualification to speak the particular truths with which they deal, but also how another (Colin, ditto) learns and thus works to gain this qualification. Analysis and discussion of the intricate ways one member 'inducted' another colleague are, however, not detailed here because of space limitations. The next section now addresses the issue of capturing real-time processes.

Capturing process: the need to audio-video-record

EM researchers scrutinise members' collaboration and coordination of activities to produce sense and 'fix' – momentarily – social or work orders, and so centrally deal with both practice and process. As noted earlier, these are also long-standing interests within MOS with, for example, Chia (1999: 224) contending that for process thinkers 'organisation is stabilizing and simple locating. The ontological act of organisation is an act of arrest-ing, stabilizing and simplifying what would otherwise be the irreducibly dynamic and complex character of lived-experience.' One claim advanced here (and elsewhere; see Samra-Fredericks 2005b; Samra-Fredericks and Bargiela-Chiappini 2008) is that it is through use of ethno-methods that members arrest, stabilise and simplify – momentarily – that complex flow and thus come to maintain that 'world in common' (Garfinkel 1967). Equally, and adding to the process scholar Alfred North Whitehead's (1929) notion of the 'fallacy of misplaced concreteness', Rawls (2001, 2008: 719) argues that if we accept that the ways 'objects and meanings are actualised (objectified) on each next occasion are empirical (seeable and hearable)', and thus not conceptual, then what we are dealing with is, instead, the 'fallacy of misplaced abstraction'. EM calls for researchers to attend to the ways concreteness is empirically accomplished and where conceptual abstractions (here, 'the market') come to be taken *as if* they were actually 'out there' and were concrete objects. So the challenge is to 'capture' and trace the intricate and sequential ways – the methods, reasoning procedures or 'sets of constitutive expectancies' which provide a 'shared founda-tion for every interaction' (Rawls 2008, 2006) – by which a mutually intelligible 'object' comes to be seen and made 'real'.

Having been exposed to the EM tradition, I found audio-/video-recordings crucial in my research, since they enabled that repeated access to and detailed study of human beings engaged in world-making. Members' talk, bodily movements and coordinated use of various tools and technologies become available for repeated, slow-motion, fine-grained study, and, alongside the visible material 'world' of documents, whiteboard screens, computer displays and so on, elusive methods and sequentially derived reasoning procedures for object construction come within an analytical purview. A characteristic of such research, then, is the reproduction and discussion of detailed analysis of fragments of transcripts. Where possible, video-stills can also highlight the coordinating, embodied nature of practice. This was apparent in a video-based study of the use of closed circuit television on the London Underground rail system by Heath and Luff (2000): workers were shown to deploy practical knowledge to 'see' on the cameras and, through subtle coordinations between each other, to anticipate the temporal flows and geographical dis-tribution of problems and put into action, for example, fine-tuned distinctions between 'crowding' and 'overcrowding'. The issue of gaining access to organisational members' everyday talk-in-interaction may, in part, also explain why empirical studies within MOS remain rare.

The invasive nature of the research (a researcher and physical recording technologies) makes concerns about confidentiality all the more understandable. For example, in the first study of a manufacturing company's senior management team, negotiations for access began in early 1987 and entry was eventually granted in the early 1990s. Who can wait that long today? Next, having accessed such rich empirical materials, we are then faced with investing a lot of time in listening to or viewing the recordings, transcribing, and under-taking detailed analysis. This can be prohibitive too. EM also remains a challenging intel-lectual approach when set against conventional thinking or theorising. Indeed, to examine and preserve the contingent details and the dynamics of situated practical interaction is counter to the 'grand theorising' and generalisation of phenomena within MOS (see Rawls 2008 for an excellent summary).

In terms of my research dealing with senior organisational members, where video-recordings were undertaken, permission was granted only to utilise 'the data' as a means to assist transcript generation (especially needed when three or more individuals spoke in fast succession, and for analytic description in terms of noting the gesture or gaze in the transcript). The recordings were then repeatedly listened to before transcriptions of the sort reproduced here were eventually generated, and it is important to note that the level of detail and some of the conventions used vary from CA approaches. Understandably, all references to members' names, the products, services, financial details, technology and so forth are also excluded from the transcripts. There are, instead, [square] brackets holding a broad description. Concerns over maintaining confidentiality and anonymity also prevent reproduction of video-stills here, as well as necessitating a broad description of the organisation from which the strip of interaction is reproduced. So, in the light of this, the organisation can be described as employing tens of thousands of employees and has a turnover of hundreds of millions of pounds sterling. In terms of spatial arrangements, the fieldwork was conducted across a set of glass-fronted, high-rise city buildings and extended over a six-month period when I sought to be there for at least one day per week. One illustrative 'slice' of members' everyday naturally occurring interaction is reproduced below; a more detailed account, with the ethnographic particulars and additional extracts, is available elsewhere (Samra-Fredericks 2005b, 2009).

One illustrative slice of members' interactional accomplishment of the strategy plan

The two focal organisational members are Peter, a director of strategy at the time of the fieldwork, and Colin (both white, mid-forties). Colin was primarily a finance 'guy' who was – as it transpired – learning to 'see' as a strategist. They sat at a small meeting table in an office. The draft document was one which Colin had most recently worked on and hence it not only provided Peter with a form of mediated access to their sought-after concept or object, but also made visible Colin's current grasp of 'seeing'. Currently this learning was accomplished in the mundane doing of the work itself and not in the mind. This artefact – the document – has a 'hybrid' status but as they worked on it they moved it from something 'private' into *making* it more public. Here, as they talked about portions of the draft text (built from prior talk-based routines of this sort), they wrote in and out various amendments arising from this talk, and then, soon after, talked about what had just been written down. In places where their talk faded off, they were undertaking solitary reading and/or writing portions of text, and in the transcripts these 'acts' were simply noted in [square] brackets. Where text is placed in single quotation marks *within* an utterance, it signals that the speaker was specifically reading out what was already written down.

	Peter	so we really need to make this (.) something *like that one* needs to be about the economic downturn and impact on market structure
	Colin	um
		(brief silence as both read)
5	Peter	what did you say on that (.) you said (.) when you say [name of division] do you mean [group name]?
	Colin	er yeah [name of company] and the organisation, the external market

	Peter	I'd think I'd call that recent trends [quietly speaks as reads] 'survival'
		[reads] it's another bit that goes in there, I think you've got it some-
10		where else but the urm the dirt cheap asset prices need to go in there
	Colin	yeah I've got that in the main body of the report and the competition
		but yeah we can out that in there as well
	Peter	I think its part of the (.) if you made that into market structure=
	Colin	=yes=
15	Peter	=what that says is (.) here's a big consolidation piece [inaudible three
		words] it's (.) consolidation [as he writes]
		(and less than a minute later. . .)
	Peter	so some of that um (.) er I would call that [brief pause] mobilising our
		strategy
20	Colin	um um right=
	Peter	=I'd call that [as he writes he slowly says] 'mobilising' (.) and I'd make
		that the last one
	Colin	sure
	Peter	in the hope that they'd got bored by then and won't read it properly (.)
25		I'd call that mobilising our strategy or a sub-heading [inaudible word]
		'business transformation' [writes as says this]

In the next section, the ways particular words/classifications are deployed to yield object construction in terms of a 'market' are touched upon.

Words, words and more words

In complex and subtle ways, Colin's turns at talk make visible the distribution of account-ability for doing the work they do, and are set against Peter's corresponding turns, which 'do' requesting and appraising of that work. Beginning with a broad description, Colin's 'um' at line 3 – a sort-of non committal continuer – is heard, given the next turn, as agreement or an instance requiring no elaboration or explanation. Then at line 7, Colin simply provides the answer to Peter's prior question and, at line 11, he elaborates on where the information has been placed and aligns it with information on 'competition', as well as adding that it is easy to move as suggested. It is only at line 13, however, that Peter begins to make explicit what *he* sees as materialising from this *highlighting* and use of *classificatory* (Goodwin 1994) language and, of course, careful ordering (line 15). As noted earlier, in Goodwin's (1994) work, forms of classificatory language and coding schemes furnish the crucial distinctions which characterise and constitute a profession or field of activity (archaeology, law and, for us, strategic management). In the excerpt, a cursory glance at language use beginning at line 2 includes two major phenomena within the field of activity known as strategic management, that is, 'economic downturn' and 'market structure'. Subsequently, we journey through the vocabulary of strategy (also pointing to the institutional relevancies and character of this encounter) which populates their world in terms of 'external markets', 'recent trends', 'survival', 'dirt cheap asset prices', 'competition', 'market structure', 'consolidation', 'mobilising our strategy' and 'busi-ness transformation'. These *words* discursively constitute a particular field of activity – strategising – where *the* core distinction revolves around the market, itself a pivotal element in 'environment' (other elements being stakeholders such as government, share-holders, the local community etc.).

Following Garfinkel's stance, this is also an occasion when information – just like 'objects, words and identities' (Rawls 2008) – is constituted as a recognisable and intel-ligible object through just these sequence orders and ways of 'making sense of a world in common'. As Rawls (2008: 722) contends, it is the relationship between the items that con-stitutes the information for those competent to read it (as in Heath and Luff's 2000 study of doctors). So when 'recent trends' and 'distressed assets' and so forth are sequentially ordered in this way (and textualised), the only recognisable or mutually intelligible object must be a 'consolidating market'. For Colin to make explicit the sequential relationship is for him to learn to make inferences appropriate to their profession and so to 'see' accord-ingly too. Clearly, where to place something – its location – is also key, together with this use of particular words or classifications; otherwise the object does not materialise as expected, which brings with it questions around objectivity and concreteness. Notably too, if the object can only be seen in 'situated social contexts by identified selves' (Rawls 2008: 723) then, perhaps, we can come to understand further the prevalence of and neces-sity for meetings and workshops too (Samra-Fredericks 2009).

Taking just one set of words for closer scrutiny – 'dirt cheap asset prices' (line 10) – two analytical points can be summarised. First, these words have a particular meaning because of where they were spoken in terms of the sequential order. It is *this* which lends mutual intelligibility to the overall object construction of 'market' as 'consolidation'. Second, these words are euphemistic, and if we were to excavate further, we could potentially make present or bring to our attention the emotional turmoil arising from people losing their jobs as this market seemingly consolidates, giving rise to those 'dirt cheap asset prices'. Taking this as a gloss where probable 'causes and effects' are left hidden, we have a morally neutral rendering which smoothes over uncomfortable or problematic aspects. Reminiscent of Garfinkel's (1974: 17) reference to talk or language use and glossing, this is perhaps one of those occasions where a member's talk – being a resource – is:

> something that while using and counting on he also glosses. This is to say that in some important ways he ignores certain features: he does not want to make a lot of it. He wants, in fact, to remove himself from that so as to recommend in the report on a world not of his doings that which for him is now available as the thing he could put together in his account of ordinary affairs.

In sum, such word use achieves two things: a distancing and reification of phenomena, and a morally neutral stance.

This exchange then, as it transpired, was one where this initial depiction of their con-solidating market emerged. There is perhaps a moment of uncertainty or a form of 'testing out' visible through something easily overlooked, the 'if'. At line 13, 'if' as a conditional qualifier does suggest the presence of other possibilities or scenarios, but what it *did* here (and notably, elsewhere too) was to mark out an occasion of not-knowingness which was, nevertheless, resolved turn by turn. In simple terms, Colin's 'yes' (line 14) latched onto Peter's prior turn and seemingly assisted this initial move from that prior 'if' (and possibili-ties) to something that 'says' it *is* consolidating (line 15). The other crucial element assisting this particular accomplishment was the sequential placing of indexed items through 'this'

and 'that', enabling Peter to arrive at a juncture where he could make explicit this important inference about the market. Further, the indexical properties of each 'this' (line 1),
'that one' or 'that' (lines 1, 5, 8, 11, 12, 13, 15, 18, 21, 22), 'there' (lines 9, 10, 12), 'here's'
(line 15) were also swiftly resolved through Peter and Colin's physical closeness. They sat
next to each other and hence Colin could 'see' what Peter was referring to (by pointing
or gesture) in the pages before them. Object construction hinged, then, on this physical
closeness, the sequential unravelling of particular indexed 'this' and 'that's as well as using
particular words to frame and guide Colin to 'see' it too. It was in this intricate and taken-
for-granted way that the 'fact' of a market consolidating is an 'accomplishment of details'
that 'exhibit order properties in their sequencing' (Rawls 2008: 706). Notably, as each minor
move laminated (Boden 1994) onto the next, then this became even more 'fixed' and 'real'
(Samra-Fredericks 2005b, forthcoming), something also traced across another study of
senior managers at work/talk where one member, in particular, guided or shaped mutual
intelligibility around two organisational weaknesses (Samra-Fredericks 2003).

In talking as they do, given this sequenced 'social organisation of referring' to the range
of 'that's briefly mentioned here, and allied with this use of particular language or words
which classify phenomena, the words themselves become clearer in terms of meaning *this*
and not that. Peter reasons out loud, drawing upon and meeting background expectations, a pattern or logic-in-use which asserts that when 'economic downturns' 'impact on
market structure' (line 2), are coded ('I'd call that. . .') under 'recent trends' (line 8) and
are linked to 'dirt cheap asset prices' (line 10) alongside information on 'competition' (line
11), it *highlights* or generates a particular reality (in terms of a market): it is a plausible 'big
consolidation piece' (line 15). And so they render that 'object as independent of the experience or perception of any one individual' (Smith 1996: 187, cited in Hindmarsh and Heath
2000: 529). It is a social economic order, no less, underpinned by this taken-for-granted
concretisation of epiphenomena known as 'the Market'.

Given space restrictions, other analytical points arising from this brief excerpt have had
to be set aside; for example, tracing features (e.g. 'I would call that', line 18), accomplishing 'learning-in-interaction' and 'identified actors' in terms of expert/strategist (Peter)
and, correspondingly, novice/manager (Colin); analysis of their choreographed deployment of embodied resources such as gaze and gesture; and the visible ways their locally
derived and emotionally imbued experiential terrain is subtly evoked (e.g. line 21–2, 24)
and made consequential too: the latter also points to the issue of account-making as the
'way that institutional constraint, power and inequality manifest in interaction' (Rawls
2008: 714). It also remains crucial to emphasise that this excerpt constitutes just one minor
move in time and space, but one where 'the market' was initially voiced or characterised
in a particular and consequential way for the next turn at talk.

Conclusion

Through talk, as well as orientating to each other's subtle moves or shifts in embodied
conduct (gesture and gaze) and tool use members do sort and settle issues which constitute 'facts' or 'truths' such as, here, a market consolidating. Meaningfulness is a socially
situated, finely tuned, interactional and sequential accomplishment, and effective practice
must also handle local contingencies, of which a crucial one, in this instance, was the
members' knowledge of other members (Samra-Fredericks 2009). To 'say' that here is

'consolidation' or to 'call' something 'recent trends' and to do so plausibly is no simple matter either. Indeed, it also brings to our attention the issue of power and critical study, often deemed to be neglected by EM and CA. In EM, the question of who can legitimately deploy particular classifications and correspondingly claim to 'see' in ways which others accept as legitimate or take for granted is opened up for empirical study in ways indicated here. EM, in sum, unremittingly pulls us back to situated actions to see what people actually do in terms of the methods they use during interaction and, from doing so, to see how power is exercised and asymmetric relations accomplished. It is, then, a study of *practice* and the constitution of *interactional effectiveness*. EM scholarship also advances our understanding of *process*. It moves beyond 'calls' to examine 'how social order is achieved; how the flux and flow of our lifeworld are rendered coherent and plausible; how individual identities are established and social entities created' (Chia 2003: 123) to empirical study of members accomplishing such 'things'. In one chapter-length offering it is, of course, inevitable that aspects of the analysis are necessarily compressed and ethnographic detailing kept to a minimum. The practical outcome here has been the purposeful selection of just one brief illustrative extract which begins to indicate the nature and scope of EM, the type of data it deals with and how, and allied forms of analysis. In doing so, its relevance for, and contribution to, what we term here the 'field' of business discourse is, hopefully, conveyed.

References

Alvesson, M. and D. Karreman (2000) Varieties of discourse: On the study of organisations through discourse analysis. *Human Relations*, 53(9): 1125–49.

Bittner, E. (1965/1974) The concept of organisation. In R. Turner (ed.), *Ethnomethodology: Selected Readings*. Harmondsworth: Penguin, pp. 69–81.

Boden, D. (1990) The world as it happens. In G. Ritzer (ed.), *Frontiers of Social Theory: The New Syntheses*. New York: Columbia University Press, pp. 185–213.

Boden, D. (1994) *The Business of Talk*. Cambridge: Polity.

Brown, B. (2004) The order of service: The practical management of customer interaction. *Sociological Research Online*, 9. http://www.socresonline.org.uk/9/4/brown.htm.

Button, G. (ed.) (1991) *Ethnomethodology and the Human Sciences*. Cambridge: Cambridge University Press.

Chia, R. (1999) A 'rhizomic' model of organisational change and transformation: Perspective from a metaphysics of change. *British Journal of Management*, 10(2): 209–29.

Chia, R. (2003) Organisation theory as a postmodern science. In H. Tsoukas and C. Knudsen (eds), *The Oxford Handbook of Organisation Theory*. Oxford: Oxford University Press, pp. 113–40.

Clegg, S., C. Carter and M. Kornberger (2004) Get up, I feel like being a strategy machine. *European Management Review*, 1: 21–6.

Drew, P. and J. Heritage (eds) (1992) *Talk at Work: Interaction in Institutional Settings*. Cambridge: Cambridge University Press.

Foucault, M. (1981) 'The Order of Discourse'. In *Untying the text: A post-structuralist reader*, R. Young (ed.). Boston: Routledge Kegan Paul, pp. 48–78.

Garfinkel, H. (1967) *Studies in Ethnomethodology*. Englewood Cliffs, NJ: Prentice Hall. (1984 edn, Cambridge: Polity.)

Garfinkel, H. (2006) *Seeing Sociologically: The Routine Grounds of Social Action*. Boulder, CO: Paradigm.

Gephardt, R. P., Jr. (1978) Status degradation and organizational succession: An ethnomethodological approach. *Administrative Science Quarterly*, 23: 552–81.

Goodwin, C. (1994) Professional vision. *American Anthropologist*, 96(3): 606–33.

Greatbatch D., P. Luff, C. Heach and P. Campion (1993) 'Interpersonal Communication and Human–Computer interaction: an examination of the uses of computers in medical consultations.' *Interacting with Computers*, 5: 193–216.

Heath, C. and P. Luff (2000) *Technology in Action*. Cambridge: Cambridge University Press.

Heath, C. and P. Luff (2007) Ordering Competition: The interactional accomplishment of the sale of Art and Antiques at Auction. *British Journal of Sociology*, 58: 63–85.

Heritage, J. (1984) *Garfinkel and Ethnomethodology*. Cambridge: Polity.

Heritage, J. (1997) Conversation analysis and institutional talk: Analysing data. In D. Silverman (ed.), *Qualitative Research: Theory, Method and Practice*. London: Sage.

Hindmarsh, J. and C. Heath (2000) Sharing the tools of the trade: The interactional constitution of workplace objects. *Journal of Contemporary Ethnography*, 29(5): 523–62.

Hindmarsh, J. and C. Heath (2007) Video-based studies of work practice. *Sociology Compass*, 1(1): 156–73.

Knights, D. and H. Willmott (1992) Conceptualising leadership processes: A study of senior managers in a financial services company. *Journal of Management Studies*, 29(6): 761–82.

Linstead, S. (2006) Ethnomethodology and sociology: An introduction. *Sociological Review* (special issue), 54(3): 399–404.

Luff, P. J., J. Hindmarsh and C. Heath (eds) (2000) *Workplace Studies: Recovering Work Practice and Informing Systems Design*. Cambridge: Cambridge University Press.

Manning, P. K. (1979) Metaphors of the field. *Administrative Science Quarterly*, 24: 660–71.

Orr, J. (1996) *Talking about Machines: An Ethnography of a Modern Job*. Ithaca, NY: Cornell University Press.

Rawls, A. W. (2001) Durkheim's treatment of practice: Concrete practice vs representation as the foundation of reason. *Journal of Classical Sociology*, 1: 33–68.

Rawls, A. W. (2006) Introduction. In H. Garfinkel, *Seeing Sociologically*. Boulder, CO: Paradigm, pp. 1–97.

Rawls, A. W. (2008) Harold Garfinkel, ethnomethodology and workplace studies. *Organization Studies*, 29(5): 701–32.

Richards, D. (2004) Introduction. *Culture and Organization* (special issue), 10(2): 101–5.

Richards, D. and C. Oswick (2004) Talk in organizations: Local conversations, wider perspectives. *Culture and Organization*, 10(2): 107–23.

Samra-Fredericks, D. (1996) The interpersonal management of competing rationalities: A critical ethnography of board-level competence for 'doing' strategy as *spoken* in the 'face' of change'. PhD thesis, Brunel University.

Samra-Fredericks, D. (2003) Strategising as lived experience and strategists' everyday efforts to shape strategic direction. *Journal of Management Studies*, 40(1): 141–74.

Samra-Fredericks, D. (2004a) Understanding the production of 'strategy' and 'organiza-
    tion' through talk amongst managerial elites. *Culture and Organization*, 10(2): 125–41.
Samra-Fredericks, D. (2004b) Managerial élites making rhetorical and linguistic 'moves'
    for a moving (emotional) display. *Human Relations*, 57: 1103–43.
Samra-Fredericks, D. (2004c) Talk-in-interaction. In G. Symon and C. Cassell (eds),
    Qualitative Methods and Analysis in Organisational Research: A Practical Guide.
    London: Sage, pp. 214–27.
Samra-Fredericks, D. (2005a) Strategic practice, 'discourse' and the *everyday* interac-
    tional constitution of 'power effects'. *Organization*, 12(6): 803–41.
Samra-Fredericks, D. (2005b) Understanding our 'world as it happens' and reconcep-
    tualising strategising as a "kinda" . . . *magic*. Paper delivered at the first *Organization
    Studies* summer workshop on theorising process, Santorini, Greece.
Samra-Fredericks, D. (2009) The interactional accomplishment of the strategic plan. In
    N. Llewellyn and J. Hindmarsh (eds), *Organisation, Interaction and Practice: Studies of
    Real Time Work and Organizing.* Cambridge: Cambridge University Press.
Samra-Fredericks, D. and Bargiela-Chiappini, F. (2008) The foundations of organizing:
    The contribution from Garfinkel, Goffman and Sacks. *Organization Studies*, 29/5:
    653–76.
Schatzki, T. (2005) The site of organisations. *Organization Studies*, 26(3): 465–84.
Silverman, D. and J. Jones (1973) Getting in: The managed accomplishment of 'correct'
    selection outcomes. In J. Child (ed.), *Man and Organisation: The Search for Explanation
    and Social Relevance.* London: George Allen and Unwin.
Silverman, D. and J. Jones. (1976) *Organisational Work: The Language of Grading/The
    Grading of Language.* London: Collier Macmillan.
Smith, D. E. (1996) Telling the truth after postmodernism. *Symbolic Interaction*, 19(3):
    171–202.
Suchman, L. (1987) *Plans and Situated Action: The Problem of Human–Machine
    Communication.* Cambridge: Cambridge University Press.
Van Mannen, J. and S. Barley (1984) Occupational communities: Culture and control
    in organizations. In J. Van Mannen and S. Barley (eds), *Research in Organizational
    Behavior: An Annual Series of Analytical Essays and Critical Reviews.* Greenwich: JAI
    Press, pp. 287–365.
Weick, K. (1969) *The Social Psychology of Organizing.* Reading, MA: Addison Wesley.
Weick, K. (1995) *Sensemaking in Organizations.* Thousand Oaks, CA: Sage.
Whalen, J., M. Whalen and K. Henderson (2002) Improvisational choreography in tele-
    service work. *British Journal of Sociology*, 53: 239–58.
Whitehead, A. N. (1929) *Process and Reality: An Essay in Cosmology*, 1979 corrected edn,
    D. R. Griffin and D. W. Sherburne (eds). New York: Free Press.
Willmott, H. (1998) Re-cognising the other: Reflecting on a 'new' sensibility in social and
    organizational studies. In R. Chia (ed.), *In the Realm of Organisation: Essays for Robert
    Cooper.* London: Routledge, pp. 213–41.

8

Corpus linguistics

Tony Berber Sardinha and Leila Barbara

Introduction

In this chapter, we present some ways in which corpus linguistics has been used in business discourse research. Our presentation reflects our experience in a large business discourse project and research group in Brazil, namely DIRECT, which has been active since 1991.

First, we define corpus linguistics as an area of language studies that is devoted to the compilation and analysis of corpora, which in turn are collections of texts and transcriptions of talk stored in computer-readable form that have been gathered for linguistic analysis. Second, we outline the three main characteristics of our approach to corpus analysis of business discourse, which are: (1) a focus on individual business genres, or socially recognisable communicative events, rather than on 'business language as a whole'; (2) the application and development of computer tools for business discourse analysis, as an aid in both the retrieval of information from and the discovery of otherwise unnoticeable patterns in electronic corpora; (3) an interface with systemic functional linguistics, as the main theoretical framework underpinning our corpus analyses, since it provides a wide range of resources for handling and interpreting discourse data.

Third, we review some of the research conducted within DIRECT that illustrates the two basic research paradigms in Corpus Linguistics, the corpus-based and corpus-driven approaches. The corpus-based approach is a type of research design in which researchers look in a corpus for linguistic or discourse characteristics defined ahead of time; it is sometimes referred to as a top-down approach. We exemplify this approach with studies on modals and business letter moves. The corpus-driven approach, on the other hand, is characterised when researchers explore the different patterns of association of units (normally words) in the corpus, without restricting what the actual patterns may be; this is sometimes also known as a bottom-up approach. We refer to corpus-driven studies that looked at a wide range of business discourse features, from pronouns in business meetings, to key words in invitation for bids, to metaphors in investment banks' conference calls. For both approaches, we show how we used computer programs for marking and retrieving discourse units, as well as for exploring corpora for lexico-grammatical patterns. We claim that both these approaches are valid and yield interesting findings.

Finally, we conclude the chapter by arguing that for a number of reasons, corpus linguistics is likely to become more popular with business discourse research, and as a result more researchers need to become acquainted with some of the tools and techniques of corpus research as well as with the theoretical consequences of adopting a corpus linguistic perspective to business discourse.

Background

The main goal of this chapter is to discuss how corpus linguistics can be used in business discourse analysis, reflecting our experience in the DIRECT project (www2.lael.pucsp. br/direct), at the Catholic University of São Paulo, Brazil. For a general introduction to the subject, the reader is referred to the standard textbooks in the area, such as Biber et al. (1998), McEnery and Wilson (2001), Kennedy (1998) and Berber Sardinha (2004); for reference on advanced topics, see McEnery et al. (2006), and for an anthology of the field, see Sampson and McCarthy (2004) and Teubert and Krishnamurthy (2007).

Broadly defined, corpus linguistics is an area of language studies that is devoted to the compilation and analysis of corpora. Corpora, in turn, are collections of texts and transcriptions of talk stored in computer-readable form that have been gathered for linguistic analysis. Hence, a selection of carefully picked examples (clauses, sentences, paragraphs) is not a corpus in this sense. A corpus needs to be made up of whole texts (both oral and written), even if one is interested in certain specific features of each text, say for instance relative clauses. It would not fit the definition of a modern corpus to collect only a sample of sentences which have relative clauses in them.

Corpus linguistics has been used in a variety of fields, such as lexicography (Sinclair 1987), language teaching (Sinclair 2004), discourse analysis (Stubbs 1996), applied linguistics (Hunston 2002), lexicology (Halliday et al. 2004), forensic linguistics (Coulthard 1993), translation (Laviosa 2002) and metaphor (Deignan 2005), among others.

This chapter will illustrate the basic approach to business corpus analysis we have developed in the DIRECT Project at the Catholic University of São Paulo, Brazil, since 1991. We will use this space to raise some possible guidelines for us to think of criteria we find, or found, interesting to follow as a community when collecting data for each specific piece of research so that we move in the direction of business corpora that can be shared. Below we outline the guiding principles of our business discourse research agenda that pertain to corpus linguistics:

  1 *Genres.* Genres are 'recognizable communicative events, characterized by a set of communicative purposes identified and mutually understood by members of the professional or academic community in which they regularly occur' (Bhatia 2004: 23). Our work has focused on the analysis of corpora of individual genres rather than on mixed corpora of 'business language', because we believe that by looking at individual genres we get closer to the use of language in social contexts. That is, professionals in business contexts do not simply use 'business language' but 'business language' in 'typified communication processes' (cf. Bargiela-Chiappini and Nickerson 2002: 278). As Halliday (2006: 296) reminds us, 'the basic unit of the corpus, however we may choose to access it, is a text', and texts are exemplars of genres. This stance is in line with an orientation in corpus linguistics that understands that textual varieties must be studied on their

own because of the wide variation that exists between them (cf. Biber 1995). This theoretical stance has an impact on our methodology of business discourse analysis in a corpus perspective, mainly on the kinds of corpora that are collected, with genre-specific corpora being preferred to mixed genre ones. A discourse analyst is usually interested in analysing specific types of language. The case of a business discourse analyst will not be different. We may want to compare different types of interactants in a specific situation, a specific company or activity in a company, a type of member of the business community in different situations and so on. As such, we, discourse analysts, can concentrate our efforts on building specific corpora so that we will eventually have a wide range of corpora reflecting a variety of genres that exist in business contexts. Ethnographic work in most social and applied social research has shown the importance of taking into account local cultures and specific situations; what speakers, participants in general as well as researchers and teachers, declare as perceived, as facts, are frequently, if not always, subjective; the increasing communication between partners from varied parts of the world demands detailed analysis of differences in culture that may cause misunderstanding. We believe our genre-specific approach can cater for this, providing 'thick descriptions' (Bhatia 2004) that link the description back to the contexts of use.

2 *Tools*. Corpus linguistics requires the use of tools to retrieve data from corpora. We have used WordSmith Tools (Scott 2004) since it offers both basic and advanced tools for handling corpus data (Berber Sardinha forthcoming). We have also striven to develop tools to automate analyses that WordSmith Tools does not offer. We have thus developed a large set of tools for corpus analysis (CEPRIL Toolbox; http://www2.lael.pucsp.br/corpora), which includes taggers, segmenters, translation aligners, parallel concordancers, and semantic and cohesion analysers, among others. Some will be discussed below. All are freely available online.

3 *Systemic functional linguistics*. Our work has been developed on the interface between corpus linguistics and systemic functional linguistics (SFL). As Halliday (2006) puts it, there is 'a natural affinity' (p. 293) between them: 'systemic linguists have always tried to base their descriptions on observable data' (p. 295) because 'systemic theory . . . readily accommodates corpus-derived findings into the ongoing elaboration of a description' (p. 296). Corpus linguistics and SFL are 'two traditions with a common ground' (Thompson and Hunston 2006b: 1), as they share some key principles: language is functional; language is probabilistic; language use is conditioned by the context of culture and situation; language studies need to be based on language produced in real situations. They are distinguished in terms of methods of analysis, as some corpus linguists tend to approach the corpus bottom up, with no a priori hypotheses, whereas the systemicist tends to bring to bear his or her hypotheses about the use of that specific language or variety in the contexts of the culture and of the situation being studied. For SFL (Halliday 1985, 1994; Halliday and Matthiessen 2004) the choices a speaker makes, among all the possible choices that a language offers, have to do with conscious or unconscious cultural and situational factors that she or he may want to express or would rather hide. And those are important

features for the discourse analyst to uncover and describe in a corpus linguistic perspective.

A central debate in corpus linguistics is whether it is only a methodology or has theory-like status. Opinions are divided on this matter. On the one hand, Biber et al. (1998), Thompson and Hunston (2006a) and McEnery et al. (2006) all argue that it is a methodology. According to McEnery et al. (2006), corpus linguistics is 'a whole system of methods and principles of how to apply corpora in language studies and teaching/learning' (p. 7). Unlike sub-fields such as phonology, morphology or semantics, which 'describe a certain aspect of language use' (p. 7), corpus linguistics methods can be 'aligned with any theoretical approach' (Thompson and Hunston 2006b: 8). On the other hand, proponents such as Sinclair (1991), Tognini-Bonelli (2001) and Hoey (2005) posit that corpus linguistics should be more than a method, since it can change the way we conceptualise the very nature of language. Sinclair (1991) has proposed the idiom principle as the chief organising principle in language, in order to account for the fact that speakers overwhelmingly reuse prefabricated lexical units rather than create original ones. A number of theories have been proposed by corpus linguists to account for corpus findings, such as linear unit grammar (Sinclair and Mauranen 2006), lexical priming (Hoey 2005) and pattern grammar (Hunston and Francis 2000). All of these theories share the common view that language is first and foremost made up of lexicogrammatic prefabricated units rather than preexisting grammatical categories that are filled with lexis, and that the ensuing patterns could not be accounted for without recourse to corpus linguistics.

In a corpus linguistic perspective, the choice of such units is probabilistic in nature (Halliday 1992) and corpus-based investigations can and should reveal this probabilistic patterning. As Halliday (2006) puts it, the corpus has theoretical status: 'data-gathering is never theory-free, and collecting, managing and interpreting corpus findings is itself a highly theoretical activity' (p. 294). In this perspective, even though corpus linguistic methods can be applied to a range of existing areas of linguistic inquiry (such as syntax or lexicology), its potential would be underestimated if it did not cause a fundamental shift in perspective about how language is organised and ultimately about what language is. As Sinclair puts it (2001), 'a corpus of any size signals like a flashing neon sign "Think again"', making it 'extremely difficult to fit corpus evidence into received receptacles' (p. 357), since 'language obstinately refuses to divide itself into the categories prepared in advance for it' (p. 358).

A related debate that surrounds corpus linguistics is the distinction between the corpus-based and the corpus-driven approaches. In a corpus-based approach, researchers start with theories that predate corpus linguistics and apply these theories to the analysis of a corpus, which means that the role of the corpus would be to provide examples of a given theory (Tognini-Bonelli 2001). In a corpus-driven approach, on the other hand, the analytic categories are not defined beforehand. The researcher starts with minimal analytic assumptions on the data and lets frequency and co-occurrence indicate salient features that deserve attention.

In what follows, we present examples of research carried out in the DIRECT project that falls broadly within the corpus-based and corpus-driven paradigms to discuss how we dealt with the challenges of doing business discourse analysis from a corpus perspective.

Table 8.1 Corpora used in the modals study (tokens refer to the total running words, and types to the total unique words)

	Brazilian	Portuguese
Meetings	10	2
Tokens	120,022	12,164
Types	8,316	1,881

Corpus-based research

In a corpus-based orientation, we may distinguish two basic kinds of search procedures for retrieving information from a corpus: word-based and tag-based.

To illustrate the first kind, we will report on a study (Barbara and Berber Sardinha 2005) in which we focused on the use of modals in Brazilian and Portuguese meetings (all held in Portuguese).

The data consisted of the corpora shown in Table 8.1.

The methodology consisted of drawing up a list of Portuguese modals (based on the relevant literature) and then concordancing the corpus for these. We used the Concord tool in WordSmith Tools to pick up all occurrences of the search words in each national variety. Once the Concord had given us all occurrences of the search string, we checked them in order to disambiguate polysemous words, such as 'achar', which also has a material sense of 'to find' in addition to being a modal ('to think'), and deleted occurrences of the latter sense. This was accomplished by first typing a letter code (for example, 'n') in the 'Set' column of the concordance to designate an unwanted line. We then sorted the concordance by the Set column (which clustered all the unwanted lines in a sequence on the screen) and rechecked every instance. Finally, we tabulated the results for each corpus and then interpreted the findings.

The second major type of corpus-based procedures is what we call tag search, which occurs when the analyst needs to retrieve occurrences of categories rather than words. To accomplish this, the corpus must be annotated in advance. Annotation is the process whereby the corpus texts are encoded with extra information. This is typically achieved by typing special tags in the body of the texts, in one of three ways:

1 manually: tags are inserted by a human being;
2 interactively: tags are inserted by a human being with the help of a computer program;
3 automatically: tags are inserted entirely by a computer program, but can be amended subsequently if necessary.

To illustrate the first kind (manual annotation), we will refer to Lima-Lopes (2005), a study of systemic functional processes in Brazilian sales promotion letters. His data consisted of 104 letters selling a wide range of products and services such as magazine subscriptions, furniture, insurance etc. The corpus amounted to 33,633 words.

In SFL, six main kinds of processes are distinguished:

1 material: processes of doing, e.g. to bring, to transfer;
2 mental: processes of feeling, e.g. to believe, to think;
3 relational: processes of being, e.g. to be, to have;
4 behavioural: processes of behaving, e.g. to watch, to evaluate;
5 verbal: processes of saying, e.g. to speak, to request;
6 existential: processes of existing, e.g. there is/are.

In view of these issues, the author tagged the entire corpus manually, and in order to do so he devised a tag set consisting of tags of the format <proc000>, where the angle brackets are called the delimiters (encapsulating the tag from the surrounding text), and the remainder (proc000) shows the main process type and sub-type. For example, <proc201> denotes a 'process type: mental, sub-type: perception'. He was then able to search the corpus for each tag (mainly using WordSmith Tools Concord), typing as a search string a tag or part of a tag. For instance, in order to retrieve the material processes, the search string was <proc100>.

A major problem with manual tagging is that the amount of data that can be handled is limited. Matthiessen (2006: 109) estimates this limit to be around 100,000 words (or 10,000 clauses).

The second type of annotation is interactive, whereby the human analyst is aided by a program that prompts him or her to enter the desired tag at the appropriate places. These programs act as an interface between the annotator and the corpus, providing facilities to ensure reliability, consistency and uniformity on the one hand and flexibility in the creation and modification of the tag set on the other. This is essentially a manual annotation process, but the actual insertion of the tags into the tags occurs in the background, hidden from clear view. In the course of the DIRECT project, we have experimented with the Systemic Coder (O'Donnell 2002), a tool for annotating texts according to systemic functional categories.

The Systemic Coder allows the user to create his or her coding scheme and save it for further use. We have used a simple tag set for transitivity, consisting of the six main process types (as shown above). After defining the coding system, the user then begins annotating the corpus. The first step is the segmentation of each text into units; we chose to segment our texts in clauses. The Coder does not segment by clause automatically (but it does so at the paragraph and sentence level). This is done by clicking the points in the text where a boundary needs to be inserted. After that, the program prompts the user to choose the option from the tag set, and then introduces the corresponding tag in the corpus, in a tidy and reliable manner. Figure 8.1 illustrates the Systemic Coder prompting the analyst to select a tag to code the clause in red letters in the upper part of the screen.

The program also enables the researcher to retrieve the tags, with the Cell Analysis option. This brings up a count of a tag and one example segment, as illustrated in Figure 8.2 (CELL is the tag, and 'members' are the segment numbers that received that particular tag).

The third type of annotation is automatic. The most common is part of speech tagging, whereby a special computer program (usually called a POS tagger) determines the grammatical category of each word in the corpus and assigns tags accordingly. As part of the DIRECT project, we have made available online two POS taggers, QTag and Tree-Tagger, for six languages (English, Portuguese, French, German, Italian and Spanish),

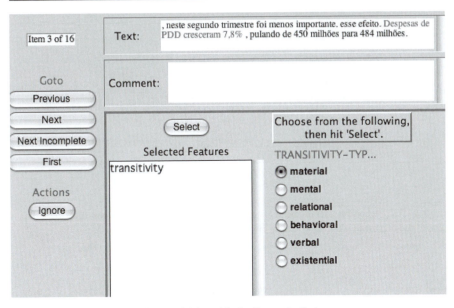

Figure 8.1 Coding a corpus for transitivity with the Systemic Coder

```
CELL: relational
Count: 6
Members: {2 5 9 10 11 16 }
Example:
neste segundo trimestre foi menos importante esse efeito.
```

Figure 8.2 Retrieval of tags in the Systemic Coder (translation from Portuguese: 'in this second quarter this effect was less important')

through the CEPRIL Toolbox. Figure 8.3 shows part of a Brazilian business conference call tagged for part of speech by the Tree-Tagger. The data are from Berber Sardinha (2008), who looked at metaphors in banking conference calls and needed to determine the word class of each potential metaphor.

The tagged files were by default tokenised and lemmatised by the tagger. Tokenisation is a process whereby the text is laid out in such a way that each token is placed on a separate line in the order in which it appears in the text, and lemmatisation is the process of assigning a root form to each word of the text. In the example, there are three columns of text, separated by tabs. The left-most column contains the conference call text; the middle column shows the part-of-speech tags (V: verb, DET: determiner, NOM: noun, PRP: preposition, ADJ: adjective); and the right-hand column presents the lemmas of each word (e.g. 'continuar', 'to continue', is the lemma of 'continuamos', 'we continue').

As can be seen, automatic tagging is advantageous, in the sense that it is speedy and generally reliable (about 97 per cent accuracy). However, it is restricted mostly to structural analysis, such as morphology and syntax. In the DIRECT project, as we mentioned, our focus has been on the interface between corpus linguistics and SFL. We have therefore

```
continuamos   V     continuar
sendo         V     ser
o             DET   o
banco         NOM   banco
com           PRP   com
o             DET   o
maior         ADJ   maior
valor         NOM   valor
de            PRP   de
mercado       NOM   mercado
entre         PRP   entre
os            DET   o
bancos        NOM   banco
brasileiros   ADJ   brasileiro
```

Figure 8.3 Text tagged for part of speech (translation from Portuguese: 'We continue to be the bank with the biggest market value among Brazilian banks')

worked towards developing automatic tools for dealing with systemic analysis. We developed three such tools, aimed at automating transitivity, appraisal and genre analysis. For reasons of space, we will comment on the transitivity tagger only.

The transitivity tagger (available in the CEPRIL Toolbox) reads an input corpus and then tags it for process types; currently it accepts Portuguese or English texts only. The aim is to automate an analysis such as the one carried out by Lima-Lopes, reported above (the author did not use it because it was not available at the time), where the system identifies each verb and labels its process type accordingly.

The transitivity tagger utilises a part-of-speech tagger as well, as a preliminary means for picking up all the verbs in the corpus. It then assigns process tags to each of these verbs, using a so-called dictionary, which is a list containing verbs and their tags. On its website, there is a dictionary available for Portuguese with 232 entries.

An excerpt from a tagged corpus (of Brazilian conference calls) follows:

> houve [Pr:existencial] uma grande recuperação de preços dos ativos no primeiro trimester; neste segundo trimestre foi [Pr:relacional] menos importante esse efeito. (translation from Portuguese: 'there was a high recovery of asset prices in the first quarter; in the second quarter this effect was less important'.)

The tags are placed immediately after each verb. In the excerpt, the process tags are [Pr:existencial] (existential process) for the verb form 'houve' (there was) and [Pr:relacional] (relational process) for the verb form 'foi' (was).

The tool also presents a listing of the frequency of processes, as well as concordances, as shown in Figure 8.4.

Corpus-driven research

In this section, we present research from the DIRECT project that illustrates the corpus-driven approach.

```
22  de e índice de basiléia em 18 , 5 % , vamos falar [Pr:verbal] um pouco mais para frente disso ; o :
23   de 4 , 65 , um pequeno crescimento , vamos falar [Pr:verbal] disso também , mais adiante . nessa :
24  mbém , mais adiante . nessa nova tela vamos falar [Pr:verbal] da demonstração de resultados . como
```

Figure 8.4 Concordance of verbal processes in a conference calls corpus

Barbara and Berber Sardinha (2007) analysed a corpus of business meetings by looking at a particular kind of collocation (Sinclair 1991): two-word clusters (also known as bigrams, two-word bundles or two-word chunks), which are recurrent combinations of two adjacent words.

The corpus was made up of ten meetings held in Brazil adding up to 120,022 words. The first step in analysing this corpus was the extraction of key words, or words that occur statistically more frequently in a corpus then in a reference corpus. The reference corpus is usually a general language corpus comprising several genres and registers, and must ideally be at least five times larger than the corpus being described (Berber Sardinha 2004). Our reference corpus was the DIRECT project's own Banco de Português, with 230,460,560 words at the time (it now comprises over 700 million), covering both written and spoken contemporary Brazilian Portuguese.

We extracted the key words with the KeyWords application in WordSmith Tools. Our immediate observation was that pronouns were particularly salient among the top key words, as Table 8.2 illustrates.

The overwhelming presence of pronouns suggests the importance of interaction in the meetings. We then decided to look at clusters formed by the key pronouns 'eu', 'gente', 'você' and 'nós'. The extraction of clusters was carried out with the NSP – Ngram Statistics Package (Banerjee and Pedersen 2003), which we made available online in the CEPRIL Toolbox. It retrieved all the two-word clusters with a frequency higher than one and computed the Mutual Information (MI) statistic, which measures the probability of two words occurring next to each other in view of their joint and separate frequencies. The MI scores indicate the degree of statistical attraction between a pair of words; the higher the score, the more attraction there is, and the lowest acceptable score is generally 3 (Stubbs 1995). We then pulled out of the list provided by NSP only those clusters with an $MI \geq 3$.

To illustrate, Table 8.3 presents some of the pronoun clusters formed with 'eu', 'I', having an $MI \geq 3$.

In systemic terms, these clusters brought to the surface the important role of the interpersonal metafunction, revealing some of the ways in which participants built relationships with one another. In addition, there was a lack of technical vocabulary among the top key words (the first technical item, 'mostruário', 'product display', appeared at position 61 in the key words table), which suggests that the meetings were not particularly information packed.

Another study that exemplifies the corpus-driven approach is Barbara and Scott (1999), who analysed a corpus of invitation for bids (IFBs) from four countries (Brazil, Bangladesh, India and Jamaica). The corpus, amounting to 49, 532 words, was bilingual, with texts written in Portuguese (Brazilian IFBs) and English (the other IFBs). Part of the study was devoted to the examination of key words, and because the corpus was bilingual, the researchers had to use two different reference corpora, one for each language. Both

Table 8.2 Key words in Brazilian meetings (all p < . 000000)

	Key word		Frequency in meetings		Frequency in reference corpus	
	Original	Translation	Number	%	Number	%
1	Eu	I	2,265	1.81	248,174	0.11
2	Pra	For	1,351	1.08	48,410	0.02
3	Gente	People	1,263	1.01	70,789	0.03
4	Então	So/then	1,095	0.87	89,223	0.04
5	Você	You (sing.)	1,068	0.85	130,921	0.06
6	É	Is	3,554	2.84	1,971,886	0.86
7	Aí	There	731	0.58	51,773	0.02
8	Tem	Has	1,529	1.22	433,609	0.19
9	Está	Is	1,465	1.17	419,868	0.18
10	Que	That (conj.)	5,765	4.61	4,981,254	2.16
[. . .] 16	Nós	We	534	0.43	64,214	0.03

Table 8.3 Pronoun clusters formed with 'eu', 'I', in Brazilian meetings

Frequency	Cluster		MI	Translation
158	Eu	acho	5.4604	I think
62	Eu	tenho	5.5972	I have
62	Eu	estou	5.6386	I am
44	Eu	vou	5.2757	I will/I go
31	Eu	posso	5.8015	I can
20	mas	eu	3.4449	But I
15	Eu	quero	5.6339	I want
15	Eu	queria	4.9924	I'd like
14	Eu	falei	5.3709	I said/told
14	deixa	eu	5.7188	Let me

reference corpora were of newspaper texts; for Portuguese, a selection of 4.9 million words from a Brazilian newspaper, and for English, 9.3 million words from a British newspaper, both published in 1994.

After retrieving the key words with WordSmith Tools, the researchers observed patterns across the key words which might indicate important characteristics of IFB st. One such pattern was the presence of modals 'shall' (English) and 'dever' (Portuguese), which performed similar functions in the bids, such as the specification of the features of bids ('bids shall contain. . .'), the definition of terms ('the term x shall mean. . .') and the statement of obligations and rules ('the bidder shall be prepared to. . .').

Besides key words, there are other procedures that may be employed in corpus-driven research. We illustrate this with a study of metaphors in a corpus of seventeen banking conference calls (98,515 tokens). Berber Sardinha (2007) developed a tool for identifying metaphor candidates (i.e. possible metaphors) in corpora which was trained on hand-coded data to notice patterns that systematically predict metaphorical expressions. This

#	Word	Tag(Prob)	Vehicle	Left Bndl	Right Bndl	Framewk	Wordclass
000001	crescimento	.9108	.9966	1.0000	1.0000	.8690	.6887
000002	segmento	.9078	1.0000	1.0000	1.0000	.8503	.6887
000003	liquidez	.9061	1.0000	1.0000	1.0000	.8421	.6887
000004	margem	.8901	.9387	1.0000	1.0000	.8235	.6887
000005	fechou	.8873	.9701	1.0000	1.0000	.7627	.7041

Figure 8.5 Metaphor candidate words in conference calls

tool (the Metaphor Candidate Identifier) is available from the CEPRIL Toolbox and works with both Portuguese and English corpora.

The tool returns a list of words in the corpus ranked by probability of metaphor use, which is reproduced in part in Figure 8.5. The column 'Tag' shows the metaphor probability of individual words.

Figure 8.5 shows that the words most probably used metaphorically in the conference calls corpus are 'crescimento' (growth), 'segmento' (segment), 'liquidez' (liquidity), 'margem' (margin) and 'fechou' (closed), all with at least an 89 per cent (.8873) chance of metaphor use. The next step was analysing each of these words in context, through concordances, which confirmed their metaphorical use in conceptual metaphors (Lakoff and Johnson 1980) such as BANKS ARE ORGANISMS ('crescimento'), FINANCES ARE LIQUID ('liquidez') and MARKETS ARE CONTAINERS ('fechou'), as well as in ontological spatial metaphors (signalled by 'segmento' and 'margem').

Conclusion

The distinction between corpus-based and corpus-driven has come under criticism from leading corpus linguists (McEnery et al. 2006), who claim that the difference has been largely overstated. According to these scholars, any corpus investigation must begin with some sort of theoretical assumption on the data, be it 'vagueness markers' or 'lexical patterns', and therefore there can be no 'pure' corpus-driven approach. For instance, Hunston's and Francis's (2000) work on a corpus-driven grammar started with the categories of verb and complementation. In addition, whenever researchers analyse data, they are consciously or unconsciously classifying it and placing it in some sort of category, which in many cases reflects preconceived theories (McEnery et al. 2006: 10).

Our own position is that the corpus-driven and corpus-based distinction should not be rigid, but a matter of degree. There is no pure version of either one, and researchers typically move from one to the other during research depending on the challenges presented by the data on the one hand and by the research goals on the other.

Corpus linguistics has grown enormously since the late 1980s. It is expected to continue to develop fast, as corpora become easier to obtain and to process automatically, computers gain more processing power, tools become more user-friendly and linguists become more attracted to technology. Corpus linguistics has caused an upheaval in language studies (Scott and Tribble 2006), but in business discourse analysis it has not made as big an impact. We believe there are two main reasons for this. One is that corpus linguistic tools in general are not attuned to the needs of discourse analysts; word frequency lists and concordances seem to decontextualise the data (Thompson and Hunston 2006b: 4). The other is that major theories of discourse do not incorporate frequency and co-occurrence, two major elements of corpus linguistics; even in SFL, there have been few attempts to add theoretical weight to these, and the tradition has been to rely on abstract categories that need to be counted by hand (Halliday 2006: 298; Matthiessen 2006; Thompson and Hunston 2006b: 5). But we think this situation is likely to change, not least because corpus analysis is not 'so much solving theoretical problems as increasing the demands that have to be made on a theory' (Halliday 2006: 298). That is, the methods and findings of corpus analysis will probably influence theories of discourse, new and old.

References

Banerjee, S. and T. Pedersen (2003) The design, implementation, and use of the Ngram Statistics Package. *Proceedings of the Fourth International Conference on Intelligent Text Processing and Computational Linguistics*: 370–81.

Barbara, L. and T. Berber Sardinha (2005) Cultural stereotype and modality: A study into modal use in Brazilian and Portuguese meetings. In G. Forey and G. Thompson (eds), *Text Type and Texture: In Honour of Flo Davies*. Liverpool: School of English, University of Liverpool, pp. 246–62.

Barbara, L. and T. Berber Sardinha (2007) Looking at business meetings from a corpus and systemic perspective. Direct Paper 54. Catholic University of São Paulo and the University of Liverpool. Available online at www2.lael.pucsp.br/direct.

Barbara, L. and M. Scott (1999) Homing in on a genre: Invitation for bids. In F. Bargiela-Chiappini and C. Nickerson (eds), *Writing Business: Genres, Media and Discourse*. New York: Longman, pp. 227–54.

Bargiela-Chiappini, F. and C. Nickerson (2002) Business discourse: Old debates, new horizons. *International Review of Applied Linguistics in Language Teaching*, 40: 273–86.

Berber Sardinha, T. (2004) *Lingüística de Corpus*. São Paulo: Manole.

Berber Sardinha, T. (2007) *Metáfora*. São Paulo: Parábola.

Berber Sardinha, T. (forthcoming) *Pesquisa em Lingüística de Corpus com WordSmith Tools*. Campinas: Mercado de Letras.

Berber Sardinha, T. (2008) Metaphor probabilities in corpora. In M. S. Zanotto, L. Cameron and M. Cavalcanti (eds), *Confronting Metaphor in Use: An Applied Linguistic Approach*. Amsterdam and Atlanta, GA: John Benjamins.

Bhatia, V. K. (2004) *Worlds of Written Discourse: A Genre-Based View*. London and New York: Continuum.

Biber, D. (1995) *Dimensions of Register Variation: A Cross-Linguistic Comparison*. Cambridge: Cambridge University Press.

Biber, D., S. Conrad and R. Reppen (1998) *Corpus Linguistics. Investigating Language Structure and Use*. Cambridge: Cambridge University Press.

Coulthard, M. (1993) On beginning the study of forensic texts: Corpus concordance collocation. In M. Hoey (ed.), *Data, Description, Discourse: Papers on the English Language in Honour of John McH Sinclair*. London: HarperCollins, pp. 86–97.

Deignan, A. (2005) *Metaphor and Corpus Linguistics*. Amsterdam and Philadelphia: John Benjamins.

Halliday, M. A. K. (1985) *An Introduction to Functional Grammar*. London: Arnold.

Halliday, M. A. K. (1992) Language as system and language as instance: The corpus as a theoretical construct. In J. Svartvik (ed.), *Directions in Corpus Linguistics: Proceedings of*

Nobel Symposium 82, Stockholm, 4–8 August 1991. Berlin and New York: De Gruyter, pp. 61–78.

Halliday, M. A. K. (1994) *An Introduction to Functional Grammar*, 2nd edn. London: Arnold.

Halliday, M. A. K. (2006) Afterwords. In G. Thompson and S. Hunston (eds), *System and Corpus*. London: Equinox, pp. 293–9.

Halliday, M. A. K. and C. M. I. M. Matthiessen (2004) *An Introduction to Functional Grammar*, 3rd edn. London and New York: Arnold.

Halliday, M. A. K., W. Teubert, C. Yallop and A. Cermáková (2004), *Lexicology and Corpus Linguistics: An Introduction*. London and New York: Continuum.

Hoey, M. (2005) *Lexical Priming: A New Theory of Words and Language*. London and New York: Routledge.

Hunston, S. (2002) *Corpora in Applied Linguistics*. Cambridge: Cambridge University Press.

Hunston, S. and G. Francis (2000) *Pattern Grammar: A Corpus-Driven Approach to the Lexical Grammar of English*. Amsterdam and Philadelphia: John Benjamins.

Kennedy, G. (1998) *An Introduction to Corpus Linguistics*. New York: Longman.

Lakoff, G. and M. Johnson (1980) *Metaphors We Live By*. Chicago: University of Chicago Press.

Laviosa, S. (2002) *Corpus-Based Translation Studies: Theory, Findings, Applications*. Amsterdam: Rodopi.

Lima-Lopes, R. (2005) Avaliação de um sistema de marcação textual aplicado à gramática sistêmico-funcional. In T. Berber Sardinha (ed.), *A Língua Portuguesa no Computador*. Campinas and São Paulo: Mercado de Letras and FAPESP, pp. 139–54.

McEnery, T. and A. Wilson (2001) *Corpus Linguistics: An Introduction*, 2nd edn. Edinburgh: Edinburgh University Press.

McEnery, T., R. Xiao and Y. Tono (2006) *Corpus-Based Language Studies: An Advanced Resource Book*. London and New York: Routledge.

Matthiessen, C. M. I. M. (2006) Frequency profiles of some basic grammatical systems: An interim report. In G. Thompson and S. Hunston (eds), *System and Corpus*. London: Equinox, pp. 103–42.

O'Donnell, M. (2002) Systemic Coder: A Text Markup Tool (Version 4.5). WagSoft Linguistic Software.

Sampson, G. and D. McCarthy (2004) *Corpus Linguistics: Readings in a Widening Discipline*. London and New York: Continuum.

Scott, M. (2004) WordSmith Tools, 4th edn. Oxford: Oxford University Press.

Scott, M. and C. Tribble (2006) *Textual Patterns: Key Words and Corpus Analysis in Language Education*. Amsterdam and Philadelphia: John Benjamins.

Sinclair, J. (1987) *Looking Up: An Account of the COBUILD Project in Lexical Computing and the Development of the Collins COBUILD English Language Dictionary*. London: Collins.

Sinclair, J. (1991) *Corpus, Concordance, Collocation*. Oxford: Oxford University Press.

Sinclair, J. M. (2001) Review of *The Longman Grammar of Spoken and Written English*. *International Journal of Corpus Linguistics*, 6(2): 339–60.

Sinclair, J. M. (ed.) (2004) *How to Use Corpora in Language Teaching*. Philadelphia: John Benjamins.

Sinclair, J. M. and A. Mauranen (2006) *Linear Unit Grammar: Integrating Speech and Writing*. Amsterdam and Philadelphia: John Benjamins.

Stubbs, M. (1995) Collocations and semantic profiles: On the cause of trouble with quantitative studies. *Functions of Language*, 2(2): 23–56.

Stubbs, M. (1996) *Text and Corpus Analysis: Computer-Assisted Studies of Language and Culture*. Oxford: Blackwell.

Teubert, W. and R. Krishnamurthy (eds) (2007) *Corpus Linguistics: Critical Concepts in Linguistics*. London: Routledge.

Thompson, G. and S. Hunston (eds) (2006a) *System and Corpus*. London: Equinox.

Thompson, G. and S. Hunston (2006b) System and corpus: Two traditions with a common ground. In G. Thompson and S. Hunston (eds), *System and Corpus*. London: Equinox, pp. 1–14.

Tognini-Bonelli, E. (2001) *Corpus Linguistics at Work*. Amsterdam and Atlanta, GA: John Benjamins.

9

Critical studies

Stanley Deetz and John G. McClellan

Introduction

Critical research offers unique ways of understanding and engaging organisational discourse. In particular, it offers the hope of understanding systems of power and domination and enabling more open forms of communication with the inclusion of a wider set of social values across a broad range of business activities.

While the term 'critical' has a broad set of meanings and is used to address an array of social issues across a variety of intellectual disciplines, it is typically used to describe works 'taking a basically critical or radical stance on contemporary society, with an orientation toward investigating exploitation, repression, social injustice, asymmetrical power relations (generated from class, gender, or position), distorted communication, and misrecognition of interest' (Deetz 2005: 86). Critical approaches to organisation studies stem from a variety of theoretical perspectives including the Frankfurt School's critique of arbitrary authority protected by myths of modernity (see Horkheimer and Adorno 1972), Habermas's (1984, 1987) demonstrations of the moral consequences of technological rationality usurping other forms of reason, and Foucault's (1972, 1980) descriptions of the normalisation of people and reality and the interrelatedness of power and knowledge. Collectively, critical researchers share a concern for understanding power relationships and language use within complex social practices with the hope of emancipating the disenfranchised and marginalised. With an interest in finding ways to generate more democratic systems of interaction incorporating the widespread interests of workers, stakeholders and members of the larger community, critical scholars take a politically sensitive and normative approach to the study of organisational discourse.

This chapter introduces critical studies of organisational discourse. The first section reviews critical discourse analysis (CDA) as a form of ideology critique. The second section considers more language-based critical analyses grounded in the 'linguistic turn' in philosophy. This perspective provides a different approach to critical work engaged in finding and promoting differences in meanings often hidden within organisational discourse. The third section explains the motivation for engaging in critical analyses of discourse, considers the methods needed, and reviews why critical researchers should make efforts to understand the organisational practices at the local level, critically assess these discourses, and attempt to transform them.

Organisational discourse and ideology critique

Since the early 1980s organisation studies scholars have emphasised the analysis of organisational discourse. These efforts have provided insight into the ways people talk in organisations as well as the resulting accomplishments of talk. Many of these studies have been descriptive and attended mostly to concrete situated discourse practices with little concern with the ethnographic context or larger social formations. Critical discourse studies, however, tend to be interested in both macro-levels of discourse and larger social contexts.

To aid in talking about larger social formations of discourse, Alvesson and Karreman (2000) distinguish between *discourse* conceptualised at the micro-level and *Discourse* at the macro-level, and many have embraced this convention. For instance, Fairhurst and Putnam (2004) distinguish between '*discourse* that refers to the study of talk and text in social practices and *Discourses* as general and enduring systems of thought' (p. 7). Critical studies tend to focus on both *discourse* as it occurs in organisations and *Discourse* at the larger, social level, focusing on the ways in which discursive formations become articulated by individuals within organisations. This type of research is important for exploring how larger discursive formations are reflected within organisational talk.

Consequently, many critical scholars have conceptualised the larger social *Discourse* in terms of ideologies hidden within organisational discourse. The term 'ideology' is used to express the presence of implicit values that direct thinking and action yet remain unknown and closed off from discussion, resulting in people's inability to understand or act in their own interests. The objective of ideology critique is to reveal the implicit values and asymmetrical power relations embedded within organisational discourse, with the hopes that transparency will engender discussion and enable people to choose more clearly in their own interest.

Mumby (1987), for instance, considers how ideological meaning formations are simultaneously produced and reproduced through symbolic forms such as organisational narratives. Arguing that 'ideology is materially grounded in the organised practices of social actors' and that 'ideology and power are inextricably tied together insofar as ideology articulates social reality in terms of the interests of the dominant social group(s)' (p. 119). Mumby shows how the telling of narratives functions to maintain and reproduce the organisation's mode of rationality that privileges those with power. Mumby directs our attention to the ways in which everyday, mundane, discursive practices create and maintain particular ideological power asymmetries among organisational participants.

In a similar way one form of CDA, a research tradition emergent in the early 1990s by scholars in Europe, engages in CDA to understand 'the role of discourse in the (re) production and challenge of dominance' (van Dijk 1993: 249). Explicit statements about the goals and aims of critical discourse analytic work can be found in Fairclough (1992, 1995), van Dijk (1993) and Wodak (1997), and a major journal founded in 1989, *Discourse and Society*, functions as an outlet for critical discourse analyses. For instance, Chiapello and Fairclough (2002) use CDA to expose ideology hidden within the new 'spirit of capitalism'. Their transdisciplinary textual analysis of the work of an influential management 'guru' exposes the 'spirit of capitalism' ideology embedded within a management text. They argue that this ideology legitimises the capitalist process by explaining what is stimulating about it, how it provides security, and how it assures justice. Their work to expose the ideological formations within this management literature results in the 'de-sacralization' of a discourse that has a 'real influence on the maintenance of dominant ideologies and on the actions of the managers who read them' (p. 207).

While there are many kinds of CDA, most research aims to make explicit and visible the masked ways that discourse functions ideologically. To make these claims, CDA research-ers presume that individual instances of discourse tend to function as the by-product of social relations, while those relations themselves are constituted, in part, by the collective instances of discourses that serve them. In CDA, dominant discursive forms relate to broader social and cultural processes and practices. The naturalised ideologies inherent in these forms legitimate their serving as agents of power relations. Because individuals are often not aware of how discourse functions in these ways, the CDA agenda is to make explicit the hidden power relations within social discourse. Thus, the connection between any given situated text and broader societal problems is of crucial concern to critical dis-course analysts.

To accomplish this agenda, Fairclough (1992) lays out an ambitious statement of the various functions and levels of discourse. He theorises a three-part relationship between discourse as text, as an instance of a discursive practice, and as a social practice. The first dimension he describes, 'discourse as text', refers to the linguistic and structural practices of any instance of text, broadly defined. Analysis of this dimension includes attention to the vocabulary, grammar, cohesion and text structure. The second dimension, the level of 'discursive practices', consists of the analysis of the production, distribution, circulation and consumption of texts. This dimension consists of a wide-ranging degree of analysis of how texts are created, moved from situation to situation, analysed and interpreted, acted on or ignored. Finally, the third dimension is of the 'discourse as an instance of social practices'. This dimension consists of the analysis of the ideological or hegemonic relationships that a text demonstrates and in which it participates.

Such an approach to language and discourse in context aims to reveal the explicit and implicit rules and power structures of social domains embodied in institutions by social power relationships and specific divisions of labour (Wodak 1997). Everyday life in organising sites is characterised by conflicts and disorders discursively, which, like con-tradictions, are often obscured and suppressed by myths and other organising symbols. Taking a critical discourse analytical perspective uncovers how structures are constantly being produced and reproduced in each specific interaction (Wodak 1997). Collectively, these works illuminate the role of organisational discourse in potentially exploiting and marginalising some organisational values, ideas, identities, practices and other discursive forms for the benefit of others. This interest in organisational discourse directs attention to the everyday use of language in organisations and how larger discursive formations are replicated through organisational talk.

However, it is possible to extend beyond this tradition by offering another way of critically engaging organisational discourse more informed by contemporary postmodern writings. In the next section we revisit the original insights of the 'linguistic turn' in an attempt to direct attention to alternative ways of studying and potentially transform-ing organisational discourse. This approach takes a strong constitutive perspective on discourse and considers a more intrinsic relationship between local everyday talk and larger social discourses within which it takes place.

Embracing the linguistic turn

The 'linguistic turn' arose in philosophy and other disciplines in the 1930s and refers to the 'turn' towards language for insight into political production of experience and social reality. The 'turn' does not just designate the centrality of discourse but also provides a reformed conception of discourse itself. From such a perspective, all personal experiences, as well as worldly objects, are inseparable from the presubjective, preobjective relationships within the constitutive activities that brought them into being (Deetz 2003). In other words, experiences and objects are not constant, static 'things', but are rather the outcome of relationships between people and the indeterminate outer space waiting to be constituted as a world through language. In the linguistic turn language replaces consciousness as the site of experience production. All seeing is a 'seeing as' and 'seeing as' is understood as discursive. In Heidegger's (2000) terms we engage the world 'languagely'.

The tradition of the 'linguistic turn' directs attention to the constitutive power of language and a concern with the processes by which 'natural' objects are discursively produced and subject positions reproduced (Deetz 2003). The result is that everything about an organisation is constituted through discourse. Organisational rules, practices, norms and other properties are developed and maintained through discursive practices (Kuhn and Ashcraft 2003) that are influenced by and intermixed with larger social and historical situated discourses. To understand discourse, then, is to understand the very way the human subject is constituted or positioned in the ongoing process of world production. While ideology critique works to expose hidden, dominant values that take precedence over alternatives, the focus here is not so much on ideological domination as on the restrictions and normalisations in the construction process and the suppression of potentially productive conflict over identities, ordering principles, knowledge and values. In other words, CDA influenced by the 'turn' focuses on the linguistic processes of creating organisation and the problems of undiscussability.

Like CDA, a constitutive perspective on organisational discourse inextricably links local practices with larger social understandings. The study of organisational discourse focuses on how local practices of talk are influenced by, supportive of or resistant to larger social discourse. Attention is turned towards the outcomes of organisational talk; to what is produced through talk. Furthermore, such critical work focuses on unmasking privileged understandings generated and supported by organisational discourse. Critical efforts embracing the ideas of the linguistic turn focus on the outcome of constitutive activities such as members' identities, rules, resources, rituals, and other factors contributing to 'organisational realities' produced through discourse. This strong constitutive perspective focuses on language use among organisational participants and directs attention towards the hidden and often tacit political contexts that shape organisations.

Boden (1994) takes this conceptual insight and shows that 'organisational talk both shapes and is shaped by the structure of the organisation itself' (p. 202). In her work, focusing on individual interactions among organisational participants is important for understanding the processes by which organisational structures are created and maintained. By focusing on organisational talk (or discourse) we can learn how 'conversational procedures invoked by members, characterised as members' practices, operate as both *interactionally* and *organisationally* relevant activities' (p. 202). Consequently, she shows how the study of organisational discourse is 'a multi layered affair, located and accomplished simultaneously at the structural, interactional and organisational levels of verbal exchange' (p. 203). She explains 'talk is not "micro" nor are organisations "macro"' (p. 214). Boden's work recognises the complexities of organisational talk and promotes the study of interrelationships among 'lower case' and 'upper case' discourse by claiming that the constitutive character of language does not have a micro/macro distinction.

Critical work embracing this strong constitutive perspective focuses on revealing taken- for-granted power relationships hidden within discursive structures that marginalise some organisational members. For instance, Martin (1990) examines a story told by the CEO of a large multinational corporation about a woman working for the company who recently had a Caesarean. Martin deconstructs this exemplary moment of organizational discourse to reveal suppressed gender conflicts hidden within the story. By systematically revealing a multitude of ways this discourse can be interpreted, she exposes hidden conflicts regarding various organisational taboos including public/private dichotomies and sexuality. Her analysis highlights 'how apparently well-intentioned organizational practices can reify, rather than alleviate, gender inequalities' (p. 339). While Martin's work exposes preferred value systems within organisational texts (fulfilling the objectives of ideology critique), her efforts of deconstruction also make explicit the processes that constitute organisation and how gender conflicts are censored within the ongoing, mundane and even well-intentioned organisational discourse. Overall, her research shows how important conflicts are suppressed in organisational discourse consequently supporting and reifying the interests of those with power. Clair (1993) in a similar fashion demonstrates how organisational discussions of women's sexual harassment experiences lead to specific discursive closure and conflict suppression.

Serious consideration of the 'linguistic turn' results in attempts to reveal the conflictual and political processes by which knowledge of social experience is created yet hidden within language and processes of institutional talk. Critical work takes on a different and valuable task. In considering how power is constituted in and by organisational discourse, it becomes impossible to separate discourse and power. And this loss of innocence directs critical researchers towards uncovering the various interpretations of meaning and exposing ideological roots embedded within the forms and structures of language itself.

Additionally, organisations become seen as the result of naturalised preferential value systems in which the original tension-filled conditions that initially created the organisation become forgotten and outcomes are seen as self-evident and natural. Thus, critical researchers recognise that what is seen as a stable 'organisation' is simply the result of a temporary arrest of organising processes leading to consistent, hierarchical, orderly centres of material arrangements created within larger discursive articulations (Broadfoot et al. 2004). Macro-level discourses-as-structures can be seen as existing only to the extent that they are endlessly reproduced in the language and knowledge resources deployed by individuals engaged in organising processes. By focusing on the concrete procedures, strategies, techniques and vocabularies individuals and institutions use to construct stable, coherent and meaningful images of reality, critical researchers can provide insight into the ways discursive formations become articulated, negotiated and deployed. These efforts can show how discourse is used to organise and pursue practical interests as well as reproduce relatively stable, sedimented social resources in interaction. As a result, analysis moves beyond the text itself to offer insights into the nature of text production and consumption and to reflect upon the societal discourses created and implicated therein.

Kinsella's (1996, 1997, 1999) studies of the Princeton Plasma Physics lab is one such case. The product of this lab was knowledge about fusion energy through the running of experiments that produced relatively small amounts of power from nuclear fusion. Large amounts of energy were required to produce fusion, thus a complicated set of instruments and readings was required to determine whether additional energy was actually produced. This meant that the 'science' itself was discursively formed, yet the active processes of knowledge construction and potential knowledge contestation were rarely explicit.

Since the lab was totally dependent on a large amount of federal grant money, that was itself dependent in large part on the public perception of scientific merit and success, organising discourse in this site always involved three very different sets of discursive resources and audiences. First, 'science talk' was essential for the practice of science and the construction of scientific knowledge inside the lab. Second, 'organisation process' talk involved the running of a rather large 'organisation' with real deadlines, pay distributions, authority relations etc. that often conflicted with the expectations and obligations of science talk as well as each other. Finally, 'big science talk' required involvement of the mass media, public perceptions of science and scientific process in order to garner more resources for the 'organisation'. In order to capture these different forms of discourse, their moments and links, Kinsella gathered documents, observations and interview data to examine science as organised work, science as epistemology and science–society relations. Big science talk often conflicted with the other two, leading Kinsella to conclude that scientists acted as bricoleurs, selecting and arranging elements from the discourses of diverse cultures (the project team, the lab, the community of physics, big science) to assemble and legitimate their projects. However, even these cultures are internally diverse, which means that scientists of all kinds and at all levels must engage in discursive work to construct and reconstruct their own legitimation (Kinsella 1996). As a result, discourse in the 'organisation' could only be understood when put in relation to all three larger discourses. The decisions on which experiments to run and when did not just appeal to different constituent needs – science needs, management needs, cultural industry needs – but required multilingual talk, since each discourse had a very different logic. Such talk evoked and appealed to conflicting self-definitions and forms of expertise. Each in turn qualified and disqualified different people in different ways; it both used and made power.

Broadfoot's (2003, 2007) work shows much the same in a very different organising setting. Her work uses ethnographic methods of participant observation and interviewing coupled with audio-taped interaction of both medical professionals and patients involved with genetic counselling interviews to examine how the discourse of the gene is transforming medicine as organised work. All three forms of empirical material – field notes, interviews and interaction transcripts – were treated symmetrically and then analysed according to CDA. Discursive themes and structures emerging from this analysis were then subjected to the dialogic technique of defamiliarisation to construct counter-texts, and work was done with negation to uncover the 'underbelly' of the discursive formations present and the dialectical tensions present in the empirical materials (Alvesson and Deetz 2000; Martin 1990).

Again, three very different discourses and sets of discursive practices come together to organise knowledge, work and self in this context. In this case, 'medical talk' appeals to and borrows from the discourse of the medical profession with its specific values, expectations and knowledge of genetic science and technologies. 'Patient talk' is connected to the larger public's and culture industry's understanding and discourse of the gene, genetic science and testing, with its own expectations and understandings. Finally, 'clinic talk' is the constant reminder that the clinic is an 'organisation' of workers, payrolls and profit margins as well as part of a larger health-care system. The end result of these discursive overlaps is a tapestry of tangled discursive threads such as clinical vs. commercial interests, the relationship between biology and biography, the need for knowledge and the preservation of mystery and, finally, the simultaneous fragmentation and integration of medicine as organised work. It is not as if each of these discursive threads and interests simply impacts differentially on the talk in the interview. Rather, all are endlessly negotiated out there as power relations shift, metaphors are mixed across discourses, interactants borrow and deploy the talk of others and misunderstandings or different understandings are let pass. These actions flow back out to their larger originating discursive sources – medical, patient or clinic – and transform our understandings of self, knowledge, technology and work as well as the larger institution of 'medicine' in a society increasingly constructed within, through and around the science of genetics. As a result, clinic and professional participants emerge as negotiators, coordinators and mediators, as the network of complexity that is medicine as organised work as well as the truly unpredictable nature of all clinical futures are revealed.

In each case, initial conflicts inherent in the formation of the organisation remain hidden and unknown, resulting in organisations being presented as unified, coherent and value-free. Thus, critical work focuses on exposing the constructed formations, protected through processes of naturalisation and various forms of discursive closure that result in making the initial politics of formation hidden or invisible (Deetz 1992). By examining the discursive processes that serve to reduce, suppress and eliminate alternative interpretations, definitions, meanings, values and vocabularies of action, critical researchers attempt to reclaim the conflicts inherent, yet invisible, within organisational discourse. Concern is placed on what is not being discussed, what is not known, and the preferred values represented in the discourse. Overall, critical research reclaims language as the producer of the very institutional forms that direct and constrain organisation, and efforts are made to make transparent the intrinsic conflicts that are treated as natural and unproblematic within organisational discourse. These critical researchers celebrate the ambiguity of the world and move the processes of resistance and indeterminacy to the forefront, where irony and play become preferred to rationality, predictability and order (see Weedon 1997). Critical efforts that embrace the linguistic turn offer hope for engendering new ways of engaging in organisational discourse that consider alternative organising practices.

Critically engaging organisation discourse

As already seen, most critical analyses of organisational discourse uses extended case studies. Moving through material sites and discursive moments, the extended case study design focuses on the discursive and material specificities of a setting but also on how these specificities vary across time and space. As a result, this research design engages the nested and interconnected nature of discursive moments, resources and procedures, vocabularies, strategies and techniques that are used by institutions and individuals to construct and sustain a coherent, stable representation of 'organisation'. In order to engage nested moments of discursive action, scholars apply a combination of ethnographic and discursive methods and practices, such as interviewing, participant observation, textual analyses and audio-taped recordings of interaction. This combination of methods captures the ways in which diverse structures of discourse, possessing systems of values, knowledge and belief, can situate themselves in organising practices in situ and the forms of language used, patterns of interaction and the routines in which 'organisation' becomes structured (Chouliaraki and Fairclough 1999; Fairclough 1992; Mokros and Deetz 1996). All empirical material (ethnographic field notes, interview and interaction transcripts and other documents) is then compared and contrasted to identify emergent meanings, discursive themes, practices and resources, illuminating instances of ambiguity, absence or silence, diversity and stabilisation, patterns of fragmentation and integration, destabilisation, fixation and orchestration (Alvesson and Deetz 2000).

A constitutive perspective on language and a critical motivation direct researchers towards understanding organisational events, critiquing them, and attempting to transform them. This requires the development of a critical approach for engaging organisational discourse. A productive critical methodology should move the researcher from 'an understanding of the constitution of experience, to an understanding of the social-linguistic structuring of experience, to an understanding of the politics of representation and experience, to an affirmation of the dialogic quality of existence' (Deetz 2003: 427). Engaging in this approach, researchers do not strive for superior insight or authoritative establishment of organisational truth; instead emphasis is placed on enabling open discourse among organisational participants. The aim is to find ways of reclaiming the inherent conflicts treated as natural and invisible in organisational life and engendering alternative forms of interaction.

Three moments of critical research

To accomplish these aims the critically sensitive researcher negotiates three important moments: understanding, distanciation and critique, and generative transformation (Alvesson and Deetz 2000). These moments of critical research encourage understanding organisational realities, countering reified aspects of organisational life, and generating new ways of thinking and talking. Each moment invites the researcher's attention towards particular aspects of discourses, and complements and informs the other moments. Thus critically sensitive researchers make efforts to place these moments in conversation. The remainder of this section reviews each critical moment and discusses particular methodological considerations inspired by each.

Understanding

Critical analysis of organisational discourse begins by attending to discourse as it is produced by real people in the concrete organisation situation. Discourse is not abstract or abstracted. Understanding discourse entails understanding the functions of an organisation as they exist and recognising the various ways in which organisational events, processes, knowledge, identity, technologies and other phenomena are formed and sustained.

This understanding is gained through careful investigation of organisational phenomena at the local level and seeing what is important in ethnographic terms. Understanding is based on understanding others as knowing actors responding in a real situation and appreciating their discourse as theirs. This moment is epistemologically connected to hermeneutics and Foucault's (1972) notion of archaeology, as it involves seeing the system of relations that make particular meanings possible.

Researchers attempting to develop an understanding of organisational events focus on local practices that directly connect the lives of real people to real organisational situations. The interpretation of discourse requires consideration of empirical material from a multitude of perspectives and careful attention to the varied meanings generated within particular aspects of organisational life. Thus, this process demands sensitivity to language, with the critical researcher remaining keenly aware of the contextual, constructive and often metaphorical character of language.

Murphy's (1998) study of airline flight attendants shows how understanding can be accomplished. Within this study, she explains how gender roles are constructed through discursive practices including regulating the use of make-up, weight requirements, and the wearing of high-heeled shoes. By exploring discourses taking place beyond direct observation of those in power, or 'hidden transcripts' (see Scott 1990), she gains an understanding of flight attendants' 'everyday tactics of resistance (e.g. not always changing shoes or wearing makeup)' (Murphy 1998: 524). On the surface it may seem that the actions of the flight attendants are aligned with the organisational policies, but Murphy's interpretative work shows the many hidden efforts to resist the dominant discourse. Her careful consideration of the complexities of organisational discourse as concrete work by flight attendants provides insight into how local practices can simultaneously enact and resist preferential meaning systems. Overall, her study illustrates how critical researchers can develop an understanding of discursive activities at the local level and expose how meanings are produced, reproduced, negotiated and resisted.

Distanciation and critique

While *understanding* tries to appreciate organisational actors and understand in their own terms the meanings and practices of organisational life as lived, critical analysis recognises that social construction always happens within relationships of power. Murphy (1998) did not stop at understanding the flight attendants' discourse; she called attention to historically and politically situated organisational policies to show how these were formed, sustained and resisted. This separation from organisational life can be accomplished by reflective analysis, which in CDA gives ideological critique, or by distanciation (recovery of the suppressed 'other'), which grants reclaimed indeterminacy and the possibility of conflict in the construction process. Both approaches to CDA aim at exposing the ways power relations are formed, reproduced and maintained.

Engaging in critique involves counteracting privileged ways of understanding organisational life. Here the reflective power of the analyst exposes and counters the domination reproduced in the discourse, aimed at a heightened consciousness on the part of society and actors. Distanciation involves reclaiming alternative practices, values and ideas marginalised by dominant, taken-for-granted ways of knowing. Here the analyst works in a more playful way to show moments of opening and closure in discourse and to reclaim lost conflicts (see Deetz et al. 2007).

These critical moves can be accomplished through Foucault's genealogy (1980), Derrida's (1976) deconstruction, or various other methods that expose domination within local discursive practices. Whichever means are employed, participating in this moment involves identifying privileged understandings complicit within the conventions and structures of organisational life. The texts, hidden within the background of a centred discourse, are recognised and articulated. This moment involves finding the processes that distort communication and articulating alternative values and meanings hidden from view.

Reflection is most often accomplished by using a theory of power and relating it to the discourse. Tompkins (1993), for instance, promotes reflection as a means of critiquing organisational practices within NASA. His work on unobtrusive control and decisional premises promotes reflection as the means for understanding the formation and consequences of organisations developing particular decisional premises. However, reflection has some difficulties. In particular, it implies that someone is capable of reflecting upon and recognising a more productive way to engage in discourse. It presumes a knowing, enlightened individual agent who has the capability to see beyond the current discourse to imagine a new way of interacting. A constitutive view of discourse, however, might go beyond this and consider the possibility that organisational participants actively, and often unwittingly, pursue the interests of others in the guise of their own (Deetz 1998).

Critique through reflection is often dependent either implicitly or explicitly on the application of normative ideals for discursive action. Habermas (1984, 1987) provides a template for critique by developing normative standards for engaging in discourse that aims at mutual understanding without systematic distortions or other powerful influences. When related to organisations, the normative ideal includes organisational discourse absent from discursive closure – or absent from procedures, policies or other practices in which organisational participants are unable to question the meanings or unaware that they could be questioned.

Thackaberry (2004), for example, demonstrates how particular organisational conflicts about safety procedures become closed off from discussion among wildland firefighters. She further illustrates how an organisational self-study has the potential to generate discursive openings; or an opportunity where firefighters are encouraged to form their own understandings of organisational policies. This moment of critique thus uses an ideal form of interaction to assess and critique current practices on the basis of normative standards.

Distanciation establishes a space for difference by deconstructing organisational discourse to reveal alternative meanings not readily apparent. This approach highlights alternative ways of understanding organisational discourse. Deconstruction allows organisational practices to have multiple, and often conflicting, meanings within particular organisational sites. For instance, Calás and Smircich (1991) deconstruct practitioner literatures to reopen the discourse of leadership. Their efforts expose the discourse of organisational leadership as seductive game – showing the limitations and constructions in prevalent understandings of leadership.

Generative Transformation

Generative transformation fulfils the activist objectives of critical research on discourse. Critical researchers engage in change by enriching and complicating organisational discourse where new concepts and practices for organisational members become possible. This might include creative euphemisms (Bourdieu 1991) or rearticulations (Laclau and Mouffe 2001; Angus 1992). Emergent discourses might resist, transform, or otherwise allow organisational participants the possibility to generate new meanings, practices, and ways of organising. Methods for encouraging generative transformations vary; however, all focus on finding ways for organisational participants to play with and invent alternative discourses that generate the possibility of discovering new ways of interacting towards a more positive future.

For instance, Gergen et al. (2004) examine 'the practical consequences of various forms of dialogue in action' (p. 40), and are intent on finding dialogic practices that might restore vitality to organisations. They attempt to find ways of encouraging what they refer to as 'generative dialogue' that can inspire 'mutually satisfying and effective organization' (p. 45). Defining generative dialogue as coherent and integrated discourse that engages difference, emphasises affirmation, includes repetitive discursive scenarios, and generates reflexivity that leads to the development of bonds among individuals, they argue that this form of talk, rather than inattention to others or blame, can promote more effective forms of organising. This focus on discourse is important because it considers how talk at the local level can have real consequences for organisational life.

Conclusion

The three moments of critical approaches to the study of organisational discourse work in a tension-filled way both to respect organisational members and organisational life as lived and to expose systems of domination and reclaim conflicts within organisational practices. By directing attention to power relationships emergent through discourse, replacing consciousness with language as a locus of analysis, intervening in the discursive systems that marginalise alternative values, and engaging in research as a communal process, the critical research project can appropriately focus on interpreting organisational events, making reified aspects of organisational life transparent, and engendering alternative forms of discourse.

References

Alvesson, M. and S. Deetz (2000) *Doing Critical Management Research*. London: Sage.
Alvesson, M. and D. Karreman (2000) Varieties of discourse: On the study of organizations through discourse analysis. *Human Relations*, 53: 1125–149.
Angus, I. (1992) The politics of common sense: Articulation theory and critical communication studies. In S. Deetz (ed.), *Communication Yearbook 15*. Newbury Park, CA: Sage, pp. 535–70.
Boden, D. (1994) *The Business of Talk: Organizations in Action*. Cambridge: Polity.
Bourdieu, P. (1991) *Language and Symbolic Power*. Cambridge, MA: Harvard University Press.

Broadfoot, K. (2003) Disarming genes and the discursive reorganizing of knowledge, technology and self in medicine. PhD thesis, University of Colorado.

Broadfoot, K. J. (2007) *Living with Genetics: Recombining Self and Health in Modern Medicine*. Cresskill, NJ : Hampton Press.

Broadfoot, K., S. Deetz and D. Anderson (2004) Multi-levelled, multi-method approaches in organizational discourse. In D. Grant, C. Hardy, C. Oswick and L. Putnum (eds), *The Sage Handbook of Organizational Discourse*. Thousand Oaks, CA: Sage, pp. 193–212.

Calás, M. and L. Smircich (1991) Voicing seduction to silence leadership. *Organization Studies*, 12: 567–602.

Chiapello, E. and N. Fairclough (2002) Understanding the new management ideology: A transdisciplinary contribution from critical discourse analysis and new sociology of capitalism. *Discourse and Society*, 13: 185–208.

Chouliaraki, L. and N. Fairclough (1999) *Discourse in Late Modernity*. Edinburgh: Edinburgh University Press.

Clair, R. (1993) The use of framing devices to sequester organizational narratives: Hegemony and harassment. *Communication Monographs*, 60: 113–36.

Deetz, S. (1992) *Democracy in an Age of Corporate Colonization: Developments in Communication and the Politics of Everyday Life*. Albany, NY: SUNY Press.

Deetz, S. (1998) Discursive formations, strategized subordination, and self-surveillance: An empirical case. In A. McKinlay and K. Starkey (eds), *Foucault, Management and Organizational Theory*. London: Sage, pp. 151–72.

Deetz, S. (2003) Taking the 'linguistic turn' seriously. *Organization: The Interdisciplinary Journal of Organization, Theory, and Society*, 10: 421–9.

Deetz, S. (2005) Critical theory. In S. May and D. K. Mumby (eds), *Engaging Organizational Communication Theory and Research: Multiple Perspectives*. London: Sage, pp. 85–112.

Deetz, S., J. MacDonald and R. Heath (2007) On talking to not make decisions: Models of bridge and fish markets. In F. Cooren (ed.), *Interacting and Organizing: Analysis of a Board Meeting*. Mahwah, NJ: Lawrence Erlbaum, pp. 225–44.

Derrida, J. (1976) *Speech and Phenomenon*. Evanston, IL: Northwestern University Press.

Fairclough, N. (1992) *Discourse and Social Change*. Cambridge: Polity.

Fairclough, N. (1995) *Critical Discourse Analysis: The Critical Study of Language*. London: Longman.

Fairhurst, G. T. and L. Putnum (2004) Organizations as discursive constructions. *Communication Theory*, 14: 5–26.

Foucault, M. (1972) *The Archaeology of Knowledge*, trans. A. S. Smith. New York: Pantheon.

Foucault, M. (1980) *Power/Knowledge*. New York: Pantheon.

Gergen, K. J., M. M. Gergen and F. J. Barrett (2004) Dialogue: Life and death of the organization. In D. Grant, C. Hardy, C. Oswick and L. Putnum (eds), *The Sage Handbook of Organizational Discourse*. Thousand Oaks, CA: Sage, pp. 39–59.

Habermas, J. (1984) *The Theory of Communicative Action. Vol. 1: Reason and the Rationalization of Society*, trans. T. McCarthy. Boston, MA: Beacon.

Habermas, J. (1987) *The Theory of Communicative Action. Vol. 2: Lifeworld and System of Society*, trans. T. McCarthy. Boston, MA: Beacon.

Heidegger, M. (2000) *Introduction to Metaphysics*, trans. G. Fried and R. Polt. London: Yale University Press. (Original work published 1953.)

Horkheimer, M. and T. Adorno (1972) *Dialectic of Enlightenment*, trans. J. Cumming. New York: Herder and Herder. (Original work published 1947.)

Kinsella, W. (1996) A 'fusion' of interests: Big science, government, and rhetorical practice in nuclear fusion research. *Rhetoric Society Quarterly*, 26: 65–81.

Kinsella, W. (1997) Communication and the construction of knowledge in a scientific community: An interpretive study of the Princeton University Plasma Physics Laboratory. PhD thesis, Rutgers University.

Kinsella, W. (1999) Discourse, power, and knowledge in the management of 'big science': The production of consensus in a nuclear fusion research laboratory. *Management Communication Quarterly*, 13: 171–208.

Kuhn, T. and K. L. Ashcraft (2003) Corporate scandal and the theory of the firm: Formulating the contributions of organizational communication studies. *Management Communication Quarterly*, 17: 20–57.

Laclau, E. and C. Mouffe (2001) *Hegemony and Socialist Strategy: Towards a radical Democratic Politics*, 2nd edn. London: Verso.

Martin, J. (1990) Deconstructing organizational taboos: The suppression of gender conflict in organizations. *Organization Science*, 11: 339–59.

Mokros, H. B. and S. Deetz (1996) What counts as real? A constitutive view of communication and the disenfranchised in the context of health. In E. B. Ray (ed.), *Communication and Disenfranchisement: Social Health Issues and Implications*. Mahwah, NJ: Lawrence Erlbaum, pp. 29–44.

Mumby, D. (1987) The political functions of narrative in organizations. *Communication Monographs*, 54: 113–27.

Murphy, A. G. (1998) Hidden transcripts of flight attendant resistance. *Management Communication Quarterly*, 11: 499–535.

Scott, J. (1990) *Domination and the Arts of Resistance: Hidden Transcripts*. New Haven, CT: Yale University Press.

Thackaberry, J. A. (2004) Discursive opening and closing in organizational self study: Culture as the culprit for safety problems in wildland firefighting. *Management Communication Quarterly*, 17: 319–59.

Tompkins, P. K. (1993) *Organizational Communication Imperatives: Lessons from the Space Program*. Los Angeles: Roxbury.

van Dijk, T. (1993) Principles of critical discourse analysis. *Discourse and Society*, 4: 249–83.

Weedon, C. (1997) *Feminist Practice and Poststructuralist Theory*, 2nd edn. Oxford: Blackwell.

Wodak, R. (1997) Critical discourse analysis and the study of doctor–patient interaction. In B. Gunnarsson, P. Linell and B. Nordberg (eds), *The Construction of Professional Discourse*. London: Longman, pp. 173–200.

10

Mediated communication

Julio Gimenez

Introduction

Mediated communication in business (MCB) has been widely investigated since the late 1980s. Research in this area can be grouped into what we can term the 'medium turn' and the 'discourse turn'. Studies in the 'medium turn' concentrated on the communication medium itself (e.g. email, fax). They mainly aimed at gaining a thorough understanding of how electronic media worked and the capabilities they offered users (e.g. Daft and Lengel 1986; Lengel and Daft 1988; Rice 1984). More recently, however, studies have brought the notion of context under consideration, giving rise to the 'discourse turn' in MCB. Among other things, this latter stream of research has pointed to the need of focusing on how medium and context interact (Lind 1999, 2001; Markus 1994; Nickerson 1999; Yates et al. 1999; among others). Later studies in the discourse turn have broadened the concept of context and have approached MCB as a discursive space where medium, physical context and users shape and are shaped by the reality of the workplace (e.g. Akar 2002; Turner et al. 2006).

This chapter first examines studies that have contributed to the development of MCB. It then analyses emerging issues in relation to MCB and how these issues have been approached and researched. It also considers the latest developments in the field and illustrates them with studies conducted in different international settings. The chapter ends by discussing possible future directions and argues for a change of focus in favour of the critical investigation of issues of power and identity in mediated business discourse.

Context: The 'medium turn' and the 'discourse turn' in MCB

In the early 1980s, research in mediated communication was motivated by the need to establish electronic media as a legitimate means of communication in business settings (Daft and Lengel 1986; Lengel and Daft 1988; Rice 1984). Daft and Lengel (1986) set out to investigate the advantages and drawbacks of computer-mediated communication (CMC) as compared to face-to-face communication in what they termed the 'channel-capacity hypothesis'. One of the major conclusions of the studies they conducted to test their hypothesis suggests that electronic media are less rich in terms of the capabilities they offer users (Daft and Lengel 1986; Lengel and Daft 1988). This feature of the media influences the choice of channel according to the content and nature of the communicative task. Thus they claimed that users would prefer electronic media for routine communication, turning to face-to-face communication for non-routine and possibly more complex communicative tasks. Studies like Lengel and Daft (1986) are representative of the 'medium turn'.

In the following decade, a second group of studies which followed the social influence theory (Fulk et al. 1990) moved away from the capacity hypothesis to make room for other, more significant variables such as corporate context and corporate culture. These early studies on the relationship between medium and context initiated the 'discourse turn' in MCB. Ferrara et al. (1990) produced one of the first investigations on the connection between context and media. They discovered that in CMC people rely more heavily on the norms of the social context to understand and respond to messages than in face-to-face communication. They concluded that the social norms of a corporation influence CMC, but this influence is later tempered to accommodate new media to the organisational social norms. Their findings clearly evidence the close interrelationship between media and context.

In her 1994 study, Markus examined the intersection between corporate culture and electronic media, arguing that the adoption of electronic media for a variety of communicative purposes is determined by corporate culture. Thus, if technology is seen as central to corporate culture, a corporation will tend to favour electronic communication regardless of the media capacity. In electronic-media-oriented corporations, Markus found that managers preferred mediated communication for both simple and complex communicative events. Markus's study thus points to the importance of examining not only media but also their context of use, including corporate culture.

Another influential study that looked at the connection between context and CMC is Louhiala-Salminen's (1997) investigation of the impact that technological advances have made on the business environment in Finland. Louhiala-Salminen found that developments in communication technology had introduced changes to the social context of the Finnish businesses she investigated. More importantly, she pointed to the fact that these changes were reflected in the language and register of the communications, which had become more informal (also see Gimenez 2000). Recognising the close connection between media, context and writer, Louhiala-Salminen approached faxes as socially constructed genres, which shape and are shaped by the practices of the business context that generates them. In a similar study on email messages written in English as a lingua franca, Kankaanranta (2006) also looked at the contextual and textual relationships in CMC, focusing primarily on emails for internal communication. Kankaanranta studied the emails in her corpus as representative of three different yet related genres: emails as 'noticeboard' for information distribution (to employees), emails as 'dialogue' for information exchange (between employees), and emails as 'postman' for document delivery by means of attachments (to and between employees). These three types of emails, Kankaanranta concluded, were crucial in supporting the communication activities of the multinational corporation she investigated. Studies like these show that written genres are windows on the discursive reality of corporations.

Along similar lines, Nickerson (1999, 2000) researched a Dutch multinational and found that CMC was very much 'embedded in the organisational practices of the corporation' (2000: 175). Nickerson examined different aspects of English use in her corpus, such as code (Dutch or English), type of situations where English was required, the communicative purposes of the messages, and their structural and lexical elements. Her research offers interesting insights into the corporate reality of multinationals in relation to written communicative practices, the role that electronic media play in them, and the status of English as an international language of communication (Bargiela-Chiappini et al. 2007). Nickerson concluded that CMC had a very active role in helping to structure both the organisational practices and the reality of the corporation she investigated.

Also influenced by the social impact of corporate communication, Lind (2001) investigated how men and women differ in their perception of CMC, in an attempt to establish a connection between gendered identities and mediated communication. She concluded that the women in her study perceived electronic media as a more satisfying medium of communication than did the men. However, their preference worked against women as the culture of their workplace preferred men's choices in relation to means of communication. Lind's study calls for a more comprehensive approach to these issues and draws our attention to the fact that the equation between context and media should also take gender and power issues into consideration (Herring 1993, 2003).

Trends and latest developments: The second phase in the discourse turn

Later studies have taken a broader perspective on discourse, focusing on the impact of electronic media on 'business discourse in context' (Harris and Bargiela-Chiappini 2003: 155). This new perspective has resulted in a second phase of the discourse turn in which studies have adopted more complex views of the roles of new media in corporate settings, incorporating political, social and economic dimensions (Akar 2002; Gimenez 2002). This need not mean that linguistic and discoursal features are no longer important. Rather, these studies propose a change of direction by looking at how political, social and economic forces that are constantly at play in business communication are formalised in the language and the discourses of the workplace.

Adopting a 'multilayered, ethnographic analysis' (Bargiela-Chiappini et al. 2007: 177), Akar (2002) has shown how the use of, and in some cases resistance to, new electronic media mirrors the tensions between local and global cultures. Akar adopts a 'macro-to-meso-to-micro' analytical approach (Bargiela-Chiappini and Nickerson 2002), which starts by examining the national culture of doing business in Turkey before considering corporate culture at the meso-level of analysis. Against this background, the author goes on to analyse the micro-features introduced by changes in communication technology. Macro-social phenomena, such as Turkey's late, state-led industrialisation process and the unique sociohistorical conditions of the country, Akar contends, 'manifest themselves in concrete ways in specific areas of business practices' (Akar 2002: 310) like the bureaucratic and hierarchical quality of their discourses. At the meso-level, Akar found a close correlation between the type and culture of the organisations she researched and the features of the discourses they produced. Thus, for example, a company with a hierarchical structure produced a highly structured and formal type of communication, whereas another company, where the American and Turkish cultures coexisted, adopted a communication style that tended to be more democratic and less formal. At the micro-level,

Akar demonstrated how the adoption of electronic media seemed to be dictated by the nature of the medium (faxes in this case) more than any other factors. Akar concludes, however, that in studies like hers it is always important to 'note that none of these factors is an independent variable; instead, they are all intertwined in many complex ways' (Akar 2002: 319).

Frameworks that combine several dimensions of analysis, like the one used by Akar, may show more clearly the complexities of the discursive reality of a corporation. Conflicts at a macro-level, such as the tensions arising from globally adopted and locally constructed identities, can be detected in the use of and resistance to new media, in certain linguistic preferences and discourse forms in corporate communication, all of which call for a multi-layered analytical approach. Gimenez (2002), for instance, investigated how these tensions permeate the very fabric of the discourses of a multinational corporation. Focusing on the communication practices between the head office based in Europe and the Argentine sub-sidiary of a multinational conglomerate, Gimenez demonstrated how the globally adopted identity of the head office conflicted with the locally constructed identity of the Argentine subsidiary. This clash resulted not only in a 'dual system' of document drafting, which included two different styles and sometimes two different codes (English and Spanish), but also, and possibly more importantly, in a 'dual identity' operating in the Argentine subsidiary; and this despite the fact that in some cases the local reality and values 'seem[ed] to override some of the globally-adopted conventions to which the head office in Europe wanted the Argentinian subsidiary local agents to adhere' (Gimenez 2002: 340).

Gimenez's (2002) study shows that issues of identity and power cannot be ignored in mediated business discourse research and should be examined at different levels. At the macro-level, the history of multinationals and the way they organise their activities to do business, i.e. their global identity, should be taken into account. In this study, the head office is defined as ethnocentric, that is, with a high concentration of power in its hands, and expecting to reduce communication to the minimum by imposing a uniform style. This style stands in sharp contrast with the local corporate culture (the meso-layer in Akar's framework) of the Argentine subsidiary, as mirrored in the comments of a local manager: 'There was no way I could make them [head office agents] see those parts were not necessary to us here. I finally decided to leave them [the parts] to put an end to the story' (Gimenez 2002: 327). At the discoursal level, there are a few interesting observa-tions to make. These comments show not only the differences in style between head office and subsidiary, linguistically realised by the use of 'them' and 'us', but also the tensions resulting from such differences: 'there was no way I could make them see. . .'. It is also interesting to see that by exercising power the head office managed to impose its style on the subsidiary ('to put an end to the story'). From a critical perspective, these comments show the locally constructed identity being silenced ('finally decided to leave them') by the power conferred on the head office by its global identity as a multinational.

More recently, Turner et al. (2006: 246) have added a new dimension to the analysis of mediated business discourse. Taking email as a legitimate communication medium, they set out to research the role and use of electronic media as 'a way of exhibiting presence within organisations' and how presence can be a tool for performance assessment. Turner and colleagues argue that the concept of 'presence' has changed from physical to virtual and is now measured by an employee's availability to appear online, either on instant messaging or by email. Visibility is further reinforced by the employees' communication competence to recognise not only 'what is said but also how it is said and through what channels' (Turner et al. 2006: 242). The authors also point to the fact that email, viewed as a tool to mark presence and visibility, can be used in relation to performance assessment. Indeed, they managed to demonstrate that managers tended to evaluate the performance of those employees who reported receiving many emails and using email more frequently in a more favourable light than the performance of those employees who reported otherwise. These observations point to the degree of embeddedness of email in corporate culture, and to the fact that it can also be used as a control mechanism.

These are three of the many examples that illustrate the need for researching the interplay between media, power and context from a more discursive perspective, possibly using research methods from the field of discourse analysis, which have been long established in disciplines like linguistics. These research perspectives may throw new light on old debates and help to highlight issues which have somehow been underresearched or gone unnoticed in the past, as the next section aims to explore.

Main issues and approaches so far

As has been discussed in the previous sections, research in MCB has generated a plethora of issues and approaches, some more revealing than others, but all equally helpful in making business discourse the exciting field of research it has now become. This section will focus on the main issues in researching business communication under the two turns identified above, while examining the analytical approaches used in researching such issues.

One of the first and central issues in the investigation of CMC has been media capacity. As already discussed, early studies concentrated on isolating the capabilities that electronic media offered users (Daft and Lengel 1986; Lengel and Daft 1988; Rice 1984). These studies used a comparative approach to investigate channel capacity by which the users' choices of media were compared along two dimensions: electronic and face-to-face communication. The obvious shortcoming of these early studies was their selective approach to the study of communication. In trying to isolate features of the media, these studies ignored more compelling factors that influenced users' choice such as context, power, identity and gender.

The second crucial issue in the studies reviewed in the previous section is the connection between media and context. Studies in what I have termed the discourse turn in MCB overcame some of the problems that early studies had experienced by taking a more socially oriented approach to examining mediated communication. Many studies in this group have used a textual analytical approach to investigate how the complex relationship between media and context is reflected in the genres analysed. For example, Louhiala-Salminen (1997) followed a textual approach to the description and analysis of the different linguistic realisations in the five distinct fax types which she identified. In a similar vein, Nickerson (1999) carried out a text-based qualitative analysis of emails in a multinational corporation to show that corporate conventions, which are part of the larger culture of the company, determine users' choice of code as well as media. Gimenez (2000) also used a textual approach to determine the emerging register patterns in emails for external communication in a UK-based export company. Helpful to our understanding of electronic media in corporate contexts as these studies have been, most of them, however, have failed to problematise the contexts which generated the data, offering them as 'unquestionable, untheorised sets of "facts"' (Blommaert 2005).

A third important issue arising from recent studies has been the incorporation of more problematic aspects of mediated business discourse such as global and local cultures. As briefly discussed before, Akar (2002) uses a multilayered, ethnographic approach to the investigation of factors that affect business communication (for a full description of this analytical model, see Bargiela-Chiappini and Nickerson 2002). Akar made interesting links between factors operating at the macro-level of analysis (national culture) and elements at the meso-level (corporate culture). These two levels of analysis provided a background to her textual analysis. Gimenez (2002) also used a mix of qualitative techniques (interviews, observations and genre analysis) to access the discursive identity of the subsidiary which he investigated.

The final issue in this section is the broader perspective of discourse that the latest research has taken. This is an important change of emphasis in studies of business communication as it has allowed researchers to incorporate a more complex reality into their analysis. Following this shift, recent studies have investigated factors such as global and local identities, their similarities and differences, and how these materialise in the discourses of, for example, multinationals. Similarly, issues like power, presence and evaluation have now started to emerge in studies of mediated business discourse (e.g. Turner et al. 2006). These new opportunities also pose new challenges. If power and identities are to be researched alongside other factors which have already found their way into mediated business discourse, a more critical perspective to examining discourse in business settings, such as critical discourse analysis (CDA; Fairclough 1989), is required. This is further explored in the following section.

Power and identity: Future directions in mediated business discourse

Mediated communication has now become a complex phenomenon and part and parcel of business reality. To explore the complexities of new issues in MCB, analytical approaches should consider not only the means of communication (e.g. email) but also the status that organisations confer upon these means. The status conferred will also encompass issues of power and corporate identity. This section of the chapter argues that to be able to examine the complexities of mediated communication in business settings, research should adopt a new, more critical perspective by which the interaction between power, identity and media can be discursively analysed. This group of studies may initiate a new turn which we may term the 'critical turn' in studies of MCB.

The investigation of identity and power and how related aspects are enacted and resisted through discourses in institutional settings is a rather complex endeavour which requires critical theoretical and analytical approaches in order to escape simplistic reductions. By the same token, researching power requires recognition of the fact that analysis is already an act of power that demands a high level of self-reflection on the part of the researcher and analyst. These principles are encapsulated in CDA, an analytical approach which has already become established in organisation and management theory (Phillips and Hardy 2002). Before briefly describing CDA as an analytical framework, the next section looks at research on power and identity in business discourse.

Identity has become a widely researched area in organisational studies, emphasising its plural, multifaceted nature. However, there has been a marked difference between how identity has been investigated in business discourse and in mediated business communication. Sveningsson and Alvesson (2003), for instance, offer a fine example of research in business discourse that investigates the processes through which 'individuals create several more or less contradictory and often changing managerial identities (identity positions)' (p. 1165). They used multiple methods and long-term fieldwork to create a case study on the managerial identities of a director of administration. They concluded that organisational discourses influence the creation of work identity as much as identity affects the creation of organisational discourses. Unlike previous work on identity which emphasised its coherent, continuous and distinctive nature (Dutton et al. 1994), Sveningsson and Alvesson defined identity as struggle for self-definition and integration; a struggle that involves contradictory and evolving discourses.

In sharp contrast to Sveningsson and Alvesson, most studies in identity and mediated communication have adopted a rather narrow approach, focusing on 'virtual identities' understood as the social and physical cues that users reveal when communicating (Walther 1995), the veracity of the information they exchange (Harasim 1993) and the gender they assume (Turkle 1995). However, it seems to me that a critical analysis of the intersection between identity and mediated business discourse may reveal other, more crucial aspects: is there a connection between corporate identity and choice of media? Do users assume different identities for different media? When corporate identity changes and evolves (e.g. after promotion), does media choice also change? These are some of the many issues relating to identity and media that can be explored through CDA.

Power has been extensively researched in business communication, especially in connection with dominance and inequality. A plethora of studies have attempted to gain a more in-depth understanding of how power and power relations affect and are affected by organisations and how all these relations materialise in organisational discourses (Alvesson 1996; Hardy et al. 2000; among many others). A related group of studies (e.g. Gabriel 2000; Rhodes 2001) have also looked at how dominating power relations that are discursively supported and circulated as the norm are contested and resisted in business communication. However, power together with its associated concepts of domination and inequality has been largely absent from studies in mediated business discourse, possibly as a result of the widespread perception of mediated communication as a 'democratic equaliser'. But when employees' performance is assessed by how frequently they use electronic media (Turner et al. 2006), the equalising nature of the media needs to be questioned. Similarly, have electronic media become a vehicle for the exercise of power in contexts where managers prefer their subordinates to use certain media for certain communicative events? These and other questions could throw some new light on the relations between power, dominance and inequality in mediated business discourse.

As already stated, when issues like power and identity involved in the production and consumption of texts and discourses are focused upon, a critical approach to investigating them is required. As mentioned above, CDA is one such approach. There have been a number of publications that have described and evaluated CDA (see, for example, Wodak and Meyer 2001 and Chouliaraki and Fairclough 1999 for descriptions and analysis, and Blommaert 2005 for a critique), but here I will follow Fairclough (1989), as it constitutes the first comprehensive study of CDA which includes an extensive treatment of questions of power and identity.

Fairclough (1989) claims that the production and consumption of texts, and discourses for that matter, is governed by the social conditions that give shape to the resources which people have access to or have been given access to, and which they put to use in the production and interpretation of texts. These social conditions serve as the context in which the interaction between the processes of interpretation and production and the formal properties of a text takes place. Thus, Fairclough explains, there is a relationship between social contexts, interactions and texts, i.e. between the three dimensions of discourse. These theoretical dimensions can be researched in three corresponding analytical stages: the description of the formal properties of the text, the interpretation of the relationship between text and interaction, and the explanation of the relationship between interaction and social contexts.

As to the operationalisation of this analytical approach, Fairclough suggests the following five steps:

1 Focus on a social problem with a semiotic aspect (e.g. how the mediated discourse identity of dominant groups gets discursively circulated as normal).
2 Identify obstacles to tackling the problem (e.g. discursive practices like this are normally 'locked' into the dominant groups, so access may become an obstacle).
3 Examine whether the problem is a logical consequence of the social order (e.g. does this problem represent reality or ideology?).
4 Identify possible ways past the problem (e.g. are there alternative representations of the reality that the problem is (mis)representing? Are there also resistant texts?).
5 Reflect critically on the analysis (e.g. how does this analysis contribute to a more in-depth understanding of the problem? Does it contribute to social change? How?).

Although in a rather sketchy fashion, this brief account has hopefully demonstrated the possibilities that CDA offers to the investigation of questions of power and identity in mediated business discourse. It is hoped that this and other critical approaches to analysing new issues in mediated business discourse will find their way into future studies.

Conclusion

This chapter has presented a brief review of the main studies that have contributed to the development of mediated discourse analysis as a research site in its own right. More specifically, it has grouped studies into the 'medium turn', which focused on the capabilities of the media, and the 'discourse turn', which investigated the multilayered connections between media, context, culture, identity and power. The chapter has also argued for the need for a new turn, the 'critical turn', in mediated business discourse which will help reveal more complex realities in relation to questions of power and identity. CDA was suggested as a possible analytical framework which may inform future developments in the field.

References

Akar, D. (2002) The macro contextual factors shaping business discourse: The Turkish case. *International Review of Applied Linguistics in Language Teaching*, 40: 305–22.

Alvesson, M. (1996) *Communication, Power and Organization*. Berlin: De Gruyter.

Bargiela-Chiappini, F. and C. Nickerson (2002) Business discourse: Old debates, new horizons. *International Review of Applied Linguistics in Language Teaching*, 40: 273–86.

Bargiela-Chiappini, F., C. Nickerson and B. Planken (2007) *Business Discourse*. Basingstoke: Palgrave Macmillan.

Blommaert, J. (2005) *Discourse*. Cambridge: Cambridge University Press.

Chouliaraki, L. and N. Fairclough (1999) *Discourse in Late Modernity: Rethinking Critical Discourse Analysis*. Edinburgh: Edinburgh University Press.

Daft, R. L. and R. H. Lengel (1986) Organizational information requirements, media richness and structural design. *Management Science*, 32: 554–71.

Dutton, J., J. Dukerich and C. Harquail (1994) Organizational images and member identification. *Administrative Science Quarterly*, 43: 293–327.

Fairclough, N. (1989) *Language and Power*. London: Longman.

Ferrara, K., H. Brunner and G. Whittemore (1990) Interactive written discourse as emergent register. *Written Communication*, 8: 8–34.

Fulk, J., J. Schmitz and C. Steinfield (1990) A social influence model of technology use. In J. Fulk and C. Steinfeld (eds), *Organizations and Communication Technology*. Newbury Park, CA: Sage, pp. 71–94.

Gabriel, Y. (2000) *Story-Telling in Organizations*. Oxford: Oxford University Press.

Gimenez, J. (2000) Business email communication: Some emerging tendencies in register. *English for Specific Purposes*, 19: 237–51.

Gimenez, J. (2002) New media and conflicting realities in multinational corporate communication: A case study. *International Review of Applied Linguistics in Language Teaching*, 40: 323–44.

Harasim, L. (1993) Collaborating in cyberspace: Using computer conferences as a group learning environment. *Interactive Learning Environments*, 3: 119–30.

Hardy, C., I. Palmer and N. Phillips (2000) Discourse as a strategic resource. *Human Relations*, 53: 1227–48.

Harris, S. and F. Bargiela-Chiappini (2003) Business as a site of language contact. *Annual Review of Applied Linguistics*, 23: 155–69.

Herring, S. (1993) Gender and democracy in computer-mediated communication. *Electronic Journal of Communication*, 3, http://www.cios.org/www/ejc/v3n293.htm. Accessed 10 October 2006.

Herring, S. (2003) Gender and power in on-line communication. In J. Holmes and M. Meyerhoff (eds), *The Handbook of Language and Gender*. Malden, MA: Blackwell, pp. 202–28.

Kankaanranta, A. (2006) 'Hej Seppo, could you pls comment on this!' Internal email communication in lingua franca English in a multinational company. *Business Communication Quarterly*, 69: 216–25.

Lengel, R. H. and R. L. Daft (1988) The selection of communication media as an executive skill. *Academy of Management Executive*, 2: 225–32.

Lind, M. R. (1999) The gender impact of temporary virtual work groups. *IEEE Transactions on Professional Communication*, 42: 276–85.

Lind, M. R. (2001) An exploration of communication channel usage by gender. *Work Study*, 50: 234–40.

Louhiala-Salminen, L. (1997) Investigating the genre of a business fax: A Finnish case study. *Journal of Business Communication*, 34: 316–33.

Markus, M. L. (1994) Electronic mail as the medium of managerial choice. *Organization Science*, 5: 502–27.

Nickerson, C. (1999) The use of English in electronic mail in a multinational corporation. In F. Bargiela-Chiappini and C. Nickerson (eds), *Writing Business: Genres, Media and Discourses*. Harlow: Longman, pp. 35–56.

Nickerson, C. (2000) *Playing the Corporate Language Game*. Amsterdam and Atlanta, GA: Rodopi.

Phillips, N. and C. Hardy (2002) *Understanding Discourse Analysis: Investigating Processes of Social Construction*. Thousand Oaks, CA: Sage.

Rice, R. E. (1984) *The New Media: Communication, Research, and Technology*. Beverly Hills, CA: Sage.

Rhodes, C. (2001) *Writing Organization*. Amsterdam: John Benjamins.

Sveningsson, S. and M. Alvesson (2003) Managing managerial identities: Organizational fragmentation, discourse and identity struggle. *Human Relations*, 56: 1163–93.

Turkle, S. (1995) *Life on the Screen*. New York: Simon & Schuster.

Turner, J. W., J. A. Grube, C. H. Tinsley, C. Lee and C. O'Pell (2006) Exploring the dominant media: How does media use reflect organizational norms and affect performance? *Journal of Business Communication*, 43: 220–50.

Walther, J. B. (1995) Related aspects of computer mediated communication: Experimental observations over time. *Organization Science*, 6: 196–203.

Wodak, R. and M. Meyer (2001) *Methods of Critical Discourse Analysis*. London: Sage.

Yates, J., W. J. Orlikowski and K. Okamura (1999) Explicit and implicit structuring of genres in electronic communication: Reinforcement and change of social interaction. *Organization Science*, 10: 83–117.

11

Negotiation studies

Anne Marie Bülow

Introduction

Negotiation can be defined as the process of communication whereby two parties seek to resolve their conflicting interests in a manner that both parties prefer to the alternative.

Only a portion of the research on negotiation deals explicitly with the discourse that the negotiators use. This chapter reviews the major contributions in the discursive field, divided into three major categories. First, studies based in pragmatics, conversation analysis and sociolinguistics are introduced, in order to demonstrate the insights that are available from negotiation transcripts analysed e.g. for speaker roles and face strategies. Second, conflict handling is treated with a review of studies based on argumentation and social constructivism. Lastly, intercultural negotiation studies are reviewed, with examples of comparative studies and their often contradictory results, particularly in studies of western and non-western participants.

Since negotiation is strategic in nature, it necessarily represents a set of overlapping goals – some of them substantive, like a good price, some relational, like trust. These goals may be complementary or in opposition. For professional business negotiators the job is to secure a settlement within their bargaining range, and to trade interests wisely. The purpose of this chapter is to ask what difference the knowledge of language use can make to this process.

Discourse may be said to be of interest because it is used:

- to present information, framed in a manner that renders it relevant and preferably attractive to the partner;
- to present offers, refusals, threats and promises that set out the available options;
- to extract information and frame the next turn in terms of expected action;
- to control the flow of topics in the dialogue and to summarise;
- to construct common ground and shared future scenarios;
- to shift the partner's perception of the parties' relative power and the value of their best available alternatives;
- to safeguard personal relations by attention to face needs, i.e. both parties' need for respect and sympathy.

   Academic studies of negotiation talk represent a number of scholarly starting points. From the management perspective, studies seek to uncover systematic connections between process and outcome; for example, is there a direct connection between the amount of information exchanged and joint gains? Social psychologists enquire into cognitive patterns such as perceptions of trustworthiness or fairness; for example, how is an image of trustworthiness built discursively? Discourse analysts look at the micro-processes of the negotiation, such as the significance of overlaps and interruptions. Teachers of business communication seek results that can be taught to improve performance: what, for example, is the effect of a non-native speaker appearing overly tentative or overly assertive?

Background

While general persuasiveness has been described for centuries, scholars of management and conflict resolution have paid detailed attention to the communication patterns of negotiation from the 1960s onwards. Thus Morley and Stephenson (1977) supplied 45 minutes' worth of negotiation transcript in order to systematise what is accomplished interactionally by different moves. Influential textbooks by Fisher and Ury (1983) and Lewicki and Litterer (1985) dedicated serious interest to the formulation of the 'yesable proposition', to the linguistic creation of climate, and to the construction of principles underlying the argumentation.

   By 1992 the field was well established: Putnam and Roloff's edited volume *Communication and Negotiation* could review substantial work on topics including speech acts, facework, argumentation, and framing and reframing.

   Recent research-based textbooks in negotiation theory are characterised by great sensitivity to discourse; excellent reviews of relevant research can be found in the reference sections of Thompson (2008) and Lewicki et al. (2006).

Methods

Studies of negotiation discourse vary widely. Types that are exemplified in this chapter include:

- studies centred on patterns of talk, typically based on conversation analysis (CA) and using short fragments of natural speech. The overview introduction by Firth (1995b) explains the basic point that within CA no assumptions are made about the speaker's strategic intention. Thus it makes sense to talk of acts such as 'threats' only if an utterance is *treated* as such by the next speaker.
- studies based on pragmatics and interaction theory. Pragmatic studies often use speech acts to investigate the management of face concerns, particularly in cross-cultural studies. Interaction studies code long sequences as acts and moves, which can then be seen to form cycles of tactical reciprocation (e.g. a threat answered with a counter-threat) or backing down (side-stepping confrontation).
- studies concerned with types of arguments and claims, typically based on rhetoric and social constructivism, and often concerned with phases of negotiations matched with types of reasons and persuasive attempts.

- studies based on social psychology, where external factors like power relations and internal factors like goal motivation underlie communicative patterns. Here the focus is on the individual negotiator and his or her conflicting goals.

Owing to the strategic nature of negotiation discourse, the scholarly approach is often transdisciplinary. Thus studies interested in the conversational distribution of power may well involve traits from CA, sociolinguistics and social psychology. Different types of data give rise to different research questions; for example, a meeting may produce data for a study of the way roles are constituted between buyer and seller, while several pairs of negotiators playing the same negotiation game will supply data for comparisons of such buyer–seller relations, also across cultures. Putnam (2005) discusses different types of research questions that present themselves to analysts working with negotiation data.

Working for agreement: studies based on pragmatics, conversation analysis and sociolinguistics

Trajectory vs. local interchanges

Whatever their starting point, negotiation theorists share an interest in the sequence of offers, rejections, concessions and information sharing. In a pioneering work, Donohue et al. (1984) coded a collection of negotiations for moves of attack, defence and integration in order to chart negotiation exchanges and to check for correlations between types of move, sides and phase structure. Their corpus included both real-life union negotiations and comparable simulations. Their results showed a bias: unions attacked much more than management, and with real money at stake, union officials attacked, rejected proposals and rejected rationale much more vehemently than they did in their role-plays.

A characteristic distribution of moves may also correlate with impressions formed by the participants. Thus Neu and Graham (1995) cross-checked types of questions, self-disclosures, admonitions and prescriptions with structural variables such as role and profit, and found that some variables in the sellers' talk co-varied with their profit level – in fact, the more the sellers spoke, the less they earned, and the less satisfaction was recorded by buyers.

Common ground

Constructing agreement on common ground is a central feature in negotiation. Being able to build a solution depends on the way the parties review what they have achieved so far. But there are curious differences in the way it is done.

There is evidence that the more formal the session, the more the negotiators feel a need for explicitness. Diez (1986) compared competitive negotiation sessions with more relaxed caucus sessions, where the same participants prepared a shared viewpoint to present to the opposite party. The data revealed not only the expected formality differences in vocabulary ('it is incumbent on the Board' vs. 'we would like you to'), but also clear differences in stating common ground. Thus in competitive sessions

> speakers would give, for example, an introductory statement on a topic, a rationale for the proposal, and implications for the other side's accepting or rejecting the

proposal. Subsequent utterances were tied specifically to these context-setting utterances. Cooperative negotiations, or caucus sessions, in contrast, often used shorthand references to common understandings. (Diez 1986: 227)

The results indicate that in formal circumstances, statements about common ground take on the function of a reasoned deduction or even a moral obligation, rather than a shared vision.

Summarising is another feature that discursively creates common ground. A study by Walker (1995) investigates the category 'formulation'. In CA, a formulation is an utterance that gives the gist of the preceding talk; in Walker's union–management talks, such summaries were associated with concessions, so that the formulations occurred as a prelude to agreement-seeking on a particular point. In contrast, other studies (Charles and Charles 1999; Bülow-Møller 2005) regard formulations as power moves used strategically to manage the conversation: stating 'where we are now' creates common ground in a way that serves the speaker's interest.

Roles

Roles are sets of rights, obligations and expectations that attach to particular positions, typically including buyers and sellers.

In routine sales encounters, sellers are expected to do the talking by seeking information and making the offers. Buyers, on the other hand, are expected to give directions, ask clarifying questions, and refuse first offers. If the relationship is well established and interdependent, the search for solutions will be discursively treated as problem-solving (Charles 1996). Interestingly, the sellers in Charles's corpus treat the role with self-respect: they do not belittle their competitors, and they show empathy with the buyer's problems.

The weight of dependence, however, decides who exactly is doing the 'selling' of an idea. If a buyer has a specific need, he may very well try to 'sell' his wish to the seller, so that the persuasion is done by the unexpected party. Such an example is found in Wagner (1995), where a florist is trying to get his normal supplier to sell him some snowdrops that the supplier has promised to another customer (original data in German, translation by Wagner):

R {buyer}:	what about snowdrops? Are we going to get any more? Are we getting one rack or what?
M {seller}:	no we are getting only one layer (.) at the moment
R:	is that *really* the best you can offer? Didn't you want me as your (.) best customer?
M:	yes, yes sure[(chuckles)
R:	[*yes*
M:	well we'll have to w(h)ait a bit (.)
R:	yes but how can I become your number one customer if you don't supply me?

(Wagner 1995: 19)

Power and solidarity

The negotiation literature is replete with studies of power in negotiations; for a recent overview of several types of power, see Kim et al. (2005). But power is only effective if it is perceived by the other party, and discourse has a major role in creating a powerful stance. Thus conversational power play includes introducing, accepting or rejecting topics, and in buyer–seller negotiations the seller will often show some deference, allowing the buyer to manage the talk.

The creation of solidarity, on the other hand, is often studied through the use of pronouns, and here the evidence is less clear. Speakers who use 'inclusive *we*' (referring to everyone around the table) create a different power stance from those who use 'exclusive *we*', referring to their own side; the distribution often follows the phase structure with exclusive *we*s in the 'claiming' phase and more inclusive *we*s towards the end, where problems are solved. Correspondingly, Neu and Graham (1995) note that sellers who use a large number of exclusive *we*s reduce buyer satisfaction.

Intuitively, attention to the partner ought to create solidarity. In her comparative study of experienced and aspiring negotiators, Planken rated the frequent use of *you* as good rapport management, as in the quotation 'If you were to take the offer on the backpacks this time, your management would surely be happy' (Planken 2005: 295). In contrast, Neu and Graham (1995) found that using 'presumptive *you*s', where the seller speaks about the buyer's presumed wishes, was another tactic that reduced buyer satisfaction. In cross-cultural comparisons, Graham (2003) treated *you*s as an explicitly aggressive feature (Brazilian negotiators held the record score in this investigation).

Commands are also complex as a confrontational category. Donohue and Diez (1985) studied imperatives and found that they were used primarily among people with a long relational history. In this way, saying 'Give me more details' remains a command, but it is also a marker of solidarity and thus more intimate than 'Could you supply more details, please.'

Face

Preserving the partner's face in negotiations is a skill of rapport management which has received attention mostly in lingua franca or cross-cultural contexts (see below). But all negotiators worry about losing face, according to Wilson (1992). They worry most about being discredited in the eyes of significant others, such as their opponent or their own constituents. In this sense facework extends much further than polite phrasing. Thus defensive facework includes avoidance of topics that are problematic and repair of threatened identity so as not to look weak or foolish. In contrast, an opponent's face is defended by allowing him or her to concede without loss of face, and by providing a fulfilling role (see Fisher and Shapiro 2005 for the role of emotions in facework).

An interesting new development concerns mediated negotiations. Most people find it is easier to say no over the telephone than face to face. But with the spread of the internet, more 'talk' now takes place through email, which provides a written record. With email, personal status has less importance, and people tend to mistrust the partner more (Thompson and Nadler 2002). Again, whereas the telephone is a relatively rich, instant medium that preserves facework, the real-time, synchronous medium of instant messenger (IM) is lean and mean. Studies that compare IM with asynchronous email (which leaves time for reflection) have found that negotiators using IM show more positive and more negative emotion, while using less thanking or apology and hence even less attention to face (Pesendorfer and Koeszegi 2006).

Conflict handling: studies based on rhetoric, social constructivism and cognition

The point of business negotiations is to solve problems of conflicting interests. Consequently, the study of how opinions are shifted in negotiation is a major field of interest.

Conflicts can be toned down if the speaker forestalls a negative reaction. As in most conversations, negotiators also tend to add an explanation if they turn down a request. Firth (1995a) quotes an exporter who refuses a demand for a price cut, adding that the price is below his cost price. Such a reason is immediately acceptable and therefore reduces responsibility. Reasoning reveals the basis on which choices are made, and as such it is discursively important in any negotiation process.

Argumentation

However, in negotiations there is never just one argument. Sets of arguments have been codified in much the same fashion as the interaction moves discussed above. Thus in a routine grievance negotiation consisting of teachers' pay talk, Putnam et al. (1990) isolated a list of stock issues (adapted from original):

- 'Harm' arguments assert (or deny) that there is a severe problem with the status quo.
- 'Inherency' arguments assert that the harm was (not) caused by structural features of the status quo.
- 'Workability' arguments assert (or refute) that a proposal would solve the problem.
- 'Implementation' arguments claim that a proposal is (un)acceptable to the side or their constituents.
- 'Disadvantage' arguments claim that a proposal will (not) create harmful consequences.

As with the phase structure, it can be shown that negotiation is a process that moves priorities: Putnam et al. found that in the early stages of this negotiation the teachers centred on harm and workability arguments, to justify their claims (e.g. they were overworked, and compensation or holidays might ease the problem), while the board members relied on disadvantage (this would ruin budgeting and planning). In the later stages, the teachers switched to implementation arguments in order to prioritise issues (higher pay would be preferable for their colleagues), while their original harm arguments could be heard in the opposite camp, as the board rationalised the settlement to themselves (perhaps the teachers really were understaffed and needed the boost).

It is noteworthy that there is a distinction between quality and quantity of argumentation. Speakers who argue a great deal are not necessarily successful: Roloff et al. (1989)

found that the more arguing there was in a dyad, the more it was likely to deadlock, as arguing was symptomatic of negotiators that fought for their own advantage and did not consider joint gains. It seems that successful negotiators frame a proposal so that the receiver can see their advantage, instead of defending a point.

Framing

The insight that the offer itself should be both attractive and legitimate has a long tradition in the literature, e.g. Fisher and Uri (1983). To be attractive to the receiver, the proposal should meet an important need, and to be legitimate, it should build on some shared norm. Discursively, this means choosing terms that resonate with the receiver's values, and selecting an appropriate frame or orientation.

The frame tends to guide disputants' selection of the information they perceive. Levin et al. (1998) in their treatment distinguish between attribute framing and goal framing. The attributes of a loaded term influence the way it is perceived: thus percentage figures for *mortality rate* are judged differently from *survival rate*, and *success rate* works differently from *failure rate*. Even though the hearer knows that *30 per cent mortality* means the same thing as *70 per cent survival*, the choice of term tends to focus the hearer's attention.

With goal framing, the issue is framed so as to provide a benefit or prevent a loss. Thus the difference between paying cash and paying by credit card can be framed as *cash discount* or *credit card surcharge*, and since most people instinctively prefer to prevent a loss rather than gain an advantage, the negative frame stimulates action more often. Metaphor and analogy referring to loss and benefit are powerful linguistic options that can function as frames that gain tacit agreement for common ground and reinforce rapport (Smith 2005).

In negotiation, an important set of frames relate to fairness (for a social psychology overview of fairness studies, see Ambrose 2002). The following extract is from a telephone conversation initiated by a factory owner who lives on an island; a crumbling bridge to the mainland has been closed to heavy traffic by the local authority, and the man is trying to negotiate compensation from the council's insurance company. The two speakers frame the conflict in distinctly different terms:

> *Black*   *[insurance manager]*: [Eaton council] were under no obligation to make good the bridge, and their failure to do so therefore cannot create a liability.
>
> *Jones*:   Of course it creates a liability. That puts people out of business because they haven't done it [. . .] I mean, you don't just, when planning permission is given, you don't just change over a blasted road to make it do heavy engineering if you like overnight, and then after 20 or 30 years they come and put a weight limit on it and put you out of business. In fact, Eaton Council if you like had the power to do that bridge and then to ask for a contribution afterwards.
>
> *Black*:   Yes, that is absolutely true, as I understand it, but having the power to do it doesn't mean they have an obligation to do it.
>
> *Jones*:   They got no obligation, no obligation to the families down there now in those houses, with the bridge deteriorating every day?

> *Black*:   No, as I understand it, Eaton Council has no obligation in respect of
>   that bridge whatsoever.
> (Bülow-Møller 2005: 49)

The 'grievance owner', Jones, first tries the legal frame, and on encountering opposition he shifts to a frame of moral obligation. Black sticks rigorously to the legal frame, thus resisting Jones's frame-shift. The lack of overlap in framing is symptomatic of this particular negotiation, which soon reached an impasse.

The international and intercultural angle

International negotiation studies have become a specialised field, with a large output for both scholars and practitioners. Their focus is normally either cross-cultural, with comparisons of national styles, or intercultural, documenting culturally based pitfalls. There are anthologies of research by Ghauri and Usunier (2003), and Gelfand and Brett (2004), while overviews include Cai and Drake (1998), Gelfand and Dyer (2000), and an authoritative review by Weiss (2004). The most frequently used parameter is that of collectivism vs. individualism, i.e. the cultural value that prioritises benefits to the collective over individual rights and gains, and vice versa.

While the majority of studies are not discourse-based, many include references to discourse categories, such as face-threatening moves or the tolerance of silence, together with more classic negotiation variables, e.g. concession behaviour or risk-taking. Studies that compare several cultures on such single parameters include work by Graham and his colleagues, summarised in Graham (2003), and Brett and her colleagues, reported in Brett (2007) and Adair and Brett (2004).

The information that is produced by this wealth of studies is complex and ambiguous; for illustration, some work on negotiations involving Chinese or Japanese partners is discussed below.

Conflict and face management

'*Harmony* is an overarching goal of human interaction among Chinese people. Chinese communicate to establish and maintain a harmonious relationship, which is characterized by mutual dependency' (Sheer and Chen 2003: 52). Practically all writers stress the importance of *guanxi*, the system of personal connections, which allows partners to count on favours from each other, and of *mianzi*, face and social capital, which dictates that conflict should be avoided.

At the same time, discourse features are found that are normally associated with aggression, among them many conversational overlaps and interruptions (Graham 2003), shaming and deception (Ghauri and Fang 2001; Brett 2007), threats, and (judged by westeners) rude persistency in asking questions (Movius et al. 2006). Obviously, different norms are at work here. For example, interruptions can be interpreted as denoting eagerness, and deception may be an attempt not to lose face before the group. Westeners deceive, too: studies that follow big company deals, such as Movius et al. (2006) and Ghauri and Fang (2001), indirectly show how it is important to build up an image of a completely trustworthy person, and at the same time exercise timely hypocrisy. Thus they make it clear that high-status officials should be treated with respect even when they are wholly ignorant of a technical matter ('I pretended he was right and smiled a lot', Movius et al. 2006: 74). Conversationally, endless questions may be asked because the Chinese admire and expect relentlessness (Graham and Lam 2003), or in order to safeguard against mistakes that a team could be blamed for later.

In comparison, work on Japanese negotiation style notes very little aggression in the sense of saying 'no' or overlap (Graham 2003), but a full capability to use threats and put-downs (Tinsley, reported in Brett 2007). Attention to face is often handled though indirectness, and since features that are absent are difficult to spot, this is a source of potential difficulty. Here follows an example from Mariott (1995), where a Japanese buyer considers a purchase of cheese from an Australian producer:

> *J*: uh uhu and eh do you have any patent in Australia or eh to produce this such
>   a such a (picks up packet of cheese)
> *A*: no we don't have any patent
> *J*: patent
> *A*: no
> *J*: but eh you have know-how of the
> *A*: yeah we have the know-how
> *J*: know-how yeh
> *A*: we have two other people making this product [. . .]
> (Mariott 1995: 118)

Mariott reports that in the interviews that followed this session the Japanese buyer admitted to having lost all interest in the product when he discovered that there was no patent. However, he did not say so, and the Australian (whose face had been protected) was clearly baffled at the inconclusiveness of the interview, as he had not perceived any difficulty.

In view of this conflicting evidence, can we say that discourse studies bear out the idea of collective cultures as based on harmony? Probably the dissonance is a question of scale. Overall, valuing a long-term, trust-based relationship may easily coexist with local power-based moves.

Participants and context

While practised negotiators interviewed for the studies above report that eastern negotiation styles have little influence on their results, everyone agrees that rules for interaction are different in terms of participation.

Where typical buyer–seller negotiations discussed in the previous sections involved two people, sales in Japan and China involve delegations making elaborate presentations to each other, mostly of information that is well known to both companies, but also to a large number of other stakeholders from local and central government. Chinese delegations are often large (Zhao 2000) and are replaced without explanation (Ghauri and Fang 2001). In both countries the negotiation teams are unlikely to have the authority to decide; the primary question of communication is therefore whether the real decision-makers can be influenced, which might involve the help of a trusted third party.

Context is therefore of paramount importance; without knowledge of the norms that adhere to a speaker's position and status, the talk will have no meaning. Even more important is the role that the speaker holds as buyer or seller. Special norms of deference to the buyer, particularly in Japan, were shown by Graham, but may be waning with the young generation; and importantly, both Brett and Okumura (1998) and Drake (2001) report from their intercultural studies that the variable of culture is not particularly influential compared to that of role. The really problematic field is that of *joint* gains: in the parallel games used by Brett and Okumura, both Americans and Japanese negotiators were capable of negotiating high joint gains intraculturally; but the mixed intercultural groups left money on the table. It can be speculated that the extra effort in negotiating with a person whose norms cannot be taken for granted stopped the necessary information exchange and resulted in both parties taking what they could get from the deal. The handling of information, then, is a substantial worry that would bear further investigation in intercultural situations.

Other cross-cultural studies

There is a substantial literature of studies of language in meetings that compares traits like directness of requests and similar features of cross-cultural pragmatics, e.g. Americans with Japanese, Israelis with Indians, Germans with Norwegians, Dutchmen with Frenchmen, Danes with Spaniards, and several other combinations. Many of these studies build on simulations, and although they can show differences in style that may potentially lead to local misunderstandings, it is encouraging to note that real business relationships seem to be different from games, with both parties accommodating each other to the extent that the cultural difference is barely relevant (Cai et al. 2000). For treatments of interlanguage discourse, see Chapters 14 and 24 in this volume, or Bargiela-Chiappini et al. (2007).

Conclusions

From this survey, it would appear that the main contribution from discourse studies is to complement findings from other disciplines on negotiation behaviour by supplying both authentic data and explanatory value. The detailed accounts of what it is that negotiators actually do when they talk themselves into agreement or impasse serve to qualify anecdotal evidence from negotiators; at the same time, analyses bring out structures and patterns of information–sharing and strategic moves that serve to explain outcomes. Even if the evidence is at times ambiguous, it represents a connection between micro- and macro-levels of research in negotiation that is long overdue.

If there is a trend to be noticed in the more recent studies, it is probably that they do not isolate the communication process; rather, they treat it as one of several factors in context, highlighting interconnections. For example, there is now a general interest among negotiation theorists in how women perform, how their ambition level changes with the resistance they encounter, and how they perform in intercultural contexts representing traditionally collectivist or individualist cultures; some of these issues manifest themselves discursively. Similarly, there is interest in technology and how the use of software changes the negotiation process, and how information technology aids or hinders the intercultural process; again, some of these concerns are tied up with communication.

For teaching purposes, the trend seems to be towards greater verisimilitude in cases.

This is likely to entail collaboration between trainers with several kinds of skills, and such collaboration can only produce more professional and more enjoyable teaching of professional negotiation skills.

References

Adair, W. L. and J. M. Brett (2004) Culture and negotiation processes. In M. J. Gelfand and J. M. Brett (eds), *The Handbook of Negotiation and Culture*. Stanford, CA: Stanford Business Books, pp. 158–76.

Ambrose, M. L. (2002) Contemporary justice research: A new look at familiar questions. *Organisational Behaviour and Human Decision Processes*, 89(1): 803–12.

Bargiela-Chiappini, F., C. Nickerson and B. Planken (2007) *Business Discourse*. Basingstoke: Palgrave Macmillan.

Brett, J. M. (2007) *Negotiating Globally*, 2nd edn, San Francisco: Jossey-Bass.

Brett, J. M. and T. Okumura (1998) Inter- and intracultural negotiations: U.S. and Japanese negotiators. *Academy of Management Journal*, 41(5): 495–510.

Bülow-Møller, A. M. (2005) Persuasion in business negotiations. In H. Halmari and T. Virtanen (eds), *Persuasion across Genres: A Linguistic Approach*. Amsterdam: John Benjamins, pp. 27–58.

Cai, D. A. and L. E. Drake (1998) The business of business negotiation: Intercultural perspectives. In M. Roloff (ed.), *Communication Yearbook* 21. Mahwah, NJ: Lawrence Erlbaum, pp. 153–89.

Cai, D. A., S. R. Wilson and L. E. Drake (2000) Culture in the context of intercultural negotiation: Individualism–collectivism and paths to integrative agreements. *Human Communication Research*, 26(4): 591–617.

Charles, M. L. (1996) Business negotiations: Interdependence between discourse and the business relationship. *English for Specific Purposes*, 15(1): 19–36.

Charles, M. L. and D. Charles (1999) Sales negotiations: Bargaining through tactical summaries. In M. Hewings and C. Nickerson (eds), *Business English: Research into Practice*. London: Longman, pp. 71–82.

Diez, M. E. (1986) Negotiation competence: A conceptualization of the rules of negotiation interaction. In D. G. Ellis and W. A. Donohue (eds), *Contemporary Issues in Language and Discourse Processes*. Hillsdale, NJ: Lawrence Erlbaum, pp. 223–37.

Donohue, W. A. and M. E. Diez (1985) Directive use in negotiation interaction. *Communication Monographs*, 52: 305–18.

Donohue, W. A., M. E. Diez and M. Hamilton (1984) Coding naturalistic negotiation interaction. *Human Communication Research*, 10: 403–25.

Drake, L. E. (2001) The culture–negotiation link. *Human Communication Research*, 27(3): 317–49.

Firth, A. (1995a) 'Accounts' in negotiation discourse: A single-case analysis. *Journal of Pragmatics*, 23(2): 199–226.

Firth, A. (ed.) (1995b) *The Discourse of Negotiation: Studies of Language in the Workplace*. Oxford: Pergamon.

Fisher, R., and D. Shapiro (2005) *Beyond Reason: Using Emotions as you Negotiate*. New York: Viking.

Fisher, R. and W. Ury (1983) *Getting to Yes: Negotiating Agreement Without Giving In.* Glenfield: Hutchinson.

Gelfand, M. J. and J. M. Brett (eds) (2004) *The Handbook of Negotiation and Culture.* Stanford, CA: Stanford University Press.

Gelfand, M. J. and N. Dyer (2000) A cultural perspective on negotiation: Progress, pitfalls, and prospects. *Applied Psychology*, 49(1): 62–99.

Ghauri, P. and T. Fang (2001) Negotiating with the Chinese: A socio-cultural analysis. *Journal of World Business*, 36(3): 303–25.

Ghauri, P. N. and J.-C Usunier (eds) (2003) *International Business Negotiations*, 2nd edn. Amsterdam: Elsevier.

Graham, J. L. (2003) Viv-à-vis: International business negotiations. In P. N. Ghauri and J.-C. Usunier (eds), *International Business Negotiations*, 2nd edn. Amsterdam: Elsevier, pp. 23–50.

Graham, J. L. and N. M. Lam (2003) The Chinese negotiation. *Harvard Business Review*, 81(10): 82–91.

Kim, P. H., L. R. Pinkley and A. R. Fragale (2005) Power dynamics in negotiation. *Academy of Management Review*, 30(4): 799–822.

Levin, I. P., S. L. Schneider and G. J. Gaeth (1998) All frames are not created equal: A typology and critical analysis of framing effects. *Organisational Behaviour and Human Decision Processes*, 76(2): 149–88.

Lewicki, R. J. and J. A. Litterer (1985) *Negotiation.* Homewood, IL: Irwin.

Lewicki, R. J., D. M. Saunders and B. Barry (2006) *Negotiation*, 5th edn. Boston, MA: McGraw-Hill.

Marriott, H. (1995) The management of discourse in international seller–buyer negotiations. In K. Ehlich and J. Wagner (eds), *The Discourse of Business Negotiation.* Berlin: Mouton de Gruyter, pp. 103–26.

Morley, I. E. and G. M. Stephenson (1977) *The Social Psychology of Bargaining.* London: Allen and Unwin.

Movius, H., M. Matsuura J. Yan and D.-Y. Kim (2006) Tailoring the mutual gains approach for negotiations with partners in Japan, China, and Korea. *Negotiation Journal*, 22(4): 389–435.

Neu, J. and J. L. Graham (1995) An analysis of language use in negotiations: The role of context and content. In K. Ehlich and J. Wagner (eds), *The Discourse of Business Negotiation.* Berlin: Mouton de Gruyter, pp. 243–72.

Pesendorfer, E. and S. Koeszegi (2006) Hot versus cool behavioural styles in electronic negotiations: The impact of communication mode. *Group Decision and Negotiation*, 15: 141–55.

Planken, B. (2005) Managing rapport in lingua franca sales negotiations: A comparison of professional and aspiring negotiators. *English for Specific Purposes*, 24: 381–400.

Putnam, L. L. (2005) Discourse analysis: Mucking around with negotiation data. *International Negotiation*, 10: 17–32.

Putnam, L. L. and M. E. Roloff (eds) (1992) *Communication and Negotiation.* Newbury Park, CA: Sage.

Putnam, L. L., S. R. Wilson and D. B. Turner (1990) The evolution of policy arguments in teachers' negotiations. *Argumentation*, 4: 129–52.

Roloff, M. E., F. E. Tutzauer and W. O. Dailey (1989) The role of argumentation in distributive and integrative bargaining contexts: Seeking relative advantage but at what cost? In M. A. Rahim and M. Afzalur (eds), *Managing Conflict: An Interdisciplinary Approach*. New York: Praeger, pp. 109–19.

Sheer, V. C. and L. Chen (2003) Successful Sino–Western business negotiation: Participants' accounts of national and professional cultures. *Journal of Business Communication*, 40(1): 50–85.

Smith, T. H. (2005) Metaphors for navigating negotiations. *Negotiation Journal*, 21(3): 343–64.

Thompson, L. (2008) *The Mind and Heart of the Negotiator*, 4th edn. Upper Saddle River, NJ: Prentice Hall.

Thompson, L. and J. Nadler (2002) Negotiating via information technology: Theory and application. *Journal of Social Issues*, 58(1): 109–24.

Wagner, J. (1995) What makes a discourse a negotiation? In K. Ehlich and J. Wagner (eds), *The Discourse of Business Negotiation*. Berlin: Mouton de Gryuter, pp. 9–36.

Walker, E. (1995) Making a bid for change: Formulations in union/management negotiations. In A. Firth (ed.), *The Discourse of Negotiation*. Oxford: Pergamon, pp. 101–40.

Weiss, S. E. (2004) International business negotiation research: Revisiting 'bricks, mortar, and prospects'. In B. J. Punnett and O. Shenkar (eds), *Handbook for International Management Research*, 2nd edn. Ann Arbor: University of Michigan Press, pp. 415–73.

Wilson, S. R. (1992) Face and facework in negotiation. In L. L. Putnam and M. Roloff (eds), *Communication and Negotiation*. Newbury Park, CA: Sage, pp. 176–205.

Zhao, J. J. (2000) The Chinese approach to international business negotiation. *Journal of Business Communication*, 37(3): 209–37.

12

Multimodal analysis

Giuliana Garzone

Introduction

The development of computer-mediated communication and the evolution of the World Wide Web have made a whole range of new multimodal options available to companies, profoundly affecting the organisation of their communication. Recourse to multimodality is not exclusive to the computer-mediated environment, as there are other areas – e.g. advertising, cinema, TV – where it is used extensively. But the inherent 'multimedianess' (Askehave and Ellerup Nielson 2004: 12–13) of hypermedia computer-mediated environments (Hoffman and Novak 1996) is particularly interesting as it offers easy access to the simultaneous and integrated deployment of different media, and consequently to the utilisation of a whole range of multimodal resources – images, sounds, animation, videos. In the computer-mediated environment, multimediality gives access to multimodality, i.e. the combined utilisation of different semiotic resources within a single communicative process (cf. also Stöckl 2004: 10). Connection to the World Wide Web offers further advantages in terms of what Kress and van Leeuwen call 'distribution' (1996/2001: 7–8, 103–10), as computer-created multimodal products are made potentially available to millions of users the world over in no time and with no additional costs.

Companies have taken advantage of such options not only to enact more effective interpersonal and interorganisational communication, but also to enhance all forms of communication contributing to corporate image-building and promotion, in the business environment proper as well as in marketing activities and in relations with customers, investors and other stakeholders.

This chapter explores the impact of the spread of new multimodal technologies on corporate communication, illustrating their effects and their potentialities. For this purpose, the website of a large US corporation, Campbell Soup, will be analysed and discussed as a representative case study. In the discussion, special attention will be given to theoretical and methodological issues raised by recourse to multimodality and web-mediated communication in terms of discursive practices, rhetorical strategies and language use.

Methodological issues

The analysis of communicative practices in multimodal computer-mediated environments involves the need to identify conceptual frameworks suitable to cope with the complexity of the multimodal semiotics associated with new multimedia constellations within which traditional forms of communication are transferred, transduced or resemiotised (Kress and van Leeuwen 1996/2001; Iedema 2003). This has prompted the production of a number of studies that discuss methodological issues associated with multimodality in different contexts, including the print media, advertising, etc.

Initially, special attention was given to the integration of visual resources into communicative acts and discursive practices (Kress and van Leeuwen 1996/2001; van Leeuwen and Jewitt 2001), extending linguistic concepts, such as those of grammar and syntax, to visual communication in a systemic-linguistic framework. This paved the way to an approach in which discourse analytical tools, originally conceived for the analysis of language use above the sentence, were further extended to make them suitable to the dynamic and complex semiosis of multimodality (Kress and van Leeuwen 1996/2001). More recently, several works based on multimodal analysis (e.g. LeVine and Scollon 2004; O'Halloran 2004; Ventola et al. 2004) have explored multisemiotic meaning generation in a number of domains – from architecture to film, from video-taping to museum organisation, from humour to scientific communication – and in many cases have contributed to the development or evolution of analytic frameworks and tools, e.g. the revision of the notion of context in computer-mediated communication (Jones 2004), and the reconsideration of the relationship between media and modes, i.e. between technologies of dissemination and technologies of representation (Jewitt 2004).

As concerns the impact of multimodality on organisational communication, it has been studied in various disciplinary areas, such as system sciences, information science and technology, and business communication studies, where in general this issue is only a secondary concern in works focused on different topics, although in some cases it is given substantial attention (e.g. Segars and Kohut 2001 on the effectiveness of the CEO's letter; Coupland 2005 and Coupland and Brown 2004 on corporate social responsibility).

So far, contributions from linguists specifically dealing with multimodality in business discourse have been relatively few, and most of them have been based on the analysis of single cases or genres (e.g. most of the studies collected in Garzone et al. 2007). In the works taking a more methodologically oriented approach, a central issue has been the viability of traditional analytical tools for use in research on web-mediated communication. In this respect, Bargiela-Chiappini (2005) insists on a stratified approach that should take account of the presentational, orientational and organisational components in multimodal communication, and emphasises the 'polyphonic' quality of multimodality, which she sees as all the more challenging for linguists and discourse analysts.

More specifically, Garzone (2002) argues that the text linguistic model (de Beaugrande and Dressler 1981) can be fruitfully applied to the analysis of multimodal and multimedia discourse, provided that it is adapted and oriented towards a more generally semiotic, rather than strictly linguistic, approach (2002: 295). Along a similar line, Garzone (2007), following some studies advocating an updating of the criteria used in genre categorization (Askehave 1999; Askehave and Swales 2001), contends that the extension of genre analysis to web-mediated discourse – whether native to the web or transduced – requires a semiotically stratified approach. Thus, genre theory (Swales 1990; Bhatia 1993) should not only incorporate the notion of medium, as suggested by Askehave and Ellerup Nielsen (2004), but also take into consideration a whole range of factors associated with hyper-textuality or hypermediality, e.g. granularity, co-articulation, multiple fruition modes (reading mode, navigating mode) and interactivity, as well as the extension of the partici-pation framework afforded by web distribution.

Taking account of these methodological contributions, the analysis in this chapter will make use of discourse analytical tools, integrating them with some elements of multimodal analysis in order to adapt them to the study of hypermedia computer-mediated communica-tion (cf. Kress and van Leeuwen 1996/2001) and its inherent properties. Recourse will also be had to notions elaborated in hypertext or hypermedia research, which has now a consolidated tradition behind it (e.g. Nelson 1981; Landow 1992; Lemke 2002). A key concept that will be assumed is that, in spite of its inherent virtuality, 'the corporate web site, as an example of organisational communication, is [to be] recognised as social action on behalf of, or treated in the name of, the members of the community' (Coupland and Brown 2004: 1326).

Within this theoretical framework, the Campbell Soup website (www.campbellsoup. com, accessed 19 March 2007) will be analysed as a particularly useful case study on account of its highly articulated structure consisting of a cluster of different websites, each with a different purpose and a different audience. In the analysis special attention will be given to the distinctive features of language use in the computer-mediated environment and to the interaction between discursive practices and other semiotic resources deployed as a function of the different objectives to be pursued in each case. Furthermore, the strategic choices concerning the general orientation and structure of the website will be examined, and we will look at how multimodal resources are modulated for the purpose of constructing a specific identity for the company on the web.

The case study

Corporate websites have been around for over fifteen years, but only in the late 1990s did marketing departments start to become really interested in the commercial and promo-tional potential of the web. The evolution in web design and in the options offered has been dramatic, in a context where web design is always pushing the boundaries of what current technology allows. A lot of progress has been made from the early days of maga-zine-style brochures, where text originally produced for the printing press was transferred to the computer environment, to the most recent trends of interactive web interfaces.

Today, websites at their simplest are relatively cheap to put up, so even the smallest firms – e.g. the corner shop or the family-run firm – can have one, albeit with radically different levels of investment and commitment. For such businesses, the internet is an excellent instrument for gaining some visibility, obtaining new customers and building their brands in ways that would never have been possible before. In this respect, web-mediated communication has brought with it an inherent element of democratisation.

Thus, websites come in radically different 'sizes', from the simple one- or two-page presentation of a small company to the vastly stratified websites of global companies rep-resenting self-contained virtual worlds, populated with music, animation, videos, games etc. The website analysed here (Figure 12.1) is complex, including separate sections each performing a different role in external corporate communication (e.g. promotion, public

Figure 12.1 Campbell Soup homepage, 18 March 2007.
Image courtesy of Campbell Soup Company

relations, direct sales). This is why its analysis can provide interesting insights into the
distinctive features of different types of website.

The Campbell Soup website relies on a complex semiotic mix, with a colourful and
eye-catching visual organisation. The graphics of the whole website, dominated by red, is
in the company's traditional style, made famous by Andy Warhol's pictures, universally
celebrated pop art works which have turned Campbell's soup cans into an icon of US
consumerism. This represents an extraordinary example of 're-use' in which an artist

has borrowed and elaborated a commercially designed object, and commercial design has reappropriated it to exploit it for promotional purposes.

The homepage provides access to the essentially informative pages included in the central section of the website ('Our Brands', 'What's New?', 'Have a Question?', etc.), and to the separate branches into which the main website splits. From here one can also get access to the localised websites of the company addressed to specific national markets – Canada, Germany Belgium, Sweden, Australia, Hong Kong, Japan and Finland – drawn up in the local languages when necessary (which will not be discussed in this chapter). Thus the homepage has the status of a global portal, being the main page that can be accessed from search engines, although some of the features it offers are mainly addressed to the US market. Given this overall structure, it emerges that the different branches are aimed at different categories of recipients, American, local or global, but also laypeople or stakeholders (as, for instance, in the 'Our Company' section, which is mainly addressed to global investors).

The website ramifies into several 'Product Websites', giving access to a number of pages each devoted to a single product, with pop-up fact sheets and catalogue-like pictures: 'Campbell's Kitchen', the recipe-and-menu branch; 'Nutrition and Wellness', providing health-related information and tips; 'Our Company', featuring corporate information; 'Labels for Education', presenting a point-bonus collection programme addressed specifically to US schools, awarding them free educational equipment; and 'Shop', a direct-sale site offering Campbell Soup gadgets and collectables. Each of these sections serves a different purpose and is addressed to different groups of users. On the basis of traditional genre theory (e.g. Swales 1990; Bhatia 1993), this is enough to classify each of them as belonging to a different genre (or subgenre).

In general, on homepages all the features that are peculiar to web-mediated communication tend to be present in the highest degree, and Campbell Soup is no exception. The deployment of multimodal resources is more extensive than in most other areas of the site. In the page as a whole the hypertextual mode clearly prevails over the textual mode, as all objects, consisting mainly of hyperlinks and menus, put the user in the position of performing prevalently navigating actions rather than reading actions (cf. Askehave and Ellerup Nielsen 2004). As for the 'very short texts' functioning as links, they are mainly nominal ('Our Brands', 'Shop', 'Campbell's Kitchen' etc.), thus presenting a stable picture of the structure of the website. Some of them also give access to podcasts of company news (e.g. a press conference) and animation (e.g. a film feature illustrating how best to open soup cans). Multimodality is also exploited to introduce an advertising component. A banner takes up the higher part of the screen transversally, where lower-sodium soup cans move in one after the other, forming a crowd, and a caption flashes ('New! Now you can enjoy the great-tasting soups you love with less sodium!'). This is matched by the presence of a slogan in the uppermost left corner of the page near the Campbell's logo: 'Nourishing people's lives everywhere, every day.'

The Campbell Soup website and its branches

Noteworthy among the different branches of the website is the 'Campbell's Kitchen' section, which is devoted to menus and recipes utilising Campbell's products ('Browse our meal ideas'). This branch tries to establish an individual relationship with the user, who can register and build up her own electronic recipe box; she can also share her recipes and experiences and even photographs with other users in the 'Share ideas and tips' area, express her views in opinion polls, put forth and discuss her ideas in the 'Blogs' and in the 'Forums'. These interactive options contribute to promoting the user's personal involvement, not only in a one-to-one relationship with the company, but also with the virtual community of Campbell consumers. In discursive terms this is reflected in the genuinely interactive organisation of this section of the website, where all short texts in links are highly interpersonal, with a prevalence of the conative function ('Share your Photos') or, occasionally, of the phatic function ('What's for Dinner Tonight?'). A strong interpersonal, dialogic orientation also characterises longer texts, both on the top page and on the lower levels of the hypertext. This applies also to the captions accompanying hyperlinks, which incidentally tend to use strongly evaluative language (Hunston and Thompson 2000):

> (1) *Share your photos*
> Share a story of your kitchen experiences! Whether a delicious meal, a nifty time-saving trick or a culinary catastrophe, people are looking to read your blogs!

Only the longer texts providing the actual recipes are organised more descriptively, following the conventions of the recipe book genre. In this specific branch, the substantial promotional component characterising other parts of the website also is oriented towards public relations, being aimed at fidelisation by enhancing the sense of belonging to a virtual community ('Campbell's Community').

A public relation component characterises the 'Nutrition and Wellness' branch too, which nevertheless differs from the section that has just been discussed in that its purpose is essentially informative, as it not only aims to provide the user with all the necessary information for the correct consumption of Campbell products, but in doing so it also contributes to building the image of a company that is highly competent and prepared to give priority to health-related issues. So it comes as no surprise that this branch is the only one in the website – except for the 'Investor Center' and 'Media Relation' sections – featuring longer and prevalently informative texts. For example, the link 'The Benefits of Maintaining a Healthy Weight' leads to a moderately long text (237 words) on a lower level of navigation:

> (2) More than ever, Americans need to make achieving a healthy weight a top priority. Recent statistics estimate that 67% of American adults are overweight or obese.
> One of the most important reasons to shed excess pounds is health. Being over-weight can increase your risk for conditions such as hypertension, type 2 diabe-tes, and stroke. If you already have one of these conditions, losing weight can help you to control it and may reduce or even eliminate your need for medications.

Here, the ideational metafunction prevails, with the thematic part of all sentences taken up by inanimate objects or by a third-person pronoun (i.e. a pronoun referring to a 'non-person' or a *persona in absentia*, according to Benveniste 1966). However, the interlocutor is still present, as in the last sentence the information given so far is brought to bear on the addressee thanks to direct address with the pronoun *you*, thus reintroducing a dialogic dimension.

One would expect a similarly informative focus to characterise the 'Our Company' branch of the website, which provides all managerial and financial information about the company ('Investor Center', 'Media Relations', 'Career Center', 'Governance' and 'Campbell Worldwide'). In general, the areas of websites aimed at providing information for financial analysts, journalists, investors and other stakeholders tend to be organised in a way that is more similar to traditional informative brochures and financial documents, and texts are made available for download in pdf format.

Many companies nowadays have evolved their communication formats in response to technological advances, taking full advantage of the affordances of the computer-mediated environment. For instance, in many cases annual company reports (ACRs) are not only made easily retrievable and dowloadable for printing, but also made accessible in HTML format, which is inherently hypertextual; so the user can surf through financial documents, co-articulating them, i.e. looking only at those parts that interest him or her in the order she or he desires (although obviously this is possible only for those sections of the ACRs that are subject to statutory obligations, e.g. not for the 10-K form for US companies, which are customarily made available in 'frozen' pdf format). Making ACRs available in a hypertextual format is an obvious response to the enlargement of the participation frame-work for financial communication made possible by web distribution, which enables it to reach not only the stakeholders to whom it was traditionally addressed, but also a virtually unlimited number of recipients, and in particular the curious potential investors as well as the lay net surfers who come across the website by pure chance; of these users the drafters of the documents take account, thus granting them the status of ratified participants. What inevitably ensues is the addition of a promotional element to financial documents, aimed at attracting the highest possible number of such casual participants.

In the case of the 'Investor Center' section, this promotional component is especially prominent; its graphic organisation is similar to that of the homepage and sometimes also has animation features (cf. the 2003, 2004 and 2005 Reports). It is also clear that the overall structure of the documents is originally conceived for the hypertextual medium rather than for print, as is shown by recourse to a powerful graphic component and the use of bullet-point lists and slogans, which in the HTML version rush in quickly one after the other like a PowerPoint presentation. The text thus organised is subsequently 'reconstructed' in the form of a continuous document for the pdf (or printed) version, which nevertheless exhibits the organisation and graphic layout typical of the hyper-media computer-mediated environment. Incidentally, this is an instance of what Bolter and Grusin (1999: 59) call *re-mediation*, i.e. the process whereby new forms of commu-nication contribute to refashioning pre-existing ones. Another interesting fact is that the 'Investor Center' offers some webcasts of presentations on company performance, each accompanied by the relevant set of slides (cf. for example the 'Second Quarter 2007 Result Conference Call'), which indicates a deliberate effort to capture the user's attention and get him or her personally involved.

But the branch of the website that stands most evidently apart is the 'Shop' branch, which is aimed at the direct sale of gadgets and collectables that exploit Campbell's brand name and the graphic design associated with it. The 'shop' metaphor qualifies it as an e-commerce website, which not only enables users to interact with the company, but also has transactional aspects, offering them the possibility of 'getting things done' in the real world by means of actions performed through the computer medium, and in particular of negotiating and performing business transactions by means of electronic events. In this way, to paraphrase Searle's words (1975), users' actions have a 'website-to-world direction of fit' (that is, they actually affect reality, bringing about changes in the real world) rather than a 'world-to-website direction of fit' (as is the case, for instance, with actions performed in computer-mediated virtual environments, e.g. in video games, which present a copy of the real world where users can do things they would never be able to do in real life). From the point of view of discourse organisation, this branch of the website is the web-mediated counterpart of the mail order catalogue, featuring pictures of the objects on sale and short descriptive texts, with the difference that here fruition is not linear and the user can work his or her way in the catalogue selectively by means of links without shuffling through it page after page. Text is used in two ways: interpersonally, imperatively inviting the user to perform certain actions (e.g. for the sale of bags: 'Bag it . . . Choose from 5 vinyl Andy Warhol inspired designs'), or ideationally, naming or describing objects on sale (e.g. 'Tomato Soup Baby Doll'). In both cases, there is a strict relationship between image and text, and the latter can be understood only in the context of the visual element. It is on this relationship that the overall cohesion of each page rests (cf. Garzone 2002).

All in all, each section of the website is representative of a web genre characterised by discursive practices which on the one hand draw normatively upon pre-existing conventional discourse types, but on the other exhibit a degree of creativity or innovation, obviously prompted by transfer to the web, i.e. by their relocation to a different order of discourse. Hence their inherent hybridity and heterogeneity, typical of discursive practices in web communication (cf. Fairclough 1995: 60–1), which are the result of the recontextualisation of social interaction and related practices in a computer-mediated environment.

The most meaningful element found in all section of the website is the constant presence of a dialogic dimension, the traces of which are perceptible in linguistic and discursive choices, as well as in the contents and in the overall organisation, where an interpersonal component is always at work. This confirms the idea that a website is a discursive space characterised by a typically social dimension, where, thanks to the inherent interactivity of the computer medium, users are assigned a role in the negotiation of meaning.

Concluding observations

Thanks to a combination of multimodal analysis and discourse analytical tools, the discussion of the Campbell Soup website has provided the opportunity to examine some of the issues involved in the utilisation of multimodal resources in computer-mediated communication in the business context. The website's main branches have been examined as instantiations of different types of corporate website, each characterised by a set of peculiar characteristics, from the transactional interactivity of e-commerce websites to the highly interpersonal and socialising features of public relations websites aimed at customer fidelisation, from the ideational focus of informative websites, exhibiting longer and more traditional texts, to the brand-new mix of informativity and promotion of online corporate investor and media centres.

The website as a whole provides a telling example of an extensive and effective use of multimodal resources. A particularly meaningful aspect is the differentiation of communicative strategies in the various branches of the site in response to one of the peculiar affordances of web-mediated communication, i.e. the possibility of addressing different audiences at the same time. The different objectives pursued in the various sections can be simultaneously achieved by adjusting and modulating semiotic and discursive resources. Each section has its own generic integrity, defined (paraphrasing Bhatia and Leung 2006: 280) as a socially constructed typical constellation of form-function correlations representing a specific communicative construct realising a specific communicative objective of the genre in question. This generic integrity is exploited to project in each case a slightly different image of the company's own identity, adjusted to the communicative purpose and the intended recipients it is addressed to. At the same time all the sections in the site contribute, together with the homepage, to the construction of an overarching corporate identity. In this specific case, the overall communicative strategy seems to be aimed at projecting the image of a corporation that, despite operating in over 100 countries throughout the world, still maintains its distinctively American identity, which has a central position in its marketing effort. This strategy is obviously the result of a deliberate choice, taking pride in American identity in spite of the wave of hostility towards US commercial power which the no-global movement has fostered world-wide.

This is all the more evident if one compares the Campbell's Soup website with those of other multinational food corporations. For instance, in Nestlé's website recourse to multimodal resources tends to be limited; its homepage stands out for being plain and unadorned, featuring only a few small pictures on a white background. There are no elements highlighting the original national identity of the company, which is represented as an international corporation characterised by competence and seriousness, engaged in a wide range of socially sensitive and research activities, with the evident aim of proving the groundlessness of its reputation for inadequate social responsibility and ruthless exploitation of poorer countries. The promotional component is also weak and becomes only less so in the localised websites of the company's subsidiaries operating in the various countries. This indicates that the company, enjoying a highly consolidated market position and relying on a wide range of globally well-established brand names, is less interested in promoting its commercial image or its products aggressively.

Against this backdrop, the Campbell's Soup website stands out for its strongly American cultural connotation deriving from the choice to present the company not as a global concern but rather as a US company operating internationally, as well as for its extensive use of visual and multimodal resources, which is strictly correlated with the strong promotional component characterising it.

Prospects for future developments

After discussing a number of methodological issues relating to the analysis of web-mediated multimodal communication in the first part of the chapter, the analysis of the Campbell Soup website as a representative case study has raised a number of considerations regarding the use of multimodality in business communication. It has also illustrated the distinctive linguistic features of textual formations in web-mediated environments and emphasised the variability of discursive practices as a function of context, participation framework and purpose.

Far from being conclusive, these findings provide indications for further work, in a sector where language- and discourse-oriented research still has a long way to go. In particular, a specially interesting area of investigation regards the strict correlation between, on the one hand, the communicative purpose of each sub-website as a function of the area of corporate communication to which it belongs, and, on the other hand, the deployment of multimodal resources and the degree of hypertextuality on which it relies. This can provide the starting point for further studies focusing on different website types and analysing a substantial number of representative samples of each of them in order to test the viability of the analytical tools employed and produce generalisations that are sufficiently reliable.

Moreover, a satisfactory taxonomy of corporate and business-oriented websites based on communicative and generic criteria is still missing, so its compilation could be included among the objectives of the systematic extension of research to a large number of websites.

With regard to factors more specifically connected with corporate communication, future research efforts could lead to a better understanding of how web-mediated communication functions, and contribute to generating models suitable for the evaluation of efficiency and effectiveness in the deployment of multimodal resources. It could also help to identify the options made available by multimodal technologies that are uniquely attractive for different types of companies, and evaluate the ways in which they can be best utilised in each case.

References

Askehave, I. (1999) Communicative purpose as genre determinant. *Hermes: Journal of Linguistics*, 23: 13–23.

Askehave, I. and A. Ellerup Nielsen (2004) Webmediated genres: A challenge to traditional genre theory. Working Paper no. 6, Aarhus: Center for Virksomhedskommunication.

Askehave, I. and J. M. Swales (2001) Genre identification and communicative purpose: A problem and a possible solution. *Applied Linguistics*, 23(2): 195–212.

Bargiela-Chiappini, F. (2005) Polyphony or pseudo-dialogue? Multimodality, hypertextuality and internet banking. In G. Del Lungo Camiciotti, M. Dossena and B. Crawford Camiciotti (eds), *Variation in Business and Economics Discourse: Diachronic and Genre Perspectives*. Rome: Officina Edizioni, pp. 101–14.

Benveniste, É. (1966) Structures de relations de personne dans le verbe. In *Problèmes de linguistique générales, I*. Paris: Gallimard, pp. 225–50. (1st edn 1946.)

Bhatia, V. J. (1993) *Analysing Genre: Language Use in Professional Settings*. London: Longman.

Bhatia, V. J. and J. Leung (2006) Corporate identity and generic integrity in business discourse. In J. C. Palmer-Silveira, M. F. Ruiz-Garrido and I. Fortanet-Gopmez (eds), *Intercultural and International Business Communication: Theory, Research and Teaching*. Bern: Peter Lang, pp. 265–85.

Bolter, J. D. and R. Grusin (1999) *Remediatio: Understanding New Media*. Cambridge, MA: MIT Press.

Coupland, C. (2005) Corporate social responsibility as argument on the web. *Journal of Business Ethics*, 62: 355–66.

Coupland, C. and A. D. Brown (2004) Constructing organizational identities on the web: A case study of Royal Dutch/Shell. *Journal of Management Studies*, 41(8): 1325–47.

Fairclough, N. (1995) *Media Discourse*. London: Arnold.

Garzone, G. (2002) Describing e-commerce communication: Which models and categories for text analysis? In P. Evangelisti and E. Ventola (eds), *TEXTUS* (*English in Academic and Professional Settings: Techniques of Description/Pedagogical Application*), XIV(2), pp. 279–96.

Garzone, G. (2007) Genres, multimodality and the World Wide Web: Theoretical issues. In G. Garzone, G. Poncini and P. Catenaccio (eds), *Multimodality in Corporate Communication: Web Genres and Discursive Identity*. Milan: FrancoAngeli, pp. 15–30.

Garzone, G., G. Poncini and P. Catenaccio (eds) (2007) *Multimodality in Corporate Communication: Web Genres and Discursive Identity*. Milan: FrancoAngeli.

Hoffman, D. L. and T. P. Novak (1996) Marketing in the hypermedia computer-mediated environment: Conceptual foundations. *Journal of Marketing*, 60(3): 50–68.

Hunston, S. and G. Thompson (eds) (2000) *Evaluation in Text*. Oxford: Oxford University Press.

Iedema, R. (2003) Multimodality, resemiotization: Extending the analysis of discourse as multi-semiotic practice. *Visual Communication*, 2(1): 25–57.

Jewitt, C. (2004) Multimodality and new communication technology. In P. LeVine and R. Scollon (eds), *Discourse and Technology: Multimodal Discourse Analysis*. Washington, DC: Georgetown University Press, pp. 184–95.

Jones, R. H. (2004) The problem of context in computer-mediated communication. In P. LeVine and R. Scollon (eds), *Discourse and Technology: Multimodal Discourse Analysis*. Washington, DC: Georgetown University Press, pp. 20–33.

Kress, G. and T. van Leeuwen (1996/2001) *Multimodal Discourse*. London: Arnold.

Landow, J. (1992) *Hypertext: The Convergence of Contemporary Critical Theory and Technology*. Baltimore, MD: Johns Hopkins University Press.

Lemke, J. L. (2002) Travels in hypermodality. *Visual Communication*, 1(3): 299–325.

LeVine, P. and R. Scollon (eds) (2004) *Discourse and Technology: Multimodal Discourse Analysis*. Washington, DC: Georgetown University Press.

Nelson, T. (1981) *Literary Machines*. Swarthmore, PA: self-published.

O'Halloran, K. (ed.) (2004) *Multimodal Discourse Analysis: Systemic-Functional Perspectives*. London: Continuum.

Searle, J. R. (1975) A taxonomy of illocutionary acts. In K. Gunderson (ed.), *Minnesota Studies in the Philosophy of Science. Vol. VII: Language and Knowledge*. Minneapolis: University of Minnesota Press, pp. 344–69.

Segars, A. H. and G. F Kohut (2001) Strategic communication through the Word Wide Web: An empirical model of effectiveness in the CEO's letter to shareholders. *Journal of Management Studies*, 38(4), 535–56.

Stöckl, H. (2004) In between modes: Language and image in printed media. In E. Ventola, C. Charles and M. Kaltenbacher (eds), *Perspective on Multimodality*. Amsterdam and Philadelphia: John Benjamins, pp. 9–30.

Swales, J. M. (1990) *Genre Analysis: English in Academic and Research Settings*. Cambridge: Cambridge University Press.

van Leeuwen, T. and C. Jewitt (2001) *Handbook of Visual Analysis*. London: Sage.

Ventola, E., C. Charles and M. Kaltenbacher (eds) (2004) *Perspectives on Multimodality*. Amsterdam and Philadelphia: John Benjamins.

13

Politeness studies

Rosina Márquez Reiter

Introduction

Ever since the publication of Brown and Levinson's (1978) 'Universals in language usage: Politeness phenomena' and its revised reissue as *Politeness: Some Universals in Language Use* (1987), politeness research has thrived. The wealth of studies in linguistic politeness that had been published almost within a decade of Brown and Levinson's (1987) seminal work on the subject led some scholars (Thomas 1995) to suggest that politeness should be seen as a subdiscipline of pragmatics (Márquez Reiter 1998). The suggestion had sufficient predictive power. This is evidenced by the array of further studies that has been published on the subject, which demonstrates the ongoing interest in the field and its widening scope as illustrated by the range of studies that make use of politeness theory to investigate various types of discourse, such as medical discourse, media talk, computer-mediated interactions (Christie 2005) and business discourse, the creation of international politeness forums (*Journal of Politeness Research*, *Estudios del Discurso de la Cortesía en Español*, www.edice.org) and the recent alternative approaches that have emerged to examine the social phenomenon.

Before we proceed to examine the studies that have been carried out into the politeness of business discourse, it is apposite to provide a working definition of politeness and to explain what kind of business discourse will be the focus of this chapter. Politeness is understood as the facework 'strategies involved in friction-free[1] communication' (Márquez Reiter 2000: 5), that is, the facework strategies employed by interlocutors to protect and/or enhance each other's need for positive and negative face (see the following section). Business discourse is broadly understood as the way in which human beings communicate in business settings to get their work done (Bargiela-Chiappini et al. 2007). Therefore the communicative behaviour of participants in service encounters, that is, in social interactions between service providers and customers in some service area (Merritt 1976), is a form of business discourse. However, the service encounters settings that have been examined (i.e. public institutions and service encounters in small shops), and, in particular, the phases of these encounters that have been investigated (i.e. mainly openings and closings) are characterised by their routine nature and thus less prone to negotiation.[2] For this reason, only those studies that have analysed aspects of politeness in negotiating discourse will form part of this chapter.

In what follows, we will briefly consider the approaches to politeness theory that have been employed to examine politeness in negotiating business discourse, with special attention to Brown and Levinson's face-saving view and the rapport management perspective, given that these two approaches, in particular the former, have been deployed to examine the bulk of research into the politeness of business discourse. The studies reported will be divided into those that have focused on spoken business discourse and written business discourse, respectively. Thus, we first discuss the studies that have examined the expression of politeness in spoken business discourse from the face-saving view and from the perspective of face as a relational concept, respectively. We then turn our attention to the studies that have focused on politeness in written business discourse and, finally, we present our conclusions.

The face-saving view

Interest in politeness as an area of pragmatic inquiry had emerged before Brown and Levinson's (1978, 1987) seminal work on the subject. Lakoff (1973) was the first scholar to investigate the expression of linguistic politeness on the basis of Grice's (1967/1975) co-operative principle. However, it appears to have been Grice's universal view of communication and its adoption by Brown and Levinson that laid the bases for the (sub-)field. Since then it has become clear that conversational participants do not just interact with one another to convey information and/or to do things but also to (re-) establish relationships. Specifically, participants deviate from the Gricean maxims of efficient communication in order to express politeness and (re-)establish interpersonal relations.

Central to Brown and Levinson's theory is the concept of face, derived from Goffman (1967) and from the English folk terms 'losing face' and 'saving face'. The theory assumes that all competent adult members of a society are concerned about their face, the self-image every member wants to claim for himself or herself and recognises others have. Politeness is thus understood as the linguistic means by which facework is achieved. On the basis of Durkheim's (1915) differentiation between negative and positive rites, Brown and Levinson distinguish between negative and positive face wants, aspects of face which the authors regard as universal. Negative face refers to basic claims of territory, freedom of action and freedom from imposition. Positive face, on the other hand, refers to the desire of being appreciated and approved by others. It is in the reciprocal interest of the participants in conversation to maintain each other's face. There are certain acts, face-threatening acts (FTAs), which by their very nature threaten the face of the participants, and their seriousness can be assessed according to three independent and culture-sensitive social variables: the social distance and the social power between the speaker and the hearer and the absolute ranking of impositions within a particular culture. In order to assess the amount of face-work or politeness required in a situation, bearing in mind the participants' needs to maintain each other's positive and negative face as well as their motivation to perform acts that may run contrary to those desires, speakers add up the values of the different social variables and choose from a set of five possible strategies to mitigate or avoid the FTAs:

1 bald on record, without redressive action – e.g. 'Shut the door';
2 positive politeness – e.g. 'Sweetie, shut the door for us, will you?';
3 negative politeness – e.g. 'I wonder if you could you shut the door';
4 off record – e.g. 'It's noisy in here, isn't it?';
5 don't do the FTA.

As one moves up the scale of strategies, from 1 to 5, the risk for loss of face, which is determined by the cumulative effect of the social variables, increases, and the more polite the strategy becomes.

Almost every aspect of Brown and Levinson's theory has been challenged. It is not within the scope of this chapter to present a detailed account of the wealth of studies that have epistemologically criticised the theory, provided empirical counter-evidence, suggested reconceptualisations of (aspects of) it or proposed alternative approaches, as this would require a whole different chapter and there is an array of studies published on this (see, for example, Bargiela-Chiappini 2003; Eelen 2001; Lakoff and Ide 2005). Moreover, the bulk of research into politeness in business discourse has made use of Brown and Levinson's approach to explain observed differences in the politeness behaviour of different cultures. Thus, in what follows it will suffice to describe briefly some of the main criticisms voiced against the theory.

Perhaps one of the most important criticisms levelled against the theory is its claim to universality. This is one of the theory's underlying assumptions, derived from the then prevalent, and to a large extent still prevalent today, universal Anglo–American understanding of pragmatics (i.e. Gricean maxims of interaction and speech act theory), and one on which key concepts such as rationality, face and the relationship between face and politeness rest.

The relevance of the concept of face for non-western cultures has come under scrutiny and remains an issue open to further empirical testing. The notion has been criticised for being individualistic, thus failing to account for politeness in cultures where there is an orientation to the group (Nwoye 1989; Strecker 1993), cultures with a strong normative rather than primarily strategic orientation behind polite behaviour (see, for example, Gu 1990; but see also Pan 1995) and cultures where politeness does not seem to be motivated by the face concerns of the participants, at least understood à la Brown and Levinson, but by their social standing in respect to others in their group (see, for example, Ide 1989; Matsumoto 1988; but see also Fukushima 2000) or by politic behaviour, that is, conventionally appropriate behaviour rather than an individual's strategic politeness (Watts 2003).

The treatment of Brown and Levinson's social variables has also been objected to. The variables, though independent in that they are explanatory rather than response variables, are not independent of each other (Holtgraves and Yang 1992; Watts et al. 1992). Some scholars have observed that one of the variables, social distance, rather than a combination of social power, social distance and ranking of imposition, was determinant of politeness (McLaughlin et al. 1983; Baxter 1984; Holmes 1990). Further, other scholars (Márquez Reiter 2000) found that social distance explained the degree of indirectness in formulating requests but that social power and imposition, in this case the severity of the offence, explained apologising behaviour; thus suggesting that the weighting of the explanatory variables put forward by the authors might vary according to the speech act under examination and providing further support for the claim that the variables are dependent on each other.

The results of studies in vast number of cultures have shown that, as predicted by Brown and Levinson, politeness is manifested across languages by means of conventional indirect forms (Márquez Reiter et al. 2005); however, the superstrategies for conveying such conventionality, namely positive and negative politeness (strategies 2 and 3 above), have been criticised for not being clear cut (Craig et al. 1986). It is common to find instances of strategy overlap, as in *Would you be an angel and fetch me a glass of water, please?*, where there is an orientation to positive politeness ('be an angel') within the essentially negative politeness strategy of conventional indirectness (Blum-Kulka et al. 1989): *Would you do X for me, please?* Further, contrary to what the theory predicts, off-record politeness forms are not always perceived as communicating politeness (Blum-Kulka 1987) and negative politeness is not always more polite than positive politeness (Baxter 1984). The analytical categories have also come under fire for being unable to account for how politeness unfolds in conversation (Penman 1990).

Some thirty years since the face-saving view of politeness was first published, and despite the criticisms levelled against it and the alternative conceptualisations of politeness that have recently emerged as result of these, Gumperz's (1987: xiii) description of Brown and Levinson's seminal work as 'the classic treatment on politeness in communication' is still valid. Furthermore, Kasper's assertion that their theory was the only which satisfied the criteria for empirical theories such as explicitness, parsimony and predictiveness (1994: 3208) cannot, as yet, be said to describe accurately the alternative approaches to politeness that have emerged since then, in spite of some of the intuitively sound theoretical claims that they make and the adoption of micro-analytic tools (e.g. conversation analysis) to examine manifestations of politeness in discourse better (Arundale 2006). It should not come as a surprise, therefore, to learn that the bulk of studies undertaken in politeness in business discourse have mainly employed Brown and Levinson's perspective.

Politeness in spoken business discourse

The studies that have investigated politeness in spoken business discourse have taken face as the key element in the expression of politeness and can be divided into face-saving studies and studies that view face as a relational concept.

Face-saving studies in spoken business discourse

Stalpers (1995) compares the realisation of the potentially face-threatening act of disagreement (Brown and Levinson 1987) and its mitigation in intracultural French and Dutch negotiations and in non-native intercultural negotiations between French and Dutch participants (see also van der Wijst and Ulijn 1995 for an analysis of simulated negotiations in French between Dutch and French negotiators). The findings reveal that disagreements in negotiations are generally mitigated, albeit not as much as in everyday conversation, thus suggesting that clarity overrides politeness concerns in business interactions. Interestingly, these results, although analysed from the face-saving perspective, seem to provide implicit support for Lakoff's (1973) conversation maxim view of politeness and suggest that business negotiations may exhibit particularly idiosyncratic discourse features.

Neumann (1997) investigates the realisation of requests, another potentially face-threatening act, in business interactions between German and Norwegian buyers and sellers negotiating in German. The results show that the Norwegians employed more indirect strategies than the Germans and that there was a considerably higher incidence of direct requests than in everyday conversation. Although not specified by the author, the latter result is in line with Stalpers's (1995) findings as far as the politeness vs. clarity requirements of business negotiations go, despite differences in the cultures and business settings examined.

Charles (1996) examines the production of face-saving hedging devices in authentic English business negotiations and concludes that their performance is bound by the role of the buyer and the seller. Fant (1992) investigates simulated negotiations between Spanish and Swedish professional negotiators. Grindsted (1997) analyses the use of joking as a strategy for creating rapport in simulated interactions between Spanish and Danish professional negotiators, and Villemoes (1995) focuses on face-work priorities in intercultural negotiations between Spaniards and Danes. These authors coincide in observing that the Spaniards made more use of laughing and joking in the context of business negotiations than their Scandinavian counterparts and that they sought more interpersonal bonding (Grindsted 1997) and exhibited more of a group orientation (Fant 1992).

Of related interest, although not explicitly focusing on the expression of politeness per se, is Bilbow's (1997) cross-cultural examination of promises and expressions of commitment, also potentially face-threatening acts according to Brown and Levinson (1987), in intercultural business meetings at a multinational airline company based in Hong Kong. The author finds similarities in the frequency with which both the Chinese and western participants employed the speech acts and differences in terms of their linguistic realisation and in the circumstances under which the acts were performed. Cross-departmental co-operation meetings had the highest incidence of promises and expressions of commitment, whereas weekly departmental meetings and brainstorming sessions exhibited fewer occurrences of the acts. He thus notes that the type of business meeting is an important factor in determining the way in which and frequency with which the acts are employed in business meetings.

While the findings of these studies reveal that the potentially face-threatening acts in the languages and business environments examined receive less 'padding' than in everyday interaction (possibly owing to concerns for efficiency in business), they cannot be considered evidence of politeness in business discourse because of the different research objectives and methodological approaches taken. Nor can these findings be generalised to the languages and business contexts under scrutiny, given the lack of representativeness of the data.

Face as a relational concept in spoken business discourse

Recent reconceptualisations of Brown and Levinson's theory as well as the alternative approaches that have emerged explicitly view face as a relational concept. Face, rather than being an individual phenomenon, is interactionally achieved in relationships with others (Arundale 2006) and best examined as a discursive phenomenon (Locher 2006).

In Spencer-Oatey's (2000) rapport management perspective, politeness is understood as one of the resources which are available to participants for managing relationships. Participants are concerned about managing face and managing sociality rights. Face has two interrelated aspects: 'quality face' and 'social identity face', and is thus related to Brown and Levinson's positive face in that it refers to the desire of individuals to be evaluated positively. 'Quality face' is the desire to be evaluated positively in terms of personal qualities, and 'social identity face' the desire to be acknowledged in our social identity roles (for example, as teacher, wife, and so on), thus accounting for the public element neglected in Brown and Levinson's interpretation of face. 'Sociality rights' comprise two interrelated aspects: 'equity rights' and 'association rights'. The former refers to our desire not to be unduly imposed upon and to receive the benefits to which we are entitled, and the latter to our belief that we are entitled to association with others. Our association with others vary according to our 'interactional' and 'affective' 'association/dissociation rights', that is, the extent of our involvement with others and the extent to which we share concerns, feelings and interests with others, respectively. Sociality rights thus account for the criticism levelled against Brown and Levinson's negative face for being inapplicable to cultures where interactions with members of the in-group and out-group vary considerably and generally follow specific interactional rules. The rapport management perspective successfully counters the criticisms made against the Brown and Levinson model, in particular with respect to the concepts of face and its negative and positive dichotomy in an attempt to explicate the motivational concerns of interlocutors. It does, however, provide little insight into its operationalisation and the strategies associated with a given motivational concern. Further research will shed light on its general applicability.

Applications of the rapport management view can be found in Spencer-Oatey and Xing's (2003) study of relational management in two Sino–British welcome meetings, and in Planken's (2005) examination of managing rapport in lingua franca sales encounters between professional and aspiring negotiators. Spencer-Oatey and Xing (2003) observe that despite similarities in the communicative behaviour of the Chinese and the British delegations at these meetings in terms of seating arrangements (chairperson was seated at the head of the table), discourse content (chairperson's welcome speech) and discourse structure (neither delegation was invited to give a return speech), differences were found in the parties' perceptions of the meetings. Specifically, the Chinese delegation that participated in the second meeting felt that the seating arrangement was inappropriate. They had expected their leader to sit directly opposite his British counterpart, since they believed that they had higher status than their British hosts as they had wrongly assumed that business with China was crucial for the company's survival. Similarly, they had interpreted their leader's lack of opportunity to give a return speech as a face-threatening act and the British speech as rather offensive in that the visitors were not sufficiently praised. On the other hand, the British reported having adopted a more informal style during Chinese visits, such as giving a return speech, as they had mistakenly assumed that the Chinese had become less concerned about protocol and formality given that the Sino delegation members had become younger over the years.

Planken (2005) examines manifestations of face-work in simulated intercultural sales negotiations in English as a lingua franca by professional negotiators and students of international business management. The author focuses on the categories of 'safe' talk topic, frequency and locus of occurrence in the initiation of interactional talk, and the use of personal pronouns as indicators of the negotiator relationship ('you' as indicator of other-orientedness, inclusive vs. exclusive 'we' as indicator of co-operativeness and professional distance respectively, and 'I' as indicator of self-orientedness). The study reveals differences in the way professionals and students build rapport in negotiating settings. Unlike professional negotiators, the students did not engage in the safe talk categories of business environments (e.g. target groups, competitors, markets, the economy, etc.), product information (e.g. product characteristics, etc.) or corporate information (e.g. company history, core activities, management, etc.). This, however, is not surprising given that the students are only *aspiring* negotiators. In addition to the differences already mentioned, the author observes differences in the frequency with which the two groups engaged in safe talk topics and the stage of the interaction where this occurred. Professional negotiators used considerably more safe talk in all the phases of the negotiation than the students, who engaged in little safe talk in the openings and closings only. Regarding the use of personal pronouns, the students underused the institutional 'we' and employed non-inclusive pronouns ('you' and 'I') particularly in the bargaining stage of the exchange. According to Planken, this made the students' discourse 'highly subjective' and hence potentially conflictive. Despite the limitations of employing a student population which is not acculturated to any given corporate institution, Planken's (2005) findings for the discourse (safe talk topics) and participatory (use of personal pronouns) domains show how Spencer-Oatey's (2000) rapport management may inform the production of teaching materials for working professionals whose native language is not English but need to communicate in English as a lingua franca, with rules for use that are frequently left untouched in the English-language classroom.

Last but not least are Holmes and Stubbe's (2003)[3] study of power and politeness in the workplace, based on Holmes's Wellington Language in the Workplace Project, and Mullany (2004, 2006). Holmes and Stubbe (2003) examine a range of authentic workplace interactions in New Zealand to investigate the ways in which people signal and negotiate their working relationships with others in terms of politeness and power. The researchers' findings as far as politeness is concerned reveal that managers tended to use more linguistically polite strategies in order to achieve their conversational goals in a consensual manner while still maintaining their authority, and that workers in the lower organisational hierarchy employed different face-work strategies with their peers from those deployed with those who had greater authority than them. Holmes and Stubbe's incisive analysis reflects the dynamic and intersubjective nature of workplace talk as conversational participants realign their identities and goals in the course of interaction; workplace roles and relationships seem to be open to negotiation in contemporary New Zealand culture. Mullany (2004, 2006) considers the importance of humour as a negotiation strategy to gain compliance in workplace business meetings, and the tactical use of small talk by female managers to create collegiality and social distance between them and males in communities of practice, respectively.

Politeness in written business discourse

As remarked earlier, research into the politeness of written business discourse has been approached from the face-saving perspective. In these studies face is (implicitly) understood as an individually rooted construct rather than being interactionally achieved. This is not surprising given the peculiarities of written vs. spoken communication, and in particular the fact that the only vehicle for the expression of politeness in written discourse is the actual language. Thus, as Pilegaard (1997: 240) notes, 'greater care is spent on adapting the text to its illocutionary purpose in written than in oral communication . . . that the deployment of politeness strategies therefore more truly reflects strategic considerations in written than in oral form'.

Graham and David (1996) contrast American faculty memos from administrators to faculty members with those written in a corporation. The study focuses on the levels of indirectness, tentativeness, indebtedness and personalisation. The results show higher levels of politeness in the university than in the corporation. This is explained by the egalitarian vision that has permeated academia. Specifically, intensified indirectness, tentativeness and indebtedness are employed in American faculties to obscure power asymmetries and thus create ambiguous messages. On the other hand, the comparatively moderated indirectness and tentativeness found in the corporate memos is geared not towards empowering subordinates but towards promoting efficiency. This study shows that the use of politeness strategies is context specific and varies according to the values of the organisation.

Pilegaard (1997) offers a text-linguistic perspective on the realisation of requests in a variety of English business letters. Her findings indicate that politeness strategies are deployed to prepare the ground for the main goal of the letter, to redress the potentially face-threatening act of requesting something from the client and to close the letter. While both positive and negative politeness strategies are frequent in the early stages of the letter to assert commonality and togetherness, negative politeness strategies, in particular conventional indirectness, dominate once negotiation has commenced, with the aim of redressing face-threat. Pilegaard's findings also reveal that sellers engage in more positive face-work than buyers, and that the more clear cut the power relationship between the buyer and the seller, the less need there is to engage in positive face-work.

Yeung (1997) examines the use of polite requests in English and Chinese business correspondence and reports that the ranking of the imposition, rather than the social power and social distance between the sender and the addressee, explains politeness behaviour. Importantly, the author claims that the face-saving view is inapplicable to the Chinese data in that other factors, such as the Chinese principle of reciprocity and the style in which the letter is written – that is, Classical Chinese vs. Modern Standard Chinese – need to be borne in mind to account for the expression of politeness in Chinese business correspondence.

McLaren (2001) investigates the politeness of self-evaluative claims which praise a company's abilities, products, qualities and the like in a corpus of French corporate brochures. Her findings suggest that the strategies deployed to redress the same type of FTA 'may vary from one part of any given text to another' (p. 187), and that the relationship between the author and the audience gradually develops throughout the text, as do the values of relative power and distance.

Kong (2006) analyses the use of accounts as a politeness strategy in internal emails within a business firm in Hong Kong. The findings indicate that accounts are more frequently used in power-asymmetrical relationships. Specifically, subordinates use accounts more often when requesting something from their superiors, and superiors justify their requests to their subordinates more frequently than peers justify requests among themselves. This is explained by the writers' awareness of the greater face threat created by power differences between employees of the firm, and by the need of postmodern enterprises to reconcile the business goal of companies and the personal goals of individuals for strategic purposes. Although not mentioned by the author, these results mirror those reported by Holmes and Stubbe (2003; see above), given that greater politeness investment is once more observed in power-asymmetrical than in power-symmetrical work relationships, despite differences between the cultures and type of discourse examined.

Chakorn (2006) contrasts request letters written in English by native speakers of English with those written by Thais in an array of Thai business contexts. Unlike other studies, which have compared the politeness patterns of English native speaker written discourse with that of non-native speakers with the aim of informing the production of English-language teaching (ELT) materials,[4] Chakorn's inclusion of English letters written by non-native speakers is motivated by the relatively recent position of Thailand as an international financial hub. This, according to the author, has resulted in an increasing trend by Thais and others to write business correspondence in English for external and internal communication both locally and abroad. The findings of the study reveal notable differences in the way in which the main request for business is introduced. Unlike native speakers of English, who tend to introduce the main request at the initial stages of the letter, Thais do so in the middle or penultimate part of the letter. In addition, the author observes that expressions of gratitude/appreciation are more prominent in letters written by Thais. She relates the first finding to the 'quasi-inductive' style noted by Hinds (quoted in Chakorn 2006) typical of Chinese, Japanese, Korean and Thai.[5] As far as the expression of politeness is concerned, Chakorn finds that letters written by Thais, including those which addressed to other Thais, are more oriented towards emotional appeals, collectivism and relationship building, whereas those written by native English speakers are more rationally induced and individualistic. Although not discussed by the author, the observed orientation towards collectivism and relationship building by the Thais may be the result of first language transfer.

Despite the fact that these studies, unlike those which have been conducted into the politeness of spoken business discourse, share a conceptual understanding of face, their findings cannot be generalised because of issues of sample equivalence, amongst others.

Conclusion

Research into the politeness of business discourse has been principally approached from the face-saving perspective (Brown and Levinson 1987). Despite differences in the cultures that have received attention both at the linguistic (language used) and corporate (type of business environment) level, as well as differences in the kind of discourse that has been examined – spoken vs. written business – the findings of extant research into the politeness of business discourse suggest that clarity motivated by efficiency supersedes politeness considerations in business interactions. Specifically, the politeness exhibited in corporate discourse has been found to be comparatively moderate in relation to that observed, for example, in academic discourse. Additionally, manifestations of politeness have been shown to vary according to the type and purpose of the business encounter (e.g. co-operation meetings vs. cross-departmental meetings), the roles assumed by the participants (e.g. buyer vs. seller), the linguistic medium (oral vs. written communication), the culture of the participants and their status in the organisation. Thus, sellers have been reported to use more positive face-work strategies than buyers, and superiors have been shown to engage in more linguistically polite strategies with their subordinates. On the other hand, those at the lower end of the organisational hierarchy have been shown to employ different politeness strategies with their peers and with those who have greater authority than they do in Hong Kong and New Zealand. Similarly, greater care in the adoption of strategic politeness strategies has been reported in written than in oral business communication owing to the former's lack of recourse to extra-linguistic features.

Overall, the findings of the studies reported in this chapter indicate that business discourse has its own idiosyncratic characteristics and that a multitude of factors, including those that have been identified by Brown and Levinson (social power, social distance and ranking of imposition), motivate the expression of politeness.

In the light of the increasing globalisation of business, the values of the organisations that have been investigated need to be unravelled in order to establish the discursive strategies that are privileged by different organisational sites and the extent to which the culture of individual members may or may not be subsumed under a corporate ethos. Research that deploys ethnographic methods may thus be a way forward. Further, given that the findings discussed above are not always comparable, it is time that we reflected on the development of the field and fine-tuned our research procedures to guarantee comparability and, ideally, replicability. In so doing, we will be in a better position to compare the findings obtained across languages and cultures, and this, in turn, will allow us to gain a more comprehensive understanding of politeness in business discourse, which will also be of value to the larger user community.

Notes

1 The term 'friction' seems to have been interpreted according to Brown and Levinson's generally 'paranoid' view of social interaction (Kasper 1994), in particular as evidenced by the operationalisation of their face-saving strategies. However, friction may arise not only when the need for independence or dissociation is threatened but also when the need for interdependence or association is not acknowledged in a given interaction where it is socially expected (e.g. a compliment).

2 See, for example, Anderson (1994), Economidou-Kogetsidis (2005), Kerbrat-Orecchioni (2005), Kong (1998), Márquez Reiter (2005, 2006, in press), Márquez Reiter and Placencia (2004), Márquez Reiter and Stewart (2008), Pan (2000) and Placencia (2004).

3 Of related interested although mainly focusing on gender issues in the workplace are Holmes and Marra (2004) and Holmes (2005).

4 See, for example, Maier (1992) and Arvani (2006).

5 But see also Thatcher (2000) and Conaway and Wardope (2004), amongst others, for an examination of 'South American' and Guatemalan business written discourse, respectively, where the same pattern has been reported.

References

Anderson, L. (1994) Accounting practices in service encounters in English and Italian. In H. Purschel, E. Bartsch and P. Franklin (eds), *Duisberger Arbeiten Zur Sprach und Kulturwissenschaft*. Bern: Peter Lang, pp. 99–120.

Arundale, R. (2006) Face as relational and interactional: A communication framework for research on face, facework, and politeness. *Journal of Politeness Research*, 2: 193–216.

Arvani, M. (2006) A discourse analysis of business letters written by Iranians and native speakers. *Asian ESP Journal*, 1: 12–23.

Bargiela-Chiappini, F. (2003) Face and impoliteness: New 'insights' for 'old' concepts. *Journal of Pragmatics*, 35: 10–11, 1453–69.

Bargiela-Chiappini, F., C. Nickerson and B. Planken (2007) *Business Discourse*. Basingstoke: Palgrave Macmillan.

Baxter, L. (1984) An investigation of compliance gaining as politeness. *Human Communication Research*, 10: 427–56.

Bilbow, G. (1997) Spoken discourse in the multicultural workplace in Hong Kong: Applying a model of discourse as 'impression management'. In F. Bargiela-Chiappini and S. Harris (eds), *The Languages of Business: An International Perspective*. Edinburgh: Edinburgh University Press, pp. 21–48.

Blum-Kulka, S. (1987) Indirectness and politeness in requests: Same or different? *Journal of Pragmatics*, 11: 131–46.

Blum-Kulka, S., J. House and G. Kasper (1989) *Cross-Cultural Pragmatics: Requests and Apologies*. Norwood, NJ: Ablex.

Brown, P. and S. Levinson (1978) Universals in language usage: Politeness phenomena. In E. Goody (ed.), *Questions and Politeness: Strategies in Social Interaction*. Cambridge: Cambridge University Press, pp. 56–310.

Brown, P. and S. Levinson (1987) *Politeness: Some Universals in Language Use*. Cambridge: Cambridge University Press.

Chakorn, O. (2006) Persuasive and politeness strategies in cross-cultural letters of request in the Thai business context. In F. Bargiela-Chiappini (ed.), 'Asian business discourse(s) Part II', *Journal of Asian Pacific Communication* (special issue), 16(1): 103–46.

Charles, M. L. (1996) Business negotiations: Interdependence between discourse and the business relationship. *English for Specific Purposes*, 15: 19–36.

Christie, C.L. (2005) Editorial. *Journal of Politeness Research*, 1(1): 1–7.

Conaway, R. and W. Wardope (2004) Communication in Latin America: An analysis of Guatemalan business letters. *Business Communication Quarterly*, 67: 465–74.

Craig, R., K. Tracy and F. Spisak (1986) The discourse of requests: Assessment of a politeness approach. *Human Communication Research*, 12: 437–68.

Durkheim, E. (1915) *The Elementary Forms of the Religious Life*. London: Allen and Unwin.

Economidou-Kogetsidis, M. (2005) Yes, tell me please, what time is the midday flight from Athens arriving? Telephone service encounters and politeness. *Intercultural Pragmatics*, 2–3: 253–73.

Eelen, G. (2001) *A Critique of Politeness Theories*. Manchester: St Jerome.

Fant, L. (1992) Scandinavians and Spaniards in negotiation. In A. Sjörgen and L. Janson (eds), *Culture and Management in the Field of Ethnology and Business Administration*. Stockholm: Stockholm School of Economics, pp. 125–53.

Durkheim, E. (1951) *The Elementary Forms of the Religious Life*. London: Allen and Unwin.

Fukushima, S. (2000) *Requests and Culture: Politeness in British English and Japanese*. Bern: Peter Lang.

Goffman, E. (1967) *Interaction Ritual: Essays on Face-to-Face Behaviour*. New York: Doubleday Anchor.

Graham, M. and C. David (1996) Power and politeness: Administrative writing in an 'organized anarchy'. *Journal of Business and Technical Communication*, 10: 5–27.

Grice, P. (1967/1975) Logic in conversation. In P. Cole and J. Morgan (eds), *Syntax and Semantics: Speech Acts 3*. New York: Academic Press, pp. 41–58.

Grindsted, A. (1997) Joking as a strategy in Spanish and Danish negotiations. In F. Bargiela-Chiappini and S. Harris (eds), *The Languages of Business: An International Perspective*. Edinburgh: Edinburgh University Press, pp. 159–81.

Gu, Y. (1990) Politeness in modern Chinese. *Journal of Pragmatics*, 14: 237–57.

Gumperz, J. (1987) Foreword. In P. Brown and S. Levinson, *Politeness: Some Universals in Language Use*. Cambridge: Cambridge University Press, pp. xiii–xiv.

Holmes, J. (1990) Apologies in New Zealand English. *Language in Society*, 19: 155–99.

Holmes, J. (2005) Leadership talk: How do leaders 'do mentoring', and is gender relevant? *Journal of Pragmatics*, 37: 1779–800.

Holmes, J. and M. Marra (2004) Relational practice in the workplace: Women's talk or gendered discourse? *Language in Society*, 33: 377–98.

Holmes, J. and M. Stubbe (2003) *Power and Politeness in the Workplace: A Sociolinguistic Analysis of Talk at Work*. London: Longman.

Holtgraves, T. and J. Yang (1992) Interpersonal underpinnings of request strategies: General principles and differences due to culture and gender. *Journal of Personality and Social Psychology*, 62: 246–56.

Ide, S. (1989) Formal forms and discernment: Two neglected aspects of universals of linguistic politeness. *Multilingua*, 12: 7–11.

Kasper, G. (1994) Politeness. In R. Asher and J. Simpson (eds), *The Encyclopedia of Language and Linguistics*. Oxford: Pergamon, pp. 3206–11.

Kerbrat-Orecchioni, C. (2005) Politeness in France: How to buy bread politely. In L. Hickey and M. Stewart (eds), *Politeness in Europe*. Clevedon: Multilingual Matters, pp. 29–44.

Kong, K. C. C. (1998) Politeness of service encounters in Hong Kong. *Pragmatics*, 8: 555–75.

Kong, K. C. C. (2006) The use of accounts as a politeness strategy in internal directive documents of business firms in Hong Kong. In F. Bargiela-Chiappini (ed.), 'Asian business discourse(s) Part II', *Journal of Asian Pacific Communication*, 16 (1): 75–99.

Lakoff, R. (1973) The logic of politeness; or minding your p's and q's. *Papers from the 9th Regional Meeting of the Chicago Linguistic Society*, 292–305.

Lakoff, R. and S. Ide (eds) (2005) *Broadening the Horizon of Linguistic Politeness*. Amsterdam: John Benjamins.

Locher, M. (2006) Polite behaviour within relational work: The discursive approach to politeness. *Multilingua*, 25: 249–67.

McLaren, Y. (2001) To claim or not to claim? An analysis of the politeness of self-evaluation in a corpus of French corporate brochures. *Multilingua*, 20: 171–90.

McLaughlin, M., M. Cody and D. O'Hair (1983) The management of failure events: Some contextual determinants of accounting behaviour. *Human Communication Research*, 9: 208–24.

Maier, P. (1992) Politeness strategies in business letters by native and non-native speakers of English. *English for Specific Purposes*, 11: 189–205.

Márquez Reiter, R. (1998) The teaching of 'politeness' in the language classroom. In I. Vázquez Orta and I. Guillén Galve (eds), *Perspectivas pragmáticas en lingüística aplicada*. Zaragoza: Anubar, pp. 291–7.

Márquez Reiter, R. (2000) *Linguistic Politeness in Britain and Uruguay*. Amsterdam: John Benjamins.

Márquez Reiter, R. (2005) Complaint calls to a caregiver service company: The case of *desahogo*. *Intercultural Pragmatics*, 2–4: 481–514.

Márquez Reiter, R. (2006) Interactional closeness in service calls to a Montevidean carer service company. *Research on Language and Social Interaction*, 39: 7–39.

Márquez Reiter, R. (in press) Intra-cultural variation: Explanations in service calls to two Montevidean service providers. *Journal of Politeness Research*.

Márquez Reiter, R. and M. Placencia (2004) Displaying closeness and respectful distance in Montevidean and Quiteño service encounters. In R. Márquez Reiter and M. Placencia (eds), *Current Trends in the Pragmatics of Spanish*. Amsterdam: John Benjamins, pp. 121–55.

Márquez Reiter, R. and M. Stewart (2008) Les interactions en site commercial à Montevideo et Edimbourg: 'engagement' (involvement) et 'considération envers les autres' (considerateness). In C. Kerbrat-Orecchioni and V. Traverso (eds), *Les interactions en site commercial: Invariants et variations*. Lyon: Ens Editions, pp. 277–303.

Márquez Reiter, R., I. Rainey and G. Fulcher (2005) A comparative study of certainty and conventional indirectness: Evidence from British English and Peninsular Spanish. *Applied Linguistics*, 26: 1–31.

Matsumoto, Y. (1988) Reexamination of the universality of face: Politeness phenomena in Japanese. *Journal of Pragmatics*, 12: 403–26.

Merritt, M. (1976) On questions following questions in service encounters. *Language in Society*, 5: 315–57.

Mullany, L. (2004) Gender, politeness and institutional power roles: Humour as a tactic to gain compliance in workplace business meetings. *Multilingua*, 23: 13–37.

Mullany, L. (2006) 'Girls on tour': Politeness, small talk, and gender in managerial business meetings. *Journal of Politeness Research*, 2: 55–77.

Neumann, I. (1997) Requests in German–Norwegian business discourse: Differences in directness. In F. Bargiela-Chiappini and S. Harris (eds), *The Languages of Business: An International Perspective*. Edinburgh: Edinburgh University Press, pp. 72–93.

Nwoye, O. (1989) Linguistic politeness in Igbo. *Multilingua*, 8: 259–75.

Pan, Y. (1995) Power behind linguistic behaviour: Analysis of politeness in Chinese official settings. *Journal of Language and Social Psychology*, 14: 462–84.

Pan, Y. (2000) Facework in Chinese service encounters. *Journal of Asian Pacific Communication*, 10: 25–61.

Penman, R. (1990) Facework and politeness: Multiple goals in courtroom discourse. *Journal of Language and Social Psychology*, 9: 15–38.

Pilegaard, M. (1997) Politeness in written business discourse: A textlinguistic perspective on requests. *Journal of Pragmatics*, 28: 223–44.

Placencia, M. (2004) Rapport-building activities in corner shop interactions. *Journal of Sociolinguistics*, 8: 215–45.

Planken, B. (2005) Managing rapport in lingua franca sales negotations: A comparison of professional and aspiring negotiators. *English for Specific Purposes*, 24: 381–400.

Spencer-Oatey, H. (ed.) (2000) *Culturally Speaking*. London: Continuum.

Spencer-Oatey, H. and J. Xing (2003) Managing rapport in intercultural business interactions: A comparison of two Chinese–British welcome meetings. *Journal of Intercultural Studies*, 24: 33–46.

Stalpers, J. (1995) The expression of disagreement. In K. Ehlich and J. Wagner (eds), *The Discourse of Business Negotiations*. New York: Mouton de Gruyter, pp. 275–90.

Strecker, I. (1993) Cultural variations in the notion of 'face'. *Multilingua*, 12: 119–41.

Thatcher, B. (2000) Adpating to South American communication patterns. In D. Bosley (ed.), *Global Documentation: Case studies in International Technical Communication*. Boston, MA: Allyn and Bacon, pp. 81–95.

Thomas, J. (1995) *Meaning in Interaction*. London: Longman.

van der Wijst, P. and J. Ulijn (1995) Politeness in French/Dutch negotiations. In K. Ehlich and J. Wagner (eds), *The Discourse of Business Negotiations*. New York: Mouton de Gruyter, pp. 313–48.

Villemoes, A. (1995) Culturally determined facework priorities in Danish and Spanish business negotiations. In K. Ehlich and J. Wagner (eds), *The Discourse of Business Negotiations*. New York: Mouton de Gruyter, pp. 291–312.

Watts, R. (2003) *Politeness*. Cambridge: Cambridge University Press.

Watts, R., S. Ide and K. Ehlich (eds) (1992) *Politeness in Language: Studies in its History, Theory and Practice*. Berlin: Mouton de Gruyter.

Yeung, L. (1997) Polite requests in English and Chinese business correspondence in Hong Kong. *Journal of Pragmatics*, 27: 505–22.

14

BELF: Business English as a Lingua Franca

Marinel Gerritsen and Catherine Nickerson

Introduction

Communication between speakers of different languages has increased exponentially in the course of the past decades in all walks of life, including in the business world. This is the case not only for internal business communication, as more and more business organisations are characterised by a multicultural, multilingual workforce, but also in external business communication, where the different stakeholders involved in the communication originate from different countries. In such commonplace situations in international business communication, whenever person A with first language A speaks to person B with first language B, there are four options available to them:

1 Both speakers use language A.
2 Both speakers use language B.
3 Person A uses his or her first language A, and Person B uses his or her first language B.
4 Person A and Person B opt for a third language, language C, that both parties are able to speak and understand well enough to communicate, i.e. they opt for a lingua franca.

The choice that is made depends on many different factors. The foreign language proficiency of the interactants plays an important role; if B does not speak A, then option 1 is not possible; likewise, if A does not speak B, then option 2 is not possible; and for option 3 to be successful, both parties must be able to understand both languages well. For option 4 to be successful, both parties must be able to use the chosen lingua franca well enough for the interaction to take place. In addition, although research has suggested that organisations may be more likely to complete transactions such as sales transactions successfully by following a strategy of accommodation (as in examples 1 and 2) rather than by using a lingua franca (as in example 4; Vandermeeren 1999), the latter remains the norm in much international business communication, more specifically in situations where the chosen lingua franca is English. Artificially created languages such as Volapük and Esperanto that were purposefully designed as a lingua franca have never played a significant role in international business, and although French, German, Spanish and Scandinavian have all been documented as being used as lingua francas (Vandermeeren 1999; Poncini 2004; Louhiala-Salminen et al. 2005), English has played an increasingly dominant role in business transactions in general around the globe over the course of the last two decades.

The role of English as an international business lingua franca is now beyond dispute (Knapp and Meierkord 2002; Mair 2003; Seidlhofer 2004; Gerritsen and Nickerson 2004; van Els 2005; Ammon 2006; Gunnarsson 2006; Jenkins 2006; Louhiala-Salminen and Charles 2006; Mollin 2006; Seidlhofer et al. 2006; Bargiela-Chiappini et al. 2007; Bjorge 2007; Rogerson-Revell 2007). In this chapter we will discuss the methodologies that have been used to investigate the use of business English as a lingua franca (BELF), i.e. in situations where speakers of two different languages opt for a third that is not a first language for either one of them. In this respect we consider BELF transactions as a special type of international business English (IBE), where IBE may be viewed as an overarching term that includes interactions between first language speakers of different varieties, between speakers of English as a second language (ESL) or foreign language (EFL), in communication with other first language speakers, and, in the special case of BELF transactions, between ESL or EFL speakers with other non-native English speakers. We recognise that much of what we discuss may also be relevant for interactions between two native speakers of English (NSE), or between an NSE and an ESL or EFL speaker, especially where participants vary in the level of expertise in a given domain, where they differ in cultural background or where they speak a different variety of English (for further discussion, see e.g. Gass and Varonis 1991; Smith 1992; Lindemann 2002). For the sake of clarity, however, we will limit most of our discussion in the rest of this chapter to BELF encounters.

BELF research is not in itself a methodology, nor indeed has it been associated with any one methodology in particular. As we will demonstrate below, it is rather, a rich area of research that has made use of a variety of different methodological approaches, each intended to reveal a different aspect of lingua franca communication. In the sections that follow, we will first discuss the nature of BELF communication, and the underlying reasons why there may be a breakdown in communication in a BELF transaction. We will then go on to highlight a number of the methodologies that have been used to investigate the use of BELF communication, i.e. observations, survey research, corpus research and experiments, and the characteristics of BELF communication that these have revealed.

Background: The nature of BELF communication

In this section, we will discuss the nature of BELF communication, and attempt to analyse what the potential communication problems are in a BELF encounter that the interactants need to be able to deal with in order to communicate successfully. Louhiala-Salminen et al. (2005) provide the following working definition of BELF:

> BELF refers to English used as a 'neutral' and shared communication code. BELF is neutral in the sense that none of the speakers can claim it as her/his mother tongue; it is shared in the sense that it is used for conducting business within the global business discourse community, whose members are BELF users and communicators in their own right – not 'non-native speakers' or 'learners'. (2005: 403–4)

While we accept this definition in principle as capturing the essence of BELF communication, we would wish to add the proviso that the fact that BELF users are also non-native speakers impacts on the interaction both in terms of the (cultural) discourse strategies that are chosen, and in the language that is used to realise them. Essentially, BELF encounters may fail where there are differences either in cultural discourse strategies between the interactants and/or in the language that is used to realise them. Generally speaking, the literature on lingua franca communication would suggest that BELF communication may fail for one of three reasons, which can occur singly or in combination: lack of comprehensibility, cultural differences and stereotyped associations. Although the literature provides numerous examples of these three phenomena, much of what is cited is anecdotal and examples specific to the business context are more difficult to find. The discussion below draws on several studies that we are aware of into BELF communication, and it can be viewed as the basis for a future research agenda to continue to investigate the causes of failure in BELF transactions in a systematic, empirical way.

Lack of comprehensibility

Comprehensibility means that the message is understood by the receiver in the way in which the sender intended, and research has shown that most comprehensibility problems occur at a lexical and grammatical level. As reported by Tajima (2004), for instance, the worst accident ever in aviation history was the crash between two Boeing 747 Jumbo Jets in Tenerife in 1977, and this was due to a communication breakdown in a BELF situation. The Dutch captain said in English 'We are now at takeoff', a phrase that was interpreted by the Spanish controller as 'We are now at the takeoff position.' What the Dutch captain meant to say, however, was 'We are now actually taking off.' The English sentence the captain uttered was an unusual phrase in English aviation terminology and this was due to interference from his native language of Dutch. Lexico-grammatical differences in BELF encounters may hopefully lead to less catastrophic results, but they may certainly occur on a regular basis. It would be a useful addition to our knowledge of BELF encounters to investigate systematically the role played by lexico-grammatical differences (see also Seidlhofer and Jenkins 2003, for a discussion on this point for lingua franca communication in general).

Cultural differences

A breakdown in communication can also be the result of underlying cultural differences between the interactants. Speakers communicate from the perspective of their own cultural background, which means that they use the communication strategies associated with that culture even if they are communicating in a language other than their own (first) language. While people may need to 'speak the same language' in such multilingual contexts, they may not necessarily 'speak the same way' (Rogerson-Revell 2007: 188) and similarly, they 'tend to interact in accordance with the socio-cultural norms which govern the use of their own first language' (Vandermeeren 1999: 275), Shaw et al. (2004) show for instance, that Europeans from Belgium, Denmark, Sweden and the UK have substantially different ideas about what is preferable and acceptable problem-solving discourse than Italians. The Belgians, Danish, Swedish and British showed a significantly greater preference for straightforward but relational dialogues than did the Italians, who preferred longer dialogues with the incorporation of additional politeness strategies. It may be the case, as a result, that the problem-solving strategies favoured by the northern Europeans are considered too direct – and therefore potentially detrimental to the communication – by the Italians. In a similar way, Bjorge (2007) shows that in BELF email correspondence, people who belong to cultures with a high power distance use more formal salutations and closing phrases (e.g. 'Dear Madam', 'Yours respectfully') than writers from low power distance cultures (e.g. 'Hi', 'Cheers'). Clearly this difference may lead to communication difficulties, because the high power distance cultures may experience the informal use of language as impolite and too personal, and the low power distance cultures may experience the formal use of language as unnecessarily distant.

A more extensive discussion on the impact of culture in BELF encounters is beyond the scope of this chapter, and the nature of intercultural encounters in business in particular is dealt with in more detail elsewhere in Chapter 24 of this volume. Later in this chapter we will discuss the extensive survey of BELF in Scandinavia by Louhiala-Salminen et al. (2005), together with the different methodologies that were used, and we will show how the Swedish and Finnish BELF partners involved in the study were aware of the underlying communication differences between them that could be attributed to culture.

Stereotyped associations with a particular accent in English

Research in foreign language acquisition has shown that it is almost impossible for EFL speakers to adopt a completely convincing NSE accent (Kellerman and Vermeulen 1995; Bongaerts et al. 2000), and the idea that EFL speakers must learn to ape NSE speakers, i.e. the type of linguistic imperialism that has been pilloried by authors such as Phillipson (1992), Pennycook (1998) and Canagarajah (1999), has been increasingly replaced by what Rogerson-Revell refers to as a 'functional realism' (Rogerson-Revell 2007). In this approach EFL is viewed as a new variety of English, rather than an imperfect approximation of an NSE variety (Kachru 1986; Ammon 1996; Alexander 1999; Jenkins 2000, 2006; van Oostendorp 2002; Louhiala-Salminen and Charles 2006; Seidlhofer et al. 2006). The English produced by an EFL speaker in a BELF interaction, then, will reflect the speaker's first language, and research shows that this may often have a negative influence on the associations that a hearer may have with that speaker, since people may associate other (unrelated) characteristics such as high or low status, high or low intelligence, and a particular professional background with a given accent. British hearers, for instance, perceive speakers of German English as less prestigious and less socially attractive than speakers of Standard English, whereas they rate French English speakers much more positively (Coupland and Bishop 2007). Likewise, when Nejjari et al. (2007) studied the effect of a slight Dutch English accent compared to the effect of (British) RP in the onset of a telephone sales talk for a Dutch asset management business, they found that RP hearers – playing the role of potential customers – attribute a much lower status to the speakers of Dutch-English they heard than to RP speakers.

Similar associations with different accents may also clearly impact a BELF encounter in either a positive or negative way. However, despite the fact that interactions between EFL speakers with different first languages are a common feature of business organisations in the twenty-first century, surprisingly little is known about the attitude that EFL speakers have towards the accents produced by other EFL speakers if they do not share the same first language. Research is urgently needed in this area. The literature on BELF interactions that we have selectively reviewed above would suggest that participants need to be aware of the impact that differences in lexico-grammatical realisations can have on their communication, they need to understand the impact of differences in accent, and they need to understand the effects of the differences in discourse strategies that different BELF speakers or writers may use to underpin the spoken or written transaction. The burgeoning of cross-border business interactions and the increase in the diverse nature of the workforce, both in multinational corporations (MNCs) and in local business environments (Louhiala-Saminen 2002), suggests that it is becoming increasingly important to understand the different factors that may play a role in whether or not BELF encounters are successful. In the remainder of this chapter, we will highlight a number of the methodologies that have been used to investigate the use of and characteristics associated with BELF.

Methodologies used in research on BELF interactions

The body of knowledge on BELF communication is based on research that has drawn primarily on four different methodologies: survey research, the analysis of a corpus, experimental research and observation. *Survey* research applied to BELF could be a survey questionnaire or set of structured interviews about the use of English world-wide in an MNC, and the problems associated with its use. The *analysis of a corpus*, could be a corpus of business meetings, email correspondence or advertising texts in which BELF is used, which a researcher then analyses to establish what the general characteristics of BELF in the corpus are. In *experimental research* a research team could devise a set of experimental procedures to establish empirically the attitudes of one set of BELF users, e.g. German BELF users, to the accent typical of a second set of BELF users, e.g. French BELF users. All three of these methods have often been used in combination with an initial period of *observation*, which is used to inform the questions in a questionnaire survey, to underpin the selection and analysis of an appropriate corpus, or to design the test items and measuring instruments in an experiment.

In the discussion below we will refer to a number of different studies and discuss the contribution that each approach has made to the existing body of knowledge on BELF communication. For survey research we will focus on Vandermeeren's work (1998, 1999) on the car component and electronics industry in five European countries, and on Charles and Marschan-Piekkari's work (2002) in an MNC. We will then discuss how survey research was combined with a corpus analytical approach in Louhiala-Salminen et al.'s (2005) study of cross-border mergers in Scandinavia. For the experimental approach (which is often prefaced by the compilation of a corpus) our focus will be on the work of the Nijmegen group (e.g. Gerritsen et al. 2000; van Meurs et al. 2004; Nickerson et al. 2005; Nejjari et al. under review; together with researchers such as Wang 2007 and van den Doel 2006).

The survey of foreign language use in European business carried out by Sonja Vandermeeren during the 1990s is a landmark study that uses the survey method as its main methodology. Data was collected in this large-scale project in the sociolinguistic tradition (e.g. Vandermeeren 1998, 1999) by asking companies in Germany, France, the Netherlands, Portugal and Hungary to fill in written questionnaires about the use of foreign languages in a variety of intercultural settings. The project aimed not only to identify patterns of language use within the target corporations, but also to establish why these patterns existed, and whether there was a link between foreign language use and export performance. In 1993 and 1994, corporations representing the car components sector and the electrical and electronics industry were surveyed in the five countries, resulting in a response from 415 corporations. The survey showed that English was in widespread use but also that other languages were used and were considered necessary by the specialist informants. For instance, 42 per cent of the French companies reported that they used German almost always in correspondence with German companies, compared to only 30 per cent who almost always used English, and likewise, although just over 30 per cent of the German companies reported that they almost always used English in correspondence with French companies, almost 25 per cent reported that they almost always used French. As Vandermeeren observes, at least for German–French written business interaction in 1993 and 1994, English did not dominate as a lingua franca and a considerable number of the corporations chose to use the first language of their business partner.

Vandermeeren discusses the relationship between the selection of BELF for all transactions and the conscious choice of not using BELF, but using the business partner's language. She suggests that at least for the French corporations that responded to the survey, the choice of German in correspondence with German business partners seemed to be associated with a better export performance than where companies had opted for English in their correspondence.

Vandermeeren's study provides a useful snapshot of the languages used as lingua franca in a particular sector in European business at the beginning of the nineties, or at least what the respondents reported to her by means of a written survey. Inherent within the survey as a methodology is the fact that the findings are based on what respondents report they are doing, and not on what they may actually be doing, such that in Vandermeeren's study, for instance, it would have been a useful addition to observe respondents as they went about their daily business, to interview them or to collect further information on language use in the form of a corpus. In more recent studies that have incorporated a survey as part of the research methodology, researchers have used other, additional methods to collect their data, for example, in Li So–mui and Mead's (2000) study of English as an international language in the textile industry in Hong Kong, observation, interviews, a survey and a corpus are used.

Two studies of lingua franca English in the Scandinavian context have been of enormous influence in defining the field of BELF research. The first of these is the 2002 study of language use at Kone Elevators by Charles and Marschan-Piekkari, and the second the 2005 study of English lingua franca use in two Nordic corporate mergers by Louhiala-Salminen et al. Charles and Marschan-Piekkari (2002) is a study which uses an extensive survey and interview investigation of middle management at Kone Elevators, an MNC with a head office in Finland. Survey data was collected to investigate the relationship between corporate language policy, i.e. the adoption of English as a corporate lingua franca in the early 1970s, and the employees' actual communication practices. One hundred and ten staff were interviewed about their use of English and the problems they experienced, representing twenty-five corporate units in ten different countries in Europe, Mexico and Asia, and this was followed by six further in–depth interviews with key people within the organisation. Despite the fact that English had been in use within the corporation for more than thirty years at the time when the study took place, the employees interviewed reported that lack of language proficiency caused problems in the communication, as did the frequent lack of a shared language among a set of interactants. Tellingly for BELF research, the employees interviewed reported that there were difficulties caused by the diversity of different Englishes that were used within the company, and perhaps most interesting of all, BEFL and (B)ESL speakers had less difficulty understanding other BEFL and (B)ESL speakers than they did their NSE colleagues, particularly the British NSEs. As a result, one of the recommendations made by Charles and Marschan-Piekkari is to raise NSEs' awareness of BEFL and (B)ESL varieties and to teach them how to communicate more effectively with those speakers. Similar findings are reported by Rogerson-Revell (2007) in her survey of participants that use IBE at a European business organisation, including BELF and NSE speakers, suggesting that this should be an area of interest for both researchers and teacher-trainers in the future.

The 2005 study by Louhiala-Salminen et al. also focuses on BELF in Scandinavian corporations. This multimethod study looks at the use of BELF in two Swedish–Finnish corporate mergers: a bank and a paper manufacturer. It combines a written question-naire survey, a set of interviews and the compilation and analysis of both a written and a spoken corpus. The study set out to investigate the use of BELF, and more specifically to identify the similarities and differences between the Swedish and Finnish employees in BELF encounters and the problems that arose between them. In this respect, it involved the collection and analysis of not only the language challenges faced by employees in using BELF on a daily basis, but also the cultural challenges they perceived. The data and methods used were varied, and this allowed the research team to build up a rich picture of BELF use within the two corporations. For instance, in the survey part of the project 920 questionnaires were circulated across the two corporations and a total of thirty-one interviews were held with key informants to verify the information reported on in the written survey. Then a corpus of four complete BELF meetings were analysed (using a discourse analytical approach), followed by the analysis of 114 BELF emails (using genre analysis), again to investigate the language and cultural challenges that had been signalled by the survey respondents and interviewees in the first stage of the project. For instance, the Finnish and Swedish employees viewed each other (and themselves) as direct (Finns) as opposed to discussive (Swedes), and this was also reflected in the discourse character-istics observed in the spoken and written corpora. An important finding of the study on BELF use in business organisations is that despite its 'neutral' status as a 'cultureless' communication instrument, 'it can be seen to be a conduit of its speaker's communication culture' (2005: 417).

Louhiala-Salminen et al.'s study is of course not the only study to use a corpus-based approach in investigating BELF: studies such as van Mulken and van der Meer's analysis of replies to customers (2005), Poncini's study of multicultural business meetings in Italy (2004), Tajima's study of interactions between pilot and controller before air traffic acci-dents (2004), Planken's discussion of BELF negotiation situations (2005), and Bjorge's study of email correspondence (2007) are all excellent examples. What sets Louhiala-Salminen et al.'s study apart, however, and suggests at the same time a fruitful area of future research, is its combination of different methodologies and analytical approaches and its focus on the role played both by language and by culture.

For the past decade, researchers at the Radboud University Nijmegen, in the Netherlands have been investigating the use of English and the effects of this use in the (non-NSE) European context. Using both *corpus* analysis and *experimental* investigation, the group has sought to establish the ways in which English has been incorporated into a variety of different business texts in the various languages spoken throughout the European Union, and then to investigate the comprehensibility of and attitudes to that English amongst the more educated population. Therefore, for instance, Gerritsen et al. (2000) look at television advertising in the Netherlands, van Meurs et al. (2004) at job advertisements, also in the Netherlands, and Gerritsen et al. (2007) at the use of English in product advertisements in Belgium, France, Germany, the Netherlands and Spain. The studies show a consistent – and increasing – use of English lexis in the business genre under investigation over a period of time, and the experimental investigations have shown that compared to the use of the local language, consumers across the EU hold neutral to negative attitudes towards the use of English. Additional investigation has shown that the use of English does not have any effect on the image of the product or the company with which it is associated, and also that, even for the highly educated sector of society, 30 per cent of the English lexis used is not at all understood. While we accept that these situations may be different in nature from the other BELF interactions we have discussed, since the national cultures involved are not in communication with each other, we also believe that this type of BELF communication will continue to increase within the European context.

Other very recent *experimental* research, both at the Radboud University Nijmegen and elsewhere, has focused on the comprehensibility of different EFL accents, and has so far provided contradictory findings. According to Nejjari et al. (under review), for instance, British NSEs are able to comprehend fully sentences uttered with a strong Dutch English accent, whereas the studies by van den Doel (2006) and Wang (2007) indicate that some EFL accents are less comprehensible for NSEs than others, depending on the first language of the EFL speaker; i.e. the more the accent resembles English the better it is understood. This is also true for ELF communication between EFL speakers with a different first language, such that the more the languages resemble each other the better the speakers understand each other. More experimental research in this field is clearly needed, especially in BELF encounters with EFL speakers of different languages.

Experimental methods clearly have their limitations. Texts are manipulated to represent a particular variable or set of variables, sacrificing authenticity in the process, and respondents may answer in a different way in an experimental setting and in real life. In an ideal situation, the data collected by means of an experiment should be complemented by data obtained in real-life situations (observation). Having said that however, experimental research is an important, perhaps crucial, approach in investigating BELF interactions, since it is only through the combination of survey, corpus and experimental investigations that we will really be able to isolate those characteristics of BELF communication that may cause a communication breakdown, and likewise, those that are not likely to do so.

Discussion and future developments

As Seidlhofer and Jenkins (2003) suggest, perhaps the most fruitful area of inquiry in lingua franca research in the future will be to develop appropriate methodologies to identify those aspects of communication that are most likely to lead to disruption in the interaction. Rather than focusing on language proficiency in general in courses designed for EFL or ESL speakers, the findings of such research could then drive teaching and training materials to focus more efficiently on those areas that are likely to cause a problem. The same would also be true for courses designed for NSEs of English in raising their awareness of BELF and other types of IBE interactions.

In this chapter, we have identified at least four areas of lingua franca communication that have as yet received little attention. The first of these is the role played by comprehensibility, and specifically what factors affect comprehensibility in either a positive or a negative way. Second, there are as yet few studies that have looked in a systematic way at the role played by different aspects of culture in BELF communication – with the exception of the European-wide project based at the Helsinki School of Economics that incorporates culture in an electronic survey of corporate communication (www.hse.fi/ckh). Third, BELF research would benefit from research that is specifically designed to identify the associations that hearers have with accents that are dissimilar to their own in business interactions, as well as with accents (in English) that are the same as their own. And finally, little has as yet been done to categorise the relative seriousness of different types of communication failures; e.g. is a lexical miscommunication less or more threatening to the communication than a cultural miscommunication related to, for example, the degree of directness used in an encounter? All four of these areas would benefit from the application of the same set of consistent methodologies to build up a picture of BELF communication around the globe.

In addition to the methodologies that we have discussed above (observation, survey research and corpus research), it would be useful to add the *focus group* as a qualitative way of investigating BELF interaction. A focus group consists of a number of people, usually around eight to ten, who are working in an organisation, for instance, where English is used. Focus groups can be used at two points in a research project. They can be used in order to determine the scope of a large research project, such that a focus group discussion on the use of BELF and the problems associated with its use can be used to underpin a set of questionnaire or interview questions. A focus group can also be used after a period of observation, a survey, a corpus analysis or an experiment have taken place. The group can then be used to discuss the findings, since the reaction of the group may shed new light on how these may be interpreted and why.

Conclusion: implications for scholarship, research and training

As we discussed in the previous section, much still needs to be done in developing appropriate methodologies for the systematic investigation of BELF. Despite some commentators' suggestions that languages such as Hindi and Chinese will steadily gain in popularity as business languages (e.g. Graddol 2004), we believe that English will continue to dominate both business lingua franca interactions specifically and international business communication in general. The work of researchers such as Briguglio (2005), Bolton (2002, 2003) and Chew (2005), for instance, shows the existing need for English in Asia, and the newly emerging interest in the English used in the business processing outsourcing (BPO) industry across Asia, i.e. in call-centre communication in countries such as India, the Philippines and China, will make a major contribution to our understanding of BELF, BESL and IBE interactions in the future (Forey and Lockwood 2006). Growth areas of business that are directly related to a nation's proficiency in English, such as the BPO industry, would clearly benefit from a battery of diagnostic tools combining observation, survey, corpus analysis, respondent surveys and focus groups, in order to improve upon the effectiveness of the communication that takes place in customer interactions.

The research findings and methodologies that we have discussed here suggest two obvious areas on which teaching and training should focus. First, it is important to raise students' awareness of the different varieties of English that are used in the business world, and along with that to facilitate their understanding of their own variety of English – be that NSE, EFL or ESL – and the impact that that variety might have on a speaker from a language background different to theirs. In this respect, we agree with Jenkins's contention that EFL should not be viewed (by trainers or teachers) as 'incorrect', but rather more as a variety of English with its own characteristics (Jenkins 2006). Second, and perhaps more importantly, teachers and trainers need to make students aware of the impact of culture. This would involve not only an awareness of the students' own culture and associated communication strategies, but also the culture and strategies used by other colleagues that they are likely to come into contact with in the process of doing business.

References

Alexander, R. J. (1999) Caught in a global English trap, or liberated by a lingua franca? Unravelling some aims, claims and dilemmas of the English teaching profession. In C. Gnutzmann (ed.), *Teaching and Learning English as a Global Language*. Tübingen: Stauffenburg, pp. 23–39.

Ammon, U. (1996) The European Union (EU – formerly: European Community): Status change of English during the last fifty years. In J. A. Fishman, A. W. Conrad and A. Rubal-Lopez (eds), *Post-Imperial English: Status Change in Former British and American Colonies, 1940–1990*. Berlin and New York: Mouton de Gruyter, pp. 241–67.

Ammon, U. (2006) Language conflicts in the European union: On finding a politically acceptable and practicable solution for EU institutions that satisfied diverging interests. *International Journal of Applied Linguistics*, 16: 319–38.

Bargiela-Chiappini, F., C. Nickerson and B. Planken (2007) *Business Discourse*. Basingstoke: Palgrave Macmillan.

Bjorge, A. K. (2007) Power distance in English lingua franca email communication. *International Journal of Applied Linguistics*, 17(1): 60–81.

Bolton, K. (ed.) (2002) *Hong Kong English: Autonomy and Creativity*. Hong Kong: Hong Kong University Press.

Bolton, K. (2003) *Chinese Englishes*. Cambridge: Cambridge University Press.

Bongaerts, T., S. Mennen and F. van der Slik (2000) Authenticity of pronunciation in naturalistic second language acquisition: The case of very advanced late learners of Dutch as a second language. *Studia Linguistica: Revue de Linguistique Generale et Comparée*, 54(2): 298–308.

Briguglio, C. (2005) Developing an understanding of English as a global language for business settings. In F. Bargiela-Chiappini and M. Gotti (eds), *Asian Business Discourse*. Bern: Peter Lang, pp. 313–44.

Canagarajah, A. S. (1999) *Resisting Linguistic Imperialism in English Teaching*. Oxford: Oxford University Press.

Charles, M. L. and R. Marschan-Piekkari (2002) Language training for enhanced horizontal communication: A challenge for MNCs. *Business Communication Quarterly*, 65(2): 9–29.

Chew, S. K. (2005) An investigation of the English language skills used by new entrants in banks in Hong Kong. *English for Specific Purposes*, 24(4): 423–35.

Coupland, N. and H. Bishop (2007) Ideologised values for British accents. *Journal of Sociolinguistics*, 11(2): 74–93.

Forey, G. and J. Lockwood (2006) 'I'd love to put someone in jail for this': An initial investigation of English in the business processing outsourcing (BPO) industry. *English for Specific Purposes*, 26(2): 308–26.

Gass, S. M. and E. M. Varonis (1991) Miscommunication in nonnative speaker discourse. In N. Coupland, H. Giles and J. M. Wiemann (eds), *Miscommunication and Problematic Talk*. Newbury Park, CAI: Sage, pp. 121–45. London and New Delhi: Sage.

Gerritsen, M. and C. Nickerson (2004) Fact or fallacy? English as an L2 in the Dutch business context. In C. Candlin and M. Gotti (eds), *Intercultural Aspects of Specialized Communication*. Berlin: Peter Lang, pp. 105–25.

Gerritsen, M., H. Korzilius, F. van Meurs and I. Gijsbers (2000) English in Dutch commercials: Not understood and not appreciated. *Journal of Advertising Research*, 40(4): 17–31.

Gerritsen, M., C. Nickerson, A. van Hooft, F. van Meurs, U. Nederstigt, M. Starren and R. Crijns (2007) English in product advertisements in Belgium, France, Germany, the Netherlands and Spain. *World Englishes*, 26(3): 291–316.

Graddol, D. (2004) The future of language. *Science*, 303: 1329–31.

Gunnarsson, B.-L. (2006) Swedish companies and their multilingual practices. In J. C. Palmer-Silveira, M. F. Ruiz-Garrido and I. Fortanet-Gómez (eds), *Intercultural and International Business Communication*. Bern: Peter Lang, pp. 243–62.

Jenkins, J. (2000) *The Phonology of English as an International Language: New Models, New Norms, New Goals*. Oxford: Oxford University Press.

Jenkins, J. (2006) Points of view and blind spots: ELF and SLA. *International Journal of Applied Linguistics*, 16(2): 138–62.

Kachru, B. B. (1986) *The Alchemy of English: The Spread, Functions, and Models of Non-Native Englishes*. Oxford: Pergamon.

Kellerman, E. and R. Vermeulen (1995) Causation in narrative: The role of language background and proficiency in two episodes of 'the frog story'. In D. Albrechtsen, B. Henriksen, I. Mees and E. Poulsen (eds), *Perspectives on Foreign and Second Language Pedagogy*. Odense: Odense University Press, pp. 161–76.

Knapp, K. and C. Meierkord (eds) (2002) *Lingua Franca Communication*. Frankfurt: Peter Lang.

Lindemann, S. (2002) Listening with an attitude: A model of native-speaker comprehension of non-native speakers in the United States. *Language in Society*, 31: 419–41.

Li So-mui, F. and K. Mead (2000) An analysis of English in the workplace: The communication needs of textile and clothing merchandisers. *English for Specific Purposes*, 19: 351–68.

Louhiala-Salminen, L. (2002) The fly's perspective: Discourse in the daily routine of a business manager. *English for Specific Purposes*, 21: 211–31.

Louhiala-Salminen, L. and M. Charles (2006) English as the lingua franca of international business communication: Whose English? What English? In J. C. Palmer-Silveira, M. F. Ruiz-Garrido and I. Fortanet-Gómez (eds), *Intercultural and International Business Communication*. Bern: Peter Lang, pp. 27–54.

Louhiala-Salminen, L., M. Charles and A. Kankaanranta (2005) English as a lingua franca in Nordic corporate mergers: Two case companies. *English for Specific Purposes*, 24: 401–21.

Mair, C. (ed.) (2003) *The Politics of English as a World Language*. Amsterdam and Atlanta, GA: Rodopi.

Mollin, S. (2006) *Euro-English: Assessing Variety Status*. Tübingen: Gunter Narr.

Nejjari, W., M. Gerritsen, M. van der Haagen and H. Korzilius (2007) Responses to Dutch-Accented English. Unpublished ms.

Nickerson, C., M. Gerritsen and F. van Meurs (2005) Raising student awareness of the use of English for specific business purposes in the European context: A staff–student project. *English for Specific Purposes*, 24(3): 333–46.

Pennycook, A. (1998) *English and the Discourses of Colonialism*. London: Routledge.

Phillipson, R. (1992) *Linguistic Imperialism*. Oxford: Oxford University Press.

Planken, B. (2005) Managing rapport in lingua franca sales negotiations: A comparison of professional and aspiring negotiators. *English for Specific Purposes*, 24(4): 381–400.

Poncini, G. (2004) *Discursive Strategies in Multicultural Business Meetings*. Bern: Peter Lang.

Rogerson-Revell, P. (2007) Using English for international business: A European case study. *English for Specific Purposes*, 26: 103–20.

Seidlhofer, B. (2004) Research perspectives on teaching English as a lingua franca. *Annual Review of Applied Linguistics*, 24: 209–39.

Seidlhofer, B. and J. Jenkins (2003) English as a lingua franca and the politics of property. In C. Mair (ed.), *The Politics of English as a World Language*. Amsterdam and Atlanta, GA: Rodopi, pp. 139–54.

Seidlhofer, B., A. Breiteneder and M. L. Pitzl (2006) English as a lingua franca in Europe: Challenges for applied linguistics. *Annual Review of Applied Linguistics*, 26: 3–34.

Shaw, P., P. Gillaerts, E. Jacobs, O. Palermo, M. Shinohara and J. P. Verckens (2004) Genres across cultures: Types of acceptability variation. *World Englishes*, 23(3): 385–401.

Smith, L. (1992) Spread of English and issues of intelligibility. In B. B. Kachru (ed.), *The Other Tongue: English across Cultures*. Oxford: Pergamon, pp. 75–90.

Tajima, A. (2004) Fatal miscommunication: English in aviation safety. *World Englishes*, 23(3): 451–70.

van den Doel, R. (2006) *How Friendly are the Natives? An Evaluation of Native-Speaker Judgements of Foreign-Accented British and American English*. Utrecht: Netherlands Graduate School of Linguistics (LOT).

Vandermeeren, S. (1998) *Fremdsprachen in europäischen Unternehmen: Untersuchungen zu Bestand und Bedarf im Geschäftsalltag mit Empfehlungen für Sprachenpolitik und Sprachunterricht*. Waldsteinberg: Heidrun Popp.

Vandermeeren, S. (1999) English as a lingua franca in written corporate communication: Findings from a European survey. In F. Bargiela-Chiappini and C. Nickerson (eds), *Writing Business: Genres, Media and Discourses*. Harlow: Longman, pp. 273–92.

van Els, T. (2005) Multilingualism in the European Union. *International Journal of Applied Linguistics*, 15(3): 263–426.

van Meurs, F., H. Korzilius and J. Hermans (2004) The influence of the use of English in Dutch job advertisements: An experimental study into the effects on text evaluation, on attitudes towards the organisation and the job, and on comprehension. *ESP across Cultures*, 1: 93–110.

van Mulken, M. and W. Van der Meer (2005) Are you being served? A genre analysis of American and Dutch company replies to customer enquiries. *English for Specific Purposes*, 24: 93–109.

van Oostendorp, M. (2002) *Steenkolen Engels*. Amsterdam and Antwerp: Uitgeverij Veen.

Wang, H. (2007) *English as a Lingua Franca: Mutual Intelligibility of Chinese, Dutch and American Speakers of English*. Utrecht: Netherlands Graduate School of Linguistics (LOT).

Part Three: Disciplinary Perspectives

15

Linguistic anthropology

Christina Wasson

Introduction

This chapter presents an overview of the contributions that linguistic anthropology has made to the study of business discourse, including a critical appraisal of significant developments and a short outline of future trends. The chapter starts by explaining the history of the discipline; it developed only in the United States as part of the uniquely American conceptualisation of anthropology as consisting of four fields, one of which was linguistic anthropology. Next, the chapter describes the discipline and what sets it apart from related areas like discourse analysis and conversation analysis. Linguistic anthropology draws on aspects of both cultural anthropology and linguistics; its practitioners engage in extensive ethnographic fieldwork as well as detailed examinations of situated language use.

The chapter then turns to linguistic anthropological research in the area of business discourse. The combination of an ethnographic and linguistic focus has enabled linguistic anthropologists to present detailed analyses of business-based communicative interactions situated in a variety of overlapping cultural contexts, from corporate cultures, to national cultures, to the subcultures of users of particular products. The chapter reviews research on five topics: (1) cross-cultural communication in the workplace, (2) narrative in institutions, (3) meetings, (4) language ideologies, and (5) design anthropology. The last topic extends the field of business discourse by considering the interactions of not just employees, but also consumers. Furthermore, researchers in this area are often employed in the private sector. We are seeing the rise of 'scholar-practitioners' who have bridged the old divide between academic research and practical business applications.

The field of linguistic anthropology

The field of linguistic anthropology is a peculiarly American phenomenon. It originated with the founder of American anthropology, Franz Boas, who, in the early 1900s, conceptualised anthropology as consisting of four fields (Stocking 1974; Hymes 1983). These four fields were: *cultural anthropology*, the study of present-day cultures around the world; *archaeology*, the study of cultures from the past; *physical anthropology*, the study of the physical evolution of humans; and *linguistic anthropology*, the study of culturally shaped communication patterns around the world. Boas's interest in language developed through his studies of Native American groups such as the Kwakiutl. As he learned more about their cultures, he found that he needed to understand their languages in order to gain insight into their worldviews. Boas's holistic conceptualisation of anthropology profoundly shaped the development of the discipline in the United States, and today most anthropologists still adhere to the ideology of the 'four-field' approach, although not all departments include members of all four fields. The American Anthropological Association endorses the four-field approach.

Linguistic anthropologists generally have training in both *linguistics* and *cultural anthropology*, and in many ways the field may be regarded as the intersection of these two disciplines. Early figures in the history of linguistic anthropology include Benjamin Lee Whorf and Edward Sapir, both of whom explored relationships between language, culture and perceptions of reality in the 1920s and 1930s (Sapir 1949; Whorf 1956).

In the 1960s and 1970s, Dell Hymes and John Gumperz moved the field of linguistic anthropology forward by shifting its emphasis to the study of situated communication and language use. Their approach was more process-oriented and ethnographic than the previous Sapir/Whorf emphasis on the collection of texts and examination of grammar and phonology. Hymes developed a model for the 'ethnography of speaking' based on the acronym SPEAKING, which stood for 'setting and scene, participants, ends, act sequence, key, instrumentalities, norms, and genre' (1962, 1974). The terms of this model made visible Hymes's focus on examining communication in the settings in which it occurred, through close ethnographic fieldwork. Meanwhile Gumperz developed 'interactional sociolinguistics'. He explored the ways in which participants in an interaction produce meaning by drawing on their shared knowledge of communicative resources. For instance, members of a community that uses two communicative codes understand what it means when someone shifts from one code to the other (Blom and Gumperz 1972). For Gumperz, a key analytical tool was the 'contextualization cue', which he defined as 'any feature of linguistic form that contributes to the signaling of contextual presuppositions' (Gumperz 1982a: 131). Such elements provide information for participants about how to interpret each other's contributions. Gumperz and Hymes together edited the groundbreaking volume *The Directions in Sociolinguistics: Ethnography of Communication* (1972).

From the late 1970s onward, Michael Silverstein emerged as a key figure for the next generation. To the Hymes/Gumperz emphasis on situated linguistic *practices*, he added a consideration of the linguistic *ideologies* which participants in an interaction use to evaluate one another's practices (Silverstein 1979, 1993). In addition, influenced by a reconsideration of Whorf's research, Silverstein initiated studies of topics such as indexicality, the ways in which texts (including spoken conversations) point to and draw on other, earlier texts (2003). In general, linguistic anthropologists since the late 1980s have become much more concerned about tying micro-level interactional phenomena to macro-level social, political and economic structures (Gal 1989; Woolard 1985; Woolard and Schieffelin 1994).

A second current strand of linguistic anthropology has coalesced around the marriage of conversation analysis with anthropological methods and concerns; key figures include Charles Goodwin, Marjorie Goodwin and Alessandro Duranti (C. Goodwin 1981; M. H. Goodwin 1990; Duranti 1994). Such scholars link detailed analysis of video-recordings and transcripts with extensive ethnographic fieldwork and a concern with relating interactional behaviours to broader cultural phenomena. In practice, many current linguistic anthropologists draw on both this latter approach and Silverstein's approach.

Linguistic anthropology did not develop as a defined field in Europe because there, the entire discipline of anthropology was equated with only one of the four American fields of anthropology, namely cultural anthropology. Furthermore, national disciplinary traditions developed somewhat differently. In Britain, for instance, anthropology was referred to as 'social anthropology', and it was characterised by a greater focus on social structures than was common among American cultural anthropologists. (The term 'ethnology' was also used to refer to cultural anthropology, both in Europe and in the United States.) The lack of a four-field approach to anthropology in Europe meant that the topics that American linguistic anthropologists explored were primarily examined by non-anthropologists in Europe.

Linguistic anthropology may be distinguished from conversation analysis and discourse analysis in several ways. First of all, what sets linguistic anthropology apart is the unique combination of ethnographic fieldwork and close attention to situated language use, including both linguistic practices and linguistic ideologies. Second, linguistic anthropology is characterised by the particular intellectual genealogy summarised above. Third, linguistic anthropology is a formal discipline, as indicated, for instance, by the fact that it has a professional association (the Society for Linguistic Anthropology) and a flagship journal (the *Journal of Linguistic Anthropology*). By contrast, conversation analysis and discourse analysis are philosophical and methodological approaches *utilised* by members of various disciplines.

Conversation analysis (CA) was originally developed by the sociologist Harvey Sacks and his students Gail Jefferson and Emanuel Schegloff (Goodwin and Heritage 1990; Sacks et al. 1974). They believed that participants in an interaction continually display to each other their own understanding of what they are doing. The goal for CA was to understand how the participants in an interaction understand the process of their interaction. To this end, CA researchers developed a number of key concepts, for instance how turn-taking happens, and a variety of interactional moves that participants were shown to make. CA researchers are known for their close analysis of recordings of naturally occurring conversations. Unlike anthropologists, they do not consider it necessary to learn more about the participants in an interaction than what is visible in the recording; they do not conduct ethnographic fieldwork such as participant observation or interviews.

At the same time, as noted above, some linguistic anthropologists have long used conversation analysis as an important part of their methodological and philosophical toolkit. As anthropologists, they generally reject CA's claim that research does not need to go beyond what is visible in the transcript, since they seek to link interactional patterns with broader cultural, political and economic phenomena. However, they value CA's profound insights into the subtleties of how participants in an interaction coordinate their contributions with one another (Goodwin and Heritage 1990).

In contrast to CA, discourse analysis (DA) is an umbrella term for a wide variety of approaches. It may be defined broadly as being '(a) concerned with language *use* beyond the boundaries of a sentence/utterance, (b) concerned with the interrelationships between language and society and (c) concerned with the interactive or dialogic properties of everyday communication' (Stubbs 1983: 1). Beyond this shared framework, however, DA encompasses a large number of diverse approaches which differ in their assumptions and

Table 15.1 Approaches to discourse analysis (Slembrouk 2006)

1 Analytical philosophy	5 Poststructuralist theory
• Speech act theory	• M. M. Bakhtin
• Principles of information exchange	6 Semiotics and cultural studies
2 Linguistics	• Semiotics and communication studies
• Structuralist linguistics	• Cultural studies
• Register studies and stylistics	7 Social theory
• Text linguistics	• Pierre Bourdieu
• Pragmatics	• Michel Foucault
• Presuppositions	• Jürgen Habermas
• Face and politeness	8 The sociology of order in interaction
• Reference	• Erving Goffman
3 Linguistic anthropology	• Interaction order
• Ethnography of speaking	• Frame analysis
• Ethnopoetics	• Footing
• Indexicality	• Face
• Interactional sociolinguistics	• Conversation analysis
• Natural histories of discourse	• Ethnomethodology
4 New literacy studies	

Source: Slembrouck (2006)

methodologies. Slembrouck (2006) organised a review of DA around the categories listed in Table 15.1.

If we follow Slembrouck's schema, we may locate linguistic anthropology within the broader field of DA. However, as the schema also indicates, DA is such a broad concept that it is not useful for drawing the kinds of distinctions that are made in this chapter. Furthermore, different readers may associate DA with different varieties of scholarship, leading to confusion. We will not, therefore, utilise the term in this chapter.

Linguistic anthropology and business discourse

The overall contribution of linguistic anthropology to the study of business discourse has been its distinctive combination of ethnographic fieldwork and close attention to situated language use, as described above. This has enabled linguistic anthropologists to present detailed analyses of communicative interactions situated in their cultural contexts. The contexts considered have ranged from organisations, to national cultures, to the subcultures of users of particular products.

Up until now, a fairly small number of linguistic anthropologists have examined business discourse. Why not more? One reason is that the overall number of linguistic anthropologists is quite small; according to the director of academic relations of the American Anthropological Association, there were approximately 600 linguistic anthropologists teaching in American universities in 2006, about 5.8 per cent of the total anthropology faculty (Terry-Sharp, personal communication, 23 July 2007). A second reason is that until recently, most American anthropologists focused their research on traditional ways of life in non-industrialized, non-Western societies. Graduate students in American anthropology programmes were advised that they would be less marketable if they studied a Western society, or indeed anything so mainstream as a corporation. For linguistic anthropologists in particular, it was important to conduct research on a non-western language. A third reason is that institutional ethnography was long left to sociologists. However, some of these limitations, at least, are dissolving. In recent years, it has become much more acceptable for graduate students to study Western, industrialized countries including the institutions of capitalism; in fact, it has become fashionable! In addition, corporations are now hiring significant numbers of anthropologists, who then conduct applied research projects with a business focus; I will return to this theme at the end of the essay.

Methodology

Linguistic anthropologists draw on methodologies from both cultural anthropology and linguistics. I will describe first data collection and then analysis.

Data collection

The hallmark of both linguistic and cultural anthropology is participant observation. Throughout the twentieth century, researchers would typically spent a year or longer in the villages where most anthropological research was done. Even now, in the new millennium, they still spend long periods of time in the field relative to researchers in other disciplines, participating in community members' daily activities, and learning what it means to act, think and feel like a 'native' (Duranti 1997). Long-term participant observation is the defining characteristic of linguistic and cultural anthropological research methods.

In addition, researchers conduct interviews with community members to find out what kinds of meanings they assign their activities, and to collect background information about the topic under investigation. These interviews range from highly structured to unstructured, with the most common format being 'semi-structured', in which the researchers start with a list of questions but extend the conversation well beyond that list by asking follow-up questions and letting study participants raise unanticipated topics. Interviews also range widely in how long they take, from a few minutes to several hours. Both participant observation and interviews are documented via careful field notes, and sometimes via recordings (Duranti 1997; Schensul et al. 1999).

Participant observation and semi-structured interviews are the two most central ethnographic techniques for linguistic and cultural anthropologists. In addition, however, they may draw on a variety of other approaches, depending on the needs of their study. For instance, they may develop kinship diagrams, map the physical environment, or conduct surveys (LeCompte and Schensul 1999b).

Linguistic anthropologists also conduct *linguistic* fieldwork by making recordings of naturally occurring discourse in the communities they are studying (Duranti 1997). This approach to data collection is similar to that of descriptive linguists and sociolinguists who research language variation. Historically audio-recordings were made; now, video is increasingly popular. The recordings are transcribed. Usually standardised spelling is used, rather than the International Phonetic Alphabet, but interactional phenomena such as pauses and overlaps between speakers may be noted. Many linguistic anthropologists have adopted conventions from CA for transcription, but this usage is not universal (Sacks et al. 1974; Psathas and Anderson 1990). For video-recordings, visual phenomena such as gestures may also be noted, depending on the goals of the study.

Data analysis

In general, linguistic anthropology, like cultural anthropology and field linguistics, follows an inductive approach to analysis. While researchers start with as much background information as they can gather before their fieldwork, they are open to exploration and discovering the unexpected. They do not design their research as a series of hypothesis-testing experiments. While they start with certain established social theories as tools for analysis, they also develop novel interpretative frameworks, and remain open to considering other social theories which might illuminate emergent patterns in their data. As Geertz stated, 'Believing, with Max Weber, that man is an animal suspended in webs of significance he himself has spun, I take culture to be those webs, and the analysis of it to be therefore not an experimental science in search of law but an interpretive one in search of meaning' (1973: 5).

The process of analysis, then, is a matter of working from the particular to the general. Researchers seek to identify patterns in the study of participants' ideas, behaviours and ways of speaking. Then they look for relationships between patterns, ultimately developing an explanatory model for the observed phenomena. In a classic text on ethnographic analysis, LeCompte and Schensul refer to this process as moving from the 'item level' to the 'pattern level' to the 'structure level' (LeCompte and Schensul 1999a: 68; Wasson 2002a).

The specific analysis techniques that researchers use vary somewhat depending on the needs of the project and the technology skills of the researcher. It would be typical to code core data documents such as transcripts of naturally occurring discourse, transcripts of interviews and field notes. Although it is possible to code by hand, qualitative analysis software like Atlas.ti makes the process much quicker, and provides powerful tools such as the ability to diagram the relationships between codes. However, some linguistic anthropologists do not rely on coding software, preferring to scan visually for and manually annotate patterns and meanings in transcripts.

The identification of patterns or codes is usually emergent, meaning that the interpretation of transcripts is an iterative process. In the case of researchers who use coding software, for instance, they develop an initial list of codes based on a preliminary perusal of the data. However, as they apply the codes to the data, they usually find themselves splitting some codes, combining others, adding new codes, and eliminating a few as well. In order to code all data consistently, they therefore have to go back a few times to apply the changes to documents that they had already coded before. The patterns being identified may be based on known concepts in linguistic anthropology (or linguistics or cultural anthropology), or they may be innovations inspired by the data at hand. The process of analysis allows researchers to identify patterns and relationships between patterns, leading ultimately to explanatory models and theory development (LeCompte and Schensul 1999a).

Although linguistic anthropologists always engage in qualitative analysis, they do not typically engage in extensive quantitative analysis.

Discussion of research themes

The rest of this chapter will be organised around five themes which constitute a chronology of developments in the linguistic anthropology of business discourse, broadly conceived. These themes all illustrate the distinctive way in which linguistic anthropologists carefully synthesise ethnographic and linguistic approaches to data collection and analysis. The following five research themes are explored: (1) cross-cultural communication in the workplace, (2) narrative in institutions, (3) meetings, (4) language ideologies, and (5) design anthropology.

The first three themes emerged first, and their findings overlapped with concurrent investigations occurring in other disciplines, although the approach and therefore also the insights of linguistic anthropologists were always distinctive. The last two themes are more particular to linguistic anthropology, and they are located at the cutting edge of the discipline.

Cross-cultural communication in the workplace

A research strand that began in the late 1970s was the investigation of cross-cultural communication in the workplace. Early work was contributed by John Gumperz and his students and associates. Gumperz examined the communication difficulties of South Asians in England. He developed the theory that cross-cultural differences in communicative practices often led to misunderstandings between co-workers, and that, because they did not recognise the true nature of their interactional difficulties, they tended to attribute their problems to national stereotypes. Gumperz laid out his theoretical framework in *Discourse Strategies* (1982a), and edited a volume of case studies, including several workplace-related chapters, in the same year (1982b). He also developed a training video for British employers (British Broadcasting Corporation 1979).

Subsequently, Laura Miller developed a large body of work in this area (1991a, 1991b, 1994a, 1994b, 1994c, 1995, 1998, 2000). She examined companies in Japan in which American and Japanese employees worked together, video-taping their everyday interactions. Her framework was strongly influenced by Gumperz. She was also one of the first linguistic anthropologists to video-tape naturally occurring interactions extensively; this allowed her to conduct fine-grained analyses of the interactions of her study participants. The communicative practices she investigated included negative assessments (2000), complimenting (1991a), listening behaviours (1991a, 1991b), indirectness (1994c) and decision-making (1994b).

At the same time, Miller also investigated communicative practices that co-workers of different nationalities used to develop group cohesion. The most striking practice she identified was the use of code-switching as a resource for building solidarity (1991a, 1995, 1994a). Usually the code-switching literature has presented the two codes involved as a 'we' code and a 'they' code – but Miller argued that 'in the case of code-switching which occurs between those of different ethnic and linguistic backgrounds, who are nevertheless bound together into a single social unit, the code-switching itself becomes the "we" code' (1991a: 100–1). In addition, drawing on her video-taped data, she explored a variety of communicative resources that co-workers used to build solidarity within groups that contained both Japanese and American members (1995, 1994a).

Benjamin Bailey continued the Gumperz-based focus on cross-cultural miscommunications, but added a political dimension to it as well (1997, 2000). He conducted research on service encounters in the US between Korean shopkeepers and African-American customers. Following the Gumperz-based framework, he identified a Korean model of interactional 'restraint' that guided the behaviour of the shopkeepers, contrasting with an African-American model of 'social involvement' that shaped the behaviour of the shopkeepers. Evidence for these models could be seen in the fact that Korean–Korean service encounters were even shorter than the interethnic encounters, while interactions between African-American store owners and customers displayed more longer, more involved social engagement than the interethnic encounters.

However, Bailey went further in his analysis by asking why communicative tensions between Koreans and Africa-Americans persisted over time, and even intensified, since one might expect that participants would learn to accommodate each other (2000). Here, he argued that participants' behaviours relating to interactional 'restraint' or 'social involvement' could become political statements of identity; 'divergent patterns of communicative behaviour in service encounters are not a *cause* of interethnic tensions, but rather a *local enactment of pre-existing social conflicts* (2000: 102–4). Bailey's interpretative move of situating these interactions in the larger political economy reflects a trend in linguistic anthropology that will be discussed further below under 'Language ideologies'.

Narrative in institutions

Charlotte Linde and Julian Orr have conducted linguistic anthropological studies of the ways in which institutions and their members use narratives (Linde 1996, 1997b, 1999, 2000a, 2000b, 2001, 2005, 2006; Orr 2000, 1996). In a review article, Linde argued that there are two approaches to the study of narrative in institutions: (1) how 'narrative is used to carry out the daily work of the institution', and (2) how narratives reproduce and maintain organisational identity, i.e. the role they play in inducting new members and helping them 'adapt to change, and deal with contested or contradictory versions of the past' (2001: 518). The studies of both Linde and Orr exemplify the strengths of linguistic anthropology by combining careful ethnographic fieldwork with close attention to language use

Orr has conducted the most extensive ethnographic research on how narratives help institutions do their daily work (1996). He examined the role of stories in the work of Xerox repair technicians. He found that the manuals that the technicians had available to them were only partly useful in resolving difficult diagnostic problems. More typically, technicians out on a call together would share stories of previous, similar cases with each other, hoping that the narratives might suggest a solution. In addition, back in the lunchroom or on other social occasions, technicians shared their 'war stories' about how they had solved difficult problems. Such storytelling was a way for newer technicians to learn, and for more experienced technicians to gain symbolic capital, 'a celebration of being a technician, able to cope with anything that either machines or customers or both can do' (Orr 1996: 139).

Both Orr and Linde have also examined ways in which narratives reproduce and maintain the identity of organisation members and the organisation itself. Orr argued that the 'war stories' of Xerox repair technicians were a key index of their membership in an occupational community (1990). Linde examined a major American insurance company, and found that agents and employees drew on a consistent set of 'nonparticipant narratives' about the history of the company that, in their retelling, reproduced and strengthened the organisational culture, or, at other times, contested dominant managerial ideologies (2000a, 2000b, 2001, 2005). This research builds on Linde's prior studies of life stories (1993).

In addition, Linde has linked narrative in organisations to the related issues of institutional memory and knowledge management. She argues that work practices are largely shared and transmitted to new members by means of stories. Institutional memory includes both texts and the ways in which they are circulated: 'the tellings of the story of how the company was founded, the current stories and rumors, the paths that rumors travel, the Friday afternoon beer busts, the jokes, etc.' (1996: 335). As anyone who has worked in an organisation knows, developing an institutional memory about work processes that outlasts particular employees is an ongoing challenge. Linde has provided recommendations on how to make systems such as knowledge management databases more effective (2001, 2006).

Meetings

A third broad area of linguistic anthropological research is the investigation of business meetings, both face to face and virtual. These studies display their disciplinary orientation in the way they pay close attention to the lived experience of corporate employees, as it is shaped by the cultures and political economies that structure their environment.

Face-to-face business meetings have been examined by Miller and Wasson. Miller has one article specifically about meetings in Japan versus the US (1994c). Furthermore, her many other publications, described above under 'Cross-cultural communication in the workplace', include analyses of interactional behaviours which may occur in meetings as well as other types of workplace encounters. These include indirectness, negative assessments and listening behaviours. While these topics might also be addressed by e.g. scholars in the field of pragmatics, Miller's linguistic anthropological approach shows in the way she combines micro-level and macro-level phenomena in her data collection and analysis. At the micro-level, Miller has extensively video-taped naturally occurring workplace interactions and analysed them for interactional patterns, as well as conducting long-term participant observation. At the macro-level, Miller situates these patterns within the context of their speakers' national culture. For instance, she argues that in Japan, a key part of the decision-making process occurs *prior* to meetings, while American business managers expect to reach decisions *during* meetings. This can lead to misunderstandings on teams with cross-cultural membership (Miller 1994c).

Wasson's (2000a) study of business meetings highlighted the political economy of the organisation as a key cultural context. Her research site was a large, high-technology multinational firm based in the United States. She explored the ways that the lived experience of managers was shaped by organisational structures and politics. Like politicians, managers were vulnerable to having their reputation damaged by saying the wrong thing to the wrong audience. For this and other reasons, managers developed a disposition to caution in many interactional circumstances. Wasson explored one linguistic manifestation of this caution by examining consensus decision-making in cross-functional teams. She found that team members were rarely insistent on holding onto a particular opinion, and indeed, easily engaged in reversals of opinion. Wasson's findings were based on sixteen months of ethnographic and linguistic fieldwork. Her analysis of linguistic practices drew on CA-oriented studies of assessments (Goodwin and Goodwin 1992) and negotiations (Maynard 1984; Firth 1995). She also considered the language ideologies related to practices of caution.

Linguistic anthropologists have also examined virtual meetings. Linde (1991) pioneered the topic by studying the introduction of new communication technologies in two workplace sites. Her study focused on how topic management varied between face-to-face and virtual meetings. She concluded that new communications technologies 'must be capable of becoming transparent: that is, the mechanics of their use must be assimilable to the rules of the conversation' (Linde 1991: 313). This is a key point for designers of such technologies.

Ruhleder and Jordan (2001) continued the technology focus with an examination of video-conferences. They found that the noticeable time lag between settings created communication challenges, since the participants automatically reacted to silences of a certain length as indirect negative assessments.

Most recently, Wasson (2004b, 2006a) conducted a study of virtual team meetings which relied on teleconferences and shared computer applications (thus avoiding the challenges of video-conferences). She discovered that most team members engaged in extensive multitasking during the meetings, for instance checking their email (Wasson 2004b). While this was widely known in corporate circles, it had never been written about in scholarly publications on virtual meetings. Her discovery thus highlighted the strength of a linguistic anthropological approach which involved extensive observation and building rapport with study participants.

More importantly, Wasson identified the fundamental change that had taken place with the advent of new communication technologies: for the first time in history, it was possible for people to be present in two or more interactional spaces at once. During virtual meetings, employees were present minimally in (1) the interactional space of the meeting and (2) their local office space. Participant structures were different in each space, and there were visual and auditory barriers between the spaces. It was this phenomenon of being in two spaces at once that made multitasking possible. Wasson was initially led to this discovery by the challenges of transcribing video-tapes of virtual meetings; Wasson (2006a) described the challenges of transcribing interactions in multiple spaces, and explored the philosophical and practical implications of this phenomenon.

Language ideologies

The unique contribution that linguistic anthropologists made to the previous three themes was their careful synthesis of ethnographic and linguistic data collection and analysis, which revealed the complexities of how life on the ground was experienced by employees in business organisations, and explored how discursive phenomena were part and parcel of that experience. However, although their approach was distinctive, linguistic anthropologists were not the only scholars who examined these themes.

The next two research themes are different in that they are more particular to developments within the field of linguistic anthropology. First we review studies of language ideologies in business settings. The concept of 'language ideologies' (or 'linguistic ideologies') is one of the key innovations that linguistic anthropology has offered social studies of language in recent years. Language ideologies may be defined as the beliefs or attitudes that speakers of a language hold towards their language (or specific varieties of it, Silverstein 1979; Irvine 1989; Kroskrity 2004). The concept connects linguistic practices with social/political structures and processes.

> Language ideologies are viewed as multiple and constructed from specific politi-
> cal economic perspectives . . . not merely those ideas which stem from the 'official
> culture' of the ruling class but rather a more ubiquitous set of diverse beliefs,
> however implicit or explicit they may be, used by speakers of all types as models
> for constructing linguistic evaluations and engaging in communicative activity.
> (Kroskrity 2004: 497)

Since studies of organisational discourse have primarily focused on linguistic *practices* until now, the concept of linguistic ideologies can significantly extend the field of business discourse by adding a complementary analysis of the *ideologies* which organisation members use to evaluate each other's talk. This analysis of ideologies is thus somewhat different from that of critical discourse studies, which primarily examines written texts rather than conversational interactions in organisations.

Wasson introduced the linguistic anthropological concept of language ideologies to an organisation studies audience through various conference presentations and publications (1998, 1999, 2001, 2002b, 2003, 2004a, 2004c). Her investigations included studies of 'enterprise language', i.e. the use of marketplace metaphors to conceptualise relationships inside the workplace; irony in organisations; and beliefs about the spread of English in corporate Europe.

Wasson (2003) provided a published introduction to language ideologies for an organisation studies audience, and a model for the linguistic anthropological analysis of language in organisations that draws on this concept. In her model, language is inserted in the middle of the traditional 'structure versus agency' duality; Wasson argues that language provides resources for both organisations and social actors. Language is, in turn, comprised of both linguistic practices and linguistic ideologies. According to the model, then, language is 'Janus-faced': one face, linguistic *ideologies*, provides resources for the organisational power structure, while another face, linguistic *practices*, offers resources to employees.

In addition, Urciuoli has examined the way in which enterprise language is being applied to higher education (2003, 2005, n.d.). She argues that neoliberal discourses are increasingly shaping college administrators' understandings of the mission of their educational institutions, as well as the perceptions of students themselves. Although this research does not take place in corporate settings, I mention it here because it applies the logic of the private sector to the field of education.

Design anthropology

Finally I turn to a cutting-edge development in the use of linguistic anthropology to analyse communicative interactions for business organisations. This theme is a bit different from the others in that it is primarily practised in applied contexts. Such practitioners are employed by large corporations and design consulting firms. They conduct ethnographic studies to understand how consumers interact with products and services, and collaborate with designers to make these products more suited to users' daily practices and the symbolic meanings they assign such artefacts.

This field is most often referred to as 'design anthropology'. As described in Wasson (2000b), the theoretical approach and methodology used in design anthropology are strongly shaped by ethnomethodology and CA, as these were being used by linguistic anthropologists, as well as activity theory as it was being used by workplace anthropologists. Early researchers discovered that theoretical frameworks focused on the analysis of face-to-face interaction could be extended to a broader analysis of people interacting both with each other *and* with artefacts and physical environments. They therefore adopted the methodological emphasis on video-taping interactions that characterised forms of linguistic anthropology shaped by ethnomethodology and CA (Brun-Cottan and Wall 1995; Suchman and Trigg 1991).

Much of the early work in this field took place at the Xerox Palo Alto Research Center. For a period of about fifteen years, in the 1980s and 1990s, a group of eight or so anthropologists worked to improve the design of Xerox products by examining how users interacted with them in the context of their everyday work practices. The leader of this group, Lucy Suchman, received her PhD in anthropology at UC Berkeley under John Gumperz.

> An obvious methodological influence from conversation analysis (CA) has been the Xerox PARC practice of using videotape to document ethnographic materials . . . More profoundly, CA and ethnomethodology have provided theoretical tools for Xerox researchers. For instance, they interpret collaborative work behaviours using the fundamental CA principle that interactions are structured as sequences in which each move incorporates the actor's interpretation of the immediately preceding moves . . . the diffusion of these ideas at Xerox PARC was furthered in the early 1990s by a yearlong visit from the eminent anthropologists and conversation analysts Marjorie Harness Goodwin and Charles Goodwin . . . They in turn invited other CA scholars, such as Emanuel Schegloff. (Wasson 2000b: 381)

The anthropologists at Xerox PARC were part of the emergent field of computer-supported co-operative work.

In the 1990s, the idea of using CA-inflected ethnographic research to understand how consumers interacted with the objects in their lives diffused widely across the field of design. 'By 1997, every major design firm claimed to include ethnography as one of its approaches' (Wasson 2000b: 382). The trend continues; there is now an annual conference, the Ethnographic Praxis in Industry Conference, and a listserv called 'anthrodesign' with 1091 members as of 31 May 2007.

The literature on design anthropology encompasses several focuses and directions, and not all of it emphasises a linguistic anthropological framework. Good examples of the genre as described here include all of the work by the anthropologists who worked at Xerox PARC (Blomberg et al. 1993, 1997; Brun-Cottan and Wall 1995; C. Goodwin 1996; Goodwin and Goodwin 1996; M. H. Goodwin 1995; Suchman 1987, 1992, 1995,

1996; Suchman and Trigg 1991; Orr 1990, 1996), as well as publications by anthropologists who worked for the closely related Institute for Research on Learning (Jordan 1996; Ruhleder and Jordan 2001; Linde 1997a). Also of interest are Sacher's (2002) semiotic perspective on design research, and the application of linguistic anthropology to market research (Sunderland and Denny 2003). The Proceedings of the Ethnographic Praxis in Industry Conference provide a good overview of the breadth of recent work (Anderson and Lovejoy 2005, 2006).

Future developments

Business discourse should not be regarded as a special application of linguistic anthropology, but rather as one of the directions that offer great promise for the field. The developments delineated in this chapter constitute important contributions to the discipline.

Looking toward the future, we may expect further developments in the linguistic anthropology of business discourse to focus especially on the two last themes described. The notion of linguistic ideologies has now become so foundational that it would be surprising to see future research that did not take this aspect of communication into account.

Furthermore, the field of design anthropology is expanding rapidly. Researchers in this area are both articulate in their theoretical framing, and creative in their application, so we can expect to see interesting work emerging from this field in the future. Cutting-edge presentations can be seen not only at the Ethnographic Praxis in Industry Conference, mentioned above, but also at design/technology conferences such as the International Conference on Ubiquitous Computing, and at applied anthropology conferences such as the Society for Applied Anthropology Annual Meeting. At the 2007 SfAA meeting, for instance, a design anthropologist from Motorola organised a session on linguistic anthropological topics; the papers included (1) a paper from anthropologists at General Motors Labs on how institutional narratives can be used for organisational change; (2) a paper from CA scholars at the Palo Alto Research Center (formerly Xerox PARC) analysing a new communication technology that promotes group interaction; (3) a paper from Motorola Labs in India examining the use of information kiosks there; and (4) results of another Motorola Labs study on a different communication technology that helped bring people closer to their family and friends (Metcalf 2007).

What makes the design anthropology research stream different from much of the other work on business discourse is that it extends the field of investigation from the world of employees to the world of consumers. Some people may argue that looking at the world of consumers is not an appropriate topic for the field of business discourse. However, I would offer the perspective that an exploration of discourse in the private sector can properly encompass both the production and consumption moments of the capitalist cycle. The main design anthropology conference was named the 'Ethnographic Praxis in Industry Conference' precisely in order to avoid this analytic split between production and consumption. In linguistic anthropology, at least, I believe that the growth area in upcoming years will be the investigation of how consumers interact with business discourses.

Conclusion

As a final note, I would like to point out that several of the key contributors to the design anthropology field (such as Linde, Orr, Jordan and Suchman) are practitioners – that is, they are employed in industry. At the same time, they are also scholars – they regularly publish in highly regarded peer-reviewed journals. In fact, we are seeing the rise of a new class of intellectuals, the 'scholar-practitioners' (Copeland-Carson 2005; Wasson 2006b). These people have bridged the old divide between theory and application. This is an exciting change in the terrain of the intellectual field. Scholar-practitioners are able to combine the insights of their extensive experience in the business world with rigorous intellectual analysis and the ability to situate their findings with regard to prior scholarship. In the field of applied anthropology, this new hybrid identity has received attention for its ability to redress the limitations of earlier research approaches (Copeland-Carson 2005; Wasson 2006b). Perhaps it can contribute to the field of business discourse as well.

Acknowledgements

I would like to express my gratitude to Francesca Bargiela for her patient and gracious editing, and to three anonymous reviewers for thoughtful comments which significantly enhanced the quality of this chapter. In addition, I thank Kathleen Terry-Sharp, director of academic relations, American Anthropological Association, and Patricia Cukor-Avila, professor, linguistics, University of North Texas, for their valuable assistance in articulating some of the points made in this chapter.

References

Anderson, K. and T. Lovejoy (eds) (2005) *Proceedings of the Ethnographic Praxis in Industry Conference*. Washington, DC: American Anthropological Association.

Anderson, K. and T. Lovejoy (eds) (2006) *Proceedings of the Ethnographic Praxis in Industry Conference*. Washington, DC: American Anthropological Association.

Bailey, B. (1997) Communication of respect in interethnic service encounters. *Language in Society*, 26: 327–56.

Bailey, B. (2000) Communicative behaviour and conflict between African-American customers and Korean immigrant retailers in Los Angeles. *Discourse and Society*, 11(1): 86–108.

Blom, J.-P. and J. J. Gumperz (1972) Social meaning in linguistic structures: Code-switching in Norway. In J. J. Gumperz and D. Hymes (eds), *Directions in Sociolinguistics: The Ethnography of Communication*. Oxford: Blackwell, pp. 409–34.

Blomberg, J., J. Giacomi, A. Mosher and P. Swenton-Wall (1993) Ethnographic field methods and their relation to design. In D. Schuler and A. Namioka (eds), *Participatory Design: Principles and Practices*. Hillsdale: Lawrence Erlbaum, pp. 123–55.

Blomberg, J., L. Suchman and R. Trigg (1997) Back to work: Renewing old agendas for cooperative design. In M. Kyng and L. Mathiassen (eds), *Computers and Design in Context*. Cambridge: MIT Press, pp. 267–87.

British Broadcasting Corporation (1979) *Crosstalk*. Videotape. London: British Broadcasting Corporation.

Brun-Cottan, F. and P. Wall (1995) Using video to re-present the user. *Communications of the ACM*, 38(5): 61–71.

Copeland-Carson, J. (2005) 'Theory-building' evaluation anthropology: Bridging the scholarship-versus-practice divide. *National Association for the Practice of Anthropology Bulletin*, 24(1): 7–16.

Duranti, A. (1994) *From Grammar to Politics: Linguistic Anthropology in a Western Samoan Village*. Berkeley: University of California Press.

Duranti, A. (1997) *Linguistic Anthropology*. Cambridge: Cambridge University Press.

Firth, A. (ed.) (1995) *The Discourse of Negotiation: Studies of Language in the Workplace*. Oxford: Pergamon.

Gal, S. (1989) Language and political economy. *Annual Review of Anthropology*, 18: 345–67.

Geertz, C. (1973) Thick description: Toward an interpretive theory of culture. In C. Geertz, *The Interpretation of Cultures*. New York: Basic Books, pp. 3–30.

Goodwin, C. (1981) *Conversational Organization: Interaction between Speakers and Hearers*. New York: Academic Press.

Goodwin, C. (1996) Transparent vision. In E. Ochs, E. A. Schegloff and S. A. Thompson (eds), *Interaction and Grammar*. Cambridge: Cambridge University Press, pp. 370–404.

Goodwin, C. and M. H. Goodwin (1992) Assessments and the construction of context. In A. Duranti and C. Goodwin (eds), *Rethinking Context: Language as an Interactive Phenomenon*. Cambridge: Cambridge University Press, pp. 147–89.

Goodwin, C. and M. H. Goodwin (1996) Seeing as situated activity: Formulating planes. In Y. Engeström and D. Middleton (eds), *Cognition and Communication at Work*. Cambridge: Cambridge University Press, pp. 61–95.

Goodwin, C. and J. Heritage (1990) Conversation analysis. *Annual Review of Anthropology*, 19: 283–307.

Goodwin, M. H. (1990) *He-Said-She-Said: Talk as Social Organization among Black Children*. Bloomington: Indiana University Press.

Goodwin, M. H. (1995) Assembling a response: Setting and collaboratively constructed work talk. In P. ten Have and G. Psathas (eds), *Situated Order: Studies in the Social Organization of Talk and Embodied Activities*. Washington, DC: International Institute for Ethnomethodology and Conversation Analysis and University Press of America, pp. 173–86.

Gumperz, J. J. (1982a) *Discourse Strategies*. Cambridge: Cambridge University Press.

Gumperz, J. J. (ed.) (1982b) *Language and Social Identity*. Cambridge: Cambridge University Press.

Gumperz, J. J. and D. Hymes (eds) (1972) *Directions in Sociolinguistics: The Ethnography of Communication*. New York: Holt, Rinehart and Winston.

Hymes, D. (1962) The ethnography of speaking. In T. Gladwin and W. C. Sturtevant (eds), *Anthropology and Human Behavior*. Washington, DC: Anthropology Society of Washington, pp. 13–53.

Hymes, D. (1974) *Foundations in Sociolinguistics: An Ethnographic Approach*. Philadelphia: University of Pennsylvania Press.

Hymes, D. (1983) *Essays in the History of Linguistic Anthropology*. Amsterdam: John Benjamins.

Irvine, J. T. (1989) When talk isn't cheap: Language and political economy. *American Ethnologist*, 16: 248–67.

Jordan, B. (1996) Ethnographic workplace studies and CSCW. In D. Shapiro, M. Tauber and R. Traunmüller (eds), *The Design of Computer Supported Cooperative Work and Groupware Systems*. Amsterdam: Elsevier, pp. 17–42.

Kroskrity, P. V. (2004) Language ideologies. In A. Duranti (ed.), *A Companion to Linguistic Anthropology*. Oxford: Blackwell, pp. 496–517.

LeCompte, M. D. and J. J. Schensul (1999a) *Analyzing and Interpreting Ethnographic Data*. Walnut Creek: AltaMira Press.

LeCompte, M. D. and J. J. Schensul (1999b) *Designing and Conducting Ethnographic Research*. Walnut Creek: AltaMira Press.

Linde, C. (1991) What's next? The social and technological management of meetings. *Pragmatics*, 1(3): 297–317.

Linde, C. (1996) Whose story is this? Point of view, variation and group identity in oral narrative: Sociolinguistic variation – data, theory and analysis. In J. Arnold, R. Blake, B. Davidson, S. Schwenter and J. Solomon (eds), *Selected Papers from NWAV23 at Stanford*. Stanford: CSLI, pp. 333–46.

Linde, C. (1997a) Evaluation as linguistic structure and social practice. In B.-L. Gunnarsson, P. Linell and B. Nordberg (eds), *The Construction of Professional Discourse*. London: Longman, pp. 151–72.

Linde, C. (1997b) Narrative: Experience, memory, folklore. *Journal of Narrative and Life History*, 7(1–4): 281–9.

Linde, C. (1999) The transformation of narrative syntax into institutional memory. *Narrative Inquiry*, 9(1): 139–74.

Linde, C. (2000a) The acquisition of a speaker by a story: How history becomes memory and identity. *Ethos*, 28(4): 608–32.

Linde, C. (2000b) Narrative in institutions. In D. Schiffrin, D. Tannen and H. E. Hamilton (eds), *The Handbook of Discourse Analysis*. Oxford: Blackwell, pp. 518–35.

Linde, C. (2001) Narrative and social tacit knowledge. *Journal of Knowledge Management*, 5(2): 160–71.

Linde, C. (2005) Institutional narrative. In D. Herman, M. Jahn and M.-L. Ryan (eds), *Routledge Encyclopedia of Narrative Theory*. London: Routledge, pp. 243–7.

Linde, C. (2006) Learning from the Mars Rover Mission: Scientific discovery, learning and memory. *Journal of Knowledge Management*, 10(2): 90–102.

Maynard, D. W. (1984) *Inside Plea Bargaining: The Language of Negotiation*. New York: Plenum.

Metcalf, C. (organiser) (2007) Session on 'Contributing to cultural understanding: Interdisciplinary applied methods for technology innovation'. Society for Applied Anthropology Annual Meeting, Tampa, FL.

Miller, L. (1991a) Consequences of Japanese and American business conversations. *Intercultural Communication Studies*, 1(1): 95–103.

Miller, L. (1991b) Verbal listening behaviour in conversations between Japanese and Americans. In J. Blommaert and J. Verschueren (eds), *Pragmatics of Intercultural and International Communication*. Amsterdam: John Benjamins, pp. 110–30.

Miller, L. (1994a) Giving good listening: Interaction and identity in Japan's bicultural workplace. *World and I*, 9(12): 221–9.

Miller, L. (1994b) Japanese and American indirectness. *Journal of Asian Pacific Communication*, 5(1 and 2).

Miller, L. (1994c) Japanese and American meetings and what goes on before them: A case study of co-worker misunderstanding. *Pragmatics*, 4(2): 221–38.

Miller, L. (1995) Two aspects of Japanese and American co-worker interaction: Giving instructions and creating rapport. *Journal of Applied Behavioral Science*, 31(2): 141–61.

Miller, L. (1998) Stereotype legacy: Culture and person in Japanese/American interactions. In Y.-T. Lee, C. McCauley and J. Draguns (eds), *Through the Looking Glass: Personality in Culture*. Mahwah, NJ: Lawrence Erlbaum, pp. 213–31.

Miller, L. (2000) Negative assessments in Japanese–American workplace interaction. In H. Spencer-Oatey (ed.), *Culturally Speaking: Managing Rapport through Talk across Cultures*. London: Continuum, pp. 240–54.

Orr, J. E. (1996) *Talking about Machines: An Ethnography of a Modern Job*. Ithaca, NY: ILR Press and Cornell University Press.

Orr, J. E. (2000) Sharing knowledge, celebrating identity: Community memory in a service culture. In D. Middleton and D. Edwards (eds), *Collective Remembering*. London: Sage, pp. 169–89.

Psathas, G. and T. Anderson (1990) The 'practices' of transcription in conversation analysis. *Semiotica*, 78(1/2): 75–99.

Ruhleder, K. and B. Jordan (2001) Co-constructing non-mutual realities: Delay-generated trouble in distributed interaction. *Computer Supported Cooperative Work*, 10: 113–38.

Sacher, H. (2002) Semiotics as common ground: Connecting the cultures of analysis and creation. In S. Squires and B. Byrne (eds), *Creating Breakthrough Ideas: The Collaboration of Anthropologists and Designers in the Product Development Industry*. Westport, CT: Bergin Garvey, pp. 175–95.

Sacks, H., E. A. Schegloff and G. Jefferson (1974) A simplest systematics for the organisation of turn-taking for conversation. *Language*, 50: 696–735.

Sapir, E. (1949) *Selected Writings in Language, Culture and Personality*. Berkeley: University of California Press.

Schensul, S. L., J. J. Schensul and M. D. LeCompte (1999) *Essential Ethnographic Methods: Observations, Interviews, and Questionnaires*. Walnut Creek: AltaMira Press.

Silverstein, M. (1979) Language structure and linguistic ideology. In P. R. Clyne, W. F. Hanks and C. L. Hofbauer (eds), *The Elements: A Parasession on Linguistic Units and Levels*. Chicago: Chicago Linguistics Society, pp. 193–247.

Silverstein, M. (1993) Metapragmatic discourse and metapragmatic function. In J. A. Lucy (ed.), *Reflexive Language: Reported Speech and Metapragmatics*. Cambridge: Cambridge University Press, pp. 33–58.

Silverstein, M. (2003) Indexical order and the dialectics of sociolinguistic life. *Language and Communication*, 23(3–4): 193–229.

Slembrouck, S. (2006) What is meant by 'discourse analysis'? http://bank.rug.ac.be/da/da.htm. Accessed 4 November 2007.

Stocking, G. W., Jr. (1974) *A Franz Boas Reader: The Shaping of American Anthropology, 1883–1911*. Chicago: University of Chicago Press.

Stubbs, M. (1983) *Discourse Analysis: The Sociolinguistic Analysis of Natural Analysis.* Oxford: Blackwell.

Suchman, L. (1987) *Plans and Situated Actions: The Problem of Human–Machine Communication.* Cambridge: Cambridge University Press.

Suchman, L. (1992) Technologies of accountability: Of lizards and aeroplanes. In G. Button (ed.), *Technology in Working Order: Studies of Work, Interaction, and Technology.* London: Routledge, pp. 113–26.

Suchman, L. (ed.) (1995) Representations of work. *Communications of the ACM* (special issue), 38(9).

Suchman, L. (1996) Constituting shared workspaces. In Y. Engeström and D. Middleton (eds), *Cognition and Communication at Work.* Cambridge: Cambridge University Press, pp. 35–60.

Suchman, L. A. and R. H. Trigg (1991) Understanding practice: Video as a medium for reflection and design. In J. Greenbaum and M. Kyng (eds), *Design at Work: Cooperative Design of Computer Systems.* Hillsdale: Lawrence Erlbaum, pp. 65–89.

Sunderland, P. L. and R. M. Denny (2003) Psychology vs. anthropology: Where is culture in marketplace ethnography? In T. D. Malefyt and B. Moeran (eds), *Advertising Cultures.* Oxford: Berg, pp. 187–202.

Urciuoli, B. (2003) Excellence, leadership, skills, diversity: Marketing liberal arts education. *Language and Communication*, 23: 385–408.

Urciuoli, B. (2005) The language of higher education assessment: Legislative concerns in a global context. *Indiana Journal of Global Legal Studies*, 12(1): 183–204.

Urciuoli, B. (n.d.) Skills and selves in the new workplace. Manuscript.

Wasson, C. (1998) Employees as 'entrepreneurs': The discursive legitimation of changing workplace relationships. Paper delivered at the Academy of Management Annual Meeting, San Diego, CA.

Wasson, C. (1999) The paradoxical discourse of 'ownership'. Invited speech delivered at the International Conference on Language in Organisational Change and Transformation, Columbus, OH.

Wasson, C. (2000a) Caution and consensus in American business meetings. *Pragmatics*, 10(4): 457–81.

Wasson, C. (2000b) Ethnography in the field of design. *Human Organization*, 59(4): 377–88.

Wasson, C. (2001) The Janus-faced power of language in organisations. Keynote speech delivered at the First International and Interdisciplinary Symposium on Communication within Organisations, Mannheim, Germany.

Wasson, C. (2002a) Collaborative work: Integrating the roles of ethnographers and designers. In S. Squires and B. Byrne (eds), *Creating Breakthrough Ideas: The Collaboration of Anthropologists and Designers in the Product Development Industry.* Westport, CT: Bergin & Garvey, pp. 71–90.

Wasson, C. (2002b) The spread of English in corporate Europe. Paper delivered at the University Mannheim Business School, Mannheim, Germany.

Wasson, C. (2003) The Janus-faced power of language in organisations. In A. P. Müller and A. Kieser (eds), *Communication in Organisations: Structures and Practices.* Frankfurt: Peter Lang, pp. 21–46.

Wasson, C. (2004a) An anthropological eye on theories of organisational irony. In U. Johansson and J. Woodilla (eds), *The Ironic Organization: Epistemological Claims and Supporting Field Stories*. Malmö: Liber AB, pp. 51–63.

Wasson, C. (2004b) Multitasking during virtual meetings. *Human Resource Planning*, 27(4): 47–60.

Wasson, C. (2004c) The paradoxical language of enterprise. *Critical Discourse Studies*, 1(2): 175–99.

Wasson, C. (2006a) Being in two spaces at once: Virtual meetings and their representation. *Journal of Linguistic Anthropology*, 16(1): 103–30.

Wasson, C. (2006b) Making history at the frontier. *National Association for the Practice of Anthropology Bulletin*, 26: 1–19.

Whorf, B. L. (1956) *Language, Thought, and Reality: Selected Writings*. Cambridge, MA: MIT Press.

Woolard, K. A. (1985) Language variation and cultural hegemony: Toward an integration of sociolinguistic and social theory. *American Ethnologist*, 12(4): 738–48.

Woolard, K. A. and B. B. Schieffelin (1994) Language ideology. *Annual Review of Anthropology*, 23: 55–82.

16

Gender studies

Louise Mullany

Introduction

As more and more women have entered the commercial domains of work since the 1970s, studies of business discourse investigating gender have rapidly increased in disciplines across the social sciences and humanities. 'Gender studies' can be utilised as an all-encompassing term to characterise such investigations. However, this definition is rather general, and in practice, gender studies from across a variety of disciplines share far more commonalities than just the choice of gender as an investigative topic.

Researchers also tend to be united by common political goals, and whilst it is important to acknowledge that gender studies of business discourse do not have to be politically motivated, in practice it is extremely unusual to find a study which is not feminist in orientation. I am defining 'feminist' here in a broad sense as the commitment to investigating social and political problems in society, with the overall aim of bringing about gender equality through academic research (Christie 2000). In following this perspective I am certainly not denying that different forms of feminism exist, from liberal to more radical perspectives, but a useful way of bringing gender studies work together is under this common political aim of gender equality. All of the studies discussed in this chapter are united by this overall goal.

Indeed, the mass influx of women into the business world has resulted in the development of a number of gender inequalities. Perhaps the most persistent of these are: lower pay for women fulfilling exactly the same role as their male counterparts, sexual objectification and harassment, and the 'glass ceiling' (Morrison et al. 1987) – the barrier that women face in reaching the higher echelons of power in commercial arenas. The 'glass ceiling' metaphor has recently been reformulated into a 'concrete ceiling' to provide a more accurate characterisation of the non-transparent and impenetrable barriers faced by women of colour in the US (Johnson 2006). The 'concrete ceiling' has also recently been used by commentators in Japan to depict the severity of the barriers faced by women in Japanese business environments (Wahlin 2007). Feminist researchers from a wide range of disciplinary backgrounds, including linguistics, sociology, social psychology, organisational studies, communication studies (organisational communication in particular), management studies, economics and business administration, have investigated the role that business discourse can play in producing, maintaining and reproducing these inequalities.

Whilst there has tended to be a dominant focus on native English speakers in Anglo-American contexts, the dramatic increase in women entering commercial workplaces is a pattern that can be observed in numerous countries across the globe. One of the most influential projects at present is the work of the Language in the Workplace team in New Zealand, which includes both English and Maori speakers. A significant proportion of their data is taken from commercial interactions, and one key area of investigation is the crucial role that gender plays in business communication (Holmes and Stubbe 2003; Holmes and Schnurr 2005; Holmes 2006). A number of other works on gender and business discourse have also recently appeared in a range of different global locations in what can now be described as a burgeoning field. These include Martin Rojo and Gómez Esteban (2005) in Spain, Thimm et al. (2003) in Germany, Yieke's (2005) work in Kenya, Bastos's (2005) work in Brazil, Metcalfe's (2006) study of international businesses in the Middle East and Eastern Europe, the work of Peck (2006) and Still (2006) in Australia, Jones's (2000) and Olsson and Walker's (2003) work in New Zealand, along with studies by Baxter (2003: 128–80), McRae (2004) and Mullany (2007) in the UK, and Tannen (1999) and Ashcraft and Mumby (2003) in the US. As Thimm et al. (2003: 531) point out, 'talk at work has received attention from feminists worldwide, reflecting the growing importance of professional communication for women in different countries'.

Interestingly, Bargiela-Chiappini et al. (2007) observe that feminist studies of business discourse, as critical, politically motivated investigations, provide a notable exception to the descriptive work which tends to dominate business discourse research. They argue that such feminist studies may well inspire future directions for business discourse investigations. It is thus the intention that, by discussing key contemporary issues surrounding gender studies of business discourse, this chapter will emphasise the benefits of taking a more political, non-descriptive approach, and thus aid in producing different directions for future business discourse research.

It is important to acknowledge that gender studies of business discourse do not just include a focus on women and femininities – whilst this is no doubt the dominant focus, and a consequence of the need to establish women and femininities firmly on the academic map, some researchers also investigate men and masculinities (Hearn and Parkin 1988, 2006), and some also examine femininities and masculinities within the same study (see Holmes and Stubbe 2003).

In addition to being united by political aims and goals, gender studies researchers have also been united in recent years by sharing theoretical approaches to conceptualising both gender and discourse(s). This phenomenon is not unique to gender studies. Indeed, within the humanities and social sciences, there is 'an increasing tendency for the same theoretical canon to be drawn upon in a range of different disciplines' (van Leeuwen 2005: 9). In gender studies of business discourse this tendency can be observed in particular through the work of Butler (1990) and Foucault (1972).

The linkage between various disciplines and linguistics has also greatly increased in recent years because of the 'linguistic turn' which has taken place in a range of disciplines including organisational and management studies, whereby researchers have turned to language and linguistic frameworks in order to enhance their analyses (Alvesson and

Kärreman 2000). This turn thus encourages interdisciplinary research by enabling one's own area of expertise to be blended together with linguistic approaches.

In what follows, I will begin by detailing the unifying theoretical approaches that business discourse and gender researchers have taken, followed by some examples of data analysis to illustrate the practical application of these theories. I will then move on to consider key methodological issues that currently occupy gender studies researchers, and conclude with directions for future research.

Theoretical approaches: Third wave feminism

The term 'third wave feminism' (Mills 2003; Baxter 2006) can be utilised collectively to refer to the theoretical perspectives which have tended to dominate gender studies in recent years. The majority of research on business discourse tends to embrace at least some, if not all, of the principles of the third wave approach. The approach can initially be classified as one where gender is viewed from a social constructionist perspective, often following Butler's (1990) work on performativity. According to Butler, gender should be conceptualised as something that is fluid and dynamic, as opposed to a fixed, static entity. Gender is therefore something that we do as opposed to something that we are.

There are countless examples of gender studies across disciplines which have drawn upon Butler's conceptualisation of performativity when examining business discourse. These include Mulholland's (2006) study of advisor–client interaction, Metcalfe's (2006) examination of multiple gender performances in international business communication, Holmes's (2000, 2006) extensive commercial data analysis from the Language in the Workplace project, and Jones's (2000) organisational communication work. Indeed, in their introduction to *Gender and Communication at Work*, Barrett and Davidson (2006: 14) highlight how their book embodies 'the nature of gender as performance' throughout. Butler's work is not without its critics (for example, see Walsh 2001), often being accused of assigning too much agency to speakers; some researchers favour a social constructionist approach without embracing Butler's notion of performativity (see Kotthoff and Wodak 1997). Nevertheless, Butler's work has been undeniably seminal for gender studies of business discourse.

In addition to the social constructionist view of gender, a third wave feminist approach also focuses on investigating localised contexts, with feminist researchers aiming to achieve fine-grained analyses of communication within very specific business contexts. Researchers from a range of different disciplines often use the communities of practice (CofP) approach to achieve this (see Metcalfe 2006; Holmes 2006). Within gender studies, a CofP is traditionally identified as follows: 'An aggregate of people who come together around mutual engagement in an endeavor. Ways of doing things, ways of talking, beliefs, values, power relations – in short – practices – emerge in the course of this mutual endeavor' (Eckert and McConnell-Ginet 1992: 464). It is an advantageous concept as it provides a unifying, coherent framework that enables gender performance in different workplace groupings to be compared with one another. The Language in the Workplace team have demonstrated how the CofP approach neatly integrates with the notion of gender as a performative construct in commercial workplace culture (Holmes and Schnurr 2005; Holmes 2006). As Holmes (2006: 13) points out, 'social constructionism is basic to the notion of the community of practice' because of its emphasis on 'process and interaction'.

In addition to a concentration on gender as a social construct and CofPs, within a third wave perspective, an examination of 'discourses' has also become popular, with investigators following Foucault's (1972: 49) oft-cited definition of discourses as 'practices that systematically form the objects of which they speak'. Mills (1997) elaborates on how such Foucauldian discourses can be identified: 'A discursive structure can be detected because of the systematicity of the ideas, opinions, concepts, ways of thinking and behaving which are formed within a particular context, and because of the effects of those ways of thinking and behaving' (Mills 1997: 17).

Foucault's work has been influential in a range of disciplines where gender studies researchers have investigated the intricacies of gender and business discourse (see Jones 2000; Brewis 2001; Fitzsimons 2002; Baxter 2003: 128–80). At first glance, Foucault's work, particularly his fluid conceptualisation of power, may seem incompatible with feminist research's clear political aim of challenging existing power structures. However, Foucault's perspectives have proved to be productive. Indeed, his view of power as a 'web' or a 'net' has been a valuable metaphorical conceptualisation (Baxter 2003: 8). It enables the differences *within* groups of women and *within* groups of men to be emphasised, and pluralised masculinities and femininities are now studied (see Coates 1999; Holmes and Schnurr 2006). It also allows gender studies researchers to move away from using the problematic and arguably now-outdated term 'patriarchy', i.e., the view that *all* men oppress *all* women. Instead, this is replaced with the pluralised notion of dominant masculinist discourses (Walsh 2001), thus enabling a more nuanced view of gender, discourse and power.

Within linguistics, 'discourse' also has a more traditional, micro-level definition as a form of analysis of 'language beyond the sentence' (Tannen 1989: 6). Business discourse researchers working within the linguistic sub-fields of discourse analysis and sociolinguistics, including Baxter (2003) and Mullany (2007), have adopted a dual definition of discourse(s), whereby 'discourse' is first contextualised in its traditional sense, as language above the level of the sentence, enabling a close textual analysis of specific linguistic discourse features to be examined. This is then followed by an integrated analysis of 'discourse(s)' in a Foucauldian sense, enabling a much broader analysis of gendered practices and gendered discourses to take place. The linguistic discourse analysis can be placed within this broader analysis, in order for the crucial role that social structuration plays in governing gendered norms and conventions to be examined.

This overall approach, incorporating textual analysis, the CofP framework and analysis of overarching gendered discourses, accords with Bucholtz's (2001: 166) argument that any investigation of discourse needs to pay attention to 'large-scale cultural forces, to local contexts of practice and to the fine details of discursive form and content'.

Gendered discourses and gender ideologies

Sunderland (2004: 20–1) has coined the term 'gendered discourses', arguing that 'gendered' is much stronger than the descriptive term 'gender-related', as it clearly emphasises that 'gender already is part of the "thing" which *gendered* describes' (emphasis in original). She fuses this definition with the Foucauldian notion of discourse to provide an overarching framework within which different types of gendered discourses, as observable systems which govern evaluations and judgements of 'appropriate' gender behaviour, can be located. Indeed, gendered discourses work as crucial regulators of behaviour in society, and it is through gendered discourses that women and men 'are represented and/ or expected to behave *in particular gendered ways*' (Sunderland 2004: 21, emphasis in original). Gendered discourses are maintained and reproduced by gender ideologies. Heller's (2001) perspective from sociolinguistics is worth considering here as she neatly brings out the connection between Foucauldian discourses and ideology. She posits that discourses 'are obviously linked to the notion of ideology, insofar as ideologies are understood as means of structuring and orienting domains of activity, and therefore inform discursive production and content' (Heller 2001: 120).

Arguably one of the most influential ways in which such Foucauldian-influenced notions of discourse have been beneficial is through drawing attention to the crucial *discourse of gender difference*. This overarching discourse is extremely important in explaining the persistence of the view that women and men are fundamentally different. In business discourse research, its importance has already been illustrated in a range of work including Brewis (2001), Olsson and Walker (2003), Cameron (2003) and Mullany (2007). The discourse of gender difference heavily emphasises and exaggerates fundamental differences between women and men in society. Sunderland (2004: 52) argues that it is ' "a significant lens" for the way people view reality, *difference* being for most people what gender is all about' (emphasis in original). This includes emphasising that there are allegedly fundamental differences in communicative strategies between women and men, which, like all aspects of behaviour, are focalised through the discourse of gender difference. This difference is a highly stereotypical notion, maintained by powerful gender ideologies.

Indeed, Cameron (2003) characterises the view that there are significant differences between women's and men's use of communicative strategies as one of the most persistent ideological perspectives on gender and language. Furthermore, 'in many versions of this ideology the differences are seen as natural, and in most, they [differences] are seen as desirable' (2003: 450). This explains the persistence of the view in wider society that women and men speak differently. It also accounts for the popular success of books which draw on gendered stereotypes of appropriate language use in businesses, including Gray's (2002) *Mars and Venus in the Workplace* (see Cameron 2007 for an excellent critique of Gray's work).

Brewis (2001) utilises the notion of the discourse of gender difference to explain gender inequalities in the organisations she studied. She concludes that the differential, unsatisfactory treatment that women receive in organisations should be perceived as 'a form of practice characteristic of the discourse of gender difference which constitutes women as irrational, emotional and subjective (and men as the opposite)' (2001: 300). Furthermore, the dominant discourse of gender difference, so persistent in societies around the world, works to emphasise *homogeneity* within *singular* categories of femininity and masculinity and stresses fundamental differences *between* women and men. These differences are often ascribed to the false but persistent perspective of biologically essentialist differences, resulting in men being perceived as 'naturally' more suited for the business world.

The third wave feminist perspective thus contrasts with earlier approaches to investigating gender and business discourse. Such earlier studies have been accused of simply cataloguing and dichotomising women's and men's speech, as well as assuming that speech differences pre-exist by taking difference to be the starting point of research (Eckert and McConnell-Ginet 2003). These dichotomies include men's assumed competitive speech style versus women's co-operative speech style, paralleled by women's alleged 'transformational' leadership style versus men's 'transactional' leadership style in organisational studies (see Trinidad and Normore 2005).

However, the findings of these earlier studies should not simply be dismissed. Indeed, they have been very influential to contemporary investigations. The dichotomous speech styles that were discovered as part of the earlier research paradigms can be justifiably viewed as part of the deeply entrenched, stereotypical expectations of gendered behaviour within societies. Ochs's (1992) theoretical notion of the indexicality of gender is invaluable here to illuminate this perspective. Ochs argues that gender can be indexed either directly or indirectly through language. Direct indexing applies to the few specific items where gender is directly encoded within the linguistic forms used, such as with the lexical items 'man' or 'women'. More commonly, gender is indirectly indexed through language use. For example, the well-founded differences between women and men's speech styles, (e.g. indirectness versus directness, mitigation of directives versus bald, on-record directives) should be viewed as being indirectly indexed with gender*ed* meaning, as women and men are constantly evaluated and assessed in the light of these differing gendered expectations. Business interactants can therefore be very differently evaluated, even when enacting exactly the same behaviour, on the grounds that they have gone beyond gendered expectations for their sex.

I will now move on to illustrate how the different facets of the theoretical framework outlined above can be brought together to produce an analysis of gender in business discourse data.

Analysis: The double bind

The overarching discourse of gender difference can be aptly used to illustrate the 'double bind' that women can face in commercial domains. If a businesswoman acts in a more stereotypically 'masculine' manner, she faces accusations of being unfeminine, aggressive and bossy. Alternatively, if she displays stereotypically 'feminine' characteristics through her speech, then she runs the risk of negative evaluation for being ineffective. This double bind has been found in gender studies research across numerous disciplines, strengthening overall arguments of the fundamental role that it can play in stopping women in middle-ranking positions within businesses from breaking through the glass ceiling. Furthermore, it does not work in reverse, i.e. men are not disadvantaged for using a stereotypically feminine style. As Appelbaum et al. (2002) point out:

> When women attempt to prove their competence by 'acting like a man' they are considered to be less than women. When there seems to be some merit in what would normally have been considered a 'female' approach, men adopt it as their own. What was seen as weak is now thought of as flexible; what was emotional now combines with the rational to bring balance. (Appelbaum et al. 2002: 45)

To illustrate further, I will focus on Amy, a woman manager who was part of an ethnographic case study that I conducted in a UK retail organisation. The first data extract is taken from an audio-recorded business meeting. Extracts 2 and 3 are taken from dyadic interviews conducted by myself. Extract 2 is an interview with one of Amy's subordinates and Extract 3 is another interview with one of her status equals. Extract 1 is taken from Amy's departmental business meeting, which she chairs:

> *Extract 1*
> (Amy is explaining departmental policy to Kirsty and Eddie)
> 1. Amy: we're going to be carrying it for more than fifteen weeks=
> 2. Karen: =yeah it's ten weeks for stock and it will be calculated
> 3.   on how many sales within five weeks
> 4. Amy: No it's longer than that Karen
> 5. Karen: Oh (.) right
> 6. Amy: It's longer

At line 4, Amy produces a direct, on-record challenge to Karen's previous utterance without any mitigation, thus performing a stereotypically masculine speech style. This is reiterated on-record again at line 6. Although on the whole the majority of Amy's utterances in this meeting are mitigated strategies, drawing upon co-operative, stereotypically feminine discourse strategies (see Mullany 2007), it is not these examples but the others where she breaks the stereotypical gendered norms to which her colleagues refer. In both interviews we were not talking about Amy in particular, but both interviewees choose to bring up Amy when discussing the topic of managers and approachability:

> *Extract 2*
> {Karen: Amy's subordinate}: Amy is a very strong character very
>   straightforward erm says what she means is very direct and it can be
>   quite an overpowering experience talking to her.

> *Extract 3*
> {Kelly: Amy's status equal}: Females are more caring generally (.)
>   naturally more nurturing they've definitely got certain qualities that are
>   different to men but some females can be real tyrants.

After the interview officially finished Kelly (Extract 3) acknowledged that she had been referring to Amy when talking of female 'tyrants'. She presents Amy as being in opposition with expectations for a 'natural' female manager who is more 'nurturing'. There is clear evidence in both extracts of negative evaluation of Amy for going against the expected gendered norm. Extract 2 aptly illustrates how this relates directly to Amy's speech style, thus providing explicit evidence of the gendered language ideology. These negative attitudes and evaluations are wholly representative of the manner in which Amy was perceived within this business by both her female and male colleagues (see Mullany 2007 for further details).

I will now move on to consider important methodological issues which are currently being debated within gender studies.

Methodological issues

The vast majority of gender studies of business discourse, including the examples taken from my own work above, have tended to use qualitative methods. This can be perceived to be a consequence of the dominance of the view that there should be a focus on local practices in order to avoid producing the same overgeneralisations about women's and men's behaviour (Eckert and McConnell-Ginet 2003; Baxter 2006). Within the sociolinguistic subdiscipline of language and gender studies, Holmes and Meyerhoff (2003) point out that the qualitative paradigm is currently the most popular. However, in order to move gender research forward, they argue that a more integrated approach, combining qualitative and qualitative methods, should be taken (cf. Swann and Maybin 2008).

Quantitative research can be very useful for identifying overall patterning in data samples, and these patterns can then be followed up by more detailed qualitative research. A good example of business discourse research which utilises such an integrated methodological approach is Koller's (2004) innovative work on gendered metaphors in business media discourse. Koller integrates the quantitative techniques of corpus linguistics (using computerised technology to look for language patterns in large banks of data) with detailed qualitative analyses of texts pinpointed by corpus searches. Her work is also notable as it expands gender studies by investigating written business discourse.

Koller (2004: 6) describes her examination of written media texts as focusing on 'secondary discourse', with these texts providing a commentary on the 'primary discourse' (spoken or written) produced in the business workplace by commercial representatives. Koller's corpus comprises business magazines in two key areas: marketing, and mergers and acquisitions, where the readership is 90 per cent male. Her integrated analysis demonstrates that masculinised war/fighting metaphors are the most frequent and the most deeply embedded metaphors within the magazine texts. Examples of this from a quantitative perspective include use of lexical items relating to physical violence, including 'blood', 'to bleed', 'bruise', 'cut-throat' and 'killer' (Koller 2004: 65). The following example gives a more contextualised, qualitative illustration of such metaphors:

> NetApp has a **fight** on its hands. Since the market up for grabs is so
> huge, it is worth the **bruises**. (Koller 2004: 101, emphasis in original)

Koller concludes that the dominance of war/battle metaphors works to exclude women by perpetuating the view that the business world is a male world. She argues that at the very least journalists should stop using such excessively violent metaphors to characterise the world of business.

In current gender studies, the qualitative paradigm still prevails. However, in order to move gender research forward, it would be beneficial not to be situated in 'armed camps' in terms of loyalty to a particularly popular methodological paradigm (Silverman 2000: 11). More integrated approaches to gender studies, through recent innovations including the techniques of corpus linguistics, should thus be explored in order to expand and develop the field. Ideally, when entering business communities and conducting empirical research, this should be negotiated in close conjunction with members of the workforce and practitioners in order to devise a methodological approach that will enable relevant and practical feedback to be given to those under study (see Mullany 2008).

Future directions: Diversifying the field

Third wave researchers have called for more diversification in future investigations, particularly in terms of shifting attention away from the discourse of white middle-class women (and men; Mills 2003). The dominant focus on this group is far from surprising as research has tended to be clustered in professional, corporate environments where this demographic unarguably prevails. Whilst there is a handful of notable exceptions, including a case study of factory discourse in the Language in the Workplace project (Holmes and Stubbe 2003), and Johnson's (2006) aforementioned study investigating African American women managers and leaders, the focus still tends to be on white middle-class women in positions of corporate power. Barrett and Davidson (2006: 2) argue that the predominance of work focusing on the 'corporate' woman tells us nothing about gender and communication in 'newer' business workplaces, including teleworking and non-managerial work. Teleworking, and customer service call centres in particular, have now become a global phenomenon. Some academics have already responded to this by investigating these arenas (Cameron 2000, 2006; Franken and Wallace 2006; Hultgren 2008).

The customer service discourse which employees are systematically trained to adopt is characterised by Cameron (2006) and Franken and Wallace (2006) as a form of 'emotional labour'. This can be further characterised as feminised discourse, bearing all of the stereotypically feminine traits of what Cameron (2006: 128) aptly describes as 'expressive language'. The mass development of call centres as commercial employers has resulted in large clusters of women working in these low-paid, menial positions. The dominance of women within this new field can been seen as heavily interlinked with the inaccurate and damaging ideology that women are biologically programmed to be better communicators than men. Cameron (2003) summarises the damage this dominant stereotypical conception can cause, simultaneously outlining the importance of producing future academic research in these newer arenas:

> Common-sense ideas about women as "naturally" skilled communicators help to naturalize the way women are channeled into low-paid and low-status service occupations – as if the issue were all about women's aptitude for the work and not at all about their greater willingness (born of historical necessity rather than choice) to accept the low pay, insecurity, and casualization which were endemic to "women's work" in the past and are now becoming the lot of many more workers. (Cameron 2003: 461–2)

The lack of prestige associated with such feminised styles of communication contributes to men's continued 'disdain' for such jobs (Cameron 2006: 132). However, as Cameron goes on to point out, this unwillingness to do work stereotypically associated with women is no longer a sustainable position for men to take, as globalisation is 'destroying alternative sources of employment' in commercial domains.

Overall, this chapter has emphasised the importance of carrying out discursive investigations of gender to assess political and social inequalities within commercial domains. Whilst the glass ceiling continues to be a persistent barrier to white middle-class women in many societies, future gender studies of business discourse need to diversify their focus. One way to achieve this is to investigate the gendered discourses of non-white, non-western women, which can be focalised through the notion of the 'concrete ceiling'. Another way forward is to investigate gender in relation to workers within businesses who occupy lower, less well-paid positions in the institutional hierarchy. This should include part-time employment in commercial organisations, positions that are traditionally less well paid, unstable and still occupied in the majority by women (EOC 2006).

Furthermore, the persistence of the problem of what Hearn and Parkin (2006: 111) refer to as 'gendered violation' at work, bullying, sexual harassment and sometimes even physical violence, also requires much deeper examination from a discourse perspective at all different levels of commercial domains, from the boardroom right down to the shop floor. Another arena that requires investigation from a gender perspective is computer-mediated communication (CMC). Whilst early visions of CMC suggested utopian ideals of 'gender-free' communication (Haraway 1985), the reality has proved very different, with initial research in this area highlighting how gender inequalities are very much alive and well in CMC (see Brosnan 2006).

In summary, all of these topics require further research in order to expand the focus on gender studies of business discourse and make it a more comprehensive field of investigation. As academics, we should look towards developing more interdisciplinary projects, drawing upon our expertise across different disciplines, to attempt to maximise the impact that we can have upon social policy-makers and practitioners in the business world.

References

Alvesson, M. and D. Kärreman (2000) Taking the linguistic turn in organizational research: Challenges, responses, consequences. *Journal of Applied Behavioural Science*, 36(2): 136–58.

Appelbaum, S., L. Audet and J. Miller (2002) Gender and leadership? Leadership and gender? A journey through the landscape of theories. *Leadership and Organization Development*, 24(1): 43–51.

Ashcraft, K. and D. Mumby (2003) *Reworking Gender: A Feminist Communicology of the Organization*. Beverly Hills, CA: Sage.

Bargiela-Chiappini, F., C. Nickerson and B. Planken (2007) *Business Discourse*. Basingstoke: Palgrave.

Barrett, M. and M. Davidson (2006) Gender and communication at work: An introduction. In M. Barrett and M. Davidson (eds), *Gender and Communication at Work*. Aldershot: Ashgate, pp. 1–16.

Bastos, C. (2005) Constructions of identity and leadership in business meetings. Paper delivered at the 3rd International Conference on Discourse and Communication in the Enterprise (DICOEN), PUC-Rio, 9 September.

Baxter, J. (2003) *Positioning Gender in Discourse: A Feminist Methodology*. Basingstoke: Palgrave.

Baxter, J. (ed.) (2006) *Speaking Out: The Female Voice in Public Contexts*. Basingstoke: Palgrave.

Brewis, J. (2001) Telling it like it is? Gender, language and organizational theory. In R. Westwood and S. Linstead (eds), *The Language of Organization*. London: Sage, pp. 283–309.

Brosnan, M. (2006) Gender and diffusion of email: An organizational perspective. In M. Barrett and M. Davidson (eds), *Gender and Communication at Work*. Aldershot: Ashgate, pp. 260–9.

Bucholtz, M. (2001) Reflexivity and critique in discourse analysis. *Critique of Anthropology*, 21(2): 165–83.

Butler, J. (1990) *Gender Trouble: Feminism and the Subversion of Identity*. New York: Routledge.

Cameron, D. (2000) *Good to Talk: Living and Working in a Communication Culture*. London: Sage.

Cameron, D. (2003) Gender and language ideologies. In J. Holmes and M. Meyerhoff (eds), *The Handbook of Language and Gender*. Oxford: Blackwell, pp. 447–67.

Cameron, D. (2006) *On Language and Sexual Politics*. London: Routledge.

Cameron, D. (2007) *The Myth of Mars and Venus: Do Men and Women Really Speak Different Languages?* Oxford: Oxford University Press.

Christie, C. (2000) *Gender and Language: Towards a Feminist Pragmatics*. Edinburgh: Edinburgh University Press.

Coates, J. (1999) Changing femininities: The talk of teenage girls. In M. Bucholtz, A. Liang and L. A. Sutton (eds), *Reinventing Identities: The Gendered Self in Discourse*. Oxford: Oxford University Press, pp. 123–44.

Eckert, P. and S. McConnell-Ginet (1992) Think practically and look locally: Language and gender as community-based practice. *Annual Review of Anthropology*, 21: 461–90.

Eckert, P. and S. McConnell-Ginet (2003) *Language and Gender*. Cambridge: Cambridge University Press.

EOC (Equal Opportunities Commission) (2006) *Sex and Power Index*. London: Equal Opportunities Commission UK.

Fitzsimons, A. (2002) *Gender as a Verb: Gender Segregation at Work*. Aldershot: Ashgate.

Foucault, M. (1972) *The Archaeology of Knowledge*. London: Routledge.

Franken, M. and C. Wallace (2006) Women's work: The language use of call centre representatives. In M. Barrett and M. Davidson (eds), *Gender and Communication at Work*. Aldershot: Ashgate, pp. 142–53.

Gray, J. (2002) *Mars and Venus in the Workplace*. New York: HarperCollins.

Haraway, D. (1985) A manifesto for cyborgs: Science technology and socialist feminism in the 1980s. *Socialist Review*, 80: 65–107.

Hearn, J. and W. Parkin (1988) Women, men, and leadership: A critical review of assumptions, practices, and change in the industrialized nations. In N. Adler and D. Izraeli (eds), *Women in Management Worldwide*. London: M. E. Sharpe, pp. 17–40.

Hearn, J. and W. Parkin (2006) Gender, violation and communication at work. In M. Barrett and M. Davidson (eds), *Gender and Communication at Work*. Aldershot: Ashgate, pp. 111–26.

Heller, M. (2001) Critique and sociolinguistic analysis of discourse. *Critique of Anthropology*, 21(2): 117–41.

Holmes, J. (2000) Women at work: Analysing women's talk in New Zealand. *Australian Review of Applied Linguistics*, 22(2): 1–17.

Holmes, J. (2006) *Gendered Talk at Work*. Oxford: Blackwell.

Holmes, J. and M. Meyerhoff (2003) Different voices, different views: An introduction to current research in language and gender. In J. Holmes and M. Meyerhoff (eds), *The Handbook of Language and Gender*. Oxford: Blackwell, pp. 1–17.

Holmes, J. and S. Schnurr (2005) Politeness, humor and gender in the workplace: Negotiating norms and identifying contestation. *Journal of Politeness Research: Language, Behaviour, Culture*, 1(1): 121–49.

Holmes, J. and S. Schnurr (2006) Doing femininity at work. *Journal of Sociolinguistics*, 10(1): 31–51.

Holmes, J. and M. Stubbe (2003) 'Feminine' workplaces: Stereotype and reality. In J. Holmes and M. Meyerhoff (eds), *The Handbook of Language and Gender*. Oxford: Blackwell, pp. 573–99.

Hultgren, A. K. (2008) Reconstructing the sex dichotomy in language and gender research: Some advantages of using correlational sociolinguistics. In K. Harrington, L. Litosseliti, H. Sauntson and J. Sunderland (eds), *Gender and Language Research Methodologies*. Basingstoke: Palgrave, pp. 29–42.

Johnson, N. (2006) *An Examination of the Concrete Ceiling: Perspectives of Ten African American Women Managers and Leaders*. Boca Raton, FL: Dissertation.Com.

Jones, D. (2000) Gender trouble in the workplace: 'Language and gender' meets 'feminist organisational communication'. In J. Holmes (ed.), *Gendered Speech in Social Context: Perspectives from Gown to Town*. Wellington: Victoria University Press, pp. 192–210.

Koller, V. (2004) *Metaphor and Gender in Business Media Discourse: A Critical Cognitive Study*. Basingstoke: Palgrave.

Kotthoff, H. and R. Wodak (1997) Preface: Gender in context. In R. Wodak and H. Kotthoff (eds), *Communicating Gender in Context*. Amsterdam: John Benjamins, pp. vii–xxv.

McRae, S. (2004) Language, gender and status in the workplace: The discourse of disagreement in meetings. PhD thesis, Milton Keynes, Open University.

Martin Rojo, L. and C. Gómez Esteban (2005) The gender of power: The female style in labour organizations. In M. Lazar (ed.), *Feminist Critical Discourse Analysis*. Basingstoke: Palgrave, pp. 66–89.

Metcalfe, B. (2006) Gender, communication and international business. In M. Barrett and M. Davidson (eds), *Gender and Communication at Work*. Aldershot: Ashgate, pp. 95–110.

Mills, S. (1997) *Discourse*. London: Routledge.

Mills, S. (2003) *Gender and Politeness*. Cambridge: Cambridge University Press.

Morrison, A., R. White and E. van Velsor (1987) *Breaking the Glass Ceiling: Can Women Reach the Top of America's Largest Corporations?* Reading, MA: Addison Wesley.

Mulholland, J. (2006) Gender and advisor–client communication. In M. Barrett and M. Davidson (eds), *Gender and Communication at Work*. Aldershot: Ashgate, pp. 84–94.

Mullany, L. (2007) *Gendered Discourse in the Professional Workplace*. Basingstoke: Palgrave.

Mullany, L. (2008) Negotiating methodologies: Making language and gender relevant in the professional workplace. In K. Harrington, L. Litosseliti, H. Sauntson and J.

Sunderland (eds), *Gender and Language Research Methodologies*. Basingstoke: Palgrave, pp. 43–55.

Ochs, E. (1992) Indexing gender. In A. Duranti and C. Goodwin (eds), *Rethinking Context: Language as an Interactive Phenomenon*. Cambridge: Cambridge University Press, pp. 335–58.

Olsson, S. and R. Walker (2003) Through a gendered lens? Male and female executives' representations of one another. *Leadership and Organization Development*, 24(7): 387–96.

Peck, J. (2006) Women and promotion: The influence of communication style. In M. Barrett and M. Davidson (eds), *Gender and Communication at Work*. Aldershot: Ashgate, pp. 50–66.

Silverman, D. (2000) *Doing Qualitative Research: A Practical Guide*. London: Sage.

Still, L. (2006) Gender, leadership and communication. In M. Barrett and M. Davidson (eds), *Gender and Communication at Work*. Aldershot: Ashgate, pp. 183–94.

Sunderland, J. (2004) *Gendered Discourses*. Basingstoke: Palgrave.

Swann, J. and J. Maybin (2008) Sociolinguistic and ethnographic approaches to language and gender. In K. Harrington, L. Litosseliti, H. Sauntson and J. Sunderland (eds), *Gender and Language Research Methodologies*. Basingstoke: Palgrave.

Tannen, D. (1989) *Talking Voices: Repetition, Dialogue and Imagery in Conversational Discourse*. Cambridge: Cambridge University Press, pp. 21–8.

Tannen, D. (1999) The display of (gendered) identities at work. In M. Bucholtz, A. Liang and L. Sutton (eds), *Reinventing Identities: The Gendered Self in Discourse*. Oxford: Oxford University Press, pp. 221–40.

Thimm, C., S. Koch and S. Schey (2003) Communicating gendered professional identity: Competence, cooperation, and conflict in the workplace. In J. Holmes and M. Meyerhoff (eds), *The Handbook of Language and Gender*. Oxford: Blackwell, pp. 528–49.

Trinidad, C. and A. Normore (2005) Leadership and gender: A dangerous liaison? *Leadership & Organization Development*, 26(7): 574–90.

van Leeuwen, T. (2005) Three models of interdisciplinarity. In R. Wodak and P. Chilton (eds), *A New Agenda in (Critical) Discourse Analysis*. Amsterdam: John Benjamins, pp. 3–18.

Wahlin, W. (2007) Women in the workplace. *J@pan.Inc*, 73, http://www.japaninc.com/mgz_sep-oct_2007_issue_women-in-the-workplace.

Walsh, C. (2001) *Gender and Discourse: Language and Power in Politics, the Church and Organisations*. London: Longman.

Yieke, F. (2005) Gender and discourse: Topic organisation on workplace management committee meetings in Kenya. Paper delivered at Theoretical and Methodological Approaches to Gender, BAAL/CUP Seminar, University of Birmingham, 18 November.

17

Sociology, narrative and discourse

Tony J. Watson

Introduction

Language has in recent years moved firmly into the centre of research and theoretical debate in organisation and management studies. The central concept used in these studies is 'organisation' rather than 'business'. This valuably recognises that there is a great deal in common between the activities which occur in private business organisations and organisations located in the public (i.e. non-commercial) sector. What I shall characterise here as a sociological concept of discourse can be seen as an invaluable addition to the analytical apparatus available for studying how work activities are patterned and organised, in business and elsewhere. However, I shall also argue that the growing interest in language and discourse by those studying organisations can lead to the danger that language, discourse, narrative and the like become overprivileged in the study of social and organisational life. There has been a growing tendency to see human realities in terms of 'texts', with those aspects of social life previously conceptualised by anthropologists and sociologists as 'structures' or 'cultures' being treated primarily as facets of language in action. The present chapter sets out to demonstrate the value of an approach to discursive aspects of business and organisations which stresses the importance of discourses but which keeps, so to speak, language and discourse in their place. To do this, attention will first be given to the nature of the so-called 'linguistic turn' in organisation studies. Some problems will then be identified and a general 'way forward' outlined. In support of this, an analytical framework will be presented, one which makes central use of the concepts of discourse and narrative. Its use will be illustrated by its application to a sample of business language 'data'.

The linguistic turn in organisation studies

The metaphor of organisation researchers 'turning' to language has been very popular both with writers who have associated themselves with such a turn and with writers arguing against such a turn (or arguing, indeed, for a 'turning back'; Reed 2005). What is rarely acknowledged in this literature, however, is that the term 'linguistic turn' has been borrowed from philosophy. Although it is even more rarely, if ever, acknowledged, the term was created by Gustav Bergmann, the ideal-language philosopher who, in his final published work, argued for 'containing the linguistic turn' – one of his worries being that philosophy was in danger of being displaced by linguistics (Bergmann 1992). So what is this 'turn' that so many people in organisation studies have apparently taken? Alvesson and Kärreman (2000a) identify it as part of a trend which has occurred within sociology, social psychology, communication theory and cultural anthropology as well as organisation theory in which scholars 'rethink and reclaim their various subjects for textual and linguistic points of view' (p. 137). Their message is that we can only understand social phenomena like societies, institutions, identities and cultures by viewing them as 'discursively constructed ensembles of texts'. This message derives from a view of language which has its roots in the insistence of philosophers like Wittgenstein (1953) and Austin (1962) that language is a form of action in the world rather than simply a device used to describe or represent the world. But it is also a message strongly informed by a worldview that goes beyond this fundamental and important insight: that of postmodernism. This can be characterised as 'a way of looking at the world which rejects attempts to build systematic explanations of history and human activity and which, instead, concentrates on the ways in which human beings go about "inventing" their worlds, especially through language and cultural innovation' (Watson 2008a: 66).

This postmodernist tendency is closely associated with the French poststructuralist tradition and its rejection of any idea of there being structures underlying human existence. Such a position is clearly adopted by Westwood and Linstead (2001: 4–5) when they argue that 'organisations exist in the text – there is no structure of boundary or bureaucratic manifestation that can be meaningfully presented as organisation. . . organisation has no autonomous, stable or structural status outside the text that constitutes it'. Although many of those writing about 'organisational discourse' do not explicitly link their position to either postmodernism or poststructuralism, they appear to work with assumptions which are not fundamentally different from poststructuralist ones. In the introduction to a major organisational discourse handbook, Grant et al. (2004b: 3) say that the term 'organisational discourse' 'refers to the structured collections of *texts* embodied in the practices of talking and writing (as well as a wide variety of visual representations and cultural artefacts) that bring organisational related objects into being as these texts are produced disseminated and consumed'. The handbook is organised within a scheme which treats texts as a 'manifestation' of discourse. Texts are the 'discursive units' which researchers study and they are constituted in several 'domains', especially those of conversation and dialogue; narratives and stories; rhetoric and tropes (2004b: 4). A position which appears to be shared by most of the organisational discourse analysts is that identified by Delbridge and Ezzamel (2005), in which 'the object of analysis and the subject engaging with that object are not separated', with the effect that' there is no sense in which reality, in the form of an object such as organisation, is "out there" with a presence that stands apart from the subject engaging with it' (p. 607).

At the heart of this style of thinking is the notion that language 'brings into being' organisations and organisational practices (to refer back to the phrase highlighted in the above paragraph), and we will reflect critically on this shortly. First, however, we need to examine how significant this trend of thinking is within organisation and management studies. And perhaps it is helpful to put this question into perspective by noting the observation, made by Heritage in *The Cambridge Dictionary of Sociology*, that 'despite the obvious significance of language as a basis of social identity and culture', the topic of language 'has not received much attention from sociologists' (Heritage 2006: 322). This makes it quite remarkable that a clear trend towards language-centred analysis is occurring in the organisational field. Bibliometric figures compiled by Pritchard (2006) show the number of scholarly papers using the terms 'discourse', 'organisation' and 'management' rising from 3 in 1988 to 79 in 2005. Pritchard closely examined the 40 most cited papers and grouped them on the basis of the methodological approach they take with regard to discourse. The largest and most significant group of papers, he says, uses 'discourse analysis' as a 'synonym for analysis of forms of knowledge and practice' – with 'management knowledge' being especially important. The primary influence on these is Foucault's approach to discourse (Foucault 1980). And this points to a key role for poststructuralist thinking in the literature – Foucault being seen by most people as the pre-eminent poststructuralist thinker within the so-called linguistic turn. The Foucauldian notion of discourse used is that neatly characterised by Howarth (2000: 9) as referring to 'historically specific systems of meanings which form the identities of subjects and objects'. Thus, again echoing the words used earlier, both organisations and human subjectivities are constituted or 'brought into being' by discourse.

Some problems with language-centred thinking

There are worthwhile and interesting forms of scholarly analysis which examine pieces of text as a means of understanding how those texts might have come about and how they function 'on the page'. Thus we have very worthy outputs of discourse analysis, rhetorical analysis, narratological analysis and so on. A problem arises, however, if these analytical means become ends in themselves when they are deployed in a context where the topic of study is not meant to be language as such but organisations, management, work practices and the like. What is required here, I suggest, is a sociological analysis of organisations, within which attention is paid to the part played by discourses, narratives or rhetoric – alongside other factors which play their parts too. What all too often happens, however, is that when a discourse analysis 'approach' is taken to organisations, organisations tend to become discursive phenomena. When a narratological perspective is applied to human identities, identities tend to become narrative phenomena. And when a rhetorical analysis is applied in a managerial context, management becomes a rhetorical process. With regard to narratives and identity, for example, Musson and Duberley (2007) note how in some studies, 'identity is revealed as an amalgam of multiple, diverse and sometimes contradictory narratives' (p. 147). A simple example of this danger, with regard to narratives and organisations, is seen in the characterisation by Currie and Brown (2003) of the 'narratological perspective' which they adopt in studying managerial processes in a health service context. 'In a sense', they say, 'organisations literally are the narratives that people author in networks of conversations' (p. 564). Again, it is language that brings social phenomena 'into being'.

This is probably the sort of thing that Spicer (2005) has in mind when he writes of a 'ghoulish idealism' arising as part of a 'headlong charge' into 'culturalist' organisation studies. At its crudest, he says, this treats corporate strategy as 'simply a discursive manoeuvre', with the labour market being 'spoken into being' and power working only through 'restrictions on how we think of the world' (p. 945). Much of the impetus for the

critique of the language-centred tendency in organisation studies has come from organisation theorists adopting a critical realist or 'relational' position (Bhaskar 1989; Mutch
1999; Mutch et al. 2006). This insists on the reality of structures, processes and causal
mechanisms which operate beneath the surface of social reality. From such a position,
Fleetwood (2005) has expressed a worry that organisation studies have been 'captured by
what is variously described as a cultural, linguistic, poststructural or postmodern turn'
(p. 198) and that this work is characterised by ontological ambiguity, an ambiguity which
needs to be rejected by a realist (as opposed to constructivist) acceptance that social entities
can exist 'without someone observing, knowing and constructing' them (p. 199).

A realist position by no means requires the abandoning of a concept of discourse.
Instead, it starts from the assumption that the world that we experience is met by us as
already 'structured' and that, as Reed (2004) puts it, 'this pre-structuring process, and
the material conditions and social structures that it reproduces, cannot be collapsed into
language or discourse' (p. 415). Our work degenerates into an 'idealist regress' if discourse is assigned 'ontological primacy' and 'explanatory sovereignty over social-material
reality and the structures or mechanisms through which it is generated, elaborated and
transformed'. Fairclough (2005), the key figure of critical discourse analysis, is similarly
critical of the 'prominent tendency' to see organisation as 'an interactive accomplishment
in organisational discourse' (p. 217).

Towards language-sensitive analysis

The way forward, I suggest, is to stop these 'turning games', and to take neither the
linguistic turn towards language-centred organisation studies nor what Reed (2004) is
now calling the 'realist turn', something that involves an embracing of the critical realists' 'hard' concept of structures as entities containing generative mechanisms and causal
powers. Explanation for critical realists involves 'revealing the mechanisms which connect
things and events in causal sequences and requires the elaboration of structures, mechanisms, powers and relations' (Ackroyd and Fleetwood 2000: 15). Such mechanisms are
'real' and have an existence independent of human understandings of them. They can be
'revealed' because they are indeed 'out there' in the same way that the ground is 'down
there' when we fly over it in an aircraft (Easton 2000). This, I suggest, is a kind of 'ghoulish realism' which matches the 'ghoulish idealism' of language-centred thinking. What
would avoid the polarisation (Watson 2006a) that is coming about between so-called realists and the constructivists/poststructuralists is the adoption of a pragmatist epistemology
– one which happily uses notions of social structure, class or capitalism but uses these as
pragmatically selected conceptual devices to help us make sense of the patterns of human
relationships, processes and understanding which human activity shapes and is shaped by.
We experience the sociological phenomena of class, race, state power and organisational
rules as if they were 'things out there' and are acting upon us. But these structural tendencies cannot be reified and given the hard ontology of machines, mechanisms and causal
powers. Instead, they have an 'as-if-ness' type of reality – a soft ontology, we might say.
We hit up against them. They seem to push us around. But without the active involvement of meaning-making human agents, on both the 'doing' and 'being done to' sides,
they would have no reality.

At first sight, it may appear that a call is being made for a pragmatist turn. This is not so. The approach being advocated – without, of course, it being cast in the language of the American pragmatist school of philosophy (Mounce 1997; Putnam 1995) – has existed within sociology ever since Marx observed that human beings 'make their own history', albeit 'not within the conditions of their own choosing', and Weber analysed the interplay between human interpretative processes and emerging patterns of structure and culture. It was the pulling together of several of these classic sociological traditions that produced Berger and Luckmann's *The Social Construction of Reality* (1971).

The concept of the social construction of reality is formally defined below (p. 233) At this point, however, it is important to stress that this is neither a vacuous idealist notion, nor a 'hard' realist one. But it is about reality – reality as the knowledge that people have of the social world and the institutional realities within which they have to live. Berger and Luckmann (1971) showed, in a broadly Weberian manner, that people 'make the social world' at the same time as their own notions of who they are and what they are doing are 'made by' the social world. People shape organisations, but the organisations in which they are involved, in part, shape them. People work, shop, are born and die in these organisations. They are 'real'. But they are not real in the sense that they are entities that we can touch, feel, hear or smell. They become real to us as we confront the institutionalised patterns of rules, norms, procedures and expectations that we take for granted as 'reality'. And that 'taken-for-grantedness' is the outcome of historically grounded processes of human interpretation of the world. We might say that it is only by putting 'constructions' on our world that we can relate to it and achieve both personal sanity and social 'order'.

This original 'social construction of reality' was intended as a contribution to the sociology of knowledge. Above all, though, it is a way of understanding social institutions and the ways in which these institutions and human meaning-making and action relate to each other (Watson 1997). It was not the language-centred style of analysis that some work labelled social construction*ist* or constructi*vist* has become (Gergen 1999). It is consistent with Fairclough's (2005) version of 'relational' analysis in which the focus is on 'relations between linguistic/semiotic elements of the social and other (including material) elements' (p. 916). And it is language sensitive, recognising that language does not, on the one hand, bring the social world 'into being' but neither does it, on the other hand, merely 'describe' the world. The implications of this are effectively brought out by Spicer (2005), who suggests that we treat language as 'part of the being organised that we set out to study'. This means, he says, that we would not give special priority to discourse, nor would we seek to write it off as a second-order event. Instead, we could look at language as 'part of the thing in itself that is studied' (p. 946).

The 'thing itself' that we are concerned with here is the organisation and the relationship between human beings and the organisations with which they are involved. Within this, we can focus on the role that language plays as 'part of' that thing. We must not, however, lose sight of the fact that organisations themselves cannot be understood as other than components of the societies in which they are located. To deal with this we need a sociological style of analysis. The sociological imagination pushes us always to move from concern with the lives of human individuals to the broader public issues and societal patterns with which these are connected (Mills 1970). Even the smallest utterance or mundane piece of dialogue can be linked back to the wider culture, social structure and processes of the society in which it takes place (Watson 2008a).

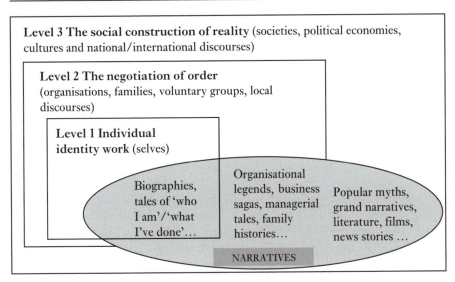

Figure 17.1 Narratives at three levels of social life

Narratives in individual identity work, the negotiation of order and the construction of reality

An analytical framework designed to link pieces of language-in-use to structural/cultural patterns at the two 'higher' levels of the 'negotiation of order' and the 'social construction of reality' is drawn in Figure 17.1. It is vital to stress that these categories are analytical ones. The levels and the concepts deployed within and across the levels are analytical devices which the sociologist can use pragmatically or instrumentally to make sense of the rich and complex actualities of lives as people live them. The dualism of individual/social context operating here is, as Fairclough (2005) puts it, an analytical dualism. It is not to embrace Cartesian dualism and treat 'individual' and 'societal' as two ontologically separate realms.

The five key concepts being used are outlined below.

1 **Discourse**: The term 'discourse' has been used in various ways in organisation theory (Alvesson and Kärreman 2000b; Grant et al. 2004a; Watson 2000), with the Foucauldian (Foucault 1980) usage being dominant. The notion is used here, however, in a sociological as opposed to a poststructuralist way with discourses being seen as 'framing' and influencing rather than determining. Further, members of societies do not simply and passively 'read' these discursive framings. They also contribute (the relatively powerful to a much greater extent than the less advantaged) to the shaping of these ideas, with their language use affecting their actions and their actions affecting their language use – and with all of this occurring within a political, economic context and within processes of conflict, contest and change. Discourses, then, are sets of concepts, statements, terms and expressions which constitute a way of talking or writing about a particular aspect of life, thus framing the way people understand and act with respect to that area of existence.

This concept of discourse, I suggest, fills a serious conceptual gap in sociology. It helps us deal with the level of social reality that mediates between that of culture at the relatively 'macro'-level and the social interactions and interpretative actions of individuals and groups at the more 'micro'-level. People's lives are influenced by a wide range of different discourses that surround them, rather than by a single overarching 'culture'. In this way we can treat discourses as the building blocks or *elements* of culture. In Figure 17.1 we see discourses located at the relatively 'global' level 3 of the model and at the more 'local' level of organisations, associations or families at level 2. At level 3 we see discourses that people across a society, or across societies, might draw upon. Examples would be discourses of democracy, mental health and business enterprise. These are referred to in the plural, it will be noted, because at any point in time, there is likely to be a variety of discourses in any one of these 'discursive eras', with links, tensions and contestation between them. Local discourses will often be variants of a wider discourse, with a focus on issues of relevance to a particular town, village, organisation or family. An example of this would be discourses of inclusion or exclusion in a geographical locality or an organisation ('locals' and 'incomers', for example, in a small town).

2 Narrative: The part played by narrative and stories in organisations has been given close attention in recent years (Czarniawska 1998; Boje et al. 2001; Gabriel 2004; Rhodes and Brown 2005). They can be linked to the concept of discourse. If discourses are elements of culture then narratives and stories can be seen as elements of discourses. They operate alongside other elements – or 'domains' as we noted Grant et al. (2004b) called them – such as tropes and rhetorical devices. The concept of narrative is a very broad one and can be defined in a generic way: a narrative is an account of a particular aspect of the world which follows a basic form of 'this, then that, then that'. We can thus have a narrative of how rainfall comes to happen or of how a baby is born. But once we move to the level of human social activities, narratives typically take on a more developed story-like form involving characters with interests, motives, emotions and moralities. In Figure 17.1 examples of narratives are seen at all three levels of the model in the shaded ellipse which is drawn across the three levels. Within the examples given here we would expect to come across cases varying from simple narratives to complex stories. To take the example of individuals' biographical narratives, we might hear from one person something like 'I was born in the house where I live; I went to the village school; I have been a farm worker all my life; when I leave this house it will be in a coffin.' But from another individual we might hear a long, complicated narrative; a story full of events, place descriptions, portraits of characters, and a series of 'twists and turns' of plot. But whichever end of the continuum from simple narrative to complex story-like narrative we hear from people, we are, in listening to them, witnessing their engagement in 'identity work'.

3 Identity work: This concept was imported into organisation and management studies in the 1990s (Watson 2008b) and is being used with increasing degrees of theoretical rigour (Alvesson and Willmott 2002; Sveningsson and Alvesson 2003; Watson 2007, 2009). It is the mutually constitutive process in which people strive to shape a relatively coherent and distinctive notion of personal self-identity and struggle to come to terms with and, within limits, to influence the various social identities which pertain to them in the various milieux in which they live their lives. Identity work brings together two aspects of 'human identity' (which is the notion of who or what a particular person is, in relation to others, and which defines the ways in which any given person is like other people and the ways in which they differ from others). First we have the 'internal' part of human identity, the individual's *self-identity*. This is the individual's own notion of who and what they are. It has to be 'worked at'. In order to be sane and effective social actors, individuals have to achieve a degree of coherence and consistency in their conception of who they are. This can only happen, however, through relating to the social world and, in particular, to *social identities*: cultural, discursive or institutional notions of who or what any individual might be. In Figure 17.1, identity work is located at level 3 of the model.

4 Negotiated order: Although individuals' identity work involves them in using discursive resources from the overall social constructed reality of their society and culture, they often utilise discursive resources that have been mediated by the middle level of social structure in, say, the organisations they work in or the families in which they have grown up. The concept of negotiated order was developed in the organisational context to refer to the ever-shifting pattern of organisational activities that has arisen or emerged over time as an outcome of the interplay of the variety of interests, understandings, reactions and initiatives of the individuals and groups involved in the organisation (Strauss et al. 1963; Strauss 1978; Watson 2001, 2006b). This concept can be applied to the 'order' of the family, ethnic group or church that the individual is associated with. In Figure 17.1, negotiated order is located at level 3 of the model.

5 The social construction of reality: This is the process in which human beings, through cultural interaction, give meaning to the world – a world that may well exist beyond language but which can only be known and communicated by people through language-based processes of cultural interpretation and sense-making. The process produces the institutions that make up societies and gives social structures legitimacy and taken-for-grantedness (Berger and Luckmann 1971). In Figure 17.1, the social construction of reality is located at level 3 of the model. These relatively global processes are fed by and feed into the processes of negotiation of order at level 2 and processes of identity work at level 1.

Narratives, discursive resources and identity work in practice

At this point we turn (!) to some actual language-in-use. The dialogue which is produced here is from a conversation between Lawrence Taylor and me. In setting up this research interview I was, in effect, inviting Lawrence to 'do' identity work by speaking to the researcher and his mini-disk recorder. Thus the dialogue that we now read is an example of both language-in-action and identity work in practice. As Lawrence speaks, he is simultaneously 'working at' his own notion of who he is and the notion he wishes to give the researcher of who and what he is. Lawrence begins,

    A: You will tell me if I go on too much won't you?

    B: How do you mean?

    A: I'm well known as a guy who can talk the hind leg off a donkey. I am Mr Motor-mouth, Mr Salesman of the Year. But John's obviously decided that I'm an interesting bloke for you to talk to. In fact, I remember the first time I met John. It was when I was in my own business, no I tell a lie, it was when I was in what was then my uncle's business – you know, before he retired and

I took it over. Anyway, we had this new fabric that we wanted to get onto the market. And Derek, that's my uncle, always used to say that you need to get close to your best customers. He used to tell us all regularly how, for the first two years of the life of the business, he kept going on just three key customers. So Derek and I went for steak and chips at this place that used to be quite popular – it is closed now, but do you remember when we all went out for steak and chips. Ordinary people were getting more affluent and, uhm. I'd always been to restaurants. I didn't think about it at the time, but I suppose my parents had always been quite well off. I remember my mother teaching me how to speak properly to waiters. One day she made me order the whole meal. I was quite young at the time, perhaps eight or nine. I was really well brought up, I suppose. I mean, it makes a difference. So I was OK taking people out like John and telling them about the wonderful new material that we were making and how his business really needed it. In the end I sold him nothing because he was going bankrupt. He only told me at the end of the meal and after two bottles of wine. Does that matter? Not at all – Derek told me I had done the right thing. But, he said, 'You could have started listening to the customer earlier in the evening and got away with just one bottle of wine.' But, well the thing is – John and I are still friends and we've helped each other out on all sorts of things.

B: So I gather that you took over your uncle's business and ran it yourself?

A: My mother didn't want me to leave school at 16 and go to work for my uncle. She came from a professional sort of family. She wanted me to be a lawyer, or an optician or uhm, uhm. No, I rather fancied 'trade' – a word she hated. She said to me one day, 'You think that with your mouth that you will make a fortune in the cloth trade' (and you should have heard the way she said 'cloth trade' – well I mean she scrunched up her eyes whenever she spoke of 'trade'). 'But if you were a barrister – just imagine how you could win cases; I'd be so proud.' But when I moved into my present job, I must tell you about. . .

B: Before you do though, Lawrence, I just need to clarify the sequence of events here. . .

A: Sorry about that. I told you that I don't half go on.

Analysis

In this small piece of text we have an example of identity work in action and an individual deploying a variety of discursive resources to rehearse who he is for the researcher and for himself. These words are a slice of his ongoing autobiographical self-shaping. To understand what is occurring here sociologically – relating action at a 'micro'-interactional level to wider societal patterns – we can deploy the range of concepts set out earlier. At the very beginning we see an expression of self-identity as Lawrence refers to himself as someone who 'goes on too much'. But this is quickly related to a social identity; a discursive resource or typification available in the societal socially constructed reality (at our model's level 3) of people who could 'talk the hind leg off a donkey'. And this is connected to two other culturally available variants of the garrulous individual,

'Mr Motor-mouth' and, perhaps rather strangely, 'Mr Salesman of the Year'. The reference here to salesmen is probably functioning to signal what is going to emerge later as Lawrence's favoured self-identity as a salesman. He then launches into Narrative 1. This first narrative runs through the dialogue and it mixes level-1 narrative elements (autobiographical storytelling) and level-2 elements (the story of the fabric business – a narrative from the business's negotiated order). There then appears Narrative 2, which crosses levels 2 and 3 with the societal narrative about businesspeople getting 'close to customers' and the organisational order of the fabric firm, where the uncle pressed on organisational members the importance of this principle. At this point, Narrative 3 is inserted; a slice of level-3 folk-social history about steak restaurants. And Narrative 4 quickly takes over from this with the story about his mother's training him in restaurant etiquette. Lawrence uses this to project a self-identity as a person who was 'well brought up' (this discursive resource connecting to a certain historically specific middle-class social identity). Almost seamlessly we are then taken into Narrative 5 and the tale of the naive but kind Lawrence failing to make sales but establishing a long-term friendship with John.

In response to the researcher's invitation to provide more information on how Lawrence came to take over his uncle's business, Lawrence goes back further in his biography and, in Narrative 6, which relates a conversation with his mother (a level-1 autobiographical tale), he draws on level-3 social identities of 'professional' workers and those in 'trade'. These social identities are part of a societal level-3 narrative, which Lawrence is indirectly alluding to, about a British social-structural division which arose historically between emerging professional workers and people in 'trade' (Watson 2008a).

Conclusion

The above piece of analysis could be characterised as an example of sociological discourse analysis. Although the conversation has been presented here in isolation, without its being linked into the wider investigation of which it is a part, it is clearly related to a broad project of applying the basic sociological insight identified early in this chapter to the relationship between the lives and identities of managers and entrepreneurs, on the one hand, and social and cultural patterns at both the organisational and the societal levels, on the other hand. I hope that the three-level model will, in its own right, be of use to others wishing to study discourse in organisations and business. But, more importantly perhaps, I hope that its use here will demonstrate the advantages of a language-sensitive form of organisational analysis. This is intended to avoid the excesses of language-centred analyses in which identities, organisations and societies are brought into being by discourses, texts and narratives. It is equally intended to avoid the tendencies of certain 'realist' reactions to the so-called linguistic turn in which processes and patterns are reified into hard structures, mechanisms, causal powers and the like. Concepts of discourse, narrative, rhetoric, social construction and the like are vital to social and organisational analysis. But their deployment does not constitute social analysis. Language is everywhere. Without language, nothing can be achieved socially. But language is not everything. As Bergmann (1992) said to the philosophers, the linguistic turn has been important. But it must be contained.

References

Ackroyd, S. and S. Fleetwood (2000) Realism in contemporary organisation and management studies. In S. Ackroyd and S. Fleetwood (eds), *Realist Perspectives on Management and Organisations*. London: Routledge, pp. 3–25.

Alvesson, M. and D. Kärreman (2000a) Taking the linguistic turn in organizational research: Challenges, responses, consequences. *Journal of Applied Behavioral Science*, 36: 136–58.

Alvesson, M. and D. Kärreman (2000b) Varieties of discourse: On the study of organizations through discourse analysis. *Human Relations*, 53: 1125–49.

Alvesson, M. and H. Willmott (2002) Identity regulation and organizational control: Producing the appropriate individual. *Journal of Management Studies*, 39(5): 619–72.

Austin, J. L. (1962) *How to Do Things with Words*. Oxford: Oxford University Press.

Berger, P. L. and T. Luckmann (1971) *The Social Construction of Reality*. Harmondsworth: Penguin.

Bergmann, G. (1992) *New Foundations of Ontology*. Madison: University of Wisconsin Press.

Bhaskar, C. R. (1989) *Reclaiming Reality*. London: Verso.

Boje, D., R. C. Alvarez and B. Schooling (2001) Reclaiming story in organization: Narratologies and action sciences. In R. Westwood and S. Linstead (eds), *The Language of Organization*. London: Sage, pp. 132–75.

Currie, G. and A. D. Brown (2003) A narratological approach to understanding processes of organizing in a UK hospital. *Human Relations*, 56: 563–86.

Czarniawska, B. (1998) *A Narrative Approach to Organization Studies*. London: Sage.

Delbridge, R. and M. Ezzamel (2005) The strength of difference: Contemporary conceptions of control. *Organization*, 12(5): 603–18.

Easton, G. (2000) Case research as a method for industrial networks: A realist apologia. In S. Ackroyd and S. Fleetwood (eds), *Realist Perspectives on Management and Organisations*. London: Routledge, pp. 205–19.

Fairclough, N. (2005) Discourse analysis in organization studies: The case for critical realism. *Organization Studies*, 26(6): 915–39.

Fleetwood, S. (2005) Ontology in organization and management studies: A critical realist perspective. *Organization*, 12(2): 197–222.

Foucault, M. (1980) *Power/Knowledge: Selected Interviews and Other Writings*. Brighton: Harvester.

Gabriel, Y. (2004) Narratives, stories and texts. In C. Hardy, C. Oswick and L. Putnam (eds.), *The Sage Handbook of Organizational Discourse*. London: Sage, pp. 61–77.

Gergen, K. E. (1999) *An Invitation to Social Construction*. London: Sage.

Grant, D., C. Hardy, C. Oswick and L. Putnam (eds) (2004a) *The Sage Handbook of Organizational Discourse*. London: Sage.

Grant, D., C. Hardy, C. Oswick and L. Putnam (2004b) Introduction: Organizational discourse: exploring the field. In C. Hardy, C. Oswick, and L. Putnam (eds), *The Sage Handbook of Organizational Discourse*. London: Sage, pp. 1–36.

Heritage, J. (2006) Language. In B. S. Turner (ed.), *The Cambridge Dictionary of Sociology*. Cambridge: Cambridge University Press, pp. 322–4.

Howarth, D. (2000) *Discourse*. Buckingham: Open University Press.

Mills, C. W. (1970) *The Sociological Imagination*. Harmondsworth: Penguin.

Mounce, H. O. (1997) *The Two Pragmatisms*. London: Routledge.

Musson, G. and J. Duberley (2007) Change, change or be exchanged: The discourse of participation and the manufacture of identity. *Journal of Management Studies*, 44(1): 143–64.

Mutch, A. (1999) Critical realism, managers and information. *British Journal of Management*, 10(4): 323–34.

Mutch, A., R. Delbridge and M. Ventresca (2006) Situation organizational action: The relational sociology of organizations. *Organization*, 13(5): 607–25.

Pritchard, C. (2006) The organization of organizational discourse. *Management Communication Quarterly*, 20(2): 213–26.

Putnam H. (1995) *Pragmatism*. Oxford: Blackwell.

Reed, M. (2004) Getting real about organizational discourse. In D. Grant, C. Hardy, C. Oswick and L. Putnam (eds), *The Sage Handbook of Organizational Discourse*. London: Sage, pp. 413–20.

Reed, M. (2005) Reflections on the 'realist turn' in organization and management studies. *Journal of Management Studies*, 42(8): 1621–44.

Rhodes, C. and A. D. Brown (2005) Narrative, organizations and research. *International Journal of Management Reviews*, 7(3): 167–88.

Spicer, A. (2005) A quiet manifesto of realism. (Review of Grant et al. 2004a.) *Organization*, 12(6): 944–7.

Strauss, A. (1978) *Negotiations*. New York: Wiley.

Strauss, A., L. Schatzman, D. Erlich, R. Bucher and M. Sabsin (1963) The hospital and its negotiated order. In E. Friedson (ed.), *The Hospital in Modern Society*. New York: Macmillan.

Sveningsson, S. and M. Alvesson (2003) Managing managerial identities: Organizational fragmentation, discourse and identity struggle. *Human Relations*, 56(10): 1163–93.

Watson, T. J. (1997) Languages within languages: A social constructionist perspective on multiple managerial discourses. In F. Bargiela-Chiappini and S. Harris (eds), *The Language of Business*. Edinburgh: Edinburgh University Press, pp. 211–27.

Watson, T. J. (2000) Discourse and organisation (review article). *Human Relations*, 53(4): 559–97.

Watson, T. J. (2001) Negotiated orders, in organizations. In N. J. Smelser and P. B. Baltes (eds), *International Encyclopedia of the Social and Behaviour Sciences*. Amsterdam: Elsevier, pp. 10965–7.

Watson, T. J. (2006a) The organization and disorganization of organization studies (review essay). *Journal of Management Studies*, 43(2): 367–82.

Watson, T. J. (2006b) *Organising and Managing Work: Organisational, Managerial and Strategic Behaviour in Theory and Practice*, 2nd edn. Harlow: Prentice Hall.

Watson, T. J. (2007) Identity work, managing and researching. In A. Pullen, N. Beech and D. Sims (eds), *Exploring Identity: Concepts and Methods*. Basingstoke: Palgrave Macmillan, pp. 135–50.

Watson, T. J. (2008a) *Sociology, Work and Industry*, 5th edn. London: Routledge.

Watson, T. J. (2008b) Managing identity: Identity work, personal predicaments and structural circumstances. *Organization*, 15(1): 121–43.

Watson, T. J. (2009) Entrepreneurial action, identity work and the use of multiple discursive resources: The case of a rapidly changing family business. *International Small Business Journal (ISBJ)*, 27(3).

Westwood, R. and S. Linstead (eds) (2001) *The Language of Organization*. London: Sage.

Wittgenstein, L. (1953) *Philosophical Investigations*. Oxford: Blackwell.

18

Pragmatics

Kenneth C. C. Kong

Introduction

> 'Then you should say what you mean,' the March Hare went on.
>
> 'I do,' Alice hastily replied; 'at least – at least I mean what I say – that's the same thing, you know.'
>
> 'Not the same thing a bit!' said the Hatter. 'You might just as well say that "I see what I eat" is the same thing as "I eat what I see"!'
>
> 'You might just as well say,' added the March Hare, 'that "I like what I get" is the same thing as "I get what I like"!'
>
> 'You might just as well say,' added the Dormouse, who seemed to be talking in his sleep, 'that "I breathe when I sleep" is the same thing as "I sleep when I breathe"!' (Lewis Carroll, *Alice's Adventures in Wonderland*)

Alice made a mistake in taking the superficial meaning of language as fixed and stable, but language is far from transparent and unambiguous. This can be regarded as one of the most difficult problems in human communication, that is, we do not say what we mean sometimes or we do not mean what we say at other times. This complicated relationship between words and meanings has intrigued linguists and philosophers alike for centuries. There are many reasons for this phenomenon, such as the need to save and protect the face needs of others or ourselves. This is precisely the premise of pragmatic approach(es) to human communication including, of course, business communication. Pragmatics can be defined as the study of language use in context, particularly focusing on the relationship between what we say and what we mean in certain contexts. The complex relationship is mediated by many factors such as social distance, power relationships, gender differences and intercultural differences. Business discourse is 'all about how people communicate using talk or writing in commercial organisations to get their work done' (Bargiela-Chiappini et al. 2007: 3). This process involves the intricate negotiation of the above-mentioned factors through the use of language. The study of business discourse also has a focus on how interactants achieve common understanding in business contexts (cf. Bremer 1996; Firth 1995). Therefore, pragmatics is a very useful and valuable tool to deal with these issues.

As pragmatics makes use of a wide range of theories and principles (from turn-taking mechanisms to politeness models), this Chapter will focus on only two important and classic concepts: speech act theory and the co-operative principle. It will be shown how these two principles work and how previous research on business discourse has been motivated and enriched by those concepts. The Chapter begins by identifying the difference between semantics and pragmatics – two branches of linguistics which show similar interest in words and meanings. Then it will move on to explain what the two concepts are about and how these concepts have informed and enriched research in business discourse.

Words and meanings: What is pragmatics?

There are two closely related branches of linguistics which deal with meaning: semantics and pragmatics. They both originated from the same motivation: the search for the complicated relationship between words and their meanings. Semantics, as Yule (1996: 4) puts it, is the 'study of relationships between linguistic forms and entities in the world; that is how words literally connect to things'. For example, semantics studies the range and field of words, that is, how many different meanings a word can entail (semantic range) and how words are related to one another (semantic field). In other words, semantic analysis, like syntactic analysis, can be performed regardless of who is using the words, where the words are uttered, what the relationship is between the addressors and addressees, etc. It is pragmatics which brings those contextual variables into analysis. Pragmatics has been defined in different ways:

> Pragmatics studies the use of language in human communication as determined by the conditions of society. (Mey 2001: 6)
> Pragmatics is the study of the relationships between linguistic forms and the users of those forms. (Yule 1996: 4)

A more sophisticated definition is provided by Thomas (1995: 22), who argues pragmatics is the study of 'meaning in interaction':

> meaning is not something which is inherent in the words alone, nor is it produced by the speaker alone, nor by the hearer alone. Making meaning is a dynamic process, involving the negotiation of meaning between speaker and hearer, the context of utterance (physical, social and linguistic) and the meaning potential of an utterance.

The definitions above all point to context sensitivity, i.e. language is never free of context and meaning is not inherent in words. The definitions also underscore the complex relationship of words and meanings, which can be uncovered only through identifying the underlying assumptions of language users as well as the cultures in which interactions take place. Austin (1975), the father of pragmatics, first developed the idea of pragmatics when he observed people can make perfect sense of each other even though language is full of imprecision and contradictions. According to Austin, language is not best described in terms of how it is used to make true statements about the world; instead language should be described in terms of actions (see below).

Pragmatics is a very useful tool[1] in business discourse research because business discourse is a site of communication where language plays a subtle role in negotiating human relationships, and hence, the outcomes of a transaction. It allows us to see why people use certain linguistic forms in some situations, but not in others. Nevertheless, since pragmatic analysis takes into consideration a range of contextual variables – from the place of interaction to the gender of the interactants – the analysis can be more subject to individual interpretation, which has to be enriched by a large database and research methodologies allowing language users to voice their views. In the following, I will turn to the two classic concepts central to the study of pragmatics: speech act theory and the co-operative principle. Both have intentionality as their central tenet. While speech act theory focuses on how utterances can perform various functions, the co-operative principle looks at how people make sense of each other and their utterances.

Speech act theory

Proposed by Austin (1975), a philosopher of language, speech act theory examines how we achieve various goals by using language. Language does not simply state or describe, but also acts. By using language, we can perform various functions. There are three levels of meaning according to Austin: locution, illocution and perlocution. Locution is the superficial realisation of a linguistic item. Illocution is the intention of the speaker/writer, while perlocution is the effect on the addressee after something is uttered. Take the sentence 'Can you send the letter by 5 p.m.?' as an example. At the level of locution, it makes use of the modal 'can', denoting the meaning of ability, and an interrogative polar sentence structure ending with a question mark, expecting a 'yes' or 'no' answer. This illustrates how different words are combined together, which in fact can be studied at the level of syntax or semantics. This is the first or 'locutionary' level of analysis, which involves analysis of the literal meaning of individual words. However, as we have already seen, the level of locution is a superficial one and the complete meaning of an utterance cannot be determined unless contextual variables are taken into consideration. This is why illocution, the second level of meaning, should be examined; it can be argued to be the most important component of speech act theory. Illocution, in simple terms, is what the speaker/writer means by using a cluster of words. The utterance 'Can you send the letter by 5 p.m.?' is a request in terms of the speaker's meaning and may not have anything to do with ability.[2] The last level of meaning is perlocution, the consequence of an act. At this level, an affirmative answer to the question is an acceptance of the request whereas a negative answer is a signal of rejection. Sometimes this can be done nonverbally by nodding or shaking one's head.

The three levels of force mentioned above can well capture the complex relationship between words and their meanings, which is not a simple one-to-one matching relationship. A prototypical meaning usually assigned to a particular linguistic item can also be realised through different linguistic items. For example, a business request for catalogues can be realised by an imperative sentence structure, such as 'Please send your catalogues to our company.' This is the most direct and obvious realisation, and does not require any guessing or inferencing from the message receiver. However, the same illocution can be performed by other sentence structures, such as a declarative sentence ('I am interested in your company('s) catalogues'). The illocutionary force of the sentence is less obvious than the first one and is an 'indirect' speech act, or what Brown and Levinson (1987) call an off-record strategy, which requires more effort from the receiver to work out the intended meaning of the addressor. While the same illocution can be performed by using different linguistic items, the same linguistic item can be used to perform various functions. For example, the modal 'can' in the sentence is used to make a request, but it can also refer to the ability of someone (such as 'The company can make more profit next year'). In short, the three abstraction levels of meaning can help us to identify the complex relationship between what something literally means and what the addressor intends.

Speech acts have been classified according to their lexical/syntactic realisations or their specific functions. Austin (1975) developed a classification of speech acts based on illocutionary verbs. This more intuitive attempt was later modified by Searle (1975). He argued that speech acts should be classified according to illocutionary point, speaker's psychological state, and propositional content, resulting in five categories of speech acts: representatives, directives, commissives, expressives and declarations, which have been more frequently used in discussing speech acts in pragmatics:

1 Representatives commit the speaker to the truth of the expressed proposition, e.g. asserting, concluding, deducing.
2 Directives are attempts by the speaker to get the hearer to do something, e.g. requesting, inviting, offering, ordering, questioning.
3 Commissives commit the speaker to some future course of action, e.g. promising, threatening, offering.
4 Expressives express a psychological state of the speaker, e.g. thanking, congratulating, apologising, welcoming.
5 Declarations effect immediate changes in the institutional state of affairs, e.g. appointing, nominating, pronouncing, resigning.

In the business world, some speech acts are used more often than others. For example, directives, i.e. asking someone to get something done, have almost become daily routines within and across institutions. Commissives are also frequently used in meetings and negotiations. Declarations are more restricted and may only be used in certain personnel situations, such as appointing and resigning. The most obvious strength of speech act theory in business discourse research is that it provides a feasible unit of analysis. Negotiation is too large as a unit of analysis whereas a particular linguistic item is too small. Speech acts have been extensively studied across and within cultures. Blum-Kulka et al.'s CCSARP (Cross-Cultural Speech Act Realization Project; 1989) is a good example of research which analysed the interlanguage and cross-cultural realisations of different speech acts, such as requests and apologies. Much research along this line has been carried out since then. For example, the Japanese culture has been regarded as indirect, modest and non-confrontational. Studies have identified the fact that Japanese and native English speakers have different preferences when making complaints and responding to them (Murphy and Neu 1996; Rinnert et al. 2006). On the other hand, speech acts can be a very useful unit of analysis even within the same culture. For example, research has been conducted as to how requests are made in different hierarchical relationships within an institution: peer-to-peer, subordinate-to-superior, and superior-to-subordinate (cf. Kong

2006). These subtle differences are crucial and form the basis of effective communication within any institution.

The co-operative principle

In speech act theory a distinction is made between what is said and what is meant, i.e. what is said and what action is performed. The co-operative principle developed by Grice (1975)[3] is an attempt to explain 'how a hearer might get from the level of expressed meaning to the level of implied meaning' (Thomas 2001: 116). In order to explain this phenomenon, Austin (1975) introduced four specific maxims and a co-operative principle. The principle adheres to the basic assumption that individuals are rational and co-operative in their conversations. This assumption is classified/ expanded upon by Grice through four specific maxims, related to truth (maxim of quality), informativeness (maxim of quantity), relevance (maxim of relation) and orderliness (maxim of manner). These maxims can take the form of imperatives as if they are 'rules' of communication:

Maxim of quality
- Try to make your contribution one that is true.
- Do not say what you believe to be false.
- Do not say that for which you lack adequate evidence.

Maxim of quantity
- Make your contribution as informative as is required (for the current purpose of the exchange).
- Do not make your contribution more informative than is required.

Maxim of relation
- Be relevant.

Maxim of manner
- Be perspicacious.
- Be brief.
- Be orderly.

Though they take the form of imperatives in Grice's presentation, these maxims are not rules that interlocutors must follow. They can be flouted, exploited at the expense of other maxims, violated, infringed, opted out of or suspended by participants who have absolutely nothing wrong with their speech and hearing. We assume that people normally follow these maxims. When people do not, this creates an implicature of the underlying meaning. It is sometimes through the violation of those assumptions that we actually co-operate, but in a different sense, of course. In fact this is the strength of the co-operative principle. Even when a maxim is violated, a special meaning (implicature) is created if we assume the co-operative principle is working. Implicature is, in other words, the hidden meaning created when a maxim is violated. Take the following conversation as an example:

Colleague A: Can you prepare another document for me?
Colleague B: What time is it now?

B's answer violates the maxim of relevance. The intention of A is obviously to request B to prepare a document for him or her, i.e. a directive. The potential answers/responses would be either 'yes' (acceptance of the request) or 'no' (rejection of it). Instead, B asks a counter-question and creates a possible implicature that it is time for him or her to leave or that he or she does not have enough time to perform the task. It can serve as an indirect way of rejecting the request. There are many reasons for violating a maxim and creating an implicature. One of the most common reasons is to reduce the face loss or 'face threat', i.e. the imposition on the hearer's status and self-esteem (Brown and Levinson 1987) created by rejecting someone's request. Providing an indirect ('off-record') response that involves implicature is one strategy for mitigating such face threat.

The co-operative principle is not without its critics. It has been argued from cognitive perspectives that the four maxims can be subsumed by one single maxim, i.e. the maxim of relevance (Sperber and Wilson 1995). Another argument is that the four maxims may not carry equal weight in different contexts. In a study in conflict management among friends, Schiffrin (1990) found that the maxim of quality is a more important element to be negotiated in argumentative talk, because the truth value of (the) statement(s) and the sincerity of the speaker matter most in arguments. On the other hand, it has been pointed out that the four maxims may not be adequate to explain the sense-making mechanisms involved in an interaction since there may be some specific assumptions unique to certain relationships and cultures (Kong 2003; Matsumoto 1989). For example, hierarchy and harmony are arguably the most important principles governing Chinese institutional communication (Gabrenya and Hwang 1996). In order to maintain the status quo in the workplace, Chinese interlocutors may not follow the co-operative principle at all. Nevertheless, the co-operative principle is still an important concept in pragmatics and can help analysts identify how people make sense of one another and negotiate meanings in contexts.

Applications of speech act theory to business discourse research

The earliest study making use of speech act theory in the workplace discourse dates back to the 1980s, when immigration caused serious problems of miscommunication between native and non-native speakers in the workplace. The studies conducted by Clyne and his colleagues (Clyne 1981, 1987, 1994; Clyne et al. 1991) compare the intercultural realisations of different speech acts in Australia and point to the importance of the awareness of underlying cultural assumptions. Although the same language, i.e. English, is used, there are both universal and specific features of language use shared by different ethnic groups. Clyne (1994) and Gumperz (1982) are good examples of systemic studies applying speech act theory in the workplace. The focus of Clyne (1994) was on complaints, directives, commissives and apologies.

In addition to academically oriented works, there have also been efforts to apply the speech act approach to the study of non-academic talk. Ewald and Stine (1983) is an early application of speech acts analysis to the teaching of business communication. Mulholland (1991, 1994), based on Searle's taxonomy of speech acts, proposed a finer classification

of speech acts in the workplace, such as accepting, accusing, dismissing and reprimand-
ing. Practical suggestions are also given to practitioners as to how these speech acts can
be performed in different situations. In the next section, I will turn to some examples of
studies focusing on the realisations of specific speech acts in the workplace.

Directives

Among the five types of speech acts, directives have received most attention in business discourse research. This is not surprising since getting jobs done can be regarded
as the single most important element of an institution; nevertheless, asking someone
to comply with a request can be regarded as the most face-threatening act (perhaps
except for the declaration act of terminating someone's employment or business relationship). Speech act has been used as an analytic unit for comparisons between diverse
cultures and different hierarchical levels within the same institution. For example,
Kong (1998) is an intercultural study of Chinese and English routine business request
letters. The study reveals that in the Chinese request letters, a deference face system
is dominant, marked by features such as an inductive introduction to a request (justification + request), an absence of face-threatening moves, and a greater proportion of
and flexibility in the use of rapport-building strategies throughout the whole text. On
the other hand, in the English letters, a solidarity face system is employed in making
routine business requests, with features such as a deductive introduction to a request,
greater emphasis on the ideational or informational content, and more frequent occurrence of face-threatening moves. The differences are argued to be due to the different
expectations of readers and writers in composing routine business request letters in
the two cultures. Nevertheless, it should be remembered that inductive and deductive
styles are not unique features of Chinese and English(-speaking) cultures, respectively.
What matters most is the writers' and readers' expectations in a particular situation
and relationship.

Besides the intercultural realisation of directives, intra-institutional requests are
also important as written directives that are circulated within an institution; these are
the most common forms of discourse in the modern organisational structure. Kong
(2006) examines the frequency, semantic type and sequencing of accounts in internal
company emails with directive elements. He found that subordinates provide justifications most frequently when they make requests to their superiors (60.6 per cent of
directives with justification). Managers tend to justify their requests to their subordinates more frequently than peers justify requests among themselves (55.2 per cent
versus 43.8 per cent). The latter finding is attributed to the dilemma faced by modern
institutions of wanting to ascertain that workers achieve institutional goals on the one
hand, and allowing individuals to operate as autonomous workers on the other hand.
Nevertheless, managers, when requesting their subordinates to do something, tend
to use more accounts that are not typically associated with justification for action; in
this way, they can exercise control while mitigating their action and without putting
their (higher) institutional status at stake. For example, justifications are usually in the
semantic category of REASON:

> *We also found that XXX is broken (REASON).* So please send it to us.

While REASON is usually used for justification purposes, the condition-related accounts which are not usually used for justification can be used by superiors in order to soften or mitigate the request:

> *If you have any queries*, you can use [brand name] online scan function to detect any virus in your computers.
> *If you need more details on their request*, Ms Fan said you could contact Director XXX (Tel. XXX) for further instruction.

In Kong's (2006) study of 250 emails written by 16 subjects in a medium-sized company in Hong Kong, it was also found that differences are exhibited in the sequencing of accounts (Table 18.1).

Pre-posed accounts are more commonly used in peer-to-peer and subordinate-to-superior groups than in superior-to-subordinate groups. The sequencing of accounts is argued to be the result of a number of factors, including coherence, agent reference and the relationship between addressor and addressee. The most interesting is the third of these, which is more closely related to the pragmatic negotiation of relationship, although this is seldom highlighted in the literature. In the following example, the agent of the purpose clause is ambiguous and it is more diffused than in the main clause. This ambiguity of reference is a useful strategy in the mobilisation of institutional control, especially when the requestor does not have legitimate power over the requestee:

> *In order to convince them to order more and provide our better service to them*, would you please send 9 units adjustable shelves (w/o logo) by TNT express to us ASAP.

Representatives

Representatives are also an important speech act in the business world. People have to state, report or assert in order to convince others of certain ideas and beliefs. Specific functions such as disagreeing, asserting oneself in job applications, and reporting have received the most attention.

Staplers (1995) made use of speech act theory as a methodology to compare the ways in which French and Dutch disagree among themselves in their own culture and the ways in which French and Dutch disagree with each other during negotiation. A list of features was found to co-occur with the so-called 'dispreferred acts' such as disagreements (Levinson 1983). The most interesting point Staplers makes is that although these features are present in disagreements, the amount of mitigation or politeness strategies is not as much as can be found in everyday situations. This phenomenon is attributed to the importance of conversational clarity over politeness considerations in the French–Dutch workplace.

Another study focused on how one makes assertions when asking for a second chance at an interview (Maier 1992). Native and non-native English speakers were asked to write an explanation letter to their potential employers after failing to show up for an interview. Applicants' letters contained a number of speech acts, including representatives asserting the merits of the applicant and the benefits to the company if the applicant were to

Table 18.1 Sequencing of accounts in different relationships

	Peer-to-peer (%)	Subordinate-to-superior (%)	Superior-to-subordinate (%)
Pre-posed	75	75	56.3
Post-posed	25	25	43.7

Table 18.2 Formal and informal language use by native and non-native speakers

Native speakers	Non-native speakers
Please accept this letter of apology for not being able to meet you yesterday for our scheduled interview.	First I want to say sorry for not attending a job interview.
The position you have opening looks quite challenging to me and I feel qualified to handle it.	I really, really want to work in your company. I had already graduated from my school. Therefore I really want to make use of my study.
I believe my qualifications and educational background makes me an excellent candidate for your open position.	I believe that I can handle this job well enough. You have already known what my background is.

Table 18.3 Inclusion of personal details by non-native speakers

Native speakers	Non-native speakers
I would like to be part of your organisation.	I have prepared and trained myself to get this job for a long time.
I remained very interested in this position.	I am very interested in your company. Working in ABC Corporation is my dream. . .. I cannot give up my dream.

be employed. It was found that native and non-native speakers adopted different degrees of formality and made different use(s) of politeness strategies. For example, non-native speakers tended to use more informal or conversational features (Table 18.2).

Although the meaning of each pair is very similar, the linguistic formulation is different. Native speakers can utilise a wider range of politeness strategies in order to soften or reinforce the tone so that the reader can accept the message more readily. Another difference is that non-native speakers tend to include more personal details when they are showing interest in a company (Table 18.3).

Lastly, reporting is also a very important speech act especially when it is aimed at a public audience by a large corporation. Hyland (1998) studied CEOs' letters included in annual reports and focused on the use of metadiscourse/metadiscursive features. The main purpose of the CEOs' letters was to project a positive personal and corporate image of a company, so as to satisfy their shareholders. The metadiscourse/metadiscursive features were classified according to two major functions: interpersonal and textual. Interpersonal features included hedges (*might, perhaps*), emphatics (*in fact, definitely*) and attitude markers (*surprisingly, hopefully*). Textual features included logical connectives (*in addition*), sequencers (*first, next*) and frame markers (*finally, my goal is*). It was argued that these metafeatures play an important role in organising and evaluating information so as to orient readers to a particular interpretation of the content.

Expressives

Among expressives, apologies have received the most attention in the cross-cultural/intercultural pragmatic literature. The speech act of apologising can be realised in different ways, such as announcing the apology, showing regret, giving reasons for having caused the impingement, acknowledging responsibility, offering repair, and promising forbearance (Cohen and Olshtain 1981; Owen 1984). In the study on letters requesting a second chance of interview mentioned above, Maier (1992) also examined the speech act of apology and concluded that natives tend to announce their apologies by using the word 'apology' whereas non-native speakers tend to use the word 'sorry', a more frequent way of making an apology in conversational English (Owen 1984).

Complaints have also received some attention in studies of expressives. Since it is difficult to obtain authentic complaint letters from companies as data because of their confidentiality, Hartford and Mahboob (2004) made use of letters to newspaper editors to identify intercultural differences in the realisation of complaints and to propose an organisational model of complaint letters. Model complaint letters to newspaper editors in self-reference/self-help books were compared with authentic letters written in Urdu, Pakistani English, Nepali English and American English. It was concluded that the authentic letters in all of these cultural and language groups share close similarities in terms of their organisation:

> Move 1: Introduction
> Move 2: Praise
> Move 3: Alerters
> Move 4: Background
> Move 5: Complaint
> Move 6: Appeals to editor
> Move 7: Request for redress
> Move 8: Suggestion
> Move 9: Justification for request/suggestion

It was also found in their study that regardless of language and cultural group, the most frequent politeness strategies found in these complaint letters were the use of the interrogative form, of passives and impersonal constructions, and of performative verbs.

Table 18.4 Use of initiated and uninitiated commissives by western and Chinese participants

Commissives	Western (%)	Chinese (%)	Total (%)
Initiated	26	33	60
Direct: Promises	18	28	46
Indirect: Commissive hints	8	5	13
Uninitiated	31	9	40
Direct: Offers	17	7	24
Indirect: Suggestory hints	14	2	16

Source: adapted from Bilbow (2002: 301)

Commissives

Bilbow (2002) studied the use of commissive speech acts in intercultural meetings in Hong Kong. This study was based on recordings of meetings conducted in English and involving Chinese and westerners in a large multinational airline corporation in Hong Kong. Both the speech acts and their lexico-grammatical realisations were compared across the two cultural groups and in different meeting types. Two main types of commissive acts were found: initiated versus uninitiated. The former can be defined as 'promises' and the latter 'offers'. Each one can be subdivided into direct or indirect realisations, resulting in four possible options (Table 18.4).

As shown in Table 18.4, generally speaking, western participants used more commissive acts, both initiated and uninitiated, than did Chinese participants (57 per cent versus 42 per cent). The most interesting difference is that western participants tended to make more use of uninitiated commissives, in the form of both direct and indirect realisations. However, Chinese participants made more use of initiated commissives owing to someone's request (33 per cent versus 26 per cent). The results are argued to be due to the western preference for spontaneity and the 'Chinese disposition in such contexts not to initiate conversation' (Bilbow 2002: 301). Another reason given by Bilbow was the linguistic disadvantage of the Chinese speakers who spoke English as their second language.

Declarations

Declarations are the least studied speech act in business discourse research, possibly because they are less frequently used than other speech acts, and they are usually restricted to more limited situations. Nie (2003) is a recent notable exception, which argues that before addressing the issue in question, Chinese business communicators have to establish proper relationships by using titles, hence defining their roles and responsibilities. This is also the case even when someone resigns from his or her position. This is argued to be the result of the two important Confucian principles: *li* (rituals/rules) and *ren* (love/benevolence). The following is the beginning of a resignation letter by a subordinate to his director: 'This humble subordinate, sheltered in the past twenty years by your honoured giant tree, always benefits from your instructions, so this humble subordinate will never forget your kindness until my teeth are decayed' (Nie 2003: 167). This inductive pattern in Chinese resignation letters marks an obvious

Table 18.5 Expectations of native English speakers in an adjustment letter

Elements	Sincerity	Insincerity
Amount written	As much as possible	As little as possible
Reasons for failure	Limited but relevant detail	Highly detailed
Apology	Single	Multiple
Solution	Offer	Don't offer

Source: adapted from White (2001: 66)

Table 18.6 Expectation of Polish speakers in an adjustment letter

Elements	Sincerity	Insincerity
Amount written	As much as possible	Too much (or too little)
Reasons for failure	Highly detailed	Limited detail
Apology	Multiple	Single
Solution	Offer	Don't offer

Source: adapted from White (2001: 67)

contrast with the direct approach in English resignation letters; nevertheless, Nie's research is based on limited data.

Applications of the co-operative principle to business discourse research

White (2001) puts Grice's co-operative principle in the context of writer–reader expectations. By analysing the responses of native English speakers to an adjustment letter (an institutional response to a complaint) written by a Polish writer, White argues that the four maxims in the co-operative principle may not be interpreted similarly in different cultures. To take the maxim of quality as an example: sincerity is a value subject to cultural variations. According to White, Table 18.5 shows what native English speakers expect when they read an adjustment letter, while Table 18.6 shows what a Polish speaker expects.

The communication will be smooth and without problems if writer's and reader's expectations converge. In the case of adjustment letters, English and Polish people tend to hold different assumptions as to what is considered sincere or insincere; in other words, they come to a different interpretation of Grice's maxim of quality. The overdetailed adjustment letter composed by the Polish writer was considered evasive and giving excuses instead of providing a solution to the problem. Nevertheless, White went on to argue that Grice's maxims are still valid but have to be adjusted for teaching purposes. He proposes using Grice's maxims as guidelines to increase students' awareness of the readers' culture and expectations. The following are sample questions that White (2001: 67–8) suggests using in teaching the genre of adjustment letters in EFL classes:

> What is the reader's main concern? In the letter of apology, this could be inconvenience, loss of business, financial loss, etc. (Maxim of Relation)

What are the constraints on meeting readers' expectations? Legal? Financial? Practical? (Maxim of Quality)

How much information is it feasible/sensible to provide? For instance, if we give too much information, is it likely to be used against us in litigation? (Maxim of Quantity)

Clyne (1994), in a similar vein, argues that Grice's maxims are useful but have to be revised when applied to other cultures. For example, Clyne argues that in content-oriented cultures, including those of many continental European and East/Southeast Asian countries, the maxim of quantity is not followed, and the rule is 'the more knowledge provided, the better' (p. 192). The maxim of quality ('Be true and don't say anything you lack evidence to support') may not be a criterion at all in Southeast Asian Chinese and Vietnamese cultures because of the presence of other dominant factors such as harmony and respect. How much information is needed (the maxim of relation) is closely related to power asymmetry in Asian cultures. What is considered as irrelevant in Anglo-Saxon cultures may be considered as relevant in Asian cultures, depending on factors such as the power difference between the addressor and addressee. The maxim of manner also has cultural variations. For example, ambiguity or vagueness is appropriate or even encouraged in academic cultures with a strong author orientation. In the light of the above problems, Clyne suggests that Grice's maxims be revised as follows:

> Quantity: A single maxim – Make your contribution as informative as is required for the purpose of discourse, within bounds of the discourse parameters of the given culture.
>
> Quality: Supermaxim – Try to make your contribution one for which you can take responsibility within your own cultural norms. Maxims: (1) Do not say what you believe to be in opposition to your cultural norms of truth, harmony, charity, and/or respect. (2) Do not say that for which you lack adequate evidence.
>
> Manner: The supermaxim can be retained in its original form – Be perspicacious. Maxims: (1) Do not make it any more difficult to understand than may be dictated by questions of face and authority. (2) Make clear your communicative intent unless this is against the interests of politeness or of maintaining a dignity-driven cultural core value, such as harmony, charity or respect. (3) Make your contribution the appropriate length required by the nature and purpose of exchange and the discourse parameters of your culture. (4) Structure your discourse according to the requirements of your culture. (Clyne 1994: 194)

A new maxim is also proposed to be included in the maxim of manner:

> In your contribution, take into account anything you know or can predict about the interlocutor's communication expectations. (Clyne 1994: 195)

The maxim of relation can be retained without changes. These revised maxims, as Clyne argues, can better accommodate the differences arising in intercultural communication.

Kong (2003) argues that instead of Grice's maxims of the co-operative principle being revised, they should be enriched by other possible maxims unique to an interactional situation, because general maxims may not be adequate to explain the sense-making mechanisms involved locally. Reliance on the four maxims may overlook other important sense-making criteria that are relevant only to a particular community or identity. For example, in network marketing interactions, the participants have both business and interpersonal relationships, as shown in the following example (Cantonese transcript; only English translations provided here).

Excerpt 1
1 N (Network marketer): My wife is fine. She's in the Mainland doing business.
2 P (Prospect): My boss is in the Mainland too, that's why I'm so busy.
3 N: Then recently do you feel tired?
4 P: Yeah, pretty much, but I can still manage. Oh right, where's your wife now?
5 N: Have you ever heard of XXX? I have been attending their health workshops. XXX are quite good.
6 P: Yeah, but I think I don't use that kind of products, I don't trust them.
7 N: No, you should try. They are really good.
8 P: Well: I don't need them.
9 N: Well: My wife said:

In turn 4 above, the prospect asks the network marketer how his wife is doing. To respond, the network marketer violates the maxim of relation by asking a seemingly irrelevant question: 'Have you ever heard of XXX (a popular brand name of network marketing products)?' Knowing about the brand name and the product's nature, the prospect can infer his friend's intention – to persuade him to buy certain products – and he rejects this selling move by denying his need for these products. The rejection is mitigated, however, through 'I think'. The marketer's continuous selling act results in the prospect's almost 'bald-on-record' blunt refusal with minimal mitigation in turn 8, which can be interpreted as a violation of the maxim of quantity. The marketer has no choice but to resume the previous topic, i.e. his wife.

On the surface, the co-operative principle is working and suffices to explain the situation. In other words, the participants co-operate with each other even when some maxims are violated and hence some implicatures are created. Nevertheless there are some prior assumptions that must hold true in order for the participants to engage successfully in sense-making. For example, how does the prospect know his friend is selling some products to him when he is violating the maxim of relation in turn 5? This could be simply a digression or mishearing of the prospect's question in the previous turn. In other words, why is the prospect certain about the exact intention of his friend? In addition, why does the network marketer stop his selling act altogether in turn 9, instead of continuing his attempt, as would be expected in unsolicited sales interactions involving strangers? Kong

(2003) argues that the maxims specific to friendship (intimacy, control, trust and positiveness) should be taken into consideration if one wants to capture the complete view of sense-making mechanisms.

Conclusion(s)

Two important concepts in pragmatics – speech act theory and the co-operative principle – have proven to be very useful in analysing universal and specific linguistic realisations of different speech functions within and across cultures. The speech act taxonomy is a useful framework upon which analysis can be based. In fact, other theoretical constructs, such as genre analysis (Swales 1990; Bhatia 1993), are useful in part precisely because they are firmly grounded in speech act theory for their emphasis on identifying the 'communication purpose' of a particular genre. Speech act theory also contributes to a better understanding of the function of language in shaping our identities in the workplace. Nevertheless, speech act theory should be applied with caution. Speech acts may be realised not only locally but globally. In other words, a letter of apology may contain a mixture of other speech acts, such as asserting and promising. Attention should also be paid to the complex interplay of macro- and micro-realisations.

Grice's co-operative principle is another useful starting point from which to investigate how communicators achieve a common understanding when they follow and violate underlying assumptions (the four maxims) of an interaction. The usefulness of the co-operative principle lies more in its ability to explain how people make sense of each other even when they appear not to be co-operating. In addition, the principle is important not only in understanding the language structure itself but also in uncovering the processes through which our identities are constructed in daily lives.

Acknowledgements

I would like to thank two anonymous reviewers for their useful suggestions.

Research was supported by Faculty Research Grant FRG/07-08/I-43, Hong Kong Baptist University.

Notes

1 It should be stressed that pragmatics is also a field of study with diverse interests and methods although this chapter focuses on the application of pragmatic concepts to workplace discourse.
2 Sometimes the meaning of ability can also be triggered in this request, for example, as a follow-up question to make sure the requestee is able to meet the deadline. I thank the reviewer for pointing this out.
3 Grice and Austin were colleagues at Oxford in the 1940s and 1950s (Thomas 2001: 116).

References

Austin, J. L. (1975) *How to Do Things with Words*, 2nd edn. Cambridge, MA: Harvard University Press.

Bargiela-Chiappini, F., C. Nickerson and B. Planken (2007) *Business Discourse*. Basingstoke: Palgrave Macmillan.

Bhatia, V. K. (1993) *Analysing Genre: Language in Professional Settings*. London: Longman.

Bilbow, G. (2002) Commissive speech act use in intercultural business meetings. *International Review of Applied Linguistics in Language Teaching*, 40(4): 287–303.

Blum-Kulka, S., J. House and G. Kasper (eds) (1989) *Cross-Cultural Pragmatics: Requests and Apologies*. Norwood; NJ: Ablex.

Bremer, K. (1996) *Achieving Understanding: Discourse in Intercultural Encounters*. London: Longman.

Brown, P. and S. Levinson (1987) *Politeness: Some Universals in Language Usage*. Cambridge: Cambridge University Press.

Clyne, M. (1981) Culture and discourse structure. *Journal of Pragmatics*, 5: 61–6.

Clyne, M. (1987) Culture differences in the organization of academic texts: English and German. *Journal of Pragmatics*, 11: 211–47.

Clyne, M. (1994) *Inter-Cultural Communication at Work*. Cambridge: Cambridge University Press.

Clyne, M., B. Martin and D. Neil (1991) Inter-cultural communication at work in Australia. *Multilingua*, 10: 251–73.

Cohen, A. and E. Olshtain (1981) Developing a measure of sociocultural competence: The case of apology. *Language Learning*, 31: 113–34.

Ewald, H. R. and D. Stine (1983) Speech act theory and business communication conventions. *Journal of Business Communication*, 20(3): 13–25.

Firth, A. (ed.) (1995) *The Discourse of Negotiation: Studies of Language in the Workplace*. Oxford: Pergamon.

Gabrenya, J. and K. K. Hwang (1996) Chinese social interaction: Harmony and hierarchy on the good earth. In M. H. Bond (ed.), *The Handbook of Chinese Psychology*. Hong Kong: Oxford University Press, pp. 309–21.

Grice, H. P. (1975) Logic and conversation. In P. Cole and J. Morgan (eds), *Syntax and Semantics. Vol. 3: Speech Acts*. New York: Academic Press, pp. 41–58.

Gumperz, J. J. (1982) *Discourse Strategies*. Cambridge: Cambridge University Press.

Hartford, B. and A. Mahboob (2004) Models of discourse in the letter of complaint. *World Englishes*, 23(4): 585–600.

Hyland, K. (1998) Exploring corporate rhetoric: Metadiscourse in the CEO's letter. *Journal of Business Communication*, 35(2): 224–45.

Kong, C. C. K. (1998) Are simple business request letters really simple? A comparison of Chinese and English business request letters. *Text*, 18: 103–41.

Kong, C. C. K. (2003) How to do business without losing friends: Negotiating friendship in conversations between network marketers and their prospects. *Language in Society*, 32(4): 487–522.

Kong, C. C. K. (2006) The use of accounts as a politeness strategy in the internal directive documents of business firms in Hong Kong. *Journal of Asian Pacific Communication* (special issue on Asian business discourse), 16(1): 75–99.

Levinson, S. (1983) *Pragmatics*. Cambridge: Cambridge University Press.

Maier, P. (1992) Politeness strategies in business letters by native and non-native speakers. *English for Specific Purposes*, 11: 189–205.

Matsumoto, Y. (1989) Politeness and conversational universals: Observations from Japanese. *Multilingua*, 8(2–3): 207–21.

Mey, J. (2001) *Pragmatics: An Introduction*. Oxford: Blackwell.

Mulholland, J. (1991) *The Language of Negotiation: A Handbook of Practical Strategies for Improving Communication*. London: Routledge.

Mulholland, J. (1994) *Handbook of Persuasive Tactics: A Practical Language Guide*. London: Routledge.

Murphy, B. and J. Neu (1996) My grade's too low: The speech act set of complaining. In M. Glass and J. New (eds), *Speech Acts across Cultures: Challenges to Communication in a Second Language*. New York: Mouton de Gruyter, pp. 191–216.

Nie, S. (2003) Resignation letter to departmental director. In Z. Feng (ed.), *A Comprehensive Reader of Social Interactions. Vol. 3*. Shanghai: Cultural Books, p. 167.

Owen, M. (1984) *Apologies and Remedial Interchanges: A Study of Language Use in Social Interaction*. Berlin: de Gruyter.

Rinnert, C., Y. Nogami and C. Iwa (2006) Preferred complaint strategies in Japanese and English. *Authentic Communication Proceedings of the 5th Annual JALT Pan-SIG Conference. May 13–14. Shizuoka, Japan: Tokai University of Marine Science*: 32–47.

Schiffrin, D. (1990) The management of a co-operative self during argument: The role of opinions and stories in arguments. In A. D. Grimshaw (ed.), *Conflict Talk*. Cambridge: Cambridge University Press, pp. 241–59.

Searle, J. R. (1975) A taxonomy of illocutionary acts. In K. Gunderson (ed.), *Language, Mind, and Knowledge*. Minneapolis: University of Minnesota Press, pp. 344–69.

Sperber, D. and D. Wilson (1995), *Relevance: Communication and Cognition*, 2nd edn. Cambridge, MA: Harvard University Press.

Staplers, J. (1995) The expression of disagreement. In K. Ehlich and J. Wagner (eds), *The Discourse of Business Negotiations*. New York: Mouton de Gruyter, pp. 275–90.

Thomas, J. (1995) *Meaning in Interaction: An Introduction to Pragmatics*. London: Longman.

Thomas, J. (2001) Conversational maxims. In J. R. Mesthrie (ed.), *Concise Encyclopedia of Sociolinguistics*. New York: Elsevier, pp. 116–21.

Swales, J. (1990) *Genre Analysis: English in Academic and Research Settings*. Cambridge: Cambridge University Press.

White, R. (2001) Adapting Grice's maxims in the teaching of writing. *ELT Journal*, 55(1): 62–9.

Yule, G. (1996) *Pragmatics*. Oxford: Oxford University Press.

19

Organisational communication

Amy M. Schmisseur, Guowei Jian and Gail T. Fairhurst

Introduction

The study of discourse in a business context has become an increasingly popular area of research, as evidenced by the number of special issues, book chapters, literature reviews and cross-disciplinary collaborations, including this *Handbook* (Bargiela-Chiappini and Nickerson 2002; Grant et al. 2004; Keenoy et al. 1997; Putnam and Fairhurst 2001). However, with such proliferation comes the need to understand and clarify the respective contributions of the disciplines doing organisational discourse research, given that their theoretical interests, assumptive bases and preferred methods may vary. The purpose of this chapter, then, is to focus on organisational communication (OC) and the discursive research initiated by a number of its scholars, several of whom have been at the forefront in casting organisations as discursive constructions (Cooren and Taylor 1997; Fairhurst and Putnam 2004).

In many countries, business discourse analysts teach organisational communication while residing in business schools. The OC discourse analyst may reside in a school of communication or liberal arts college – primarily, though not exclusively, in the United States. Both business discourse and OC scholars are likely to share some antipathy towards a psychological paradigm (for example, leadership psychology) and quantitative methods as the most appropriate way to study communication in organisations (Bargiela-Chiappini and Nickerson 2002; Fairhurst 2007). Both also recognise the interdisciplinary possibilities associated with the term 'discourse' rather than 'communication.' However, as this chapter will show, OC discourse scholars prefer the term 'organisational' to 'business' discourse and entertain some distinct concerns from business discourse with respect to how organisation and communication processes are conceptualised. Again, our aim is to clarify and, hopefully, encourage more interdisciplinary dialogue. With these objectives in mind, we first offer an overview of the field of organisational communication and its orientations to discourse studies, followed by a brief review of the organisational communication discourse research and a discussion of how OC scholars view both the organisation–discourse and communication–discourse relationships. We then conclude with a brief commentary on the scholarly and practical implications of pursuing interdisciplinary discourse research.

Organisational communication

As a subdiscipline within the larger field of communication studies, OC is grounded in both the social sciences and humanities (vis-à-vis the study of rhetoric). The term 'organisational communication' was not officially coined until the 1960s, although its roots really originated a decade earlier out of a need for basic communication skills training for US supervisors in a post-World War II era (Redding 1985). Since that time, the field has evolved from a focus on managerial interests to a multiperspective field with an interdisciplinary identity that is eclectic in its approach to theories, methods and research (Mumby 2007). In addition to organisational discourse, OC scholars study communication networks and roles, information processing and group decision-making, leadership, organisational climate and culture, power and politics, organisational identity and image, complex adaptive systems, and communication technologies, among others. Discourse analysts often join with media scholars, rhetoricians and social scientists to form communication studies programmes.

As a set of empirical phenomena, OC is often cast as a primary or secondary process. Most social scientists outside of the field of communication studies cast it as a secondary social process, where communication is only one of several processes or an outcome of one or more traits, states, emotions or cognitive processing styles that influences message behaviour. Scholars outside of the field are also more likely to cast communication as a simple act of transmission, as reflected in the Shannon and Weaver (1949) model and the conduit metaphor (Axley 1984). Those using this model conceive of organisations as stable entities engaged in information processing and dissemination in order to meet institutional goals and objectives.

However, for OC discourse scholars, communication is a primary social process and as much a site of meaning construction and negotiation as an act of transmission. Meaning-centred communication models have been heavily influenced by the linguistic turn in the social sciences in which language is constitutive of reality, not merely reflective of it, and language is performative of social action (Austin 1962; Bochner 1985; Wittgenstein 1953). As such, in varying degrees (depending upon one's theoretical orientation), OC discourse scholars are likely to do the following.

Problematise issues of meaning. For example, what does it mean to cast organisational cultures as systems of shared meanings, or to cast leadership as the management of meaning with shared meaning the presumed goal (Eisenberg and Riley 2001; Fairhurst 2001; Putnam 1983)? Is shared meaning possible or do communicators merely act *as if* they share meaning (Ellis 1995)? Is shared meaning necessary for coordinated action (Eisenberg 1984, 1990)? Are issues of power always central to the management and negotiation of meaning (Deetz 1992)?

Pursue relational over individual unit of analyses. OC discourse scholars are more likely to reject communication as a simple act of transmission where individual senders or receivers are the unit of analysis. Instead, these scholars often pursue a transactional model of communication in which senders and receivers are encoding and decoding messages simultaneously such that a time order is indiscernible and the *relationship* between communicators is the unit of analysis. As such, meaning is always co-defined and may be contested and resisted.

Pursue process over static forms of human systems. OC discourse scholars are more likely to see the limits of survey research, in which retrospective summarising judgements are gathered, to study relationships. Such methods are prone to reified views of the relationship. By contrast, as people position themselves with respect to one another through language in social interaction, relationships evolve from message patterns and evolving communication systems. Theoretically what constitutes a 'system' could be a leadership relationship, a work unit (such as a team, department or plant) or a whole organisation. All are predicated on the more process-oriented view that systems emerge over repeated interactions that evolve into multilevelled orders of pattern (Bateson 1972).

View context as multilayered and dynamic. OC discourse scholars question the notion of a stable context, citing Bateson (1972), who noted that each action is '*part* of the ecological subsystem called context and not as the product or effect of what remains of the context after the piece which we want to explain has been cut from it' (p. 338, emphasis in the original). However, levels of context go beyond immediately preceding utterances to include identities, relationships, groups, organisational cultures and sociohistorical influences reflexively interrelated at given moments in time.

Problematise agency amidst constraint. Many OC discourse analysts adopt the more general ethnomethodological argument of Garfinkel (1967) that action is organised from within – meaning that actors are knowledgeable agents, who reflexively monitor the ongoing character of social life as they continuously orient to and position themselves vis-à-vis specific norms, rules, procedures and values in interaction with others. However, critics question whether such a view exaggerates the role of agency, especially when considering the impact of power and politics, that is, how agency becomes constrained by material forces such as the brute facts of a physical world (for example, buildings, mountains and texts; Cooren 2001; Taylor and Van Every 2000), science's putative objective procedures (Edwards 1997), or macro-social contexts of institutions and power relations (Deetz 1992; Mumby 2001). Critical scholars charge that inattention to material forces leaves discursive approaches prone to *relativism* (Reed 2000), such that reality is just what actors define it to be, and *discoursism*, in which the organisation collapses into discourse irrespective of the material conditions that constrain it (Conrad 2004).

Problematise discourse as operating on more than one level. OC discourse analysts study discourse in wide-ranging ways. This includes the study of text and talk in social practices, what Alvesson and Kärreman (2000) call little 'd' *d*iscourse; the study of general and enduring systems of thought, termed big 'D' *D*iscourse; and all points in between. Viewed as a local accomplishment, *d*iscourse embodies cultural meanings, and the details of language use and talk-in-interaction are its central concerns. Talk-in-interaction involves the sending and receiving of messages, the conversing or 'doing' of organisational *d*iscourse, whereas text is the 'done' or the material representation of *d*iscourse in spoken or written terms. As such, texts have unique properties such as the capacity to absorb, influence and transform other texts and thus produce intertextual meaning (Fairclough 1995; Fairclough and Wodak 1997). They also endure and generate meaning independent of their author(s) (Cooren 2001). By contrast, *D*iscourses are formed by constellations of ideas, talk patterns, logics and assumptions that constitute objects and subjects and order and naturalise the world in particular ways (Foucault 1980, 1995). Culturally standardised *D*iscourses such as those involving managerialism, entrepreneurialism, masculinity and femininity are institutionalised forms of intelligibility that supply linguistic resources to communicating actors (Shapiro 1992).

With these orientations in mind, we now turn to an overview of current OC discourse research. We then seek to problematise the discourse-organisation and discourse-communication relationships.

Organisational communication discourse research: An overview

As mentioned above, OC discursive research employs diverse discourse theories and methods. In the discussion below, we make no attempt to be exhaustive, given space limitations. However, our purpose is to give the reader a sampling of OC's diverse research efforts, divided roughly into the study of *d*iscourse as language and interaction, *D*iscourse as a system of thought, and multiple levels of *d*/*D*iscourse (for a more comprehensive review, see Putnam and Fairhurst 2001).

Language and interaction view of discourse

A large body of OC research studies *d*iscourse as language and interaction (little 'd' discourse) to understand how actors construct emotions, attitudes, identities, work relationships, organisational problems and knowledge, and organising processes. However, several subgenres are distinguishable in the OC literature, including interaction analysis (Fairhurst 2004), conversation analysis (Boden 1994) and speech act schematics (Cooren 2001).

For example, interaction analysis involves the categorisation of *d*iscourse units into a predefined set of codes. It is a quantitative approach to *d*iscourse analysis that draws from message functions and language structures to assess the frequency and types of verbal communication (Fairhurst 2004). Coding enables analysts to study the sequences and stages of interaction, their redundancy and predictability, and the link between interaction structure and context (Putnam and Fairhurst 2001). Various forms of interaction analysis have been used to study leader–member control sharing in mechanistic versus organic systems (Fairhurst et al. 1995), bargaining and negotiation (Putnam and Wilson 1989) and technology appropriation (DeSanctis and Poole 1994), among others.

Conversation analysts eschew coding schemes and a priori analytic concepts like control. Emphasis is given to how actors use various interactional methods and procedures to produce their activities and make sense of their worlds (Sacks 1992). OC conversation analysts follow Boden's (1994) lead in emphasising the ethnomethodological ties to conversation analysis. For example, Pomerantz et al. (1997) found that spatial positioning, word choice and ambiguity play a critical role in shaping identities and managing impressions in hospital settings. Cooren (2004) examined the co-production and co-completion of utterances in board member discussions to assess whether 'collective minding' (Weick and Roberts 1993) could be achieved in seemingly mundane situations such as board meetings. Fairhurst (2007) and Fairhurst and Cooren (2004) analysed the distributed nature of leadership in a high-reliability organisation through turn-taking and membership categorisation.

Speech act schematics focuses on the performative nature of language through speech acts such as directives, assertives, commissives, expressives and so on (Austin 1975; Searle 1979); however, emphasis is given to the sequential order of speech acts in episodic encounters (Cooren 2001). Research using this approach has examined coalition-building during ecological controversies (Cooren and Taylor 2000), the management of public town council meetings (Robichaud 2003) and parliamentary commissions (Cooren and Taylor 1998), among others.

Drawing more generally from the above traditions, a number of OC *d*iscursive studies refer to *d*iscourse as the communication that takes place during the organising process and the associated meanings shaped through retrospective sense-making. Taking a broadly constructionist stance, these analyses regard *d*iscourse as a type of organisational sense-making that helps shape meanings for key organisational events such as crises (Seeger and Ulmer 2002), downsizings (Fairhurst et al. 2002) and job loss (Buzzanell and Turner 2003), to name a few. Other studies focus more directly on the role of narrative in constructing discursive realities. For example, Browning's (1992) investigation of technical communication sheds light on the ways in which lists and stories serve to structure organisations. Lucas and Buzzanell (2004) examine how the occupational narratives of miners serve to construct a sense of pride about their work as well as redefine notions of success as traditionally defined by white-collar work, while Fairhurst (2007) examines the role of narrative in constructing leader–member exchanges of high, medium and low quality.

Finally, Schneider (2001) studies the construction of organisational knowledge through exploring the interrelationship between talk and writing. Her findings suggest that the practice of note-taking and the interaction of text and talk involved with the interviewing process build 'legitimate' knowledge necessary for credible decision-making in organisations.

Discourse as a system of thought

Although clearly different, both critical and postmodern/poststructuralist perspectives contribute to the study of *D*iscourse as a system of thought (Alvesson and Deetz 1996). For example, more critical research emphasises *D*iscourse as systems of power/knowledge displayed through culturally standardised interpretative frames, such as workplace health promotion *D*iscourse (Zoller 2003a, 2003b) or the *D*iscourse of 'appropriate technology' (Ganesh 2003). *D*iscourses are not only historically anchored, boundary spanning, and manifest in linguistic and extra-linguistic practices, but constitute workers' subjectivities, establish and naturalise managerial control, and discipline the productive body.

Other strains of critical research examine the formation of a *D*iscourse as an assembly of others within a unique historical context. For instance, Medved and Kirby (2005) reveal that the corporate mothering *D*iscourse, which often marginalises women's role as caregivers, is formed 'at the confluence of three distinct yet interrelated streams of *D*iscourse: ideologies of mothering in relation to the public or private spheres, the contemporary privileging of the organisation, and feminist debates on motherhood' (p. 461). Likewise, in his study of a Princeton laboratory, Kinsella (1999) argues that power and knowledge are disseminated and emerge as action when both the technical claims and counter-claims of a scientific community converge with *D*iscourses surrounding the social norms and expectations governing a particular culture.

Drawing from poststructuralism, other studies focus on how the intersection of several *D*iscourses offer actors a 'space of action,' a term used by Daudi (1986) to refer to individuals' 'striving for freedom, for autonomy and for personal interest' (p. 124). When individuals rebel against the ways a *D*iscourse defines them, a space is created between the hegemonic attempts of a *D*iscourse to affix meaning and whatever meaning potentials constitute resistance (Fleming 2005; Mumby 1997, 2005). As subjects experience something lacking in a *D*iscourse to which they have been linked, they have room to resist within a competitively structured discursive field. For example, Holmer-Nadeson (1996) demonstrated how a group of women service workers at a public university exploited the contradictions within patriarchal, bureaucratic and capitalistic *D*iscourses to resist and counter-identify with the organisational roles ascribed to them. Harter et al. (2006) examined the *D*iscourse of members belonging to a non-profit organisation that provided employment opportunities to individuals with disabilities. Although disabilities *D*iscourse is most often characterised by a sense of exclusion and inferiority, their analysis revealed a set of counter-narratives that ultimately resisted these traditional *D*iscourses and promoted a community of integration and inclusion instead.

Multiple levels of d/Discourse

Increasing amounts of OC discourse research suggest the interplay of *d*iscourse and *D*iscourses at multiple levels. Consider Zorn et al.'s (2000) study of organisational change and managerialist *D*iscourse, which embodied the *d*iscourse of organisational development programmes, various concepts and language from popular business press and academic *D*iscourses, and cultural *D*iscourses regarding the larger fascination with change in contemporary society.

Much OC discursive research focuses on gender as omni-present and constitutive of organising at multiple levels (Ashcraft and Mumby 2004). For example, Buzzanell and Liu (2005) uncovered a number of contradictions and ironies in women's accounts regarding their maternity leave. Using a poststructuralist feminist analysis, these researchers were able to unveil the instability of individuals' language, including the various subjectivities and constitutive elements of their sense-making discourse. Fairhurst (2007) examined gender-based *D*iscourses of difference, including the exclusion of women executives from the 'alpha' category in executive coaching *D*iscourses, while demonstrating one female CEO's use of emasculating matriarchal language and argument that left little doubt as to her 'alpha-ness'. Finally, Ashcraft and Mumby (2004) led the way in OC work on the construction of masculinity in, for example, their in-depth feminist communicology of the airline pilot.

Drawing from Fairclough (1993), critical discourse analysis (CDA) focuses on the dialectical and often opaque relationship between micro-level discourses (spoken or written language use) and more macro-levels or 'orders of discourse' involving the 'totality of discursive practices of an institution, and relationships between them' (p. 135). Livesey (2002) used CDA in her analysis of a social report published by the Royal Dutch/Shell Group. She argues that while some may have interpreted the corporate *d*iscourse as an attempt to regain hegemonic control, such *d*iscourse appeared indicative of the ongoing struggle within the organisation to reconcile economic and ecological goals – a process that transformed the organisation. Using the critical linguistics of Fowler (1981, 1986), Brenton (1993) analysed a challenge to religious authority and the resulting legitimation attempt, demonstrating the ways in which language can achieve ideological control and conversational implicature can be exploited to created double binds for those in power.

The relationship between discourse and the organisation

OC scholars have had a long-standing concern with challenging positivist reifications of the organisation, asking *not* what is communicative about organisations, but what is organising about communication (Cooren and Taylor 1997; McPhee and Zaug 2000; Putnam 1983; Smith 1993). Its discourse analysts entered the debate with Fairhurst and Putnam's (2004) literature review of organisations as 'discursive constructions', in which they demonstrated analysts' varied orientations to the relationship between discourse (broadly defined) and organisation: object, becoming and grounded-in-action. Discourse through the object orientation sees the organisation as a pre-formed object with discursive features and outcomes, while the becoming orientation conceptualises the organisation as in a perpetual state of becoming based on the organising properties of discourse (for example, how people position themselves with respect to one another through language). Finally, the grounded-in-action orientation attempts to resolve dualistic conceptions of micro-macro-concerns and agency/ structure by conceptualising organisation at the level of social practices and discursive forms. The authors assert that all three orientations are necessary stances for discourse analysts in order to capture the complexity of the organisation–discourse relationship.

However, there have been several interesting issues associated with this debate, including McPhee and Zaug's (2000) critique of the becoming orientation, in which they question how the organising properties of discourse beget the complex form 'organisation'. Instead, they call on OC scholars to explore membership negotiation, organisational self-structuring, activity coordination and institutional positioning as four key processes constitutive of organisations. Taylor and Cooren (1997) likewise address a key issue in the object orientation, concerning how the voices of the many within a collective translate into the voice of the organisation. Taylor and Van Every (2000) go on to describe human systems as intrinsically binary, in which the activity of individuals or the system as an object is emphasised. Depending upon whether activity or the system is emphasised, communication is either interactive speech mediated by text or an intertext mediated by interactive speech.

The relationship between discourse and communication

The relationship between discourse and communication is a complex one both inside and outside the field of organisational communication. Presumably, communication is of interest to discourse scholars of all stripes, although interest in human interaction varies, as the distinction between *d*iscourse and *D*iscourse makes clear. Scholars who study *D*iscourse are less concerned with the details of social interaction and more concerned with the linguistic resources, or what discursive psychologists label the 'interpretative repertoire' (Potter and Wetherell 1987), of social actors. However, there is also substantial disagreement over the terms 'communication' and 'discourse'. For example, in writing about conversation analysis' emphasis on talk-as-action, Edwards (1997) viewed it as antithetical to what he called a 'communication model', in which communication is cast strictly as a means of expressing speaker intentions and an act of transmission. Yet most communication theorists in the discipline of communication neither endorse a strict transmission model of communication, nor equate the study of communication with speaker intentionality and its transmission aspects (Craig 1999).

Contra Edwards (1997), some organisational communication theorists like Taylor (personal communication, May 2002) actually prefer the term 'communication' to 'discourse' because the latter term obscures the relationship between interactive speech and text, a relationship that Taylor believes explains the way the organisation emerges in communication (Taylor and Van Every 2000). Finally, the organisational discourse literature appears relatively unconcerned with communication issues over the putatively endless deferral of meaning in the poststructuralist debate (Derrida 1988; Ellis 1995) and how tightly coupled linguistic practices are with meaning (Alvesson and Karreman 2000). Both issues are instrumental in answering the question, 'how is communication brought off?'

Moving forward

Given the debate occurring in the business discourse literature, perhaps a third relationship to query concerns that of 'business' versus 'organisational' discourse. Bargiela-Chiappini and Nickerson (2002) rightly predict the critical OC scholars' response to 'business discourse' as evocative of a 'symbiotic relationship with the corporate world' (Mumby and Stohl 1996: 56), one that potentially marginalises concerns with deep structure power and politics (Deetz 1992). The current research in business discourse appears to have its greatest affinity with the language and interaction (little 'd' *d*iscourse) OC scholars, who emphasise the more surface aspects of power. However, as business discourse further crosses disciplinary boundaries with organisational communication, critical management and others, attention to more deeply embedded structures of power should be increasingly evident.

If OC discourse scholars can further sensitise business discourse analysts to power issues, perhaps the latter can influence OC scholars to increase the amount of their intercultural work, which pales in comparison to business discourse. Work by Cheney and colleagues (Cheney 1999; Ganesh et al. 2005) stands out as a notable exception. While there are a number of intercultural communication scholars, most cannot capture the complexities of the organisational context without some grounding in the organisational sciences. Closer interaction between OC and business discourse scholars should influence the former to tackle the complexities of intercultural, organisational discursive research, which is so much needed in an increasingly global society.

Nowhere is this need greater than in the education of business management professionals, whose orientations towards communication are often to ignore or minimise it (Fairhurst 2005). More recently calls have been made for business schools to focus more attention on the required skills of a profession (Bennis and O'Toole 2005), including communication. Yet, even with the growing interest in 'soft skills' in some top business programmes today, there remains little instruction or learning on how our discourse creates systems of meaning and, thus, action in organisations. Perhaps, as Holt (1998) suggests, managers need to become discourse analysts – trained in their sensitivity to language, the sequential flow of social interaction, the interpretative repertoires that *D*iscourses make available to communicating actors, and the multiple levels of context that call forth the need for linguistic precision and variety. Perhaps if such knowledge were acquired and ultimately put into practice, managers would be more confident in navigating the politicised aspects of work life and more adept in handling the communicative challenges brought on by a multicultural and largely distributed workforce.

Finally, with work such as Bargiela-Chiappini and Nickerson (2002) and this *Handbook*, the writers on business discourse are signalling ferment in the field of unprecedented proportions. Despite practical limitations, scholars have called for stronger research communities characterised by multidisplinary perspectives (e.g. Goswami 1999). Indeed, we must reconsider our respective disciplines and their boundaries to focus on our common need for multifaceted, multimethod, multidisciplinary and multicultural research that would better capture the discursive and communicative complexities of organisational life in the twenty-first century. This *Handbook* is a welcome addition in this regard.

References

Alvesson, M. and S. A. Deetz (1996) Critical theory and postmodernism approaches to organizational studies. In S. R. Clegg, C. Hardy and W. R. Nord (eds), *Handbook of Organization Studies*. London: Sage, pp. 191–217.

Alvesson, M. and D. Kärreman (2000) Varieties of discourse: On the study of organisations through discourse analysis. *Human Relations*, 53(9): 1125–49.

Ashcraft, K. L. and D. K. Mumby (2004) *Reworking Gender: A Feminist Communicology of Organizations*. Thousand Oaks, CA: Sage.

Austin, J. (1962) *How to Do Things with Words*. Oxford: Oxford University Press.

Austin, J. (1975) *How to Do Things with Words*, 2nd edn. Cambridge, MA: Harvard University Press.

Axley, S. R. (1984) Managerial and organisational communication in terms of the conduit metaphor. *Academy of Management Review*, 9: 428–37.

Bargiela-Chiappini, F. and C. Nickerson (2002) Business discourse: Old debates, new horizons. *International Review of Applied Linguistics in Language Teaching*, 40(4): 273–86.

Bateson, G. (1972) *Steps to an Ecology of the Mind*. New York: Ballantine.

Bennis, W. G. and J. O'Toole (2005) How business schools lost their way. *Harvard Business Review*, 83: 96–104.

Bochner, A. P. (1985) Perspectives on inquiry: Representation, conversation, and reflection. In M. L. Knapp and G. R. Miller (eds), *Handbook of Interpersonal Communication*. Beverly Hills, CA: Sage, pp. 27–58.

Boden, D. (1994) *The Business of Talk: Organisations in Action*. Cambridge: Polity.

Brenton, A. L. (1993) Demystifying the magic of language: Critical linguistic case analysis of legitimation of authority. *Journal of Applied Behavioral Science*, 21: 227–44.

Browning, L. (1992) Lists and stories as organizational communication. *Communication Theory*, 2(4): 281–302.

Buzzanell, P. M. and M. Liu (2005) Struggling with maternity leave policies and practices: A poststructuralist feminist analysis of gendered organizing. *Journal of Applied Communication Research*, 33: 1–25.

Buzzanell, P. M. and L. H. Turner (2003) Emotion work revealed by job loss discourse: Backgrounding-foregrounding of feelings, construction of normalcy, and (re)instituting of traditional masculinities. *Journal of Applied Communication Research*, 31(1): 27–57.

Cheney, G. (1999) *Values at Work: Employee Participation Meets Market Pressure at Mondragon*. Ithaca, NY: Cornell University Press.

Conrad, C. (2004) Organizational discourse analysis: Avoiding the determinism–volunteerism trap. *Organization*, 11: 427–39.

Cooren, F. (2001) *The Organizing Property of Communication*. Amsterdam and Philadelphia: John Benjamins.

Cooren, F. (2004) The communicative achievement of collective minding: In-depth analysis of a board meeting excerpt. *Management Communication Quarterly*, 17(4): 517–51.

Cooren, F. and J. R. Taylor (1997) Organization as an effect of mediation: Redefining the link between organization and communication. *Communication Theory*, 7: 219–60.

Cooren, F. and J. R. Taylor (1998) The procedural and rhetorical modes of the organizing dimension of communication: Discursive analysis of a parliamentary commission. *Communication Review*, 3: 65–101.

Cooren, F. and J. R. Taylor (2000) Association and dissociation in an ecological controversy: The great whale case. In N. W. Coppola and B. Karis (eds), *Technical Communication, Deliberative Rhetoric, and Environmental Discourse: Connections and Directions*. Stamford, CT: Ablex, pp. 171–90.

Craig, R. (1999) Communication theory as a field. *Communication Theory*, 9: 119–61.

Daudi, P. (1986) *Power in the Organisation*. Oxford: Blackwell.

Deetz, S. A. (1992) *Democracy in an Age of Corporate Colonization: Developments in Communication and the Politics of Everyday Life*. Albany, NY: SUNY Press.

Derrida, J. (1998) *Limited Inc*. Evanston, IL: Northwestern University Press.

DeSanctis, G. and M. S. Poole (1994) Capturing the complexity in advanced technology use: Adaptive structuration theory. *Organization Science*, 5: 121–47.

Edwards, D. (1997) *Discourse and Cognition*. London: Sage.

Eisenberg, E. (1984) Ambiguity as strategy in organizational communication. *Communication Monographs*, 51: 227–42.

Eisenberg, E. (1990) Jamming: Transcendence through organizing. *Communication Research*, 17: 139–64.

Eisenberg, E. and P. Riley (2001) Organizational culture. In F. Jablin and L. L. Putnam (eds), *The New Handbook of Organizational Communication: Advances in Theory, Research, and Methods*. Thousand Oaks, CA: Sage, pp. 291–322.

Ellis, D. G. (1995) Fixing communicative meaning: A coherentist theory. *Communication Research*, 22: 515–44.

Fairclough, N. (1993) Critical discourse analysis and the marketization of public discourse: The universities. *Discourse & Society*, 4: 133–68.

Fairclough, N. (1995) *Critical Discourse Analysis: The Critical Study of Language*. London: Longman.

Fairclough, N. and R. Wodak (1997) Critical discourse analysis. In T. A. van Dijk (ed.), *Discourse as Social Interaction*. London: Sage, pp. 258–84.

Fairhurst, G. (2001) Dualisms in leadership research. In F. M. Jablin and L. L. Putnam (eds), *The New Handbook of Organizational Communication: Advances in Theory, Research, and Methods*. Thousand Oaks, CA: Sage, pp. 379–439.

Fairhurst, G. (2004) Textuality and agency in interaction analysis. *Organization*, 11: 335–54.

Fairhurst, G. T. (2005) Reframing the art of framing: Problems and prospects for leadership. *Leadership*, 1: 165–85.

Fairhurst, G. (2007) *Discursive Leadership: In Conversation with Leadership Psychology.* Thousand Oaks, CA: Sage.

Fairhurst, G. and F. Cooren (2004) Organizational language in use: Interaction analysis, conversation analysis, and speech act schematics. In D. Grant, C. Hardy, C. Oswick, N. Philips and L. Putnam (eds), *The Sage Handbook of Organizational Discourse.* London: Sage, pp. 131–52.

Fairhurst, G. T. and L. Putnam (2004) Organizations as discursive construction. *Communication Theory*, 14: 5–26.

Fairhurst, G., S. G. Green and J. A. Courtright (1995) Inertial forces and the implementation of a socio-technical systems approach: A communication study. *Organisation Science*, 6: 168–85.

Fairhurst, G. T., F. Cooren and D. J. Cahill (2002) Discursiveness, contradiction, and unintended consequences in successive downsizings. *Management Communication Quarterly*, 15(4): 501–40.

Fleming, P. (2005) Metaphors of resistance. *Management Communication Quarterly*, 19: 45–66.

Foucault, M. (1980) *Power/Knowledge: Selected Interviews and Other Writings 1972-1977.* New York: Pantheon.

Foucault, M. (1995) *Discipline and Punish.* New York: Vintage and Random House.

Fowler, R. (1981) *Literature as Social Discourse: The Practice of Linguistic Criticism.* Bloomington: Indiana University Press.

Fowler, R. (1986) *Linguistic Criticism.* Oxford: Oxford University Press.

Ganesh, S. (2003) Organizational narcissism: Technology, legitimacy, and identity in an Indian NGO. *Management Communication Quarterly*, 16(4): 558–94.

Ganesh, S., H. M. Zoller and G. Cheney (2005) Transforming resistance: Critical organizational communication meets globalization from below. *Communication Monographs*, 72: 169–91.

Garfinkel, H. (1967) *Studies in Ethnomethodology.* Englewood Cliffs, NJ: Prentice Hall.

Goswami, D. (1999) Afterword: Teaching and research directions for international professional communication. In C. R. Lovitt and D. Goswami (eds), *Exploring the Rhetoric of International Professional Communication: An Agenda for Teachers and Researchers.* Amityville, NY: Baywood.

Grant, D., C. Hardy, C. Oswick and L. Putnam (2004) Introduction: Organizational discourse: Exploring the field. In D. Grant, C. Hardy, C. Oswick and L. Putnam (eds), *The Sage Handbook of Organizational Discourse.* Thousand Oaks, CA: Sage, pp. 1–36.

Harter, L. M., J. A. Scott, D. R. Novak, M. Leeman and J. F. Morris (2006) Freedom through flight: Performing a counter-narrative of disability. *Journal of Applied Communication Research*, 34(1): 3–29.

Holmer-Nadesan, M. (1996) Organizational identity and space of action. *Organization Studies*, 17(1): 49–81.

Holt, G. R. (1998) Talk about acting and constraint in stories about organizations. *Western Journal of Communication*, 53: 374–97.

Keenoy, T., C. Oswick and D. Grant (1997) Organisational discourses: Texts and contexts. *Organisation*, 4: 147–57.

Kinsella, W. J. (1999) Discourse, power, and knowledge in the management of 'big science': The production of consensus in a nuclear fusion research laboratory. *Management Communication Quarterly*, 13(2): 171–208.

Livesey, S. M. (2002) The discourse of the middle ground: Citizen Shell commits to sustainable development. *Management Communication Quarterly*, 15(3): 313–49.

Lucas, K. and P. M. Buzzanell (2004) Blue-collar work, career, and success: Occupational narratives of Sisu. *Journal of Applied Communication Research*, 32: 273–92.

McPhee, R. D. and P. Zaug (2000) The communicative constitution of organization: A framework for explanation. *Electronic Journal of Communication*, 10: 1–16.

Medved, C. E. and E. Kirby (2005) Family CEOs: A feminist analysis of corporate mothering discourses. *Management Communication Quarterly*, 18(4): 435–78.

Mumby, D. K. (1997) The problem of hegemony: Reading Gramsci for organizational communication studies. *Western Journal of Communication*, 61: 343–75.

Mumby, D. K. (2001) Power and politics. In F. M. Jablin and L. L. Putnam (eds), *The New Handbook of Organizational Communication: Advances in Theory, Research, and Methods*. Thousand Oaks, CA: Sage, pp. 585–623.

Mumby, D. K. (2005) Theorizing resistance in organisation studies: A dialectical approach. *Management Communication Quarterly*, 19: 1–26.

Mumby, D. K. (2007) Organizational communication. In G. Ritzer (ed.), *The Encyclopedia of Sociology*. Oxford: Blackwell, pp. 3290–9.

Mumby, D. K. and C. Stohl (1996) Disciplining organizational communication studies. *Management Communication Quarterly*, 10(1): 50–72.

Pomerantz, A., B. J. Fehr and J. Ende (1997) When supervising physicians see patients. *Human Communication Research*, 23: 589–615.

Potter, J. and M. Wetherell (1987) *Discourse and Social Psychology*. London: Sage.

Putnam, L. L. (1983) Organizational communication: Toward a research agenda. In L. L. Putnam and M. E. Pacanowsky (eds), *Communication and Organizations: An Interpretive Approach*. Beverly Hills, CA: Sage, pp. 31–54.

Putnam, L. L. and G. Fairhurst (2001) Discourse analysis in organizations. In F. M. Jablin and L. L. Putnam (eds), *The New Handbook of Organizational Communication*. Thousand Oaks, CA: Sage, pp. 78–136.

Putnam, L. L. and S. R. Wilson (1989) Argumentation and bargaining strategies as discriminators of integrative outcomes. In M. A. Rahim (ed.), *Managing Conflict: An Interdisciplinary Approach*. New York: Praeger, pp. 121–41.

Redding, W. C. (1985) Stumbling toward identity: The emergence of organizational communication as a field of study. In R. D. McPhee and P. K. Tompkins (eds), *Organizational Communication: Traditional Themes and New Directions*. Beverly Hills, CA: Sage, pp. 15–54.

Reed, M. I. (2000) The limits of discourse analysis in organization analysis. *Organization*, 7: 524–30.

Robichaud, D. (2003) Narrative institutions we organise by: The case of a municipal administration. In B. Czarniawska and P. Gagliardi (eds), *Narratives We Organise By*. Amsterdam: John Benjamins, pp. 37–53.

Sacks, H. (1992) *Lectures on Conversation. Vols 1 and 2.* Oxford: Blackwell.

Schneider, B. (2001) Constructing knowledge in an organization: The role of interview notes. *Management Communication Quarterly*, 15(2): 227–55.

Searle, J. R. (1979) *Meaning and Expression: Studies in the Theory of Speech Acts.* Cambridge: Cambridge University Press.

Seeger, M. W. and R. R. Ulmer (2002) A post-crisis discourse of renewal. *Journal of Applied Communication Research*, 30(2): 126–42.

Shannon, C. and W. Weaver (1949) *The Mathematical Theory of Communication.* Urbana: University of Illinois Press.

Shapiro, M. (1992) *Reading the Postmodern Polity.* Minneapolis: University of Minnesota Press.

Smith, R. C. (1993) *Images of Organizational Communication: Root Metaphors of the Organization–Communication Relationship.* Washington, DC: International Communication Association.

Taylor, J. R. and F. Cooren (1997) What makes communication 'organizational'? How the many voices of a collectivity become the one voice of an organization. *Journal of Pragmatics*, 27: 409–38.

Taylor, J. R. and E. Van Every (2000) *The Emergent Organization: Communication as its Site and Surface.* Mahwah, NJ: Lawrence Erlbaum.

Weick, K. E. and K. H. Roberts (1993) Collective mind in organizations: Interrelating on flight decks. *Administrative Science Quarterly*, 38: 357–81.

Wittgenstein, L. (1953) *Philosophical Investigations.* Oxford: Blackwell.

Zoller, H. M. (2003a) Working out: Managerialism in workplace health promotion. *Management Communication Quarterly*, 17(2): 171–205.

Zoller, H. M. (2003b) Health on the line: Discipline and consent in employee discourse about occupational health and safety. *Journal of Applied Communication Research*, 31 (2): 118–39.

Zorn, T. E., D. J. Page and G. Cheney (2000) Nuts about change: Multiple perspectives on change-oriented communication in a public sector organization. *Management Communication Quarterly*, 13(4): 515–66.

20

International management

Rebecca Piekkari

Introduction

As a field of study, international management deals with inter-firm and intra-firm processes that span national, cultural, geographical and linguistic boundaries. It centres on questions associated with multinational corporations (MNCs), international strategy, international human resource management, cross-cultural management, leadership and the general environment in which international management is practised. More specifically, the field focuses on headquarters–subsidiary and inter-subsidiary relationships, control and coordination within the MNC as well as between firms. It is a sub-field of international business and very much an English-language domain thanks to its roots in the Anglophone USA (Chapman et al. 2004).

While communication has not been the primary focus of international management scholars, international management processes contain a strong communicative element. For example, the implementation of foreign subsidiary control builds on effective communication between the parties involved. Spreading shared practices across the subsidiary network, introducing a new organisational structure with reporting lines, agreeing upon budgetary controls and submitting monthly reports all require a great deal of consultation and discussion between headquarters and the subsidiaries. Yet recent textbooks on managing the modern multinational do not discuss communication challenges per se but rather more specific questions such as knowledge transfer between subsidiary units (e.g. Forsgren et al. 2005; Johnston 2005).

A growing strand of research in international management has, however, established the importance of language in international management processes (Barner-Rasmussen and Björkman 2007; Brannen 2004; Brock et al. 2000; Buckley et al. 2005; Marschan-Piekkari et al. 1999b; Sunaoshi et al. 2005; Welch et al. 2005). As Luo and Shenkar (2006: 322) argue, '[i]t is via language that MNC executives develop their strategies and policies, disseminate and implement them'. In this stream of research, the view of language has shifted from an operational issue to a more strategic one (Luo and Shenkar 2006; Marschan et al. 1997).

This chapter looks at MNCs and takes communication in the common corporate language as its starting point. More specifically, the purpose of the present chapter is to explore the broader implications of using a common corporate language (i.e. an internal working language) for managing people in multinationals. This chapter is concerned with the everyday spoken and written usage of languages such as English and French in the MNC, as opposed to discourses which can be understood as 'framing devices, systems of shared meaning' used in speaking or writing about a particular subject matter (Tietze et al. 2003: 78). It aims to show the potential of cross-fertilisation between the fields of international management and international business communication.

The remainder of the chapter is structured as follows. First, the discussion builds on recent conceptualisations of the MNC as a multilingual organisation (Barner-Rasmussen and Björkman 2007; Janssens et al. 2004; Luo and Shenkar 2006). Second, the role of the common corporate language is defined, and its choice and rationale in this multilingual corporate environment are debated. Third, three types of effects of the common corporate language are identified: communicative, career and organisational effects. Throughout the chapter I will refer to my own and empirical studies by others in order to provide real-life company examples.

Common corporate language and the multinational corporation

The organisational context in which international management is practised has a lot to offer for communications research. Recently, the MNC has been conceptualised as a multilingual organisation (Barner-Rasmussen and Björkman 2007; Janssens et al. 2004) or a multilingual community (Luo and Shenkar 2006). According to this view, an MNC consists of headquarters and subsidiary units, which are spatially separated and often embedded in different language environments. Consequently, internal communication often involves crossing language boundaries and operating at the interface between several language, including those of the home country and the host country, the corporate language and 'company speak'. For example, an MNC may use English as its common corporate language but infuse it with abbreviations, expressions and vocabulary that distinguish this company from others. Formally, the common corporate language tends to occupy the most important position in the organisational hierarchy of languages. It is used in board meetings, reporting, internal management meetings, management training and development as well as in corporate communications more generally. The common corporate language is also used in inter-subsidiary communication (e.g. emails) when at least one person who does not speak the local subsidiary language is addressed, involved or potentially affected by the communication (Blazejewski 2006).

Definition, rationale and choice of a common corporate language

Many MNCs, such as ABB, Electrolux, General Electric, Nokia and Phillips, use a common corporate language in an attempt to reduce language diversity and facilitate in-house communication between units (Feely and Harzing 2003; Marschan-Piekkari et al. 1999a; Nickerson 2000). Given the prominent role of English in international business, it is not surprising that companies often opt for English in order to standardise internal language use (Marschan-Piekkari et al. 1999a). Sørensen (2005) defines a common corporate language as an administrative managerial tool, which is derived from the need of an international board of directors and top management in an MNC to run global operations.

Luo and Shenkar (2006: 325) specify that a common corporate language (they use the term 'parent functional language') 'is chosen to facilitate global coordination, streamline intra-network communication, and bolster transferability of information, knowledge and expertise'. Basically, the common corporate language is intended to increase efficiency by overcoming misunderstandings, reducing costs, avoiding time-consuming translations and creating a sense of belonging and cohesion within the firm (Marschan-Piekkari et al. 1999a; Sørensen 2005). It can also be seen to influence the corporate identity and image (Piekkari et al. 2005). Finally, the designation of a common corporate language may also be regarded as a value-infused control mechanism to support and strengthen the corporate culture (Blazejewski 2006). From this perspective, it can be viewed as an attempt by head-quarters to monitor its foreign operations (Marschan-Piekkari et al. 1999b; SanAntonio 1987).

Researchers in the fields of international management and international business communication have addressed the question of a common corporate language both conceptually and empirically. Some of the conceptual work has focused on managing and organising language diversity within the MNC (Feely and Harzing 2003; Janssens et al. 2004; Luo and Shenkar 2006). For example, Luo and Shenkar (2006) discuss the overall language strategy of the MNC and introduce terms such as 'language choice' and 'language design'. They argue that the language system of the MNC 'needs to be designed to balance global integration with local adaptation in line with corporate strategy and an evolving global environment' (Luo and Shenkar 2006: 322). This view builds on the assumption that top management is willing and able to make a decision regarding the language strategy of the firm.

A number of qualitative studies have empirically investigated the actual choice of the common corporate language in European MNCs. A case study of the Finnish-based Kone Corporation showed how the use of English was very much an outcome of an emergent strategy as the company started to expand internationally through acquisitions (Marschan-Piekkari et al. 1999a). In a study of Siemens, the globally operating engineering company headquartered in Germany, both English and German were used in the internal communication (Fredriksson et al. 2006). Although top management had made attempts to introduce English as the common corporate language of Siemens, several different languages continued to be used within the organisation, with German and English as the dominant ones. The interviews conducted in different Siemens units revealed that there were even opposing perceptions of which language – German or English – had been chosen as the official language. The researchers' interpretation was that the common corporate language had been intentionally left ambiguous and was allowed to solve itself in an emergent manner in order to avoid provoking emotional reactions from either the German or the non-German parts of Siemens. Thus, it was concluded that one strategy of managing language diversity may in fact be non-management in the form of conscious ambiguity and lack of top management intervention (Fredriksson et al. 2006).

Cross-border mergers and acquisitions offer another organisational context which brings the choice of the common corporate language to the fore. Language considerations are closely intertwined with the power balance and degree of influence between the previously separate organisations (Louhiala-Salminen et al. 2005; Welch et al. 2005). For example, Scandinavian Airlines (SAS), which is a pan-Scandinavian organisation originating in Sweden, Denmark and Norway, did not formally appoint a common corporate language, partly because of an attempt to maintain the power balance between the three nations (Bruntse 2003). Alongside English, Scandinavian languages were extensively used within SAS, which was characteristic of its internal communication, as Bruntse explains. Another example of a cross-border merger is the Nordic financial institution MeritaNordbanken (today Nordea), which first introduced Swedish as the common corporate language between the Swedish and Finnish merging organisations, but later changed it into English as the company continued to expand internationally (Louhiala-Salminen et al. 2005; Piekkari et al. 2005). Thus, language choice is intertwined with pragmatic as well as political considerations.

To sum up, the discussion portrays several perspectives regarding the choice of a common corporate language. On the one hand, it has been suggested that companies make an explicit management decision based on rational considerations. On the other hand, the use of a common corporate language may be an emergent process, an outcome of political power play or even non-management.

Effects of the common corporate language

Three different types of effects of the common corporate language may be identified: communicative, career and organisational effects. The categories are not mutually interdependent but overlapping, as the effects build on each other. The first two categories of effects are primarily examined at the individual level of analysis while the organisational effects shift the discussion to a more aggregate level of analysis. They will be discussed below.

Communicative effects

Empirical studies have investigated the use of a common corporate language in international companies and identified its limitations (Louhiala-Salminen and Charles 2006; Louhiala-Salminen et al. 2005). For example, Andersen and Rasmussen (2004) investigated the role of language skills in corporate communication among Danish firms and their subsidiaries in France. They explain that although the common corporate language is English, 'the day-to-day communication between headquarters and the subsidiary has to be organised in French due to lack of English speaking personnel in the French subsidiary' (Andersen and Rasmussen 2004: 237). Additional support is provided in a recent survey of seventy Danish firms. In this study, Sørensen (2005) found that English is used alongside local languages, as most documents are translated into and from English. He labels English a 'transit language' operating as a bridge between various local languages (Sørensen 2005: 70).

The expected gains of a common corporate language are often associated with improved internal communication. Consider English as the common corporate language. Once all company memoranda and reporting are produced in English, a wider access to corporate communications is ensured. From a top management perspective, English is often perceived as a truly 'common' corporate language, as top management themselves have a good command of English and have been socialised into the Anglo-Saxon management discourse taught at business schools and on MBA courses (Tietze 2004). In this sense, top managers of MNCs often represent a fairly coherent group of transnational elites who are integrated through language use.

However, the imposition of a common corporate language may influence patterns of informal communication in unforeseen ways. In particular, lower-level employees or older-generation managers in foreign subsidiaries, whose English skills are likely to vary, are inclined to speak only their local language. In Blazejewski's (2006) case study of a German-owned subsidiary in Japan, English was introduced as a common corporate language as part of a transfer of organisational practices from Germany to the Japanese subsidiary. Blazejewski found a divide between groups of Japanese staff, namely young English-speaking junior managers and the older-generation middle management. 'The older generation felt increasingly excluded from the MNC communication network, particularly from the informal network connecting the young English-speaking Japanese colleagues with the local expatriates and parent company representatives' (Blazejewski 2006: 85). She explains that with English as the common corporate language, the danger of information asymmetries and misunderstandings increased. One of her interviewees exemplified this by describing how emails written in rather poor English turned into 'verbal missiles' used in a battlefield between the Japanese and the French subsidiary of the German MNC (Blazejewski 2006: 85). At the same time, the need for closer and more direct interaction with expatriates and other foreign colleagues had grown sharply in the Japanese subsidiary. The young English-speaking managers were instrumental in filtering information coming from the parent company or other subsidiaries (Blazejewski 2006). Similar findings were identified in previous research by SanAntonio (1987) and Marschan-Piekkari et al. (1999a: 386) who termed these individuals 'language nodes'.

While individuals develop and maintain personal relationships in various languages, so do foreign subsidiaries. One of the key subsidiary responsibilities is to communicate local market knowledge to the rest of the firm. From this perspective, subsidiaries take on an interpreter role by providing contextual understanding of local conditions (Ferner 2000). A case study of knowledge-sharing in MNCs showed how subsidiaries formed language based-clusters, such as English-, German-, Spanish- and Swedish-speaking clusters, when interacting with each other (Mäkelä et al. 2007). These language-based clusters consisted of persons who had a common mother tongue or who shared the facility to operate in a given language. The case evidence demonstrated that despite English being the common corporate language in all three MNCs, several other languages were used alongside English to share knowledge informally. The ease of knowledge-sharing was explained by homophily, a tendency to interact with similar others (Mäkelä et al. 2007). A survey of foreign-owned subsidiaries in China and Finland provides additional support for the crucial importance of fluency in a common language for the development of close inter-unit relationships (Barner-Rasmussen and Björkman 2007).

Thus, it is obvious that the mere designation of a language – whether English or any other – as the common corporate language does not improve individuals' skills in itself. Given that language proficiency among different groups of personnel will vary, it takes time before the necessary level of language competence has been achieved through, for example, corporate training efforts and new recruitment policies. Therefore, the benefits of standardising language use in cross-border communication cannot be reaped over night. At the same time, new markets may be entered, and some of the existing operations may be closed down or divested, making the overall level of language competence within the MNC organisation highly unstable and dynamic (Fredriksson et al. 2006).

Career effects

An imposed corporate language may influence individual career paths, as some employees will master it while others will have to decide whether to invest the time and energy in order to learn it. For those who possess the necessary skills, language competence may be a strategic career asset that opens up career opportunities which would not otherwise exist (e.g. Bloch 1995; Marschan-Piekkari et al. 1999a). For outsiders, the choice of the common corporate language may also shape the company image among potential recruits in terms of its attractiveness as a potential employer (Piekkari et al. 2005). Once a common corporate language is in place, it becomes a requirement for being admitted to corporate training and management development programmes, potential international assignments and promotion, thus affecting individual career opportunities (Marschan-Piekkari et al. 1999a).

In Blazejewski's (2006) study of the Japanese subsidiary within an MNC based in Germany, the global recruitment practices and corporate management training schemes were adjusted to meet the new requirements of English as the corporate language. Blazejewski found that very few Japanese managers had been sent on corporate training courses, because of their limited skills in English. The privileging of English had also led to a situation in which some young but rather inexperienced Japanese junior managers considerably enhanced their positions within the internal power structure of the firm vis-à-vis older-generation Japanese managers (Blazejewski 2006: 85). It was obvious that their English skills opened up direct communication lines to the local expatriates and other international managers. Consequently, language skills and with them an information surplus became 'new important power bases in the Japanese organisation, supplanting the more traditional fundament of power drawing from seniority, formal position and techno-logical expertise' (Blazejewski 2006: 88). Supporting evidence was found in a study of an American-owned subsidiary in Japan which followed a very strict English-only language policy (SanAntonio 1987).

The study by Blazejewski (2006) also powerfully demonstrates how one key manager in the local subsidiary can effectively block the implementation of a parent company practice to prioritise English in recruitment. According to the view of the Japanese human resources manager, Japanese 'graduates often *either* possess the required technical expertise *or* they speak English in a sufficient way' (Blazejewski 2006: 86). Thus, adher-ing to the recruitment criteria of the parent company would have led to a biased selection of employees with language skills *only*. The human resources manager himself belonged to the group of non-English speakers and by refraining from adjusting to the corporate language policy he also secured his own, individual interests.

In a cross-border merger between the Finnish Merita Bank and the Swedish Nordbanken, the two financial institutions formed MeritaNordbanken (now Nordea). In conjunction with the restructuring, Swedish was introduced as the common corporate language. An ethnographic case study of the Finnish part of the organisation shows that many Finns had to operate professionally without adequate skills in the new common cor-porate language (Piekkari et al. 2005). The findings show how career paths and promotion opportunities became partly language-dependent. Those Finns whose mother tongue was Swedish or who were fluent in Swedish became key persons in the new organisation. Others who were solely Finnish speaking escaped to those parts of the merged organisation in which Swedish was not used. Clearly, competence in the common corporate language shaped, steered and even diverted individual career paths. In MeritaNordbanken the introduction of Swedish as the common corporate language operated as a glass ceiling, preventing promising individuals with management talent from advancing in their careers and reaching the top echelons of the organisation (Piekkari et al. 2005). Many of these career effects tend to remain invisible to top management, which is likely to be competent in the common corporate language within the MNC.

Organisational effects

As mentioned previously, one of the purposes of introducing a common corporate language is to integrate the culturally, nationally and linguistically scattered MNC. Such a decision, when made explicitly, is likely to change habitual communication practices within the MNC dramatically. Moreover, it carries with it certain values which may be used to strengthen and support the corporate culture (Blazejewski 2006). The previous discussion on communicative and career effects showed, however, that individual differences in language competence may provide some organisational members and personnel groups with a language advantage. In contrast, limited competence in the common corporate language may exclude employees from critical exchanges of information. Building on these insights, the broader organisational effects in terms of cohesion, integration or disintegration can be identified.

Much of the qualitative work cited in this chapter shows that the implementation of the common corporate language decision is not a quick fix; rather, it tends to be problematic. For example, Blazejewski (2006) concludes that while on the surface the Japanese subsidiary had implemented English as a common corporate language, there was strong resistance in the form of a hidden conflict among subsidiary staff. Her study demonstrates how imposing English as the common corporate language created high levels of frustration and strained interpersonal relationships, particularly between employee generations within the Japanese subsidiary. Moreover, there was an increasing feeling of isolation and growing distance between the Japanese subsidiary and its German parent company (Blazejewski 2006). In a similar vein, the inability to operate effectively in the common corporate language created islands in the Finnish MNC, Kone Corporation (Marschan-Piekkari et al. 1999b). Instead of integrating the MNC, the common corporate language seems to cause disintegrating effects.

The disintegrating effects were very visible in the case study of MeritaNordbanken (Piekkari et al. 2005). The common division into 'us' and 'them', which tends to prevail in many mergers and acquisitions, followed language-based groups alongside the traditional organisational boundaries of the acquired versus the acquiring organisation. As top managers did not have a realistic understanding of the level of language competence within the organisation, the strong emotional reactions among Finnish-speaking employees took them by surprise. The findings show how Swedish as the common corporate language unintentionally undermined the integration efforts that were being introduced within the new organisation (Piekkari et al. 2005). As Blazejewski (2006: 86) observes, 'the growing internal split between those who speak English and those who do not has already become apparent in the interviewees' use of an "us/them" dichotomy to denote emerging language-based internal barriers'.

Conclusions

The present chapter is a review of recent communications research in international management. While early research on MNCs was concerned with formal and informal communication in headquarters–subsidiary and inter-subsidiary relationships (e.g. Hulbert and Brandt 1980; Leksell 1981), more recent work has shifted its focus on specific research themes such as knowledge transfer and social capital within the MNC. In this chapter, an explicit choice was made to introduce a growing stream of research that has looked at the broader implications of communicating in a corporate language for multinational management. The discussion shows that the introduction of a common corporate language may affect career considerations of staff and the organisational cohesion of the MNC. These effects go beyond the purely communicative function of the common corporate language.

The main contribution of international management stems from examining the common corporate language in its natural context. First, international management scholars have extensively studied the *organisational context* – the MNC and its inner workings. It is an organisational arena characterised by power and political games, which is important to appreciate. Second, international management brings to the fore the *multinational and multilingual context* of business exchanges today. The crossing of language boundaries is at the very heart of managing people in MNCs. Third, following on from this, the field puts language and communication issues in their *strategic business context*. Combined with qualitative research methods, the study of the common corporate language-in-use demonstrates the broad managerial implications that range from the individual and his or her immediate workplace to the corporation in its entirety.

References

Andersen, H. and E. S. Rasmussen (2004) The role of language skills in corporate communication. *Corporate Communication: An International Journal*, 9(2): 231–42.
Barner-Rasmussen, W. and I. Björkman (2007) Language fluency, socialization and inter-unit relationships in Chinese and Finnish subsidiaries. *Management and Organisational Review*, 3(1): 105–28.
Blazejewski, S. (2006) Transferring value-infused organisational practices in multinational companies: A conflict perspective. In M. Geppert and M. Mayer (eds), *Global, National and Local Practices in Multinational Corporations*. Basingstoke: Palgrave Macmillan, pp. 63–104.
Bloch, B. (1995) Career enhancement through foreign language skills. *International Journal of Career Management*, 7(6): 15–26.
Brannen, M. Y. (2004) When Mickey loses face: Recontextualization, semantic fit and the semiotics of foreignness. *Academy of Management Review*, 29(4): pp. 593–616.
Brock, D., D. Barry and D. Thomas (2000) Your forward is our reverse, your right, our wrong: Rethinking multinational planning processes in light of national culture. *International Business Review*, 9(6): 687–701.

Bruntse, J. (2003) It's Scandinavian: Dansk-svensk kommunikation i SAS (Danish–Swedish communication in SAS). Master's dissertation, Institute for Nordic Philology, University of Copenhagen.

Buckley, P. J., M. J. Carter, J. Clegg and H. Tan (2005) Language and social knowledge in foreign-knowledge transfer to China. *International Studies of Management & Organisation*, 35(1): 47–65.

Chapman, M., H. Gajewska-De Mattos and C. Antoniou (2004) The ethnographic international business researcher: Misfit or trailblazer? In R. Marschan-Piekkari and C. Welch (eds), *Handbook of Qualitative Research Methods for International Business*. Cheltenham and Northampton, MA: Edward Elgar, pp. 287–305.

Ferner, A. (2000) The underpinnings of bureaucratic control systems: HRM in European multinationals. *Journal of Management Studies*, 37(4): 521–39.

Feely, A. and A. Harzing (2003) Language management in multinational companies. *Cross-Cultural Management: An International Journal*, 10(2): 37–52.

Forsgren, M., U. Holm and J. Johanson (2005) *Managing the Embedded Multinational: A Business Network View*. Cheltenham and Northampton, MA: Edward Elgar.

Fredriksson, R., W. Barner-Rasmussen and R. Piekkari (2006) The multinational corporation as a multilingual organisationl: The notion of a common corporate language. *Corporate Communications: An International Journal*, 11(4): 406–23.

Hulbert, J. and W. Brandt (1980) *Managing the Multinational Subsidiary*. New York: Praeger.

Janssens, M., J. Lambert and C. Steyaert (2004) Developing language strategies for international companies: The contribution of translation studies. *Journal of World Business*, 39(4): 414–30.

Johnston, S. (2005) *Headquarters and Subsidiaries in Multinational Corporations: Strategies, Tasks and Coordination*. Basingstoke: Palgrave.

Leksell, L. (1981) *Headquarter–Subsidiary Relationships in Multinational Corporations*. Stockholm: Gotab.

Louhiala-Salminen, L. and M. Charles (2006) English as the lingua franca of international Business communication: Whose English? What English? In J. C. Palmer-Silveira, M. F. Ruiz-Garrido and I. Fortanet-Gomez (eds), *Intercultural and International Business Communication: Theory, Research and Teaching*. Bern: Peter Lang, pp. 27–54.

Louhiala-Salminen, L., M. Charles and A. Kankaanranta (2005) English as lingua franca in Nordic corporate mergers: Two case companies. *English for Specific Purposes*, 24(4): 401–21.

Luo, Y. and O. Shenkar (2006) The multinational corporation as a multilingual community: Language and organisation in a global context. *Journal of International Business Studies*, 37(3): 321–39.

Mäkelä, K., H. K. Kalla and R. Piekkari (2007) Interpersonal similarity as a driver of knowledge sharing within multinational corporations. *International Business Review*, 16(1): 1–22.

Marschan, R., D. E. Welch and L. S. Welch (1997) Language: The forgotten factor in multinational management. *European Management* Journal, 15(5): 591–8.

Marschan-Piekkari, R., D. E. Welch and L. S. Welch (1999a) Adopting a common corporate language: IHRM implications. *International Journal of Human Resource Management*, 10(3): 377–90.

Marschan-Piekkari, R., D. E. Welch and L. S. Welch (1999b) In the shadow: The impact of language on structure, power and communication in the multinational. *International Business Review*, 8(4): 421–40.

Nickerson, C. (2000) Playing the corporate language game: An investigation of the genres and discourse strategies in English used by Dutch writers working in multinational corporations. PhD thesis, University of Utrecht, Amsterdam.

Piekkari, R., E. Vaara, J. Tienari and R. Säntti (2005) Integration or disintegration? Human resource implications of a common corporate language decision in a cross-border merger. *International Journal of Human Resource Management*, 16(3): 333–47.

SanAntonio, P. M. (1987) Social mobility and language use in an American company in Japan. *Journal of Language and Social Psychology*, 6(3–4): 191–200.

Sørensen, E. S. (2005) Our corporate language is English: An exploratory survey of 70 DK-sited corporations' use of English. Master's dissertation, Faculty of Language and Business Communication, Aarhus Business School.

Sunaoshi, Y., M. Kotabe and J. Y. Murray (2005) How technology transfer really occurs on the factory floor: A case of a major Japanese automotive die manufacturer in the United States. *Journal of World Business*, 40(1): 57–70.

Tietze, S. (2004) Spreading the management gospel – in English. *Language and Intercultural Communication: Multilingual Matters*, 4(3): 175–89.

Tietze, S., L. Cohen and G. Musson (2003) *Understanding Organisations through Language*. London: Sage.

Welch, D. E., L. S. Welch and R. Piekkari (2005) Speaking in tongues: Language and international management. *International Studies of Management & Organisation*, 35(1): 10–27.

21

Management communication

N. Lamar Reinsch, Jr

Introduction

Management communication is a relatively new academic field, and one of several that encourage scholarship focused on business discourse. In this chapter I sketch a history of management communication as an offshoot of business communication and as related to the emergence of MBA (Master of Business Administration) degree programmes in the USA. I also provide a brief description of current conditions before turning to a discussion of management communication research.

With regard to research I (1) review some of the historically important studies of managerial communication behaviour, a research focus that began in Europe and migrated to the USA; (2) acknowledge the range, quality and some apparent omissions of more recent research; (3) argue that management communication would benefit from increased emphasis on scholarship, particularly the scholarships of integration and discovery (Boyer 1990); and (4) note that (at least in the USA) an emphasis on the scholarships of teaching and application (Boyer 1990), and the typical career paths of management communication lecturers in leading business schools, hinder the development of the field.

Historical background and current activities

I define the discipline of management communication as the study of the communicative behaviours of managers, within the evolving context of human organisations, in order to facilitate societal benefit, organisational performance, and the individual achievements of current and would-be managers. In this approach, I build on the work of others (e.g. Smeltzer 1996; Smeltzer and Thomas 1994) and call attention to some of the challenges faced by the field.

Management communication was called into existence to improve the communication abilities of would-be managers. It emerged in the USA concomitant with the growth of postgraduate MBA degree programmes (Knight 1999). Management communication is, perhaps, most accurately seen as an offspring of business communication (Reinsch 1996; cf. White-Mills and Rogers 1996). It evolved to meet the needs of persons enrolled in MBA programmes, young men – and, later, young women – who had already completed a university degree and accumulated several years of work experience.

When postgraduate business programmes began to develop – the Tuck school at Dartmouth College was established in 1900 – they frequently included some instruction in written communication. Over time that instruction evolved to include more material on oral communication (e.g. the briefing and the team meeting) and, in some cases, to create additional courses (Munter 1989, 1990). Today, around the world, many postgraduate business programmes include one or more required or elective courses in communication (Knight 1999, 2005).

Some US textbooks provide exposition with illustrations (e.g. Hynes 2008; Penrose et al. 2004); others emphasise cases (e.g. Hattersley and McJannet 2008; O'Rourke 2006). The most enduring management communication text appears, however, to have been Mary Munter's *Guide to Managerial Communication* (2005). And some management communication instructors select their textbooks from the available trade books (e.g. Alred et al. 2006; Long 2004; Morgan 2003).

A proliferation of courses and instructional materials does not, however, mean that management communication has a secure place in every MBA curriculum. A number of highly ranked MBA programmes in the USA operate without any formal instruction in communication. Furthermore, business schools that have communication programmes sometimes abandon or reduce them to pursue other objectives. And revisions of MBA curricula can produce results like those at 'School A' (Kleiman and Kass 2007).

'School A' set out to develop a 'proactive mission-based' MBA curriculum (Kleiman and Kass 2007: 85). The developers articulated a clear mission statement; identified the tasks that MBAs should be able to perform; specified the knowledge, skills and abilities (KSAs) that MBA students should acquire in school; and created a set of courses designed to teach the most important KSAs. The list of desired courses included 'Managerial Communication Skills' (Kleiman and Kass 2007: 94). The course description stated:

> The goal of this course is to help students develop the skills that a manager needs to effectively communicate with various stakeholders and build and sustain a productive workforce. The students learn how to communicate in a supportive and persuasive manner, manage conflict, build and lead a team, and produce effective presentations and written reports. (Kleiman and Kass 2007: 101)

However, 'when the proposed slate of courses was shown to the full faculty, [some of] the . . . professors balked'; it turned out that none of the business school professors 'felt competent to teach . . . [managerial communication skills] and feared that their attempts to do so would jeopardize their careers' (Kleiman and Kass 2007: 94).

As illustrated by this episode, MBA programmes in the USA have a conflicted relationship with management communication. The manifest needs of students regularly stimulate MBA programmes to re-emphasise communication. And then, periodically, either professors or deans conclude that tenure-track business school professors should not teach management communication. Thus, at many of the highly ranked business schools in the USA where competition for rankings is most intense, communication education either is omitted or is delivered by persons employed as part-time, adjunct or non-tenure-track professors. And, in many cases, the persons in these irregular instructional positions lack political clout, teach very large numbers of students, and spend uncounted hours giving feedback on individual assignments.

As a result of the emphasis on teaching, most management communication scholars in the USA have less time and energy than colleagues in other business disciplines to contribute to their field's intellectual capital. In fact, management communication professors who succeed in earning tenure at some of the more highly rated universities in the USA do so by directing their research efforts away from management communication (e.g. Yates and Kelly 2007: 434).

The evolution of *Management Communication Quarterly* (*MCQ*) provides another window on the history of management communication in the United States. The idea for *MCQ* emerged from conversations in the early and mid-1980s within the Management Communication Association, an informal organisation of persons who teach communication in some of the leading business schools in the USA. As the idea took shape, the planners envisioned *MCQ* as a multidisciplinary journal, publishing work in management communication, organisational communication, corporate communication and related areas. Over time, however, *MCQ* became in reality – but not in name – a journal of organisational communication (Miller 2007). So, for example, the journal can now publish a spirited exchange on the topic 'Whither management communication?' in which all the authors write about 'organisational communication' (Barker 2006).

The evolution of *MCQ* away from management communication and towards organisational communication was probably inevitable, given the relative levels of maturity of the two fields when *MCQ* began (Miller 1996), the inherent difficulty of maintaining a multidisciplinary journal across sequential editorial transitions, and the need for a strong outlet for research in organisational communication, a field sometimes undervalued by its originating field, speech communication. Perhaps the most accurate summary would be to say that the management communication community wasn't ready for *MCQ*.

Today, members of the management communication academic community find intellectual nourishment in professional associations and scholarly periodicals. The professional associations include the (still informal) Management Communication Association, the Association for Business Communication (the MBA Consortium Interest Group) and the Academy of Management (the Organisational Communication and Information Systems Division). Research related to management communication (not necessarily about management communication per se) appears in a number of periodicals within the broad fields of management and communication. Examples include the *Journal of Business Communication* and *Business Communication Quarterly*, both of which have their editorial policy controlled by the Association for Business Communication. Other examples are *Management Communication Quarterly* and the *Journal of Business and Technical Communication*, both independent journals published by Sage.

So, is management communication a discipline? Historically a discipline was defined in terms of intellectual features; more recently it has been described as a social construction, a construction based on professional associations and research outlets. Shelby incorporated both perspectives in describing a discipline as defined by '(a) a community of scholars with shared interests, (b) a research focus, (c) a coherent body of knowledge linked to theory, and (d) a commitment to communicating knowledge' (1996: 99). Against this standard, the management communication butterfly is only a caterpillar. An enduring community of scholars shares research and teaching interests. But management communication research lacks both a unifying focus and a significant and coherent body of theory-based knowledge.

Research focus, methods and results

Published research that touches on the communication of managers is voluminous, particularly within the fields of management and communication. Only a small portion of that research, however, deals with the issue that should be central to management communication: discovering the means of persuasion that a manager may use to further organisational goals and benefit organisational stakeholders (cf. Aristotle 1991: 36).

Building on the work of others (Smeltzer 1996; Smeltzer and Thomas 1994), I argue that the field of management communication should focus on the communicative behaviour of managers within the context of human organisations and do so with a goal of benefiting society, organisations and individuals. Speaking approvingly of organisational objectives may open me to accusations of managerial bias, said to infect many aspects of organisational studies (Mumby and Stohl 1996: 55–8). I would argue, however, that educating managers and would-be managers calls for supporting the goals of an employing organisation, without losing sight of the individual's and the organisation's responsibilities to society. This focus describes, I think, the central interests of the management communication community in the USA. It also provides a foundation for thinking about the development of management communication scholarship.

Boyer has argued that scholarship can be placed in four categories: discovery, integration, application and teaching. The scholarship of discovery aims to develop new knowledge (1990: 17). The scholarship of integration 'seeks to interpret, draw together, and bring new insight to bear . . . [,] fitting one's own research – or the research of others – into larger intellectual patterns' (1990: 19). The scholarship of application asks questions such as 'How can knowledge be responsibly applied to consequential problems?' (Boyer 1990: 21). The scholarship of teaching makes available to others the results of discovery, integration and application.

Viewed through the lens of Boyer's categories, the management communication academic community in the USA emphasises the scholarship of teaching and the scholarship of application. Both teaching and application are, however, dependent on the scholarships of synthesis and discovery. Historically, some of the most important discovery research relevant to management communication – research that provides a foundation for the field – emerged as management scholars used surveys, diaries and direct observation to describe the activities of managers at work. The following paragraphs review some of those studies, organised around three questions.

What do managers do?

The earliest studies that contribute to our understanding of management communication described the work of managers. Previous treatments had – on the basis of anecdotal observation – claimed that managerial work consisted of several functions such as planning, organising, coordinating and controlling. The newer studies aimed at more concrete and granular descriptions.

One of the earliest was a diary study of nine directors of Swedish companies (Carlson 1951). Results showed that managers were frequently interrupted and rarely alone. A decade and a half later, Stewart (1967, 1976) collected data from 160 senior and middle managers in the UK. The managers she studied spent an average of 43 per cent of their time in informal discussions, 7 per cent in committee meetings, 6 per cent in telephone conversations and 4 per cent in social activity, for a total of 60 per cent of their time engaged in interpersonal communication.

In the USA, Mintzberg (1973, 1975) – building on the European work – directly observed the activities of eight North America managers, five in the initial study and three in a follow-up study. He noted that the managers read and wrote, and spoke and listened, with considerable frequency (1973: 250–1). He observed managers spending about one-third to one-half of their time communicating with subordinates and about one-third of their time communicating with persons outside the organisation (1973: appendix C). In his conclusions, Mintzberg described ten managerial roles, several of which (e.g. 'liaison', 'disseminator', 'spokes[person]') called attention to communication (1973: ch. 4).

About a decade later, Kotter observed and interviewed fifteen general managers in the USA. He noted that general managers spent up to 90 per cent of their time interacting with others, not only subordinates and bosses but also customers, suppliers and even apparently 'relatively unimportant outsiders' (1982: 80).

These studies revealed a significant mismatch between anecdotal descriptions of management and the activities of working managers and, as a consequence, transformed academic thinking.

In what ways do managers communicate?

The studies cited in the previous section provided information about the ways in which managers communicated. First, the studies noted that managers communicated orally. Mintzberg, for example, explained the preference for face-to-face or telephone interaction as an indication that managers need timely information (1975: 166), a need that renders the carefully prepared written report stale before it arrives. Second, the studies also reported a good deal of variation from manager to manager. Mintzberg attributed the differences to environment, job demands, personality traits and situational variables (1973: ch. 5; cf. Kotter 1982: 98; Luthans and Larsen 1986).

Other studies addressed managerial communicative activities more directly and specifically (e.g. Luthans and Larsen 1986: 162). Managers make speeches (Beason 1991); serve as chairperson for meetings (Bilbow 1998); read books (Pagel and Westerfelhaus 2005); write memos, letters and reports (Smeltzer and Thomas 1994); intervene with troubled supervisors (Hopkins 2001); gather information (Barnard 1991); lead change (Harrison and Young 2005); consult with others (Salk and Brannen 2000); and increasingly do all these things in multicultural contexts (Rogers and Lee-Wong 2003). Managers also adopt and adapt genres as audiences, expectations and cultures change (Yates 1989a, 1989b).

Does communication influence performance?

As scholars acquired better descriptions of managerial behaviour, their attention shifted to a related issue (e.g. Bray et al. 1974): which of the various behaviours might account for differences in effectiveness?

Boyatzis (1982) used data from more than 1,000 managers to identify four clusters of managerial competencies: goal and action management, leadership, human resource management, and focus on others. Several of the competencies related to communication. For example, the leadership cluster included the oral presentation competency, defined as speaking and asking questions in arenas ranging from one-on-one to an 'audience of several hundred' (1982: 105). And several of the competencies with communication elements were positively associated with managerial performance; the relationship between oral presentation competence and managerial performance was particularly strong (1982: 108, 116).

Boyatzis also distinguished between a threshold competency and a competency. He designated an element as a threshold competency if increments beyond a certain level were not associated with improved performance: examples included logical thought (in the leadership cluster) and the ability to communicate positive regard (in the human resource cluster). On the other hand, abilities such as oral presentation ability, conceptualisation, and management of group processes were identified as competencies; that is, more ability was associated with better performance even when the manager's level of ability was already high.

In another extended research effort (as summarised by Luthans et al. 1988), Luthans and his colleagues (e.g. Luthans and Larsen 1986; Luthans et al. 1985) used participant observation, interviews and surveys of subordinates to collect data on 457 managers. They grouped managerial activities into four categories: (1) communication activities (exchanging information, handling paperwork); (2) traditional management activities (planning, decision-making, controlling); (3) networking activities (interacting with outsiders, socialising/politicking); and (4) human resource management activities (motivating/reinforcing, disciplining/punishing, managing conflict, staffing, developing).

Luthans and his colleagues defined individual success as 'an index of the speed . . . of promotion' (Luthans et al. 1988: 3). They defined unit effectiveness with a combination of subordinate satisfaction, subordinate commitment, and the qualitative and quantitative performance of the manager's unit (1988: 64). Thus, success concerned a manager's personal advancement, and effectiveness concerned the productivity of a manager's unit. After identifying the most and least successful managers and the most and least effective managers, the authors calculated the amount of time that managers spent in various activities. They found that the most rapidly promoted managers emphasised networking (48 per cent) and communicating (28 per cent). On the other hand, the managers leading the most productive units emphasised communicating (44 per cent) and human resource management (26 per cent).

Other evidence indicates that a manager's communicative skilfulness – not just allocation of time – is important. For example, Shipper found that both unit performance and morale were related to a manager's mastery of the arts of clarifying goals, encouraging upward communication, providing feedback and recognising performance (Shipper 1991; Shipper and White 1999).

More detailed analyses using the individual as the unit of analysis have linked personal communication abilities – for example, persuasiveness, cognitive differentiation, perspective-taking, listening, media selection and audience adaptation – to personal success (Russ et al. 1990; Suchan 1998; Suchan and Colucci 1989; Sypher et al. 1989; Sypher and Zorn 1986; Turner et al. 2006; Zorn and Violanti 1996). Other studies have demonstrated a link between a manager's personal communication abilities and unit performance (Alexander et al. 1992; Penley et al. 1991).

Studies using the company as the unit of analysis have also shown that communication practices and training relate to organisational performance. For example, Baum et al. (1998) collected vision statements from CEOs of 183 entrepreneurial firms. They assessed the vision statements both on content (explicit commitment to growth) and on other attributes including brevity and clarity. They also conducted interviews to learn whether employees believed the company had a vision and whether the CEO had communicated the vision. The results showed that both vision content and vision attributes (clarity, brevity, etc.) had direct effects on growth. However, 'the indirect effects through vision communication were more important . . . [A]lthough a vision affects performance directly [apparently by guiding management decisions], it is more likely to affect performance if employees know about it and understand it' (1998: 51–2). Similarly, in a study of branch managers in a Canadian bank, Barling et al. (1996) found that leadership training (designed to help managers communicate higher expectations, clarify the organisational mission and coach employees) enhanced employee commitment to the organisation and produced significant increases in loan sales during a subsequent year.

Research supports, therefore, a number of conclusions. We know that managers spend a lot of time communicating, sometimes as much as 90 per cent of the workday. We know that many managers use multiple media. We know that senior managers communicate with many persons who perform a variety of roles both inside and outside of the organisation. We know that individual managers differ considerably in their communication practices – for example, Stewart (1967) identified various clusters of managers as 'emissaries', 'writers', 'discussers', 'trouble shooters', and 'committeemen'. And we know that communication behaviours and skilfulness make a difference in personal success and in unit effectiveness, and we have some ideas about which behaviours are sometimes relevant and what sort of differences they can make.

However, some of our information is growing dated, reflecting neither contemporary communication technologies nor organisational forms. The studies that locate communication behaviours in a comprehensive matrix of managerial practice are now twenty or more years old (e.g. Luthans et al. 1988). And, in general, our information is neither as comprehensive nor as holistic as we might wish.

Managers work within organisations, social environments created by humans and, therefore, 'artificial' (Simon 2001). Because such environments evolve, and because they seem to be evolving rapidly during the current era of corporate responsiveness to environmental issues, globalisation and metastasising communication technologies (e.g. Reinsch et al. 2008), even the most basic questions should be re-examined periodically. How do contemporary managers communicate? How does communication influence performance in contemporary organisations?

Excellent research completed in recent years identifies a number of personal communication abilities that can affect personal success and managerial effectiveness. That research needs scholarly assessment and synthesis. In their study of reading, Pagel and Westerfelhaus called the relevant literature 'not only fragmented and incomplete but . . . also inconclusive and sometimes contradictory' (2005: 422), a description that applies to the entire field of management communication (e.g. the type of listening that has been linked to success and effectiveness differs from study to study and the differences have not been satisfactorily explained).

Future developments

Management communication remains a perennial pedagogical need in MBA curricula; its future as a teaching area seems assured. A 1988 study of business education in the USA found the graduate not well prepared in terms of 'communication (in the broad sense of being able to get meaning across and to be persuasive)' (Porter and McKibbin 1988: 122). More recently, a *Wall Street Journal* article (Alsop 2004) described US MBAs as deficient in communication abilities. Some students and graduates lacked facility in the local language ('English isn't their native language'), a problem of insufficient fluency. Others made 'spelling and grammar errors . . . [or used a] casual tone suitable for emails between friends', a problem of insufficient professionalism. Still others were – in language that sounded like the 1988 study – 'unable to write even the simplest of arguments', a problem of insufficient effectiveness. This third area – effectiveness – is the appropriate focus for management communication pedagogy. What most managers and would-be managers need is not declarative knowledge about how managers communicate, although such information is highly valuable to the pedagogue and may be helpful to the student, but, rather, experiences that allow them to learn to sharpen their personal communication abilities.

The future of the field of management communication depends, therefore, on whether scholars develop a substantive body of theory-connected knowledge. If the field emphasises only teaching and application, members of the management communication community are likely to remain employed in irregular positions, working directly or indirectly for business schools that grant them little status and little research support. If the field can supplement its pedagogy and application with synthesis and discovery, it may yet become a butterfly.

Implications for Pedagogy and Research

Management communication is most likely to make a substantive and enduring contribution as a genuinely interdisciplinary field by seeking synthesis rather than mere 'disciplinary juxtaposition' (Gardner 2006: 55). Hydrogen and oxygen gases can either merely mix as gases or they can combine to form a liquid, water. The goal should not be to mix management and communication but to develop a new field, management communication, with a focus on genuine synthesis in every realm of scholarship including teaching, application, integration and discovery.

The scholarship of teaching

Teaching will be central to management communication so long as individual managers are less effective than they, and their employers, want them to be; in other words, forever. The field should – and generally does – cultivate and celebrate the scholarship of teaching.

However, the rapid pace of change in the world of business implies that teachers in both universities and corporate settings will need to monitor changes in managerial behaviour in order to remain relevant. Furthermore, recognising that organisational contexts constantly evolve implies that the educational task does not consist only of helping the student to develop a finite list of identified skills. Rather, the educational task consists of helping the student to develop habits of thought that will allow him or her to assess the rhetorical dimensions of a new technology or a new organisational structure, to identify emerging problems and solve them creatively (Reinsch and Turner 2006).

The scholarship of application

As a field that borrows much of its intellectual capital, management communication emphasises the scholarship of application, the deployment of knowledge to solve managers' problems. 'Learning from the management literature', the subtitle of a fine recent paper (Berry 2006), suggests a continuing series of papers in which scholars could explore the managerial communication implications of research in other fields. Such scholarship will require scholars who understand both the source literature (e.g. management, communication, information technology etc.) and the field of management communication; when completed it will have value for both the university lecturer and the corporate trainer.

The scholarship of integration

Management communication needs studies that aggregate and evaluate relevant research. Excellent models of such work can be found in other fields, particularly in organisational communication (e.g. Jablin and Putnam 2001). However, there seem to be only a few such papers directly relevant to management communication (e.g. Smeltzer and Thomas 1994) and only a few attempts to articulate macro-level theories of management communication (e.g. Shelby 1988, 1991). If management communication is to overcome the condition of being fragmented, incomplete, inconclusive and contradictory, it will need to give more attention to the scholarship of synthesis.

The scholarship of discovery

While management communication is a narrow field with an appropriate emphasis on application and teaching, the field needs both integration and discovery. In the past much of the discovery scholarship that has been useful to management communication has been conducted by scholars affiliated with other fields such as management or organisational communication. But some research questions (e.g. the role of the memorandum in the emergence of American management; Yates 1989a, 1989b) may interest primarily management communication scholars. And many questions central to management communication – for example, identification of personal communication abilities that contribute to unit performance – are not likely to be explored thoroughly, holistically and systematically except by management communication scholars.

Conclusion

Collectively managers do much to shape the quality of human life in the modern world, affecting the daily lived experience of their subordinates, colleagues, suppliers, and customers. Management communication – a field focused on understanding and improving communicative behaviour in the managerial context – can contribute to the performance of managers and to the quality of life for all those whose lives they touch; that is, for all of us.

Managers do their work by communicating, and many of them are neither as effective nor as successful as they could be. That deficiency defines the need for management communication pedagogy. But the effectiveness of management communication pedagogy will depend, in the long run, on the quality of other dimensions of management communication scholarship.

References

Alexander, E. R., III, L. E. Penley and I. E. Jernigan (1992) The relationship of basic decoding skills to managerial effectiveness. *Management Communication Quarterly*, 6: 58–73.

Alred, G. J., C. T. Brusaw and W. E. Oliu (2006) *The Business Writer's Handbook*, 8th edn. Boston, MA: Bedford and St Martin's.

Alsop, R. (2004) How to get hired: We asked recruiters what M.B.A. graduates are doing wrong. Ignore their advice at your peril. *Wall Street Journal*, 22 September.

Aristotle (1991) *On Rhetoric: A Theory of Civic Discourse*, trans. G. A. Kennedy. New York: Oxford University Press.

Barker, J. R. (ed.) (2006) Forum: Whither management communication? *Management Communication Quarterly*, 19: 635–66.

Barling, J., T. Weber and E. K. Kelloway (1996) Effects of transformational leadership training on attitudinal and financial outcomes: A field experiment. *Journal of Applied Psychology*, 81: 827–82.

Barnard, J. (1991) The information environment of new managers. *Journal of Business Communication*, 28: 312–24.

Baum, J. R., E. A. Locke and S. A. Kirkpatrick (1998) A longitudinal study of the relation of vision and vision communication to venture growth in entrepreneurial firms. *Journal of Applied Psychology*, 83: 43–54.

Beason, L. (1991) Strategies for establishing an effective persona: An analysis of appeals to ethos in business speeches. *Journal of Business Communication*, 28: 326–46.

Berry, G. R. (2006) Can computer-mediated asynchronous communication improve team processes and decision making? Learning from the management literature. *Journal of Business Communication*, 43: 344–66.

Bilbow, G. T. (1998) Look who's talking: An analysis of 'chair-talk' in business meetings. *Journal of Business and Technical Communication*, 12: 157–97.

Boyatzis, R. E. (1982) *The Competent Manager: A Model for Effective Performance*. New York: Wiley.

Boyer, E. L. (1990) *Scholarship Reconsidered: Priorities of the Professorship*. Princeton, NJ: Carnegie Foundation for the Advancement of Teaching.

Bray, D. W., R. J. Campbell and D. L. Grant (1974) *Formative Years in Business: A Long-Term AT&T Study of Managerial Lives*. New York: Wiley.

Carlson, S. (1951) *Executive Behaviour: A Study of the Work Load and the Working Methods of Managing Directors*. Stockholm: Strömberg.

Gardner, H. (2006) *Five Minds for the Future*. Boston, MA: Harvard Business School Press.

Harrison, C. and L. Young (2005) Leadership discourse in action: A textual study of organizational change in a government of Canada department. *Journal of Business and Technical Communication*, 19: 42–77.

Hattersley, M. E. and L. McJannet (2008) *Management Communication: Principles and Practice*, 3rd edn. Boston, MA: McGraw-Hill and Irwin.

Hopkins, K. M. (2001) Manager intervention with troubled supervisors: Help and support start at the top. *Management Communication Quarterly*, 15: 83–99.

Hynes, G. E. (2008) *Managerial Communication: Strategies and Applications*, 4th edn. Boston, MA: McGraw-Hill and Irwin.

Jablin, F. M. and L. L. Putnam (eds) (2001) *The New Handbook of Organizational Communication: Advances in Theory, Research, and Methods*. Thousand Oaks, CA: Sage.

Kleiman, L. S. and D. Kass (2007) Giving MBA programs the third degree. *Journal of Management Education*, 31: 81–103.

Knight, M. (1999) Management communication in US MBA programs: The state of the art. *Business Communication Quarterly*, 62(4): 9–32.

Knight, M. (2005) Management communication in non-U.S. MBA programs: Current trends and practices. *Business Communication Quarterly*, 68: 139–79.

Kotter, J. P. (1982) *The General Managers*. New York: Free Press.

Long, L. (2004) *The Power of Logic in Problem Solving & Communication*. Marietta, GA: SCC.

Luthans, F. and J. K. Larsen (1986) How managers really communicate. *Human Relations*, 39: 161–78.

Luthans, F., S. A. Rosenkrantz and H. W. Hennessey (1985) What do successful managers really do? An observation study of managerial activities. *Journal of Applied Behavioral Science*, 21: 255–70.

Luthans, F., R. M. Hodgetts and S. A. Rosenkrantz (1988) *Real Managers*. Cambridge, MA: Ballanger.

Miller, K. I. (ed.) (1996) Management, business, organizational, and corporate communication: A discussion of our disciplines. *Management Communication Quarterly* (special issue) 10.

Miller, K. I. (2007) Steps (and missteps?) during the adolescence of *MCQ*. *Management Communication Quarterly*, 20: 437–43.

Mintzberg, H. (1973) *The Nature of Managerial Work*. New York: Harper & Row.

Mintzberg, H. (1975) The manager's job: Folklore and fact. *Harvard Business Review*, 53: 49–61.

Morgan, N. (2003) *Working the Room*. Boston, MA: Harvard Business School Press.

Mumby, D. K. and C. Stohl (1996) Disciplining organizational communication studies. *Management Communication Quarterly*, 10: 50–72.

Munter, M. (ed.) (1989) *Emerging Perspectives in Management Communication*. St Louis, MO: American Assembly of Collegiate Schools of Business.

Munter, M. (1990) What's going on in business and management communication courses? In M. Kogen (ed.), *Writing in the Business Professions*. Urbana, IL: Association for Business Communication, pp. 267–78.

Munter, M. (2005) *Guide to Managerial Communication: Effective Business Writing and Speaking*, 7th edn. Upper Saddle River, NJ: Prentice Hall.

O'Rourke, James S., IV (2006) *Management Communication: A Case-Analysis Approach*, 3rd edn. Upper Saddle River, NJ: Prentice Hall.

Pagel, S. and R. Westerfelhaus (2005) Charting managerial reading preferences in relation to popular management theory books: A semiotic analysis. *Journal of Business Communication*, 42: 420–48.

Penley, L. E., E. R. Alexander, I. E. Jernigan and C. I. Henwood (1991) Communication abilities of managers: The relationship to performance. *Journal of Management*, 17: 57–76.

Penrose, J. M., R. W. Raspberry and R. J. Myers (2004) *Business Communication for Managers: An Advanced Approach*, 5th edn. Mason, OH: South-Western.

Porter, L. W. and L. E. McKibbin (1988) *Management Education and Development: Drift or Thrust into the 21st Century?* New York: McGraw-Hill.

Reinsch, N. L., Jr. (1996) Business communication: Present, past, and future. *Management Communication Quarterly*, 10: 27–49.

Reinsch, N. L., Jr. and J. W. Turner (2006) Ari, r u there? Reorienting business communication for a technological era. *Journal of Business and Technical Communication*, 20: 339–56.

Reinsch, N. L., Jr., J. W. Turner and C. H. Tinsley (2008) Multicommunicating: A practice whose time has come? *Academy of Management Review*, 33: 391–403.

Rogers, P. S. and S. M. Lee-Wong (2003) Reconceptualizing politeness to accommodate dynamic tensions in subordinate-to-superior reporting. *Journal of Business and Technical Communication*, 17: 379–412.

Russ, G. S., R. L. Daft and R. H. Lengel (1990) Media selection and managerial characteristics in organizational communication. *Management Communication Quarterly*, 4: 151–75.

Salk, J. E. and M. Y. Brannen (2000) National culture, networks, and individual influence in a multinational management team. *Academy of Management Journal*, 43: 191–202.

Shelby, A. N. (1988) A macro theory of management communication. *Journal of Business Communication*, 25: 13–28.

Shelby, A. (1991) Applying the strategic choice model to motivational appeals: A theoretical approach. *Journal of Business Communication*, 28: 187–212.

Shelby, A. (1996) A discipline orientation: Analysis and critique. *Management Communication Quarterly*, 10: 98–105.

Shipper, F. (1991) Mastery and frequency of managerial behaviors relative to sub-unit effectiveness. *Human Relations*, 44: 371–88.

Shipper, F. and C. S. White (1999) Mastery, frequency, and interaction of managerial behaviors relative to subunit effectiveness. *Human Relations*, 52: 49–66.

Simon, H. A. (2001) *The Sciences of the Artificial*, 3rd edn. Cambridge, MA: MIT Press.

Smeltzer, L. R. (1996) Communication within the manager's context. *Management Communication Quarterly*, 10: 5–26.

Smeltzer, L. R. and G. F. Thomas (1994) Managers as writers: A meta-analysis of research in context. *Journal of Business and Technical Communication*, 8: 186–211.

Stewart, R. (1967) *Managers and their Jobs: A Study of the Similarities and Differences in the Ways Managers Spend their Time*. London: Macmillan.

Stewart, R. (1976) *Contrasts in Management. A Study of Different Types of Managers' Jobs: Their Demands and Choices*. London: McGraw-Hill.

Suchan, J. (1998) The effect of high-impact writing on decision making within a public sector bureaucracy. *Journal of Business Communication*, 35: 299–327.

Suchan, J. and R. Colucci (1989) An analysis of communication efficiency between high-impact and bureaucratic written communication. *Management Communication Quarterly*, 2: 454–84.

Sypher, B. D. and T. E. Zorn, Jr. (1986) Communication related abilities and upward mobility: A longitudinal investigation. *Human Communication Research*, 12: 420–31.

Sypher, B. D., R. N. Bostrom and J. H. Seibert (1989) Listening, communication abilities, and success at work. *Journal of Business Communication*, 26: 293–303.

Turner, J. W., J. A. Grube, C. H. Tinsley, C. Lee and C. O'Pell (2006) Exploring the dominant media: How does media use reflect organizational norms and affect performance? *Journal of Business Communication*, 43: 220–50.

White-Mills, K. and D. P. Rogers (1996) Identifying the common and separate domains of business-management-organizational communication. *Journal of Business Communication*, 33: 353–61.

Yates, J. (1989a) The emergence of the memo as a managerial genre. *Management Communication Quarterly*, 2: 485–510.

Yates, J. (1989b) *Control Through Communication: The Rise of System in American Management*. Baltimore, MD: Johns Hopkins University Press.

Yates, J. and C. Kelly (2007) The beginnings. *Management Communication Quarterly*, 20: 432–36.

Zorn, T. E. and M. T. Violanti (1996) Communication abilities and individual achievement in organizations. *Management Communication Quarterly*, 10: 139–69.

22

'Race' and management communication

Patricia S. Parker and Diane S. Grimes

Introduction

> [E]veryone in this social order has been constructed . . . as a racialized subject. (Carby 1992: 193)

> [In the study of organisations] the prefix "white" is usually suppressed, and it is only other racial groups to which we attach prefixes. (Nkomo 1992: 489)

This chapter foregrounds 'race' as a central issue in management communication theory, research and practice in the global economy. We begin with the above quotations to emphasise our focus on (1) race as a socially constructed phenomenon that has political and economic expedience and material consequences but no biological basis, and (2) the silences and concealment surrounding whiteness and white privilege that have persisted in the management literature (Omi and Winant 1994). We acknowledge that as co-authors of this chapter, what we present here is influenced by our own racialised subjectivities – as African American (Patricia) and white (Diane) women academics in organisational communication studies. For both of us, but in different ways, race has significant meaning in our daily lives, and we bring those standpoints to bear in considering race in management discourses. Also, we have both called attention to the silence around race in management research (Grimes 1996, 2001, 2002; Parker 2001, 2003, 2005). Indeed, although there *has* been a sustained critique in the management communication literature of organisations as fundamentally 'gendered', more than sixteen years after Stella Nkomo's (1992) groundbreaking call for a rewriting of 'race in organisation', the issue of organisation and management as fundamentally 'raced' still has not been adequately addressed (Ashcraft and Allen 2003). The trend is to study race in ways that reinforce western universalistic paradigms, maintain whiteness as the status quo, and fail to question the limits and controlling influences of these paradigms (see critical reviews by Ashcraft and Allen 2003; Grimes 2001, 2002; Parker 2003).

In contrast, our focus in this chapter follows an emerging stream of thought in management studies that draws upon postcolonial and critical race theories to illustrate the continuing legacy of western colonial constructions of race and to apply methodologies that 'decolonise' management scholarship. Postcolonial theory and criticism recognise that 'the neocolonial world order of our times is extremely unfair and unjust' and that 'achieving true freedom and justice requires a genuine global decolonization . . . that is strongly committed to contesting and subverting the unquestioned sovereignty of Western categories – epistemological, ethicomoral, economic, political, aesthetic, and the rest' (Prasad 2003: 7). Similarly, critical theories of race, including the racial formation approach (Omi and Winant 1994; Winant 2000), critical race theory (CRT; Williams 1997) and the interrogating whiteness approach (hooks 1990; Grimes 2001, 2002), reveal race as a sociohistorical construction and work to unmask the often obscured articulations about race that (re)produce unequal social arrangements. These perspectives are considered 'decolonising' because they highlight the persistence of colonising forms of racial difference and hierarchy in contemporary organisations and global markets (Essed 1991, 2005; Prasad 2003), and provide tools for seeing how race, though often hidden, 'operates at different levels and is open to interpretation and articulation by diverse actors in varied spaces' (Kothari 2006: 10). They also demonstrate the social construction of racial categories and their connections to other categories of (gendered, classed, sexual, embodied) difference (Essed 2005; Gunaratnam 2003).

The purpose of this chapter, then, is to attend to concepts and methodologies that reveal the hidden, persistent articulations about race in management discourses. The chapter unfolds in four parts, beginning with a discussion of the obstacles to 'seeing' race in management studies. The second section provides a critical framework for studying race and management communication and defining important concepts for researching race as a social construction. In the third section we introduce postcolonial and critical theories of race as tools for 'seeing' race in management communication theory, research, and practice. The chapter concludes with a discussion of future directions for management communication scholarship.

Not seeing race in mainstream management discourses

In management studies race generally has not been treated as a social construct, and rarely are the historic foundation and systemic character of contemporary racial oppression considered (Feagin 2006). One reason for this lapse is the dominant trend to research race as a demographic variable without considering historical and cultural (macro-)discourses and everyday dynamic (micro-)processes that reproduce racialised arrangements. The variable analytic approach has been critiqued for its reliance on neopositivist methods that treat groups of people as the passive object of scientific methods (such as experiments, questionnaires and interviews) proclaimed to be neutral and representative of an objective reality (Alvesson and Due Billing 1997). This is a trend Nkomo pointed to in 1992 and it continues at present, fuelled by current demands for social science research based on this type of evidence (Lincoln 2005). Race in this approach serves as an unproblematic proxy for entire groups of people (e.g. identified as white, black/African American, Latino/a, Asian American etc.) and ignores the complex cultural patterns and dynamic processes that reproduce race.

For example, recently a spate of studies has revealed race to be a persistent factor in recruitment and hiring decisions. In a much-publicised US study, researchers randomly assigned traditionally white- or black-sounding names to identical resumés. As measured by the number of employer requests for call-backs, the study found that having a white-sounding name added an advantage equivalent to eight years' experience (Bertrand and Mullainathan 2003). Another study revealed that race accounted for differences in employment opportunities for applicants with criminal records. Black applicants were less than half as likely to receive consideration by employers as their white counterparts. Remarkably, black applicants with no criminal record were less likely to be hired than white applicants with prior felony convictions (Pager 2003). Both of these studies reveal the very real consequences of race, but do not provide a theoretical basis for questioning the reproduction of persistent racial hierarchies.

Another reason race has not been adequately addressed in the management literature is the reliance upon race-neutral perspectives in the emerging global economy. Increasingly, management is seen as occurring in supposedly non-racialised global spaces where communities are 'networks of markets', and where 'capital flows reflect the purportedly 'color-blind' imperatives of profit maximization . . . and race-neutral laws of supply and demand' (Iglesias 2002: 312). This trend reflects past and current imperialist views of leadership and management that focus on conquering, managing, or neutralising difference and assuming a western-centric model of leadership (Parker et al. 2006). Additionally, it illustrates the race-neutral perspective underlying the neoliberal approach to global markets. This approach perpetuates a colonising process that conceals the (re)creation and reinforcement of a racial social order that privileges western norms of whiteness (Iglesias 2002; Kothari 2006). Researching race in the global context requires attention to these processes.

Theories and concepts for decolonising management discourse

Racial formation, racialisation, racial ideology and representation are important concepts for understanding the social construction of race. Space precludes us from going into extended detail. However, there are several thorough treatments on these topics (Bonilla-Silva 2006; Feagin 2006; Murji and Solomos 2005; Winant 2000). We introduce these concepts here because they are useful in explaining postcolonial theorising and critical theories of race and their application to seeing race in management discourse.

Racial formation

Racial formation is a theoretical approach that presents race as a central organising principle in contemporary society (Omi and Winant 1994; Winant 2000). It alerts us to 'racial projects' whereby racial categories are formed, transformed, destroyed and reformed, through structural, institutional and discursive means (Omi and Winant 1994). The meanings and manifestations of race differ across time and place, yet always unfold in the everyday, are always political, and are 'open to many types of agency from the individual to the organisational, from the local to the global' (Winant 2000: 182). Stated more simply, 'race is a product of human social and historical processes that have arbitrarily (but purposefully) created categories of people that are positioned differently in society' (Parker and Mease in press). A European invention during the age of 'Enlightenment', the understanding of race we have inherited took shape with the rise of a world political economy. The categories 'black' and 'white' grew out of the consolidation of racial slavery and were later maintained through a colour line that perpetuated this exploitative, race-based economic system (Omi and Winant 1994). Bonilla-Silva (2007) points to a current racial formation when he argues that politically expedient racial categories are now emerging, proposing the hierarchical categories of 'white', 'honorary white' and 'black'. The anchor that allows some groups to move towards whiteness is still a blackness viewed as inferior to and diametrically opposed to whiteness (Bonilla-Silva 2006; Feagin 2006).

Racialisation

Closely related to racial formation, racialisation is an ideological process that signifies the extension of racial meaning to a previously racially unclassified relationship, social practice or group (Murji and Solomos 2005; Omi and Winant 1994). 'Immigration, the media, political discourses, crime and policing, housing and residential patterns, and poverty are among the leading topics or issues analysed in terms of racialization in the United Kingdom [and in the United States]' (Murji and Solomos 2005: 1). As we discuss later, management discourses intersect with these racialised topics and issues in ways that perpetuate racial hierarchies in hiring, promotion and other organisational practices.

Racial ideology

Bonilla-Silva (2003: 9) describes racial ideology as 'racially based frameworks' used by dominant race(s) to explain and justify the status quo and subordinated race(s) to challenge it. Each race's frameworks reflect its group-based experiences and interests, but only the dominant group's framework is known by all. Subordinated groups have not only to offer an alternative framework (based on experiences that are often unheard) but must challenge the very 'common sense' of the dominant groups (Bonilla-Silva 2003: 9–10). Two common frameworks that promote this type of uncritical dominant racial ideology are *colour-blind racism* (or race neutrality) and the *ethnicity paradigm*. Colour-blind racism is grounded in a structural definition of racism conceptualised as: 'culturally sanctioned beliefs which, regardless of the intentions involved, defend the advantages whites have because of the subordinated positions of racial minorities' (Wellman 1977: xviii). Colour-blind racism, then, 'explains contemporary racial inequality as the outcome of nonracial dynamics' such as market dynamics, naturally occurring phenomena and group cultural limitations (Bonilla-Silva 2003: 2). Similarly, the ethnicity paradigm is a racial framework that discursively erases race and racial histories and presumes that cultural groups vary in their ability, propensity or desire to assimilate into the dominant white culture (Nkomo 1992: 492–7). It is assumed that any lack of assimilation is the fault of the ethnic group and not due to mainstream exclusion or hostility.

Representation

The ideology of representation is a key mechanism thorough which racial ideologies are reproduced and maintained. Representational ideology is 'the belief that theories are attempts to accurately describe and represent reality as it is in itself' (Kwek 2003: 125). Representations created in mainstream culture often rely on essentialism, or reducing phenomena to a concrete, observable, limited and supposedly innate form so that it is more easily engaged and controlled. Power and domination are inextricably tied to

Table 22.1 Methodologies for decolonising management research, theory and practice

Postcolonial theory and criticism	Critical theories of race	
	Critical race theory	Interrogating whiteness
Challenge the west's creation of a subordinated Other	Challenge legal justifications for sustaining white supremacy	Challenge discourses, images and practices that protect and advantage whiteness
Expose and critique 'Othering' through representational practices	Expose and critique 'colour-blind' racism and claims of race neutrality	Expose and critique discourses that normalise whiteness
Centre Others' alternative histories and self-representations	Centre the voices, experiences and realities of the oppressed	Centre the self-reflexive voices of white people critiquing white privilege

representation practices: 'whoever represents the world, appropriates reality for him/herself, and by appropriating it, dominates it, thereby constituting it as an apparatus of power' (Kwek 2003: 127, summarising Marin). The issue of who has the power to circulate which meanings to whom (Hall 1985) is a central concern in decolonising management discourses.

Methodologies for decolonising management discourses

In what follows we discuss postcolonial and critical theories of race as productive tools for revealing the silences and concealment surrounding race and management (see Table 22.1). The frameworks presented are influenced by a range of disciplines and perspectives, including subjectivist epistemologies – black feminism/womanism, queer theory, Latina/o critical theory and others – that emerged from the experiences and knowledge systems of groups marginalised by the dominant Western-centric paradigm (Ladson-Billings 2000). Our framework is not meant to be comprehensive of the range of interpretations possible in postcolonial and critical race theory (or theories). Rather we highlight some fundamental claims and strategies that we believe are helpful in exposing, critiquing and countering the dominating influences of oppressive racial ideologies and discourses. We invite the reader to investigate these ideas further.

Postcolonial theory and criticism

Prasad (2003: 7) characterises postcolonial theory as a 'set of productively syncretic theoretical and political positions' that creatively employ concepts, epistemological perspectives and multiple approaches from various scholarly fields. Postcolonial analyses can 'alert us to the fact that the imperialist lens that greatly influenced the West's perception of the non-West during the colonial era is, arguably, still actively shaping and controlling the non-West in numerous domains today' (Kwek 2003: 130). Colonising influences are revealed through critiques of racialised histories that discursively produce and try to silence the west's inferior 'Other' (Said 1978), as well as the creative resistance strategies through which subordinated ('Othered') groups seek to decolonise the social order (Fanon

1967). Specifically, strategies for decolonising management discourses would focus on (1) critiquing and revealing racialised representations in management theory and practice; (2) giving voice to alternative histories of the Other (Kwek 2003: 131); (3) 'offering analytical categories and representational approaches for subordinated groups to represent themselves in "their own terms"' (Calas and Smircich, cited in Kwek 2003: 130); and (4) the pervasiveness of the dominant discourse in its ability to marginalise and silence (Kwek 2003: 130).

Critical theories of race advance decolonising methodologies because they stand in opposition to the mainstream views of ethnicity-oriented paradigms that discursively erase race and racial histories. We examine CRT, in its more contemporary form, and interrogating whiteness as two critical theories of race that are particularly useful methodologies for decolonising management discourse.

Critical race theory

CRT emerged from a movement of critical legal scholars interested in studying and transforming the relationship between law, race, racism and power in society (Williams 1997). However, in its more contemporary form CRT encompasses a range of disciplines and spaces where racism is institutionalised and where critical coalitions are formed against it (Valdes et al. 2002). The theory posits that 'because [racism] is so enmeshed in the fabric of the U.S. social order, it appears both normal and natural to people in this society . . . Therefore, the strategy for those who fight for racial social justice is to unmask and expose racism in all of its various permutations', including claims of neutrality and colour-blindness (Ladson-Billings 2000: 264). CRT looks at issues such as the contradiction between the egalitarian and democratic ideals of the USA and its racist history and present (Bell 2000; Williams 1997), and the history of and legal justification for legal and material advantages that accrue to whiteness (Harris 1993; Lipsitz 1998). CRT methodologies include storytelling as a primary means for exposing the experience of multiple and intersecting oppressions of racism, sexism, homophobia, xenophobia and others. These features of CRT – exposing claims of 'normal racism', challenging legal justifications for sustaining white supremacy, and giving voice to the experiences and realities of the oppressed – can be applied to our understanding of raced management practices.

Interrogating whiteness

To address systems of racial privilege and oppression fully, we must address the perpetuation of white privilege as a taken-for-granted norm. Interrogating whiteness (hooks 1990) has the goal of making whiteness and white privilege visible, exploring its consequences and the ways it is normalised. A set of 'linked dimensions', whiteness is (1) 'a location of structural advantage', (2) 'a place from which white people look at ourselves, at others, and at society', and (3) a set of unmarked and unnamed social practices (Frankenberg 1993: 1). Whiteness is the primary means through which racialised and power-laden relationships are reproduced and sustained in management discourses.

Interrogating whiteness, then, is an activity 'that involves critical reflection about whiteness and privilege and the implications of living in a race-centered society' (Grimes

2001: 139). It requires investigating how white people protect their own 'normal' status. It asks white people to examine behaviours or beliefs that contribute to racism, even in the absence of racist intention. In interrogating whiteness, not only do we need to make whiteness visible, we need to scrutinise actively *how* words, images and practices encountered in everyday societal situations serve to protect and advantage white people and limit the life choices of marginalised others.

Future directions: Decolonising race and management discourse

Because race structures and impacts organisations in ways that are not well understood, every area of management scholarship and practice could benefit from new questions informed by critical theories of race and postcolonial perspectives. In this section we focus on literature that draws upon postcolonial and critical theories of race (as summarised in Table 22.1) to provide future directions for unmasking the hidden articulations about race in management theory construction, research and practice.

Seeing race in management theory construction

Decolonising management theory begins with the recognition that knowledge production in the current global context is itself a 'racial project' that continues to recreate and advance the west's reliance on a subordinated Other. The task for management scholars, then, is to levy challenges to this racial project, and several management and organisational communication scholars have begun to do so. Kwek's (2003) postcolonial critique of the cross-cultural management literature reveals the underlying logics of representation that impose western cultural dimensions upon the very reality they seek to describe. He argues that cross-cultural studies 'become Western tools for colonization . . . preemptively preventing other cultures from having a voice in their own representation' (p. 122).

Focusing on racialisation processes, Ashcraft and Allen (2003) use a critical race framework to expose the ways in which whiteness is normalised in the field of organisational communication by considering its foundational textbooks. They observe how 'the normative power of organised whiteness' is preserved, even as these foundational texts purportedly attend to issues of race (Ashcraft and Allen 2003: 5). This is accomplished, for example, by treating race as a discrete variable that only becomes relevant in certain circumstances, and essentialising race by conflating it with 'cultural' or 'international differences'. Equating race with national cultures makes race doubly invisible because it also assumes national cultures have no diversity within them, and leaves the impression of a homogenous, race-neutral culture.

My work (Parker 2001, 2005) uses a black feminist standpoint approach to demonstrate how mainstream leadership theories advance idealised images of white feminine and masculine models of leadership as the universal, race-neutral way of viewing leadership. These models discursively erase the racialised and colonising histories that connect them to white middle-class norms, values and experiences, casting others as deficient, devalued or non-existent leaders. My work centres the histories, voices and experiences of African American women executives to deconstruct and redefine two raced, gendered and supposedly diametrically opposed notions of leadership – collaboration and instrumentality – common in the management literature. I then present a both/and approach to leadership from the perspectives of African American women executives: 'Situated at the intersection of race, gender, and class oppression within dominant-culture society, the contours of Black women's voices are simultaneously confrontational (in response to different interests) and collaborative (in response to shared interests)' (Parker 2001: 72). One goal of my work is to 'demonstrate the importance of placing marginalized groups at the center of analysis to disrupt the silences that devalue their contributions to knowledge production' (2005: 91).

I (Grimes 2002) build theory by introducing the interrogating whiteness perspective (2001, 2002). My work focuses on hidden discourses about race that reinforce white privilege. I use the perspective to critique management discourses, both academic management discourses that are not 'about' race (2001) and managing diversity discourses that *mask* and/or *recentre* whiteness. *Masking* fails to acknowledge differences sustained by whiteness, emphasising that people are 'all the same' in ways that ignore the difficulties and discrimination that people of colour encounter. *Recentring* whiteness acknowledges difference without fully challenging the hierarchies associated with those differences.

Seeing race in management research

Researching race in management studies as a decolonising activity involves 'excavating marginalized, oppositional scholarship' that challenges and interrupts, rather than becoming 'complicit with, oppressive and racist forms of knowledge production' (Gunaratnam 2003: 8). Decolonising research methodologies create opportunities for the co-creation of knowledge through collaboration with research participants throughout the research process. For example, Su and Yamamoto (2002) provide a personal (Su's) account of coalition building with Thai and Latina garment workers in Los Angeles to advocate an approach that involves scholars and subordinated communities. Similarly, Boje reflects on his time living and doing volunteer consulting in a predominantly black public housing community (Boje and Rosile 1994). He eventually learned to use the researcher and expert roles to assist residents on their own terms.

Centring the voices and histories of marginalised Others, including their own, is the central project of decolonisation, and many scholars are using this approach in critical studies of race, management and organising (Allen 1995; Essed 1994; Parker 2001, 2005; Pierce 2003). A related approach in critical race studies is centring the voices of white people to reveal racialisation processes. Two key research tactics are used in management studies: (1) centring the self-reflexive voices of white people critiquing white privilege (Alderfer 1982; Feagin and Mckinney 2003; Grimes 2001; Ramsey 1994), and (2) revealing the processes of normalising whiteness in white people's everyday discourses (Essed 2005; Tilbury and Colic-Peisker 2006). Alderfer (1982) was one of the first to express concern about the lack of attention to whiteness in organisation studies and to call for white people to critique white privilege. Also, in her personal account, Ramsey (1994) reflects on her changing awareness as she took a job at a predominantly black university, and notes an incident in which she keeps referring to 'the three racial groups' in a study she is discussing with an African American colleague while he patiently keeps referring to 'four'. She shares with readers her shock of awareness that she is not counting whites as a racial group.

Other scholars have centred white people's everyday discourses to reveal processes of normalising whiteness. For example, Tilbury and Colic-Peisker (2006) explore a number of discursive devices used by employers when talking about employment market issues for migrants in Australia. The employers used rhetorical discourses embedded within broader racist discourses to deflect attention from their own possible culpability in discriminating against 'visibly different' refugees and new migrants. This latter approach – centring voices to reveal the construction of whiteness – has implications for management practice. As researchers and practitioners, we must do our own 'work' on racial issues before we can presume to train those in organisations in any useful way (Grimes 2001). Furthermore, the task of management educators is to draw attention to the discursive concealment of whiteness and model a process of surfacing it (Macalpine and Marsh 2005).

Seeing race in management practices

Decolonising management practice focuses on the racialised spaces where macro-level discourses are revealed in micro-practices. It involves unmasking racialised arrangements that reproduce subordinated 'Others' in everyday rituals such as recruitment, hiring and workplace interactions. The implications for teaching and training are clear: to challenge the problematic aspects of 'Othering' we must be able to recognise the sites and contours of its processes. Scholars have focused on mechanisms of exclusion – especially during recruitment and job entry – as prime instruments of 'Othering'. For example, my (Parker 2003) reading of the literature on African American women's experiences in the US labor market revealed subtle exclusionary practices that result in job segregation (e.g. only 'allowed' entry into certain jobs) across levels – working-class, management and executive. These practices are linked to pervasive stereotyping grounded in historical representational discourses applied exclusively to African American women.

Puwar (2001) illustrates this pattern of exclusion by analysing a somatic norm in the British civil service that is invisibly white, male and middle-class. The somatic norm grows out of a 'global [racial] contract formed within the history of colonialism' (Puwar 2001: 64). Black upper-level civil servants are 'Space Invaders' because their bodies are literally out of place. She argues that according to the normative image, the Space Invaders 'belong' in 'wild' spaces, yet are moving within a space that represents the pinnacle of Reason. In interviews, the black civil servants reported white response to their presence as including dissonance and disorientation, infantilisation and invisibility, and hyper-surveillance. Both Puwar's theorising of the somatic norm as a legacy of colonisation and the particular responses it engendered would be useful starting places for seeing race in management practices.

Essed (2005) shifts her gaze from exclusion to sameness in her study of what she calls *cultural cloning*, or the preference for sameness in high-status professions and in corporations. She observes that candidates for the professions are selected through networking and according to their closeness to a normative (preferred) image. It is a process of systemic ordering that perpetuates whiteness and white privilege in society and organisations. Reinforcing Essed's thesis, researchers have pointed to employers' attempts to 'de-race' workers' bodies in the quest for race-neutral sameness. For example, Byrd and Tharps (2001) report that during the late 1990s over a thousand African American women, mostly front-line workers in the service or hospitality industries, were fired or reprimanded because of 'bans on cornrows' (p. 107). Cornrows, a braided hairstyle with roots in African culture, were deemed 'not fit for the "corporate" image' (Byrd and Tharps 2001: 107–8). A more recent 'de-racing' project is the French ban on religious headwear targeting Muslim women.

Finally, other scholars have used an interrogating whiteness perspective to investigate how privilege and domination unfold and are normalised in everyday organisational life. Macalpine and Marsh (2005) highlight the taken-for-grantedness of whiteness through discourses of neutrality among public-sector managers and professionals. Silence about ethnicity (racialised identities) means that talk about ethnicity is 'transgressive' and silence about whiteness masks white power through normalising whiteness. Silencing operates as a hegemonic discourse, policed through embarrassment, which perpetuates inequalities and conceals white power.

Pierce (2003) introduces 'racing for innocence' as a discursive practice in contemporary corporations that disavows accountability for racist practices at the same time that everyday racism is practised. She compares the narratives of African American male lawyers who left a corporate legal department with the white male lawyers who stayed. Focusing on an African American man – Randall Kingsley – Pierce argues that the white men, by virtue of their social location, cannot see how they contributed to the hostile climate that forced Randall to leave the firm. 'What he experiences as systemic unrelenting forms of indifference, derision and exclusion, the white lawyers insist are isolated individual events' (p. 66). Pierce demonstrates that the narratives of both the white lawyers and Randall Kingsley empirically support the systemic account of why Randall left the firm. As shown in Pierce's study, a company might boast about its affirmative action programme but fail to address the difficulties marginalised people encounter in their organisational experiences.

These studies point to particular discursive practices – cultural cloning, reproducing 'Space Invaders', racing for innocence, silence about racial issues, normalisation of whiteness, and policing through embarrassment – that link micro- and macro-aspects of a racialised social structure (Winant 2000). Management theory, research and practice must draw attention to these hidden discursive practices and bring them to awareness and scrutiny.

Conclusion

In this chapter we have introduced critical theories of race and postcolonial theory as useful methodologies for addressing race in management discourse. We have focused on the importance of the critique of problematic assumptions as well as taking seriously the self-representations and experiences of dominated groups. We have tried to make clear the consequences of continuing to ignore race in management discourses. Important questions to continue pursuing include: what 'work' do persisting racial distinctions (coupled with their invisibility) do in management discourse? Further, what is it that encourages us to see race as simple or irrelevant, at best, or not to see it at all? We have given one, necessarily partial, response to those questions. We hope our chapter inspires others to continue this important work.

References

Alderfer, C. (1982) Problems of changing white males' behavior and beliefs concerning race relations. In P. S. Goodman (ed.), *Change in Organizations: New Perspectives on Theory*. San Francisco: Jossey-Bass, pp. 122–65.

Allen, B. J. (1995). 'Diversity' and organizational communication. *Journal of Applied Communication Research*, 23: 143–55.

Alvesson, M. and Y. Due Billing (1997) *Understanding Gender and Organizations*. Thousand Oaks, CA: Sage.

Ashcraft, K. L. and B. J. Allen (2003) The racial foundation of organizational communication. *Communication Theory*, 13(1): 5–38.

Bell, D. (2000) Affirmative action: Anther instance of racial workings in the United States. *Journal of Negro Education*, 69: 145–9.

Bertrand, M. and S. Mullainathan (2003) *Are Emily and Greg More Employable than Lakisha and Jamal? A Field Experiment on Labor Market Discrimination*. Cambridge, MA: National Bureau of Economic Research.

Boje, D. and G. A. Rosile (1994) Diversities, differences and authors' voices. *Journal of Organizational Change Management*, 7(6): 8–17.

Bonilla-Silva, E. (2003) *Racism without Racists: Color-Blind Racism and the Persistence of Racial Inequality in the United States*. New York: Rowman & Littlefield.

Bonilla-Silva, E. (2006) *Racism Without Racists: Color-Blind Racism and the Persistence of Racial Inequality in the United States*, 2nd edn. New York: Rowman and Littlefield.

Bonilla-Silva, E. (2007) Color-blind present, Latin America-like future: Racial stratification in 21st century Amerika. Paper delivered at the 13th Annual Academic Conference, Moore Undergraduate Research Apprenticeship Program, University of North Carolina at Chapel Hill, July.

Byrd, A. and L. Tharps (2001) *Hair Story: Untangling the Roots of Black Hair in America*. New York: St Martin's Press.

Carby, H. (1992) The multicultural wars. In G. Dent (ed.), *Black Popular Culture*. Seattle: Bay Press, pp. 187–99.

Essed, P. (1991) *Understanding Everyday Racism*. Newbury Park, CA: Sage.

Essed, P. (1994) Contradictory positions, ambivalent perceptions: A case study of a Black woman entrepreneur. In K. Bhavnani and A. Phoenix (eds), *Shifting Identities, Shifting Racisms: A Feminism and Psychology Reader*. London: Sage, pp. 99–118.

Essed, P. (2005) Gendered preferences in racialized spaces: Cloning the physician. In K. Murji and J. Solomos (eds), *Racialization: Studies in Theory and Practice*. New York: Oxford University Press, pp. 227–47.

Fanon, F. (1967) *The Wretched of the Earth*, trans C. Farrington. Harmondsworth: Penguin.

Feagin, J. R. (2006) *Systemic Racism: A Theory of Oppression*. New York: Routledge.

Feagin, J. R. and K. D. McKinney (2003) *The Many Costs of Racism*. Lanham, MD: Rowman and Littlefield.

Frankenberg, R. (1993) *White Women, Race Matters: The Social Construction of Whiteness*. Minneapolis: University of Minnesota Press.

Grimes, D. S. (1996) 'When and where I enter': Adding in Black women's insights to critique organization studies. PhD thesis, Purdue University, West Lafayette.

Grimes, D. S. (2001) Putting our own house in order: Whiteness, change, and organization studies. *Journal of Change Management*, 14(2): 132–49.

Grimes, D. S. (2002) Challenging the status quo? Whiteness in the diversity management literature. *Management Communication Quarterly*, 15(3): 381–409.

Gunaratnam, Y. (2003) *Researching Race and Ethnicity: Methods, Knowledge, Power.* Thousand Oaks, CA: Sage.

Hall, S. (1985) Signification, representation, ideology: Althusser and the post-structuralist debates. *Critical Studies in Mass Communication*, 2: 91–114.

Harris, C. (1993) Whiteness as property. *Harvard Law Review*, 106(8): 1707–91.

hooks, b. (1990) *Yearning: Race, Gender, and Cultural Politics.* Boston, MA: South End Press.

Iglesias, E. M. (2002) Global markets, racial spaces, and the role of critical race theory in the struggle for community control of investments: An institutional class analysis. In F. Valdes, J. Culp and A. P. Harris (eds), *Crossroads, Directions and a New Critical Race Theory.* Philadelphia: Temple University Press, pp. 310–36.

Kothari, U. (2006) An agenda for thinking about 'race' in development. *Progress in Development Studies*, 6(1): 9–23.

Kwek, D. (2003) Decolonizing and re-presenting culture's consequences: A postcolonial critique of cross-cultural studies in management. In A. Prasad (ed.), *Postcolonial Theory and Organizational Analysis: A Critical Engagement.* New York: Palgrave, pp. 121–46.

Ladson-Billings, G. (2000) Racialized discourses and ethnic epistemologies. In N. K. Denzin and Y. S. Lincoln (eds), *The Sage Handbook of Qualitative Research* 2nd edn. Thousand Oaks, CA: Sage, pp. 257–78.

Lincoln, Y. (2005) Institutional review boards and methodological conservatism: The challenge to and from phenomenological paradigms. In N. K. Denzin and Y. S. Lincoln (eds), *The Sage Handbook of Qualitative Research* 3rd edn. Thousand Oaks, CA: Sage, pp. 165–82.

Lipsitz, G. (1998) *The Possessive Investment in Whiteness: How White People Profit from Identity Politics.* Philadelphia: Temple University Press.

Macalpine, M. and S. Marsh (2005) 'On being white: There's nothing I can say': Exploring whiteness and power in organizations. *Management Learning*, 36(4): 429–50.

Murji, K. and J. Solomos (eds) (2005) *Racialization: Studies in Theory and Practice.* New York: Oxford University Press.

Nkomo, S. M. (1992) The emperor has no clothes: Rewriting 'race in organizations'. *Academy of Management Review*, 17: 487–513.

Omi, M. and H. Winant (1994) *Racial Formation in the United States: From the 1960s to the 1980s*, rev. edn. New York: Routledge.

Pager, D. (2003) The mark of a criminal record. *American Journal of Sociology*, 108: 937–75.

Parker, P. S. (2001) African American women executives within dominant-culture organizations: (Re)conceptualizing notions of collaboration and instrumentality. *Management Communication Quarterly*, 15(1): 42–82.

Parker, P. S. (2003) Control, power, and resistance within raced, gendered, and classed work contexts: The case of African American women. *Communication Yearbook*, 27: 257–91.

Parker, P. S. (2005) *Race, Gender, and Leadership: Reconceptualizing Organizational*

Leadership from the Perspectives of African American Women Executives. Mahwah, NJ: Lawrence Erlbaum.

Parker, P. S. and J. Mease (in press) Beyond the knapsack: Disrupting the production of white racial privilege in organizational practices. In L. A. Samovar, R. E. Porter and E. R. McDaniel (eds), *Intercultural Communication: A Reader.* Belmont, CA: Thompson.

Parker, P. S., S. A. Dempsey and K. Krone (2006) Organizational leadership as global activism: Lessons from transnational feminist networks. Paper delivered at the annual meeting of the National Communication Association, November.

Pierce, J. L. (2003) 'Racing for innocence': Whiteness, corporate culture, and the backlash against affirmative action. *Qualitative Sociology,* 26(1): 53–70.

Prasad, A. (2003) *Postcolonial Theory and Organizational Analysis: A Critical Engagement.* New York: Palgrave.

Puwar, N. (2001) The racialised somatic norm and the senior civil service. *Sociology,* 35(3): 651–70.

Ramsey, J. (1994) A different way of making a difference: Learning through feelings. *Journal of Organizational Change Management,* 7(6): 59–71.

Said, E. (1978) *Orientalism.* New York: Vintage.

Su, J. and E. K. Yamamoto (2002) Critical coalitions: Theory and praxis. In F.Valdes, J. Culp and A. Harris (eds), *Crossroads, Directions, and a New Critical Race Theory.* Philadelphia: Temple University Press, pp. 379–92.

Tilbury, F. and V. Colic-Peisker (2006) Deflecting responsibility in employer talk about race discrimination. *Discourse and Society,* 17(5): 651–76.

Valdes, F., J. M. Culp and A. P. Harris (2002) *Crossroads, Directions, and a New Critical Race Theory.* Philadelphia: Temple University Press.

Wellman, D. (1977) *Portraits of White Racism.* Cambridge: Cambridge University Press.

Williams, P. (1997) *Seeing a Color-Blind Future: The Paradox of Race.* New York: Noonday Press.

Winant, H. (2000) Race and race theory. *Annual Review of Sociology,* 26: 169–85.

23

Business communication

Leena Louhiala-Salminen

Introduction

Like business discourse (BD) scholars, business communication (BC) researchers focus on text and talk in the context of business. The two disciplines share a lot, and the concepts overlap to a large extent. However, in the rapidly changing business context – and for that matter in the academic context as well – it is worthwhile considering the two notions and the relationship between them.

At present, the discipline of BC seems to be gaining momentum. Today's complex business environment, with its new technologies, new structures, multiple languages and multiple cultures, has acknowledged the salient role of communication in business activities in general, and international activities in particular; simultaneously, a growing need to know more about communication-related issues sparks new research. There is wide interest in BD and its context.

Whether a research project falls within the framework of BC or that of BD is often a matter for the researchers to decide; they must situate themselves in the research community. In their book *Business Discourse* Bargiela-Chiappini et al. (2007: 3) write as follows: 'Business discourse is all about how people communicate using talk or writing in commercial organisations in order to get their work done. In this book we will view business discourse as social action in business contexts.' Comparing this characterisation with what seems to constitute BC research today, we can note two things. First, BC has the same focus as BD, i.e. how people communicate to get their work done. Second, in addition to this micro-level view of individuals communicating, BC is also interested in how companies reach their targets through communication, i.e. the macro-perspective.

Another aspect in which BC and BD seem to differ is the size of the target in focus. Both disciplines look at text and context, but BC seems to target a wider range of textual and contextual issues, while BD focuses more directly on text and uses context to explain linguistic phenomena. In other words, what is seen as context in BD research may very well be the focal point of a BC study; for example, survey findings about the views of business practitioners may be contextual data for a BD researcher, whereas they may be the actual object of investigation in a BC research project.

This chapter will present a view of BC in the corporate environment of the 2000s and discuss the concept especially from the perspective of current developments in global business. It will also indicate areas where BD and BC scholars share issues and suggest lines of BC research that could contribute to BD research projects. First, some historical developments will be presented, with a review of earlier considerations on the disciplinary status of BC. Then the focus will shift to the specific trends in the corporate environment of the 2000s that seem to be strengthening the discipline. The purpose of the chapter is to show the evolution of BC from a skills-oriented, detail-focused subject to a significant discipline, actively engaged in research on a wide range of topics.

Background

The history of science shows that new disciplines always struggle for status. Achieving coherence in disciplinary objects and theories takes time, and requires a fair amount of argumentation, counter-argumentation, conceptualisation, research activities and applied work. In the field of communication, the discussion of disciplinary status started in the 1930s. Donsbach (2005) refers to a speech made by Ferdinand Tönnies, the president of the German Sociological Association, in 1930, in which he questions the position of communication (then called 'press research') as a new discipline: 'Why would we need press research within sociology? We don't need a chicken or duck science within biology.' Communication today enjoys the status of an established academic discipline, yet discussion about its 'identity' continues.

Although the scope of BC is more limited than that of communication, the 'identity crisis' has been no less serious. This may be partly due to the dyadic nature of the field; on the one hand, BC is a practical, skills-oriented subject taught in university programmes and also supports an extensive consultancy business; on the other hand, it is an object of serious academic inquiry. BC could be regarded as a subdiscipline of communication, i.e. a 'duck/chicken science' that has grown out of communication However, BC can also be seen as one of the business disciplines; it is increasingly researched and taught in business schools and is gaining more attention and importance among business practitioners. It draws from communication studies and theories, but also from rhetoric, discourse analysis, conversational analysis, management, psychology and sociology, to name a few

The research traditions of BC in the USA stem from rhetoric. (For a vivid metaphorical account of the neglected and lonesome Business Communication and her mother, the former beauty queen Rhetoric, see Reinsch 1996: 27.) In Europe, as argued by Charles (1998: 85), BC studies are deeply rooted in a multicultural and multilingual reality; European research has emerged from the needs of foreign language learning and teaching, and much of BC scholarship has been conducted within such frames as business English (BE) or English for specific purposes (ESP).

Considering the varied base and, indeed, the great variety of lenses that are used to examine BC issues, it is no wonder that the question of identity emerges. Since the early 1990s, the discussion has been lively, and in 1998 the *Journal of Business Communication* devoted an entire issue to discipline formation. In that issue, Graham and Thralls (1998: 7) argue that the desire to legitimise the work done and to show that BC is a coherent, knowledge-producing field, instead of a mere skills-based approach, has produced intense and sustained self-reflection among BC scholars. The rapidly changing business environment of the 2000s has made self-reflection even more intense, and, as this chapter argues, has also resulted in a wider view of BC as a discipline.

Discussing disciplinarity in general, Mumby and Stohl (1996: 52) refer to a shared set of paradigmatic assumptions as vital; although various and competing theories may emerge, they usually develop out of a common set of epistemological, ontological and methodological assumptions. Graham and Thralls (1998) present more specific disciplinary criteria, such as a shared goal for research and the existence of common journals, associations and institutional sites. As regards a 'shared goal for research' for BC, there seems to be a general understanding of the utilitarian goal of developing and disseminating knowledge that increases the effectiveness and efficiency of business operations. The goal of effectiveness is embedded in Reinsch's 1996 definition of BC, where he conceptualises BC as 'the scholarly study of the use, adaptation and creation of languages, symbols and signs to conduct activities that satisfy human needs and wants by providing goods and services for private profit' (Reinsch 1996: 28). Ten years later, Reinsch and Turner (2006) elaborated the scope of the definition further, emphasising the processual nature of communication and referring to the fact that BC is increasingly conducted in crosscultural and/or virtual environments. They also elaborate the restriction to 'activities . . . for private profit' by referring to what they call 'profit-motivated (efficiency-seeking) exchange of goods and services'. However, the underlying principle of effectiveness and a distinct focus on language remain the same.

BC also meets the criteria of discipline identification that call for the existence of common public sites, i.e. professional organisations and journals where scholarship is legitimised and defined. The Association for Business Communication is currently the best-known internationally active organisation, and its two journals, The *Journal of Business Communication* (focusing on research) and *Business Communication Quarterly* (focusing on pedagogy), were ranked as top business and management communication journals by two recent surveys (see Rogers et al. 2007; Lowry et al. 2007). Nevertheless, the existence of only a few institutional sites of its own still make BC an 'orphaned' field to some extent, as was argued by Hagge (1986). Although BC is housed in a variety of academic institutions, it now increasingly operates in business schools and thus coexists and more or less co-operates with other business disciplines. In addition, academia has been interested in establishing programmes and professorships in BC, or more specifically, in BC in international contexts. Two European examples are the master's program in corporate communication at the School of Business of the University of Aarhus in Denmark, and the master's and doctoral programmes in international BC at the Helsinki School of Economics.

Furthermore, a discipline quite obviously ought to have a shared object of study. Locker (1998: 16) defined the object 'which we teach, research and attempt to define as *communication in the workplace*' (emphasis added). She argued that BC is at least an 'emerging' discipline, and stressed the interdisciplinary nature of this scholarship; she (1998: 15) noted that a discipline can emerge in its own right by virtue of the ways in which it selects from and interprets its parent disciplines. Locker's wide perception of the shared object includes all kinds of organisations. In the present complex operating environment, *communication in the workplace* might, however, seem a somewhat restricted object; much of today's communication is in fact distributed across various organisational and national borders rather than literally 'in' the workplace. For example, current BC scholarship includes studies that investigate various communication processes such as collaborative writing. (For an extensive account of recent work in this area, see Lowry et al. 2004.)

In addition to BC, there are other domains of communication that can claim the label of 'communication in the workplace' as their object of study. Miller (1996) talks about the four subdisciplines at the crossroads between communication and organisational life: (1) management communication, (2) organisational communication, (3) corporate communication and (4) BC. The perceived characteristics of the four 'neighbours' have been extensively discussed in earlier work (e.g. Argenti 1996; Kalla 2006; Louhiala-Salminen 1999a; Mumby and Stohl 1996; Reinsch 1996; Rogers 1996, 2001; Shelby 1993, 1996; Smeltzer 1996). However, a brief introduction to the neighbouring domains will follow, since it seems that understanding the relationship between BC and BD also requires knowledge of the main traditional characteristics of management, organisational and corporate communication.

Management communication, as the name suggests, investigates and teaches present and future managers. The goal is to increase the effectiveness and efficiency of the communicative activities of managers, or, as Kalla (2006: 128) puts it, to increase 'the development of the knowledge sharing skills of managers'. *Organisational communication* seeks to understand how the context of the organisation influences communication processes (Miller 2003: 1) and how people in the organisation ascribe meanings to messages; it is also interested in how meanings are distorted or changed when messages are exchanged in both formal and informal networks (Tourish and Hargie 2004: 10). While in 1996 Mumby and Stohl (1996: 56) explicitly distance themselves from the utilitarian goals of some communication research, and also from their colleagues in business and management who 'exist in a symbiotic relationship with the corporate world', in 2004 Tourish and Hargie (p. 10) include the effectiveness of communication among the key issues of their research. The third 'neighbour', *corporate communication*, has evolved from what used to be known as public relations ('shielding top managers from bullets thrown at them from outside the boundaries of the organisation'; Argenti 1996: 75) to a business function responding to the challenges of the rapidly changing environment. Argenti and Forman (2002: 4) define corporate communication as the corporation's voice and the images it produces of itself to its various audiences. Today, corporate communication is increasingly seen as a holistic concept, including both company-external and company-internal communication; some scholars would even use the term interchangeably with 'business communication'.

The domains discussed above have a lot in common. Although the emphasis may differ, I would argue that the four fields seem to *con*verge rather than *di*verge (see also Rogers 2001) in the research arena of the 2000s. Rogers argues that a single, unified disciplinary identity is in fact of less importance than the richness that is gained from interdisciplinarity. Drawing from various fields, and crossing borders to fields previously foreign to us, are a necessity for today's researchers, whether they work within the frame of BC or that of BD.

The impact of current business trends on business communication research

The context of BC in the 2000s, i.e. the entire business community, has undergone fundamental change processes at an extremely fast pace. Three trends stand out. First, technology has taken gigantic leaps; second, business structures have changed. The third trend, globalisation, overlapping and intertwined with the other two, is an issue affecting all society but particularly the business world. The impact of globalisation is felt not only in large, multinationally operating companies, but to a great extent in small and medium-sized businesses as well.

The next three subsections will focus on the effects of the above changes in business on the work conducted and planned within BC.

Technology

Advancing (or, perhaps, simply 'changing') technology does not only alter the ways in which BC is conducted; it changes the actual communication and also affects the organisation. As an example of a major organisational change, Reinsch and Turner (2006: 342; see also Louhiala-Salminen 1999a) mention the impact of wordprocessing software on the number of secretarial jobs. Yates (1989, 2005) has shown that even before computers, 'technologies' such as carbon paper and vertical files contributed to new approaches in management and produced new organisational structures.

As an example of technology affecting what and how business communicates, consider the developments in sending written interpersonal business messages. Before the fax revolution (Louhiala-Salminen 1997) at the end of the 1980s, the dominant genre in written communication was the business letter (for an extensive volume on genre variation in business letters, see Gillaerts and Gotti 2005). The fax machine not only made communication faster, but also affected format and language. Some messages that would have earlier been communicated over the telephone were now faxed. This happened especially in cross-border contacts between non-native speakers of English, as it was often easier to write a fax than to discuss an issue on the phone (for a more thorough discussion, see Louhiala-Salminen 1996, 1999a, 1999b; Louhiala-Salminen and Kankaanranta 2005). The 'fax era' in communication did not last long. Although the pace at which email has conquered the scene has not been equally rapid in all parts of the world (see Zhu 2005), most north European companies no longer use the fax. Email has not only taken over the tasks previously done by fax, but has also assumed tasks from other media, e.g. face-to-face interaction or the telephone. Kankaanranta's (2005) study on internal communication in a multinational company shows how different email genres are used to conduct global business operations (see also Nickerson 2000).

In the past two decades, genre-based approaches to technology-induced changes in BC have been common. Both scholars who represent 'pure' communication research as opposed to a more linguistic perspective (e.g. Yates and Orlikowski 1992; Orlikowski and Yates 1994) and scholars whose work could be regarded as either BD or BC research (e.g. Akar and Louhiala-Salminen 1999; Gimenez 2000; Kankaanranta 2005; Louhiala-Salminen 1997, 1999a, 1999b; Louhiala-Salminen and Kankaanranta 2005; Nickerson 2000; Poncini 2005; Zhu 2005) have through genre analysis produced valuable knowledge for business research and practice. Today, new technological solutions continuously give rise to new BC genres, and research should keep up with the developments. An example of a potential research object is the recent tendency of businesspeople to use decks of slides from visual presentations (e.g. PowerPoint) to replace written reports (see also Turner and Reinsch 2007).

Technology has changed BC and its context in many ways. For example, mobile phones and laptop computers are personal gear that enable multitasking. Imagine a team in their weekly meeting around a large, round table; the participants sit behind their laptop screens, sometimes lifting their eyes above the computer and discussing an issue, but most of the time either taking notes or writing messages and doing other planning or reporting tasks. Multitasking is to some extent familiar to business communicators of all times, but modern technology seems to make it more frequent (Turner and Reinsch 2007). More research is, however, needed to evaluate its effectiveness. A study by Rubinstein et al. (2001) showed that their subjects lost time when they had to switch from one task to another. Rubinstein et al. (2001: 770) talk about human 'executive control' that involves two stages, i.e. goal-shifting (as applied to the meeting example above: 'I am now turning my attention from this email to this quarter's budget, item three on the agenda') and rule activation (as applied to the meeting example above: 'I am turning off the rules for emailing and turning on the rules for meeting behaviour'). One might, of course, argue that while some time is lost in switching from one task to another, overall efficiency might, however, increase as several other tasks are performed during the meeting.

Further recent technological changes that affect BC in the 2000s include the use of electronic media that free people from being tied to their desks, virtual service organisations, call centres in distant locations, and the use of digital cameras built into mobile phones or located on top of computer screens (Reinsch and Turner 2006: 43). All these new contexts are producing new kinds of BD that call for research. In addition, internet blogs and other sites are new arenas of communication that will significantly affect advertising and probably also other areas of BD.

Business structures

The second conspicuous trend in the contemporary business community is sweeping structural change. In the earlier environment, the borders of the operating business unit were clear; company A operated (buying or selling, usually) and thus communicated with company B. Today, businesses increasingly operate as units within a network of companies (A–B–C–D–E–F), where every unit has a specific task in relation to the entire network and the tasks of the other units.

The forms of traditional co-operation started to change when specialisation increased and systemic product/service offerings became common. This led to 'core business thinking', and companies started to outsource their operations. The greater degree of specialisation also led to fierce competition, which then forced companies to seek alliances and partners and start forming networks (see, for example, Möller and Halinen 1999).

In recent research on business networks, communication seems to have emerged as one of the key issues; it has been addressed through management, knowledge-sharing and intercultural relations. For example, Möller and Svahn (2004: 219) referring to Li et al. (2002), argue that advancing globalisation is forcing firms to engage in alliances and networks with partners from widely diverse cultural backgrounds. However, if the differences in the cultural orientation are managed in a balanced manner, performance may even improve. It is fairly obvious, and also confirmed by the literature (e.g. Svahn 2004; Tuusjärvi 2003), that networks must be characterised by openness, trust and continuous development of relations. These can only be achieved through communication; since no formal organisation with rules and formal structures exists, maintaining a network requires continuous communication and shared knowledge. In 1995 Grandori and Soda (1995: 184–5) defined a business network as follows: 'A network is a mode regulating interdependence between firms . . . which is based on a cooperative "game" with partner-specific communication.' It seems that this 'partner-specific communication' is one of the key issues that future BD and BC researchers could investigate, since a lot needs to be communicated, but more and more selectively. Network members must consider what to disclose to their closest strategic partners, how to disclose it, and how this differs from what is conveyed to the other members in the network.

Globalisation

Globalisation is not a new phenomenon. Friedman (2005; see also Thomas 2007) claims that globalisation began in 1492, with Columbus opening trade between the Old World and the New World. Friedman further argues that we have now entered a new era, Globalisation 3.0, where not only countries and companies but also individuals collaborate and compete globally. This makes the impact of current globalisation on companies and employees extremely strong. For BC, globalisation brings entirely new challenges as regards communication flows, media, cultural considerations and, above all, language; what used to be 'BC in language X' is now 'BC in (some form of) English'.

Charles (2007) writes that globalisation depends on people having access to a shared language facility. In the past few decades, it has become widely accepted that the lingua franca of international business is English, which can also be seen in the extent to which companies increasingly choose English as their official corporate language. The majority of international business is done in English (for a discussion, see Louhiala-Salminen et al. 2005), but not in native-speaker English. More often than not none of the communicating parties has English as their mother tongue. Lesznyak (2002), Mauranen (2003) and Seidlhofer (2002), among others, refer to these instances of language use as ELF (English as a lingua franca) communication. To focus specifically on business ELF situations, and to explore issues related to the English used in contemporary globalised BC, Louhiala-Salminen et al. (2005) coined the term BELF, business English as a lingua franca. BELF refers to English used as a 'neutral' and shared communication code for the function of conducting business. In this definition, two particular aspects are central: the role played by the speakers of this code and the domain of its use. First, taking BELF to be a functioning tool for communication means that the role of communicators is that of language users in their own right – not the 'non-native speakers' or 'learners' of second language research. Second, the 'B' in BELF emphasises the fact that business is the domain where the code is used. The reference point in any linguistic comparison must be in the domain of business. So far, we know little of the characteristics and possible cultural connections and implications of BELF.

Overall, BC scholars agree that language matters, but we need more research to find out how and why it matters. Over the years, various methods have been used to investigate language (e.g. Poncini 2004; Charles 1995; Planken 2005; Clifton 2006), and most researchers seem to accept the use of multiple methods to investigate the various sides of a research problem. However, as is usual in all research, all methodological choices are not unanimously supported , as is evidenced by a recent debate on the merits of micro-analytical studies in examining communication (see McPhee et al. 2006; Cooren 2006).

In addition to language, globalisation has highlighted the importance of studies investigating culture. Thomas (2007: 269) points out the significance of intercultural communication, and Jameson (2007) calls for a broader conception of cultural identity that does not privilege nationality but consists of several components, and is negotiated through communication. Concerns with culture – or rather 'culture' – are shared among BC and BD scholars. Cultural issues have been examined by several prominent BC researchers, e.g. Jameson (2007), Scollon and Scollon (2001), Varner (2000) and Beamer (1995).

Conclusion

This chapter has discussed the notion of BC and some of the key contextual factors in the business environment. Efforts have been made to illustrate differences and similarities between the approaches assumed in BD and BC research.

To conclude, I would like to conceptualise BC as an integrated 'umbrella' concept covering all formal and informal communication within a business context, using all possible media, involving all stakeholder groups, operating both at the level of the individual employee and at that of the corporation. Depending on the issue at hand, BC studies focus either on text or context, or they use multiple methods to look at both. From this perspective, the 'traditional' neighbouring disciplines could all be placed under the BC umbrella, and a specific situational emphasis assumed when an issue needed to be considered from the management, corporate or organisational point of view. Also, the individual perspective of BD referred to at the beginning of this chapter – 'how people communicate using talk or writing in commercial organisations in order to get their work done' – as I see it, would be placed under the BC umbrella.

The purpose of the chapter has also been to show that the present view of BC as a widely active business research discipline is justified. Like those of other business disciplines, the ontological and epistemological assumptions of BC are built on a basic understanding of the effectiveness of operations as the targeted state. Also, as BC seems to be gaining importance in both academia and the world of practice – for example, communications directors increasingly sit at board tables and businesses assess the impact of effective communications on the bottom line – its status as a subdiscipline of business is emerging. Further, BC is often housed in business schools, it draws from various business fields, and it looks at similar issues to those of international business research (e.g. organisational effectiveness in cross-border mergers and acquisitions), marketing (e.g. change of brand strategy) and management (e.g. strategy implementation process). However, even as a business discipline BC has a unique perspective of its own, i.e. communication as the prerequisite for any business, and text – words, sentences, utterances – as the prerequisite for any communication.

References

Akar, D. and L. Louhiala-Salminen (1999) Towards a new genre: A comparative study of business faxes. In F. Bargiela-Chiappini and C. Nickerson (eds), *Writing Business: Genres, Media and Discourses*. London and New York: Longman, pp. 207–26.

Argenti, P.A. (1996) Corporate communication as a discipline: Toward a definition. *Management Communication Quarterly*, 10(1): 73–97.

Argenti, P. A. and J. Forman (2002) *The Power of Corporate Communication: Crafting the Voice and Image of Your Business*. New York: McGraw-Hill.

Bargiela-Chiappini, F., C. Nickerson and B. Planken (2007) *Business Discourse*. Basingstoke: Palgrave Macmillan.

Beamer, L. (1995) A schemata model for intercultural encounters and case study: The emperor and the envoy. *Journal of Business Communication*, 32(2): 141–61.

Charles, M. (1995) Organisational power in business negotiations. In K. Ehlich and J. Wagner (eds), *The Discourse of International Negotiations*. Berlin: Mouton de Gruyter, pp. 151–74.

Charles, M. (1998) Europe: Oral business communication. *Business Communication Quarterly*, 61(3): 85–93.

Charles, M. (2007) Language matters in global communication. *Journal of Business Communication*, 44(3): 260–82.

Clifton, J. (2006) A conversation analytical approach to business communication: The case of leadership. *Journal of Business Communication*, 43(3): 202–19.

Cooren, F. (2006) Arguments for the in-depth study of organizational interactions. *Management Communication Quarterly*, 19(3): 327–40.

Donsbach, W. (2005) The identity of communication research. *Journal of Communication*, 56: 437–38.

Friedman, T. (2005) *The World is Flat*. New York: Farrar, Straus & Giroux.

Gillaerts, P. and M. Gotti (2005) *Genre Variation in Business Letters*. Bern: Peter Lang.

Gimenez, J. (2000) Business email communication: Some emerging tendencies in register. *English for Specific Purposes*, 19(3): 237–51.

Graham, M. and C. Thralls (1998) Connections and fissures: Discipline formation in business communication. *Journal of Business Communication*, 35(1): 7–13.

Grandori, A. and G. Soda (1995) Inter-firm networks: Antecedents, mechanisms and forms. *Organization Studies*, 16(2): 183–214.

Hagge, J. (1986) Business communication, the orphaned discipline: A historical review of business communication teachers' perception of their field's place in the college curriculum. In D. Andrews (ed.), *Proceedings of the 51st ABC International Convention*. Los Angeles: Association for Business Communication, pp. 168–77.

Jameson, D. (2007) Reconceptualizing cultural identity and its role in intercultural business communication. *Journal of Business Communication*, 44(3): 199–235.

Kalla, H. (2006) Integrated internal communications in the multinational corporation. PhD thesis, Helsinki, Helsinki School of Economics.

Kankaanranta, A. (2005) 'Hej Seppo, could you pls comment on this!' Internal email communication in lingua franca English in a multinational company. PhD thesis, University of Jyväskylä, Centre for Applied Language Studies. http://ebooks.jyu.fi/solki/9513923207.pdf.

Lesznyak, A. (2002) From chaos to the smallest common denominator: Topic management in English lingua franca communication. In K. Knapp and C. Meierkord (eds), *Lingua Franca Communication*. Frankfurt: Peter Lang, pp. 163–94.

Li, J., L. Karakowsky and K. Lam (2002) East meets east and east meets west: The case of Sino–Japanese and Sino–West joint ventures in China. *Journal of Management Studies*, 38: 841–63.

Locker, K. (1998) The role of the Association for Business Communication in shaping business communication as an academic discipline. *Journal of Business Communication*, 35(1): 14–49.

Louhiala-Salminen, L. (1996) The business communication classroom vs. reality: What should we teach today? *English for Specific Purposes*, 15(1): 37–51.

Louhiala-Salminen, L. (1997) Investigating the genre of a business fax: A Finnish case study. *Journal of Business Communication*, 34(3): 316–33.

Louhiala-Salminen, L. (1999a). From business correspondence to message exchange: The notion of genre in business communication. PhD thesis, Jyväskylä, University of Jyväskylä.

Louhiala-Salminen, L. (1999b) 'Was there life before them?' Fax and email in business communication. *Journal of Language for International Business*, 10(1): 24–42.

Louhiala-Salminen, L. and A. Kankaanranta (2005) 'Hello Monica – kindly change your arrangements': Business genres in a state of flux. In P. Gillaerts and M. Gotti (eds), *Genre Variation in Business Letters*. Bern: Peter Lang, pp. 55–84.

Louhiala-Salminen, L., M. Charles and A. Kankaanranta (2005) English as a lingua franca in Nordic corporate mergers: Two case companies. *English for Specific Purposes* (Special issue), 24(4): 401–21.

Lowry, P., A. Curtis and M. Lowry (2004) Building a taxonomy and nomenclature of collaborative writing to improve interdisciplinary research and practice. *Journal of Business Communication*, 41(1): 66–99.

Lowry, P., S. Humphreys, J. Malwitz and J. Nix (2007) A scientometric study of the perceived quality of business and technical communication journals. *IEEE Transactions on Professional Communication*, 50(4): pp. 352–78.

McPhee, R., K. Myers and A. Trethewey (2006) On collective mind and conversational analysis. *Management Communication Quarterly*, 19(3): 311–26.

Mauranen, A. (2003) Lingua franca englanti: Tuntematonta kieltä? In M. Koskela and N. Pilke (eds), *Kieli ja Asiantuntijuus*. Jyväskylä: AfinLA, pp. 117–34.

Miller, K. (1996) Who are we and what are we doing? *Management Communication Quarterly*, 10(1): 3–4.

Miller, K. (2003) *Organizational Communication: Approaches and Processes*. Belmont, CA: Wadsworth.

Möller, K. and A. Halinen (1999) Business relationships and networks: Managerial challenge of network era. *Industrial Marketing* Management, 28: 413–27.

Möller, K. and S. Svahn (2004) Crossing east–west boundaries: Knowledge sharing in intercultural business networks. *Industrial Marketing Management*, 33: 219–28.

Mumby, D. K. and C. Stohl (1996) Disciplining organizational communication studies. *Management Communication Quarterly*, 10(1): 50–72.

Nickerson, C. (2000) *Playing the Corporate Language Game: An Investigation of the Genres and Discourse Strategies in English Used by Dutch Writers Working in Multinational Corporations*. Amsterdam: Rodopi.

Orlikowski, W. and J. Yates (1994) Genre repertoire: The structuring of communicative practices in organizations. *Administrative Science Quarterly*, 39: 541–74.

Planken, B. (2005) Managing rapport in lingua franca sales negotiations: A comparison of professional and aspiring negotiators. *English for Specific Purposes*, 24(4): 381–400.

Poncini, G. (2004) *Discursive Strategies in Multicultural Business Meetings*. Bern: Peter Lang.

Poncini, G. (2005) Constructing an international event in the wine industry: An investigation of emails in English and Italian. In P. Gillaerts and M. Gotti (eds), *Genre Variation in Business Letters*. Bern: Peter Lang, pp. 205–31.

Reinsch, L. (1996) Business communication: Past, present, and future. *Management Communication Quarterly*, 10(1): 27–49.

Reinsch, L. and J. Turner (2006) Ari, R U there? Reorienting business communication for a technological era. *Journal of Business and Technical Communication*, 20(3): 339–56.

Rogers, P. (1996) Disciplinary distinction or responsibility? *Management Communication Quarterly*, 10(1): 112–23.

Rogers, P. (2001) Convergence and commonality challenge business communication research: Outstanding researcher lecturer. *Journal of Business Communication*, 38(1): 14–23.

Rogers, P., N. Campbell, L. Louhiala-Salminen, K. Rentz and J. Suchan (2007) The impact of perceptions of journal quality on business and management communication academics. *Journal of Business Communication*, 44 (4): 403–26.

Rubinstein, J. S., D. E. Meyer and J. E. Evans (2001) Executive control of cognitive processes in task switching. *Journal of Experimental Psychology: Human Perception and Performance*, 27(4): 763–97.

Scollon, R. and S. Scollon (2001) *Intercultural Communication: A Discourse Approach*. Oxford: Blackwell.

Seidlhofer, B. (2002) The shape of things to come? Some basic questions about English as a lingua franca. In K. Knapp and C. Meierkord (eds), *Lingua Franca Communication*. Frankfurt: Peter Lang, pp. 269–302.

Shelby, A. (1993) Organizational, business, management, and corporate communication: An analysis of boundaries and relationships. *Journal of Business Communication*, 30(3): 241–67.

Shelby, A. (1996) A discipline orientation: Analysis and critique. *Management Communication Quarterly*, 10(1): 98–105.

Smeltzer, L. (1996) Communication within the manager's context. *Management Communication Quarterly*, 10(1): 5–26.

Svahn, S. (2004) Managing in different types of business nets: capability perspective. PhD thesis, Helsinki, Helsinki School of Economics.

Thomas, G. F. (2007) How can we make our research more relevant? Bridging the gap between workplace changes and business communication research. *Journal of Business Communication*, 44(3): 283–96.

Tourish, D. and O. Hargie (2004) The crisis of management and the role of organizational communication. In D. Tourish and O. Hargie (eds), *Key Issues in Organizational Communication*. London: Routledge, pp. 1–16.

Turner, J. and L. Reinsch (2007) The business communicator as presence allocator. *Journal of Business Communication*, 44(1): 36–58.

Tuusjärvi, E. (2003) Multifaceted norms in SMC export cooperation: A discourse analysis of normative expectations. PhD thesis, Helsinki, Helsinki School of Economics.

Varner, I. (2000) The theoretical foundation for intercultural business communication: A conceptual model. *Journal of Business Communication*, 37(1): 39–57.

Yates, J. (1989) *Control through Communication: The Rise of System in American Management*. Baltimore, MD: Johns Hopkins University Press.

Yates, J. (2005) *Structuring the Information Age: Life Insurance and Technology in the Twentieth Century*. Baltimore, MD: Johns Hopkins University Press.

Yates, J. and W. Orlikowski (1992) Genres of organizational communication: A structurational approach to studying communication and media. *Academy of Management Review*, 17(2): 299–326.

Zhu, Y. (2005) *Written Communication across Cultures: A Sociocognitive Perspective on Business Genres*. Amsterdam: John Benjamins.

24

Intercultural communication

Ingrid Piller

Introduction

In the context of globalisation, intercultural communication has become ubiquitous in contemporary business communication and the importance of preparing business graduates for communication in the global village has become a truism (Goby 2007). Friedman (2006) pithily distinguished between three stages of globalisation: Globalisation 1.0 was driven by countries internationalising; Globalisation 2.0 was driven by companies internationalising; and Globalisation 3.0 is driven by individuals internationalising themselves. Intercultural communication research is both a response to globalisation and simultaneously a facet of globalisation, and I will therefore organise this chapter around three different phases in intercultural communication research, which coincide rather neatly with Friedman's phases of globalisation – not necessarily chronologically, but in terms of their key research concerns. It is the purpose of this chapter to provide an overview of the field of intercultural communication research, particularly as pertinent to business communication.

The emergence of the field of intercultural communication studies dates from the 1940s and researchers were initially focused on nationals of different countries interacting with each other. I will call this phase 'Intercultural Communication 1.0'. As regards cross-cultural business communication, the most influential author in 'Intercultural Communication 1.0' is the Dutch psychologist Geert Hofstede, whose large-scale comparisons of a small set of five cultural values in different countries continues to inspire research in intercultural communication. In the 1980s a new focus started to emerge and researchers began to investigate communication in international corporations; I will dub this research 'Intercultural Communication 2.0'. In my review, I will particularly highlight research with multinational companies in Central Europe and Scandinavia. In the next section I will move on to the most recent phase of intercultural communication research – research where the locus of intercultural communication is the individual. In 'Intercultural Communication 3.0' I will introduce research that deals with individuals who are employed specifically to communicate interculturally, as is the case for call centre operators. While the research foci on nations, companies and individuals emerged at different times, each new focus combined with the previous one, and today all three foci co-exist. Indeed, not only do they co-exist but they also overlap and inform each other, and it is this overlap that I will explore in the final section on future developments.

Before I move on, a brief terminological clarification is necessary: 'intercultural communication' and 'cross-cultural communication' are sometimes used interchangeably. However, it is more useful if 'intercultural communication' is used for communication between members of different cultures and 'cross-cultural communication' is used for research that compares communication in different cultures (Gudykunst 2000; Piller 2007b; Scollon and Scollon 2001; Spencer-Oatey and Kotthoff 2007). I will follow this usage if it is necessary to distinguish between interactive and comparative research. If it is not, I will use Intercultural Communication in capitals as the superordinate term.

Intercultural Communication 1.0

Intercultural Communication 1.0 with its focus on the nation as the locus of cultural difference is strongly influenced by the work of the Dutch psychologist Geert Hofstede (Hofstede 2001; Hofstede and Hofstede 2005). In the late 1960s and early 1970s, Hofstede worked as a psychologist for IBM and in this role he gained accessed to questionnaire data collected from more than 100,000 IBM employees in 40 countries in the 1960s. Hofstede's work is characterised by three basic assumptions: (1) the country in which a person lives is the key determinant of their cultural orientation; (2) the key problem in intercultural communication is that people from different countries have different value orientations; and (3) these value orientations can be measured and quantified. Hofstede initially (in the 1980 first edition of Hofstede 2001) distinguished four value orientations, namely power distance, individualism, masculinity and uncertainty avoidance. After further data collection in China, Hofstede later added a fifth dimension, namely long-term orientation.

The power distance index refers to the level of inequality in a society and the degree to which the unequal distribution of power is accepted by members of that society. The individualism index refers to the level of connection in a society and whether individuals are expected to fend for themselves or to act as members of a group. The masculinity index refers to the degree to which gender roles are differentiated in a society. The uncertainty avoidance index refers to the level to which a society accepts uncertainty and ambiguity and to what degree it tries to control uncertainty and ambiguity through the imposition of explicit rules. Finally, the long-term orientation index deals with the extent to which a society values thrift and perseverance versus attendance to more short-term goals such as fulfilling social obligations (more detailed definitions can be found in Hofstede 2001 as well as on his website at http://www.geert-hofstede.com). On the basis of the data from IBM employees, Hofstede has calculated a score for each of these indexes for fifty countries and three regions (Arab World; East Africa; West Africa). As an example, I am quoting the description of China from Hofstede's website:

> Geert Hofstede analysis for China has Long-term Orientation (LTO) the highest-ranking factor (118), which is true for all Asian cultures. This Dimension indicates a society's time perspective and an attitude of persevering; that is, overcoming obstacles with time, if not with will and strength. . . . The Chinese rank lower than any other Asian country in the Individualism (IDV) ranking, at 20 compared to an average of 24. This may be attributed, in part, to the high

level of emphasis on a Collectivist society by the Communist rule, as compared to one of Individualism. The low Individualism ranking is manifest in a close and committed member 'group', be that a family, extended family, or extended relationships. Loyalty in a collectivist culture is paramount. The society fosters strong relationships where everyone takes responsibility for fellow members of their group.... Of note is China's significantly higher Power Distance ranking of 80 compared to the other Far East Asian countries' average of 60, and the world average of 55. This is indicative of a high level of inequality of power and wealth within the society. This condition is not necessarily forced upon the population, but rather accepted by the society as their cultural heritage. (http://www.geert-hofstede.com/hofstede_china.shtml; accessed 4 February 2008)

Hofstede's work has been immensely influential, particularly in management studies and the literature on international management, and has spawned a large body of inter-cultural communication advice manuals, both in books and on the internet, with titles such as *Hidden Differences: Doing Business with the Japanese* (Hall and Hall 1987), Beyond Chocolate: *Beyond Chocolate: Understanding Swiss Culture* (Oertig-Davidson 2002) or 'Communication with Egyptians' (Begley 2003). At the same time, Hofstede has also been widely criticised on a number of fronts (e.g. McSweeney 2002; Roberts and Boyacigiller 1984). Critics of Hofstede's work have pointed out a number of flaws in his argument, but I will here concentrate on two main problems, which his work shares with most work in Intercultural Communication 1.0, namely overgeneralisation and essentialism.

Overgeneralisation relates to the fact that findings with one group of people in a country – IBM staff in Hofstede's work – are generalised to the population as a whole and the reduc-tion of these findings to numbers suggests a scientific precision which hardly captures the complexity of life in a country. We may well ask what, say, male, middle-class, educated professional city-dwellers in a country have in common with illiterate, female, landless country-dwellers in the same country. Nothing much, I should think. These overgenerali-sations from a few hundred survey respondents to a whole population of millions of people only make sense if one subscribes to an essentialist view of culture. In this view culture is not a social phenomenon that people share but rather 'the software of the mind . . . our mental programming' (Hofstede and Hofstede 2005). An essentialist view of culture sees national culture as a stable attribute of a person, in the same way that gender and race are often seen as fairly stable attributes.

Consider the following excerpt from a country profile for Germany from an Intercultural Communication advice website which relies heavily on Hofstede's work:

- *The German thought process* is extremely thorough, with each aspect of a project being examined in great detail.
- *German citizens do not need or expect to be complimented. In Germany, it is assumed* that everything is satisfactory unless the person hears otherwise.
- *Germans are able to consume large quantities of beer* in one evening. (http://www.cyborlink.com/besite/germany.htm; accessed 5 March 2007; emphasis added)

In this text, the existence of a specific German 'software of the mind' – 'the German thought process' – is assumed. Indeed, 'Germanness' extends beyond being a trait of the mind to being a physical characteristic ('Germans are able to consume large quantities of beer in one evening'). These mental and physical traits of Germanness are assumed to go hand in hand with German citizenship – it is unclear where this would leave the hundreds of thousands of German residents who do not have German citizenship (cf. Hansen-Thomas 2007; Piller 2001). Indeed, by equating 'German citizens' with 'in Germany', German residents who are not German citizens are systematically removed from the landscape of contemporary Germany. This particular country profile thus – unwittingly? – buys into a view of German national identity as inherited, based on *ius sanguinis*, the law of blood relationships, rather than *ius solis*, the law of residence.

Intercultural Communication 2.0

Intercultural Communication 2.0 sees as the locus of culture not the nation but rather 'the diversity of the globalized business community' (Charles 2007: 266). Its proponents explicitly reject the essentialism of Intercultural Communication 1.0 and draw on social constructionism to conceptualise cultural membership. Social constructionist (or poststructural) approaches are characterised by an emphasis on 'doing culture' as opposed to 'having culture' – as memorably expressed in Brian Street's paper, 'culture is a verb' (Street 1993). This focus on the process of 'doing intercultural communication' usually goes hand in hand with a different methodological orientation. Intercultural Communication 1.0 typically relies on quantitative methods to analyse data from large populations (cf. Hofstede's 100,000 IBM employees). The data from these populations is mostly gathered through multiple-choice questionnaires. These obviously have the advantage of being able to produce data from a large number of respondents. However, at the same time, this data cannot include but a very limited number of generic items. Researchers in this paradigm will not be able to find out anything that they have not asked. Poststructuralist approaches, on the other hand, tend to adopt ethnographic methods such as participant observation, recordings of interactions and semi-structured interviews with participants, or a combination of these. These produce 'rich' data that lends itself to 'thick descriptions' (Geertz 1973) of local contexts. For obvious reasons these approaches are well suited to an exploration of intercultural communication in a specific context such as a company. At the same time, it is also obvious that they would be unsuitable for the description of a national culture.

A key question for Intercultural Communication 2.0 is what participants in an interaction actually orient to: 'Instead of imposing outsider categories, linguistic anthropology induces analytic categories that participants either articulate or presuppose in their action, and it insists on evidence that participants themselves are presupposing categories central to the analysis' (Wortham 2003: 2). Thus, the key analytic question of Intercultural Communication 2.0 is no longer how members of different cultures interact. Rather, the key question becomes what categories people in a given context – for instance, employees in an international company – orient to: what does culture mean to them? What does difference mean? What does communication mean? And do any of these categories actually matter to them? For instance, in a study with eight Finnish–Swedish post-merger companies, Vaara (2000) found that 'culture', or more specifically cultural differences between Finns and Swedes, was not something that existed outside specific discursive contexts. In these companies, 'culture' was selectively used as a discursive resource to

explain problems: 'organisational actors often find cultural differences convenient attribution targets. Consequently, failures or unsuccessful experiences are often purposefully
attributed to cultural differences, while successes are explained by other factors, such as
the management's actions' (Vaara 2000: 105).

Thus, the shift in focus from Intercultural Communication 1.0 to Intercultural
Communication 2.0 has also brought with it a theoretical and analytic shift. This has
resulted in a further shift in the view of 'communication'. Intercultural Communication
1.0 places a strong emphasis on attitudes, beliefs, values, value orientations and thought
patterns. There is also a relatively strong interest in nonverbal communication. However,
attention to the role of language use, including multilingual language use, language learning and linguistic proficiency, is relatively underdeveloped. Therefore, Intercultural
Communication 1.0 can make strange and surprising reading for a linguist. Some of the
most widely read textbooks in Intercultural Communication (e.g. Chaney and Martin
2004; Gudykunst and Mody 2001; Jandt 2006; Lustig and Koester 2005; Martin and
Nakayama 2003; Samovar et al. 2007; Ting-Toomey and Chung 2004; Varner and Beamer
2005) give short shrift to language and languages. By contrast, a linguist would consider
natural languages the most important aspect of human communication, and Intercultural
Communication 2.0 studies show that language choice and language proficiency clearly
matter to social actors, i.e. international companies and their employees.

When companies go international – as is the case in cross-border mergers or when an
international company sets up a subsidiary in a new market – they basically have three
linguistic options (Vandermeeren 1998). They may bring in language professionals, i.e.
translators and interpreters, to facilitate communication between staff with different
linguistic backgrounds. Alternatively, they may rely on some staff members, usually staff
members based in the subsidiary, to accommodate speakers of the majority partner's
language, in which case communication will be between native speakers and non-native
speakers. A third option is the choice of a lingua franca (see Chapter 14 in this volume).
All these options may co-exist within one single company and oftentimes do.

The need for language services can be a significant cost factor, as Nekula and Šichová
(2004) found in a study with around 400 Czech subsidiaries of Austrian, German and
Swiss companies (out of a total of over 2,000 such subsidiaries operating in the Czech
Republic at the time of the research). More than half of these companies had an 'official
company language' policy. The majority of these were officially monolingual in German
(55 per cent), English (16 per cent) or Czech (9 per cent); the remainder had either English
and German as their official languages (15 per cent) or Czech and German (5 per cent).
However, despite these official language policy decisions, 18 per cent of all the surveyed
companies employed internal translators or interpreters, and the percentage increased
with the size of the company: of the large companies with more than 500 employees,
40 per cent employed language professionals. Additionally, 58 per cent of the surveyed
companies regularly outsourced translating and interpreting services to external providers (47 per cent of small companies, 66 per cent of medium-sized ones and 70 per cent of
large companies). On the basis of their findings, Nekula and Šichová (2004) estimate that
the language costs for the 2,000 Czech joint ventures with German-speaking companies
must have been 3.3 billion euros between 1989 and 2003. These are the direct costs of
using language services only. However, Nekula and Šichová (2004) are quick to point
out that the indirect costs of language differences in multinational companies are even

higher. What the researchers could not calculate are losses resulting from lack of control over external communication, from the non-availability of timely information to production staff, or from negative stereotyping and lack of rapport between staff members from different linguistic backgrounds.

In a study of the language practices of the Finnish multinational Kone, Marschan-Piekkari et al. (1999) considered 'softer' language factors whose cost cannot be easily calculated. The researchers conducted fieldwork in 25 units of the company in 10 countries and interviewed a total of 110 employees at top management (24), middle management (57) and operating level (29). Kone's official company language is English but middle management and lower-level employees were not necessarily able to use English. Sixty-five per cent of the interviewees identified language as a key concern in internal communication in the multinational company, and they did so from three different perspectives. First, most of the employees saw language as a barrier to both technical and non-technical information exchanges. Language as barrier manifested itself in a number of ways: for instance, employees could not engage in the kind of horizontal relationship-building across units encouraged by the company; or Spanish middle managers had relatively few opportunities to meet with headquarters, because Finnish top managers avoided Spain because the staff there were less proficient in English than in other European countries; or staff members with limited English could not attend in-house training courses in Finland.

Second, some participants mentioned that language acted as a facilitator. This was true of staff members who were more proficient in English than their peers. Some staff members with English facility accrued significant advantages. A Spanish operative with good English, for instance, was sent to represent his unit at training courses and in meetings, even if he did not have functional responsibility for the issue at stake. Third, language was identified as a source of power, with employees proficient in three languages – English as the company language, Finnish as the company's 'home language' and the language of the subsidiary country – being in the most advantageous position of being able to access a wide range of information, to network across the company and to act as go-between for others.

The power that can accrue to proficient speakers and the disempowering effects of some language choices over others is also apparent in another study of a merger between a Finnish and a Swedish bank (Vaara et al. 2005). When it was decided that the company language would be English, many of the Finnish managers felt as though part of their professionalism had been taken away. Marschan-Piekkari et al. (1999) point out that, in effect, a multinational company's language policy coupled with the proficiencies of staff can result in an alternative 'shadow structure' that de facto supersedes the formal organisational structure of the company (see also Chapter 20 in this volume).

Intercultural Communication 3.0

Friedman (2006) sees Globalisation 3.0 as characterised by individuals 'going global' and competing – and collaborating – globally. Indeed, the Intercultural Communication 2.0 research I featured above (Marschan-Piekkari et al. 1999; Vaara et al. 2005) portrays individuals within companies whose linguistic repertoires provide them with challenges or opportunities within their organisations. 'Intercultural Communication 3.0' is characterised by the commodification of language and communication skills. Multilingual proficiency, communicative facility or cultural authenticity have become key aspects of some individuals' business activities, and their access to economic resources has come to be played out on the terrain of intercultural communication. For employees in the multinational companies described above, intercultural competence in the form of proficiency in English, Finnish and the local language worked to their advantage – in terms of increased networking opportunities, accelerated promotion or enhanced access to information. Lack of proficiency in English, on the other hand, denied other individuals access to those same resources. Intercultural communication skills can thus be converted into economic gain. Intercultural Communication 3.0 research has responded to these new challenges by adopting theoretical approaches informed by the political economy of language. They draw on the work of the French sociologist Pierre Bourdieu (1990, 1991, 1993) to explore how linguistic and cultural capital can be transformed into economic capital in the context of Globalisation 3.0.

How have language and communicative abilities come to be tied to the ability of individuals to engage in business activities? In an economy characterised by agriculture, primary extraction and production, it does not really matter what the language background of workers is and which other languages they may or may not speak (Piller and Pavlenko 2007). However, in an economy where business activities centre on knowledge, information and services, language and communication become a part of people's job, something they may be remunerated for. The term 'language work' describes jobs where a substantial aspect of the work consists of language-related tasks. Examples include language teaching, translating and interpreting or call centre work. The term 'language work' is modelled on Hochschild's (2003) term 'emotional labor', which this researcher used to describe the demands on flight attendants to be friendly as part of their job, even with aggressive, overly demanding or obnoxious customers. Research into Intercultural Communication 3.0, with its focus on 'where language fits in the daily experiences of people working and living in the shifting conditions of the new economy' (Heller 2005: 1), is relatively new. As an illustration of this trend, I will now review research into language work in Indian call centres.

Mirchandani (2004) and Pal and Buzzanell (2008) conducted fieldwork with Indian call centre workers whose work consists of taking calls from or making calls to North America for a range of global companies. Inbound calls usually deal with service inquiries such as computer problems, credit card statements or travel bookings, and outbound calls are usually made to market a product or service. India, with its recently installed long-distance fiber cables, comparatively low wages and pool of well-educated English speakers, has experienced a boom in call centres in the early years of the twenty-first century. Pal and Buzzanell (2008) cite the following growth indicators: between 2002 and 2003, the revenue of Indian call centres grew 59 per cent to $2.3 billion. The number of foreign companies outsourcing to India increased from 60 in 2000 to 800 by the end of 2003 (a 1,200 per cent increase). Overall, in 2007, call centres employed an estimated 600,000 Indians. However, this boom is expected to slow or even move on to another country as Indian graduates are increasingly finding better jobs (Thanawala 2007).

Both Mirchandani's (2004) and Pal and Buzzanell's (2008) research demonstrates how call centre work becomes intimately tied up with operators' identities: all of the workers' interviewed had received 'accent reduction classes', which were meant to 'neutralise' their Indian accent so that they would be understood by their American clients. In addition they adopted English names and were required to familiarise themselves and stay up to date with everyday knowledge of the American middle class. One call centre operator said: 'We have cross-cultural training. Even little things like Starbucks, Central Park . . . the nitty gritties like that are important' (Pal and Buzzanell 2008: 44f). Training was also provided in the actual scripting of an interaction, and a high level of standardisation was imposed on the interactions that operators could engage in with clients. The level of regulation of interactions is apparent in the following account of another operator:

> This is our script, we have to go through this. Thank you for choosing [name of American company]. My name is Tanya [assigned pseudonym]. May I have your first and last name. Thank you. May I call you by your first name? Thank you very much. How are you doing today? . . . These are the typical statements that we have to say – Great. Thank you. Excellent. Wonderful job. These are the power words. We have to use those words in our scripts. (Mirchandani 2004: 361)

Operators found that the high level of scripting of interactions removed their autonomy, deskilled their work and made it tedious. However, it was not only in the workplace that call centre operators took on new identities. Their job had a significant impact on their identities outside of work as well. Because of the time difference between India and North America, call centre operators mostly work night shifts, and this fact severely constrained their family and home life: rather than socialising with family and friends during 'normal' hours, the workers' social activities revolved around the workplace, sometimes to such an extent that they described their colleagues as family and their workplace as home (Pal and Buzzanell 2008).

Call centre jobs are sometimes touted as wonderful opportunities for Indian graduates to advance in the global economy (e.g. Friedman 2006: 28). However, most of the participants in the research conducted by Mirchandani (2004) and Pal and Buzzanell (2008) expressed cynicism about their work, which they considered a dead end and 'not a career', and which they were treating as providing them with pocket money while pursuing tertiary education. They were very aware that North American call centre operators with significantly lower qualifications earn a much higher salary, and expressed resentment at business practices which they considered exploitative. Most were planning to leave call centre work as soon as they were ready to start a family or as soon as a better job opportunity came up (see also Thanawala 2007).

Future developments and implications

In this chapter I have tied my overview of Intercultural Communication in business contexts to globalisation. In the same way that three different aspects of globalisation can be distinguished depending on whether the main drivers are nations, companies or individuals, three different strands of Intercultural Communication can be distinguished depending on whether nations, companies or individuals are considered the locus of intercultural communication. Of course, these three strands are mostly not as clearly demarcated as my account of three different phases of Intercultural Communication may have suggested. In the following I will indicate six areas of future development where

Intercultural Communication 1.0, 2.0 and 3.0 will have to combine in order to meet the challenges posed by the object of inquiry: intercultural communication as an object in motion in the fast-changing global economy.

Dynamic perspectives on national culture

Nation states are not going to go away any time soon, and many people on this globe are shaped in their predispositions by one nation or other and may have a strong sense of affiliation with a nation. However, instead of treating national culture as a given, Intercultural Communication will need to see the nation as a discursive construction that social actors draw upon in selective ways (see Vaara 2000). It has become a key question for Intercultural Communication research 'who invokes "culture" when, where, how and for what purposes' (Piller 2007b: 210).

Multicultural perspectives on companies

One of the consequences of the strong focus on the nation has been that cultural and linguistic diversity within companies in one location has been often obscured and rendered invisible. However, in many multinational companies today it is not only nationals from the home country interacting with nationals from the subsidiaries, but additionally migrants from other backgrounds are likely to be employed as well. In German business, for instance, the 60,000 companies run by Turkish nationals have become major economic players – in 2004, they employed 350,000 staff and generated 30 billion euros in revenue (Sollich 2004). Kemal Şahin, one of the tycoons of German industry and the recipient of the German 1997 Manager of the Year award, for instance, is Turkish-born. Companies and businesspeople such as these are routinely overlooked in Intercultural Communication advice manuals. As long as Intercultural Communication continues to reproduce official ideologies of national belonging, it remains complicit in rendering diversity invisible instead of describing and interpreting it.

Industry-specific perspectives on language work

It makes a difference for workers in the global marketplace whether language and communication is one of their core competencies and whether they work in an industry whose core business is communication. Symbolic industries such as tourism in particular are in need of greater attention from Intercultural Communication. Tourism often invokes cultural stereotypes to market local authenticity while at the same time standardising communication, thus leaving employees in a double-bind situation where the imperative for authenticity competes with the imperative for standardisation (Heller 2003). At the same time, language and communication skills are similarly commodified, as in the call centre industry (Piller 2007a).

Sociolinguistic perspectives on intercultural communication

Intercultural Communication advice manuals and training courses are full of cultural stereotypes where culture and behaviour are mistakenly linked in a cause-and-effect relationship. A good example is the stereotype of 'the silent Finn' (Tulviste et al. 2003), where silence is often explained as a result of cultural values. Indeed, Finns were often silent in the Finnish–Swedish company described by Vaara et al. (2005). However, this had nothing to do with the fact that they valued silence – on the contrary, they were pained by their silence and felt it compromised their professional identity. The reason for their (relative) silence was lack of proficiency in the company language, Swedish. Intercultural Communication clearly needs a more sophisticated understanding of natural language interaction, particularly multilingual interactions, as developed in interactional sociolinguistics and related ethnographic approaches, in order not to mistake language problems for cultural problems.

Critical perspectives on Intercultural Communication

Multilingualism is not the only aspect of intercultural communication that the field often-times tends to overlook. 'Culture' is too often treated as an explanatory concept rather than one that is itself in need of explanation; as a consequence, another possible explanatory – inequality – is overlooked. However, no human interaction is free from power relationships, and inequality in intercultural communication may result from sociostructural factors (such as who acquires whom in a merger situation), roles and positions within an organisation (such as supervisor–supervisee relationships) and access to cultural and linguistic resources (Marschan-Piekkari et al. 1999).

Training perspectives on intercultural communication

The main determinant of language proficiency is which and how many (and in some countries, unfortunately even today, whether) languages are taught in schools (Werlen 2008). Considering the direct and indirect costs of language work described by Nekula and Šichová (2004) and others, language policies in education are significant for intercultural business communication. A good example of language planning for intercultural communication can be found in the Council of Europe's Common European Framework for Languages (Council of Europe 2001). Language planning for intercultural communication also needs to include the provision for language training in adult migrant education, where Australia's Adult Migrant English Program provides a good model (Lo Bianco 2008; Martin 1998).

References

Begley, P. A. (2003) Communication with Egyptians. In L. A. Samovar and R. E. Porter (eds), *Intercultural Communication: A Reader*. Belmont, CA: Thomson Wadsworth, pp. 87–93.

Bourdieu, P. (1990) *The Logic of Practice*. Cambridge: Cambridge University Press.

Bourdieu, P. (1991) *Language and Symbolic Power*. Cambridge: Polity.

Bourdieu, P. (1993) *Outline of a Theory of Practice*. Cambridge: Cambridge University Press.

Chaney, L. H. and J. S. Martin (2004) *Intercultural Business Communication*, 3rd edn. London: Pearson Education.

Charles, M. L. (2007) Language matters in global communication: Article based on ORA lecture, October 2006. *Journal of Business Communication*, 44(3): 260–82.

Council of Europe (2001) *Common European Framework of Reference for Languages*. www.coe.int/t/dg4/linguistic/Source/Framework_EN.pdf. Accessed 11 March 2008.

Friedman, T. L. (2006) *The World is Flat: The Globalized World in the Twenty-First Century*. London: Penguin.

Geertz, C. (1973) *The Interpretation of Cultures: Selected Essays*. New York: Basic Books.

Goby, V. P. (2007) Business communication needs: A multicultural perspective. *Journal of Business and Technical Communication*, 21(4): 425–37.

Gudykunst, W. B. (2000) Methodological issues in conducting theory-based cross-cultural research. In H. Spencer-Oatey (ed.), *Culturally Speaking: Managing Rapport through Talk across Cultures*. London: Continuum, pp. 293–315.

Gudykunst, W. B. and B. Mody (eds) (2001) *Handbook of International and Intercultural Communication*, 2nd edn. London: Sage.

Hall, E. T. and M. R. Hall (1987) *Hidden Differences: Doing Business with the Japanese*. Garden City, NY: Doubleday.

Hansen-Thomas, H. (2007) Language ideology, citizenship, and identity: The case of modern Germany. *Journal of Language and Politics*, 6(2): 249–64.

Heller, M. (2003) Globalization, the new economy, and the commodification of language and identity. *Journal of Sociolinguistics*, 7(4): 473–92.

Heller, M. (2005) Language, skill and authenticity in the globalized new economy. *Noves SL: Revista de Sociolingüística*. http://www.gencat.cat/llengua/noves. Accessed 12 August 2008.

Hochschild, A. R. (2003) *The Managed Heart: Commercialization of Human Feeling*, 20th anniversary edn. Berkeley: University of California Press.

Hofstede, G. H. (2001) *Culture's Consequences: Comparing Values, Behaviors, Institutions, and Organizations across Nations*, 2nd edn. Thousand Oaks, CA: Sage.

Hofstede, G. H. and G. J. Hofstede (2005) *Cultures and Organizations: Software of the Mind: Intercultural Cooperation and its Importance for Survival*, 2nd edn. New York: McGraw-Hill.

Jandt, F. E. (2006) *An Introduction to Intercultural Communication: Identities in a Global Community*, 5th edn. London: Sage.

Lo Bianco, J. (2008) Language policy and education in Australia. In S. May and N. H. Hornberger (eds), *Encyclopedia of Language and Education. Vol. 1: Language Policy and Political Issues in Education*. New York: Springer, pp. 343–53.

Lustig, M. W. and J. Koester (2005) *Intercultural Competence: Interpersonal Communication across Cultures*, 5th edn. Boston: Allyn & Bacon.

McSweeney, B. (2002) Hofstede's model of national cultural differences and consequences: A triumph of faith – a failure of analysis. *Human Relations*, 55(1): 89–118.

Marschan-Piekkari, R., D. Welch and L. Welch (1999) In the shadow: The impact of language on structure, power and communication in the multinational. *International Business Review*, 8(4): 421–40.

Martin, J. N. and T. K. Nakayama (2003) *Intercultural Communication in Contexts*, 3rd edn. New York: McGraw-Hill.

Martin, S. (1998) *New Life, New Language: The History of the Adult Migrant English Program*. Sydney: NCELTR.

Mirchandani, K. (2004) Practices of global capital: Gaps, cracks and ironies in transnational call centres in India. *Global Networks*, 4(4): 355–73.

Nekula, M. and Šichová, K. (2004) Sprache als Faktor der wirtschaftlichen Integration [Language as a factor in economic integration]. *brücken*, 12: 317–35.

Oertig-Davidson, M. (2002) *Beyond Chocolate: Understanding Swiss Culture*. Basel: Bergli Books.

Pal, M. and P. Buzzanell (2008) The Indian call center experience: A case study in changing discourses of identity, identification, and career in a global context. *Journal of Business Communication*, 45(1): 31–60.

Piller, I. (2001) Naturalisation language testing and its basis in ideologies of national identity and citizenship. *International Journal of Bilingualism*, 5(3): 259–77.

Piller, I. (2007a) English in Swiss tourism marketing. In C. Flores and O. Grossegesse (eds), *Wildern in luso-austro-deutschen Sprach- und Textgefilden: Festschrift zum 60. Geburtstag von Erwin Koller* [Roughing it in the Linguistic and Textual Wilds of Portuguese, Austrian and German: Festschrift for Erwin Koller on the Occasion of his 60th Birthday] Braga: Cehum – Centro de Estudos Humanísticos, pp. 57–73.

Piller, I. (2007b) Linguistics and intercultural communication. *Linguistics and Language Compass*, 1(3): 208–26.

Piller, I. and A. Pavlenko (2007) Globalization, gender, and multilingualism. In H. Decke-Cornill and L. Volkmann (eds), *Gender Studies and Foreign Language Teaching*. Tübingen: Narr, pp. 15–30.

Roberts, K. and N. Boyacigiller (1984) Cross-national organizational research: The grasp of the blind man. In B. M. Staw and L. L. Cummings (eds), *Research in Organizational Behavior. Vol. 6*. Stamford, CT: JAI Press, pp. 423–75.

Samovar, L. A., R. E. Porter and E. R. McDaniel (2007) *Communication between Cultures*, 6th edn. New York: Thomson Wadsworth.

Scollon, R. and S. W. Scollon (2001) Discourse and intercultural communication. In D. Schiffrin, D. Tunnen and H. E. Hamilton (eds), *The Handbook of Discourse Analysis*. Oxford: Blackwell, pp. 538–47.

Sollich, R. (2004) Türkisch und unverzichtbar [Turkish and indispensable]. *DW-World. de*. http://www.dw-world.de/dw/article/0,2144,1186742,00.html. Accessed 2 August 2005.

Spencer-Oatey, H. and H. Kotthoff (2007) Introduction. In H. Kotthoff and H. Spencer-Oatey (eds), *Handbook of Intercultural Communication*. Berlin and New York: Mouton de Gruyter, pp. 1–6.

Street, B. (1993) Culture is a verb. In D. Graddol, L. Thompson and M. Bynam (eds), *Language and Culture*. Clevedon: Multilingual Matters, pp. 23–43.

Thanawala, S. (2007) India's call-center jobs go begging. *Time*. http://www.time.com/time/business/article/0,8599,1671982,00.html. Accessed 11 March 2008.

Ting-Toomey, S. and L. C. Chung (2004) *Understanding Intercultural Communication*. Los Angeles: Roxbury.

Tulviste, T., L. Mizera, B. De Geer and M.-T. Tryggvason (2003) A silent Finn, a silent Finno-Ugric, or a silent Nordic? A comparative study of Estonian, Finnish, and Swedish mother–adolescent interactions. *Applied Psycholinguistics*, 24: 249–65.

Vaara, E. (2000) Constructions of cultural differences in postmerger change processes: A sensemaking perspective on Finnish–Swedish cases. *M@n@gement*, 3(3): 81–101.

Vaara, E., J. Tienari, R. Piekkari and R. Säntti (2005). Language and the circuits of power in a merging multinational corporation. *Journal of Management Studies*, 42(3): 595–623.

Vandermeeren, S. (1998) *Fremdsprachen in europäischen Unternehmen: Untersuchungen zu Bestand und Bedarf im Geschäftsalltag mit Empfehlungen für Sprachenpolitik und Sprachunterricht* [Foreign Languages in European Companies: Studies in the Language Use and Language Needs in Business with Recommendations for Language Policy and Language Teaching]. Waldsteinberg: Heidrun Popp.

Varner, I. and L. Beamer (2005) *Intercultural Communication in the Global Workplace*, 3rd edn. New York: McGraw-Hill.

Werlen, I. (2008) *Sprachkompetenzen der erwachsenen Bevölkerung in der Schweiz* [Language Competence of the Adult Swiss Population]. Swiss National Fund. http://www.nfp56. ch/d_projekt.cfm?Projects.command=download&file=22_02_2008_03_49_04-Schlussbericht-Werlen.pdf&name=Werlen.pdf. Accessed 11 March 2008.

Wortham, S. E. F. (2003) Linguistic anthropology of education: An introduction. In S. E. F. Wortham and B. Rymes (eds), *Linguistic Anthropology of Education*. Westport, CT, and London: Praeger, pp. 1–29.

Part Four: Localised Perspectives

25

Japan

Hiromasa Tanaka

Introduction

In the new global economy, Asia's presence has grown substantially. Although Japan's status as the premier Asian economic power is being challenged by other countries, Japan will remain a major economy for many years to come. The Japanese society itself has undergone a considerable change under the influence of globalisation. With new business strategies, including the formation of international alliances with non-Japanese companies, there has been an increase in contact situations between Japanese and non-Japanese. As a result the role of English as lingua franca has become significant.

A substantial body of research on Japanese business discourse has developed around this dynamic change. Researchers from various disciplines have investigated intercultural business situations. Theoretical, speculative and empirical research of business discourse involving Japanese has thus accumulated. This chapter reviews Japanese business discourse research evolving from this socioeconomic change. The first section provides an overview of past research on business discourse in a wide range of business contexts. It first examines linguistics and communication studies that investigate intercultural business interaction. Reference is also made to management and organisation studies that highlight Japanese cultural attributes and Japanese management preferences potentially affecting business discourse. In the second section the author presents an exemplary study of Japanese business discourse research which empirically illustrates some of the issues dealt with by previous research.

Context

Being geographically and culturally located on the periphery of the world business map, Japan had limited exposure to English except for written documents. Early academic research on business communication up to the 1990s, therefore, focused on lexical and systematic features of written documents (Nakasako 1998). Intercultural contacts took place mainly in processes of international trade. Since trade documents tend to be formulaic and highly technical, the function of English was considered to be that of an apolitical tool

(Seargeant 2005). However, the issue of whether or not English for business was culture-free became controversial after intercultural contacts increased (Kameda 2001).

Japan's rapid economic growth increased outward investment from the 1980s, which heightened the need for research on intercultural spoken discourse. In order to account for the cultural influence, earlier research emphasised national cultural differences. Nakajima (1993) uses cultural dimensions developed by Hofstede (1980) to account for the difference between Japanese and American business people. Nakajima argues that Japanese indirect speech can cause communication breakdown with American counterparts (p. 9). Although Nakajima's study highlighted the substantiality of cultural influences in business communication, her study was not based on empirical data from actual work sites.

Yamada's book-length study (1992) was significant because it is one of the earliest studies that analysed empirical data. She examines American and Japanese bankers' meetings recorded in their offices in the USA. Another contribution of Yamada's research to the field is its focus on the sociolinguistic elements of business communication, based upon knowledge provided by linguistic studies on intercultural communication involving Japanese (LoCastro 1987; Maynard 1986). The data consist of three types of internal meetings: a meeting held by American participants, an intercultural meeting using English, and a meeting held by Japanese participants using Japanese. Yamada reflects on the cultural influences on the interlocutors' sociolinguistic behaviour, such as topic management, turn-taking and back-channelling. For example, by examining the participants' turn distribution data, Yamada argues that American participants aim for independence by taking more frequent turns when the topic case is under their responsibility, while Japanese aim to achieve interdependence by taking equally frequent turns. She concludes that both Japanese and Americans needed to understand each other's interactional goals.

Yamada attempts to elucidate underlying cultural assumptions within the frame of Japanese cultural uniqueness that researchers of *Nihonjinron* or theories on the Japanese discussed in the 1970s. Yamada refers to Nakane's study (1970) to explain the group orientation of Japanese. Nakane developed her theory from the analysis of Japanese community-based social structure. Nakane argues that the society assumes loyalty from below and benevolence from above. Yamada also uses Doi's (1971) notion of Japanese interdependency to account for the Japanese participants' relation-oriented talk. Doi introduced *amae*, referring to a reciprocal, interdependent relationship, as a key concept for understanding Japanese psychology. Similarly, special attention was paid to the role that culture plays by researchers who examined business discourse in the Japanese language. Jones (1995) found that a high value was placed on interpersonal harmony by a native speaker of Japanese in her study of negotiation in a Thai educational institute. Yotsukura's (2003) large-scale research on Japanese business interaction on the telephone provides empirical evidence of the cultural beliefs and expectations that Japanese speakers bring into their conversations. These findings warrant a closer look into the question of whether Japanese speakers potentially transfer such cultural assumptions into English communication.

Japan exceeded the United States in GNP per person in 1977. The Japanese cultural uniqueness emerging from *Nihonjinron* was used to explain the strength of the Japanese economy when Japan became one of few eastern competitors to western 'developed' countries in the world economy. Observation of the Japanese management system through western perspectives generated 'the myth of Japanese uniqueness' (Dale 1986). It was often argued that Japanese culture, ethics and psychological orientation were unique and so different that the Japanese management system and businesspeople's behaviour are not easily understood by non-Japanese (Mouer 1988). However, some researchers challenged the idea of Japanese national uniqueness and focused on the management system itself. Vogel (1979) argued that the Japanese management system, including seniority-based compensation, participatory decision-making and long-term employment, was a key to explaining Japan's economic growth. Johnson (1982) pointed to government intervention, and argued that Japanese economic strength was nurtured in specific political and economic environments. Johnson's study suggests that the Japanese management system is not merely a system but a reification of a complex business ideology (Ishizawa 1997: 73).

Following this new line of argument, two significant anthropological studies were undertaken by Sumihara (1993) and Kleinberg (1999). Both studies use data from Japanese companies' subsidiaries located in the United States. They found that Japanese collective decision-making practices created friction between Japanese and American participants. The observations point to the difficulty of translating Japanese business ideology into a local workplace where English, imbued with different business ideologies, is spoken.

Marriott (1995) demonstrated the complexity of intercultural business contact situations where different cultural assumptions, communication strategies and business ideologies interplay. Marriott investigates topic management in Japanese–Australian dyadic negotiations. She examines three dimensions of interaction – linguistic, sociolinguistic and sociocultural – and found different topic management strategies adopted by Japanese and Australians. The analysis revealed that the Japanese buyer's strategic topic introduction did not convey the intended message to the Australian buyer. Marriott's follow-up interview found that the participants' socioeconomic behaviour triggered communication breakdown. The Australian buyer's lack of knowledge about the Japanese participatory decision-making style also caused the Australian's misinterpretation of the Japanese seller's inconclusive response to the Australian's proposal. Marriott's use of multiple data collection methods and multilayered analysis proved to be effective in exploring complex interactional issues.

One of the limitations of these studies is that the participants were mostly Japanese business expatriates who were specially trained or highly educated. This issue became problematic when the influx of foreign investment increased contact situations between Japanese and non-Japanese in the domestic workplace after the beginning of the twenty-first century (Okabe 2005); not only highly educated expatriates but also general employees needed to interact in English. This change required researchers to pay careful attention to local and regional perspectives (Bargiela-Chiappini 2006).

Compared with expatriates, company employees working in Japan are more diverse in their profiles, including their linguistic competence, level of education and attitudes towards foreign businesspeople. Befu (1987) and Noguchi (1995) have brought a political perspective to the study of Japan and challenged the monolithic view of Japanese national cultural characteristics as described in earlier research. Befu (1987) argues that group orientation and emphasis on harmony are part of the ideology that the government of nation-state Japan strategically implemented. On the same line, Noguchi (1995) argues that the Japanese characteristics were not developed through Japan's long history; rather they were by-products of the government's economic policy based on the regime of 'national socialism' that was established in the 1940s in order for the Japanese empire to overcome political and economic difficulties. These arguments suggest that frequently discussed

'Japanese otherness' is a situational result of the discursively constructed socioeconomic system. Furthermore they negate the homogeneity of Japanese individuals; the degree of influence from this socioeconomic system may vary depending on the individual's hierarchical position in an organisation, gender, age and local contexts.

Observation of English use in Japan suggests a need to revise the view of Japanese as a static and monolithic cultural group with unique national characteristics. Miller (1994, 1995) shows evidence of critical diversity among Japanese businesspeople. Miller's study provides, as far as the author recognises, the first empirical documentation of business discourse between Japanese and Americans in a domestic business setting. In her articles, Miller criticises the simple dichotomies used in earlier research. She lists six (1994) and twenty-two (1995) dimensions that show reification of opposite characteristics defining Japanese and Americans. The list includes nonverbal and verbal, indirect and direct, circular discourse and linear discourse continua. Miller's analysis is an attempt to deconstruct these stereotypes. Miller demonstrated how the interaction was influenced by institutional power relations, the participants' perceived objectives of the meetings, and pragmatic transfer.

Pragmatic transfer in intercultural business discourse is the focus of Fujio's study (2004) that investigates a one-hour meeting between a US manager, a Japanese manager and a Japanese junior staff member at a US company operating in Japan. Fujio shows the Japanese use of 'yes' to be as a sign of listening rather than a sign of agreement as argued in Mulholland (1997: 101). Silence was perceived negatively by the American, while Japanese analysts read it as a display of shame for making mistakes in English. Furthermore, Fujio goes on to challenge the stereotypical notion of Japanese indirectness in intercultural communication by reporting on instances of direct speech by the Japanese manager and of indirect speech by the American manager, and attributes these behaviours to contextual factors.

The heterogeneity of the Japanese is in evidence also in Sunaoshi (2005). Her study looks at Japanese and American workers' interactions in a factory in the American South. The participants are high school graduate workers rather than managers with distinguished educational records. Sunaoshi's data shows that the Japanese workers' uses of available communicative resources to compensate for their limited English competence are counter-stereotypical behaviours to the 'taciturn and receptive Japanese'. She interprets the Japanese workers' technical superiority as a display of power over the American workers. Consequently, the American workers concentrated on listening to what the Japanese were trying to say. Sunaoshi argues that frequently discussed Japanese unique characteristics were in fact not Japanese national characteristics but a result of interaction between historical and contextual factors. It is interesting that the effective use of visual aids and gestures by Japanese factory management had already been discussed by Potoker (1993) as a way of enhancing communication within diverse cultural environments. The similarities of findings from the two worker-focused studies and the differences between these and other research looking at managers or bankers indicate that it is necessary to distinguish between types of workplace discourses rather than labelling them all as one 'Japanese business discourse'.

Kawai (2007) echoes Sunaoshi by arguing that the use of English must also be analysed through multiple perspectives. Kawai's research investigates the Japanese government's and public discourses on English. She criticises the instrumental view of English as a neutral communication tool. She further argues that language should be viewed from historical, political, economic and cultural perspectives. This argument can be applied to business communication research, since we are all aware that the complexity of current business communication develops within social constraints, cultural traditions, and the constant conflict between globalisation and local identities (Seargeant 2005).

Using a critical analytic approach, Tanaka (2006) uncovers the penetration of American business ideology into a meeting where English was used as the corporate language. Tanaka's study suggests that weak linguistic competence can become a source of exclusion. A similar relation between language selection and institutional power was identified by Chingprasertsuk (2005). Her quantitative study examines interactions between Japanese managers and Thai workers in Thailand. Chingprasertsuk's factor analysis reveals that Japanese expatriates do not utilise nonverbal communication, in spite of the generally insufficient Japanese linguistic competence of their counterparts, Thai employees. Moreover, Chingprasertsuk illustrates the tendency of Japanese expatriates to enforce Japanese business ideology. The studies of Tanaka and Chingprasertsuk suggest a dynamic relation between language (choice) and power.

These studies suggest that power relations between speakers are produced and reproduced through institutional hierarchy, the speaker's command of language, and technical superiority. Findings from recent research do not negate the cultural effect on business discourse; nevertheless, they indicate that multiple elements interrelate and influence business discourse.

Study of an intercultural meeting

The present study illustrates the effects and consequences of using English as a lingua franca in Japanese business contexts. In this study, I intend to provide some concrete examples of issues that past research on Japanese business discourse has highlighted, such as communication breakdown triggered by different business ideologies (see Kleinberg 1999; Marriott 1995; Sumihara 1993) and different sociolinguistic behaviour (Fujio 2004; Mulholland 1997; Yamada 1992).

Background

The study was carried out in 1998–9 as part of a large-scale needs analysis project administered in a Japanese company, Namori Corporation (pseudonym), at the time when it was about to enter an international alliance with non-Japanese companies. I was asked to lead the project, which aimed to identify the English training needs of employees required to function in multicultural meetings. On the basis of the analysed needs, a training programme was designed, which has been running at Namori since 2000.

Methodology

In order to capture the employees' complex needs, a multilayered approach, which investigated sociolinguistic, pragmatic and discursive elements, was chosen. The meeting data as well as pre- and post-meeting interviews data were audio-recorded and later transcribed.

In addition to the transcripts, my field notes, feedback by meeting participants, and non-participants' feedback on my findings were used in the analysis.

The audio-recorded meeting data, consisting of an IT meeting 1 hour and 40 minutes in length, and a 5-hour-and-10-minute-long personnel meeting held in 1998, were analysed. In order to examine the sociolinguistic layer of the interaction (see Yamada 1992), I focused on the participants' turn distribution, back-channelling and turn-taking strategies. Turn distribution has been examined as an indicator of cultural influence on business discourse (Du-Babcock 2006; Yamada 1992). Back-channelling refers to short messages such as 'yes' and 'uh-huh', which the person who has the turn acknowledges without relinquishing his or her turn (Yngve 1970: 574). Back-chanelling was selected as a focus of the analysis since past studies (LoCastro 1985; Tanaka 2006) describe how Japanese speakers' transfer of first language (L1) back-channel behaviour triggered problematic situations. Turn-taking strategies emerged as potentially significant during the analysis.

In order to elicit the underlying assumptions and the historical/institutional contexts of the participants, unstructured interviews and the participants' feedback as well as their colleagues' feedback were analysed. The feedback data were collected during the training programme where I shared my analysis of the meeting data with Namori employees.

Discussion

The pre-meeting interviews with training managers revealed their concerns about the less-active participation of Namori staff in previous alliance meetings, and their potential disempowerment. Table 25.1 shows the scores for turns and back-channelling in the IT meeting; Table 25.2 lists the scores for the personnel meeting. The data shows that the numbers of turns taken by Namori participants were relatively fewer than those taken by representatives of other partner companies.

However, it should be noted that each cultural group showed variety. There were non-Japanese participants who talked as little as some Japanese participants, whilst Yuuki and Tomoki took a fair proportion of the total turns.

Business ideology: discrepancy of evaluation

Post-meeting interviews revealed participants' conflicting evaluations of the overall meeting and the less active participation of the Namori employees. A fairly positive evaluation was given by an IT meeting participant: 'It [little participation] may slow down the meeting. But a quick answer is not always a good answer. They probably need to think. I understand' (Ian).

Others commented negatively. Ruth expressed her concern about Namori employees' minimal participation. 'It was an issue and wasn't raised as an issue. But it continues to be an issue.' Other negative voices include, 'It's a lot of time and money to attend a meeting. Waste of time and money if nobody says anything' (Maarten).

On the contrary, interviews with Namori participants showed their satisfaction with the IT meeting. Yuuki, who took the largest number of turns of any Namori employee in the meeting, did not see other Namori participants' silence as a problem. 'Kochira kara teian wo dasu to iu koto dattan de yokattan dewa nai ka to omoi masu. [We were supposed to present our proposal. I think it was fine.]' The two participants who took no turns in

Table 25.1 Turn-taking and back-channelling in the IT meeting

Participant	Cultural background	Total turns	Number of back channels
Maarten	Northern Europe	57	11
James	North America	65	4
Akira	Japan	0	0
Michio	Japan	0	0
Toru	Japan	4	0
Shin	Japan	2	1
Ruth	Oceania	40	2
Hans	Northern Europe	2	0
Ian	North America	12	2
Dean	North America	14	0
Yuuki	Japan	15	0
Shilpa	Oceania	9	2
Santi	Southeast Asia	2	0
Sataphorn	Southeast Asia	0	0
Peter	North America	106	3
Total		328	25

Table 25.2 Turn-taking and back-channelling in the personnel meeting

Participant	Cultural background	Total turns	Number of back channels
Kate	North America	75	3
Antonio	South America	30	1
Tomoki	Japan	13	0
Michael	Oceania	23	0
Terachai	Southeast Asia	20	1
Glenda*	North America	14	2
Udo	Northern Europe	63	3
Steve	North America	51	3
Andy*	Northern Europe	33	4
Jose	South America	5	0
Carmen	Southeast Asia	23	2
Tom	North America	22	1
Marc	Northern Europe	43	3
Total		415	23

*Attended the morning session only

the meeting also said that the meeting was successful. They seemed to be satisfied with the fact that Yuuki's presentation conveyed the message which was based on their consensus prior to the meeting.

I argue that the discrepancy in evaluation comes from the differently perceived goals of the meeting. Interview data from the Namori participants to the IT meeting and from the participants' feedback indicates that the taken-for-granted assumption of a meeting in the discourse of Namori seems to be that a meeting is a place to convey information to others, or to collect information. Michio, one of the two directors, said, 'Joho atsume to iu koto de. Minna ni. . . narubeku ooku no hito ni nani ga okotte iru ka nama no joho wo motte oite moraitai. [They attended the meeting to collect information. I want everyone to come face to face with the real information of what is actually happening.]' In the feedback, several participants confirmed that, in Namori, meetings were often a place to convey information. This comment indicates that the Namori employees' perception of a meeting relates to the Japanese participatory decision-making system.

In contrast, James's comment indicates that he viewed a meeting as a creative place where everybody contributes to the exchange of knowledge. '[When Japanese participants are silent], I can't read them. I'm confused. No contribution sometimes frustrates me' (James).

The data presented here indicates that the variation in the participants' evaluation was partly due to the difference of perceived meeting objectives that could be influenced by local business discourse.

Sociolinguistic behaviour: strategic use of back-channelling

In this study, I found a strategic use of back-channelling by some non-native speakers in order to 'empower themselves'. The frequency of participants' back-channelling was counted using 15 minutes of each meeting. The data was collected from 13:40 to 13:55 in the IT meeting and from 13:20 to 13:35 in the personnel meeting. In the IT meeting, the total number of back-channels Maarten voiced was 11, which was the largest number, followed by James's 4. The Japanese participants only voiced one, while non-Japanese participants voiced 24 (Table 25.1).

In the personnel meeting, the difference between the Japanese participant and others was unremarkable. Andy, a non-native speaker from Northern Europe who talked most frequently in the morning meeting, voiced four back channels, the largest number, followed by Udo, Marc, Steve and Kate. Tomoki did not utter any back channels (Table 25.2).

The data provides counter-evidence to the results of previous studies. Maynard (1986) and Yamada (1992) showed that Japanese produced more frequent back-channelling than Americans. The findings of the present study can be attributed to the degree of anxiety caused in the participants by lack of confidence in their own linguistic ability.

Maarten stood out by his frequent back-channel behaviour. Some of Maarten's back channels were audible. The following two excerpts are taken from the IT meeting data.

Excerpt 1
(1) Peter: We don't have to have data.
(2) Maarten: OK. Fine.

Excerpt 2
(3) Peter: Chair of the sponsor(???)sign [that] (???).
(4) Maarten: [OK].

Post-meeting interviews revealed that Maarten used his back-channelling intentionally. 'Maybe I try to demonstrate my presence. . .by, maybe, saying so.' Andy was more conscious about voicing his back channels. He explained this as: 'Continuous voice of "I am here", everyone tries to show that they are there.' For Andy, back-channelling behaviour functioned as a verbal sign of his presence.

I argue that sociolinguistic behaviours such as back-channelling are 'universal' communication strategies which are acquired naturally by non-native speakers through their use of English in the exercise of business. More frequent back-channelling by Japanese participants could have made their presence stronger and, therefore, could have empowered them.

Turn-taking strategies: delayed participation

While analysing the data, I noticed that the Namori employees tended to take turns after listening to everyone. On the other hand, some western non-native speakers showed a different turn-taking strategy. Udo used the analogy of a glass of water to explain his turn-taking strategy. 'I usually talk with a half-filled water glass and while I am talking the glass becomes full.' He starts with an incomplete utterance and by co-constructing with other participants he completes his message. Excerpt 3, taken from the personnel meeting, shows how Udo applies such a method.

> **Excerpt 3**
> (5) Marc: Could I just make a comment? Our responsibility is to utilise the channels that are affordable to us.
> (6) Udo: But (.) that(.) er(.)that leaves us the second
> (7) Terachai: (.)element?
> (8) Udo: second element we have. That is (???)

Udo co-constructs the message. He throws in an incomplete turn and waits for someone to help form it. Tomoki's speech in the same meeting showed a contrasting strategy. He sounded sufficiently self-prepared to talk about his idea. Out of his thirteen self-selected turns taken in the meeting, he only talked twice in the morning. According to my field notes, he seemed to concentrate on listening to others and grasping the context while preparing what to say. As soon as the afternoon session began he took a turn. When he opened his mouth Tomoki sounded well-prepared.

> **Excerpt 5**
> (9) Tomoki: May I say something?
> (10) Kate: Yes.
> (11) Tomoki: A thing I have concern is that it's very good material for cross-cultural situation. Maybe they are looking at the different direction. This is my first comment. My second comment, people are not familiar with this kind of training.

Tomoki went on for a few more sentences. Tomoki's comments sounded better prepared than Udo's. I would call the two different styles of forming speech 'perfection by self-construction (Tomoki)' and 'perfection by co-construction (Udo)'. In the former style, Tomoki spent time listening and understanding the situation, took more time to make his speech relevant to the discussed issue and structured it in two points, while in the latter style, 'perfection by co-construction', Udo just said 'but', took some time to think about what he should say, and continued with 'that leaves us the second. . .' and again searched for an appropriate word.

This case demonstrates the reality of multicultural meetings at various levels. The analysis shows that the participants' different objectives were based on their differing business ideologies and resulted in discrepant evaluations of the meetings. The Namori participants' sociolinguistic behaviour was evaluated differently, which may create a certain type of power relation between participants. The results of this research indicate that awareness of the complex interplay between non-native speakers' linguistic constraints, power and management ideologies is essential when English is chosen as a lingua franca within a multicultural organisation.

Future developments

As discussed in the first part of this chapter, there have been a number of studies that examined business discourse involving Japanese and westerners, in particular Americans. In retrospect, the movement of the international economy centred on Japan is characterised by an expansion from activities focused on the USA to activities that encompass Asia (Cabinet Office Government of Japan 2004). However, to date there has been little research on business discourse between Japanese and non-Japanese from other Asian countries. Although the choice of language may or may not always be English, such business contact situations will increase and will become a crucial area for further investigation. Furthermore, it will be mandatory to investigate business discourse in multinational settings rather than bi-national settings only. Such discourse may involve even more diversified actors including Africans, Europeans, South Americans, etc.

Finally, relational talk or social talk is a discourse mode that has received increasing attention in recent years. Corpus-based studies of workplace language (Holmes and Stubbe 2003; Koester 2004) have revealed the critical role of relational talk and challenged the conventional view that such talk is purposeless and unimportant. So far, however, this area of business discourse in Japan has not been sufficiently explored. One of the few studies on Japanese relational talk is Ide (2005), which compares service encounters in the United States and greetings in Japan. Ide discusses the similarity and differences of the role of small talk and greetings in Japanese and American contexts and argues that greetings in Japanese contexts fulfil the phatic function that small talk plays in American contexts. Her argument points to the potential inadequacy of applying the notion of 'politeness' developed by western academics to intercultural encounters that involve Japanese and possibly other Asian businesspeople. Further work is needed to explore relational talk in business discourse involving Japanese.

Conclusion

The overview of Japanese business discourse research has shown that there has been continuous change in business discourse. As the study discussed in this chapter has sought

to demonstrate, it is impossible to prescribe universally appropriate discursive strategies
to be applied in business interaction. However, the multilayered approach adopted in the
study is a first step towards dealing with the complexity of business discourse on sites
where multinational participants meet (Bargiela-Chiappini et al. 2007: 177). Importantly
for future developments, recent Japanese business discourse research shows that the sociolinguistic behaviour of the interactants is influenced not only by the language selected,
but also by underlying business ideologies, which are embedded in the discourse of the
participants themselves.

References

Bargiela-Chiappini, F. (2006) (Whose) English(es) for Asian business discourse(s)?
Journal of Asian Pacific Communication, 16(1): 1–24.
Bargiela-Chiappini, F., C. Nickerson and B. Planken (2007) *Business Discourse*. Basingstoke:
Palgrave Macmillan.
Befu, H. (1987) *Ideorogii to shite no nihon bunka ron*. Tokyo: Shiso no kagaku sha. Cabinet
Office Government of Japan (2004) www5.cao.go.jp/zenbun/wp-e/wp-je04/04-
00400.html. Accessed 3 March 2007.
Chingprasertsuk, P. (2005) A study of business communication problems between Thai
and Japanese businesspeople. In H. Okazaki (ed.), *Kyosei jidai wo ikiru Nihongo kyoiku*.
Tokyo: Bonjinsha, pp. 349–76.
Dale, P. N. (1986) *The Myth of Japanese uniqueness*. New York: St Martin's Press.
Reprinted 1991.
Doi, T. (1971) *Amae no kozo* [The Anatomy of Dependence]. Tokyo: Kobundo.
Du-Babcock, B. (2006) An analysis of topic management strategies and turn-taking
behavior in the Hong Kong bilingual environment. *Journal of Business Communication*,
43: 21–42.
Fujio, M. (2004) Silence during intercultural communication: A case study. *Corporate
Communications*, 9(4): 331–9.
Hofstede, G. (1980) *Culture's Consequences: International Differences in Work-Related
Values*. Beverly Hills, CA: Sage.
Holmes, J. and M. Stubbe (2003) *Power and Politeness in the Workplace: A Sociolinguistic
Analysis of Talk at Work*. London: Longman.
Ide, R. (2005) Small talk to aisatsu. In S. Ide and M. Hiraga (eds), *Koza shakai gengo gaku
dai ikkan*. Tokyo: Hitsuji Shobo, pp. 198–215.
Ishizawa, Y. (1997) *Nihonjinron: Nihonjinron no keifu*. Tokyo: Maruzen Library.
Johnson, C. (1982) *MITI and Japanese Miracle*. Stanford, CA: Stanford University
Press.
Jones, K. (1995) Masked negotiation in a Japanese work setting. In A. Firth (ed.), *The Discourse
of Negotiation: Studies of Language in the Workplace*. Oxford: Pergamon, pp. 141–58.
Kameda, N. (2001) The implication of language style in business communication: Focus
on English versus Japanese. *Corporate Communications*, 6(3): 144–9.
Kawai, Y. (2007) Japanese nationalism and the global spread of English: An analysis of
Japanese government and public discourse on English. *Language and Intercultural
Communication*, 7(1): 37–55.
Kleinberg, J. (1999) Negotiated understanding: The organizational implication of a

cross-national business negotiation. In S. L. Beechler and A. Bird (eds), *Japanese Multinationals Abroad: Individual and Organizational Learning*. New York: Oxford University Press, pp. 62–91.

Koester, A. J. (2004) Relational sequences in workplace genres. *Journal of Pragmatics*, 36: 1405–28.

LoCastro, V. (1987) Aizuchi: A Japanese conversational routine. In L. E. Smith (ed.), *Discourse across Cultures*. London: Prentice Hall, pp. 101–13.

Marriott, H. (1995) The management of discourse in international seller–buyer negotiations. In K. Ehlich and J. Wagner (eds), *The Discourse of Business Negotiation*. Berlin: Mouton de Gruyter, pp. 103–26.

Maynard, S. K. (1986) On back-channel behavior in Japanese and English casual conversation. *Linguistics*, 24(6): 73–105.

Miller, L. (1994) Japanese and American indirectness. *Journal of Asian Pacific Communication*, 5(1 & 2): 37–55.

Miller, L. (1995) Two aspects of Japanese and American co-worker interaction: Giving instructions and creating rapport. *Journal of Applied Behavioral Science*, 31(2): 141–61.

Mouer, R. E. (1988) Reviewed work(s): *The Myth of Japanese Uniqueness. Pacific Affairs*, 61(4): 691–3.

Mulholland, J. (1997) The Asian connection: Business requests and acknowledgements. In F. Bargiela-Chiappini and S. Harris (eds), *The Language of Business: An International Perspective*. Edinburgh: Edinburgh University Press, pp. 94–116.

Nakajima, S. (1993) Demonstrating miscommunication problem between American and Japanese businessmen through video. Paper delivered at the Annual Eastern Michigan University Conference on Languages and Communication for World Business and the Professions.

Nakane, C. (1970) *Tate shakai no ningen kankei*. Tokyo: Kodansha.

Nakasako, S. (1998) Japan. *Business Communication Quarterly*, 61(3): 101–6.

Noguchi, Y. (1995) *1940 nen taisei*. Tokyo: Toyokeizaishinposha.

Okabe, Y. (2005) The cost and benefit of using Japanese as means of communication in Japanese companies. *Japan Academy of International Business Studies Bulletin*, 11: 118–21.

Potoker, E. (1993) Management and training across cultures: Importance of non-verbal communication strategies – A case study. Paper delivered at the Annual Eastern Michigan University Conference on Languages and Communication for World Business and the Professions.

Seargeant, P. (2005) Globalization and reconfigured English in Japan. *World Englishes*, 24(3): 309–19.

Sumihara, N. (1993) A case study of cross-cultural interaction in a Japanese multinational corporation operating in the United States: Decision-making processes and practices. In R. R. Sims and R. F. Dennehy (eds), *Diversity and Differences in Organization: An Agenda for Answers and Questions*. Westport, CT: Quarum Books, pp. 135–48.

Sunaoshi, Y. (2005) Historical context and intercultural communication: Interactions between Japanese and American factory workers in the American South. *Language in Society*, 34: 185–217.

Tanaka, H. (2006) Emerging English-speaking business discourse in Japan. *Journal of Asian Pacific Communication*, 16(1): 25–50.

Vogel, E. F. (1979) *Japan as Number One: Lessons for America*. Cambridge, MA: Harvard University Press.

Yamada, H. (1992) *American and Japanese Business Discourse*. Norwood, NJ: Ablex.

Yngve, V. H. (1970) On getting a word in edgewise. *Papers from the Sixth Regional Meeting of the Chicago Linguistic Society*. Chicago: Chicago Linguistic Society, pp. 567–78.

Yotsukura, L. A. (2003) *Negotiating Moves: Problem Presentation and Resolution in Japanese Business Discourse*. Amsterdam: Elsevier.

26

China

Yunxia Zhu and Lan Li

Introduction

This chapter offers a critical overview of research about Chinese business discourse conducted in Greater China, which includes mainland China, Hong Kong and Taiwan. On the one hand, these countries/regions share strong Chinese traditions rooted in Confucian philosophy, which promotes unity and harmony. On the other hand, the rapid development of globalisation and the market economy has exposed Chinese business practitioners to western influences with their focus on individualism and competition. In particular, mainland China is catching up swiftly as an important player in the world economy since joining the World Trade Organisation (WTO) in December 2001. Accordingly, the business discourse used in Greater China paradoxically reflects both Confucian values and the western influence of marketing practices. This interesting combination of contrasting values has inspired research on Chinese business discourse and business communication (Goodman and Wang 2007; Li et al. 2001; Cheng and Mok 2006) covering cultural values in various Chinese communities. There are also some comparative studies showing the distinctions in cultural and discursive features between the Chinese and their business counterparts (Courtis and Hassan 2002; Hsu 2004; Ralston et al. 1997; Scollon and Scollon 1991, 2001; Spencer-Oatey and Xing 1998; Orton 2000; Young 1994). Some studies have focused on written business discourse (Cheng and Mok 2006; Cheung 2006a, 2006b; Courtis and Hassan 2002; Kong 2006; Ulijn and Li 1995; Yeung 1997; Zhu 1997, 2000, 2005), while others have probed into the spoken domain (Du-Babcock 2005, 2006; Bilbow 1997; Pan 2000). However, the specific perspectives through which researchers have approached the study of discourse also vary, which is worth our attention in this chapter.

Specifically, this review is composed of a brief outline of the methodology, followed by four main sections. The first of these sections provides a glimpse of the historical study of Chinese business discourse, which also reflects the traditional approach in the history of Chinese discourse study. The second section revolves around intercultural communication and contrastive discourse studies, which represent a strong trend in research since the late 1980s. The third section looks at business discourse research as applied to the area of business and management studies and notes the increasing importance of discourse approaches in these and other disciplines. As Bargiela-Chiappini, Nickerson, and

Planken (2007) point out, business discourse study is an interdisciplinary area overlapping a number of fields, among which we found that business and management studies are quite prominent. The final section concludes with reflections on future research directions based on our preliminary review of existing research on Chinese business discourse.

Methodology

The research method is based on a literature search of published works in the areas of business communication and discourse analysis. However, it needs to be noted that the review is not an exhaustive review of all the published works. Rather it reflects the general tendencies of research, which include the historical study of Chinese business discourse, intercultural communication and the multidisciplinarity of business discourse. A historical review is essential for Chinese business discourse study as China has a long history of using business or administrative discourse, although it has never become a mainstream interest in Chinese discourse studies (Li 1990; Zhu 1999). We will focus on intercultural communication and multidisciplinarity and review significant research findings relating to these aspects; we will also highlight various contributions the researchers have made to the understanding of Chinese business discourse.

Historical studies of Chinese business discourse

A number of studies have been conducted in both English and Chinese on the evolution of business discourse in relation to social and political changes. For example, Zhang (2006) offered a historical review of the development of *gongwen* (official-letter genres), *yingyong wen* (practical genres) and international business genres. He pointed out that these genres were created to meet the social, political and economic needs of Chinese society. The author especially alluded to the fact that in traditional official-letter writing, Chinese business discourse is characterised by attentiveness to politeness principles. Chinese business discourse was influenced by English business writing. The earliest western influence on Chinese business writing started during the Opium War in 1841 when Chinese enterprises had to adapt to a more competitive business environment. Accordingly, the term *yingyong wen* was introduced for the first time to reflect everyday business practices. More forms of *yingyong wen* such as *gongwen* were introduced during the 1870s and 1880s, including *mingling* (orders), *tongzhi* (circulars) etc. These types of business discourse have gone through regularisation processes following the economic reform in China. A greater emphasis is now placed on the use of *pingxing* (writing between equals) genres.

These studies echo Zhu's (2000) findings on the development of Chinese business discourse after Mao came to power. Zhu used a diachronic approach to study the thematic development of genres in mainland China in response to the social and economic changes over the period. Bargiela et al. (2007) categorised Zhu's approach as theme-based. While agreeing about the themes, Zhu's findings also reflect a more traditional Chinese diachronic approach often used for analysing written discourse (Liu 1959).

According to Zhu (2000), the event that had the greatest impact on Chinese written discourse is the economic reform of 1978. Zhu further divided Chinese written discourse into two periods: the pre-reform period and the post-reform period. Zhu found that more *shangxing* (a subordinate writing to a superior) and *xiaxing* (a superior writing to a

subordinate) genres were used in the pre-reform period and more *pingxing* genres have
been used since the reform period and up until today. For example, Zhu found that business companies before 1978 tended to use *qingshi* (requests) and *pifu* (official approval) as
important means of communication through the commercial goods distribution system
of the government. After 1978, companies started to use the *pingxing* sales promotional
letters to communicate with other companies. The change in discourse patterns towards
a more horizontal relationship clearly reflects the reader–writer relationship in a more
competitive business environment.

Intercultural communication and Chinese discourse

Culture and business discourse

One of the focal research interests in Chinese business discourse is the contrastive study of
language and communication (Connor 1996; Kaplan 1966) and intercultural communication (Hofstede 1991; Scollon and Scollon 2001).

For example, Kirkpatrick (1991) analysed thirty authentic request letters sent to Radio
Australia and identified a pattern which starts with a preamble and then moves on to the
request. This information sequence reflects an indirect politeness ritual. According to
Kirkpatrick, Chinese indirectness can also be related to the Chinese grammatical pattern
of *yinwei* (because) and *suoyi* (therefore), a complex sentence structure which places the
reason before the statement. This inductive sequence appears to be significantly different
from that of English, which tends to begin with a main statement followed by reasons.

Kirkpatrick's contribution lies in his emphasis on the relationship between logic, language and culture. A related study on information sequences was conducted by Young
(1994) observing simulated business meetings in which American students negotiated
with Chinese students. Young's study indicates that the inductive sequence is very
common in the spoken discourse of Chinese students.

Researchers have found that in the business context, linguistic forms relating to face-
keeping and harmony are important Chinese politeness strategies, and this issue is often
discussed in a cross-cultural context (Bilbow 1995; Gunthner 1993; Ulijn and Li 1995).
Kong has promoted the study of information sequences in his analysis of business request
letters (1998) and internal emails (2006). He found that the justification elements are
related to politeness strategies and often appear in the propositions preceding a face-
threatening act. He argued that in business transactions, the propositions that come before
and after a request may be as important as the request itself (Kong 1998: 110). Kong
(2006) also conducted a systematic discourse study in which 250 internal directive emails
were analysed according to the semantic accounts of reason, condition, purpose, result,
attribution, concession and manner, in order to illustrate indirectness in business interactions. He calculated the frequency differences in the use of justifications in three types
of relationship – peer to peer, subordinate to superior and superior to subordinate – and
found that the politeness behaviours are not necessarily related to the Chinese ideology
of hierarchy, which stipulates absolute respect for power and authority. He noted that
differences among the groups are attributable to politeness and mitigation of potential
face-threat; his findings also highlight 'the equal concern of the Chinese employees for
hierarchy and harmony in the workplace' (Kong 2006: 98). Protection of face in business

correspondence is also highlighted by Cheng and Mok's (2006) research on emails, in which they found that Hong Kong Chinese professionals have a general preference for choosing an inductive rhetorical strategy, an indirect way of organising discourse, when writing face-threatening business texts (Cheng and Mok 2006: 43).

Further contrastive research can be found in Li (1996) and Zhu and Hildebrandt (2003), who argued that the difference between English and Chinese business writing is actually related to the philosophical underpinnings of rhetoric and persuasion in each cultural tradition. They took a contrastive approach to compare the western and eastern rhetorical traditions and pointed out that Chinese culture, under the influence of Confucian philosophy, stresses both *qing* (emotion) and *li* (reason), while western cultures tend to emphasise logos (reason) in the Aristotelian philosophical tradition. Zhu and Hildebrandt's views coincide with Sheng's (2003) discussion on Chinese *li* (reason) and *lijie* (politeness rituals); *lijie* is also the application of *qing* and is used to indicate appropriate levels of politeness. Sheng analyses some business writing excerpts to identify cases lacking in *li* (reason) or *li* (politeness), and points to the importance of 'expression of feelings and friendship' (Sheng 2003: 62).

A number of other contrastive rhetoric studies were conducted in Hong Kong, which were inspired by the bilingual context. As one of the most important international financial centres in the world, Hong Kong attributes its economic success to bilingual business communication. Business letters, one of the most common communication forms, have been investigated by a number of scholars. Chinese and English sales letters are found to possess similar communicative purposes, social functions, structural moves and steps (Cheung 2006a), and both inductive and deductive patterns are used by people of both eastern and western cultural background (Kong 1998). Although Cheung asserted that the cultural differences are attributed to frequent reference to social issues by westerners and less frequent use of pressure tactics by Chinese, Yeung's (1997) business discourse comparison revealed a more convincing factor: linguistic politeness. He employed the three factors of Brown and Levinson's (1987) framework, namely imposition, social distance and relative power, but found that they do not appear to work for the Chinese data, because 'the Chinese seem to have a somewhat different system for the choice of politeness strategies which is not accurately reflected by the factors postulated by Brown and Levinson' (Yeung 1997: 520). Yeung argues that on-record appropriateness and the principle of reciprocity are the factors preferred by Chinese in the selection of politeness strategies. Although comparative studies of business letters are limited in terms of scale, scope and methodology, they reflect discursive similarities and differences, and can pave the way for more extensive research in this genre.

Cross-cultural genre studies

The annual report of a company exemplifies corporate rhetoric and is widely seen as a promotional genre, designed to construct and convey a corporate image to stockholders, brokers, regulatory agencies, financial media and the investing public. Courtis and Hassan (2002) compared English and Chinese annual reports in Hong Kong and found that bilingual narrative reporting differs with regard to reading ease. The indigenous language versions are easier for the general public to read than their English versions. Their research employed both Flesch's (1964) Reading Ease formula for English and Yang's (1971) formula for Chinese, both counting the number of syllables in a 100-word text, but failed to capture the discourse features of the annual reports. Therefore Courtis and Hassan (2002: 409) admitted that 'discourse analysis and other linguistic approaches may be more suitable' as analytical tools. In the light of developing analytical tools, Hyland (1998) applied the metadiscourse functional approach of Crismore et al. (1993) in an analysis of CEOs' letters in corporate annual reports. Hyland (1998) identified 250 metadiscourse markers in the data and a comprehensive and pragmatic description framework covering different categories of functions under textual metadiscourse and interpersonal metadiscourse. These findings show that metadiscourse is central to imparting confidence and convincing investors that the company is pursuing sound and effective strategies (Hyland 1998: 224).

Zhu (1997, 2005) made an attempt to broaden the sociocultural dimension of contrastive rhetoric by marrying it with the genre tradition (Bakhtin 1986; Miller 1984; Swales 1990). She examined three genres – Chinese sales letters, sales invitations and faxes – and compared them with the same typology of document in English. She also used intercultural dimensions, genre analysis and incorporating both Chinese and New Zealand managers' views, which represents an important contribution to contrastive rhetoric. As Derrida (1992) points out, it is essential to compare cultures with a dual perspective and let all the voices of target cultures be heard. For example, Zhu (2005) found that compared to the New Zealand managers, Chinese managers paid a lot more attention to politeness rituals such as using appropriate forms of respect for the reader. Zhu's research is an example of combining genre analysis with intercultural communication, which she categorises as cross-cultural genre studies.

Other contrastive studies

Speech act theory has been applied to the study of Chinese business discourse. Beamer (2003) applied speech act theory to analyse English business letters written by Chinese professionals to the English company of Jardine and Matheson in the nineteenth century. Beamer challenged some research findings which claimed that in intercultural communication, Chinese prefer indirectness. She noticed little indirectness in her collection of business letters, including the majority of requests. However, she did find that the collectivistic values of the Chinese culture appear to affect indirectness and directness in correspondence. Beamer's research advanced discourse knowledge about business letters written in a second language, implying that writing genres in different languages may point to the relationships between language and culture (Kaplan 1966). For example, if the texts were written in Chinese, would the writer still prefer the 'direct' approach?

Research on written business discourse also goes beyond genres to include other areas such as brand names (Huang and Chan 2005), an important topic in marketing communication. Huang and Chan classified 5,089 Chinese brand names in 21 product categories according to both linguistic and cultural criteria. Among the linguistic parameters, they included syllable and tone patterns, compounding structures, and semantic patterns relating to positive connotations. This analysis provided detailed insights on specific strategies Chinese marketers use to advertise their products. Huang and Chan also found that cultural influence is reflected in the selection of semantic fields and the choice of words for brand names relating to fortune and prosperity. This culture-specific word choice differs significantly from the branding in the west, which indicates an absence of similar brand name preferences. However, the marketers also vary their linguistic strategies in line with different customer groups. For example, unconventional and imaginative terminologies are used for promoting cars and computers to well-educated, middle-class people.

Spoken business discourse studies

Spoken business discourse has also increasingly attracted researchers' attention. A few spoken business corpora have been compiled in Mainland China and Hong Kong (Bilbow 1995; Sheer and Chen 2003; Cheng 2006; Du-Babcock 2005, 2006) with audio- and/or visual recordings and transcriptions, covering service encounters, workplace telephone calls, business meetings, job and placement interviews, presentations, announcements and conference presentations. Diverse research methodologies have been applied to their analysis. For example, Li et al. (2001) used conversation analysis to illustrate the workings of the key cultural concept of 'harmony' at business meetings in the final stage of negotiation. They argued that the speaker's responsive treatment of the prior turns in business conversation provides clear evidence of his or her interpretative process and practical reasoning, and therefore the cause of understanding, non-understanding and misunderstanding can be traced by discourse markers such as *shi-bu-shi* (literally yes-no-yes), *duiduidui* (right right), *shi/jiushi* (yes/that's right) and *haohao* (good good). Li et al. show that Chinese speakers can work together to achieve conversational coherence, which in turn contributes to a harmonious relationship.

Researchers tend to draw comparisons between westerners and Chinese when analysing spoken discourse in bilingual settings. Chinese indirectness deriving from 'face' and politeness issues has been identified in several research projects but interpreted differently by researchers from different cultural backgrounds. Bilbow (1997) reported his observation of various speech acts at a range of business meetings in Hong Kong. There was a significant difference between direct and indirect commissive speech acts used by Chinese managers and western expatriates. Bilbow ascribed this to contrasts between Confucian and western philosophies. More recent research can be found in Yeung (2003), who compared the discourse patterns of leadership style from twenty bank meetings in Australia and in Hong Kong. She found both Chinese and westerners demonstrated self-consciousness of authority in directive phrases, formulaic requests for opinion and question forms signalling non-imposition. Hong Kong Chinese showed a higher degree of openness by using more bipolar and multiple-choice questions and tended to invite subordinates' participation in decision-making, while Australian managers exhibited a distinctive consultative mode by using leading and loaded questions to enlist support from subordinates.

Business discourse and business and management studies

Business discourse is playing an increasingly important role in management and business studies. More and more researchers have begun to pay attention to discourse as an additional perspective on business issues. Publications on Chinese business discourse also appear in management training manuals, such as that by Pan et al. (2002), who examined the written and spoken discourse of Finnish, Hong Kong and Chinese managers in intercultural interactions. On the basis of their findings the authors developed a training package for global managers to enhance their cultural sensitivity and knowledge.

Zhao (2000) adopted the content analysis method to analyse fourteen Chinese text-books on negotiation, and complemented this method with ethnographic interviews with business managers with negotiation experience. For example, Zhao discusses communication strategies in business negotiation such as creating atmosphere and resolving conflicts, and relates these strategies to Chinese cultural values. Although limited in his data and research method, Zhao has made an original contribution by incorporating managers' perspectives in research on business negotiation.

More focus on discourse analysis in the area of Sino–western business negotiation can be found in Li (1999), Ghauri and Fang (2001), Graham and Lam (2003) and Sheer and Chen (2003). Sheer and Chen analysed the interview discourse of both Chinese and western managers, which can be seen as a further contribution to incorporating managers' perspectives into the study of cross-cultural negotiations. These researchers' interest is in identifying the interface of social practice, culture and negotiation in interviews. Their study also adds insightful findings into contrastive studies of intercultural negotiations. The successful strategies of Chinese negotiators focused primarily on rational, professional approaches while those of westerners centred on coping effectively with Chinese social values. Sheer and Chen incorporated extracts from interviews; for example, they include an anecdote about a Chinese business woman's experience meeting her French host for the first time. She became upset because her host did not shake hands with her. Only later did the Chinese business woman learn that French men tend to shake hands with women who offer their hand first.

Zhu et al. (2006) examined the genre of business executives' success stories about how they managed relationship-building with customers. Their innovative use of the story genre delineates an effective means of constructing meanings in different cultural contexts. The four 'cultures' they examined included China, New Zealand, India and South Africa. For example, they found positive connotations in the Chinese executives' vocabulary of interpersonal relations, which included terms such as *jianli* (construct) and *fazhan* (develop), rather than the derogative *gao guanzi* (manipulate relationships) as reported in earlier research. The discourse perspective therefore affords insights in to how different cultures define and construct business relations.

Summary and conclusion

In sum, Chinese business discourse, although built upon a tradition of written discourse studies, is now at the stage of being exposed to multiple discourse approaches. Both diachronic and historical patterns, as well as the influences of western approaches, were found to apply to Chinese business discourses.

First of all, we found that the historical approach is used to study the dynamic nature and evolution of Chinese business discourse. This approach is particularly relevant today when Chinese discourse is undergoing dramatic changes, as signalled for example in the emergence of new patterns of interpersonal interactions in business contexts.

Second, significant findings have been reported in intercultural communication research. Recent years have witnessed more research effort in this field as China has become an increasingly important player in the world market. Two strands have been identified: one is the continuation of the contrastive study of linguistic forms and the impact of Chinese cultural values on the use of these forms. The second strand is cross-cultural genre studies which explore and compare Chinese written genres with those of English. The use of the genre approach also provides understanding about the discursive knowledge mobilised by the discourse community.

Third, the multidisciplinary nature of Chinese business discourse reflects the tendency of business discourse research in general (Bargiela-Chiappini et al. 2007). This tendency seems to have strengthened after the introduction of discourse analysis in business and management studies (Philips et al. 2004). As shown in our discussion, analysis and incor-poration of managers' own discourses and perspectives can provide more in-depth under-standing of business and managerial issues from a practitioner's viewpoint.

The above research tendencies have implications for future research in the area of business discourse in China. The historical approach will continue to be relevant to the reflection on discursive developments in the fast-changing business and technological contexts of China. Cultural factors will remain a strong dimension for further research. It is interesting to note that in the globalised context, Chinese cultural values are still playing an important role in business discourse formation and development. Future research may need to address more complex issues relating to specific incorporation of both traditional Chinese culture and western influences. More attention also needs to be paid to the study of spoken discourse through the application of diverse analytical methods. Finally, more collaborative exchanges need to be encouraged among research-ers within Greater China, since we are all contributing to the same field of business discourse.

Acknowledgements

Thanks are given to Francesca Bargiela and the three reviewers for their valuable com-ments and input into our earlier drafts.

References

Bakhtin, M. M. (1986) The problem of speech genres. In C. Emerson and M. Holquist (eds), *Speech Genres and Other Late Essays*. Austin: University of Texas Press, pp. 60–102.
Bargiela-Chiappini, F., C. Nickerson and B. Planken (2007) *Business Discourse*. Basingstoke: Palgrave Macmillan.
Beamer, L. (2003) Directness in Chinese business correspondence of the nineteenth century. *Journal of Business and Technical Communication*, 17(2): 201–36.
Bilbow, G. T. (1995) Requesting strategies in the cross-cultural business meeting. *Pragmatics*, 5(1): 45–55.
Bilbow, G. T. (1997) Spoken discourse in the multicultural workplace in Hong Kong: Applying a model of discourse as 'impression management. In F. Bargiela-Chiappini and S. Harris (eds), *The Languages of Business: An International Perspective*. Edinburgh: Edinburgh University Press, pp. 21–48.
Brown, P. and S. Levinson (1987) *Politeness: Some Universals in Language Usage*. Cambridge: Cambridge University Press.

Cheng, W. and E. Mok (2006) Cultural preference for rhetorical patterns in business writing. *Hong Kong Linguist*, 26: 69–80.

Cheung, M. (2006a) Producing and communicating electronic sales messages in Hong Kong: Insights from a discourse study and from industry practitioners. *Proceedings of the 5th International Conference of the European Association of Languages for Specific Purposes*: 108–18.

Cheung, M. (2006b) A discourse analysis of Chinese and English sales letters in Hong Kong. *Proceedings of the 5th International Conference of the European Association of Languages for Specific Purposes*: 142–50.

Connor, U. (1996) *Contrastive Rhetoric: Cross-Cultural Aspects of Second-Language Writing*. Cambridge: Cambridge University Press.

Courtis, J. and S. Hassan (2002) Reading ease of bilingual annual reports. *Journal of Business Communication*, 39(10): 394–413.

Crismore, A., R. Markkanen and M. Steffensen (1993) Metadiscourse in persuasive writing: A study of texts written by American and Finnish university students. *Written Communication*, 10(1): 39–71.

Derrida, J. (1992) *The Other Heading: Reflections on Today's Europe*, trans P.-A. Brault and M. B. Naas. Bloomington and Indianapolis: Indiana University Press.

Du-Babcock, B. (2005) An investigation of individual and small-group behavior decision-making: A cross-cultural approach. *Proceedings of the Association for Business Communication 7th European Convention*: 1–10.

Du-Babcock, B. (2006) An analysis of topic management strategies and turn-taking behaviour in the Hong Kong bilingual environment: The impact of culture and language use. *Journal of Business Communication*, 43(1): 21–42.

Flesch, R. (1964) *The ABC of Style: A Guide to Plain English*. New York: Harper and Row.

Ghauri, P. and T. Fang (2001) Negotiating with the Chinese: A socio-cultural analysis. *Journal of World Business*, 36(3): 303–25.

Goodman, M. B. and J. Wang (2007) Tradition and innovation: The China business communication study. *Journal of Business Strategy*, 28(3): 34–41.

Graham, J. and M. N. Lam (2003) The Chinese negotiation. *Harvard Business Review*, 81(10): 82–91.

Gunthner, S. (1993) *Diskursstrategien in der interkulturellen kommunikation*. Tübingen: Niemeyer.

Hofstede, G. H. (1991) *Cultures and Organisations: Software of the Mind*. New York: McGraw-Hill.

Hsu, C. F. S. (2004) Sources of differences in communication apprehension between Chinese in Taiwan and Americans. *Communication Quarterly*, 52: 370–94.

Huang, Y. Y. and A. K. K. Chan (2005) The role of language and culture in marketing communication. *Journal of Asian Pacific Communication*, 15(2): 257–85.

Hyland, K. (1998) Exploring corporate rhetoric: Metadiscourse in the CEO's letter. *Journal of Business Communication*, 35(2): 224–45.

Kaplan, R. B. (1966) Cultural thought patterns in inter-cultural education. *Language Learning*, 16: 1–20.

Kirkpatrick, A. (1991) Information sequencing in Mandarin in letters of request. *Anthropological Linguistics*, 33(2): 183–203.

Kong, C. C. K. (1998) Are simple business request letters really simple? A comparison of Chinese and English business request letters. *Text*, 18(1): 103–41.

Kong, C. C. K. (2006) Accounts as a politeness strategy in the internal directive documents of a business firm in Hong Kong. *Journal of Asian Pacific Communication*, 16(1): 77–101.

Li, D. (ed.) (1990) *Caijng yingyong xiezuo* [On the Writing of Practical Documents in Finance and Economics]. Beijing: Zhongguo Caizheng Jingji Chubanshe.

Li, W., H. Zhu and Y. Li (2001) Interpersonal harmony and textual coherence in Chinese business interaction. *Multilingua*, 20(3): 285–310.

Li, X. (1996) *'Good Writing' in a Cross-cultural Context*. Albany, NY: SUNY Press.

Li, X. (1999) *Chinese–Dutch Business Negotiations: Insights from Discourse*. Amsterdam: Rodopi.

Liu, X. (1959) *The Literary Mind and the Carving of Dragons*, trans. W. Y. C. Shih. New York: Columbia University Press.

Miller, C. R. (1984) Genre as social action. *Quarterly Journal of Speech*, 70: 151–67.

Orton, J. (2000) *Keys to Successful Intercultural Communication between Partners in Australian–Chinese Joint Ventures*. Richmond: Australia China Business Council.

Pan, Y. (2000) Facework in Chinese service encounters. *Journal of Asian Pacific Communication*, 10(1): 25–61.

Pan, Y., R. Scollon and S. W. Scollon (2002) *Professional Communication in an International Setting*. Oxford: Blackwell.

Phillips, N., T. B. Lawrence and C. Hardy (2004) Discourse and institutions. *Academy of Management Review*, 29(4): 635–52.

Ralston, D. A., D. H. Holt, R. H. Terpstra and K. C. Yu (1997) The impact of national culture and economic ideology on managerial work values: A study of the United States, Russia, Japan, and China. *Asia Pacific Journal of Management*, 14(1): 1–20.

Scollon, R. and S. W. Scollon (1991) Topic confusion in English–Asian discourse. *World Englishes*, 10(2): 113–25.

Scollon, R. and S. W. Scollon (2001) *Intercultural Communication: A Discourse Approach*, 2nd edn. Oxford: Blackwell.

Sheer, V. C. and L. Chen (2003) Successful Sino–western business negotiation: Participants' accounts of national and professional cultures. *Journal of Business Communication*, 40(1): 50–85.

Sheng, M. (2003) Reason and 'politeness': The appropriate styles for writing business letters [Shangwu xinhan xiezuo zhong de deti tan]. *Journal of Lixin Accounting Institute Quarterly*, 17(3): 60–3.

Spencer-Oatey, H. and J. Xing (1998) Relational management in Chinese–British business meetings. In S. Hunston (ed.), *Language at Work*. Clevedon: British Association for Applied Linguistics in association with Multilingual Matters, pp. 31–55.

Swales, J. (1990) *Genre Analysis: English in Academic and Research Settings*. Cambridge: Cambridge University Press.

Ulijn, J. M. and X. Li (1995) Is interrupting impolite? Some temporal aspects of turn-taking in Chinese–western and other intercultural business encounter. *Text*, 15(4): pp. 589–627.

Yang, S. J. (1971) A readability formula for Chinese language. PhD thesis, University of Wisconsin.

Yeung, L. (2003) Management discourse in Australian banking contexts: In search of an Australian model of participation as compared with that of Hong Kong Chinese. *Journal of Intercultural Studies*, 24(1): 47–63.

Yeung, L. N. T. (1997) Polite requests in English and Chinese business correspondence in Hong Kong. *Journal of Pragmatics*, 27(4): 505–22.

Young, L. W. L. (1994) *Crosstalk and Culture in Sino–American Communication*. Cambridge: Cambridge University Press.

Zhang, Z. (2006) The historical development of international business writing [Guoji shangwu yinyongwen de lishi yange]. *International Business Studies (Guoji shangwe yanjiu)*, 4: 57–61.

Zhao, J. (2000) The Chinese approach to international business negotiation. *Journal of Business Communication*, 37(3): 209–36.

Zhu, Y. (1997) A rhetorical analysis of Chinese sales letters. *Text*, 17(4): 543–66.

Zhu, Y. (1999) Genre dynamics Exhibited in the development of sales 'tongzhi' (circulars). *Text*, 19(2): 281–306.

Zhu, Y. (2000) Rhetorical moves in Chinese sales genres, 1949 to the present. *Journal of Business Communication*, 37(2): 156–72.

Zhu, Y. (2005) *Written Communication across Cultures: A Sociocognitive Perspective on Business Genres*. Amsterdam: John Benjamins.

Zhu, Y. and H. Hildebrandt (2003) Greek and Chinese classical rhetoric: The root of cultural differences. *Asia Business and Marketing Communication*, 14(2): 90–114.

Zhu, Y., P. Nel and R. Bhat (2006) A cross-cultural study of communication strategies for building business relationships. *International Journal of Cross-Cultural Management*, 6(3): 319–41.

27

Korea

Yeonkwon Jung

Introduction

Not long ago, the global giant retailers Wal–Mart and Carrefour decided not to continue doing business in Korea. Their decision was mainly due to problems in adapting to the emotional, sensitive and shifting nature of the Korean business environment. Unless foreign companies give prominent consideration to the local culture, successful business can hardly be expected. A cultural analysis of business can offer an approach which makes it easy and quick to understand unfamiliar cultures and makes communication with them more efficient. In this respect, the acquisition of intercultural business communication skills is of crucial importance for successful international business.

Following the claim that a proper understanding of cross-cultural differences is significant background knowledge for successful international business, this chapter investigates linguistic and non-linguistic phenomena in the Korean business context based on cultural values using authentic business communication data. Studies on cross-cultural communication tend to be fragmentary accounts of cause-and-effect variables, and superficial, in that they tend to conventionalise values across cultures (Gesteland 1999; Hofstede 1994). To overcome this problematic issue, this chapter discusses the identified cultural values *within* context. This approach is expected to show that many of the established beliefs about Korean culture need to be examined. In this chapter, the notion of face is highlighted, because it is one of the most significant personality attributes affecting interpersonal interaction and is a construct of the social and personal self shaped by cultural values in Korea. According to Brown and Levinson (1987: 61), face is 'the public self-image that every member wants to claim for himself'. However, it is necessary to note that the notion of *self* varies across culture. Korean expressions of 'face' are interpreted as positive public image. Since people in collectivist societies are sensitive to face because they are more gregarious, group-oriented or relation-focused than westerners, one's self-image depends very much on how one is looked on by others. Therefore, public evaluation of self is strongly perceived by the individual, producing feelings of saving face and losing face. The concepts of positive and negative face from Brown and Levinson's (1987) model of politeness may be essential in dealing with facework reflected in communication strategies (for politeness purposes, in particular).

Positive face is defined as wants to be desirable to others, while negative face is defined as wants not to be impeded by others. Brown and Levinson call certain kinds of acts 'the face-threatening acts (FTAs)' that challenge face wants. Some acts (e.g. request, order) impose on the hearer's negative face by showing that the speaker gets the hearer to do something. Other acts (e.g. disagreement, complaint) threaten the hearer's positive face by indicating that the speaker does not share the hearer's wants. This chapter will show how Korean business professionals manage facework in business situations within the communication rules or cultural values.

After an outline of Korean cultural values and recent trends, and an account of the data, the first section investigates business communication behaviours in Korea in the light of cultural values. It examines the collective nature (the use of terms showing collectivism; the practice of mixing business with entertainment), the hierarchical nature (absolute subordination to superiors; apology as a power play), and the indirect nature (saying 'no' indirectly; gift giving for future requests) of Korean business communication. The following section explores exceptions running counter to cultural values in terms of numerous factors affecting the decision-making process such as the choice of address terms and subject pronouns, sensitivity to power, degree of imposition and rhetorical structure. This chapter claims that communication patterns depend on the specific organisational context, and concludes with implications for pedagogy and future research.

Before embarking on the analysis, I would like to provide a brief description of Korean cultural values and recent trends in Korean business communication, followed by a description of the data used in this chapter.

Korean cultural values and recent trends in Korean business communication

Alongside the entire moral value system and lifestyle, Korean business practices and customs are deeply influenced by cultural values. For example, the nature of the hierarchical order is the underlying cause of the predominantly vertical nature of the relationships in Korean business organisations. Koreans are sensitive to indirectness. They have a tendency to avoid openly expressing their opinions or feelings even in business contexts. The collectivistic nature of Korean society causes strong family ties to be extended to the work environment, so that the work organisation can function very much like a family. This collective nature creates an effect on Korean management practices. A few *kulup* (a group of affiliated companies) advocate the *inhwa* style of management (e.g. LG Electronics). *Inhwa* 'human harmony' is a concept that incorporates both loyalty on the part of employees, and maternal concern and behaviour on the part of employers towards their workers.

Despite remarkable economic growth in Korea led mainly by *kulup*, very little research has been conducted on Korean business communication until relatively recently (Kenman 2006). This is apparently because the discipline of business communication is still *new* in Korea, and therefore not academically prestigious. In view of this local situation, it is perhaps optimistic to expect active work on Korean business communication abroad. (cf. some exceptions: Jung 2002, 2005a, 2005b; Park et al. 1998; Thomas 1998). Consequently, the lack of academic popularity of Korean business communication makes it extremely difficult to keep track of previous work or major transitions in Korean business communication. Because of

Table 27.1. The number of pieces of data in the study

	Conversation	Correspondence	Interview	Business meeting	Total
Food	3	4	1	0	8
Pharmaceutical	3	3	1	0	7
Joint-venture	0	0	0	1	1
SME	2	0	1	0	3
Total	8	7	3	1	19

the limited previous or current work on Korean business communication, introductory work like this chapter is forced to adopt a synchronic approach.

Data

The data for this study comprises spoken and written data sets of Korean business interactions (i.e. conversation, interdepartmental meeting, correspondence) and interviews, collected from four Korean companies: (1) a private food company producing curry, instant food, vegetable oil products and canned tuna fish; (2) a private pharmaceutical company specialising in the export and import of both finished pharmaceuticals and raw materials; (3) a private joint-venture company producing display products like LCD panels for computer monitors, notebook PCs, mobile phones and TVs; and (4) a small and medium size enterprise (SME) making insurance products and selling them to big insurance companies. Details of the data are shown in Table 27.1.

In order to investigate the different realisation of cultural values depending on corporate cultures, this study looks at Korean companies with different corporate cultures. While the food company and SME have an oriental-style corporate culture, the joint-venture company has a western-style corporate culture (see Chen 2004 for key features of western and Asian corporate cultures). The pharmaceutical company is located in an intermediate space on the continuum but it is closer to western-style corporate culture.

In Korea, contacting an unknown person directly without going through an intermediary is viewed with suspicion and it is hard to establish credentials. When you wish to begin a business relationship with someone in Korea, it is very important to be introduced to that person by a third party known to both parties. I was able to gain access to the companies through this process. Data collection was carried out through multiple visits to each company, although the duration of stay varied across the companies. For example, the discourse activities in the food and the pharmaceutical companies (the international sales division, in particular) were observed in one complete working day, including a drinking session after work. For reasons of confidentiality, however, limited information was accessible. In the case of business meetings, in particular, I was allowed to inspect business interactions which are not directly relevant to core business talk (e.g. setting up an in-house English programme). Since the heads of the divisions had already let employees know what I would do in the office, they pursued their business work with little attention to my presence. During my observation, language was noted for business activities. When recording spoken data was not possible, I made notes as precisely as possible. Some of the material in the study (business correspondence, in particular) is drawn from my work on Korean business communication (Jung 2002).

During the first visit, I also conducted interviews and asked about the management of routine business, corporate culture, communication media, and so on. During the subsequent visits, I asked follow-up questions based on my initial analysis of the data. E-mail correspondence was also exchanged with informants to ask additional questions.

In the examples given, a detailed context or background information for each is provided, and if necessary the preceding or following talk for each is also included. Otherwise, a single unit of discourse is shown, especially in the case of the data from less rich media (e.g. letters).

Business communication behaviours in Korea in the light of cultural values

This section investigates the collective, hierarchical and indirect nature of Korean business communication by looking at (1) conceptual usages (terms carrying human network, kin terms, the 'we' pronoun) and actions (mixing business with entertainment) to create solidarity; (2) the function of power in proposing an opinion, playing a game and making an apology; and (3) the way of saying 'no' indirectly and the aim of gift giving.

The collective nature of Korean business communication

The use of terms showing collectivism

Numerous Korean terms carry the sense of interdependence and interrelatedness based on collectivism. For example, terms like *hakyen* 'school ties', *ciyen* 'regionalism' and *hyelyen* 'ties of kinship' function as basic units of many social activities in Korea. School ties are especially strong in the workplace, often approaching the importance of blood ties. Large companies often hire from the same schools, forming generational layers based on longevity and perpetuating the junior–senior relationship throughout working lives, which contributes to co-operation, loyalty and diligence in attitudes and performance (De Mente 2004). These generational layers of alumni groups may facilitate communication and co-operation among the companies. *Inyen* 'human ties' (from Buddhist doctrine) also connotes the collectivistic nature of Korean human relationships. If *inyen* between interactants exists, they consider themselves in-group members. However, if they no longer have *inyen*, Koreans may be cold to the other party: as B says in example 1, *polcangtapwassney* 'It is all over with them'. The reason why B says so also seems to be because he tries to minimise face loss by indirectly saying that we do not need you either, so goodbye. Likewise, B tries to *justify* this bad situation using a fatalism-related term, *inyen*, to save his or his company's face.

Example 1
[Korean company O, which supplies OEM products to American company O, faces difficulties because of the American company's unexpected notification. A subordinate reports on this to his superior]
A: *mikwuk Osanun Oceyphwum kongkup kyeyyak yencangul wenchi anhko isssupnita*

'American company O does not want to extend the contract to supply product O'
B: *wuliwanun inyeni kekikkacinka pokwun. polcangtapwassney*
'We may have no further human ties with them. It is all over with them'

Regarding address terms in the Korean workplace, in general, the inferior may use title + last name or title only to the superior (e.g. *kwacangnimkkeyse sayngsankyeyhoykul hyepuy hwu cay cocenghay cwusiki palapnita* 'I hope you, *kwacangnim* "head of department", will revise the production plan after discussing with us'). However, due to the collectivistic nature of Korean society, Koreans commonly use kin terms even between non-siblings. Besides creating solidarity, kin terms can be used to mitigate FTAs. In example 2, two FTAs (the complaint *nemwuhasipnita* 'It's unfair' and the rejection *ike italkkaci sencek moshayyo* 'I cannot ship this within this month') are redressed by a kin term, *hyengnim* 'brother'.

Example 2
[A junior argues with a senior about a possible date for shipping Korean products to the local dealer in Vietnam]
A: *kimtayli, mwucoken italanulo sencekhayya toyntanikka*
'Deputy Kim, you have to ship this within this month'
B: *hyengnim nemwuhasipnita. ike italkkaci sencek moshayyo*
'Brother, it is unfair. I cannot'

The use of the 'we' pronoun also demonstrates the collective nature of Korean business communication. Koreans prefer to use 'we' instead of 'I'. Using 'I' or 'my' may give the impression that the speaker is arrogant. It may also be consistent with the lack of a sense of possessiveness stemming from collectivism in many Asian languages (Mulholland 1997). *Wulipwuse* 'our department' and *cehuy* 'we' in example 3 and *tangsa* 'our company' in example 4 support the 'we-orientation'. In particular, *tangsa* is used to present the speaker as part of a powerful group to the hearer. By adopting the speaker-oriented noun phrase, the speaker tends to support and strengthen both a corporate identity and the speaker-orientation already established through the use of exclusive 'we' emphasising 'we + powerful' over 'I + powerful' (Akar 1998).

Example 3
[B complains about his senior's request for delaying the delivery date of goods]
A: *mikwukken, ipen chwumal chwulko yeycengicanha. kuntay chwulkoilcalul icwuman nucchweto toylkka?*
'Regarding the job of export to the US, this weekend was supposed to be the delivery date. However, will it be OK to delay for two weeks?'
B: *chwulko cwunpi ta machwessnunteyyo. wulipwuseeysenun yocum 2 myenguy inweni thoycikhan sangthayla koyngcanghi pappun epmwusokey ppalli cakepul hay tulyessnuntey cehuylosenun maywu hwangtanghapnita*
'We finished the work quickly to meet the delivery date in spite of being very busy due to the retirement of two people in our department. Your request for delaying the date causes us trouble'

Example 4

[A businessperson objects to a business partner's request for an extension of the settlement condition]

tangsanun D/A cokenul pwulhehana, kwisawanun yeyoycekulo D/A coken 60il kyelceycokenul swuyonghay on pa isssupnita. kulena, 120 dayslouy yencangun tang-salosenun tocehi swuyonghaki elyewun ceyanioni, tangsauy ipcangul kolyehaye kicon kelaycokenul kyeysok yucihaye cwusintamyen kamsahakeysssupnita

'We, *tangsa*, generally reject D/A conditions but we will make an exception and accept the D/A 60 day settlement condition. But, since an extension of 120 days is difficult to accept at all, I would appreciate it if you would consider our situation and continue with the existing contract'

The matter of using 'we' or impersonalising a subject through *tangsa* might also be relevant to face-saving purposes. Assessing the agent for the FTA permits a decision about who gets the blame (i.e. who will be responsible and losing face?). For example, in examples 3 and 4, agents use *cehuy* and *tangsa* to avoid the responsibility for the complaint, *maywu hwangtanghapnita* and the rejection, *tocehi swuyonghaki elyewun ceyanioni*, respectively.

The practice of mixing business with entertainment

The term 'hospitality culture' in reference to Korea means the practice of mixing business with the pleasure of entertainment. Entertaining and being entertained are essential parts of building a close relationship with Korean businesspeople. Before negotiating and entering into a business deal, Korean businesspeople socialise a great deal with potential partners and clients in order to establish a trusting relationship. This socialising is considered part of the 'work relationship', although no actual 'work' as it is understood in the west may be completed. The following episode from an interview at the Korean food company shows how important relationship-building can be in Korean business negotiation (Thomas and Inkson 2003).

Example 5

Sales manager O was introduced by his friend to Mr O. Mr O was planning to open a family restaurant and looking for a supplier to make a bulk order of product O from a food company. Manager O wanted to win a contract and he came across the fact that Mr O had recently started to play golf. When Mr O visited manager O in his office to check on the product price and other related issues, they talked about golf in addition to business. They naturally made an appointment to play golf a week later. When they met for golf, they also talked about private things like each one's family stories and hobbies. They also started talking about an order during the golf session. Without checking on the prices of product O from other firms, Mr O signed a contract with manager O the following day.

In example 5, manager O pays particular attention to creating a background relationship, which makes agreement more likely, emphasising the social side of the situation over the task side. The participants seem to consider the work relationship and the personal relationship to be the same concept. If they distinguish between the two relationships, each one's positive face is likely to be damaged, because separating them creates a calculating image. This may support the claim that Korean business negotiation sometimes begins after the contract.

The practice of mixing business with entertainment is also prominent inside the company. Events important to individual employees are acknowledged with drinks for co-workers (e.g. when employees buy a new car or house) and your membership in a workplace automatically makes you important to your co-workers. This acknowledgement can be a signal of having *nwunchi*. Koreans value *nwunchi* 'reading the other's face or feelings (lit. eye measures)' not to hurt others' feeling or face. Being skilled at *nwunchi* is one of the most important business assets one can have, and such people are highly valued because they are the ones who help keep a workplace peaceful and collective. In example 6, the speaker shows his explicit interest in the hearer's promotion and requests that they buy something to drink or eat to celebrate his promotion. On this occasion, the request serves the function of creating solidarity, because to ask for something in return for congratulations is a behaviour *giving* the requestee face (i.e. doing something to enhance someone's reputation or prestige). Probably that is why B immediately accepts A's request with no hesitation.

Example 6

[A requests something to drink or eat to celebrate B's promotion]
A: *sungcinul cinsimulo chwukhahayyyo. sungcinthek encey naylkenciyo?*
'Heartfelt congratulations on your promotion. When will you treat me to celebrate your promotion?'
B: *ung, komapta. comankan nal hanpen capca*
'Yes, thank you. Let us make an appointment'

Besides noticing something good, however, the speaker may also notice something bad that has happened to the hearer. It is customary for Korean businesspeople to contribute a set percentage of their salary to help a colleague undergoing a difficult situation (e.g. family death). In example 7, the speaker identifies with the hearer's hurt feelings brought about by the bad news (i.e. failing to get a promotion). A propositive sentence (i.e. *cyenyekey swulhancan hapsita* 'Let's go for a drink in the evening') follows the acknowledgement of bad news. In Korea, if someone proposes something to eat or drink, it is a promissive action to treat the addressee to build up solidarity between the two. Accordingly, this propositive act plays a significant role in empathising and restoring the hearer's positive face, which had already suffered due to the bad news.

Example 7

[A businessperson recognises that his colleague has failed to get a promotion]
kyengkipwucinulo manhun pwuntuli sungciney nwulaktoyncila nemwu sinkyengssusici masiko cyenyekey swul hancan hapsita
'Since many people fail to get a promotion at this time because of industrial downturn, do not worry about failing to get a promotion too much. Let us go for a drink in the evening'

In general, eating lunch or drinking after work is an extension of business in Korea. It is not a personal choice but an obligatory communal act. In example 8, typical Koreans, like A and B, have difficulty in understanding Mr O's (A&B's colleague) preference for eating alone.

> **Example 8**
> [A and B gossip about Mr O during business lunch]
> A: *papmekule kal ttay Ossinun way kathi kaci anhcyo*
> 'When we go for lunch, why do we leave Mr O out?'
> B: *ku salam honca pap meknunkel cohahay*
> 'He prefers to eat alone'
> A: *cengmal huyhanhan salamineyyo*
> 'Oh, he is extremely weird'

Since personal disclosure of face-threatening information is normally limited to those with whom trust has been established and proven, this kind of gossip will meet A and B's positive face wants (see Deal and Kennedy 2000 for the positive side of gossip in the workplace). However, the unclear distinction between private and public is most probably an imposition on independent people like Mr O, and negative face may be threatened.

The hierarchical nature of Korean business communication

Absolute subordination to superiors inside and outside the workplace

Korean companies (even some universities) function very much like army or marine corps squads. Differences in rank within organisations of all kinds are taken seriously and the behaviour of people on all levels is regimented as it is in military life. The vertical arrangements in organisations tend to make it difficult for people in companies to communicate. Therefore, *horizontal* two-way communication between power unequals is unlikely to be familiar and comfortable. In example 9, a subordinate's proposal is not accepted by a superior.

> **Example 9**
> [A superior assigns overtime work to subordinates, and then a subordinate proposes a problem about overtime work to A, the superior]
> A: *ipwa, kyeyhoykpota cakepi 4il nucchwecyesse. pamsaymcakep hayya hal kes kathuntay*
> 'Look, we are four days behind the schedule. We should put everyone on overtime'
> B: *manil kulemyen, swutanghako ilcengul cocenghayya hal kes kathunteyyo*
> 'If we did that, the wages and salary bill would shoot up. You will also have to rearrange this schedule to make up the lost time'
> A: *sinipila mwel moluna pontay halamyen haci mali manha*
> 'Don't say that. Just do it'

In public conversations, individual views and opinions must yield to the protection of face and the observance of status differences. Since a subordinate's proposal of a problem to a superior can be interpreted as a direct confrontation of the superior's positive face, the superior immediately attacks the subordinate. The superior's strong rejection of the proposal also aims to prevent other subordinates from joining B.

Likewise, subordinates or subcontractors are not supposed to challenge superiors or contractors even outside the workplace (e.g. during playing games). They have a tendency to lose a game intentionally to please superiors or contractors as the following piece of interview data shows.

Example 10
It has become popular to do business on the golf course in Korea. To lose a golf game to please an opponent who is your senior or contractor is very common. It is an underlying rule which you should always follow.

Apology as a power play

Normally superiors rarely express certain acknowledgements, like apologies. In general, an inferior apologises to a superior on the basis of power differences, because an apology implies an acknowledgement of the apologiser's lesser power over the apologee. Because of their strong tendency to avoid overt apologies, superiors tend to make apologies indirectly in numerous ways. Example 11 does not show any overt apology in order to mitigate the force of request and the requestee's negative face is saved. But merely acknowledging the superior's imposition on the inferior (i.e. 'each person in charge') through understanding and acknowledging the addressee's current difficult situation (i.e. *pappun epmwu* 'busy work') implies an apology. The superior's acknowledgement of the subordinate's current difficult situation is also likely to meet the subordinate's positive face wants.

Example 11
[A superior requests that each person in charge meet the schedule]
pappun epmwueyto kak tamtangcakkeyse cokum sinkyeng sse cwusyese ilcengey chaci-lepsi cinhayngtoyl swu isskey pwuthaktulipnita
'In spite of the busy work, I ask each person in charge to pay a little bit more attention to meeting the schedule without any delays'

The indirect nature of Korean business communication

Saying 'no' indirectly

Due to the prevalent tendency to indirectness in Korea, instead of saying 'no', one may use an expression such as *himtulkekathay* 'It seems difficult' in example 12. In example 13 a reason, *caykoka namaissci anhsupnita* 'It is out of stock', is given to minimise the other's positive face loss, and the main clause carrying the agent's refusal, *ttalase ceysitoyn kakyekulo napphwumi pwulkanunghapnita* 'Therefore, it is impossible to supply at the suggested price', is omitted (thereby avoiding a direct confrontation).

Example 12
[B rejects A's request to pay the commission due to the finance team's circumstances]

A: *khemisyen kumcwuanulo cipwulhayla*
'Pay the commission within this week'
B: *himtulkekathay. caymwuthimeyse com nuceciketun*
'It seems difficult. The commission from the finance team has been slightly delayed'

Example 13
[A does not accept the addressee's request to reconsider their price]
kakyekul inhahay tallanun kwisauy yokwunun alkeysssupnita. cennyento pwunuy ceyphwumilamyen ceysitoyn kakyekulo napphwumi kanunghaciman yukamsulep-keyto tangsaeynun caykoka namaissci anhsupnita. icem tangsauy ipcangul yangcihay cwusiki palapnita
'I can understand your request for a price reduction. If it is last year's product, it is possible to supply at the suggested price, but I'm afraid it is out of stock. I hope you understand our situation'

Gift giving for future requests

When offering a gift, the gift-giver may say *yaksohaciman patacwuseyyo* 'This is nothing good but please take it' to be modest. Likewise, in example 14, the gift-giver downplays his gift (i.e. *chwukha senmwul* 'congratulatory gift') with an adjective *cocholhan* 'small'.

Example 14
[A subcontractor sends a gift to his contractor to congratulate him on his promotion]
cicemcangnimuy yengcenul chwukhatulimye, cocholhan chwukha senmwulul taykulo ponaytulyesssupnita
'Congratulations on your promotion to branch manager. I have sent a small congratulatory gift to your home'

However, it may be more than a small gift and, in fact, a bribe. We can easily assume this in that the gift-giver sends his gift to the recipient's home, not his office. Nevertheless, giver and receiver would not consider the gift as bribery, because to give something more than a small gift is an underlying business norm for both of them. Korean businesspeople may have a different view of what is ethical from people in western societies. In example 15, an interview with an employee from the SME clarifies this.

Example 15
We regularly offer expensive gifts, such as beef rib sets, gift vouchers, and even cash, to contractors. The price of each item ranges from 150,000 to 500,000 won (US$140–500). The quality and quantity of each gift is highly dependent on to whom you are giving the gift and what it is for. Normally recipients do not show their modesty in receiving gifts.

In this case, the gift-giver, SME, gives gifts to the recipient, contractors, to put others in debt in order to prepare the way for a future request. So the act of giving gifts can reduce the possibility that a future request will be rejected. Therefore, the gift's face-saving can be used as leverage by the gift-giver to sway the recipient into granting its request. Since gift giving can be a power play in the Korean business context, the recipients who are normally higher in status do not make great efforts to save their face by showing modesty but take gifts without hesitation, as shown in example 15. In this case, power seems to supersede face-saving.

Korean business communication from the intra-cultural communication view

The previous section shows us that cultural values significantly affect verbal and non-verbal business communication in Korea. However, one may ask whether this view of culture is easily reconciled with the data from Korean business communication, because exceptions running counter to cultural values are also found.

First, Koreans are generally warm-hearted, but limit their feelings to those with whom they are close. They tend to be exclusive and discriminatory to outsiders (e.g. an insurance agent in example 16). In example 16, B seriously threatens A's face by treating A as *capsangin* 'miscellaneous merchant' and baldly asking A to get out. It may be natural for B to threaten A's positive face, because of the possibility of A's failure to meet B's negative face wants. Furthermore, we can also assume that the reason why B is so disrespectful and discriminatory against someone located on a low level in the hierarchy is to emphasise the degree of his power and dignity in front of his subordinates in his office.

> **Example 16**
> [A, an insurance agent, visits an office for the promotion of a new life insurance package to B, head of department]
> A: *sillyeyhaciman say pohemsangphwumul sokayhaytulilye hapnita*
> 'Excuse me, but I would like to introduce a new life insurance package'
> B: *capsangin chwulipkumcilanun ke mos pwasseyo? ese nakayo.*
> 'Didn't you read the sign on the door? No soliciting in this office. Get out'

Second, Korean businesspeople are not always hierarchical. Although a superior is very unlikely to make an overt apology, a top executive's overt apology is exceptionally made in certain situations. For instance, Jung (2007) relates how Asiana Airlines' CEO formally made an overt apology to stakeholders during a press conference in the wake of a pilots' strike. Although the CEO's apology may be interpreted as an acknowledgement of responsability for causing trouble, it is generally considered a method of crisis management to show 'responsible leadership' (Baum 2006) and to restore corporate face.

In example 17, an interdepartmental meeting also demonstrates that the hierarchical nature of Korean culture is not necessarily applicable to the Korean workplace. First, the participants in units 4 and 5 use an egalitarian address form, *-nim* 'Mr/Ms', which does not imply hierarchical differences. Not exercising arbitrary personal power using *-nim* is an effort to create a horizontal communication infrastructure, facilitating internal communication. Second, although in general decision making does come from the values of a culture (Beamer and Varner 2001) and traditionally, senior managers have the authority to make decisions on their own, in unit 5 the senior manager tries to rely on the consensus approach to decision-making among interest groups (i.e. discussing with staff before making a final decision). Finally, it is of interest to see that the Korean meeting did not begin with small talk. They rushed straight into business talk.

Example 17
[A senior manager is having a business meeting with the managers from each department of a joint-venture operation to discuss the issue of the new English programme in the company]

1 Senior manager: *chespenccay isswuin sanay yenge phulokulaymey kwanhay yeykihatolok hakeyssupnita. enupwun mence hasikeyssupnikka?*
'We will discuss the first issue related to the new in-house English programme. Who is going first?'

2 Marketing and sales manager: *meymo patko pwusewentulhako kwanlyenan-keneykwanhan mithingul kacyessupnita. pwusewen motwu mwuyeksehancaksen-gkwa cenhwahoyhwaey kwansimul poyessupnita*
'There was a meeting with my staff to figure out the needs to improve their English as I got the memo. My staff wanted to learn about business letter writing and telephone conversations'

3 Manufacturing manager: *cehuykyengwueyn, sayngsanlaineyissnun hankwukinkwa oykwukin notongcakaney yenge tayhwaka yecenhi elyepsupnita*
'In my case, Korean workers on the production line still have problems in communicating with their international counterparts in English'

4 R&D manager: *O-nim uykyeney tonguyhapnita. yecenhi hankwukinkwa oykwukkunlocakaney uysasothong mwunceyka isssupnita*
'I agree with **O-***nim* (manufacturing manager). Communication problems still exist between Korean and international staff in the office'

5 Senior manager: *kulem O-nimi ceyanhasin ankentaysin yenge uysasothong-mwunceypwuthe nonuyhanunkey ettehkeyssupnikka? talunuykyenepsusinciyo? . . . yey. onul hoyuykkuthnako pon ankenul pwusewentulkwa sanguyhas-inhwu kyelkwalul allyecwusikipalapnita. uykyen swulyemhwu kyelcengtholok hakeyssupnita*
'OK. Then why don't we primarily focus on improving our staff's English conversation skills instead of business letter writing and phone conversation, **O-***nim* (marketing and sales manager) suggests. Any other opinions on this? . . . OK then, after discussing this issue with your staff after today's meeting, please let me know what the results are. Once I get the overall results, I will see what we can do'

Notwithstanding hierarchism, Korean businesspeople are not always indirect. Due to the goal-oriented characteristic of a company, the speaker's wants or needs are able to override face concerns about the hearer in order to achieve the corporate goal. In example 18, even though a request is made by the subcontractor, it is done directly using the modal suffix -*eya*, which denotes necessity and obligation. In addition, the future tense *hal* 'will do' strongly supports the requester's intent to avoid disagreement with the requestee. The function of the future tense in a request is to show that making a request is typical or normal in this transactional stage so that the requester deserves compensation from the requestee. In this respect, the subcontractor also tries to save the contractor's positive face by seeking agreement with the contractor, although it may threaten the contractor's negative face.

Example 18
[Because of the sudden cancellation of an order from a contractor, a subcontractor expects some financial losses. Therefore, the subcontractor requests compensation for losses from the contractor]
manil chwisosi kwisaeyse sonsil palsayngey tayhan posangi isseya hal kesulo salyetoypnita
'If you cancel, I think you should compensate us for our losses'

Traditional Korean rhetorical structure is inductive-oriented (Eggington 1987). However, this rhetorical structure does not always apply to Korean business writing. In the following Korean business letter from the Korean pharmaceutical company, bad news is conveyed baldly by placing it towards the very beginning of the text (unit 2) instead of holding it back until later. This is because corporate culture is bad-news sensitive. Since people in the pharmaceutical company deal with people's health and illness at work, they are relatively sensitive to bad news. They give bad news as quickly as possible, because 'bad' may become 'worse'. That is why the bad news giver (normally of lower status) does not make great efforts to avoid threatening the other's face by being more indirect in the report.

Example 19
[A writer does not accept a business partner's request to recall an item because the partner has stored the item wrongly]

Text	Function
1 *annyenghasipnikka*	Greetings
'How are you doing?'	
2 *kwisaeyse ponaycwusin saymphulul silhemhan kyelkwa cwungtayhan pokwansanguy silswuka issesstanun kesi tangsauy kyenhayipnita*	Giving bad news
'The results of an experiment with the sample you have sent show us that there has been a serious problem in storing the item'	
3 *pon phwummokun ikhi asinun pawa kathi sepssi 10 to ihauy senulhan kosey pokwanhayeya hantanun cemun ceyphwumpocangey cenghwakhi myengkitoye isssupnita*	Reason
'As you know, it is specified clearly in the product's packaging that you should store this item at a temperature below 10 degrees Celsius, and away from direct sunshine'	

4 *kulentey, kwisaeyse ponayon saymphulul kemsahan*
    kyelkwa, sepssi 50 to isanguy kooney cangsikan pan-
    gchihayssulttayuy   kyelkwawa   kathun   kyelkwalul
    poiko isssupnita
    'However, the results of an experiment with the
    sample show us that you stored the item at a tem-
    perature above 50 degrees Celsius'

5 *inun kwisauy kelaycheeyse pon phwummokuy pokwan-*
    cokenlul   mwusihan   chay   pokwanhaye   palsaynghan
    mwunceylo   ceyphwumuy   phwumcilisang   mwunceyka
    aniki ttaymwuney
    'Since it happens not because of the quality of the
    product but because of your business partner's
    unreliable stock control'

6 *kwisakelaycheuy   panphwumyochengun   swuyonghal*
    swu epssumul allyetulipnita
    'We are unable to accept your business partner's
    request to recall the item'

7 *iwa   kwanlyenhan   silhemkyelkwalul   chempwuhaoni*
    chamcohasyese   kwisauy   kelaycheey   thongpohay
    cwusikipalapnita
    'I am enclosing the results of an experiment on
    this, I hope you will inform your business partner
    of them'

Giving bad news

Reason

Disagreement

Request

Concluding remarks

This chapter is an initial investigation into cultural values and their application to Korean
business communication. Cultural values still significantly affect the (non-)linguistic
phenomena of the contemporary Korean business world, in that a considerable amount
of emotional display is permitted in Korean companies. However, it is true that Korea
is undergoing a cultural change. Furthermore, Korean companies are developing their
own unique corporate cultures. For example, lately *kulup* have shown the tendency to
change their traditional hierarchical corporate culture into a horizontal one to adapt
easily to global work environments. In the case of joint-venture operations, in particular,
they encourage innovation in corporate culture to facilitate communication with foreign
employees. Many of them choose English as a business lingua franca for internal and
external communications.

In general, the corporate culture is embedded in the national culture. However, 'cultural priorities' which are influenced by the specific organisational context (Beamer and
Varner 2001) also demonstrate that Korean businesspeople are not necessarily collective,
hierarchical and indirect in the workplace. In other words, the western values of individualism, egalitarianism and directness can take priority over eastern ones. It depends
on various factors (e.g. corporate culture, business transactional stage, crisis management
style, etc.), affecting the decision-making process, the choice of address terms and subject
pronouns, sensitivity to power, degree of imposition and rhetorical structure. This may

not be necessarily consistent with the claim by Holtgraves and Yang (1992) and Ambady et al. (1996) that South Koreans weight the power and distance variables heavily in determining variation in linguistic behaviour. It is important to remember that proper cultural values should be determined *within context*. For pedagogical purposes, therefore, besides general aspects of a culture, intercultural business communication instructors need to know what is 'appropriate' in a given business context for effective communication training (Swales 2000).

The following suggestions may be made as guidelines for future research. Since communication patterns depend on the specific organisational context, more cases of various situations can offer more reliable knowledge on Korean culture. For example, since the government exercises considerable influence over business matters in Korea, research on communication patterns in government agencies or heavily government-controlled organisations will be meaningful. Also, in-depth intercultural studies on cultural values are needed to build on the present research undertaken partly from a cross-cultural communication perspective.

References

Akar, D. (1998) Patterns and variations in contemporary written business communication in Turkey: A genre study of four companies. PhD thesis, University of Michigan.

Ambady, N., J. Koo F. Lee and R. Rosenthal (1996) More than words: Linguistic and nonlinguistic politeness in two cultures. *Journal of Personality and Social Psychology*, 10(5): 996–1011.

Baum, H. (2006) *The Transparent Leader: How to Build a Great Company through Straight Talk, Openness, and Accountability*. New York: HarperCollins.

Beamer, L. and I. Varner (2001) *Intercultural Communication in the Global Workplace*, 2nd edn. New York: McGraw-Hill Irwin.

Brown, P. and S. Levinson (1987) *Politeness: Some Universals in Language Use*. Cambridge: Cambridge University Press.

Chen, M. (2004) *Asian Management Systems*, 2nd edn. London: Thomson.

Deal, T. E. and A. A. Kennedy (2000) *Corporate Culture: The Rites and Rituals of Corporate Life*. New York: Basic Books.

De Mente, B. L. (2004) *Korean Business Etiquette*. Boston, MA: TuttlePublishing.

Eggington, W. (1987) Written academic discourse in Korean: Implications for effective communication. In U. Connor and R. Kaplan (eds), *Writing across Languages: Analysis of L2 Text*. Reading, MA: Addison Wesley, pp. 153–68.

Gesteland, R. (1999) *Cross-Cultural Business Behavior: Marketing, Negotiating, and Managing Across Culture*. Copenhagen: Copenhagen Business School Press.

Hofstede, G. (1994) *Cultures and Organizations*. London: HarperCollinsBusiness.

Holtgraves, T. and J. Yang (1992) Interpersonal underpinnings of request strategies: General principles and differences due to culture and gender. *Journal of Personality and Social Psychology*, 62: 246–56.

Jung, Y. (2002) The use of (im)politeness strategies in Korean business correspondence. PhD thesis, University of Edinburgh.

Jung, Y. (2005a) The rhetorical structure in Korean business writing. In M. Gotti and P. Gillaerts (eds), *Genre Variation in Business Letters*. Bern: Peter Lang, pp. 347–68.

Jung, Y. (2005b) Power and politeness in Korean business correspondence. In F. Bargiela-Chiappini and M. Gotti (eds), *Asian Business Discourse(s)*. Bern: Peter Lang, pp. 291–312.

Jung, Y. (2007) Asiana Airlines' image restoration strategies. Paper delivered at the 7th Asia-Pacific Conference of Association of Business Communication, City University of Hong Kong.

Kenman, L. (2006) A look at Korean business communication. Paper delivered at the 71st Annual Convention of the Association of Business Communication, San Antonio, Texas.

Mulholland, J. (1997) The Asian connection: Business requests and acknowledgements. In F. Bargiela-Chiappini and S. Harris (eds), *The Languages of Business: An International Perspective*. Edinburgh: Edinburgh University Press, pp. 94–114.

Park, M., W. T. Dillon and K. L. Mitchell (1998) Korean business letters: Strategies for effective complaints in cross-cultural communication. *Journal of Business Communication*, 35(3): 328–45.

Swales, J. (2000) Language for specific purposes. *Annual Review of Applied Linguistics*, 20: 56–76.

Thomas, D. C. and K. Inkson, (2003) *Cultural Intelligence*. San Francisco: Berett-Koehler.

Thomas, J. (1998) Contexting Koreans: Does the high/low model work? *Business Communication Quarterly*, 61(4): 1080–99.

28

Vietnam

Chye Lay Grace Chew

Introduction

Little research has been conducted to date on modern business communication and business discourse in Vietnam. A domain of the field, intercultural business communication (IBC), has thus yet to attract as much attention as the increase in economic transactions between Vietnam and the world warrants. As an initial step towards locating Vietnam on the business discourse map, this chapter, therefore, emphasises the understanding of the Vietnamese culture as a way of enhancing cultural literacy in this era of globalisation. By doing so, it hopes not only to broaden and deepen understanding of the topic but also to stimulate the development of research in business discourse.

This chapter begins by examining the cultural characteristics of the Vietnamese and the implications of these characteristics in IBC through two surveys. The first is a survey conducted online in the year 2007 on the perceptions of Vietnamese by foreigners and vice versa; the second presents a literature review of English-language academic journal and book publications outside Vietnam from the 1980s up to this publication. The content of this chapter is based on the recognition that culture is a dynamic force influencing many dimensions of the business milieu which is itself established on the bedrock of sociocultural values. It argues that a prerequisite to understanding or researching the business discourse of a community is the mastery of cultural and linguistic competence, contingent on a multidisciplinary approach that involves shifting from a central study of discourse to subjects in both business and the social sciences. Furthermore the chapter proposes that understanding the factors and characteristics that differentiate the worldview of the Vietnamese from that of non-Vietnamese is also essential for the understanding IBC in Vietnam.

The chapter begins by highlighting the importance of building trust and relationship – the underlying factor for all successful business partnership in a country where a legal infrastructure is still in the stage of development. Acquiring cultural and linguistic competences is regarded not only as a means to achieving better business relations, but also as beneficial for the divergent needs of business globalisation. This emphasis on the essentiality of building trust, establishing relations and being culturally and linguistically competent is followed by a discussion on the perceptions by Vietnamese and non-Vietnamese of one another, and then by a literature review classified under the main headings of salient Vietnamese cultural values and categories.

This study uses content analysis to examine existing literature and materials related or relevant to IBC. Resources include dissertations from economics, human resource management, leadership, markets and organisational management. Surveys, email interviews and participation observation of 149 respondents in the business sector conducted inside and outside Vietnam from March 2004 to December 2007 supplied useful and current data, accompanied by secondary information from anthropology materials. While certain perceptions by the non-Vietnamese of the Vietnamese, such as their family orientation, lack of trust of foreigners and national pride (e.g. Engholm 1995: 214–16; quadrant B in the survey below) support the published cultural values and thoughts in the literature, the survey also reflects many less widely published views on the Vietnamese, such as their talkativeness and opportunistic tendencies. Additionally, the Vietnamese perception of themselves as not being collective adds new perspectives to the view, often taken for granted, that the Vietnamese, being Asians, are group-oriented, and signals for more research to be undertaken. To conclude the chapter, brief suggestions for further investigations into areas yet unexplored in IBC, Vietnam, are made.

The need for cultural and linguistic competence in relationship-building

The forces of market socialism, replacing doctrinaire socialism, have encouraged the Vietnamese to be competitive and seek profit aggressively so as 'to catch up with the rest of world' (Schultz II et al. 2006: 670) under the national slogan of 'a strong country with rich citizens' (*dân giàu, nu'ó'c mạnh*). Vietnam's renovation reform, Doi Moi, ratified in December 1986, opened up the country to the west, paving the way for its gradual integration into the global economy. Top investors in Vietnam today are South Korea (24.4 per cent of the total Foreign Direct Investment (FDI) inflow), Singapore (18.7 per cent), the British Virgin Islands (12.1 per cent) and Taiwan (8.4 per cent; *Wall Street Journal* 2007). The upward trend in foreign arrivals (Xinhua News Agency 2007) accentuates the need to expedite mutual understanding of differences between Vietnam and the world. One such difference is 'culture', which if not well understood, affects effective communication and business.

Vietnam is regarded as a high-context culture in which internalised rules of behaviour and communication dominate. However, whether Vietnam falls into the same category as China, Japan and India, as a society with highly internalised behavioural rules and subdued expression of emotions and feelings, requires investigation (Gannon 2001: 29). Functioning within Vietnam, nevertheless, requires the cultivation of a ready understanding of the subtle workings of culture, because society holds a different meaning and attitude towards things explicitly uttered or written, among which is the business contract, an agreement commonly understood to be enforceable between parties in western law. Social and work dynamics rest on trust and relationships. Relationship-building is a time-consuming investment involving linguistic and cultural competences that require much informal face-to-face communication. E-mailing and telephone calls are not the accepted way to build relationships in Vietnam. A different sense of time application is thus invoked when 'doing the right thing' and 'how you do things' are more highly prioritised than 'doing things right' (Ashwill with Diep

2005: 92–3). Once relations are forged, the emphasis on maintaining business relationships and reputation shapes the way firms endorse contracts and act when contracts are reneged. In a society without established legal institutions, firms are willing to renegotiate the contract following a breach and not to retaliate for fear of damaging relations with other firms in the industry (Mcmillan and Woodruff 1999). In short, a right, time-nurtured relationship is often the way to business success, or, as succinctly expressed in this observation, 'the shortest distance between two points is not a straight line' (Borton 2004: 205).

While possessing cultural and linguistic competence is important, economic realities often determine which set of cultural and linguistic competence should be acquired – a question evoked in the research of Wang and Hsiao (2002). Reliance on FDIs for development means that the power structure is tilted in favour of the foreign investors. Thus, an employee with competence in the culture and language of the major foreign investors of the company will tend to reap greater rewards. However, some, like Napier (2006), will argue that mutual learning should not be overlooked, regardless of which culture holds the economic power.

Current publications which support IBC in Vietnam contain interesting observations but have not systematically surveyed foreigners' perceptions of the Vietnamese and Vietnamese perceptions of themselves and 'others'. As expatriate and Vietnamese managers and businessmen manage cultural differences and synergise the diverse thinking and actions of multicultural teams and networks in an increasingly globalising environment, the awareness of these perceptions illuminates 'blind spots' and cultural strengths and weaknesses, while highlighting potential conflicts and harmony.

Vietnamese perceptions: 'self' versus 'other'

'Who are the foreigners?' is a question whose answers will offer clues to understanding the Vietnamese worldview. The Vietnamese generally classify 'foreigners' into 'Asians' (*người Châu Á*) or 'easterners'(*người Phương Đông*) and 'westerners'(*người Phương Tây*). All foreigners may be colloquially called *Tây*, literally 'westerners', because the early image of a 'foreigner' (*người nước ngoài*) was *người da trắng* ('white-skinned person').

Hesitation and contention exist regarding whether dark-skinned foreigners or blacks are *Tây* ('westerners', 'foreigners') or not, although the term *Tây đen*, literally 'black westerners/foreigners', is widely understood. When twenty-three Vietnamese were asked via email how blacks should be classified, the answers ranged from putting them outside the *Tây*-group to it depending on whether their places of origin are developed or not. Blacks are sometimes regarded as *người nước ngoài* ('foreigners'), other times not. Educational level and behaviour have also been cited as criteria for their qualification as *Tây*. Briefly, the taxonomy of the 'other' is often differentiated by 'colour' (race) and/or connoted by historical and racial attitudes.

The Chinese in Vietnam were referred to as *khách trú* ('guests'), as many were initially long-time sojourners. They are still colloquially or sometimes pejoratively called *người tàu* ('people on boats') as a result of their arrivals and exits from the country in the late 1970s to the early 1980s on *tàu* (boats). *Ba tàu* (literally 'third Chinese') is a term said to have resulted from the keenness of the Chinese to show their humility by indicating that they were occupying a lower social position than the Vietnamese, *hai Việt*, meaning 'second

Vietnamese'. The current most predominant term to refer to the ethnic Chinese is *Hoa*, meaning 'ethnic Chinese'.

A preliminary investigation on how Vietnamese perceive the non-Vietnamese has been conducted using Bergmann's (1994) exercise, based on the Johari Window (Schneider and Barsoux 2003: 17). Forty-five Vietnamese professionals – engineers, junior and senior managers, and entrepreneurs – participated in a survey conducted online in November 2007. They were asked: '(1) what do you think of your own people?', and 'what do you think about foreigners?' Simultaneously twenty-five foreign professionals also responded to a short survey with the questions: '(1) what do you think of the Vietnamese'; and '(2) how do you think the Vietnamese see Asians/Westerners?' The non-Vietnamese comprised one Belgian doctor; thirteen managers, seven of them Singaporeans and six Japanese, out of which ten were senior managers; a Singaporean technical superintendent; a Malaysian production manager; an English artist; an American entrepreneur and two consultants; a Canadian psychologist; an Australian corporate trainer/lecturer; a Swiss aid-organisation founder and an aid officer; and a Thai diplomat. The Asian respondents were asked how the Vietnamese see Asians, and westerners were asked how they think the Vietnamese view westerners; however, four respondents with considerable experience of living and working with the Vietnamese shared their views on the Vietnamese perceptions of both Asians and westerners.

The surveys were structured; part of a question and answer from Bergmann's survey were shown to respondents to guide them in the presentation of their answers. Respondents were free to express their opinions in their own words. Because of space constraints, only descriptions of the highest frequency are reflected in Table 28.1. Close synonyms or expressions with similar meanings are grouped together and counted. Opposing perspectives of a particular group are placed side by side and separated by the word 'vs.'. For example, in quadrant A, the 45 Vietnamese respondents described themselves as 'hard-working' 47 times, using words like 'industrious', 'tenacious' and repetitions with other synonyms. Immediately beside the entry is 'lazy (1)', indicating the expression 'lazy' as being used once. The Vietnamese perceptions of non-Vietnamese are classified into views on Asians and on westerners (quadrant C), the way Vietnamese will group foreigners. The figures in parentheses indicate the number of respondents.

Quadrants A and C show the heterogeneous views among Vietnamese, some of which are contradictions. The Vietnamese see themselves more positively than negatively, and are more contradictory and negative in their perceptions of Asians than of westerners. Two Vietnamese respondents wrote that Vietnamese generally 'do not highly regard Asians as much as westerners'. Among Asians, the Vietnamese tend to look down on Cambodians, Laotians and Burmese, whose overall development makes the Vietnamese feel secure, with the exception of the Singaporeans (Frobenius; Lee and Fuchida in 2007). In Asia, South Koreans are viewed by the Vietnamese with disdain for being 'brutish, uncouth', the Chinese 'with great suspicion' and Japanese 'with respect and even awe' (Frobenius in email surveys, 2007). The Vietnamese are keen to learn from the Japanese and the Koreans, while believing that the Vietnamese will outdo both of them one day (Joe in email surveys, 2008). The Vietnamese also tend to look down on darker-skinned Asians, e.g. Indonesians, Indians and Pakistanis (Lee in email surveys, 2007). In specific cases, the Asian individual or group with whom a Vietnamese respondent works directly influences the respondent's views on Asians; e.g. a Vietnamese who has worked with Singaporeans

Table 28.1. Vietnamese perceptions of themselves and of 'others'

The Vietnamese	
A Consider themselves to be: (45 respondents)	*B Are perceived by foreigners as being:* (25 respondents)
• Industrious, diligent, tenacious (47) vs. lazy (1)	• Hardworking (14); women are hardworking (1)
• Not punctual (13)	• Family-oriented (7) and thus unmeritocratic (1)
• Friendly (14)	• Quick learners (3)
• Intelligent (11)	• Condescending towards dark-skinned Asians (3)
• Altruistic, kindhearted (7) vs. doing things for own benefit (3)	• Greedy; opportunistic (3)
• Steadfast, dauntless, firm (6)	• Not creative (3) especially in solving abstract problems; creative in practical life solutions (1)
• Keen to learn (6)	• People who take advantage of foreigners (2); seeing westerners as 'idealistic fools' (1)
• Trustworthy (7) vs. untrustworthy (2)	• Persistent, quietly determined (2)
• Brave; heroic (5)	• Doing things their own way; changing terms of agreement without notification/discussion (2)
• Not collective or united (5) vs. collective (3)	• Friendly (5)
• Adaptable (4)	• Nationalistic; proud of Vietnam's achievements; thinking that Vietnam will not lose out to Japan or Korea (3)
• Hospitable (4)	• Outspoken (2)
• Nosy (4)	• Talkative (2)
• Honest (4)	• Not punctual (2)
• Peace-loving (4)	• Courteous (2)

The Vietnamese perceive foreigners to be:	
C On Asians (40 respondents; 5 abstained)	*D On westerners* (45 respondents)
• Discreet (20)	• Punctual (19)
• Industrious, diligent (13)	• Straightforward (including in business) (13)
• Inquisitive (nosy) (7) vs. not nosy (2)	• Good planners (12)
• Planning ahead (5) vs. not planning (1)	• Respectful of individualism (10)
• Emphasising collectivity (5)	• Professional, efficient (9)
• Respectful of ethnic traditions (4)	• Open-minded (8)
• Family-oriented (4)	• Accurate, concrete (7)
• Respectful of social hierarchy (3)	• Wealthy, big spenders (4) vs. not as rich as many think (1)
• Critical of others (3)	• Respectful of creativity, creative (4)
• Punctual (3) vs. not punctual (3)	• Living freely (3)
• Intelligent (3)	• Romantic, passionate (3)
• Poor and miserable (2)	• Disciplined (3) vs. lazy (2)
• Mostly living in developing nations, like Vietnamese (2)	• Sexually liberal (2)
• Not open-minded (2); conservative (2)	• Entertaining loose family ties (2)
• Not straightforward; undecided between 'yes' and 'no' answers (2)	• Independent (2)

and Europeans describe both groups as having 'good quality work', 'professionalism' and 'planning', which is unlike the way perceptions of the Asians and westerners are normally entrenched in the minds of the Vietnamese.

What the Vietnamese see as strengths in westerners often reflect what the Vietnamese perceive as their own weaknesses; e.g. two respondents indicated that the social discipline of westerners is what Vietnamese lack, and 'western' professionalism receives high regard. That Vietnamese see Asians as being the same as them (quadrant C) is another point observed by a non-Vietnamese respondent. A Japanese manager also sees the Vietnamese as having the same mindscape as the Japanese. A paradox surfaces from the Vietnamese perceptions of themselves as not being 'group-oriented' and 'working better independently than in a group' (quadrant A: 'Not collective or united'). To the Vietnamese, living and working together does not necessarily mean having a common focus. It is said that the wartime focus for many was to follow a 'leader' rather than acting as a 'team', whereby team members understood, and worked jointly with initiative to achieve, the common goal (Vu and Napier 2000: II, 9). Foreigners who have lived or worked in Vietnam were more ready to point out the negative attributes of the Vietnamese than were foreigners who have working relations with the Vietnamese but who have not lived in Vietnam. For example, the description of Vietnamese being outspoken belies one of the common observations of Vietnamese being ambiguous and indirect (e.g. Brower 1980). These divergent views provide us with a balanced picture of foreigners' perceptions of the Vietnamese while stimulating further questions such as in what contexts can and/or may a Vietnamese be forthright.

Salient Vietnamese values in publications

In recent years, courses on report writing, business etiquette, business presentations and information technology have made their way into undergraduate and graduate business English courses at major universities in Hanoi and Ho Chi Minh City. However, social psychology, discourse studies and intercultural communication are not yet an integral part of business education in Vietnam. English-language IBC essays, business guides and research only gradually increased after 1991 (e.g. Cam 1994; Nguyen 1994), a few years after Vietnam actually opened its doors, but business discourse publications remain sparse. Outside Vietnam, research in Vietnamese values that would be relevant for modern business appeared in the 1990s.

Thanks to the approaches, theories and methodologies shared among the fields that inform IBC (Bargiela-Chiappini and Nickerson 2003), works in the humanities and social sciences are sources for groundwork (e.g. Jamieson 1995; McLeod and Nguyen 2001). A multidisciplinary approach offers more profound cultural insights than the single-subject approach. History and geography, for instance, inform us that despite the common historical heritage of a core culture and mutually intelligible dialects of a language, North and South Vietnam have different historical experiences, climates, developmental patterns, psychological dispositions and dietary habits (e.g. Janse 1944: 11–14; Engholm 1995: 5–6; Lewis 2006: 480–1). Having this knowledge enables one to make or understand the hypothesis that northerners, southerners and even central Vietnamese (the way Vietnamese often distinguish themselves) have dissimilar value orientations when intra-country comparisons are made (Ralston et al. 1999). However, empirical data and research from other fields such as those that inform on the mobility and regional economic development of Vietnam are required to verify the hypothesis.

Communication cues: eye contact, face, smile and ambiguity

From 1975 to 1985, when the world suddenly had to manage the massive outflow of Vietnamese 'boat people', information useful for IBC can be found in social psychology and educational literature featuring the Vietnamese in North America (e.g. Alexander et al. 1976; Duong 1975; Kelly 1978; MSM 1979; Nguyen 1979; Penner and Tran 1977; Vuong 1976). The subjects of these studies were immigrant refugee students and counselling patients.

Brower (1980) provides cultural information, such as Vietnamese attitudes towards sex roles and the individual/family relationship, to assist the counsellor in establishing rapport with the patient and minimising miscommunications and transference dangers. Brower advises against using the young person as interpreter in a school setting where the Vietnamese expect adult authority. In cases when an interpreter is unnecessary, explicit communication may pose a challenge as what is heard is not what is expected. She uses the 'yes-means-no' example as an illustration of the ambiguous communication style of the Vietnamese, further cautioning that culture has specific interpretations for speech variations and nonverbal cues. She explains, for example, how a loud voice and a hearty greeting may not be appreciated; a quiet and dignified voice and manner instead are expected (1980: 648), the contrary causing the Vietnamese to lapse into a silence of embarrassment. A Vietnamese smile, she further explains, can reflect stoic behaviour in adversity, anger, embarrassment, rejection and other emotions. Eye contact is another area where the American and Vietnamese cultures differ, as looking directly at a person with whom they are speaking is a sign of disrespect and rudeness in Vietnamese culture (p. 648). Vietnamese upbringing regards the concealment of stress as stoic pride (p. 649), and the family's honour, pride and traditions as more important than the feelings of the individual (p. 650).

Brower points out, however, that Vietnamese society is heterogeneous, and the previous socioeconomic status of the refugees, which is related to their educational level, cross-cultural experience, degree of urbanisation and ethnic background, are factors that contribute to the 'differences' among Vietnamese (1980: 650). The counsellor is advised to learn as much as possible about a culturally different client so as to 'empathize with differences, to learn the latent messages in intercultural communications' (Alexander et al. 1976: 91, cited in Brower 1980: 650).

Despite the target audience being education professionals, businesspeople can benefit from Brower (1980). On the other hand, Engholm (1995: 214), observing from the commercial sector, differs in view from Brower: 'They're [the Vietnamese are] openly aggressive where other Asians might be more passively aggressive; they can be forthright and rancorous while most Asians are implicit in expression and afraid of giving offense.' The Vietnamese differs from the Japanese and the Chinese in valuing harmony, protecting 'face' and personal honour; 'unlike the Japanese who will bow to you and think to themselves what a jerk you are, the Vietnamese will tell you directly', writes Engholm (p. 214). He further admonishes the reader that mutual respect is essential and a foreigner should 'command respect'. The Vietnamese will not accept condescending behaviour from foreigners, as they are proud of having driven out foreign invaders (pp. 215–16). Politeness is thus paramount, and little white lies are usually preferable to being offensive (p. 216).

On ambiguity in Vietnamese speech, when 'face' and conflict-avoidance concerns are dismissed in close relationships, what results is direct communication (Vu and Napier 2000: 8). But the Vietnamese 'saving face' concept is more complex than merely 'embarrassing an individual – personally in front of others', write Vu and Napier (2000: 8). Two sides exist: (1) an 'involvement' side, which shows care and concern for another person and his or her development, and thus negative feedback for poor performance may be given within the group; and (2) an 'independent' side, which does not get too close but 'respects the distance of others', such as when someone loses 'face' to an 'outsider' (ibid.). Negative feedback such as harsh criticism when given to an in-group member shows care and concern.

Indirect speech is not unique to Vietnam. Indirectness may be more effective and polite in enhancing acceptance for a proposal rather delivering acceptance with alacrity. Borton (2004: 207–8) suggests that for extracting the 'real' content, it is necessary to listen for the negatives in positive responses or, alternatively, to ask the conversation partner for the first step towards formulating a solution for a certain problem. Another suggestion is to listen and observe how the responses are uttered or not uttered, or seek confirmation using *chắc chắn* 'certainly' help to ascertain certainty (Chew 2005). Non-Vietnamese, unaware of such communicative styles, have cast aspersions on the Vietnamese, as Clyne (1994) informs us.

Sociocultural values: harmony, kinship, politeness, respect, trust and relationships

Cultural values and categories featured prominently in IBC-related works after the 1990s. Information is found in diverse fields ranging from anthropology to management. In IBC, Clyne's (1994) research, which focuses on the communicative breakdowns when English is used in intra-organisational interaction by multiethnic groups of workers in industrial and manufacturing industrial settings in Australia, stands out. It appears from this study that Central and Southern European immigrants are doubtful of the integrity and trustworthiness of Vietnamese workers, classified as 'Southeast Asians', and describe them as people who 'do not understand, regardless of "how hard you try" '. The Vietnamese are further seen by the European immigrants as a people who 'say yes, and then they don't do it' (p. 151). Clyne interprets the problem as lying in the hidden and unexamined expectations about discourse and the culture-based implications of communicative behaviour that influence discourse interpretations.

While Clyne has made keen observations about Vietnamese communicative style (1999: 191), he has not examined the lexical semantics of Vietnamese promises. Chew (2005), contrastingly, combines lexical semantics with cultural and social realities to analyse the strategic social functions of *được* 'OK', 'possible', 'can', an auxiliary denoting agreement, and discovers that the possible explanations for what is interpreted by non-Vietnamese as the empty promises of the Vietnamese lies in the undetermined range of probabilities in the meaning of *được*, which are imperceptible by non-native intuitions. *Được* is explorative, as it sets the starting point for communication that could be furthered to reach a more conclusive result, explicitly lexicalised by *chắc chắn được* 'certainly OK', 'possible', 'can'.

Chew (2005) affirms the significance of affect in Asian business contexts, demonstrated by the tolerance for ambiguity, politeness and face concerns related to the preservation of harmony. She shows the 'other side of the story' by illustrating how impoliteness is reflected in service transactions when threats to profits are perceived. The root causes of impoliteness stem from the most 'inauspicious' amount of goods during shop-opening time, and the need for the Vietnamese vendor to distinguish herself from the foreigner by not yielding to the latter's unattractive offer in price negotiation. Readers are informed of Vietnamese business beliefs, such as not to show up for appointments and interviews on dates associated with ill fortune such as the 5th, 11th and 23rd of every lunar calendar (pp. 237, 251). This reflects the uncontrollable gods of fortune in Vietnamese belief; but the arrangement made by the gods can be controlled, coaxed, modified or precluded by innumerable methods of augury, one of which is *đốt viá*. The Vietnamese believe that an individual has three ethereal spirits, *hồn*, and five corporeal spirits, *phách* or *viá*. The corporeal spirits can be 'heavy' or 'vicious' and embark on journeys to impede a business or an affair. For example, the spirit of the first customer who does not make a purchase is believed to become errant in the shop. A short exorcising ritual, *đốt viá*, performed by burning a piece of paper or cloth, is accompanied by an incantation in the shop or around the products that the customer has touched to salvage business.

Apparently the Vietnamese worldview constructs a concept of fate and destiny different from that of the west. The former also regards the family as the crux of social interactions, linking the past to the present through the observance of patrilineal obligations and traditional celebrations that foster cosmic unity among the tutelary gods and spirits, the living and the dead (Chew 1998: 1). This has provided a sense of continuity in human relationships that could begin in the village(s) of their ancestors, thus giving parents potent influence over their offspring and enforcing familial obligations – although these are changing.

In a village, emotional relationships that enhance the value of equality and solidarity emphasise the importance of greetings, helping one another and compromising, if requested (Malarney 2002: 129–30). Good relationships today continue to be articulated on the basis of mutual help and compromises, with intimate ones involving 'mutual understanding' (*sự hiểu nhau*), 'emphathy' (*sự thông cảm*) and 'emotions/sentiments' (*tình cảm*). The fundamentals of personal relationships and business relationships are not clearly distinguished in Vietnam, as doing business with people who belong to the same established social network is preferred. The economic life of the Vietnamese is confined to the family, with trust shared among only a few acquaintances (Turner and Nguyen 2005). At the workplace, the preference for informal consultation with discussion of details and consensus-building over the 'manager-makes-the-move' approach (Borton 2004) produces a faint resemblance of the *tình làng* 'spirit of the village' that is prized in the village commune. However, this preferred management decision-making and communication style contradicts the high power distance that is indicated by cultural indices (e.g. Hofstede and Hofstede 2005). In other words, a suitable management style depends on the context as well as the size and type of the business.

Apart from understanding cultural practices, linguistic competence helps unlock the thoughts and values which may not be revealed in everyday life; however, the ability of interlocutors to use each other's language often leads to more misunderstandings than a situation where a common language is absent. Linguistic and cultural competence thus serves to minimise the misunderstandings.

The importance of 'good speech' (including greetings) for establishing congenial relationships in Vietnam is echoed in the adages *lời nói chẳng mất tiền mua* 'polite words cost nothing' and *lời chào cao hơn mâm cỗ* 'a word of greeting is greater than a tray at feast', while respect can be linguistically conveyed by the usage of such phrases as *xin phép* 'please allow me to . . .', final polite particle *ạ*, the appropriate address terms, such affective interjections as *vâng* and *dạ*, utterance tone and other strategies.

Vietnamese pronominal references, which are mostly kinship terms, distinguish associations with the echelons on the paternal and maternal branches, and in the manner their usage is attuned to the age, sex, degree of intimacy and relative social status of the interlocutors to convey communicative meanings and functions. The right pronominal usage establishes the level of respect accorded to age and the social status, thus defining the position and structure in a relationship (e.g. Coulmas 2005: 85). Social hierarchy and organisation, moral obligations and polite language usage are bound concepts. Older people or people in higher authority or positions, for instance, may not feel the need to say 'thank you' (or 'sorry') to those they consider as their junior or subordinate. To do so is tantamount to self-demotion (*hạ mình*) because a junior or subordinate has an obligation or duty to serve them (Do, p.c., cited in Bargiela-Chiappini et al. 2007: 138). The verb *biếu* 'to give' used in presentations of gifts to someone higher in the social hierarchy is said to connote the expected giving of a gift, as the verb 'binds the giver and receiver in a moral relationship', contrary to the verb *cho* 'to give' which is normally used (Malarney 2002: 131).

The notions of 'tact' also reflect gulfs between cultures that restrain emotive displays and those that show them, according to Bolinger (1982: 530, cited in Janney and Arndt 1992: 27). 'Tact', like politeness, arises from history and is shaped by it (Watts et al. 1992: 13). In Vietnam, foreigners may be irked by what they consider tactless queries from the Vietnamese in new encounters about their age, marital status and family (e.g. 'How old are you?', 'Are you married?', 'Do you have children?', 'What does your husband do?') without realising that the availability of such information puts the Vietnamese at a comfortable level of interaction with the foreigner (Chew 2005: 237; Borton 2004: 204). Such queries inform a phatic communion style that has its origin in small, close-knit, family-oriented agrarian communities where denizens notice and judge the well-being of others by superficial yardsticks such as physical size, appearance and family.

The benefits of cultural and linguistic competencies: discordant voices

Cultural values continued to be pursued as research topics in the 1990s (e.g. Houston 2002; Lewis 2006), but the economic trajectory after the year 2000 saw an increase in research on managerial practices and entrepreneurs (e.g. Büchel and Lai 2001; Chang 2005; Truong 2006; Turner and Nguyen 2005). Among them, the work of Wang and Hsiao (2002) highlights the significance of acquiring twinned cultural and linguistic competence in multinational enterprises, while Napier (2006) argues against the unilateral flow of learning from foreign investors to Vietnamese workers.

Wang and Hsiao (2002) address the issue of linguistic and cultural competence in cross-cultural management-labour communication by examining social capital and human resource practice in Taiwan overseas enterprises, tangentially reflecting the diversities within 'Confucian Asia' and the impact of globalisation on human resource practices in multinational enterprises. Reality shows that competency in the culture and language of the party that stands in the stronger power position, i.e. the employers, fetches greater premiums than otherwise, although training in the local language and culture is required. The discussion develops into the rationale for hiring Chinese professionals (Chinese nationals) rather than the Vietnamese, Taiwanese and ethnic Vietnamese Chinese in Taiwanese firms overseas. In North Vietnam, where the ethnic Chinese population is smaller than that of the South, Vietnamese graduates of Chinese studies at the universities are deemed to be better candidates than ethnic Chinese Vietnamese, because of their ability to speak more 'standard Chinese' as a result of receiving more formal education in Chinese. Besides, ethnic Vietnamese managers do not have ethnic tensions with local workers. Ethnic Chinese, while being the best candidates for interpretation posts, have lower political status in Vietnam and are thus discounted as social capital. Having the 'Taiwan experience' is a more prized attribute than being merely an 'ethnic resource' – in this resembling Japanese multinationals, which value 'Japan experience' in their non-Japanese recruitment candidates (2002: 357, 359). Chinese professionals, with working experience in Taiwanese SMEs located in Mainland China, speak a common language and have similar management styles to the Taiwanese form of social capital (pp. 359–60), and are not only cheaper to employ than Taiwanese professionals but are further commended for being good enforcers of the rules set by the Taiwanese management.

An egalitarian view comes from Napier (2006), who argues against the normal expectation that knowledge transfer of learning and technology should flow from foreigners to the Vietnamese. The usefulness of cultural knowledge in guiding business actions resonates through her article. She points out that foreign managers, while working with the Vietnamese, can tap site-specific knowledge such as knowing who the key players are in the ministry and how decisions are made within ministries, and broad non-site-specific knowledge, such as dealing with tensions and turmoil, learning to learn quickly and becoming a cultural adaptor. The author warns of value clashes, such as in the case of Coca-Cola's curtailed advertising campaign in 1996. Coca-Cola's building of its image coincided with the Vietnamese government launch of a campaign against social vices at that time. The company's successful advertising aroused fears that children would be distracted from their studies for activities such as socialising which challenged traditional expectations. In addition, the traditional Vietnamese lack of trust of foreigners still exists, unless the Vietnamese feel that there is a valuable bilateral exchange of information or help.

Conclusion

Vast opportunities remain in IBC, Vietnam, for investigation. The contexts for polite and impolite speech, communication issues in joint ventures and service deliveries, negotiation styles and behaviours between Vietnamese and non-Vietnamese, the use of English in multinationals, inter- and intra-regional business communications, gender management communication, and the synergy of traditional and modern values are just some examples. Vietnam is rapidly transforming and there is a need to conduct fresh research.

Overall the perceptions of the Vietnamese by non-Vietnamese and vice versa offer us a sense of the Vietnamese national identity – how the Vietnamese distinguish themselves from non-Vietnamese – and the hidden expectations and possible prejudices that both groups may hold of and about one another. The common heuristic exercise conducted for this chapter attempts to stimulate further questions in the psychological dimension. Clyne's (1994) publication on communicative behaviour at work in multicultural Australia warrants similar investigation in Vietnam. It should be noted, however, that the Vietnamese do not represent 'Southeast Asians', a term under which linguistic, cultural, political and religious diversities are subsumed.

Chew (2005) highlights the fact that lexical semantics can contribute to intercultural understanding. She further shows how identifying the factors that predispose an individual to certain linguistic and communicative behaviours enhances empathy and mitigate culture shock, and that contentions can arise in the politeness evaluation within the same cultural group. These works highlight the usefulness of interpreting thoughts and ideas expressed in language by scrutinising the underlying cultural conduit, thus underscoring the essentiality of this twin competence. Another rationale for acquiring these competences is based on the tendency of the Vietnamese to use adages, allusions, metaphors and idioms to explain life's phenomena, to direct thought and action or to enliven a conversation (Borton 2004; Le et al. 2007: 117) – a legacy of prominence in literature and philosophy endemic in the Chinese model (cf. Le et al. 2007: 117).

A word of caution should be added about citing Chinese or Confucian influence as an explanation for current phenomena. The Vietnamese reliance on personal relationships and the subsequent impediment to the development of the institutions of a market economy have been attributed to Confucianism (Nguyen et al. 2005), but so has the rapid modernisation of the five capitalist 'tigers' of Asia (Hofstede and Bond 2001: 5–21). It helps to explain the relationship between the philosophical dialectics and the named phenomenon in greater detail.

We can expect the gradual integration of Vietnam into the global economy to modify traditions and to create internal and external pressures for reform and the strengthening of legal agencies, simultaneously kindling changes in contracting, relationship- and trust-building and communication in its entirety. Despite the paucity of works on IBC in Vietnam, other disciplines have availed for valuable information. More publications have broached the topic of values and cultural characteristics than that of the emotional or psychological component of communication; hypotheses remain to be proven and the paradoxical angles of the 'rules of thumb' in practice warrant persistent investigations. The current small pool of publications gives rise to a wellspring of interesting questions, and researchers require linguistic and cultural competence to find the answers. Fundamentally this research approach focuses on gaining competence in the indigenous language and culture, and challenges the perception of English as the universal commercial language. It thus disregards the Anglo-centric norms in conducting business as supreme.

Acknowledgement

I thank the editor, the anonymous reviewers and Michelle Noullet for useful comments; members of VSG, University of Washington, for good information; and Poh Swee Lian and her team at the Hon Sui Sen Memorial Library for kind assistance with resources.

References

Alexander, A. A., F. Workneh, M. H. Klein and M. H. Miller (1976) Psychotherapy and the foreign student. In P. Pederson, W. J. Lonner and J. G. Draguns (eds), *Counselling across Cultures*. Honolulu: University Press of Hawaii, pp. 82–97.

Ashwill, M. A. and T. N. Diep (2005) *Vietnam Today: A Guide to a Nation at a Crossroads*. Yarmouth, ME, London: Intercultural Press.

Bargiela-Chiappini, F. and C. Nickerson (2003) Intercultural business communication: A rich field of studies. *Journal of Intercultural Studies*, 24(1): 3–15.

Bargiela-Chiappini, F., O.-O. Chakorn, C. L. G. Chew, Y. Jung, K. C. C. Kong, S. Nair-Venugopal and H. Tanaka (2007) Eastern voices: Enriching research on communication in business: A forum. *Discourse & Communication*, 1(2): 131–52.

Bergmann, A. (1994) *The 'Swiss Way of Management'*. Paris: Eska.

Bolinger, D. (1982) Intonation and its parts. *Language*, 58: 505–33.

Borton, L. (2004) Working in a Vietnamese voice. In M. P. Sheila (ed.), *International Management: Insights from Fiction and Practice*. Armonk, NY: M.E. Sharpe, pp. 203–13.

Brower, I. C. (1980) Counseling Vietnamese. *Personnel and Guidance Journal*, 58(10): 646–53.

Büchel, B. and X. T. Lai (2001) Measures of joint venture performance from multiple perspectives: An evaluation by local and foreign managers in Vietnam. *Asia Pacific Journal of Management*, 18: 101–11.

Cam, N. (1994) Barriers to communication between Vietnamese and non-Vietnamese. In X. T. Nguyen (ed.), *Vietnamese Studies in a Multicultural World*. Melbourne: Vietnamese Language and Cultural Publications, pp. 65–71.

Chang, K. C. (2005) Relationship quality and negotiation interdependence: The case study of international defect claim. *Total Quality Management*, 16(7): 903–14.

Chew, C. L. G. (1998) Tet celebrations unite. *Straits Times*, Life! Section, 30 January: 1.

Chew, C. L. G. (2005) The functions of *được* ('*OK*'; '*possible*'; '*can*') in business communication in Vietnam. *Journal of Asian Pacific Communication* (special issue) 15(2): 229–56.

Clyne, M. (1994) *Inter-Cultural Communication at Work: Cultural Values in Discourse*. Cambridge: Cambridge University Press.

Coulmas, F. (2005) *Sociolinguistics: The Study of Speaker's Choice*. New York: Cambridge University Press.

Duong, T. B. (1975) *Vietnamese in the U.S.* Arlington, VA: Center for Applied Linguistics.

Engholm, C. (1995) *Doing Business in the New Vietnam*. Englewood Cliffs, NJ: Prentice Hall.

Gannon, M. J. (2001) *Cultural Metaphors: Readings, Research Translations, and Commentary*. Thousand Oaks, CA: Sage.

Hofstede, G. and H. M. Bond (2001) The Confucius connection: From cultural roots to economic growth. In M. J. Gannon (ed.), *Cultural Metaphors: Readings, Research Translations, and Commentary*. Thousand Oaks, CA: Sage, pp. 31–50.

Hofstede, G. and G. J. Hofstede (2005) *Cultures and Organizations: Software of the Mind*. New York: McGraw-Hill.

Houston, R. (2002) Health Care and the silent language of Vietnamese immigrant consumers. *Business Communication Quarterly*, 65(1): 37–47.

Jamieson, N. L. (1995) *Understanding Vietnam*. Berkeley and Los Angeles: University of California Press.

Janney, R. W. and H. Arndt (1992) Intracultural tact versus intercultural tact. In R. J. Watts, S. Ide and K. Ehlich (eds), *Politeness in Language: Studies in its History, Theory and Practice*. Berlin and New York: Mouton de Gruyter, pp. 21–41.

Janse, O. R. T. (1944) *The Peoples of French Indochina*. Washington, DC: Smithsonian Institute.

Kelly, P. L. (1978) Vietnamese students on a small college campus: Observations and analysis. Paper delivered at the meeting of the National Association of Foreign Student Affairs, Ames, Iowa State University.

Le, C. T., C. Rowley, Q. Truong and M. Warner (2007) To what extent can management practices be transferred between countries? The case of human resource management in Vietnam. *Journal of World Business*, 42: 113–27.

Lewis, R. D. (2006) *When Cultures Collide: Leading across Cultures*, 3rd edn. Boston, MA: Nicholas Brealey International.

McLeod, M. W. and T. D. Nguyen (2001) *Culture and Customs of Vietnam*. Westport, CT: Greenwood Press.

Mcmillan, J. and C. Woodruf (1999) Dispute prevention without courts in Vietnam. *Journal of Law, Economics, & Organization*, 15(3): 637–58.

Malarney, S. (2002) *Culture, Ritual and Revolution in Vietnam*. London: Routledge Curzon.

MSM (Minister of State Multiculturism, Canada) (1979) *A Guide to Working with Vietnamese Refugees*. Douglas Pike Collection; Unit-03. Vietnam Archive, Texas Tech University.

Napier, K. N. (2006) Cross-cultural learning and reverse knowledge flows in Vietnam. *International Journal of Cross-Cultural Management*, 6(1): 57–74.

Nguyen, D. L. (1994) Indochinese cross-cultural communication and adjustment. In X. T. Nguyen (ed.), *Vietnamese Studies in a Multicultural World*. Melbourne: Vietnamese Language and Cultural Publications, pp. 44–63.

Nguyen, N. B. (1979) *Personal Communications*. Arlington, VA: Public Schools Intake Center.

Nguyen, V. T., M. Weinstein and A. D. Meyer (2005) Development of trust: A study of interfirm relationships in Vietnam. *Asia Pacific Journal of Management*, 22: 211–35.

Penner, L. A. and A. Tran (1977) A comparison of American and Vietnamese values system. *Journal of Social Psychology*, 101: 187–204.

Ralston, D. A., V. T. Nguyen and N. Napier (1999) A comparative study of the work values of North and South Vietnamese managers. *Journal of International Business Studies*, 30(4): 655–72.

Schultz, C. J., II, D. Dapice, A. Pecotich and H. D. Doan (2006) Vietnam: Expanding market socialism and implications for marketing, consumption, and socioeconomic development. In A. Pecotich and C. J. Schultz II (eds), *Handbook of Markets and Economies*. Armonk, NY: M. E. Sharpe, pp. 656–87.

Schneider, S. C. and J.-L. Barsoux (2003) *Managing across Cultures*, 2nd edn. Harlow: Financial Times.

Truong, Q. (2006) Human resources management in Vietnam. In A. Nankervis, S.

Chatterjee and J. Coffey (eds), *Perspectives of Human Resource Management in the Asia Pacific*. Sydney: Pearson Education, pp. 231–52.

Turner, S. and P. A. Nguyen (2005) Young entrepreneurs, social capital and *Doi Moi* in Hanoi, Vietnam. *Urban Studies*, 42(10): 1693–710.

Vu, V. T. and N. Napier (2000) Paradoxes in Vietnam and America: 'Lessons Earned' – Part I, II, III. *Human Resource Planning*, 23(1, 2, 3): pp. 7–8, 9–10, 9–10.

Vuong, G. T. (1976) *Getting to Know the Vietnamese and their Culture*. New York: Frederick Unger.

Wall Street Journal (2007) Vietnam today. Special advertising section, 3 October: 9.

Wang, H. Z. and H. H. M. Hsiao (2002) Social capital or human capital? Professionals in overseas Taiwanese firms. *Journal of Contemporary Asia*, 32(3): 346–62.

Watts, R., S. Ide and K. Ehlich (1992) *Politeness in Language: Studies in its History, Theory and Practice*. Berlin and New York: Mouton de Gruyter.

Xinhua News Agency (2007) Vietnam lures more foreign arrivals in first 9 months. http://www.trade.hochiminhcity.gov.vn/data/ttth/2007/04-10-2007_0.6058111584998322.html. Accessed 5 October 2007.

29

Malaysia

Shanta Nair-Venugopal

Introduction

Most of the business discourse research in commercial and other institutional settings in Malaysia has focused to date on discourse genres and related aspects of communication in contexts of situated language use (Morais 1994; Le Vasan 1996; Salbiah 1996; Nair-Venugopal 1997; Kaur 1997; Anie 1998; Arumugam 1998; Ting 2001; Puvenesvary 2002; Sargunan 2005; Hadina and Rafik-Galea 2005; Yuen 2007) against the background of English as the normative language of business. Others, namely, Zubaida (1997), Paramasivam (2004) and Jaganathan (2006), examined power, power and politeness, and interactional style and social identity respectively. Zubaida studied email discourse, Paramasivam business negotiations, and Jaganathan business meetings.

In this chapter, I report on attitudes to language use in a commercial setting by revisiting an organisation that was first investigated thirteen years ago, to provide a current perspective. Specifically it is the attitudes of trainers in a bank owned by the same organisation that are examined in relation to their rhetoric on the acceptability of localised forms of language use. Banks are some of the most conservative types of commercial organisations in Malaysia because the finance industry is highly regulated. Thus the views expressed by its trainers may be taken to be a barometer of the discourse on English in Malaysian business. It is against this background that I discuss this research and its implications for the use of localised English in Malaysian business while revisiting some of the ramifications of such use in two other contexts from an earlier large-scale study (Nair-Venugopal 1997).

Context

The dominant role and status of English during British colonial rule in Malaya changed with the movement towards independence (Merdeka) in 1957. Subsequent language policy changes reoriented the legal status of English to 'second most important language' relative to Malay as part of Malaysia's nation-building project. Formed in 1963, Malaysia comprises the eleven states of Peninsular Malaya, and Sabah and Sarawak on the island of Borneo. Nevertheless, English remained as the normative choice in Malaysian business and the dominant discourse on it is prescriptive. This is in spite of the complexity of linguistic diversity in Malaysia that routinely juxtaposes localised English with models of 'standardised English'. However, despite the colonial legacy of English in corporate business, banking and finance, and the traditional dominance of the Chinese 'dialects' in local Chinese business enterprise, Malay has now emerged as a competing code in Malaysian business. This is the result of the combined effects of the national educational policy and the New Economic Policy (NEP, 1971), which is a socioeconomic restructuring affirmative action programme aimed at reconstituting the demographic composition of the Malaysian workplace to reflect ethnic population ratios.

In many respects, the emphasis on English at the workplace is artificial because everyday communication in Malaysia is typified by alternation between competing codes and the integration of elements from a variety of languages. Using two or more different languages in a single interaction is normal linguistic behaviour for Malaysians. Moreover, despite the pervasiveness of the localised variety or Malaysian English in many domains of use, including the public, 'efforts are being made to inculcate the use of standardised English in formal settings, such as political speeches, the education system, print media, and lectures' (Singh et al. 2002: 153). These are fuelled by the government's belief that Malaysia's ability to compete in the 'new' and knowledge economies of globalisation will be determined partly by the competence of its workforce in standardised English. It has already identified deficiencies in the quantity and quality of English-language proficiency among workers as an impediment to attaining economic success. This message is constantly iterated in the local media as a lack of prerequisite communication skills for both the Malaysian and global workplace. The unemployment of thousands of graduates from local universities is even blamed on their lack of English-language skills, although it could well be argued that the government's policy of education for the masses has not matched market demand and produced unemployable graduates. We see the cultural politics of the elitist 'worldliness of English in Malaysia' (Pennycook 1994) being overtaken by the political economics of a neediness for English.

Scope of the study

Taking discourse to be both language in use and the language used to express ideas, I take business discourse to be both 'language at work' (Bargiela-Chiappini et al. 2007) – i.e. how people communicate, using talk or in writing, to get their work done as situated language use in business organisations – and language that is used to 'talk about' language at work. I also view business discourse as social action that is communicated through language. While it is important to examine business discourse as 'language at work', it is equally important to study 'talk about' language at work itself, which is the focus of this chapter. In this case it is business that is the context. Context is crucial as positions are more specifically communicated in situ as social action that constitutes social reality.

The prevailing discourse governing language and communication in Malaysian business may be viewed as ideological since it is prescriptive about what constitutes 'corporate' language use. The rhetoric of corporate management is one of 'great expectations' with regard to an idealistic or abstract linguistic 'standard', while it is one of rejection for the new forms of spoken and written literacy that have developed on the ground in business organisations. These are a sociolinguistic consequence of the national educational policy of using Malay as the medium of instruction in national schools and publicly funded universities. Additionally, rather generalised perceptions and idealistic, even unrealistic expectations about English persist.

I take the position that localised forms of English are new forms of functional literacy at work. This is a countervailing stance to the dominant discourse on English in Malaysian business, which rejects the viability of localised English, spoken and written in its 'un-English' ways (with its implications for normativity and intelligibility) and ignores the pragmatic relevance of contextualised language for local business. However, local business information is invariably conveyed in the 'local' language, in this case, Malaysian English (ME). Marked by language acculturation and code alternations that are realised as code switches and mixes, borrowings and crossings, it has evolved to serve localised language and communication needs. It is, nevertheless, invariably conflated with the portmanteau word Manglish in common parlance, which evokes the 'mangling' of English, rather than acknowledges that ME is the localised variety. Often, Manglish is used to describe 'poor', 'broken' or 'mixed-up' English.

Issues of relevance

Local diversity, global connectivity and English

In examining critical aspects of the new global capitalism, Gee (2000) points out that centralised command systems have effectively been displaced by distributed systems as, for instance, in the forms of automated machines, computers, organisational structures, the media and science; so much so that 'there is no centre . . . no discrete individuals', 'only assemblies of skills' (p. 47). These are stored in a person for a specific project, reassembled for other projects and shared with others within 'communities of practice'.

Such skills would include English-language skills too, for analogically, the 'centre' has broken in Anglophone English-language monopoly too. With the emergence of competing and multiple alternatives that cross linguistic borders, projecting both local diversity and global connectivity, 'something paradoxical is indeed happening to English. At the same time as it is becoming a lingua mundi, a world language, and a lingua franca, a common language of commerce, media and politics, English is also breaking into multiple and increasingly differentiated Englishes, marked by accent, national origin, subcultural styles and professional or technical communities' (Cope and Kalantzis 2000: 6) as specific language skills. This global mutation of English into multiple or 'multivocal Englishes' (Singh et al. 2002) strikes at the very heart of the relevance of standardised English vis-à-vis English as a localised language that serves the language and communication needs of the localised workplace, and it comprises the communicative competence of its 'non-native' users.

Indeed this fragmentation of English into many new, world or multiple Englishes (of which ME is an identifiable variety), clearly negates the notion of a global (Crystal 1997) or international English (Smith 1983), for it is variation that lies at the very heart of the notion of any language that has a global reach and influence. This renders the focus in global English on 'international intelligibility rather than a specific variety' (Graddol 2006: 93) untenable as a pedagogical goal. Yet it appears unlikely that governmental (and parental) demand for global English will diminish anywhere in the near future (ibid.). Nevertheless, the spread of a global English-based communication has exposed the myth of a global or international English.

The reality of contextualised language needs to be acknowledged and embraced. As Gee (2000: 63) argues, all language is meaningful only in and through the contexts in which it is used, on the basis of shared experiences and information. It is inexplicit until listeners and readers fill it out on the basis of the experiences they have had and the information they have gained in socioculturally significant interactions with others in communities of practice. Such contextualised language, presumably, includes the influence of cable network television, popular print and electronic media, websites on the internet, and the cell phone's short messaging service (SMS) as everyday experiences of language use and meaning-making. ME is an example of such language use in 'communities of practice' such as those of schools, businesses and neighbourhoods in Malaysia.

The 'native speaker' today is the expert 'second' language user for whom English is part of an inherited identity from birth. English is used as a local language – as contextualised language for communication with elites, peers and other members of the wider local speech community by an innovative appropriator without '"the tradition inspired" standardized nuances of another language or culture' (Khubchandani 1997: 91).

Malaysian English as localised English

The earliest study of ME (Tongue 1979), although largely anecdotal, identified a common English language variety, Singapore-Malaysian English (ESM), for both Singapore and Malaysia, distinguishing between a 'formal' and 'informal' style, with the prediction that ME would diverge from that of Singapore. A more comprehensive, empirical study of English in Singapore and Malaysia (Platt and Weber 1980) identified two varieties, MEI and MEII, and the existence of a number of sub-groups, by comparing ESM to a post-Creole continuum. Morais (1994) referred to these two varieties as well in examining verbal interactions in a Malaysian business setting. Benson (1990), however, critiqued Platt and Weber (1980) for comparing the varietal range of English in Singapore and Malaysia to the tripartite lectal structure of the post-Creole continuum. He contended that ME had evolved from the English used by the colonial expatriates. However, it appears more likely that it was Standard British English (SBrEng), or the near-native variety taught in schools during British colonial rule, which was the main precursor of ME, and that this variety differentiated into the subvarieties that spilled over into the domains of friendship in the playgrounds, into homes and the workplace. An in-depth empirical study (Baskaran 1987) showed that the substrate languages, particularly Malay, influenced the syntax of ME. Baskaran demonstrated that ME was a new variety of English in an 'un-English' context, as its structural features were distinctive, systematic and consistent despite its division into the acrolect, mesolect and basilect of the post-Creole continuum. Departing from earlier studies that had relied on the discredited post-Creole continuum, Nair-Venugopal (1997) identified a functional model of interaction as language choice for communication in Malaysian business.

Localised English in Malaysian business

In presenting this functional model of interaction, Nair-Venugopal (1997) described the verbal repertoires of individuals in the workplace settings of two large Malaysian business organisations as comprising:

- three subvarieties of the localised variety or ME;
- Malay speech inclusive of colloquial and Bazaar Malay (Bahasa Pasar);
- code-switching (CS) into Malay and English;
- code-mixing (CM) of English and Malay;
- the mixing of informal referents with formal referents and register in English.

ME was a clear constituent of the verbal repertoires of the individuals in the two business contexts investigated, which demonstrated the evolution of English as a local language. These subvarieties, namely Educated Malaysian English (EME), Colloquial Malaysian English (CME) and 'Broken' Malaysian English or Pidgin, were spoken in ethnically distinctive ways as 'ethnolects' of ME (Nair-Venugopal 2000a, 2000b, 2003, 2006).

There is evidence from Yuen (2007) that localised forms of English in written communication in business contexts are also competing with standardised forms. However, it appears to be one thing to speak of a local variety in the workplace but quite another to write the 'local language' into the business context. I was informed repeatedly by gatekeepers that business is not only about profit making, but also about applying best practices and standards, and about maintaining a corporate image that is dependent on consistent quality, and that included language use. Hence, standardised English was the natural choice for corporate Malaysian business. But linguists know that the business context, like any other, is not exempt from the vagaries of language change and that all variation is susceptible to innovative and creative language appropriation. The question to ask is not whether this scenario exists in Malaysian business but whether localised English is accepted as an indelible part of its linguistic scenery.

Attitudes to localised forms

Research context

When I first began to observe and study language use in Malaysian business contexts in the early 1990s, I became aware that language use on the ground in Malaysian business contexts did not match the language ideals held by gatekeepers, stakeholders and the political establishment, as revealed in Nair-Venugopal (1997). Others (Puvenesvary 2002, 2003; Ting 2001, 2002) have described this tension between standardised and localised English, but in more politically correct, prescriptive terms, as a 'mismatch' of skills. In revisiting the research site, I noticed no appreciable change to the institutional imperatives or rhetoric regarding a policy of English 'first and best'. While the discourse on poor English-language proficiency appeared to have given way to some tolerance, the tension over linguistic differences was replaced by ambivalence, while the rhetoric was ambiguous.

To confirm these tentative indications of attitudinal change, four trainers from the bank owned by the organisation that I first investigated thirteen years ago were subjected to a structured interview. For some control and comparison (and additional points of view), a female freelance management consultant for a state-owned corporation and a male academician trainer for a leading bank were subjected to the same. The four in-house trainers, three females and one male, work in the bank's centre for organisational development, and train almost all levels of employees in the bank on knowledge-building, work skills and personal development. They were in their early forties, thus representing a generation of Malaysian professionals who had received their education mainly, but not wholly, in Bahasa Malaysia (BM), the national language. The assumption was that they would probably be less dogmatic about English-language use than the two older respondents, who represented a generation that had been educated in English. The management consultant was fifty-five years of age and the academician fifty. All six respondents spoke as experts in their areas of training but assumed other identities too in the course of the interviews. Responses to a mix of fifteen yes/no and open-ended questions ranging from organisational language policy or philosophy to personal views and experiences in training were elicited. These questions were from a set that had been administered previously and subsequently refined for the study. Re-entry to the financial institution and access to the bank's training sessions was not easy but previously established contacts made the visits possible and pleasant.

The interviews

I discuss the attitudes of the trainers to localised English with regard to its acceptability vis-à-vis standardised English. By attitudes I mean responses arising from the evaluations individuals make of preferences or dispreferences for things, which they may or may not react to emotionally or behaviourly, and which may implicate values and beliefs (Gardner 1985). As the structured interview does not measure attitudes directly as a questionnaire does, the responses to the questions are taken to be expressions of attitudes.

The four bank trainers are referred to as A, B, C and D. Recordings were not allowed this time round, so I made verbatim notes of the responses. Doubts and points of ambiguity were clarified later. The management consultant is referred to as W and the academician trainer as M. As these two respondents worked in different and distant locations, their interviews were conducted via the internet and their responses counter-checked by phone.

As the bank's employees, the four trainers behaved as expected of designated custodians of the corporate mission and vision of the bank. Initially, they were rather guarded, presumably to safeguard either the bank's corporate image or their reputations as English-using elites. It is not uncommon for individuals in interviews and self-reports to say what they think others want to hear them say, that is, what might be politically correct rather than critical. Conversely, the researcher also tends to see what is said as a reflection of what is 'out there' rather than an interpretation to be jointly produced by both parties (Briggs 1986). I focus on those responses that best illustrate the rhetoric to try to capture the nuances.

The bank's four trainers reported that although there was no written policy on English, they were informed by superiors, at some point in their employment, that English was the language of business in the organisation. In contrast, the normative status of English was spelt out in the bank that M serviced, while in the corporation that hired W, English was tacitly accepted as the normative language. According to the bank's trainers, all levels of management staff were aware of the institutional imperative regarding English except, perhaps, those in the lower echelons, such as the drivers, cleaners and tea-ladies, for whom it probably did not matter anyway. Office and despatch 'boys' were an exception as they were always in contact with employees from other levels. Yet, in spite of the normative status of English, the four affirmed that they interspersed English with Malay in their training sessions, citing the following reasons:

> A: because she (the trainer) knows them (audience) best;
> B: needs to ensure that whatever (language) is used is used to impart knowledge;
> C: because it doesn't say Malay cannot be used;
> D: can use Malay to check comprehension for comprehension checks.

In contrast, the bank that M serviced was unambiguous. All training had to be in 'standard' or 'proper English'. As for W, she 'clearly understood' that English was the main language to be used for dealing with partners, clients and suppliers and for training.

With regard to the bank's stance on language choice and use, the bank's trainers' views were mixed, as is evident in the responses below. C and D reflect a more predictable corporate stance, while A and B, although ambiguous about Malay, are less dogmatic about English as first choice.

> A: flexible enough; given leeway although the corporate language is English;
> B: no problem switching to BM as and when necessary;
> C: executives should have good communications skills in English because English is a corporate language;
> D: English will be first and best choice.

Meanwhile M reported that it was difficult to adhere consistently to the use of English because low-level trainees lacked 'confidence in using English'. However, for W it was 'necessary', even 'good' to use English 'as most meetings and organisational communications were in English', reflecting the corporation's language practices.

With regard to which languages they considered useful for training purposes, apart from trainer D the bank trainers acceded to the potential of Malay and Chinese as languages for training. This admission of the usefulness of other languages, in the face of trainer adherence to English for training purposes, indicates the polarisation between institutional imperatives and local decisions taken by trainers on the ground.

> A: mixture of both but prefer competence in English; now production skills are poor because of Malay in schools;
> B: maybe Chinese or BM may be even more useful, say in rural areas, but English is more useful for corporate training;
> C: depends on the audience, sometimes more proficient in BM, but start with English and use BM for certain words; prefer English for technical training;
> D: prefer English for training needs, i.e. banking systems.

M found that 'using ME was most effective in creating a conducive atmosphere for learning'. As training was about imparting knowledge, he felt that the best option was to use a language that the trainees were 'comfortable with'. W opined rather unexpectedly that 'a mixture of English and Malay' would be 'more practical' for mid-level

participants; that Malay was even 'necessary' to explain 'complex concepts' or 'management jargon'.

The bank's trainers indicated that they had independence in choosing the language
for training purposes, but C added that that did not mean the outright use of Malay in
the bank, although no one had told her that that was not possible either. However, they
concurred that although they were 'particular' about the kind of English they used, they
invariably bent the rules to accommodate to the audience's proficiency and were 'always
guided by the training task'; that is, 'getting the message across [sic] always more important than the language per se'. These remarks are reminiscent of those of trainers in the
earlier large-scale study as well (Nair-Venugopal 2000a). For M it was the trainees who
ultimately determined language choice, for although the training task was always fixed, he
would 'make changes' if he felt he was not making much head way imparting knowledge.
W, meanwhile, stressed that although English was the first choice, she was 'always sensitive' to training needs.

As for their personal code choices, the four trainers indicated a preference for local
repertoires of English, as seen below:

> A: ME or 'communicative' English;
> B: EME;
> C: simplified English with an emphasis on communication;
> D: EME that all can follow.

M said his could range from 'standard' to localised English, for he saw language use only
as a means to an end. W emphasised the use of 'formal, grammatically correct English'.

Lastly, the bank's trainers concurred rather predictably that language was the most
important factor in effective training and communication in the bank. Nevertheless, they
believed that technology would enhance the training process and that e-learning programmes such as those employed by the bank might eventually replace the trainer. It is
equally likely that technology may even compensate for language deficit, as observed by
Pan et al. (2002: 4). However, while both M and W acknowledged the value of technology in
training, they maintained that language was a critical medium. Additionally, M mentioned
learning outcomes, training venues and trainer–trainee rapport as important variables.

Finally, and rather illuminatingly, the bank's trainers declared that communication
skills were more than a language issue. Yet communication skills are routinely conflated
with English-language skills in the Malaysian workplace, which echoes establishment
views. In alluding to the national policy of education that reaches out to the masses, they
contended that although lower university entry qualifications may have produced recruits
who were far less proficient in English, many were very well versed in work matters.
These recruits lacked communicative confidence in English rather than knowledge of
work matters. This confirms another observation of trainees in the large-scale study
(Nair-Venugopal 2000a) too.

Trainer A, the most proficient and fluent of the four in English, was the most empathetic to the language deficit of the trainees. According to her, the gap between the
English-language competencies of the current recruits to the organisation and that of
recruits ten years ago had grown wider, although she did not see low English-language
proficiency as a reflection of poor cognitive or communicative skills. She was thus open to

the idea of training in Malay. Trainers B and C were not against using Malay either, but D maintained that banking systems' training had to be in English or it would 'compromise' 'knowledge content training'.

Reflections

The disjuncture between the ideals of normative English-language use and actual language use on the ground are quite apparent. First, while W toed the corporate line, M conceded to the realities of language change in the workplace, despite being an older, English-educated Malaysian. Second, although all four bank trainers claimed to be speakers of standardised English, B, C and D displayed departures from its norms. Uncontroversially, however, all four saw themselves as speakers of ME, reflecting current language realities in Malaysia. Significantly, the respondents confirmed what appears to be a paradox of language and communication in Malaysian business: that while the rhetoric of the gatekeeping echelons of senior management displayed a preoccupation with establishing and maintaining 'standard', 'good', 'proper', 'correct' and even 'quality' English, such norms were not always present or put into place by trainers. In serving the corporate goals of the organisation, trainers are also gatekeepers, but they were more 'sociopragmatically savvy' (Nair-Venugopal 2003: 16) than senior management in being sensitive to issues on the ground. The latter's concerns about maintaining a desirable corporate image in the organisations' dealings with the public was inevitably based on the assumption that a particular type of English symbolised 'good' service', which was equated with an idealised 'standard'. But as Cope and Kalantzis (1997) argue, using 'productive diversity' as a metaphor for culture in a model for work and management, corporate culture can thrive on linguistic diversity too. Bargiela-Chiappini and Harris (1997) also show how different languages 'work' in businesses worldwide. In Malaysian business contexts, this linguistic diversity consists of the repertoires of subvarieties of ME, standard, colloquial and bazaar Malay, CS into Malay and English, CM of English and Malay, the mixing of informal with formal referents and workplace register, and speaking in ethnically distinctive ways as 'ethnolects' (Nair-Venugopal 2000a, 2000b).

Workplace communication in Malaysia clearly demands a plurilinguistic agenda, given the language ecology of Malaysia business contexts, but it continues to be assailed by the rhetoric of standardised English as *the* language of even local business interactions. Instead of harnessing the potential capacity of the linguistic diversity of the workforce, the backbone of that potential has been broken by the belief that achieving a competitive edge in a globalised economy depends considerably on the value-addedness of English. But even as English becomes the undisputed lingua franca of work in the world, its value-addedness may not be sustainable. Even without a competitive edge in English, the Japanese and the Koreans have managed to maintain their economic competitiveness, while the Vietnamese, Cambodians and Laotians have very successfully attracted large foreign investment funds for development. Even China, an economic giant, is not yet a nation of English users.

Concluding remarks

Graddol (2006: 17) expounds the view that English today is a near-universal basic education skill. So language proficiency may be linked with other skills and abilities to make English yet another type of functional literacy at work. Heller (2005) suggests there may even be a tension between treating language as a technical, value-added skill that is easier to measure and evaluate, and as a kind of innate talent that is not only hard to manage, but may even be scarce or non-replicable. Hence, while talent, variability and authenticity are marks of multilingualism and new economic freedoms, skill, standardisation and commodification are not. Additionally, if the ideas and practices associated with the teaching of English as a foreign language are a declining paradigm accompanied by a declining reverence for 'native speakers' of English as the gold standard (Graddol 2006: 68), it is not too far-fetched to suggest that localised English can replace standardised English.

The potential for such a trajectory is evident in Malaysian business as attested by the trainers. In the Malaysian workplace, an artificial polarisation exists between ME as a model of localised English, and standardised models of English, empowering users of the latter and disadvantaging the former. Senior and top management as gatekeepers of practices, systems and policies need to stand back and admit that there are issues of language and communication to be addressed in these contexts. Graddol (2006: 83) concedes that within traditional EFL methodology, there is an inbuilt ideological positioning of the student as an outsider and failure however proficient she becomes. If EFL is indeed designed to produce failure, how much more counter-productive is it for graduates of public universities that use Malay as a medium of education to be expected to produce standardised English on demand, as new recruits to the Malaysian workforce? Such enforcement cannot reduce the tensions of 'language at work'. Accepting ME as a model of localised English can result in workplace literary practices that will.

ME can be incorporated into national workplace communication training programmes as an aspect of current literacy practices in the Malaysian workplace. As contextualised language, it reflects and represents English-language competence in the Malaysian workplace. As a localised model of language and communication, it can help in specifying the minimum level of English-language skills for new recruits to the workforce. Charles and Marschan-Piekkari (2002), cited in Bargiela-Chiappini et al. (2007: 115), found that non-native-English-speaking employees had less apparent difficulty understanding other non-native-English-speaking employees than native speakers, while House (2003) observed that miscommunication only occurred in the interactions of multilingual speakers with native speakers. It appears then that native speakers fail to communicate because they view their norms as universally applicable and variation as deviation. These findings only reinforce the argument that a localised variety like ME can serve language and communication needs in the workplace because it matches the communicative competence of its 'non-native' users. Significantly, ME enhances intracultural communication in the Malaysian workplace because it matches its linguistic reality.

Finally, if this minimal level of English-language competence is incorporated into the communication training programmes, such as those organised by the Ministry of Human Resources and related agencies, more realistic expectations and targets regarding English-language use and competence in the Malaysian workplace can be met. Training programmes in ME will help to bridge the gap between standardised English and local literacy practices and linguistic behaviour. Conversely, blind faith in the relevance of a global linguistic norm for local workplace practices is repressive and non-productive.

References

Anie, A. (1998) English in industry: A study of language choice in two electronics firms in Malaysia. PhD thesis, Universiti Malaya, Kuala Lumpur.

Arumugam, D. (1998) Communication among the safety management team on a construction site. MA dissertation, Universiti Malaya, Kuala Lumpur.

Bargiela-Chiappini, F. and S. Harris (eds) (1997) *The Languages of Business: An International Perspective*. Edinburgh: Edinburgh University Press.

Bargiela-Chiappini, F., C. Nickerson and B. Planken (2007) *Business Discourse*. Basingstoke: Palgrave Macmillan.

Baskaran, L. (1987) Aspects of Malaysian English syntax. PhD thesis, University College, University of London, London.

Benson, P. (1990) A language in decline? *English Today*, 6(4): 19–23.

Briggs, C. (1986) *Learning How to Ask: A Sociolinguistic Appraisal of the Role of the Interview in Social Science Research*. Cambrige: Cambridge University Press.

Cope, B. and M. Kalantzis (1997) *Productive Diversity*. Sydney: Pluto Press.

Cope, B. and M. Kalantzis (2000) Multiliteracies: The beginnings of an idea. In B. Cope and M. Kalantzis (eds), *Multiliteracies: Literacy Learning and Design of Social Futures*. London: Routledge, pp. 43–68.

Crystal, D. (1997) *English as a Global Language*. Cambridge: Cambridge University Press.

Gardner, R. C. (1985) *Social Psychology and Second-Language Learning: The Role of Attitudes and Motivation*. London: Arnold.

Gee, J. P. (2000) New people in new worlds: Networks, the new capitalism, and schools. In B. Cope and M. Kalantzis (eds), *Multiliteracies: Literacy Learning and Design of Social Futures*. London: Routledge, pp. 43–68.

Graddol, D. (2006) *English Next*. London: British Council.

Hadina, H. and Rafik-Galea, S. (2005) Communicating at the workplace: Insights into Malaysian electronic business discourse. In F. Bargiela-Chiappini and M. Gotti (eds), *Asian Business Discourse(s)*. Bern: Peter Lang, pp. 121–43.

Heller, M. (2005) Paradoxes of language in the globalised new economy. Plenary paper delivered at the International Conference on Global Communication, Cardiff, July.

House, J. (2003) English as a lingua franca: A threat to multilingualism? *Journal of Sociolinguistics*, 7(4): 556–78.

Jaganathan, T. (2006) Talk at work: Interactional style and social identity in face to face interactions in the Malaysian workplace. MA dissertation, Universiti Kebangsaan Malaysia, Bangi.

Kaur, M. (1997) Discourse strategies for argumentation for work-related communication: A comparison between Malay and Australian business/economics students. Phd dissertation, Macquarie University, Sydney.

Khubchandani, L. M. (1997) *Revisualizing Boundaries: A Plurilingual Ethos*. New Delhi: Sage.

Le Vasan, M. (1996) System and process in computer mediated discourse: A case study of business communication in a Malaysian corporation. PhD thesis, Universiti Malaya, Kuala Lumpur.

Morais, E. (1994) Malaysian business talk: A study of the patterns of conflict and non-conflict in verbal interactions. PhD thesis, Universiti Malaya, Kuala Lumpur.

Nair-Venugopal, S. (1997) The sociolinguistics of code and style choice in Malaysian business settings: An ethnographic account. PhD thesis, University of Wales, Cardiff.

Nair-Venugopal, S. (2000a) *Language Choice and Communication in Malaysian Business*. Bangi: Penerbit UKM/UKM Press.

Nair-Venugopal, S. (2000b) English as sociolect and ethnolect in Malaysian business discourse. In H. M. Said and N. K. Siew (eds), *English is an Asian Language: The Malaysian Context*. Kuala Lumpur and Sydney: Persatuan Bahasa Moden Malaysia and Macquarie Library, pp. 78–89.

Nair-Venugopal, S. (2003) Malaysian English, normativity and workplace interactions. *World Englishes*, 22(1): 15–29.

Nair-Venugopal, S. (2006) An interactional model of Malaysian English: A contextualised response to commodification. *Journal of Asia Pacific Communication* (special issue), 16(1): 51–75.

Pan, Y., Scollon, S. W. and Scollon, R. (2002) *Professional Communication in International Settings*. Oxford: Blackwell.

Paramasivam, S. (2004) The play of power and politeness in negotiation discourse: A case study. PhD thesis, Universiti Kebangsaan Malaysia, Bangi.

Pennycook, A. (1994) *The Cultural Politics of English as an International Language*. London: Longman.

Platt, J. and H. Weber (1980) *English in Singapore and Malaysia*. Kuala Lumpur: Oxford University Press.

Puvenesvary, M. (2002) 'Welcome to the real world': A comparative study of the orientation to the evaluation of business correspondence by ESL instructors and business practitioners and its implications for teaching and assessment. PhD thesis, University of Melbourne, Australia.

Puvenesvary, M. (2003) English language proficiency at the workplace: Expectations of bank officers in Malaysia. *Asian Englishes*, 6(2): 64–81.

Salbiah, S. (1996) The genre and genre expectations of engineering oral presentations related to academic and professional contexts. PhD thesis, Stirling University.

Sargunan, R. A. (2005) Customer–supplier relationships in communication skills training: Ironing out the grey areas. *Journal of Communication Practices*, 2(1): 111–28.

Singh, M., P. Kell and A. Pandian (2002) *Appropriating English: Innovation in the Global Business of English Language Teaching*. New York: Peter Lang.

Smith, L. (1983) *Readings in English as an International Language*. London: Pergamon.

Star (2002) UMNO's stand. 11 May.

Ting, S.-H. (2001) Language choice in multilingual and organisational settings: The case of Sarawak, Malaysia. PhD thesis, University of Queensland, Australia.

Ting, S.-H. (2002) Is English needed in a Malay workplace? *RELC Journal*, 22(1): 143–50.

Tongue, R. (1979) *The English of Singapore and Malaysia*. Singapore: Eastern Universities Press.

Yuen, C. K. (2007) Ringing the changes: A study of language variation and use in the business correspondence of executives in a financial institution in Malaysia. PhD thesis, Universiti Kebangsaan Malaysia, Bangi.

Zubaida, S. A. A. (1997) Language and power: A critical analysis of email text in professional communication. PhD thesis, University of Lancaster.

30

Brazil

Lúcia Pacheco de Oliveira

Introduction

This chapter presents a review of the academic discussion on business discourse in Brazil. This review contextualizes academic research on business communications, relating it to local socioeconomic conditions, to the development of the area of applied linguistics and to implementation of genre studies. The chapter also aims at discussing research challenges for the improvement of discursive practices in the Brazilian entrepreneurial context.

A review on academic business discourse research in Brazil indicates that its history is relatively recent, originating in the 1990s. Its starting point can be associated with the first steps towards establishing a bridge between linguistic studies and those traditionally focused on work. Until the 1990s, language sciences had shown little interest in those questions related to work, although language activities and work activities can be seen as strictly tied, as both transform the social environment and play important roles in exchanges and negotiations among human beings (Souza-e-Silva 2002: 61–2).

The tendency to approximate these two areas of study can be attributed to a new paradigm in linguistic studies in Brazil which, in the 1980s, brought to the fore the importance of context in language studies. On the basis of this new paradigm, language studies emphasised the need to consider situational and cultural aspects in discourse (Halliday and Hasan 1989) and to study their influence on language use. Discourse analyses considering different contexts were developed, including those related to business communication. In this chapter, most of the academic research to be presented will follow the sociocultural approach to language, that is, language viewed as influenced by sociohistorical conditions and also viewed as an important element in the construction of reality.

In Brazil, this sociocultural approach to language, however, has been associated with different theoretical and methodological perspectives in academic business discourse research. Some theoretical bases for these studies come from the adoption of the interdisciplinary paradigm used in France, referring to the relation between language and work. On the other hand, some other studies on business discourse found their theoretical bases in the sociointeractional paradigm developed in the USA after the ideas of the linguist anthropologist John Gumperz, the sociologist Ervin Goffman and the sociolinguist Dell Hymes (Ribeiro and Garcez 1998; Pereira 2002b). This approach to discourse is interested in the study of interaction as it develops and builds social meanings in face-to-face encounters.

Adding to these theoretical perspectives and totally in accordance with a sociocultural approach to language, the ideas of Bakhtin (1992) have been highly influential in the study of business discourse, especially through the notions of dialogism and interdiscursiveness. Another way of looking theoretically at business discourse has been through the study of genres, which have been seen as rhetorical structures (Swales 1990), social processes (Martin 1997) or linguistic sets of features (Biber 1988) and analysed according to different methodological perspectives: move analysis, systemic-functional analysis and multidimensional analysis.

These varied theoretical and methodological approaches to research in business communication have conferred on this area of study a flexible and comprehensive analytical paradigm in Brazil. The fact that most of the research is done by linguists and applied linguists has conferred on another important characteristic: that of being discursive, that is, mostly based on oral and/or written discourse analysis of language that construes social experience in the Brazilian sociocultural entrepreneurial context.

Following the sociocultural approach to language and focusing mainly on discourse research, whose main interest has been to examine interaction in speech events such as meetings, conversations or interviews, as well as written genres used in business discourse communities, this chapter unfolds according to the following objectives: (1) to contextualise the academic discussion of business discourse in Brazil; (2) to illustrate some recent research on discourse genres used in the Brazilian business context; and (3) to present research challenges and implications related to the improvement of business discourse practices in Brazil.

In order to develop some understanding of business discourse in Brazil it is necessary to focus on a number of issues that are related to both local academic conditions and socio-economic scenarios, as well as disciplinary, linguistic and methodological perspectives. Some topics related to these issues form the bases for the discussion to be presented in this chapter.

Local academic conditions

Business is language and it engenders both professional and social exchange. As such, it involves real-world language problems, which have been the focus of study of applied linguists. Therefore, research developments in the area of business discourse are frequently related to developments in the area of applied linguistics. In Brazil, as this area grew and consolidated during the last decade of the twentieth century, the academic discussion on business discourse also increased. Postgraduate programmes in applied linguistics, such as LAEL (Applied Linguistics and Language Studies) at the Catholic University of São Paulo, implemented projects and lines of research interested in language, discourse and society. One of these, the DIRECT project ('Towards the Language of Work'), was established in 1991 aiming at the study of language in the professions. Within the scope of the project, a large corpus of texts produced in business contexts has been compiled and analysed according to different methodological approaches (Chapter 8 in this volume).

Other applied linguistics projects initiated exchange and partnerships with academic communities of different countries, which created conditions for the study of business discourse across different cultures. One of these projects, developed by researchers from three universities in Brazil – the Catholic University of Rio de Janeiro (PUC-Rio), the Catholic University of São Paulo (PUC/SP) and the Federal University of Juiz de Fora (UFJF) – and researchers from one university in Portugal – the University of Lisbon – includes studies that focused on discourse and social practices in Brazilian and Portuguese enterprises, contrasting business meetings across two varieties of the same language: Brazilian and European Portuguese (Oliveira et al. 1999a). This academic cooperation project was financed by the Coordination for the Qualification of Higher Education Professionals (CAPES/Brazil), which is a funding agency of the Brazilian Ministry of Education (MEC, BR), and by the Institute of Scientific and Technological International Cooperation (ICCTI/Portugal), a funding agency of the Portuguese Ministry of Science and Technology (MCT, PT).

Several research studies that were developed within the scope of this project investigated Brazilian and Portuguese cultural contexts in terms of the discursive relationship of participants in organisations. One of these studies focused on leadership styles in Brazilian business meetings (Bastos 2001); another described topic construction in meetings for advertising campaigns (Matheus 2002). Theses, dissertations and research articles were produced with the aim of exploring interaction in business meetings, such as the analysis of how cooperation operates among Portuguese businessmen (Gago 2002), how employees of different types of Brazilian enterprises perceive their participation in internal meetings (L. P. Oliveira et al. 2005) and how social practices related to workers' attitudes in meetings are inscribed in the Portuguese entrepreneurial context (Silvestre and Marques 2005). Also as part of this project, some research focused on other genres in organisations, such as translated reports and written documents (Santos 2001). The relationship with the teaching of business English was also established through research developed according to the English for specific purposes (ESP) approach (Vian 2003). One of the main results of such projects was the planning and realisation of the first conference on 'Discourse, Communication and the Enterprise' (DICOEN) in 2001, held in Lisbon, where results of the research of this academic co-operation project were exchanged between Brazilian and Portuguese researchers (Oliveira 2001; Silveira 2001; Barbara 2001). A further result of the same project was the publication of a book (M. C. L. Oliveira et al. 2005) that includes the translation into Portuguese of representative international research on business discourse.

Another important project that put forth the research on business discourse in Brazil was the academic link that gathered researchers from Brazil and France, including, on the Brazilian side, the following universities: PUC/SP, PUC-Rio, UFRJ and the State University of Rio de Janeiro (UERJ). On the French side, this project included researchers from the University of Provence-Aix-Marseille and the University of Rouen (Souza-e-Silva and Faïta 2002). The Brazilian team of researchers was mainly formed by linguists, while the French group was interdisciplinary, reflecting an established tradition in studies in language and work. Most of the research developed by the French scholars within the scope of this project followed the francophone tendency to focus on the relation between language and work (cf. Chapter 32 in this volume). On the Brazilian side, however, the object of study was generally interaction at work treated under diverse theoretical and methodological perspectives, including Bakhtinian dialogic and interdiscursive views and sociointeractional approaches. On the French side, research developed by human scientists from the areas of philosophy, education and linguistics brought contributions to the role played by language in several work activities.

Focusing on language activities in work situations, research developed within the scope of the project examined, for example, the house organ, an internal monthly newspaper that circulates within the company, and proposed discussions on the role of the linguist in the enterprise (Souza-e-Silva and Machado 1998). Other studies focused on different themes, such as the construction and reconstruction of identities in service encounters and meetings (Bastos 2002; Pereira 2002a). This project also included analysis of the interaction between technicians, engineers and ergonomists in business meetings to discuss the modernisation of an oil refinery (Duarte et al. 2002). The traditional way of focusing on the relation between language and work, which proposes the study of language *at* work, language *about* work or language *as* work, was revisited by Nouroudine (2002) in the volume published with most of the academic production of this French–Brazilian academic link (Souza-e-Silva and Faïta 2002). The study of language *at* work would focus, for example, on the verbal interaction that takes place as an activity develops; language *about* work corresponds to the study of language that is used to talk about work activities, that is, language that describes or comments on work situations; finally, a third approach is the study of language *as* work in situations in which language activities assume strategic functions centred on the challenges of the realisation of work.

Besides these three traditional approaches, which are represented in business discourse research developed in Brazil, a fourth has been discussed in the academic Brazilian scene since around the year 2000. This fourth approach proposes that the use of language in pedagogical contexts, such as the activity of a teacher in the classroom, should be viewed as discourse produced by professional communicators (Scollon and Scollon 1995: 3). In that sense, teaching is viewed as work and teachers are included among those professionals (e.g. lawyers, doctors etc.) for whom communication is at the heart of their professional activities. Such an approach represents the most recent perspective in terms of academic research on pedagogical discourse, imputing to it the status of professional discourse to be examined with the same theoretical and methodological tools applied to business discourse. Some examples of this new approach are reported in Machado (2004) and also explored by Miller (2001), who focused on the discourse of teacher consultancy, and Borges (2007), who analyses the discursive backstage of English teachers who act as academic supervisors in a language school.

Socioeconomic and political scenarios

Socioeconomic and political changes in the Brazilian scenario created specific needs that favoured conditions for the development of research on business discourse. The stability of the economic and political systems in the late 1990s, together with a renewed disposition towards international businesses, generated interest in foreign companies in establishing branches into the country. The privatisation of the public sector accelerated the entrance of foreign staff into the Brazilian entrepreneurial context, as well as contact with new organisational cultures. International business practices had to adapt to these recent conditions.

In order to study international business discourse practices brought by these new conditions, some important work has been developed in oral and written cross-cultural

interactional practices, involving different genres and business areas. Garcez (1993) analysed successive business meetings between American leather importers and Brazilian
exporters. During the interactions, misunderstandings were interpreted as different
cultural ways of making the point in negotiations. While Brazilians need to refer to the
sociocultural and economic context before they actually present the main point, such as
the price of products in a purchase negotiation, Americans expect that the point be made
immediately, without any delay or further explanation.

The same need to create a context to present information before writing has been identified in the written compositions of university students (Oliveira 2002), a finding which
reinforces the view that these differences found in oral interactions and written texts
between Americans and Brazilians can be attributed to cultural influences in discourse.

Another, contrastive study using a multidimensional approach examined different business genres, such as emails, professional letters and recommendation letters,
according to involvement features, such as the use of first and second person pronouns,
evaluative adjectives and adverbs, private verbs, hedges, etc. (Biber 1988, 1995; Oliveira
forthcoming). This study concluded that for both the recommendation and professional
letters American writers show more involvement than Brazilians. On the other hand,
emails showed the opposite tendency, tending towards involvement in Portuguese.
Although the sample examined in the study was not very large (N = 90 texts), the results
seem to reinforce the view that cross-cultural and cross-genre variation can be identified
in English and Portuguese.

Although in Brazil most cross-cultural business studies have focused on the comparison of Portuguese- and English-speaking contexts, a special emphasis has also been given
to the study of cultural differences in organisations in Brazil and Portugal. Drawing from
a previous study by Hofstede (1997), in which he described several cultural dimensions
identified in one corporation across fifty-three countries, a synthesis of the variation of
Brazilian and Portuguese organisations along these dimensions was presented with comments (Oliveira et al. 1999b). The study showed, for example, that Brazilian enterprises
tended towards hierarchy, and were more apt to face risks and to deal with uncertainty
than the Portuguese ones.

Disciplinary, linguistic and methodological perspectives

As the study of language use in business contexts includes both aspects of linguistic and
social structure (McGroarty 2002), academic research in this area has been highly interdisciplinary. In Brazil, joint initiatives by linguists and researchers in the areas of anthropology, sociology, psychology and administration have generated a more comprehensive view
of business discourse, consolidated in international meetings such as the 3rd DICOEN
Conference, held in Rio de Janeiro in 2005.

The study of language in professional contexts also overlaps with the area of language
for specific purposes (LSP) and ESP. In Brazil, such studies first emphasised reading in
university contexts (Celani et al. 2005); however, a more recent and broader approach to
ESP has reinforced the study of business discourse within this area, especially through
the study of genres.

The importance given to genre studies in the Brazilian educational context in recent
years, in terms of both teaching and research, has also impacted on the academic discussion

of the area of business discourse in Brazil. The emphasis given to the study of genres in schools, which occurred as a consequence of the implementation of the National Curricular Parameters for Primary and Secondary Education by the Brazilian Ministry of Education (PCN/MEC), has engendered the development of a variety of teaching materials as well as academic research that resulted in postgraduate theses and dissertations. This importance given to genres impacted on the academic discussion on business discourse and led into many publications focusing on the description and analysis of several genres, including those used in business contexts (Marcuschi and Xavier 2005; Karwoski et al. 2006; Meurer and Motta-Roth 2002). Different theoretical backgrounds have inspired some of these business discourse studies, such as systemic-functional linguistics (Almeida 2002; Vian 2003; Ikeda 2001) and corpus linguistics (Oliveira forthcoming). Different methodologies have also been applied, such as move analysis and multidimensional analysis.

The business meeting, a genre more frequently studied under interpretative methodologies with a focus on the interaction between participants, was also studied with the help of a multidimensional analysis to identify dimensions of variation concerning the perceptions of Brazilian employees and managerial staff towards internal meetings in different types of organisations (L. P. Oliveira et al. 2005). Based on the analysis of 102 questionnaires responded to by employees and managers from 6 Brazilian organisations situated in the city of Rio de Janeiro, 2 of them being mostly owned by the federal government, 7 dimensions of variation were quantitatively identified following a multidimensional analysis (Biber 1988). These dimensions are:

1 orientation towards participative communication and democratic speech distribution;
2 orientation towards the group vs. orientation towards formal distancing;
3 orientation towards competitive work vs. orientation towards hierarchical organisation;
4 orientation towards direct action vs. orientation towards dissimulation;
5 orientation towards co-operative communication and public acceptance;
6 orientation towards contextualised communication vs. shared communication;
7 orientation towards open position negotiations vs. negotiations with categorical positions.

Variation of the organisations along these dimensions showed that not only the size of the companies but also their status as 'private or government owned' contributed to the different perceptions of meetings. In large governmental enterprises, for example, communicative practices in these events were characterised as less collaborative, more hierarchical and conflict-dissimulating. On the other hand, communications in smaller, privately owned companies were seen to be more participative, with more collaborative exchange of ideas among the participants and openness in the discussion of business issues. This study, although not centred on the analysis of discourse, added some points to the description of business meetings in the Brazilian context, as it used a specific methodological approach to genre analysis and showed employees' reflections on their own corporate behaviour.

New organisational scenarios

New conditions characterise the entrepreneurial context in Brazil. The first is related to the organisational redesign of Brazilian enterprises (Chapter 6 in this volume). The usual, familiar and hierarchical structuring of Brazilian organisations, predominant in the past century, has rapidly given way in the twenty-first century to a new structure most frequently found in privately owned companies. Under this new structure the image of the powerful company owner may disappear and a council representing the shareholders will hold decision-making power. These new enterprises are more in unison with international changes that are happening around the globe, exemplified by fusions, mergers and joint ventures which are tangible examples of globalisation in the organisational context (Bargiela-Chiappini 2005: 22).

These operational and financial changes require adaptations in the individual behaviour of those immersed in these environments and may also call for ample changes in the internal communication of organisations. To accommodate this less hierarchical structure, people from different sectors in the enterprise have to be called to participate in meetings, their positioning being expected (Chapter 6 in this volume) rather than rejected. As an example, a young executive may be in charge of representing the company in important business transactions and she or he may be called to give her or his position to the company councillors. Along with these changes, language skills, in both oral and written business discourse, and expertise in new genres will be required from the employees as they participate in new social actions (Miller 1994). Academic research on these new scenarios and changing behaviours will probably need to be developed, for example the interactional impact of young executives' discourse during council meetings, generally composed of more traditional and older shareholders.

At the same time, these newly structured and stronger companies offer professionals more opportunities to develop their business careers, within their own organisations or outside them, in other positions which may be available in the market. In order to preserve staff within the organisation, those in power will have to pay attention to the work conditions they offer and will even tend to review their own perspectives on how to communicate with their employees, aiming at involving and pleasing them. A sudden need to involve and please those already in office and a search for new rhetorical ways to attract and persuade those willing to move from one organisation to another will have to be attended to. These new perspectives may also affect communication between people with different hierarchical positions in the organisation, that is, the way bosses and employees interact. In the traditional structuring, communication would be managed from the higher positions to the lower ones; in the redesigned organisations, more collaborative management implies the participation of all hierarchical levels (Souza-e-Silva 2002: 61) in communication practices.

Another noticeable change in the Brazilian entrepreneurial context is related to the previous predominance of oral communication over the production of written documents. Traditionally, much of the exchange in an organisational context could be carried out orally, especially in small corporations, and fewer documents were written. This condition has been changing, maybe as a response to influences coming from other organisational and social cultures, usually more bureaucratic, or to new practices that are introduced in the companies as they incorporate foreign staff. Consequently, new genres are required to register information in an attempt to facilitate communication between people from differ-ent language backgrounds who can follow more comfortably the unfolding of business if it is accompanied and supported by written texts. Reports, research memoranda, proposals and other types of documents seem to be more prominent in Brazilian organisations each day (Souza-e-Silva 2002: 61).

Challenges and implications for research

The academic discussion of business discourse research in Brazil faces some chal-lenges, such as the need to create more effective communication channels between the academy and the enterprise. If these discursively distinct groups try to make meaning out of each other's discourse, new links will be established, and the findings of academic research will have more opportunities to reach back to the scenarios where actual business discourse practices occur. In Brazil, these challenges are aggravated by a specific language problem: the striking differences between the complexity of academic written discourse in Portuguese (Oliveira 1999) and language used in other domains, such as business discourse. Brazilian researchers, especially applied linguists who produce most of the research on business discourse within the academic context, will possibly turn their interests in the near future towards the issues that have been creating difficulties for the transposition of the results of their studies to the business context (Oliveira 2006).

Another important challenge for Brazilian researchers has been the publication of research in international journals. As illustrated in this chapter, much research has been produced and published in Brazil about business communication. However, most of the theses, dissertations and academic articles have been written in Portuguese, a language that although spoken by millions of people around the world is not frequently accessible to the international academic community. At the same time, many Brazilian researchers, especially those who are just starting their academic careers, feel intimidated by the need to submit papers in English to international journals. In order to resolve this conflict, a new perspective needs to be considered. Yamuna Kachru, who sees the growth and impor-tance of all knowledge produced in the 'Expanding Circle' – that is, in countries where English is fast becoming a dominant second language in several fields including education, science, technology and business (Kachru 1999: 76) – proposes that, in order to facilitate the spread of this knowledge to the rest of the world, 'instead of putting all the responsibil-ity on the writers from the wider English-using world, it is desirable that the readers from the Inner Circle countries [which consists of native English-speaking countries] be willing to share the responsibility of making meaning' (Kachru 1999: 85). The adoption of such a perspective would indeed stimulate all those researchers in the Brazilian context to make their academic production available to the international scenario.

A final implication is related to theoretical and methodological approaches to business discourse analysis in Brazil. Should flexible and diversified approaches be maintained; that is, should different traditions of research enlighten this field? There is no clear answer to this question as research has to be free and attend to the demands of the communities where it is developed. However, we can analyse the issues implied in such a discussion. On the one hand, flexibility generates a variety that is rich but which makes it difficult to provide a precise characterisation of research trends. In this chapter, for example,

I have tried to show most of the theoretical and methodological tendencies present in the Brazilian context and to exemplify them through the studies developed by as many researchers as possible. However, because of the vastness of the scope to be covered, I am sure some representative research will have been left out. On the other hand, it is quite satisfying that such a variety of theoretical and methodological approaches be used in Brazil because it shows that Brazilian researchers in the area of business discourse are in unison with different perspectives developed in other cultural contexts and in several disciplinary scenarios.

This interdisciplinary and interdiscursive perspective of Brazilian business discourse research in Brazil is also coherent with the area where it first started, i.e. applied linguistics. Until the present moment most of this research is still developed by researchers who work in this area. And, as applied linguists are concerned with real-world language problems, they will possibly focus their research on the challenges related to the development of business discourse research in Brazil in the near future, such as the discursive relation between the academy and the business context and the internationalisation of nationally produced research.

References

Almeida, P. M. C. (2002) Atendimento de *check-in* de companhia aérea: Análise sistêmico-funcional de um gênero discursivo do português. MA dissertation, Department of Letters, Rio de Janeiro, Catholic University of Rio de Janeiro (PUC-Rio).

Bakhtin, M. (1992) *Estética da Criação Verbal*. São Paulo: Martins Fontes.

Barbara, L. (2001) Use and omission of personal pronouns in BP and in PP. Paper delivered at the Discourse, Communication and the Enterprise Conference, Lisbon, October.

Bargiela-Chiappini, F. (2005) Gerenciamento, cultura e discurso em administração internacional. In M. C. L. Oliveira, B. Hemais and B. L. Gunnarsson (eds), *Comunicação, Cultura e Interação em Contextos Organizacionais*. Rio de Janeiro: Papel Virtual Editora, pp. 19–42. (First published in M. Stroinska (ed.) (2001) *Relative Points of View: Linguistic Representations of Culture*. New York: Berghahn Books.)

Bastos, C. R. P. (2001) Estilo discursivo de liderança gerencial em atividades de fala problema-solução em reuniões empresariais. PhD thesis, Department of Letters, Rio de Janeiro, Catholic University of Rio de Janeiro (PUC-Rio).

Bastos, L. C. (2002) Construção e reconstrução de identidade em interações de trabalho. In M. C. P. Souza-e-Silva and D. Faita (eds), *Linguagem e Ttrabalho: Construção de Objetos de Análise no Brasil e na França*. São Paulo: Editora Cortez, pp. 159–74.

Biber, D. (1988) *Variation across Speech and Writing*. Cambridge: Cambridge University Press.

Biber, D. (1995) *Dimensions of Register Variation: A Cross-Linguistic Comparison*. Cambridge: Cambridge University Press.

Borges, E. A. V. B. (2007) Afinal, o que as suprevisoras acadêmicas fazem? Explorando o *backstage* de uma comunidade de prática. MA dissertation, Department of Letters, Rio de Janeiro, Catholic University of Rio de Janeiro (PUC-Rio).

Celani, M. A. A., A. F. Deyes, J. L. Holmes and M. R. Scott (2005) *ESP in Brazil: 25 Years of Evolution and Reflection*. São Paulo: Editora PUC/SP & Mercado das Letras.

Duarte, F. J. C. M., V. C. Rodrigues and D. Lima (2002) A construção da ação ergonômica no projeto de modernização de refinaria de petróleo: Análise das interações entre operadores, engenheiros e ergonomistas. In M. C. P. Souza-e-Silva and D. Faïta (eds), *Linguagem e Trabalho: Construção de Objetos de Análise no Brasil e na* França. São Paulo: Editora Cortez, pp. 209–35.

Gago, P. C (2002) A cooperação em uma reunião portuguesa de negociação. PhD thesis, Department of Letters, Rio de Janeiro, Catholic University of Rio de Janeiro (PUC-Rio).

Garcez, P. M. (1993) Point-making styles in cross-cultural business negotiation: A micro ethnographic study. *English for Specific Purposes*, 12(2): 103–20.

Halliday, M. A.K. and R. Hasan (1989) *Language, Context, and Text: Aspects of Language in a Social-Semiotic Perspective*. Oxford: Oxford University Press.

Hofstede, G. (1997) *Cultures and Organizations: Software of the Mind*. New York: McGraw-Hill.

Ikeda, S. N. (2001) Establishing condition in speech in a managerial meeting. Paper delivered at the Discourse, Communication and the Enterprise Conference, Lisbon, October.

Kachru, Y. (1999) Culture, context and writing. In E. Hinkel (ed.), *Culture in Second Language Teaching and Learning*. Cambridge: Cambridge University Press, pp. 75–89.

Karwoski, A. M., B. Gaydeczka and K. Brito (eds) (2006) *Gêneros Textuais: Reflexões e Ensino*. Rio de Janeiro: Editora Lucerna.

McGroarty, M. (2002) Language uses in professional contexts. In R. Kaplan (ed.), *The Oxford Handbook of Applied Linguistics*. Oxford: Oxford University Press, pp. 262–74.

Machado, A. R. (ed.) (2004) *O Ensino como Trabalho: Uma Abordagem Discursiva*. Londrina: Editora da Universidade de Londrina.

Marcuschi, L. A. and A. C. Xavier (eds) (2005) *Hipertexto e Gêneros Digitais:Novas Formas de Construção do Sentido*. Rio de Janeiro: Lucerna.

Martin, J. (1997) Analysing genre: Functional parameters. In F. Christie and J. Martin (eds), *Genres and Institutions: Social Processes in the Workplace and School*. London: Cassell, pp. 3–39.

Matheus, A. A. (2002) Estruturas de participação em reuniões empresariais realizadas entre um cliente da categoria *shopping center* e uma empresa prestadora de serviços da área de publicidade. MA dissertation, Department of Letters, Rio de Janeiro, Catholic University of Rio de Janeiro (PUC-Rio).

Meurer, J. L. and D. Motta-Roth (eds) (2002) *Gêneros Textuais ePráticas Discursivas*. São Paulo: EDUSC.

Miller, C. (1994) Genre as social action. In A. Freedman and P. Medway (eds), *Genre and the New Rhetoric*. London: Taylor & Francis, pp. 23–42.

Miller, I. K. (2001) Researching teacher consultancy via exploratory practice: A reflexive and socio-interactional approach. PhD thesis, Lancaster University.

Nouroudine, A. (2002) A linguagem: Dispositivo revelador da complexidade do trabalho. In M. C. P Souza-e-Silva and D. Faita (eds), *Linguagem e Trabalho: Construção de Objetos de Análise no Brasil e na França*. São Paulo: Editora Cortez, pp. 17–30.

Oliveira, L. P. (1999) Cross-cultural complexity level variation in written discourse styles.

Paper delivered at the American Association for Applied Linguistics Conference (AAAL), Stamford, USA.

Oliveira, L. P. (2002) Explicitação do contexto em textos de alunos brasileiros e americanos. *Palavra*, 8: 102–16.

Oliveira, L. P. (2006) Grammatical metaphor in research articles: Linguistic and disciplinary contrasts. Paper delivered at the American Association for Applied Linguistics and the Canadian Association for Applied Linguistics Conference (AAAL/CAAL), Montreal, Canada.

Oliveira, L. P. (forthcoming) Involvement variation in the writing of academics: A cross-cultural analysis of three genres. *International Journal of Corpus Linguistics*.

Oliveira, L. P., M. C. L. Oliveira and M. G. D. Pereira (2005) Práticas comunicativas e variação cultural em reuniões empresariais brasileiras: Percepções e reflexões. In M. C. L. Oliveira, B. Hemais and B. L Gunnarsson (eds), *Comunicação, Cultura e Interação em Contextos Organizacionais*. Rio de Janeiro: Papel Virtual Editora, pp. 211–48.

Oliveira, M. C. L. (2001) Language, technology and late modernity: A study of interaction in a call center. Plenary speech delivered at the Discourse, Communication and the Enterprise Conference, Lisbon, October.

Oliveira, M. C. L., E. Pedro and L. Barbara (1999a) Discurso e prática sócio-cultural em empresas luso-brasileiras. Project presented to the Coordination for the Qualification of Higher Education Professionals (CAPES/Brazil) and the Institute of Scientific and Technological International Cooperation (ICCTI/Portugal), Rio de Janeiro, Brazil, and Lisbon, Portugal.

Oliveira, M. C. L., M. G. D. Pereira and L. P. Oliveira (1999b) Brasil e Portugal: Até que ponto iguais, até que ponto diferentes. Paper delivered at the 6th Conference of the International Association for Studies of Portuguese (AIL), August. http://www.geocities.com/ail_br/ail.html.

Oliveira, M. C. L., B. Hemais and B. L. Gunnarsson (eds) (2005) *Comunicação, Cultura e Interação em Contextos Organizacionais*. Rio de Janeiro: Papel Virtual Editora.

Pereira, M. G. D. (2002a) Construção da identidade gerencial masculina no jogo interpessoal das emoções em uma reunião empresarial. In M. C. P. Souza-e-Silva and D. Faita (eds), *Linguagem e Trabalho: Construção de Objetos de Análise no Brasil e na França*. São Paulo: Editora Cortez, pp. 175–91.

Pereira, M. G. D. (2002b) Interação e discurso: Estudos na perspectiva da sociolingüística interacional/áreas de interface. *Palavra*, 8, 7–25.

Ribeiro, B. T. and P. Garcez (eds) (1998) *Sociolingüística Interacional: Antropologia, Lingüística e Sociologia em Análise do Discurso*. Porto Alegre: AGE Editora.

Santos, V. B. P. (2001) 'No' in organizational documents: The negative form as evaluation. Paper delivered at the Discourse, Communication and the Enterprise Conference, Lisbon, October.

Scollon, R. and S. W. Scollon (1995) *Intercultural Communication*. Oxford: Blackwell.

Silveira, S. B. (2001) Mediation strategies in institutional confrontation setting. Paper delivered at the Discourse, Communication and the Enterprise Conference, Lisbon, October.

Silvestre, M. C. and A. Marques (2005) Company meetings: Gender perceptions and attitudes beyond the dominance and difference theories. Paper delivered at the III Discourse, Communication and the Enterprise Conference, Rio de Janeiro, September.

Souza-e-Silva, M. C. P (2002) A dimensão linguageira em situações de trabalho. In M. C. P Souza-e-Silva and D. Faïta (eds), *Linguagem e Trabalho: Construção de Objetos de Análise no Brasil e na França*. São Paulo: Editora Cortez, pp. 61–76.

Souza-e-Silva, M. C. P and D. Faïta (eds) (2002) *Linguagem e Trabalho: Construção de Objetos de Análise no Brasil e na França*. São Paulo: Editora Cortez.

Souza-e-Silva, M. C. P. and A. R. Machado (eds) (1998) Interação em situação de trabalho: A política de comunicação do jornal interno de uma instituição privada. the *ESPecialist*, 19 (special issue).

Swales, J. (1990) *Genre Analysis*. Cambridge: Cambridge University Press.

Trompenaars, F. and C. Hampden-Turner (1998) *Riding the Waves of Culture: Understanding Diversity in Global Business*. New York: McGraw-Hill.

Vian, Jr., O. (2003) O ensino de inglês instrumental para negócios, a lingüística sistêmico-funcional e a teoria de gêneros/registro. the *ESPecialist*, 24(1): 1–16.

31

Spain

Estrella Montolío and Fernando Ramallo

Introduction

Until very recently, the research conducted in Spain on business discourse has been the preserve of specialists based in the faculties of economic and business science and in business colleges. Only over the past few years has the analysis of authentic data been undertaken in linguistics. In fact, the unresolved issue and priority task now, in this field of research, is to design and obtain a sufficiently representative corpus of documents and real interactions acquired in organisations that will allow researchers to carry out empirical studies (Bargiela-Chiappini et al. 2007).

To date, this field of knowledge has, generally, been linked either with drafting manuals, guides, etc. on communications management in organisations or, alternatively, and increasingly so since the late 1990s, with teaching Spanish as a foreign language for specific purposes, taking into account the tremendous development of Spanish as an international language and, as a result, the needs of thousands of non-native Spanish students to learn how to use it in business contexts.

This chapter provides a critical review of the research in business discourse conducted in Spain, based on the analysis of the Spanish language of Spain's organisational and commercial contexts. The chapter is divided into three main sections and a brief conclusion. The first section opens with a review of the contributions on business interaction from a Spanish cultural perspective. The chapter highlights the fact that, unlike in other cultural traditions, academic researchers have only recently focused their attention on this issue. It goes on to show how, in fact, this field of research is currently reaching a consolidation stage in Spain.

We then review published works that analyse language uses in business contexts, underlining those which have made the most important contribution to the understanding of business interactions in the Spanish context. The chapter also shows the state of current research, describing the most relevant projects and the areas most frequently investigated while pointing out the main weaknesses. The section on future developments evaluates the future potential for business discourse research in Spain.

In summary, the chapter concludes that in view of the increasing strategic and economic importance of Spanish-speaking areas, business discourse should be taken into greater consideration by researchers studying communication in professional environments. Business discourse should be considered because of the need in the professional community for a solid description of the linguistic and pragmatic characteristics of the documents drafted in these contexts. Such a description is a necessary part of improving the design of these documents in the future. Furthermore, it is necessary to provide the numerous students of Spanish as a foreign language in professional environments with an accurate description of the language used in this field.

Background

The literature on business discourse in Spain shows two clear trends. There is a distinction to be made between, on the one hand, the work written by academics, based in business schools or universities (generally in the faculties of economics and management, psychology or communication sciences), which deals with theoretical frameworks grounded in their respective disciplines and which they use in their analyses, and on the other hand, work lacking any rigorous theoretical grounding, which can be termed 'airport bookshop information' or 'self-help style communication books'. The latter will not be covered in this review.

Focusing now on the academic literature, a further distinction can be drawn between work focusing on communication as an organisational feature, and a more recent and smaller literature centring on the analysis of the discourses in communicative events taking place in organisations. To date, the latter is attributable to a small number of linguists.

In turn, studies which include a linguistic dimension can be divided into two broad fields. On the one hand, those which include descriptive-type studies of the more frequent linguistic uses (grammatical, textual, genre, register and so on) in organisations. On the other hand, there is an increasing number of studies on teaching 'Spanish for business' to students of Spanish as a foreign language (E/FL), which understand Spanish business discourse as a particular type of discourse in the context of Spanish for specific purposes (ESP).

Communication in organisations: non-linguistic studies

There are numerous publications on several aspects of communication in organisations. They are the work of professionals mainly from the fields of public relations, marketing and advertising, communication sciences, journalism and audiovisual communication, psychology and economy and management.

In the majority of such works, there is a widespread omission of the theories, concepts or descriptive tools particular to linguistics, which is surprising when we consider that it is mainly through language that communication takes place. Other works, significantly less numerous, draw from linguistic theories, although always in conjunction with other analytical perspectives. An example of this is Alberto Pérez's (2001) encyclopedic work on communication strategies.

Works that make selective use of linguistic analytical frameworks and categories are, among others, the collection of articles by Bel Mallén (2004) on communication management; the handbooks by García Jiménez (1998), Ongallo (2000) and Pozo Lite

(2000) on internal communication and its management; the work of Sotelo Enríquez (2001) on institutional communication; and the more general volumes on communication in organisations by Martín Martín (1997), Piñuel Raigada (1997), Putnam et al. (2002) and Díez Ferreiro (2005). The collective volume edited by Losada Díaz (2006) deserves special mention for its comprehensive nature, covering several aspects of communication management in organisations, such as communicative auditing, corporate image, financial communication, etc. What all the works mentioned have in common is that they lack any linguist among their authors or editors.

Other works deal with communication tangentially, by studying other aspects of organisations. For example, Manuel and Martínez Vilanova (1995) look at negotiation strategies; Vilallonga (2003) describes the qualities that should be found in a good coach; Pérez-Fernández de Velasco (1996) describes management by processes, while some of the chapters in Vara et al. (2006) analyse communication in crisis situations. All of these studies give some consideration, albeit extremely peripheral, to communication strategies and mechanisms in organisations. Finally, attention is given to the recent work by Fernández Rodríguez (2007) on the ideology underlying company management and direction manuals produced by management gurus. This work is grounded on Sociology, particularly applying the discipline of 'Critical Managerial Studies'.

Discussion

In the following section, we present a brief description and appraisal of the most relevant works conducted from a linguistic perspective. Because of the brevity of this review, only works published in Spain or dealing with the peninsular variety of Spanish will be considered. This selection necessarily excludes research carried out on other geographical varieties of Spanish.

Works with a linguistic perspective

Studies of Spanish in business organisations have focused on describing the discursive genres and the different linguistic resources required to develop work activity in each sector. This includes designing documents, establishing a corporate style and standardising conflicting or new aspects of communication (e.g. terminology, punctuation, abbreviations, capital letters and other graphic resources etc.). The purposes and procedures for deployment of such knowledge vary considerably amongst training professionals, and include, for example, establishing standards and prescriptions, developing corporate images etc.

The economic sector and the type of organisation (public or private, small or large) engender important differences in the communicative needs and in the type of discourses produced. Generally speaking, more attention is paid to the linguistic aspects by companies whose product is basically discursive, e.g. the media, consultancy firms or lawyer's practices. In this regard, the different customer service areas in large corporations are those which, as could be expected, show a greater interest in the quality of the communicative inputs generated for their customers. On this issue, some regional autonomous communities in Spain have drawn up communication training manuals aimed at professionals in public administration whose task it is to provide customer service (Llacuna 1999). Furthermore, companies which develop highly regulated activities (industrial plants, pharmaceutical laboratories, banking and financial activity) have more needs for documentation than other businesses.

In order to meet the needs of business communication in Spain, rather than developing 'national' research projects, numerous Anglo-Saxon handbooks have been translated and adapted. The genres whose description has attracted most interest have been those circulars and calls for tender. It is in this latter field that there has been an attempt to find solutions for the most frequently arising problems (Botta 1994; Garrido 1994; López Nieto and Mayo 2001; Pastor 1994). Some of this published research includes genres which are much less described in the Spanish tradition, such as protocol models (congratulations, invitations), and, particularly, technical models (reports, standards, instruction manuals).

In the work just mentioned, reflections on language models, on the characteristics of the specialised audience and on the particularities of business communication are still infrequent. Worth mentioning also are Delisau (1986) and Sanz and Fraser (1998) – the latter analysing computer-mediated communication; the handbook by Portocarrero and Gironella (2001); and the analysis of specialised discourses by Golanó and Flores-Guerrero (2002). There is a need for more research on verbal communication in organisations, which is currently limited to the genre of presentations in public (see Merayo 1998).

Given the lack of specific guidelines for companies, it is common to use general writing manuals or journalistic style books, such as that of the Agencia EFE (a Spanish news agency), or those by the newspapers *ABC*, *La Vanguardia*, *El País*, *El Periódico de Catalunya* or *La Voz de Galicia*. Over the last few years, the strategy of drafting a company style manual has become a common practice in an attempt to standardise and regulate written communication, particularly in large or multinational companies such as La Caixa or La Caixa de Catalunya, but also in lawyers' practices such as the 2005 Garrigues Practice, and in some consultancy agencies.

The growing interest in linguistics by LSP (languages for specific purposes) specialists is echoed in the publication of a volume edited by Alcaraz et al. (2007) on professional and academic languages. This book includes only one chapter communication in business, which is restricted to aspects of intercultural communication. Lacorte's volume on applied linguistics in Spanish includes a general chapter on Spanish in work contexts (Cassany et al. 2007), with a section on Spanish in companies.

More relevant to business discourse are articles by Cassany (2003, 2004). In the latter, two discursive classifications are presented based, respectively, on the organisation's flowchart (formal/informal, horizontal/vertical etc.) and the communicative functions (technical-scientific discourses, organisational, commercial and protocol discourses).

Mention should be made here of the research carried out by Montolío (2006a, 2006b). In the first of these studies, an analysis is made of a case that illustrates the emerging role for professional development which, in the technological areas, is closely linked to communicative skills, especially those involving writing, because of the structural role of email communication. In the second study, Montolío analyses an aspect of communication that had never been investigated before, namely that of the argumentative strategies used by large corporations. The author looks at the argumentative strategies used by a small but growing presence in large Spanish companies, the Department of the Customer's Ombudsman. In Montolío (2007, 2008a, 2008b), the linguistic and sociopragmatic characteristics are described as well as the rhetorical strategies of a professional genre of great strategic and economic relevance, namely reports drafted by the consultants.

Using critical discourse analysis and ethnographic observation, Morales-López et al. (2005) and Prego-Vázquez (2007) have observed the management of communicative conflict in employee–client interactions in companies. They analyse the discursive reper-cussions of a change of management in a public service (in this case, a water company), from a municipal company to a semi-private firm. In the context of the professionalisation of management, the authors analyse the linguistic resources (e.g. politeness strategies, argumentative structures etc.) deployed in solving the conflicts arising in the interactions between consumers using the service and company employees. This research has had a practical spin-off, which has seen the authors becoming involved in making suggestions on the improvement of communication by managers in private companies (Morales-López et al. 2006).

One dimension of special interest in the linguistic studies of Spanish organisations is that of genre and communicative styles, an area which has been researched by Martín Rojo and his collaborators. Their work has provided a distinctive contribution to the analysis of the communicative styles of women managers. Analysis of the discursive practices and social representations that arise and circulate on the role of women in the workplace (Martín Rojo and Gómez Esteban 2003, 2004) shows that the relationship between male management models and female leadership roles is fraught with problems. The com-municative style traditionally associated with women, based on models of more indirect, democratic management, appears to be delegitimised not only by the men but also by the women themselves. When women assimilate a male, dominant, authoritarian communi-cative style, their move is rejected by the majority. In other words, 'women always have to "pay" for having power in the work context' (Martín Rojo and Gómez Esteban 2004: 77). These findings reflect women's difficult access to managerial positions in Spanish companies. According to statistics published by the Woman's Institute in 2006, only 9 per cent of the top positions and the directorships in large companies are held by women (Instituto de la Mujer 2007).

Sociolinguistic studies have been carried out on Spanish advertising in several bilin-gual regional communities within the Spanish state. For example, Ramallo and Rei Doval (1997) analyse the attitudes of consumers in Galicia towards the use of Spanish and also the discourse of men in twenty-seven companies in terms of the commercial value of competing languages.

Finally, the language of tourism (Calvi 2000, 2006) should be included in a review of Spanish business discourse, given the critical importance that the tourist sector has in the Spanish economy.

Research with an intercultural orientation

An intercultural analytical approach has been adopted in numerous areas of research which are grounded in linguistic analysis. One topic of such research is the differences in cultural conventions affecting written genres (Jansen and van Erkel 1996). Conversely, research into intercultural pragmatics in Spanish negotiations has shed light on the pecu-liarities of the Spanish negotiator. This intercultural perspective has been developed by Scandinavian Hispanists since the late 1980s, especially following the work of Lars Fant. A few of the studies use simulated negotiations (e.g. Bravo 1999; Fant 1989, 1992; Fant and Grindstead 1995; Grindsted 1997; Pair 2000; Villemoes 2003), although more recently, real interactions have also made an appearance (Kjaerbeck 2005; Fant 2006). Bravo (1999) analyses politeness management between Spanish and Swedish negotiators and the ways they use both verbal and nonverbal resources, for example laughter. Each group projects a different social image which, to a large extent, reflects cultural conditioning. Using conversation analysis, Fant (2006) proposes a series of five 'conversational dimensions' pertaining to intercultural negotiation – intensity, proximity, competitiveness, co-operativeness and self-assertiveness. Finally, Kjaerbeck (2005), under the INES project (International Negotiations in Spanish), examines the argumentative structure of emerging narrations in the field of negotiation, relating it to the construction of identities.

Simulated intercultural negotiations are analysed also by Ulijn and Verweij (2000). In their case, a detailed analysis is offered of the form and function of questions in business encounters between Dutch and Spaniards. The differences found are related to the cultural differences in managing queries and uncertainty arising in the course of negotiations.

It is a well known fact that advertising appeals to cultural preferences; hence the importance of investigating the intercultural management of advertising communication (Hooft 2006; Hooft and Wiskerke 2008). Hoeken et al. (2003) have taken the standardisation–adaptation debate as a starting point for intercultural communication in advertising, and have concentrated on the preferences expressed by Spaniards in the production of persuasive texts, in comparison with similar texts from Belgium, France and the Netherlands.

The intercultural approach is vital for business communication research, although it is essential to overcome the limiting essentialist notion of 'one state = one culture'. In the case of Spain, highly diverse cultural realities live side by side, which means that intercultural research should be based on a multicultural corpus that makes it possible to draw comparisons between different regions (Villemoes 2003).

Research with a pedagogic orientation: 'Business Spanish' for students of Spanish as a foreign language

In view of the expansion in recent years of the teaching and learning of Spanish as a foreign language at international level, and likewise, in view of the importance that the different fields of specialised knowledge are acquiring in the current knowledge society, it is expected that teaching Spanish for specific purposes will receive a considerable boost.

On the other hand, in the light of the unquestionable commercial interest that large Spanish-speaking areas such as Central and South America, as well as the large Hispanic community in the USA, hold for international business, it is equally expected that 'business Spanish' should rank high with students of Spanish as a foreign language (see for example the reports of the CIEFE International Congress of Spanish for Specific Purposes: Bordoy et al. 2000; Antonio et al. 2003).

Various manuals have been published presenting the learner with the characteristics of the most representative professional genres. These are necessarily simplified descriptions, which emphasise terminology and often use contrived data. The leading publishing houses in E/FL have catalogues with manuals of this type adapted to the different levels of competence in Spanish. General treaties have also been published, specifically aimed at E/FL teachers, for example the series Business Spanish (Arco/Libros) and the volumes by Felices Lago (2003), Tomás (2004) and Cabré and Gómez de Enterría (2006).

Future developments

Business discourse research has a promising future in Spain. The fact that linguistics has started to get to grips with the field has promoted a better awareness of the object of the study. It is still early days to talk about schools of thought, although there are research groups whose priorities include the description and analysis of the linguistic-communicative processes involving managers in companies. Although research in the area is promising, it is as yet in its infancy. There is a need to broaden the corpuses of authentic oral and written texts. This will make it possible to work from perspectives related to discourse analysis such as pragmatics, politeness, interactional analysis, conversation analysis and critical discourse analysis.

Furthermore, since quality has become a priority business objective, research is required that evaluates the quality of communication. It is also appropriate in future research projects for linguists to become involved with managers, thus enabling them to gain first-hand knowledge of the communicative characteristics of the production context. In this way, linguists will be able to (1) access the managers' discursive knowledge of their work environment, and (2) minimise, where possible, an analyst's interpretation which ignores context. Also, it is essential to foster a multimodal approach to business discourse, incorporating multiple dimensions of sense-making in the analysis of complex texts, especially in the field of e-commerce.

Discourse analysts should act in synergy with specialists in the other disciplines who are also involved in researching communication in the corporate field, such as economists, sociologists and psychologists.

One significant piece of information which allows us to assess the development of the field of 'business discourse' in Spain emerges from collegial exchange at conferences. In particular, we refer to the Second International Conference on 'Discourse, Communication and the Enterprise', held in November 2003 at the University of Vigo in northwest Spain. At this event, over fifty papers were presented: only eight came from Spanish researchers, and out of these, only three dealt with Spanish (Ramallo et al. 2006).

One particularly interesting line of research is the bilingualism of the regions within the Spanish state. In communities where Spanish comes into contact with autochthonous languages, such as Galician, Catalan or Basque, bilingual corpuses are needed that have been gathered in bilingual environments. The analysis of code-switching, code alternation, politeness phenomena linked to language shift and to other phenomena arising from languages in contact can shed light on the diversity of business genres in these contexts, especially negotiations.

Moreover, in terms of linguistic variation, it is appropriate for future research to focus on the consequences of the coexistence of multiple geographic varieties of Spanish in urban centres, due to the recent, widespread phenomenon of immigration from South America.

Conclusion

Throughout this chapter, we have sought to give a general overview of the situation of research related to the use of Spanish in business contexts in Spain. We have highlighted the fact that we are looking at a field of study with many dimensions and that the linguistic one remains underdeveloped. Only recently has there been a change in the orientation of research, away from business Spanish for the LSP community and towards projects grounded in linguistics. Initial projects using a corpus of Spanish business discourses, which includes oral and written genres, have made it possible to conduct analysis from a pragmatic-discursive perspective.

In view of the relevance of Spanish world-wide, the collection of data in actual business contexts will also benefit the field of Spanish for specific purposes and of Spanish as an international language.

References

Alberto Pérez, R. (2001) *Estrategias de comunicación*. Barcelona: Ariel.

Alcaraz, E., J. Mateo and F. Yus (eds) (2007) *Lenguas profesionales y académicas*. Barcelona: Ariel.

Antonio, V. de., R. Cuesta, A. van Hooft, B. de Jonge, J. Robisco and M. Ruiz (eds) (2003) *Español para fines específicos: Actas del II CIEFE* (Amsterdam 2003). Madrid: Ministerio de Educación y Ciencia.

Bargiela-Chiappini, F., C. Nickerson and B. Planken (2007) *Business Discourse*. Basingstoke: Palgrave Macmillan.

Bel Mallén, J. I. (ed.) (2004) *Comunicar para crear valor: La dirección de comunicación en las organizaciones*. Pamplona: EUNSA.

Bordoy, M., A. van Hooft and A. Sequeros (eds) (2000) *Español para fines específicos: Actas del I CIEFE (Congreso Internacional de Español para fines específicos)* (Amsterdam 2000). Madrid: Ministerio de Educación, Cultura y Deporte.

Botta, M. (1994) *Comunicaciones escritas en la empresa*. Barcelona: Granica.

Bravo, D. (1999) '¿Imagen 'positiva' vs. imagen 'negativa'?: Pragmática sociocultural y componentes de *face*'. *Oralia*, 2: 155–84.

Cabré, M. T. and J. Gómez de Enterría (2006) *Lenguajes de especialidad y enseñanza de lenguas: La simulación global*. Madrid: Gredos.

Calvi, M. V. (2000) *Il linguaggio spagnolo del turismo*. Viareggio: Baroni.

Calvi, M. V. (2006) *Lengua y comunicación en el español del turismo*. Madrid: Alianza.

Cassany, D. (2003) Comunicación escrita en la empresa: Investigaciones, intervenciones y ejemplos. *Anagramas*, 2: 33–51.

Cassany, D. (2004) Explorando los discursos de las organizaciones. *Foro Hispánico*, 26: 40–60.

Cassany, D., C. Gelpí and C. López Ferrero (2007) El español en contextos laborales. In M. Lacorte (ed.), *Lingüística aplicada del español*. Madrid: Arco/Libros, pp. 449–79.

Delisau, S. (1986) *Las comunicaciones escritas en la empresa*. Barcelona: De Vecchi.

Díez Ferreiro, S. (2005) *Técnicas de comunicación en la empresa*. Vigo: Ideaspropias Editorial.

Fant, L. (1989) Cultural mismatch in conversations: Spanish and Scandinavian communicative behaviour in negotiations settings. *Hermes: Journal of Linguistics*, 3: 247–65.

Fant, L. (1992) Scandinavian and Spaniards in negotiation. In A. Sjögren and L. Janson (eds), *Culture and Management: In the Field of Ethnology and Business Administration*. Stockholm: Swedish Immigration Institute and Museum/Stockholm School of Economics, Institute of International Business, pp. 125–53.

Fant, L. (2006) National cultural norms or activity type conventions? Negotiation talk and informal conversation among Swedes and Spaniards. *Synaps*, 19: 1–22.

Fant, L. and A. Grindstead (1995) Conflict and consensus in Spanish vs. Scandinavian negotiation interaction. *Hermes: Journal of Linguistics*, 15: 111–41.

Fernández Rodríguez, C. J. (2007) *El discurso del management: tiempo y narración*. Madrid: Centro de Investigaciones Sociológicas.

Felices Lago, Á. M. (ed.) (2003) *Cultura y negocios: El español de la economía española y latinoamericana*. Madrid: Edinumen.

García Jiménez, J. (1998) *La comunicación interna*. Madrid: Díaz de Santos.

Garrido, C. (1994) *Manual de correspondencia comercial moderna*. Barcelona: De Vecchi.

Golanó, C. and R. Flores Guerrero (2002) *Aprender a redactar textos empresariales*. Barcelona: Paidós.

Grindsted, A. (1997) Joking as a strategy in Spanish and Danish negotiations. In F. Bargiela-Chiappini and S. Harris (eds), *The Language of Business*. Edinburgh: Edinburgh University Press, pp. 159–82.

Hoeken, H., C. van den Brant, R Crijns, N. Domínguez, B. Planken and M. Starren (2003) International advertising in western Europe: Should differences in uncertainty avoidance be considered when advertising in Belgium, France, the Netherlands and Spain? *Journal of Business Communication*, 40(3): 195–218.

Hooft, A. van (2006) El valor añadido de los anglicismos en la publicidad española: El impacto y la valoración social de las voces inglesas en los anuncios de la revista *Elle*. In M. V. Calvi and L. Chierichetti (eds), *Nuevas tendencias en el discurso de especialidad*. Frankfurt: Peter Lang, pp. 219–43.

Hooft, A. van and L. Wiskerke (2008) El fracaso de tres logotipos internacionales como comunicadores de los valores corporativos. In M. V. Calvi, G. Mapelli and J. Santos López (eds), *Lingua, culture, economia: Communicazione e pratiche discursive*. Milan: Franco Angeli, pp. 289–98.

Instituto de la Mujer (2007) Instituto de la Mujer, Ministerio de Igualdad. http://www.migualdad.es/mujer. Accessed April 2007.

Jansen, C. and A. J. van Erkel (1996) Instructional documents in Spanish and Dutch: Do they really differ? In T. Ensink and C. Saur (eds), *Reaserching Technical Documents*. Groningen: University of Groningen, pp. 69–86.

Kjaerbeck, S. (2005) Narratives in talk-in-interaction: Organization and construction of cultural identities. In B. Preisler, A. Fabricius, H. Haberland, S. Kjaerbeck and K. Risager (eds), *The Consequences of Mobility*. Roskilde: Roskilde University, pp. 45–57.

Llacuna, J. (1999) *Curso de comunicación y atención al ciudadano: Nivel básico y nivel medio*. Seville: Junta de Andalucía.

López Nieto, F. and F. Mayo (2001) *Escriba esa carta!* Barcelona: Gedisa.

Losada Díaz, J. C. (ed.) (2006) *Gestión de la comunicación en las organizaciones*. Barcelona: Ariel.

Manuel, F. and R. Martínez Vilanova (1995) *Comunicación y negociación comercial*. Madrid: ESIC.

Martín Martín, F. (1997) *Comunicación en empresas e instituciones: De la consultora a la dirección de comunicación*. Salamanca: Ediciones de la Universidad de Salamanca.

Martín Rojo, L. and C. Gómez Esteban (2003) Discourse at work: When women take on the role of manager. In G. Weis and R. Wodak (eds), *Critical Discourse Analysis: Theory and Interdisciplinarity*. London: Palgrave, pp. 241–71.

Martín Rojo, L. and C. Gómez Esteban (2004) The gender of power: The female style in labour organizations. In M. Lazar (ed.), *Feminist Critical Discourse Analysis*. London: Palgrave, pp. 61–89.

Merayo, A. (1998) *Curso práctico de técnicas de comunicación oral*. Madrid: Tecnos.

Montolío, E. (2006a) De técnicos informáticos a gestores de proyectos informáticos: La comunicación escrita como factor crítico de desarrollo profesional. El caso de los informáticos de *la Caixa*. In F. Ramallo, A. M. Lorenzo and X. P. Rodríguez-Yáñez (eds), *Discourse and Enterprise: Communication, Business, Management and other Professional Fields*. Munich: Lincom, pp. 23–36.

Montolío, E. (2006b) Estrategias argumentativas en las corporaciones: El caso de la Oficina del Defensor del Cliente de ENDESA. In N. Alturo, J. Besa, O Bladas and N. Nogué (eds), *L'Argumentació*. Barcelona: Promociones y Publicaciones Universitarias, pp. 181–208.

Montolío, E. (2007) Advising without committing: The use of argumentative reservation in texts written by consultants. In S. Sarangi and G. Garzone (eds), *Discourse, Ideology and Specialized Communication*. Bern: Peter Lang, pp. 251–75.

Montolío, E. (2008a) El informe de consultoría: Un género textual para la toma de decisiones. In M. V. Calvi, G. Mapelli and J. Santos López (eds), *Lingua, culture, economia: Communicazione e pratiche discursive*. Milan: Franco Angeli, pp. 213–28.

Montolío, E. (2008b) Consultors i lingüistes: Quan el producte de l'empresa és un text. *Llengua, Societat i Comunicació*, 6 (special issue), available at http://www.ub.edu_/cusc/LSC/articles/montolio.pdf

Morales-López, E., G. Prego-Vázquez and L. Domínguez-Seco (2005) Interviews between employees and customers during a company restructuring process. *Discourse & Society*, 16(2): 225–68.

Morales-López, E., G. Prego-Vázquez and L. Domínguez-Seco (2006) *El conflicto comunicativo en las empresas desde el análisis del discurso*. Coruña: Universidade da Coruña.

Ongallo, C. (2000) *Manual de comunicación: Guía para gestionar el conocimiento, la información y las relaciones humanas en empresas y organizaciones*. Madrid: Dykinson.

Pair, R. le (2000) Communication strategies: Politeness in Spanish requests. In R. Geluykens and K. Pelsmakers (eds), *Discourse in Professional Contexts*. Munich: Lincom, pp. 143–65.

Pastor, E. (1994) *Escribir cartas*. Barcelona: Difusión.

Pérez-Fernández de Velasco, J. A. (1996) *Gestión por procesos: Reingeniería y mejora de los procesos de la empresa*. Madrid: ESIC Editorial.

Piñuel Raigada, J. L. (1997) *Teoría de la comunicación y gestión de las organizaciones*. Madrid: Síntesis.

Portocarrero, M. and N. Gironella (2001) *La escritura rentable: La eficacia de la palabra en la empresa*. Madrid: SM.

Pozo Lite, M. (2000) *Gestión de la comunicación en las organizaciones: Casos de empresa*. Pamplona: Ediciones de la Universidad de Navarra.

Prego-Vázquez, G. (2007) Frame conflict and social inequality in the workplace: Professional and local discourse struggles in employee/customer interactions. *Discourse & Society*, 18(3): 295–335.

Putnam, L., J. Costa and F. J. Garrido (2002) *Comunicación empresarial*. Barcelona: Gestión 2000.

Ramallo, F. and G. Rei Doval (1997) *Vender en galego: Comunicación, empresa e lingua en Galicia*. Santiago: Consello da Cultura Galega.

Ramallo, F., A. M. Lorenzo and X. P. Rodríguez-Yáñez (eds) (2006) *Discourse and Enterprise: Communication, Business, Management and other Professional Fields*. Munich: Lincom.

Sanz, G. and A. Fraser (1998) *Manual de comunicaciones escritas en la empresa*. Barcelona: Graó.

Sotelo Enríquez, C. (2001) *La comunicación institucional*. Barcelona: Ariel.

Tomás, J. M de (2004) La enseñanza del español comercial. In J. Sánchez Lobato and I. Santos Gargallo (eds), *Vademécum para la formación de profesores: Enseñar español como segunda lengua (L2)/lengua extranjera (LE)*. Madrid: Segel, pp. 1149–63.

Ulijn, J. M. and M. J. Verweij (2000) Questioning behaviour in monocultural and inter-cultural technical business negotiations: The Dutch–Spanish connection. *Discourse Studies*, 2(2): 217–48.

Vara, A., J. R. Virgili, E. Giménez and M. Díaz (eds) (2006) *La comunicación en situación de crisis: Del 11-M al 14-M*. Pamplona: Ediciones de la Universidad de Navarra.

Vilallonga, M. (2003) Cualidades de un buen *Coach*. In M. Vilallonga (ed.), *Coaching directivos: Desarrollando el liderazgo. Fundamentos y práctica del coaching*. Barcelona: Ariel, pp. 89–110.

Villemoes, A. (2003) How do southern Spaniards create the conditions necessary to initiate negotiations with strangers? *Hermes: Journal of Linguistics*, 31:119–34.

32

Francophone research

Laurent Filliettaz and Ingrid de Saint-Georges

Introduction

In the Francophone literature, the term 'business discourse' is seldom used to describe the domain of applied linguistics devoted to the study of work (Bargiela-Chiappini et al. 2007). Instead, authors usually refer to their area of research in a more general way, as being related to 'language and work' (*langage et travail*). This reflects the fact that research on business discourse in the Francophone area tends to be affiliated with a disciplinary field called 'work analysis' (*analyse du travail*) or 'activity analysis' (*analyse de l'activité*), namely an interdisciplinary domain of research and counselling practices not originally linked to language sciences but to which linguistics has contributed in an important way during the past few years.

From a theoretical point of view, 'work analysts' are primarily interested in understanding the complexities of contemporary forms of work. They also share an interest in implementing organisational changes, and in contributing to the personal development of workers in their professional environments. The orientation taken is thus not to study work from a managerial perspective (with a focus on explicit rules or evaluations that would be prescribed by the management), but from the point of view of ordinary workers responsible for acting in the workplace.

The goal of this chapter is to introduce the area of 'language and work' (*langage et travail*) developed within this Francophone tradition, and to discuss some of its main findings. To do so, we begin by contexualising the 'language and work' paradigm historically. Next, we describe some of the methodological orientations of that field and some of its findings. And finally, we discuss some of the methodological and epistemological implications of studying jointly language and work for applied linguistics today.

From business to work: the Francophone perspective

'Work analysis' is a label for a disciplinary field that began to develop in the Francophone area in the early 1960s and encompasses research, training and consulting activities that progressively proposed a renewed approach to the problem of labour. The field's original aim was to help manual labourers cope with new work contingencies associated with modern forms of the industrial economy. Among work analysts, one common assumption is that in order to 'transform' situations at work which appear problematic, researchers must first attempt to 'understand' these situations in all their complexities (Guérin et al. 1997). To reach such a detailed understanding, they draw concepts and methodologies from psychology (Dejours 1999; Clot 1999), French ergonomics (Ombredane and Faverge 1955; Daniellou 1996), economics, sociology and linguistics. They also study the workers' activities as they are accomplished in concrete work environments such as the manufacturing industry, the nuclear industry, or various service-oriented firms or institutions.

An important theoretical distinction brought forth through this study of actual work practices is the observation that a gap necessarily exists between 'prescribed work' (*le travail prescrit*) and 'accomplished work' (*le travail réel*). 'Prescribed work' refers to a task as it is supposed to be done and as it might be conceived by managers. In contrast, 'accomplished work' refers to real action as it is actually performed (or not) by workers in concrete production conditions. Work analysts do not aim at bridging the gap between these two distinct poles and find solutions to help workers accomplish work as it is prescribed by organisations. On the contrary, they view these poles as complementary elements of the workplace and necessary components of the workers' personal or professional development. In this perspective, work analysts do not privilege the work of managing instances or rely exclusively on the idea of 'business'. Rather, they focus on the workers and their ordinary activities, examine the creativity they show when faced with problematic situations, the strategies they deploy to adapt to organisational changes or the way they cope with psychological strains.

We have outlined in detail some salient properties of the Francophone approach to work analysis because, since the 1980s, a number of linguists have begun to contribute actively to its research programme, with a specific interest in investigating the use and impact of language in workplace settings. The Language and Work Network (Réseau Langage et Travail; see http:www.langage.travail.crg.polytechnique.fr) did pioneering work in this domain. It is a group bringing together specialists from various disciplines (labour psychology, organisational sociology, sociolinguistics, discourse analysis, anthropology, economics) interested in the role of language in professional environments. The contributions of this network can be found in several collective books, which summarise the major results accomplished in the field so far (e.g. Boutet 1995; Grosjean and Lacoste 1999; Borzeix and Fraenkel 2001; Pène et al. 2001). Interested readers will find in Borzeix and Fraenkel (2001) the most recent and complete overview of the studies conducted so far by this network.

Because of space constraints, the abundant research produced by this network cannot be presented here in any exhaustive fashion. Four important orientations can nevertheless be highlighted. They are discussed below.

The status of language in contemporary work organisations

Through the detailed analysis of activity in workplace settings, the Language and Work Network has investigated the changing place of language in the contemporary workplace. Researchers have first observed that language and other forms of semiotic mediations are becoming increasingly central in the workplace (e.g. reading control screens, sending computerised instructions etc.) even in jobs where direct manual manipulation and physical engagement were intensely used in the past. They have also pointed to the growing importance of language in a service-oriented economy: while tasks are becoming ever more complex, they also occur in environments that are more multilingual and multicultural than in the past (Boutet and Gardin 2001; Zarifian 2001). And finally, they have brought to light the emergence of a 'reflexive turn' in the workplace. Beyond the usual requirement that workers perform their work adequately, there seems to be a growing tendency to ask them also to be able to account for their work and to put into words their skills in the contexts of training programmes or evaluation procedures. All these observations point to the increasing role of language in work activities and call for the study of its functions as a key dimension of professional practice.

Addressing concrete issues and problems arising in different professional settings

A second prominent characteristic of the approach proposed by the Language and Work Network has consisted in responding to calls from various professional groups (public administration, transportation industry, hospitals etc.) with the view of acting upon problematic situations in order to transform them (e.g. improving service quality, developing on-the-job training practices, improving motivation and personal development at work etc.). Since the nature of the issues for which their expertise is required is highly complex, researchers with this orientation have chosen to combine linguistic approaches with nonlinguistic methodologies. They have thus contributed to building bridges between the field of linguistics and that of labour studies.

The forms of language used at and about work

A third orientation has been concerned with the textual and linguistic properties of oral and written discourses in the workplace. Some studies have, for instance, focused on work situations where language is central, such as in team meetings, face-to-face interactions, gatekeeping encounters etc. In contrast, others have analysed situations where language is only part of a larger stream of nonverbal activities. Relying on empirical material documenting actual language use in the workplace, researchers have analysed various forms of discourse using a vast array of methodological tools, from those classically used in business discourse research in the Anglo-Saxon tradition (e.g. pragmatics, conversation analysis, interactional sociolinguistics, ethnography of communication or corpus linguistics) to approaches anchored more specifically within the Francophone discourse analytical tradition (e.g. Benveniste's and Culioli's theory of enunciative operations; Pêcheux's or Foucault's studies of discursive formation).

The functions of language in the workplace

More generally, the Francophone Language and Work Network has reflected upon the uses of language at work, providing different taxonomies for these uses (Lacoste 1995, 2001). Briefly summarised, it proposes that language simultaneously fulfils *pragmatic*, *contextual*, *relational* and *cognitive* functions. First, language plays a *pragmatic* role in the workplace in the sense that it allows workers to accomplish and evaluate specific units of action. Language also fulfils *contextual* functions, enabling workers to interpret situations as well as to coordinate, plan or orient activities or participation within workplace environments. Language has, moreover, *relational* functions. It mediates social networks, power relations or identity construction. Finally, it also fulfils *cognitive* functions, allowing, among others, collective reasoning, problem-solving, knowledge transmission and construction, memorisation, and the spreading of information.

The initial founders of the Language and Work Network have clearly played a prominent role in structuring the Francophone field of business discourse. Other researchers have, however, contributed to its development over the years too. In the next section, we describe briefly some lines of investigations pursued by this larger circle of researchers. Their work often shares many epistemological assumptions with the pioneering work of the Language and Work Network, but without necessarily claiming affiliation to it.

Some methodological orientations and empirical findings

One classical way to categorise research is to examine the types of linguistic phenomena on which the authors focus. Do they focus on situations where language is a central dimension of work? Or do they focus on research interviews or other methodologies for accessing individual or collective representations of work? Depending on the perspective, a distinction can be made between research interested in 'language *at* work', 'language *about* work' and a combination of both. We explore these three dimensions in the following subsections. Again, the existing literature cannot be reviewed exhaustively in this chapter. We thus propose a few pointers for each orientation, detailing briefly the methodological tools used for the analyses, the kinds of professional domains investigated and the main findings published so far. Interested readers can refer to Filliettaz and Bronckart (2005) for a more detailed overview of relevant empirical studies.

Researching the field of language 'at' work

Of the three orientations mentioned above, the field of language 'at' work has probably been the most fertile since the late 1980s. Traditionally set within the frames of ethnomethodology, sociolinguistics or the micro-sociology of Erving Goffman, the research aimed at developing a better understanding of the relations between discourse practices and work activities. Different issues have been addressed in this area.

Coordination and co-operation in collective activities

This theme has been investigated in a vast array of professional settings, ranging from surgical operations (Mondada 2001, 2004a) to nursing (Grosjean and Lacoste 1999), museum design (Mondada 2005a), industrial production (Filliettaz 2005a), team meetings (Mondada 2004b, 2006; Filliettaz 2007) and research meetings (Mondada 2005b). These studies have paid special attention to the use of technological tools in the accomplishment of work. More specifically, they have reflected on the complexities of professional practices when they are collectively accomplished. As shown empirically, coordinating activities is a complex endeavour, for at least three reasons that have been clearly identified by many Francophone authors:

1   Coordination results from the local and sequential organisation of interactions, and from the multimodal resources available to accomplish such interactions. Studies show, for example, that workers cannot rely on verbal utterances alone to coordinate participation at a local level. They need to combine a variety of semiotic and material resources, such as gestures, movements in space, the manipulation of objects etc. These resources do not necessarily exist prior to their actual use but emerge as constructions that workers produce jointly in and through their situated interactions.
2   Workplace interactions are multifocused. In most professional settings, workers are constantly engaged in multiple tasks, whether alternatively or simultaneously.
3   Coordination does not occur exclusively in locally situated actions but also at an institutional level. Grosjean and Lacoste (1999) show, for example, that while an important part of nurses' work consists in engaging in situated joint actions (such as caring for patients, having coordination meetings with other nurses etc.), their work involves engagement beyond the local here and now. It requires, among other aspects, examining the *trajectory* of care for each patient and weaving links between local situations and the history of the patient in the institution.

Negotiation and decision-making

Grosjean and Mondada (2005) bring together studies describing negotiation processes in different professional environments (service encounters, public administration, shops etc.). The collective volume shows that deliberating practices are central in many professional activities. It also stresses the importance of studying such practices from a linguistic perspective. Other authors focus more specifically on the cognitive aspects of decision-making within groups. Detailed analyses of verbal exchanges are used to describe the mechanisms of collective reasoning. Theoretically, these studies borrow tools and concepts from interactional psychology, conversation analysis and speech act theory. The data relates to the study of coordination meeting in industrial settings (Grusenmeyer and Trognon 1995), negotiations and decision-making in hospital talk (Trognon and Kostulski 1996), and the study of genetic counselling sessions (Trognon and Batt 2006).

Interpersonal relations and identities

Studies addressing this theme focus primarily on service encounters, whether in retail stores (Kerbrat-Orecchioni and Traverso 2008; Kerbrat-Orecchioni 2001; Traverso 2001; Dumas 2005; Doury 2001; Filliettaz 2002, 2004a, 2004b, 2005b, 2006), call centres (Boutet 2006) or housing management (Cooren and Robichaud 2006). They highlight the view that interpersonal relations at work are often asymmetric and that language plays an important role in managing this asymmetry (Laforest and Vincent 2006). Moreover, researchers investigating this field often describe the difficulty for professionals in enacting the role of expert in service encounters, particularly when clients challenge this expertise or when contradictory institutional demands are made upon them. Another fruitful area in the analysis of service encounters can be found in studies on politeness conducted at the University of Lyon 2 by Catherine Kerbrat-Orecchioni and her team. Studies concerned with analysing interpersonal relations and identities have contributed to discuss the distinction between 'functional communication' and 'relational communication'. Detailed empirical observations grounded in various professional settings show that exchanges that appear to be primarily goal-oriented can also be seen as opportunities for the construction of identities and the establishment of interpersonal relations. Conversely, exchanges that might appear on the surface to be about establishing relations (chatting, humour etc.) can serve other functional goals required by the situations at hand.

The linguistic properties of talk at work

A few studies in a vaster field of investigation can be selected to illustrate this issue. Boutet (2005) argues, for instance, that professional discourse genres differ from ordinary language use, and display specific linguistic properties on the syntactic, lexical or prosodic level. Falzon (1989) and Condamines and Vergely (2005) examine such a genre in the 'operational talk' used in airplane cockpits, highlighting some of the stable syntactic patterns used by navigating staff in managing aircraft work. In a different context, Boutet (2001) studies lexical creativity shown in certain professional settings and examines how workers transform technical vocabulary specific to their professions through metaphorical uses. Finally, Grosjean (1993) describes the prosodic features of midwives' talk in the delivery room. The findings in these articles stress the impact that work situations have on the organisation of talk. They provide empirical evidence for the claim long made by variationists that linguistic codes are not homogeneous or universally shared entities. They demonstrate that, on the contrary, linguistic forms are shaped by the uses that social and professional communities make of them.

Writing in the workplace

Three major strands of research can be highlighted here. A first orientation consists in focusing on written communication between institutions and their general audience. Clerc and Kavanagh (2006) report, for example, on a research programme formulating guidelines to help the government of Québec communicate better with its citizens through the improvement of administrative documentation, websites, and other official documents. A second orientation includes numerous studies analysing 'procedural texts' (e.g. prescriptions or instructions). Often associated with international standardisation procedures (e.g. the International Organisation for Standardisation – ISO) or oriented towards quality control, procedural texts increasingly develop in all kinds of work environments, beyond the industrial field where they originally appeared (Veyrac 2001; Pène 2001). More innovative perhaps is a third orientation, which concentrates on the writings workers spontaneously produce in the course of their activities. Fraenkel (2001) thus shows that written texts are not static or fixed units in the workplace. They are caught in the dynamics of groups at work and undergo transformations in the course of the complex trajectories to which they are subjected. Fraenkel thus reflects on the links between the 'acts of inscriptions' and the 'written forms' which are left as traces by these acts. Overall, the study of the uses of writing in the workplace is an invitation to re-examine the relations between texts and work. Texts have ceased to be viewed strictly as external to work activities (prescribing it, guiding it or supporting it). In fact, these studies show that they are deeply interwoven with professional practices and constitute one of the means through which work is accomplished on a local and situated level.

Researching the field of language 'about' work

In addition to researching language 'at' work, an important group of Francophone authors have also investigated the discourse of workers 'about' their work. Labour psychologists, for example, have used different *interviewing* methodologies in order to understand workers' professional practices better, or to induce changes in these practices. Different interviewing methodologies have been experimented with over the years. They come with different labels such as the 'explanation interview' (*l'entretien d'explicitation*; Vermersch 1994), the so-called 'instruction to a counterpart interview' (*l'instruction au sosie*; Clot 2001), or the 'self-confrontation interview' (*l'entretien en auto-confrontation simple ou croisée*; Clot 1999; Faïta 2001; Kostulski 2004). These techniques do not necessarily share the same epistemological assumptions but they have certain common goals. For instance, they seek to produce one effect in particular: self-reflexivity regarding one's own practices. Interviews conducted in this perspective are seen as moments where, engaging in self-reflexivity, workers can become more aware of their own practices. This, in turn, is seen as a source of learning and development for the worker. In such interactional settings, workers become able to entertain alternative views about work practices, in particular views that are seldom expressed in more routine workplace interactions.

During the past few years, the interviewing techniques mentioned above have been applied in various professional settings (urban transportation system, the nuclear industry, teaching and education, public services etc.) and have led to several findings. First, they have contributed to a stress on the idea that language functions as a key mediation for representing and interpreting work. Considering that work is not a 'transparent activity', interviews are a tool for self-reflexivity. However, putting one's work into words is not an easy task to accomplish. Boutet (1995) notes from that point of view that the *discourse genres* available to describe one's own professional experience are very few compared, for example, with the prescribing and evaluative genres that can be found in managerial discourse. Researchers interested in language 'about' work thus insist that spaces of deliberation should be developed where workers can reflect on their practices with others, and find how 'ways of doing things' might differ. Therefore, they endow language 'about' work with a unique mediating capacity to help groups and individuals learn from experience. For a more detailed discussion related to these interviewing techniques, we recommend a collective book recently edited by Plazaola Giger and Stroumza (2007).

Combining multiple methodological orientations

Some studies combine an interest in both language *at* work and language *about* work, and have developed specific methodologies to support it.

Carcassone and Servel (2005), for example, are interested in the professional identity of insurance counsellors, and examine several types of data to investigate it. They thus compare the image of professional counsellors as it is displayed in institutional documents, with the role insurers claim for themselves in interviews, and the roles they enact in their interactions with clients. Analysing the different images produced, the authors show that while the roles counsellors claim for themselves in interviews largely match the identity profiles found in institutional documents, their manner of enacting it with clients differs considerably. The authors attribute the gap in their data set between represented and enacted roles to change in progress in the institution studied.

De Saint-Georges (2003) similarly combines analyses of various forms of discourse in her study of work in an institution providing training for low-skilled unemployed youth. She examines institutional documents, video-recordings of situated activities, and audio-recordings of meetings evaluating the activities, with the aim of developing an understanding of 'anticipatory discourses' (plans, projects, intentions, prescriptions, scheduling etc.) within the institution. Set within a critical discourse analytical framework, the study explores the roles of anticipatory discourses in funnelling or constraining activities. It explores the effects of anticipatory mechanisms on the local level of planning and enacting work, but also, on a larger scale, for professional conversion and re-engagement (de Saint-Georges 2004). It discusses too how preferred organisational futures are negotiated and undesirable ones are challenged (de Saint-Georges 2005).

Research in the Language, Action, Training (*Langage, Action, Formation*) team at the University of Geneva has also been very productive in combining an interest in investigating the role of language both 'at' work and 'about' work. Under the supervision of Jean-Paul Bronckart, the team's focus over the last few years has been on understanding the role played by language in accomplishing and interpreting work in various professional settings, such as nursing, the pharmaceutical industry and teaching (Bronckart et al. 2004a 2004b, forthcoming; Filliettaz and Bronckart 2005; Revaz and Filliettaz 2006). At each site, the researchers have collected several types of data: procedural documents, audio-video-recordings of actual activities, interviews with workers before or after their productive activities. Analysis of the data has identified recurrent patterns of talk about work and details of its linguistic features. It has also shown that instances of such talk (e.g. describing situated actions, describing recurrent practices etc.) cut across the three professional settings examined and appear in a variety of discourse types. On a more general level, the research conducted in this area has contributed to discussing in a more detailed way the relations between discourse competencies and professional skills (Bulea and Bronckart 2007).

Conclusion

In this chapter, we have introduced the reader to some of the main questions and approaches existing in the Francophone area of research on language and work. While we have only been able to provide a few pointers to a vast literature, this brief review has allowed us to discuss some of the possible links between the Francophone tradition and the Anglo-Saxon field of business discourse. For some aspects, the two fields overlap. They address similar issues (coordination, identity, power relations, professional discourse genres etc.) or rely on similar methodological frameworks for data analysis (conversation analysis, interactional sociolinguistics, speech act theory, pragmatics etc.). But the two traditions also differ quite importantly, as when the spotlight is cast on 'workers' primarily, on their first person account of their activities rather than on 'business' and the institutional level of organisations.

To sum up, three additional observations can be made following the review of the most salient Francophone research on language and work:

1 One important accent might be on how the concept of 'action' has structured the theoretical discussions in the Francophone literature. Many studies have high-lighted the usefulness of studying organisations through a semiology of action, which describes organisational activities in terms of action units. The importance of the concept of 'action' may be linked to a more general underlying interest which cuts across the Francophone body of research: beyond investigating the complex functioning of modern workplaces, researchers show a more global interest in better understanding human activity.

2 Generally speaking, the study of professional settings has also greatly renewed the themes and issues addressed by applied linguistics. If linguists are increasingly focusing attention on topics such as polylogues, gestures, multimodality, multiactivity, temporal dynamics etc., it is partly because these issues constitute prominent features of professional practices. Goffman (1959) warned us long ago that the classical model of face-to-face interaction is not complex enough to account for ordinary verbal exchanges, and invited researchers to focus instead on the study of richer 'social encounters'. One just needs to observe work-in-action to be made aware of the fact that simplified theorisations of social interactions do not account adequately for the complexities found in work environments. The Francophone research, by analysing work in its linguistic dimensions, has also contributed to renewing the theoretical and methodological discussions about language in general.

3 Finally, in their analyses of professional environments, Francophone researchers have often gone beyond descriptive approaches to work practices. Instead, they have sought to contribute to the transformation of professional settings by using research findings as a means to induce organisational change and transformation. Boutet (2005, 2006) reminds us that taking a 'transformative' approach requires careful consideration of the ethical implications. Workers hold positions and develop in their professional environments. Analysing their activities thus puts them and the groups they belong to in the spotlight. In this context, the role of the linguist cannot be that of the mere observer. Participation in the work sphere, whether as an actor or an observer, necessarily contributes to the construction of non-neutral relationships, which also have social implications. This critical dimension has been recently discussed by many authors in the field of business discourse (Bargiela et al. 2007: 23ff). It is equally important in the Francophone area of research on language and work.

References

Bargiela-Chiappini, F., C. Nickerson and B. Planken (2007) *Business Discourse*. Basingstoke: Palgrave Macmillan.

Borzeix, A. and B. Fraenkel (eds) (2001) *Langage et travail: Communication, cognition, action*. Paris: CNRS.

Boutet, J. (ed.) (1995) *Paroles au travail*. Paris: L'Harmattan.

Boutet, J. (2001) Les mots du travail. In A. Borzeix and B. Fraenkel (eds), *Langage et travail: Communication, cognition, action*. Paris: CNRS, pp. 189–202.

Boutet, J. (2005) Genres de discours et activités de travail. In L. Filliettaz and J.-P. Bronckart (eds), *L'analyse des actions et des discours en situation de travail: Concepts, méthodes et applications*. Louvain-la-Neuve: Peeters, pp. 19–35.

Boutet, J. (2006) Travail langagier en centres d'appel: Comment être un expert sans le dire? In M. Laforest and D. Vincent (eds), *Les interactions asymétriques*. Québec: Editions Nota Bene, pp. 15–32.

Boutet, J. and B. Gardin (2001) Une linguistique du travail. In A. Borzeix and B. Fraenkel (eds), *Langage et travail: Communication, cognition, action*. Paris: CNRS, pp. 89–111.

Bronckart, J.-P., E. Bulea and I. Fristalon (2004a) Les conditions d'émergence de l'action dans le langage. *Cahiers de linguistique française*, 26: 345–69.

Bronckart, J.-P. and Groupe LAF (eds) (2004b) *Agir et discours en situation de travail*. Cahiers de la Section des Sciences de l'Education, 103. University of Geneva.

Bronckart, J.-P., E. Bulea and L. Filliettaz (forthcoming) Les processus de construction des actions et de leurs représentations en situation de travail. In S. Canelas-Trevisi (ed.), *Langage, objets enseignés et travail enseignant en didactique du français*. Grenoble: Ellug.

Bulea, E. and J.-P. Bronckart (2007) La saisie des compétences dans l'interprétation de l'activité de travail. *Bulletin suisse de linguistique appliquée*, 84: 143–71.

Carcassone, M. and L. Servel (2005) Rôle représenté et rôle joué: L'activité des techniciens Conseil. In L. Filliettaz and J.-P. Bronckart (eds), *L'analyse des actions et des discours en situation de travail: Concepts, méthodes et applications*. Louvain-la-Neuve: Peeters, pp. 79–98.

Clerc, I. and E. Kavanagh (2006) *De la lettre à la page Web: Savoir communiquer avec le grand public*. Québec: Publications du Québec.

Clot, Y. (1999) *La fonction psychologique du travail*. Paris: PUF.

Clot, Y. (2001) Clinique du travail et action sur soi. In J.-M. Baudouin and J. Friedrich (eds), *Théories de l'action et education*. Brussels: De Boeck, pp. 255–77.

Condamines, A. and P. Vergely (2005) L'expression du dysfonctionnement technique dans la navigation aérienne: Une approche de linguistique de corpus. In L. Filliettaz and J.-P. Bronckart (eds), *L'analyse des actions et des discours en situation de travail: Concepts, méthodes et applications*. Louvain-la-Neuve: Peeters, pp. 177–97.

Cooren, F. and D. Robichaud (2006) Globaliser et disloquer en situation d'interaction. In M. Laforest and D. Vincent (eds), *Les interactions asymétriques*. Québec: Editions Nota Bene, pp. 113–32.

Daniellou, F. (1996) *L'ergonomie en quête de ses principes*. Toulouse: Octarès.

Dejours, C. (1999) *Le facteur humain*. Paris: PUF.

Doury, M. (2001) Une discussion dans un commerce d'habitués. In F. Cicurel and M. Doury (eds), *Interactions et discours professionnels: Usages et transmission*. Paris: Presses de la Sorbonne Nouvelle, pp. 119–34.

Dumas, I. (2005) L'interdépendance actes de langage/gestes praxiques dans les interactions de commerce et de service. In L. Filliettaz and J.-P. Bronckart (eds), *L'analyse des actions et des discours en situation de travail: Concepts, méthodes et application*. Louvain-la-Neuve: Peeters, pp. 115–31.

Faïta, D. (2001) Genres d'activité et styles de conduite. In A. Borzeix and B. Fraenkel (eds), *Langage et travail: Communication, cognition, action*. Paris: CNRS, pp. 263–84.

Falzon, P. (1989) *Ergonomie cognitive du dialogue*. Grenoble: Presses universitaires de Grenoble.

Filliettaz, L. (2002), *La parole en action: Eléments de pragmatique psycho-sociale*. Québec: Editions Nota Bene.

Filliettaz, L. (2004a) Interaction, cognition et identités situées: Une analyse praxéologique des transactions de service. *Bulletin de Psychologie*, 57(1): 61–4.

Filliettaz, L. (2004b) The construction of requests in transactional settings: A discursive approach. In C. Gouveia, C. Silvestre and L. Azuaga (eds), *Discourse and Communication in the Enterprise*. Lisbon: Ulices, pp. 79–97.

Filliettaz, L. (2005a) Discours, travail et polyfocalisation de l'action. In L. Filliettaz and J.-P. Bronckart (eds), *L'analyse des actions et des discours en situation de travail: Concepts, méthodes et applications*. Louvain-la-Neuve: Peeters, pp. 155–75.

Filliettaz, L. (2005b) Mediated actions, social practices and contextualization: A case study from service encounters. In S. Norris and R. Jones (eds), *Discourse in Action: Introducing Mediated Discourse Analysis*. London: Routledge, pp. 100–9.

Filliettaz, L. (2006) Asymétrie et prises de rôles: Le cas des réclamations dans les interactions de service. In M. Laforest and D. Vincent (eds), *Les interactions asymétriques*. Québec: Editions Nota Bene, pp. 89–112.

Filliettaz, L. (2007) Gestualité et (re)contextualisation de l'interaction dans des réunions de relève de poste en milieu industriel. In L. Mondada (ed.), *Interacting bodies/ Le corps en interaction: Proceedings of the 2nd ISGS Conference, Lyon, June*. http://gesture-lyon2005.ens-lsh.fr/.

Filliettaz, L. and J.-P. Bronckart (eds) (2005) *L'analyse des actions et des discours en situation de travail: Concepts, méthodes et applications*. Louvain-la-Neuve: Peeters.

Fraenkel, B. (2001) La résistible ascension de l'écrit au travail. In A. Borzeix and B. Fraenkel (eds), *Langage et travail: Communication, cognition, action*. Paris: CNRS, pp. 113–42.

Goffman, E. (1959) *The Presentation of Self in Everyday Life*. New York: Doubleday.

Grosjean, M. (1993) Polyphonie et positions de la sage-femme dans la conduite de l'accouchement. In J. Cosnier, M. Grosjean and M. Lacoste (eds), *Soins et communication: Approches interactionnistes des relations de soins*. Lyon: Presses universitaires de Lyon, pp. 121–58.

Grosjean, M. and M. Lacoste (1999) *Communication et intelligence collective: Le travail à l'hôpital*. Paris: PUF.

Grosjean, M. and L. Mondada (eds) (2005) *La négociation au travail*. Lyon: Presses universitaires de Lyon.

Grusenmeyer, C. and A. Trognon (1995) L'analyse interactive des échanges verbaux en situation de travail cooperative: L'exemple de la relève de poste. *Connexions*; 65: 43–62.

Guérin, F., A. Laville, F. Daniellou, J. Duraffourg and A. Kerguelen (1997) *Comprendre le travail pour le transformer: La pratique de l'ergonomie*. Montrouge: ANACT.

Kerbrat-Orecchioni, C. (2001) *Je voudrais un p'tit bifteck*: La politesse à la française en site commercial. In F. Cicurel and M. Doury (eds), *Interactions et discours professionnels*. Paris: Presses de la Sorbonne nouvelle, pp. 105–18.

Kerbrat-Orecchioni, C. and V. Traverso (eds) (2008) *Les interactions en site commercial.* Lyon: Presses universitaires de Lyon.

Kostulski, K. (2004) Développement de la pensée et du rapport à l'autre dans une interaction. *Cahiers de linguistique française*, 26: 113–31.

Lacoste, M. (1995) Parole, action, situation. In J. Boutet (ed.), *Paroles au travail.* Paris: L'Harmattan, pp. 23–44.

Lacoste, M. (2001) Peut-on travailler sans communiquer? In A. Borzeix and B. Fraenkel (eds), *Langage et travail: Communication, cognition, action.* Paris: CNRS, pp. 21–53.

Laforest, M. and D. Vincent (eds) (2006) *Les interactions asymétriques.* Québec: Editions Nota Bene.

Mondada, L. (2001) Intervenir à distance dans une opération chirurgicale: L'organisation interactive d'espaces de participation. *Bulletin suisse de linguistique appliquée*, 74: 33–56.

Mondada, L. (2004a) *You see here?* Voir, pointer, dire: Contribution à une approche interactionnelle de la référence. In A. Auchlin, M. Burger, L. Filliettaz et al. (eds), *Structures et discourse: Mélanges offerts à Eddy Roulet.* Québec: Editions Nota Bene, pp. 433–53.

Mondada, L. (2004b) Temporalité, séquentialité et multimodalité au fondement de l'organisation de l'interaction: Le pointage comme pratique de prise de tour. *Cahiers de linguistique française*, 26: 269–92.

Mondada, L. (2005a) L'exploitation située de ressources langagières et multimodales dans la conception collective d'une exposition. In L. Filliettaz and J.-P. Bronckart (eds), *L'analyse des actions et des discours en situation de travail: Concepts, méthodes et applications.* Louvain-la-Neuve: Peeters, pp. 135–54.

Mondada, L. (2005b) *Chercheurs en interaction.* Lausanne: Presses polytechniques et universitaires romandes.

Mondada, L. (2006) L'ordre social comme un accomplissement pratique des membres dans le temps. *Médias et culture*, 2: 85–119.

Ombredane, A. and J.-M. Faverge (1955) *L'analyse du travail.* Paris: PUF.

Pène, S. (2001) Les agencements langagiers de la *Qualité.* In A. Borzeix and B. Fraenkel (eds), *Langage et travail: Communication, cognition, action.* Paris: CNRS, pp. 303–21.

Pène, S., A. Borzeix and B. Fraenkel (eds) (2001) *Le langage dans les organisations: Une nouvelle donne.* Paris: L'Harmattan.

Plazaola Giger, I. and K. Stroumza (eds) (2007) *Paroles de praticiens et description de l'activité: Problématisation méthodologique pour la formation et la recherche.* Brussels: De Boeck.

Revaz, F. and L. Filliettaz (2006) Actualités du récit dans le champ de la linguistique des discours oraux: Le cas des narrations en situation d'entretien. *Protée*, 32(2–3): 53–66.

de Saint-Georges, I. (2003) Anticipatory discourse: Producing futures of action in a vocational program for long-term unemployed. PhD thesis, Washington, DC, Georgetown University.

de Saint-Georges, I. (2004) Actions, médiations et interactions: Une approche multimodale du travail sur un chantier. *Cahiers de linguistique française*, 26: 321–42.

de Saint-Georges, I. (2005) Discours, anticipation et action: Les constructions discursives de l'avenir dans une institution de formation par le travail. In L. Filliettaz and J.-P. Bronckart (eds), *L'analyse des actions et des discours en situation de travail: Concepts, méthodes et applications.* Louvain-la-Neuve: Peeters, pp. 201–19.

Traverso, V. (2001) Syrian service encounters: A case of shifting strategies within verbal exchange. *Pragmatics*, 11(4): 421–44.

Trognon, A. and M. Batt (2006) Comment une relation médecin–patient symétrique favorise-t-elle le maintien d'une conviction? In M. Laforest and D. Vincent (eds), *Les interactions asymétriques*, Québec: Editions Nota Bene, pp. 33–47.

Trognon, A. and K. Kostulski (1996) L'analyse de l'interaction en psychologie des groupes: Économie interne et dynamique des phénomènes groupaux. *Connexions*, 68: 73–115.

Vermersch, P. (1994) *L'entretien d'explicitation*. Paris: ESF.

Veyrac, H. (2001) Aperçu de la variété des fonctions des consignes dans le monde du travail. *Pratiques*, 111/112: 77–92.

Zarifian, P. (2001) *Objectif competence*. Paris: Editions Liaisons.

33

Kazakhstan

Eleonora D. Suleimenova and Gulmira G. Burkitbayeva

Introduction

In this chapter we will, first, look at the language planning process in Kazakhstan, at its driving forces, its history, and its progress over the years. Business discourse in Kazakhstan has been shaped, and continues to be shaped, under the influence of three languages: Kazakh, Russian and English.

Second, we will discuss the extent to which each of the three languages (Kazakh, Russian and English) participates in business discourse in Kazakhstan. During the seventy years of the Soviet period, business communication in Kazakhstan was conducted in Russian. Encouragement and regulation of Kazakh language use since the independence of Kazakhstan has re-established the rights and multiple functions of the Kazakh language. The use of Kazakh has become widespread in business communication, gradually occupying more and more space along with Russian and English.

Third, we will touch upon the issue of whether the Kazakh language has sufficient linguistic and demographic resources to reach its potential for business discourse. Examination of the history of the formation of Kazakh business discourse shows that there exists a long tradition of Kazakh use in business communication, with its own genres and linguistic means. Meanwhile, Kazakh business discourse experiences specific difficulties due to the lack of appropriate language and communicative competence on the part of people working in state administration, business etc.

Fourth, we will present an overview of the long, albeit checkered, history of business discourse in Kazakhstan. The most salient point of the language planning process in the country is a political directive on trilingualism (Kazakh, Russian and English). This directive has been announced as a national educational objective at Kazakhstani schools and universities. Given the conditions inherent to globalisation and a free-market economy, general knowledge of three languages is considered as a guarantee of economic competitiveness.

Fifth, we will consider features and peculiarities of Russian and English business discourses. Considering the fact that Russian and English business discourses are characterised by their more developed language resources and sets of genres, and are studied in more depth by researchers, it would be reasonable for Kazakhstani linguists to apply this acquired expertise to the analysis of Kazakh business discourse.

Lastly, we will present our conclusions. Business discourses in Kazakh, Russian and English possess different genres and function in diverse spheres of usage. Their interplay in modern Kazakhstan and the changes that are expected in their distribution (or redistribution) within the intersection zones of the business communicative area require further analysis of their linguistic singularities and interactive potential.

Background

The formation of business discourse in Kazakhstan has taken place over a long period of time subject to the direct influence of the peculiarities of the country's language situation, which has also defined linguistic sharing in business discourse.

Modern Kazakhstan is a multilingual society[1] with 126 registered languages of different families and structural types (Suleimenova et al. 2007: 262). These languages exhibit different levels of potential for functioning in business discourse. This stems from a number of circumstances, the most important of which are:

- Ethno-demographic differences: Kazakhs constitute 53.4 per cent of the country's population, Russians 30.0 per cent, other ethnic groups 16.6 per cent. At the same time, 16.6 per cent of the population speaks 124 languages (other than Kazakh or Russian), 68 per cent of which are spoken by fewer than 1,000 people (Suleimenova et al. 2007: 281).
- Essential changes in the balance between Kazakhs and non-Kazakhs in the make-up of the population (in 1989 Kazakhs constituted 39.7 per cent; in 1999, 53.4 per cent; in 2004, 57.7 per cent). These changes are explained, on the one hand, by the natural increase of Kazakhs (75.1 per cent) and a positive migration balance (24.9 per cent) and, on the other hand, by a decrease in the number of Germans, Russians, Ukrainians, Byelorussians etc. in the country (Sultanov 2006: 503–6).
- Internal migration processes (urbanisation) in all regions of the country, which have changed the ratio between urban and rural population. This has led to an increased number of Kazakhs whose primary language is Kazakh in the ethnic structure of cities and, consequently, in administrative, educational and financial institutions, different types of enterprises, markets, services etc.
- The high degree of Kazakh and Russian language competence exhibited by the country's population as a whole, which has made these two languages the *main 'actors' of the ethno-language situation*. The overwhelming majority of languages, excluding Kazakh and Russian, have become the languages of much less numerous peoples.

All these factors taken together have determined the functional language distribution in Kazakhstan. The language situation has turned out to be clearly centred on two demographically and communicatively powerful partners – Kazakh and Russian – which are used in practically all spheres of communication. If we turn to the area of business communication in Kazakhstan, we will also observe that English has its own definite sphere of usage, sometimes supplanting other languages.

Business discourse in contemporary Kazakhstan has been shaped, and continues to be shaped, under the influence of three languages: Kazakh, Russian and English. The presence of three languages in the common communicative area of business discourse gives rise to the questions considered in this chapter. These are:

- How does the official language planning put into practice in Kazakhstan today regulate the participation of Kazakh, Russian and also English in the business discourse of Kazakhstan?
- Can one speak about Kazakh business discourse, and what are the prerequisites for its functioning in practice?
- What are the modern verbal and nonverbal relations characterising Kazakh, Russian and English business discourses in Kazakhstan?

Taking into account the complexity of the questions above and considering the fact that the most heavily investigated areas are Russian and English business discourses, which possess developed language resources and the necessary set of genres, the main focus of this chapter is the formation of a Kazakh business discourse, from its inception through to its current spread due to language planning.

Language planning and business discourse in Kazakhstan

In this section, we consider the question of how language planning[2] in Kazakhstan influences the participation of Kazakh in business communication. Some of the most vivid facts demonstrating the effectiveness of language planning in spreading the use of the Kazakh language in business communication and leading to noticeable changes in the Kazakhstani language situation are summarised below.

With the foundation of the sovereign Republic of Kazakhstan there arose an urgent need for a solution to the country's problems of state and ethnic identity (Suleimenova and Smagulova 2005). Questions of language became highly politicised. This pertained especially to the choice between Russian and the native Kazakh language in business communication.

Russian, as the language of the former Soviet state system, operated in all spheres of communication, with the exception of different forms of national art and literature. It was represented in all its forms: codified literary language, spoken language, common language, social dialects etc. The Russian language had a popular historical and cultural tradition of use among the population, which exhibited a high level of Russian language competence.

This was not the case for the Kazakh language. During the seventy years of the Soviet period, Kazakh was practically eliminated from all spheres of communication. This absence was especially pronounced in business communication, which was conducted in Russian. This is why the new language policy of sovereign Kazakhstan has sought to re-establish the rights and multiple functions of the Kazakh language. To this end, it was necessary first to establish a legal framework that would safeguard both Kazakh and Russian. The Kazakh language was defined as a state language. Russian, meanwhile, was particularised in the following way: 'In state organisations and local self-governing bodies, the Russian language is used officially together with the Kazakh language.'[3]

The different status of Kazakh and Russian defined the priorities and imperatives fundamental to planning the expansion of the Kazakh language. Revival of the use of Kazakh in the spheres from which it had been displaced during the Soviet period began. First and foremost, this concerned business discourse in state administration, business activities, office work etc.

In 2005, some essential amendments were added to the president's 7 February 2001 decree 'On the State Program of Language Functioning and Development for the Years 2001–2010', regulating the sphere of business discourse in the country, and a government resolution 'On Extending Spheres of the State Language Usage in State Organizations' was adopted. Since then, in accordance with paragraph 2 of article 7 of the Constitution of the Republic of Kazakhstan, a planned, sequential, stage-by-stage transfer of office work, record-keeping and statistical, financial and technical documentation into Kazakh has begun, which is to be completed by 2010. The stages of this transfer were fixed for all regions of the country, different ministries, committees, administrations, local representative and executive bodies etc.

Currently, in accordance with the transfer, office work is carried out entirely in the Kazakh language in several areas of the country which exhibit a considerable concentration of ethnic Kazakhs (Southern Kazakhstan, Qyzylorda, Western Kazakhstan, Almaty etc.). The most successful transfer of office work into Kazakh has been implemented in the various ministries. In Kazakhstani embassies, materials as well as documents pertaining to consular services are presented only in Kazakh, the state language (KazInform 2005). The functioning of official and business Kazakh in upper-level government administration, for example, in the Majilis (lower house of parliament) and the Senate, however, has not yet achieved the desired level.

Nevertheless, the positive dynamic of the Kazakh language's expansion into the spheres of official and non-official business communication is very real. Thus, if we compare the changes that took place over two years in the requirements for specialists in the Ministry of Finance, the Committee on Automobile Roads and Construction, the Ministry of Transportation and Communication, the Committee for Standardisation and Certification of the Ministry of Economy and Trade, the Committee of Intellectual Property Rights of the Ministry of Justice and so on, we notice that in advertisements recruiting candidates for administrative and state positions in the newspaper *Kazakhstanskaya Pravda*, the requirement for knowledge of Kazakh increased from 13 per cent in 2002 to 100 per cent in 2004 (Sarybay 2006: 150–4).

In order to understand the process of language planning, it is important to note differences in public opinion: on the one hand, the impatient expectation of language planning's swift success in spreading the Kazakh language in business communication manifested by one part of population and, on the other hand, the irritation and displeasure at the tough regulations of the expansion of the Kazakh language in office work. At the same time, there has been a gradual easing of initial emotional reactions to changes in the language situation and to the different language planning measures. The population has become more conscious of and more motivated to learn Kazakh. People have also begun to understand that the inertia of language processes is an objective factor that should be considered in language planning and that changes in language functioning cannot be decreed, nor can they happen overnight.

Different social and age groups possess different language abilities. Children born and brought up in sovereign Kazakhstan are a new generation of young Kazakhstanis for whom the state language is a reality. The public tolerance that is manifest in Kazakhstan is a result of concerted effort to establish agreement and co-operation.

Language planning thus far – redefining the status of Kazakh and Russian, encouraging the expansion of Kazakh and regulating its spread in business communication – has been quite successful. The use of the Kazakh language has become widespread in business communication, gradually occupying more and more space in common with Russian.

Kazakhstan: three languages, three business discourses

The participation of three languages in the business discourse of today's Kazakhstan requires separate commentaries for each language. In this section, the political and linguistic prerequisites of business discourse formation and the contribution of Kazakh, Russian and English are considered.

The most important point of language planning in the country is a political directive on trilingualism (Kazakh, Russian and English). This directive has been announced as a national educational objective and has become the basis of a special programme of intensive English study at Kazakhstani schools and universities. Given the conditions inherent to globalisation and a free-market economy, general knowledge of three languages is considered a guarantee of competitiveness both for the country as a whole and for each of its citizens.

All the above serves to explain the following distribution of Kazakh, Russian and English in business discourse:

- With the help of targeted government regulation, the use of Kazakh in the spheres of official and non-official business communication has grown considerably. This process can be considered a manifestation of the successful expansion of Kazakh business discourse.
- In many respects, Russian business discourse continues to preserve its position, both in the range of its genres and in the extent of communicative functions. It has even extended its boundaries to include numerous foreign companies and firms.
- English business discourse, which occupies a leading position among foreign languages in business communication with international partners and organisations, is now an active component of business communication in Kazakhstan.

The functioning of Kazakh, Russian and English in business discourse undoubtedly requires more detailed consideration. A knowledge of the traditions and general usage of these languages is crucial to understanding the peculiarities of Kazakh, Russian and English and how they operate in business communication.

The Kazakh language was, until recently, practically excluded from business communication and was rarely used as the language of important business documents or official business negotiations. Irrespective of communication content, the roles and status of participants, and the nature and site of social relations, the business community in Kazakhstan was not oriented towards the use of the Kazakh language. On the contrary, for the course of seven decades, the discourse community was shaped by the influence of the Soviet business communication experience, which levelled the usage of any culturally-marked components of business discourse.

Russian, with its rich arsenal of linguistic means, formed and developed on the territory of the Soviet Union and strongly supported by Soviet language policy, was the main language of business. The Russian language imposed its structure and typology, as well as the usage of its different units, genres and communicative strategies. The speech and communicative competence of business discourse participants, irrespective of their nationality, was formed within the frame of Russian business discourse, and that frame was involuntarily transferred to Kazakh business discourse. This resulted in practically all participants in business discourse in the country acquiring the stable habit of conducting business communication exclusively in Russian.

The English language entered the sphere of business communication with Russian (very rarely with Kazakh) when it became the working language of modern businesses, including numerous joint ventures and foreign companies (Burkitbayeva 2006: 5).

As already mentioned, the transfer of office work, record-keeping and statistical, financial and technical documentation into Kazakh is taking place at various speeds and with varying rates of success. While state institutions and organisations in different regions of the country conduct office work in both Kazakh and Russian, most private companies and firms continue to use only Russian. Meanwhile, foreign companies and companies in which foreigners serve as partners use English and Russian in communication.

Business discourse in Kazakhstan, as in many other countries, is considerably influenced by the English language. One can easily track this influence in the high demand for English-speaking specialists in the labour market. For instance, according to an investigation conducted by Sarybay for the newspaper *Novoye Pokoleniye* (16 May 2003), knowledge of English was a requirement in 98 of 101 advertisements for the positions of manager, engineer, operator, secretary, accountant and administrator. Moreover, 40 per cent of the advertisements placed in this newspaper in 2003 were published in English (Sarybay 2004: 130–5). The activities of more than fifty embassies and representative offices of foreign countries, 700 foreign enterprises and 1,500 representative offices of international companies require that business communication be conducted in English. English functions as the lingua franca in intercultural communication between local and foreign practitioners. The increased number of English-speaking professionals and interpreters/translators in Kazakhstan is due to the scale of international co-operation, of which the country's investment policy is an effective tool.

The speed and scale at which English business discourse, which has the highest communicative rating in international business communication, is spreading have led to a situation in which Kazakh and Russian business discourses are quite aggressively influenced by English. English business discourse, being in many respects more developed and stable and possessing more advanced and established forms and the means of different genres, often proves to be dominant and more highly demanded, displacing not only Kazakh but also Russian.

Thus business discourses in Kazakh, Russian and English possess different genres and function in diverse spheres of usage. They are characterised by complicated interrelations of mutual influence. Their interplay in modern Kazakhstan and the changes that are expected in their distribution (or redistribution) within the intersection zones of the business communicative area require further analysis of their linguistic singularities and interactive potential.

Resources and potentiality of Kazakh business discourse

The current practice of language planning regulating the expansion of the spheres of business discourse, unprecedented on a global scale, raises a reasonable question about the preconditions of its realisation for the Kazakh language.

This question has two important aspects. First, it touches upon doubts as to whether the Kazakh language possesses all the necessary resources and potentiality to serve as a business discourse. The second aspect concerns uncertainty as to whether there are a sufficient number of participants in Kazakh business discourse capable of conducting professional business communication using all its functions and genres. Let us consider each aspect separately.

The Kazakh language has a long literary tradition and possesses all the means necessary for carrying out both official and everyday business communication, written and oral. The versatile character of the Kazakh language is demonstrated by the history of business communication in Kazakh, which has a long and continuous tradition not limited to the Soviet period. This versatility is also evidenced by modern genres of Kazakh business discourse, which are diverse and quite developed (see the next section).

The official business style of the Kazakh written language is characterised by 'exactness', standardisation, use of words in their dictionary meaning, lack of figurative and evaluative language, impersonal character of exposition, a special system of clichés, terms and set expressions, conventional symbols and abbreviations, a distinct compositional structure etc.[4] These are all features to be found across styles in Kazakh. They are described in monographs and dissertations, textbooks and dictionaries.[5]

The situation is different, however, if we examine the everyday language of business interactions. 'Russification', which was the official ideology of Soviet language policy, has had a considerable impact on the essential features of business discourse in Kazakhstan:

- Documents were kept in the spirit of Soviet communication culture and, as such, were supranational.
- Documents connected with state administration were, as a rule, centrally compiled and regulated.
- The originals of documents were compiled in Russian; documents in Kazakh were, with very few exceptions, translated from Russian.
- Oral official business communication as well as everyday business communication was conducted mostly in Russian.

All of these factors led to a situation in which the participants of business communication used only Russian business discourse and did not have appropriate knowledge of the official business style of the Kazakh language. Contemporary participants in Kazakh-language business communication find themselves in a difficult situation: not only do they have to master a *new* language and gain cultural competency in the field of business communication in the context of a discourse community that includes society, government, administration, companies, different markets, competitors and so on; they must also use this *new* language to overcome existing traditions and their own stereotypes in the use of text types and genres of business discourse, create *new* communicative situations, change customary communicative behaviour and display a non-characteristic communicative initiative in forming a *new* discourse community and acquiring *new* business qualifications.

Another factor that compounds the complexity of the current situation is the linguistic division of the ethnic Kazakh population into two groups: those who speak the Kazakh language and the considerable number of so-called Russian-speaking Kazakhs, some of whom speak no Kazakh at all, while others have only a conversational knowledge of the language. This division of Kazakh society is connected not only with the dominant language, but also with behavioural patterns, value orientations, preferences and degrees of immersion in the native culture. These differences are so significant that one can speak of two 'subcultures', namely the different mentalities of the Kazakhs whose dominant language is Kazakh and those Kazakhs whose dominant language is Russian. Specifically, Europeanised (oriented towards the Russian culture), Russian-speaking Kazakhs working in state institutions experience particular difficulties because of their lack of proficiency in the Kazakh language and cannot become full participants in Kazakh business discourse, slowing down the process of its expansion.

Thus, at present, Kazakh business discourse, while it possesses sufficient language resources for its proper functioning, experiences specific difficulties due to the lack of appropriate language and communicative competence on the part of a considerable number of people working in state administration, business and so on.

Kazakh business discourse: a short history

In this section we consider the sources of Kazakh business discourse and the linguistic peculiarities of its formation.

The sources of contemporary Kazakh business discourse reach back to such widely known genres as wills (*osiet*), orders (*buiryk*), decrees (*zharlyk*), business letters (*iskeri khattar*) and so on, which exhibit rather stable language forms in Old Turkic written documents dating as far back as the tenth and eleventh centuries (Aidarov 1986; Balakayev 1959; Ibatov 1966; Issayev 1989; Kordabayev 1964; Kuryshzhanov 2001; Mambetova 2005; Yergaziyeva 1972; and many others).

In the eighteenth and nineteenth centuries, different types of business letters, decrees, instructions and orders (*iskeri khat*, *yarlyk*, *amir yarlyk*, *farman/firman*) issued by khans and amirs were widely used in Kazakh business discourse. These documents exhibit a strong Arabic and Persian influence, and also the influence of Tatar, which at that time was more developed; very often translators, clerks and document-compilers were Tatars, Bashkirs or mullahs. Numerous epistolary documents in the form of correspondence between Kazakh khans, sultans, senior representatives and Russian administrative institutions also appeared during this time (Yergaziyeva 1972: 8–9). Kazakh business documents of this period were not stylistically uniform. The texts made abundant use of Turkic, Arabic, Persian and Tatar vocabulary. Moreover, they were characterised by complex syntactic constructions and were not easily intelligible to the general population.

During the second half of the nineteenth century, the language of Kazakh business documents was, on the one hand, undergoing the general processes of normalisation and standardisation and, on the other hand, subject to the influence of Russian business discourse as a result of Russia's increased influence on Kazakhstan. Such standard and widely used words and expressions as 'I order' (*buyiramyn*), 'I prepare' (*tagayindaimyn*), 'the so-called' (*atalmysh*), 'below/above shown' (*tomendegi/zhogary korsetilgen*), 'named above' (*zhogaryda atalgan*), 'will be legitimised' (*bekitiledi*), 'to the name' (*atyna*), 'to sign' (*kol koyu*) and many others can be found in business documents (orders, decrees, applications, declarations and so on) from this time. They are still in use. Significant efforts for normalisation and standardisation of the Kazakh literary language were made by the Kazakh Enlightenment figures Abay Kunanbayev and Ibray Altynsarin. Their works reflected the administrative-business and oral-business language of the second half of the nineteenth century, with many borrowings from Russian: barrister (*advokat*), military governor (*askeri gubernator*), law (*zan*), party (*partiya*), court (*sot*), volost (*bolys* – the smallest administrative division of tsarist Russia), head of an *uyezd* or administrative unit (*oyaz nachalnigi*), *katalazhka* or prison (*katelechke*), *uyezdnyi* or head of an *uyezd* (*oyaznoi*), mediator (*bitimshi*), interpreter/translator (*tilmash*), application (*shagym*), to get a rank (*shen alu*) and so on (Yergaziyeva 1972: 9). During this same period, the following terms, words and word-combinations of the official business style were spread: order (*zharlyk*), work (*kyzmet*), registration (*tirkeu*), expenses (*shygyn*), book of stocktaking (*khysab dapteri*) and so on. It is typical that in early documents a significant phonetic transformation of words borrowed from Russian is observed: military governor (Kazakh[K]: *uayennyi kubrnator* – Russian[R]: *voennyi gubernator*); advisor (K: *sauetnik* – R: *sovetnik*); society (K: *obschestua* – R: *obschestvo*); official (K: *chinobnik* – R: *chinovnik*); exhibition (K: *bistabka* – R: *vystavka*) and so on.

The beginning of the twentieth century, according to Syzdykova (1984: 25), was marked by a further development of genres (correspondence *–katynas kagazdar*; resolutions – *kauly-kararlar*; references – *minezdeme*; agreements – *shart*; orders – *buyryk*; decisions – *okim* and so on), the process of business term creation, the regularisation of cliché expressions and constructions and a tendency towards use of standard syntactical constructions.

During the Soviet period, when state administration changed fundamentally, genres in official business communication were developed and diversified, the vocabulary of business documents was enlarged, semantic changes occurred and the grammatical structure was improved. Particularly intensive Kazakh-language business communication developed in collective and state farms, *aul* (small village) councils, regional and *oblast* (district) organisations, offices and so on, where office work was conducted exclusively in Kazakh. In cities, codification of the linguistic forms of written business communication, including all business and office documents, minutes, resolutions, decrees and orders of state institutions, took place; different business documents took shape according to fixed rules and standards. Moreover, it was the internal resources of the Kazakh language that served as sources of business language enrichment; for example, meeting – *zhinalys*, decree – *kauly*, seal – *mor*, copy – *nuska*, chairman – *tor-aga*, secretary – *khatshy*, vacation – *demalys*, break – *uzilis*, census – *sanak* and so on. Other sources of business Kazakh enrichment included loan translation; combined borrowing; translation and borrowings directly from Russian or from other languages by means of Russian (for example, minutes – *protocol*, document – *akti*, archives – *arkhiv*, package – *paket*, number – *nomer*, telephone – *telefon*, journal – *zhurnal* and so on); the formation of the main lexico-semantic and thematic groups (designation of positions, titles, degrees, names of institutions, departments, ministries, organisations, enterprises); abbreviations fully borrowed from Russian (for example, *gorono* – a municipal department of national education, *gorfo* – a municipal department of finance, *oblsobes* – an *oblast* department of social security, *KazGY* – Kazakh State University) and so on (Yergaziyeva 1972: 14–17).

At the same time, the policy of 'Russification' became very destructive for Kazakh business discourse because it entailed a dramatic reduction of Kazakh language use in the spheres of official and everyday business communication; there was an interruption in the tradition of business text creation and the use of Kazakh-language resources; many age-old Kazakh units previously used in business documents disappeared from the active vocabulary. Kazakh business documents were compiled as secondary sources (as the result of translation); this is especially true of business documentation from the centre (Moscow). Many unnecessary borrowings from Russian appeared; lexical and syntactical loan translation became active in Kazakh. Very often interpreters/translators replaced actual discourse participants. Similarly, translated texts were inferior in quality to the Russian originals because of their secondary nature. Moreover, the conception of the participants of business communication changed; they became non-national personalities deprived of national and cultural identity, and even the texts of Kazakh business discourse became nationally impersonal.

Contemporary Kazakh business discourse is developing rapidly and much research is being devoted to the processes and speech strategies of the Kazakh language; for example, the research of N. I. Yergaziyeva and A. T. Yesetova (2004) on lexical and stylistic peculiarities; B. S. Ashirova (2004) on terms and term formation; M. K. Mambetova (2005) on clichés and cliché constructions as a main constituent of an official business style; L. S. Duisembekova (2008) on the language of official business documentation; G. A. Birali (2004) on the influence of Kazakh culture on the process of learning business Kazakh; and many others.

Thus, the preceding examination of the history of the formation of Kazakh business discourse shows that, first, there exists a long tradition of Kazakh use in business communication, with its own genres and linguistic means; second, this tradition ceased to develop and, to some degree, this has predetermined the difficulties inherent in the functioning of Kazakh business discourse today; and third, Kazakh business discourse, being constantly and actively supported by the government, is quickly developing and forming its own discourse community.

Features of Russian business discourse in Kazakhstan

Russian business discourse in Kazakhstan has features that are similar to those of business discourse in Russia. In this section we selectively report on studies examining Russian business discourse in comparison with its Kazakh counterpart.

Russian business discourse, both in Russia and in Kazakhstan, is going through a period of genre renewal (resumé, fax, email, video- and tele-conferencing and so on) and is experiencing the appearance of new speech models and strategies. This is currently being studied in Kazakhstan from the perspective of general problems and the role and functions of business communication (Bakirova 2004); linguistic analysis of genres of business discourse, such as the business letter (Salkhanova 2006); argumentation utilised in business letters (Baimurunova 2002); requirements for texts in the official business style, included in a multimedia appendix to an electronic textbook (Tzoy 2006); and so on.

Special attention is being given to comparative studies of the interaction between Kazakh and Russian business discourses. Yerezhepova (2002) has conducted a pragma-linguistic comparison of the peculiarities of decrees as a distinct genre of business discourse in Kazakh and Russian. The common features of decrees in Kazakh and Russian, Yerezhepova asserts, are mainly connected with the fact that Kazakh texts are often not originals, but rather translations from Russian.

The decree as a genre of business discourse has its own constitutive features that must be present irrespective of the language in which the decree is presented: 'discourse as an abstract scheme is constructed, in each particular act, on a concrete language material, has specific content of businesslike character and is expressed in the form of this or that genre, in a particular business situation involving real participants of business communication' (Burkitbayeva 2005: 51). Therefore, some of the features of Kazakh-language decrees treated by Yerezhepova as common to decrees in both Russian and Kazakh should be explained not by the influence of Russian business discourse but as common (universal) features of the decree as a genre of business discourse. Such common features include, for example, standard formal and structural (compositional) characteristics and design of a decree; general functions of titles (nominative, informative, pragmatic, instructional); wide use of nominative units expressing specific objects (for example, 'founding of honorary diploma' – K: *Kurmet diplomyn tagayindau* – R: *uchrezhdeniye Pochetnogo diploma*; 'approval of regulations' – K: *yerezheni bekitu* – R: *utverzhdeniye pravil*; 'insertion of amendments' – K: *ozgerister engizu* – R: *vneseniye izmeneniy*; 'approval of conception' – K: *Tuzhyrymdamany makuldau* – R: *odobreniye Kontseptsiyi*); wide use of imperative forms ('I decree' – K: *kauly etemin* – R: *postanovlyayu*; 'to bring in' – K: *engizilsin* – R: *vnesti*; 'to appoint' – K: *tagayindau* – R: *naznachit'*; 'to receive' – K: *kabyldau* – R: *prinyat'*; and so on) connected with a strict demand to implement the decree in question; the use of cliché forms and cliché constructions (Yerezhepova 2002: 22). By virtue of its fundamental purpose, which requires that it be a compulsory and commanding genre, the decree is possibly one of the genres of business discourse which is less likely to show cultural distinctiveness.

Features of English business discourse in Kazakhstan

Insufficient research in the area of business discourse in the Kazakh and even Russian languages forces Kazakhstani linguists to turn to the varied and rich work of foreign researchers writing on English business discourse in order to apply their expertise to Kazakh business discourse. The aim of this section is to present a survey of studies on English business discourse in Kazakhstan.

At present Kazakh researchers are examining the following issues, among others: the ontology of business discourse and its genres (Burkitbayeva 2005); the functioning and semantics of nominative phrases in business correspondence (Aitureyeva 2006); the role of connecting words in the syntactic and semantic organisation of business texts (Zhambulatova 2006); lexical and syntactic means of designating communicators in business communication (Omarova 2007); syntactic features of business correspondence (Tolengutova 2008); and issues of intercultural communication (Shokhayeva 2006; Sabitova and Issina 2002).

Among these studies, Burkitbayeva's (2005) research on English business discourse should be specially noted. This work presents English business discourse as a sum of interrelated linguistic, cognitive, extra-linguistic and other features inseparably connected with business discourse production, functioning and comprehension. This treatment allows the author to analyse methodologically defining problems of business discourse ontology, interaction and genres; to include in her investigation a conceptual analysis of the notions of 'text' and 'discourse'; to study the interrelation of an official business style and business discourse; to investigate business discourse from the point of an interactive model of communication, 'intradiscursive' analysis; and also to consider business discourse within a modern theory of genres. The problem of differentiation between the notions of 'text' and 'discourse' (text = discourse, text vs. discourse, text and discourse) is solved by Burkitbayeva in the following way: relations between text and discourse cannot be qualified as either equality or identity or symmetrical or contrary relations. Discourse is a wider notion than text and the relation between the two concepts can be defined in terms of set theory as one of inclusion (text $\subset$ discourse). An analogous transfer of the features of the official business style to business discourse has made it possible to establish an actual absorption by business discourse of all essential formal and functional features of the official business style. The ontological study of English business discourse is carried out on the basis of a number of parameters (extra-linguistic and interactional context, language features), all of which are systematically described in a list of collective and distributive descriptors and reflected in a matrix model of business discourse analysis. This model has been successfully used to analyse different types and genres of English business discourse. The next stage is to verify the model with respect to interactive genres of Kazakh and Russian, English and Russian, English and Kazakh Business Discourses (Burkitbayeva 2005).

As the theory and practice of modern management came to Russia and Kazakhstan from the west, Russian and Kazakh business discourses are currently experiencing intensive penetration by English corporate jargon. Western-educated Kazakhstani specialists play a significant role in this process (3,000 young specialists study in the USA, Great Britain and other countries each year as part of the 'Bolashak' state programme alone). They constitute an emerging trilingual (Kazakh, Russian, English) group of managers, financiers, accountants and so on.

Conclusions

At this stage, the features of business discourse in Kazakhstan lie in the co-functioning of business communication in Kazakh, supported by the state; the continuation of business communication in Russian; and the introduction of American/European business communication into Kazakh and Russian business discourses, characteristic of western companies hiring young, western-educated Kazakhstani professionals. These forms of business communication cannot actually be observed in their pure form and are often mixed.

All aspects discussed in this chapter in answer to the questions posed in the introduction can be considered as positive developments in Kazakh business discourse:

1 A positive dynamic can be observed in the process of the expansion of the social functions of the Kazakh language from national language to state language.
2 Kazakh is being successfully implemented for use in written and spoken communication in business, with relatively stable communicative practices and its own set of genres (e.g. decrees, resolutions, agreements, reports, business letters etc.)
3 A growing number of qualified practitioners are able to conduct complex professional communication in Kazakh.

Furthermore, the Kazakh language already has a developed formal business writing style, one of the functional styles of the codified literary language, which is an adequate and valuable resource.

The presence of sufficient language resources for Kazakh business discourse is, however, commingled with the objective difficulties arising from its full implementation as an active discourse and caused by the absence of linguistic and communicative competence among a considerable number of employees in the state and business sectors. Nevertheless, the functional distribution of languages in contemporary Kazakhstan has changed: in accordance with the status of Kazakh as a state language, both government planning concerned with the propagation of Kazakh in business communication and all users of Kazakh and Russian are attempting to change the prevailing distribution of languages in favour of Kazakh. In this sense we can say that Kazakh and Russian, being partners in business communication, have, in a sense, found themselves in a state of opposition. On the one hand, Russian continues to be widely used in business communication; on the other hand, the directive on the dominant use of Kazakh in business communication contributes to the rapid spread of Kazakh, primarily in the bureaucratic sphere.

All these issues are awaiting attention by researchers, as business discourse is not only texts created in communicative situations; it is also what shapes the situation itself, from which genres of business discourse emerge, as well as interactants that are both linguistically and discursively competent operators in a multicultural environment.

Notes

1 The main ethnic groups in Kazakhstan are Kazakhs and Russians. Other ethnic groups are Ukranians, Byelorussians, Uzbeks, Germans, Koreans, Uyghurs, Tatars and others.
2 Language planning is understood as voluntary, concrete activities (attempts) to influence definite subjects of people's language behaviour with the purpose of changing language functioning, language structure regulation, creation of language learning conditions, and spreading a language within or outside state borders through political, educational, economic, public and linguistic institutions. Status language planning is a purposeful legislative regulation of language status, i.e. its legal status, rank as a juridical object, language position in a social system, which are defined by national and/or international legislative acts (Suleimenova et al. 2007: 163, 211, 286–7).
3 Constitution of the Republic of Kazakhstan 1993; Constitution of the Republic of Kazakhstan 1995; Law of the Soviet Socialist Republic of Kazakhstan on Languages in Kazakh SSR – Almaty, 1989; Law of the Republic of Kazakhstan on Languages in the Republic of Kazakhstan – Almaty, 1997.

4 These features of the official business style were defined by the outstanding soviet linguist I.R. Galperin (Galperin 1981: 312–13).

5 The process of describing the official business style is actually the process of standardisation of this sub-language level. Different specialists, among them linguists, teachers, editors and journalists, participate in the process of language planning,. It should be mentioned here that a scientific and lexicographic normative description of the Kazakh language was preceded by the compiling of different textbooks and manuals on business Kazakh (Akhanova et al. 2002a, 2002b; Aldasheva and Burkitbayeva 2002; Aldasheva et al. 2003, 2004; Suleimenova et al. 2005; and so on).

References

Aidarov, G. (1986) *Көне түркі жазба ескерткіштерінің тілі* [The Language of Old Turkic Literary Monuments]. Almaty: Gylym.

Aitureyeva, A. (2006) Functioning and semantics of noun phrases in business correspondence. Current Issues of Discourse: Theory and Practice. *4th Annual CA ABC Conference, 23–4 February, Almaty*, pp. 121–3.

Akhanova, D. K., A. M. Aldasheva, Z. K. Akhmetzhanova, K. K. Kadasheva, and E. D. Suleimenova (2002a) *Ресми-іскери қазақ тілі: Бірінші-үшінші деңгей* [The Official and Business Kazakh Language: Parts 1–3]. Almaty: Arman-PV.

Akhanova, D. K., A. M. Aldasheva, Z. K. Akhmetzhanova, K. K. Kadasheva and E. D. Suleimenova (2002b) *Ресми-іскери қазақ тілі: Грамматикалық түсініктеме* [The Official and Business Kazakh Language: Grammar Guide]. Almaty: Arman-PV.

Aldasheva, A. M. and G. G. Burkitbayeva (2002) *Іскерихаттар: Business Letters: Анықтамалық оқу құралы* [Business Letters: Manual]. Almaty: Legion.

Aldasheva, A. M., Z. K. Akhmetzhanova, K. K. Kadasheva and E. D. Suleimenova (2003) *Ресми іс қағаздары: Мемлекеттік қызметшілерге арналған анықтамалық* [Official Documents: A Guide for State Officials]. Astana: Arman-PV.

Aldasheva, A. M., Z. K. Akhmetzhanova, K. K. Kadasheva and E. D. Suleimenova (2004) *Қазақ тілі: Ресми қарым-қатынас, іс қағаздар тілі* [The Kazakh Language: The Language of Official and Business Documents]. Almaty: Arman-PV.

Ashirova, B. S. (2004) *Нормативті-жарлықшы құжаттар лексикасының арасалмағы* [Peculiarities of decree documents vocabulary]. Communication at Work: Issues and Challenges. *2nd Annual CA ABC Conference, 23–4 January, Almaty*, pp. 80–4.

Baimurunova, A. K (2002) *К вопросу о способах аргументации в деловом письме* [On ways of argumentation in a business letter]. World of Language and Business Communication. *1st Annual CA ABC Conference, 16 November, Almaty*, pp. 140–6.

Bakirova, G. Z. (2004) *Деловое общение, его функции и значение* [Business communication, its functions and meaning]. Communication at Work: Issues and Challenges. *2nd Annual CA ABC Conference, 23–4 January*, Almaty, pp. 3–7.

Balakayev, M. (1959) *Синтаксис словосочетания и простого предложения* [Syntax of Word-Combination and Simple Sentence]. Almaty: Gylym.

Birali, G. A. (2004) *Ұлттық-мәдени ерекшеліктерді тілді оқыту процесінде игерудің кейбір жолдары* [Some issues of national and cultural peculiarities in the process of language teaching]. *Communication at Work: Issues and Challenges. 2nd Annual CA ABC Conference, 23–4 January, Almaty*, pp. 89–92.

Burkitbayeva, G. G. (2005) *Деловой дискурс: онтология и жанры* [Business Discourse: Ontology and Genres]. Almaty: Gylym.

Burkitbayeva, G. G. (2006) *Текст и дискурс: Типы дискурса* [Text and Discourse: Types of Discourse]. Almaty: Daik-Press.

Duisembekova, L. S. (2008) *Проблемы функционирования казахского языка в системе государственного управления Республики Казахстан* [Problems of the Kazakh language functioning in the system of government management]. Problems of Language Preservation during Globalization Period. *7th International Symposium, Kazan State University, July 2–5, Kazan, Tatarstan.*

Galperin, I. R. (1981) *Stylistics.* Moscow: Vysšaja Škola.

Ibatov, A. (1966) *Қазақ тіліндегі есімдіктер тарихынан* [From the History of Kazakh Pronouns]. Almaty: Gylym.

Issayev, S. (1989) *Қазақ әдеби тілінің тарихы* [The History of the Kazakh Literary Language]. Almaty: Gylym.

KazInform (2005) Astana. http://www.inform.kz/index2.php?lang=eng&select=archiv e&section=606&page=582&y=&d=00&m=00.

Kordabayev, T. (1964) *Тарихи синтаксис мәселелері (15–18 ғасырлар материалдары бойынша)* [Some Issues of Historic Syntax (Fifteenth to Eighteenth Centuries]. Almaty: Gylym.

Kuryshzhanov, A. (2001) *Ескі түркі жазба ескерткіштері* [Old Turkic Literary Monuments]. Almaty: Gylym.

Mambetova, M. (2005) *Ресми-іскери клише тұлғалардың семантикасы және қызметі* [Semantics and use of official and business cliché units]. PhD thesis, Almaty.

Omarova, Z. K. (2007) *Способы обозначения коммуникантов в деловом общении (на материале деловых писем английского языка)* [Means of communicators' signification in business communication (explored in English business letters)]. PhD thesis, Almaty.

Sabitova, M. T. and G. I. Issina (2002) *Перевод как важный способ межкультурной коммуникации* [Translation/interpreting as an important means of intercultural communication]. World of Language and Business Communication. *1st Annual CA ABC Conference, 16 November, Almaty*, pp. 176–80.

Salkhanova, Z. K. (2006) *Деловое письмо: признаки и некоторые особенности* [The business letter: its features and some peculiarities]. Current Issues of Discourse: Theory and Practice. 4th Annual CA ABC Conference, 23–4 February, Almaty, pp. 146–9.

Sarybay, M. S. (2004) *О роли английского языка и должности переводчика в современной казахстанской организации (по материалам объявлений о вакансиях переводчиков в прессе)* [On the role of the English language and an interpreter position in a Modern Kazakhstani organization]. *Communication at Work: Issues and Challenges. 2nd Annual CA ABC Conference, 23–24 January*, pp. 130–5.

Sarybay, M. S. (2006) *Языки делового общения в Республике Казахстан* [The languages of business communication in the Republic of Kazakhstan]. In *Current Issues of Discourse: Theory and Practice. 4th Annual CA ABC Conference, 23–4 February 2006*, pp. 150–4.

Shokhayeva, K. K. (2006) *Ағылшын және қазақ іскерлік тілдерінің стильдік ерекшеліктері* [Stylistic features of English and Kazakh business languages]. Current Issues of Discourse: Theory and Practice. *4th Annual CA ABC Conference, 23–4 February, Almaty*, pp. 157–60.

Suleimenova, E. D. and Z. S. Smagulova (2005) *Языковая ситуация и языковое планирование в Казахстане* [Language Situation and Planning in Kazakhstan]. Almaty: Kazakh Universiteti.

Suleimenova, E. D., A. M. Aldasheva, D. K. Akhanova and Z. B. Aldash (2005) *Ресми-іскери тіл: қазақша-орысша тіркесімдер сөздігі. Официально-деловой язык: казахско-русский словарь сочетаемости* [Official and Business Language: Kazakh-Russian Dictionary of Phrases]. Almaty: Arman-PV.

Suleimenova, E. D., N. Z. Shaimerdenova, Z. S. Smagulova and D. K. Akanova (2007) *Словарь социолингвистических терминов* [Dictionary of Sociolinguistic Terms]. Almaty: Kazakh Universiteti.

Sultanov, B. (ed.) (2006) *Демографический ежегодник регионов Казахстана: Статистический сборник* [Demographic Year-Book of Kazakhstani Regions: Statistical Collection]. Almaty: Agency on Statistics.

Syzdykova, R. (1984), *XVIII–XIX гг. Қазақ әдеби тілінің тарихы* [History of the Kazakh Language, eighteenth to nineteenth centuries]. Almaty: Mektep.

Tolengutova, A. S. (2008) *Структурно-семантические и прагматические особенности сложноподчиненного предложения в деловом тексте (на материале английской коммерческой корреспонденции)* [Structural-semantic and pragmatic peculiarities of a complex sentence in business texts (on the basis of English commercial correspondence)]. PhD thesis, Almaty.

Tzoy, A. S. (2006) *Требования к текстам официально-делового стиля, включенным в мультимедийное приложение электронного учебника* [Requirements for texts in the official business style, included in a multimedia appendix to an electronic textbook]. Current Issues of Discourse: Theory and Practice. *4th Annual CA ABC Conference, 23–4 February, Almaty*, pp. 160–1.

Yerezhepova, S. K. (2002) *Официально-деловой стиль в казахском и русском языках: прагмалингвистический аспект* [Official and business Style in Kazakh and Russian: Pragmalinguistic aspect]. PhD thesis, Almaty.

Yergaziyeva, N. I. (1972) *Формирование и развитие официально-деловой речи в казахском языке* [Formation and development of Kazakh official and business language]. PhD thesis, Almaty.

Yergaziyeva, N. I. and A. T. Yesetova (2004) *Принципы разработки учебно-методического комплекса по практическому курсу казахского языка для студентов* [Principles of educational and methodical basis for Kazakh textbook design (for students)]. Communication at Work: Issues and Challenges. *2nd Annual CA ABC Conference, 23–4 January, Almaty*, pp. 44–9.

Zhambulatova, Z. (2006) *Роль коннекторов в синтактико-семантической организации делового текста (на материале английского языка)* [The role of connecting words in the syntactic and semantic organization of business texts) (on the material of the English language)]. Current Issues of Discourse: Theory and Practice. *4th Annual CA ABC Conference, 23–4 February, Almaty*, pp. 129–32.

Conclusions

34

Future horizons: Europe

Mirja Liisa Charles

Introduction

It is a considerable challenge to write a piece focusing on the future of business discourse research in Europe, or, indeed, any other specific locality. The challenge arises from two main sources: first, geographical delimitation; and second, subject delimitation. These challenges, of course, concern most contributors to this volume, but may well still be worth briefly examining here.

The first, geographical, challenge has to do with our current advanced state of globalisation, where it is virtually impossible to restrict a piece of research in geographical terms. A geographical delimitation presents us with the paradox of saying that something is 'local', i.e. specific to a certain location – in this case, Europe – though it is essentially open and available to the whole world. In our world of 'virtual' research, and virtual communication channels, how can any one piece of research be characterised as 'local', i.e. geographically limited? Indeed, the meaning of the word 'local' has to be queried. What makes research European? Must Europe be the point of production – i.e. the place where the researcher operates, and the location of his or her institutional affiliation? Or is it the object of the research which is 'local'? Or even perhaps the place of publication? Obviously, none of these definitions is, in itself, adequate.

The second challenge – the challenge provided by the subject delimitation – has to do with the fact that 'business discourse' is an unwieldy research area that has changed over time, in step with developments in research philosophies, approaches and business circumstances. In this chapter, the term 'business discourse' is taken to cover all texts and communication taking place in businesses. In the multifaceted business world of today, business discourse is thus an umbrella term covering a variety of texts (both written and oral) and communication processes. Some researchers prefer to group themselves under 'communication studies' rather than 'discourse studies'; cases in point are scholars in the fields of corporate, managerial, employee, change or crisis communication. However, whatever their categorisation, the field and its scholars are becoming more focused, while simultaneously branching out into new methodologies and disciplines.

With the above challenges in mind, the best this chapter can do is to adopt an extremely simple solution: in trying to reach towards the future horizons of European business discourse research, this chapter will first reach out to the past in order to identify viable trends and traditions in the research that has been done in European universities and other research institutions, and then project to the future. The chapter starts with a brief discussion of what is arguably the biggest challenge currently facing business, and thus business discourse research: an increasingly sophisticated process of globalisation. With the help of Friedman's (2006) theory of globalisation, it then looks back into how our research field has developed, and suggests trends, foci and achievements which will surely prove instrumental for creating and shaping its future. Finally, that historical overview leads to a discussion of the pillars on which future business discourse research can be built.

The globalisation process as a challenge

In the twenty-first century, globalisation is a truism that applies to most spheres of life. It has penetrated all aspects that here interest us: business is globalised; by definition, therefore, business discourse is globalised; and finally, business discourse research is globalised. Yet, because of the sheer magnitude of the concept, and the way it affects our lives at all levels, it is difficult to comprehend and digest it fully.

A point of entry into understanding globalisation as a process is offered by Friedman (2006). According to Friedman, globalisation is not a new phenomenon that has recently emerged; it has been around for a while, and developed through stages. Friedman divides the process into three stages. In the first stage, he claims, globalisation concerned countries; in the second stage, it concerned companies; in the third, it is individuals that globalise. Drawing parallels with more traditional terms used in business, Friedman's stage 1.0 would seem to approximate the more familiar term 'foreign trade'. At this stage, globalised business was fairly well structured and manageable; international business discourse was not seen as a major concern for all individuals; it basically only concerned those who chose careers in foreign trade.

Friedman's 'globalisation stage 2.0' would seem to describe what in corporate speech is referred to as 'internationalisation', or 'going international'. At this stage, businesses woke up to the fact that they faced greater requirements in overseas performance, and keener international competition. Companies became multinational, and recognised the accompanying wide variety of communication needs, which now encompassed virtually all corporate activities – not just the import and export functions. Business discourse was now being produced for a global market; it embraced most employees in globally operating companies.

'Globalisation stage 3.0.' lacks an easy parallel. This is because what it refers to is a new development for which no adequate description existed until now. Although all Friedman's stages were fuelled by technology, in this third stage technology is the driving, dynamic force to an unprecedented degree. The emergence of this stage of globalisation saw technology being brought down to the level of the individual, in the form of laptops, software, mobile phones and easy access to internet. As Friedman points out: 'every person now must, and can, ask: Where do *I* as an individual fit into the global competition and opportunities of the day, and how can *I*, on my own, collaborate with others globally?' (2006: 11; emphasis in original).

Globalisation now affects individuals functioning in their own, local environments. However, as Friedman points out, it is not globalisation reaching out to the local, or the individual; it is the local – the individual – becoming global. This he refers to as the 'glo-balisation of the local' (2006: 507–8). The challenge of globalisation, then, is: How can 'local' European business discourse research become 'global'? The answer is simple: by strengthening and building on the most viable trends which have been carried through from its strong research tradition. This strategy should see us through into what might eventually be described as 'globalisation stage 4.0' – whenever and whatever that might be. This chapter argues that, at its core, European research has always had global trends. These trends will next be briefly explored.

The past that leads to the future

In Europe, it all started from linguistics; linguists developed methodology which focused on discourse, i.e. text, rather than their traditional forte, sentences, words, meanings and sounds. The year 1975 was a breakthrough. In that year, Sinclair and Coulthard (1975) produced their pioneering framework for analysing classroom interaction. In its emphasis on units above the level of the sentence, their work was related to the work already done by continental text grammarians (e.g. van Dijk 1972). Importantly, the emphasis was on the main organisational forces that governed discourse; of these, one of the most important ones was the purpose for which text was produced – i.e. functions rather than sentences. The main philosophical home was speech act theory, largely developed in America (Austin 1975; Searle 1969), though based on ideas already presented in 1934 by the German lin-guist Bühler (1934; also Firth 1957). Accordingly, a dynamic view of language emerged: things were done through language; business was done through language, discourse.

This view of language/discourse as organised, dynamic activity was very quickly sup-plemented by European linguists with ideas borrowed from (mostly) American sociolin-guists and ethnographers like Hymes (1972, 1986) and Gumperz (1982). Sociolinguistics allowed discourse analysts to look at the social and demographic variables which impacted on text. Likewise, in analyses of spoken discourse, conversation analysis soon caught on in Europe, with Heritage (Heritage and Atkinson 1984) and Drew (1984) contributing substantially to the theory and methodology carved out by the American researchers Schegloff, Sacks and Jefferson (Schegloff and Sacks 1974; Sacks et al. 1974). Influenced by sociology and ethnography, conversation analysis gave researchers of spoken interac-tion a systematic theoretical framework and a toolkit for studying the way interaction was organised, and meanings jointly created, in conversation. These developments resulted from co-operation between different disciplines, and between scholars from different parts of the world.

Meanwhile, pragmatics was encouraging linguists to look closely at situational and contextual variables in the production of discourse. In this vein, and based on the work of American philosopher Grice (1975), Brown and Levinson (1987) broadened the field of linguistic analysis towards yet another discipline – anthropology. Their description of 'politeness strategies' inspired (and still inspires) scholars, though proving to be a some-what unwieldy instrument.

Equipped with these approaches and methodologies, European linguists very soon turned their attention to what became known as the study of languages for specific pur-poses (LSP; Dudley-Evans 1998). LSP is, in many respects, a very European approach: It arose from the everyday reality of a multilingual European environment in which there was a constant and increasing need for focused and efficient foreign language teaching and training. The aim of LSP was to identify the essence of the language used for various 'specific' purposes, and therefore to identify what language learners should be taught. The language used for business was, right from the beginning, seen as one of the highly specific and important areas (Dudley-Evans and St John 1996). LSP inspired copious research outside the English-speaking world, particularly in Germany, Austria and Scandinavia (e.g. Alexander 1988; Engberg 1997; Trosborg 1997).

While some LSP researchers homed in on terminology as the specific feature of a language used for specific purposes, others examined the way business context shaped discourse. Thus, a significant research approach gained prominence: genre analysis. John Swales's groundbreaking work on academic discourse (1981, 1990) inspired his pupil Vijay Bhatia (working in UK in the early 1980s) to branch off from his initial interest in legal English (e.g. Bhatia 1983) into a genre analysis of professional – including business – discourse (Bhatia 1993). Combining various contextual and organisational perspectives on discourse, genre analysis started to explore ways in which discourse communities created texts for their own, specific purposes in contexts which were becoming increasingly complex (e.g. Nickerson 2000, 2005).

These achievements – and many others – established multidisciplinarity and international (global) co-operation as firm features of European business discourse research. Much of the research was produced in 'globalisation stages 1.0 and 2.0'. During 'stage 1.0', the everyday discourse of export and import staff was studied; crucial and challenging situations were identified, and the discourses described. As a result, research abounded in negotiations (e.g. Lampi 1989; Firth 1995; Charles 1996; Charles and Charles 1999; Vuorela 2005a, 2005b), meetings (e.g. Williams 1988; Bargiela-Chiappini and Harris 1997; Poncini 2004), business letters (e.g. Ylijokipii 1994), faxes (e.g. Akar and Louhiala-Salminen 1999), and reports (Gunnarsson et al. 1997). These studies supplemented the more terminology-oriented LSP research, and together they provided a basis for the language training of corporate staff. With this discoursal knowledge, businesses entered 'stage 2.0'.

'Globalisation stage 2.0.' was accompanied by an increasing research focus on the business context and communication processes. It is therefore only natural that, roughly at this stage, business communication research landed in Europe from America. Still largely drawing on their linguistic research tradition, several European business discourse researchers now started to see themselves as 'business communication' researchers. They examined the way business processes were created and managed through discourse and communication. Researchers coming from established business disciplines like management and marketing further contributed to multidisciplinarity.

These developments led the way to 'globalisation stage 3'. Nickerson and Planken (Chapter 1 in this volume) report on studies which are clearly being carried out in the spirit and context of 'stage 3.0'. In addition to the work they discuss, however, there is still a lot to be done, as each stage of globalisation is characterised by new ways of doing business – and they need to be studied from the discourse point of view. For example, electronic shopping has been around for a while, but so far few studies have been done on its discourse (see, however, Laine 2004); discourse on internet and in other new media are, as yet, little explored (see, however, e.g. Bargiela-Chiappini 2005, on internet discourse, and Garzone et al. 2007, on web genres and multimodality). Although some work has recently been done on emailing (e.g. Gimenez 2000, 2006; Kankaanranta 2005), there is a great need for more, in order to understand the significant role that this form of text has in modern business. Also, outsourced call centres located in, for example, India are a prime example of developments affecting individuals. There, new dimensions for telephone communications appear, which beg for description from the business discourse perspective. With the accepted and recognised impact that context has on discourse, how are these new discourses affected by their truly global nature? Are they 'cultureless', which basically only means that they are not recognisably of any one particular national culture – or are we speaking of a 'business culture'? Clearly, culture as a concept needs to be revisited. Or should it be ditched? Is the new global business discourse cultureless? Some current research on business english as a lingua franca (BELF) argues that the 'new' global business discourse is an amalgamation of the cultures of its users, currently in a state of flux (e.g. Louhiala-Salminen et al. 2005; Louhiala-Salminen and Charles 2006; Charles 2007). As Nickerson and Planken (Chapter 1 in this volume) point out, a wealth of research topics lies here.

Throughout its development, globalisation has been driven by the need of companies to be competitive. Business discourse research has to address the issue of corporate competitiveness. In 'stage 3.0', we can see new ways of gaining a competitive edge in global business emerging. Cases in point are networking, and various alliances and partnerships. The discourse of business networks, for example, has yet to be explicated (see, however, Spencer-Oatey 2000a, 2000b). In all, the 'business context' must be seen in a more focused light, in terms of different ways of operating and creating a competitive edge.

Interestingly, not only is the world of business discourse research globalised through global objects of research, but the everyday life of business discourse scholars is now truly globalised. Research has always been, to some extent, global, but now more so than ever before. Researchers form a global discourse community. Advanced technology has been accompanied by increasing mobility and instantaneous dissemination of research results. Research findings, challenges and developments are being shared online. Trends, ideas and influences are increasingly mixing. It is virtually impossible, and, indeed, irrelevant, to try to decipher the geographical origins of new ideas; what is still important, however, is the identification of the individual who has combined those ideas in a particular, idiosyncratic manner. The best research knowhow and expertise can be pooled through global research networking – a bright future, with potential for increasing standards of scholarship. However, with this rise in research standards comes increasing competition and rivalry, problems involving plagiarism and copyright on the net – all challenges that need to be addressed.

And so to 'globalisation stage 4.0'?

The above brief historical survey has demonstrated some trends in European business discourse research which have equipped Europe to meet the challenges of what may, at some point, be referred to as 'globalisation stage 4.0'. First, there has been openness and willingness to take on board, and be inspired by, research from different parts of the world. Second, there is the pragmatic applicability of the research, stemming from close co-operation with companies, and a close link with practical training and educational needs. These are strands of motivation that run through our history. Two other basic trends, however, still deserve brief descriptions: (1) the way in which European research is grounded in the multilingual and multicultural environment from which it stems and for which it is created (for a discussion see Charles 1998), and (2) the tendency to look towards different fields of research, and an ability to adapt, modify and expand on knowledge created in a wide range of disciplines, with different methodologies and theoretical frameworks. Although this last characteristic has certainly already been pointed out, it still needs to be emphasised. I will therefore next briefly attempt to show how these last two characteristics can be expected to help Europe take on the challenges of the future (for a global review of future trends, see Suchan and Charles 2006).

The European research environment: multiple languages – or one lingua franca?

According to the UNESCO world cultural report (2000), there are forty-eight official languages in Europe. At the time of writing, the European Union has twenty-three official languages. All EU member states have the right to operate in their own native tongue, and all major EU documentation has to be produced in all of the official languages of the Union; the EU is also committed to producing the necessary interpreter and translator services. What counts as an 'official language' – or even 'a language' – is debatable, of course, but what is significant in this European situation is that the number of languages (however defined) shows no signs of diminishing. Moreover, if we link language to national culture, the number of 'cultures' in Europe does not seem to be on the decrease either. Quite the contrary: small(ish) cultural groups, with their own languages, are becoming increasingly assertive; witness developments in the Balkans and Spain, for example. To this desire to uphold national languages and national cultures, European scholars are responding. Business discourse research on the more minor languages in world business abound; on the other hand, the role of English as a lingua franca is being increasingly researched (see Chapter 14 in this volume).

Although healthy in many ways, the tradition of studying the business discourse of a small language, nation or culture faces a predicament. Should these studies on, say, Flemish and Finnish – to name just a couple of the relatively minor languages from the point of view of world business – be published in the local language, to benefit the local language community maximally and to uphold the viability of the local language? Or should they be published in English, to benefit the global business and research community maximally? Currently, both are happening. There are thriving and well-established journals publishing research in 'local' languages (e.g. *Hermes: Journal of Language and Communication Studies*, published in the various Scandinavian languages by Aarhus School of Business, Denmark; and *Virittäjä*, published in Finnish by Kotikielen seura, Helsinki, Finland). Likewise many scholars publish in a local language, with the bulk of their work dealing with that language. The problem is that, because of severe language restrictions, this research is being read in geographically limited regions only. In spite of the localisation of the language, these journals are, nevertheless, profoundly affected by globalisation. This is because the articles mostly deal with topics that are globally interesting; likewise, the theories and methodologies used, as well as the background literature referred to, are global. These articles are therefore cases of bringing the 'global' into the 'local'. With the emphasis on the value of a multilingual Europe, these local publications are likely to remain a feature of European research, with a significant, though limited, role to play. However, with increasing pressures in European academia to publish in high-ranking international journals, it – sadly – looks as if publications written in local languages are going to be fewer in the future. Economic power – publishing clout – is becoming increasingly important and is starting to dominate in research. It is likely to dictate in favour of the use of English. To maintain a multilingual Europe in the future, scholars will need to make a special effort to do research in, and on, a wide range of languages.

This desire to maintain a range of languages on the business discourse scene is sometimes taken to be in direct conflict with the spread of the use of the global lingua franca, English. In this 'lingua franca or local language' debate, questions arise concerning language choice in business discourse, but also questions concerning the nature of English used as a lingua franca. What, for example, is the 'division of labour', in a globally operating multinational, between local languages and English? Will the use of English continue to gain momentum, to a point where it will eventually suppress the use of other languages for the purposes of doing business? Some research (e.g. Louhiala-Salminen 2002) would seem to indicate that there is a role for both: while the 'hard' side of business – money issues, terms, i.e. the actual business of selling and buying – is done in English, the 'soft' side of business – i.e. the relationship-building and rapport creation – is more successfully done in the local language. Also, according to a survey done in two Scandinavian-based multinationals, 80 per cent of in-house communication took place in the mother tongue, and only 20 per cent in the official corporate language, English (Louhiala-Salminen 2002). Likewise, code-switching, where speakers switch between the 'official' English and local languages, abounds, as situations and the mix of speakers change. To delve deeper into issues like these, we need scholars who are multi- or bilingual, so that they are able to analyse both 'local' language discourse and English lingua franca discourse. Clearly, this is a niche for European researchers.

Disciplinary variation

As a result of input from a wide variety of disciplines, European research is in a position to provide a multiple perspective on business discourse. For this disciplinary co-operation to continue to be successful, however, the conceptual relationship between business and discourse will have to be revisited, and tenets taken for granted will have to be re-examined. Despite the emphasis that this chapter has given to linguistic research, it is clear that linguistics nowadays has joined forces particularly with disciplines like management, marketing and communication studies for examining business discourse. This multidisciplinarity is proving particularly useful, with research in, for example, corporate communication coming to the fore (e.g. Frandsen and Johansen 2007). It is asking useful questions such as: is discourse shaped by the nature of business (as linguistics would often have it) – or is it the other way round, i.e. is business shaped by the nature of its discourse (as, for example, critical management studies would have it)? These are profound questions which affect the very basis of our discipline: what is it that we are researching – text or business processes? Does 'business discourse research' as a discipline (if it may be so called) belong to the sphere of linguistics or is it really a part of business studies? As we have seen, the linguistic research tradition starts with the examination of text, and through that, learns about how business is carried out, how sales are done and deals negotiated. Other disciplines, like management, organisational studies, even communication studies, tend to start from business processes and what companies aim or want to achieve, and from there proceed to looking at how – and indeed whether – the discourses involved support these aims. In their differences, however, the various disciplinary perspectives are not contradictory; rather, they supplement each other, and give fuller insight into both business operations/management and business discourse. As Nickerson and Planken (Chapter 1 in this volume) point out, a much-needed critical approach is emerging.

Summary and conclusions

This chapter has looked at developments in business discourse research from the perspective of globalisation processes. It has argued that, because of its focus on changing discourses in a changing environment, findings from business discourse research have provided the business community with tools that have facilitated the globalisation process. Not surprisingly, however, the chapter has simultaneously identified advancing globalisation as a major challenge.

The chapter argues that Europe is well poised to take on the challenge of the future – 'globalisation stage 4.0'? European research strengths have developed over the years, and now give a firm foundation for future work. Its international tradition, embracing as it always has scholars coming to Europe from all over the world – and Europeans going elsewhere – to share and develop ideas, has prepared the European research community to tackle the requirements of global business while maintaining a local identity. Its firm grounding in the multilingual and multicultural European environment offers rich insight into a multifaceted world of business activities carried out in both local languages and the global lingua franca – English. The multidisciplinarity and the mix of multiple methodologies (as exemplified in this volume) which European scholars have embraced over the years mean that there is the methodological expertise required to tackle wide-ranging research, as also the motivation to discover new, emerging research issues. Indeed, this multidisciplinarity is being encouraged by the EU, which tends to fund research projects which examine issues from a variety of perspectives and disciplinary points of view. Likewise, the close links between research and foreign language teaching ensure that our field plays a part in further enhancing globalisation.

The intellectual capital accumulated through past research now allows us to broaden the scope of discourse research – to see discourse as communication, and communication as utterly basic and integral to business operations (see Chapter 23 in this volume). To do justice to the multifaceted phenomenon of 'business discourse', research will increasingly have to be done in global, often virtual, project teams, where a variety of expertise is represented, and geographical borders eliminated. Technological developments and the fluidity of patterns and agendas in global business must be accompanied by parallel developments in research: increasing methodological and conceptual flexibility, disciplinary co-operation and multimethod research will result in insightful grounding of research in both global and local environments. With increasing technological sophistication, the current qualitative emphasis in our field can be supplemented by quantitative studies of corpora, and increasing use of computer software as an analytical tool. This opens up great potential.

With changes in the global business scene, our research field will also change – as it should. Increasingly, business discourse is being referred to as business communication.

How does that affect our disciplinary status? However named, I hope that business discourse researchers will continue to be the practically oriented, applied scholars that we, to date, take pride in being. For this, we must continue to work with companies, helping them to shape up to their developing environments at a very practical level. Likewise, the link with pedagogical and training needs should be maintained. These two requirements will help us in our future research endeavours, and feed new insights into our work, thus benefiting the whole extended business discourse community on its way to take on the challenges of 'globalisation stage 4.0'.

References

Akar, D. and L. Louhiala-Salminen (1999) Towards a new genre: A comparative study of business faxes. In F. Bargiela-Chiappini and C. Nickerson (eds), *Writing Business: Genre, Media and Discourse*. London: Longman, pp. 207–26.

Alexander, R. J. (1988) Examining the spoken English of students of European business studies: Purposes, problems and perspectives. *System*, 16: 41–7.

Austin, J. L. (1975) *How to Do Things with Words*, 2nd edn. Cambridge, MA: Harvard University Press.

Bargiela-Chiappini, F. (2005) In memory of the business letter: Multimedia, genres and social action in a banking website. In P. Gillaerts and M. Gotti (eds), *Genre Variation in Business Letters*. Bern: Peter Lang, pp. 99–122.

Bargiela-Chiappini, F. and S. Harris (1997) *Managing Language: The Discourse of Corporate Meetings*. Amsterdam and Philadelphia: John Benjamins.

Bhatia, V. K. (1983) Simplification v. easification: The case of legal texts. *Applied Linguistics*, 4(1): 42–54.

Bhatia, V. K. (1993) *Analysing Genre: Language Use in Professional Settings*. London and New York: Longman.

Brown, P. and S. C. Levinson (1987) *Politeness: Some Universals in Language Usage*. Cambridge: Cambridge University Press.

Buhler, K. (1934) *Sprachtheorie*. Jena: Gustav Fisher.

Charles, M. L. (1996) Business negotiations: Interdependence between discourse and the business relationship. *English for Specific Purposes*, 15(1): 19–36.

Charles, M. L. (1998) Europe: Oral business communication. *Business Communication Quarterly*, 61(3): 85–93.

Charles, M. L. (2007) Language matters in global communication. *Journal of Business Communication*, 44: 260–82.

Charles, M. L. and D. Charles (1999) Sales negotiations: Bargaining through tactical Summaries. In M. Hewings and C. Nickerson (eds), *Business English: Research into Practice*. London: Longman, pp. 71–82.

Drew, P. (1984) Speakers' 'reportings' in invitation sequences. In J. M. Atkinson and J. Heritage (eds), *Structures of Social Action: Studies in Conversation Analysis*. Cambridge: Cambridge University Press, pp. 129–51.

Dudley-Evans, T. (1998) *Developments in English for Specific Purposes*. Cambridge: Cambridge University Press.

Dudley-Evans, T. and M. J. St John (1996) *Report on Business English: A Review of Research and Published Teaching Materials*. Princeton: Educational Testing Service.

Engberg, J. (1997) *Konventionen von Fachtextsorten*. Tübingen: Günter Narr.

Firth, A. (1995) *Discourse at Work: Negotiating by Telex, Fax and Phone*. Aalborg: Department of Languages and Intercultural Studies, Aalborg University.

Firth, J. R. (1957) *Papers in Linguistics 1934–1951*. Oxford: Oxford University Press.

Frandsen, F. and W. Johansen (2007) The apology of a sports icon: Crisis communication and apologetic ethics. *Hermes: Journal of Language and Communication Studies*, 38: 85–104.

Friedman, T. L. (2006) *The World is Flat: A Brief History of the Twenty-First Century*. New York: Farrar, Straus & Giroux.

Garzone, G., P. Catenaccio and G. Poncini (eds) (2007) *Multimodality and Webgenres in Corporate Communication*. Bern: Peter Lang.

Gimenez, J. (2000) Business email communication: Some emerging tendencies in register. *English for Specific Purposes*, 19(3): 237–51.

Gimenez, J. (2006) Embedded business emails: Meeting new demands in international business communication. *English for Specific Purposes*, 25(2): 154–72.

Grice, H. P. (1975) Logic and conversation. In P. Cole and J. L. Morgan (eds), *Syntax and Semantics III: Speech Acts*. New York: Academic Press, pp. 41–58.

Gumperz, J. (1982) *Discourse Strategies*. Cambridge: Cambridge University Press.

Gunnarsson, B.-L., P. Linell and B. Nordberg (1997) Introduction. In B.-L. Gunnarsson, P. Linell and B. Nordberg (eds), *The Construction of Professional Discourse*. London: Longman, pp. 1–11.

Heritage, J. and M. Atkinson (1984) Introduction. In M. Atkinson and J. Heritage (eds), *Structures of Social Action*. Cambridge: Cambridge University Press, pp. 1–15.

Hymes, D. (1972) Towards ethnographies of communication: The analysis of communicative events. In P. P. Giglioni (ed.), *Language and Social Context*. Harmondsworth: Penguin, pp. 21–44.

Hymes, D. (1986) Directions in sociolinguistics. In J. J. Gumperz and D. Hymes (eds), *The Ethnography of Communication*. Oxford: Blackwell.

Kankaanranta, A. (2005) 'Hej Seppo, could you pls comment on this!' Internal email communication in lingua franca English in a multinational company. Jyväskylä: Centre for Applied Language Studies. http://ebooks.jyu.fi/solki/9513923207.pdf. Accessed 21 March 2007.

Laine, P. (2004) Language of interaction in online shopping. PhD thesis, University of Vaasa, Linguistics 26, Applied Linguistics. http://lipas.uwasa.fi/julkaisu/acta/acta123.pdf. Accessed 31 March 2007.

Lampi, M. (1989) *Linguistic Components of Strategy in Business Negotiations*. Helsinki: Helsinki School of Economics.

Louhiala-Salminen, L. (2002) *Communication and Language Use in Merged Corporations: Cases Stora Enso and Nordea*. Helsinki: Helsinki School of Economics – Heseprint.

Louhiala-Salminen, L. and M. Charles (2006) English as the lingua franca of international business communication: Whose English? What English? In J. C. Palmer-Silveira, M. F. Ruiz-Garrido and I. Fortanet-Gomez (eds), *Intercultural and International Business Communication*. Bern: Peter Lang, pp. 27–54.

Louhiala-Salminen, L., M. Charles and A. Kankaanranta (2005) English as a lingua franca in Nordic corporate mergers: Two case companies. *English for Specific Purposes*, 24(4): 401–21.

Nickerson, C. (2000) *Playing the Corporate Language Game*. Amsterdam: Rodopi.

Nickerson, C. (2005) Are you being served? A genre analysis of American and Dutch company replies to customer inquiries. *English for Specific Purposes*, 24(1): 93–109.

Poncini, G. (2004) *Discursive Strategies in Multicultural Business Meetings*. Bern: Peter Lang.

Sacks, H., E. A. Schegloff and G. Jefferson (1974) A simplest systematics for the organization of turn taking for conversation. *Language*, 50(4): 696–735.

Schegloff, E. A. and H. Sacks (1974) Opening up closings. In R. Turner (ed.), *Ethnomethodology*. Harmondsworth: Penguin, pp. 233–64.

Searle, J. R. (1969) *Speech Acts*. Cambridge: Cambridge University Press.

Sinclair, J. and R. M. Coulthard (1975) *Towards an Analysis of Discourse*. Oxford: Oxford University Press.

Spencer-Oatey, H. (2000a) Rapport management: A framework for analysis. In H. Spencer-Oatey (ed.), *Culturally Speaking: Managing Rapport through Talk across Cultures*. London: Continuum, pp. 11–46.

Spencer-Oatey, H. (ed.) (2000b) *Culturally Speaking: Managing Rapport through Talk across Cultures*. London: Continuum.

Suchan, J. and M. L. Charles (2006) Business communication research: Past, present, and future. *Journal of Business Communication*, 43: 389–97.

Swales, J. (1981) *Aspects of Article Introductions*. Birmingham: University of Aston, Language Studies Unit.

Swales, J. (1990) *Genre Analysis: English in Academic and Research Settings*. Cambridge: Cambridge University Press.

Trosborg, A. (1997) *Rhetorical Strategies in Legal Language: Discourse Analysis of Statutes and Contracts*. Tübingen: Narr.

UNESCO (2000) UNESCO world cultural report, 2000. http://www.unesco.org/culture/worldreport/htmleng/stat2/table6.pdf. Accessed 31 March 2007.

van Dijk, T. A. (1972) *Some Aspects of Text Grammars*. The Hague: Mouton.

Vuorela, T. (2005a) How does a sales team reach goals in intercultural business negotiations? A case study. *English for Specific Purposes*, 24(2): 65–92.

Vuorela, T. (2005b) Laughing matters: A case of humour in multicultural business negotiations. *Negotiation Journal*, 21: 105–30.

Williams, M. (1988) Language taught for meetings and language used in meetings: Is there anything in common? *Applied Linguistics*, 9(1): 45–58.

Ylijokipii, H. (1994) Requests in professional discourse: A cross-cultural study of British, American and Finnish business writing. PhD thesis, Helsinki, Suomalainen Tiedeakatemia.

35

Future horizons: North America

Ronald E. Dulek and Margaret Baker Graham

Introduction

Business discourse is alive, well and undergoing constant flux in North America. Sometimes this flux leads to standardisation, as Jones's (2007) study of corporate web home pages documents. At other times it involves continuous change and moderate confusion, as Bluedorn et al. (1999) note in their assessment of polychronicity. No matter what the outcome, however, these ongoing changes will provide material for academic scholars to analyse for decades to come.

An equally interesting and highly pertinent question for researchers in business discourse, and a question extremely relevant for North American researchers where business discourse falls under the rubric of business or professional communication, deals with where these changes in business discourse will be studied. In particular, will business and professional communication continue to emerge as a separate and distinct discipline within North American universities? Or will it be subsumed further into other disciplines such as communications, English or management? The answers to these questions are important since they determine not just whether these studies will appear in traditionally field-specific journals such as the *Journal of Business Communication* and the *Journal of Business and Technical Communication* but also whether these studies will be centred on business discourse, with ancillary management and professional implications, or whether on management and professional situations, with ancillary business discourse implications.

This chapter will attempt to provide answers to the above listed issues by examining the future of North American professional communication through the lenses of two divergent theories. The first of these, the theory of constraints, will reveal five key constraints that the field faces as it tries to develop into a fully fledged academic discipline. These constraints must be understood and overcome for the field to develop academically. The second of these theories, the theory of opportunity, involves an analysis of three key opportunities that the field holds. Capitalising on these opportunities, we have become convinced, can help the field overcome the aforementioned constraints and continue to develop into a viable and highly valuable academic discipline.

Background

Deborah Andrews's excellent earlier chapter in this book (Chapter 3) assesses the field's present position astutely. She hits the target precisely when she describes the field as sitting 'at the crossroads of many disciplines' in North America. This crossroads location provides enormous opportunities for the field to develop, along with equally serious threats. Let us briefly extend Andrews's crossroads metaphor to clarify the purpose of this chapter and this *Handbook*. We will then comment further on her chapter before pursuing additional analysis of the field.

North American crossroads can be places where people meet, exchange ideas and experiences, and sometimes remain to build wonderful places for others to examine. Some of our finest North American cites, including Chicago, St Louis, Québec, Toronto and Winnipeg, are located at key geographical crossroads. In other instances, however, North American crossroads become places with cheap restaurants, tawdry motels and unsightly petrol stations. One need only look at the intersection of Highways 30 and 41 in Northern Indiana – an area long promoted as the 'Crossroads of America' – to see what can happen. Modern travellers do their utmost to avoid this crossroads for both aesthetic and safety reasons. Ideally, this analysis, along with those by Andrews and others in this *Handbook*, will provide valuable insights for helping the field of business discourse in North America and throughout the world develop into valued pieces of property rather than tawdry, abandoned rest stops.

A second benefit of Andrews's excellent study is that she provides a comprehensive overview of the field's present condition. She precisely identifies the main communication associations as well as the primary journals in the field. Her comments on the field's history are also well done and thorough, although her observation that specific research attention to communication in business in the USA is usually seen as dating from World War II needs a minor addition. While she is correct that the field began receiving traditional research attention post-World War II, it is also important to note that the study and teaching of business communication – then called business writing – have been practised as an academic 'field of study' in North America since before World War I. The early work of Alta Guinn Saunders (1926) demonstrates these earlier origins. Douglas and Hildebrandt's (1985) collection of essays on the history of business writing extensively documents the field's historical background. Even without this minor addition, however, Andrews's observations are on target and accurate. Even more importantly, her comments pave the way for this chapter to look forward with regard to the future of business communication in North America.

The field truly is at a crossroads – and it needs to choose its future direction carefully. The field faces serious future threats, but it also has enormous opportunities. The field's scholars need to help it overcome the threats and take advantage of the opportunities if they want to see the land of business discourse flourish. This chapter, along with the others in this *Handbook*, seeks to help guide the field along the path of opportunity. It will do so by analysing the field's future prospects both as an academic discipline and as a field of potentially fertile academic research. Through this process we hope, as we have already mentioned, to guide the field towards becoming a valued location for academic study and career development.

Methodology

To conduct the analysis, we adapted and applied two theoretical frames not previously used within business communication research: the theory of constraints and the theory of opportunity.

The first of these tools, the theory of constraints, derives from work done by Eliyahu Goldratt in the late 1970s and early 1980s. Goldratt designed the theory primarily for application to manufacturing facilities. It quickly emerged, however, as an accompaniment to Deming's total quality management movement (1982). Goldratt and Cox's premise, developed in *The Goal: A Process of Ongoing Improvement* (1986), was to apply Liebig's Law of the Minimum to manufacturing facilities.

The Law of the Minimum states that a system's output is limited by the scarcest resource (Liebig, 1855). Thus, an abundance of resources will not guarantee growth if the availability of a necessary resource is limited. Stated simply, the availability of that limited resource determines the growth rate. An excess of other resources makes no difference.

Goldratt applied the same logic to manufacturing facilities. He recognised that a manufacturing facility can produce no more than the key production constraint allows. The scarcest resource sets the pace for the entire system.

When combined with Deming's continuous improvement model, Goldratt's theory of constraints delivers ongoing improvement in the production process. Application of the theory works because as the productivity in one link increases, another link emerges as the new impediment. Management's focus must then shift to this new location and impose another improvement process upon it.

The theory of opportunity, the second theoretical frame that we plan to apply to North American business communication, derives from the field of entrepreneurial studies. Initially, researchers explored the concept of opportunity recognition as an essential quality of successful entrepreneurs (Stevenson et al. 1985). They brought together data and perspectives from a variety of different disciplines, ranging from cognitive psychology to behavioural economics, to explore the opportunity concept (Bhave 1994). Ultimately, these researchers built the field of opportunity recognition into a viable, essential part of entrepreneurship research (Venkataraman 1997).

Building on the above-mentioned work in opportunity recognition, while adding some additional work of their own, Ardichvili et al. (2003) developed the theory of opportunity identification, later and hereafter referred to as the theory of opportunity, as a means for researchers to understand and explore 'the process of opportunity identification/ recognition and development' (p. 121). Essentially, the theory contends that opportunities develop from three primary conditions: (1) the presence of key personal traits; (2) the establishment of vital social networks; and (3) the accumulation/acquisition of prior knowledge of the field. When these ingredients are present, the probability of entrepreneurial opportunity being developed increases enormously.

Ardichvili et al. further deconstruct the theory of opportunity by exploring key characteristics within each condition. Thus, qualities such as creativity and optimism are essential within personal traits. Additionally, ties, actions, partnerships and an inner circle are necessary within social networking. And, finally, an understanding of markets, customer problems and ways to serve customers is a vital ingredient of prior knowledge.

Both the theory of constraints and the theory of opportunity provide interesting and, we think, highly relevant ways to examine the future of business communication in North America. Both provide ways to assess the future consequences of our present condition. Both tools should provide insights to help us build the field into an attractive location where future scholars may choose to visit and reside.

Theory of constraints analysis

We have identified five constraints that will shape the field's research and disciplinary development over the next ten to fifteen years. We selected these constraints through targeted interviews as well as through a thorough review of the field's literature. This list of constraints is certainly not all-inclusive. Nor do we necessarily believe that we have identified the single most important constraint. Rather, we contend only that each of these constraints must be dealt with for the field of business communication to continue to develop and prosper within North American universities. We will leave it to other scholars to identify and explore additional constraints.

Constraint 1: the interdisciplinary nature of the field

The field has spilled much ink debating whether business communication is or is not a North American discipline. Can a field that is made up of pieces of management, rhetoric and linguistics – to name a few of the disciplines – count as its own discipline?

Some twenty-six years ago Daniel (1983) claimed the field lacked legitimacy. Hagge (1986) followed on and labelled it an 'orphaned discipline'. These two critiques have been met with over two decades of counter-claims to prove disciplinary status. Some of the best arguments and discussions on this point include Gieseleman (1989), Russell (1991), Rentz (1993), Shaw (1993), Shelby (1993, 1996), Argenti (1996), Reinsch (1996), Rogers (1996) and Locker (1998).

The overall consensus of the above-mentioned discussions is that business communication is a discipline from the perspective of having academic journals, one or more professional associations, reference groups such as editors and peer review boards, and graduate offerings in institutions of higher learning. However, the field fails the 'discipline test' if the criterion of having a singular research methodology is imposed. It is important to add, we believe, that fields such as English literature, philosophy, history, marketing and management also fail by this criterion. No matter what point of view one takes about disciplinary status, however, no one debates that the field is interdisciplinary. The field contains fragments of management, rhetoric, linguistics and other disciplines. Overall, our field's representatives take pride and see value in its interdisciplinary nature. Recently, many of our scholars have praised this point, including Wardrope (2001), Barton (2001), Locker (1994), Lowry et al. (2004), Du-Babcock (2006), Graham (2006a) and Dulek (2006). With this praise ringing in one's ears, then, one might inquire: 'Why label the field's interdisciplinary nature as a constraint?' The answer is simple. The interdisciplinary nature of our field is one of several impediments to the field's research productivity. Forman and Markus (2005) make this point clearly when they observe: '[T]he rhetoric encouraging interdisciplinary research has far outstripped the study of such undertakings' (p. 81). Stated simply, we talk about interdisciplinary research more than we do it. Rhetoricians tend not to stray into management theory, and management researchers equally avoid rhetorical theory.

We must, however, additionally add that this focused, field-specific approach has important benefits. In fact, it makes total sense from a strategic publication standpoint. For as Forman and Markus observe, getting interdisciplinary research accepted for publication in highly ranked journals is a high-risk endeavor. Focused, field-specific research is much easier to place.

Constraint 2: methodological consistency

A field that is truly interdisciplinary inevitably encounters this second constraint – that is, the researchers within the various specialist segments employ their preferred types of methodology. Graham (2006a) observes this phenomenon when she notes that researchers in the multidisciplinary field of business communication have a variety of methodological skills. The results of this methodological amalgam is that no one, overarching, totally accepted methodology emerges. Thus, the field's members are in almost unanimous agreement about the need to do more research (Reinsch 1996), but there is little or no agreement about the methodologies to be employed when doing this research. Over the past several years, the *Journal of Business Communication* has moved from a heavy emphasis on quantitative research to publishing more or less an equal number of quantitative and qualitative studies (Graham 2006b). This shift reflects the multifaceted research skills that our scholars bring to the field. Debates about the value of quantitative versus qualitative research therefore ensue (Smeltzer 1993), along with discussions regarding the value of applied research (Rogers 2001) as opposed to theory-building research (Smeltzer and Suchan 1991). This latter approach ultimately, of course, serves as a conduit for the former. Bargiela-Chiappini and Nickerson (2001) acknowledge this direction in noting that the useful applications of today emerge from medium- and long-term theoretical research of the past. Graham (2006a) further unites the two forces under the labels of mission and curiosity-based research.

Finally, it is important to mention that location frames methodology. In other words, the aforementioned preference for quantitative versus qualitative methods as well mission versus curiosity-based research changes markedly with the discipline in which the researcher is employed. Locker (1998) makes this point clearly when she notes that the methodology preferred depends largely on whether one works within administrative sciences, business, English, education or communication departments. We will explore the importance of these frames later in our discussion about journal rankings. For now, suffice it to say that location frames methodology.

Constraint 3: salary and tenure

Salaries of business communication academics are significantly lower than those of peers in other disciplines. The validity of this constraint is more than anecdotal – it is documented within publications of the Association to Advance Collegiate Schools of Business (AACSB) as well as through various university publications of salaries. In fact, internal surveys conducted by AACSB document that starting salaries for assistant professors of business communication are 40–50 per cent lower than those in traditional business disciplines such as management and marketing. Published salaries in the *Cavalier Daily* (http://www.Cavalierdaily.com/features/salaries/bydepartment) further support these distinctions within business schools. This discrepancy also carries over into a number of English departments where staff report instructors in business communication receive higher teaching loads and approximately 50 per cent lower pay than assistant professors in traditional disciplinary tracks.

This salary discrepancy is significant when considered from a theory of constraints perspective. Stated simply, the salaries paid in business communication provide a natural impediment to the types of people drawn to the profession. If we assume that economic interests have some influence on career decisions, it then becomes apparent that staff drawn to the field of business communication either are not economically motivated or are driven to the field by other causes.

Closely related to the issue of business communication salary is the status of tenure. Locker (2003) suggests that tenure for business communication staff is more prevalent in English departments than in schools of business. She posits that the willingness to offer tenure positions develops from English departments' often close association with technical communication: 'Tenure track positions in technical communication in English departments abound; in sad contrast, many positions for business communication faculty – especially at prestigious universities – are non-tenure track' (p. 125).

Combining the above observation with Beard and Williams's findings that business schools are home to 60 per cent of the courses taught in business communication, as opposed to 16 per cent in English departments (Beard and Williams 1993: 274), we feel safe to observe that within North American universities tenured positions in business communication are certainly less available than they are in more traditional academic disciplines.

Taken together, the salary levels and the tenure status indicate a significant constraint within the field of business communication in North America. If we assume that there is a correlation between salary, tenure track positions and status within a field – probably a spurious assumption in some fields but an accurate one in many others – then the above-mentioned findings demonstrate that the field faces serious problems in terms of the academic status afforded to it.

Constraint 4: journal rankings

A recent trend in North American universities, and especially in colleges of business, has been the creation of preferred publication listings. The premise behind these lists is that higher-ranked journals are more difficult to publish in and therefore, by implication, such journals contain better research and better fulfil a school's academic research mission. And, of course, the scholars who publish research in these journals purportedly have significantly higher academic prestige for having done so. (We do not defend the logic of this description.) Other purposes for such rankings include: guidance for promotion and tenure decisions; feedback to editorial boards about the academic community's view of the research it publishes; feedback to researchers as to where to submit their research; and information for academics and practitioners about the influence of a journal (Vokurka 1996; Zivney and Reichtensein 1994).

DuBois and Reeb (2000) note that journal rankings derive from two general approaches:

(1) surveys of academics and administrators about the importance of such rankings; and (2) citation counts detailing how many times research from a particular journal is cited by other scholars. Needless to say, these efforts are distinct attempts to quantify otherwise 'cloudy' concepts such as prestige.

The end result of this ranking phenomenon is that a number of schools, particularly business schools, now have precise lists of journals in which staff members are encouraged to publish. These lists help to determine merit raises, promotion and tenure decisions (DuBois and Reeb, 2000). Generally these lists are divided into categories such as A, B and C, or tier 1, tier 2 and tier 3.

We examined eleven journal lists from research universities within North America. None of the lists included any business communication journal as an elite/tier 1 publication. Three of the eleven list sets included business communication journals as 'alternative' or 'tier 2' publications, with one of these three listing the *Journal of Business Communication* as an example of a respected specialist journal. One other list mentioned *Management Communications Quarterly* as an 'acceptable' outlet for publication. No lists mentioned *Journal of Business and Technical Communication*, *Business Communication Quarterly* or any other journals listed in Debby Andrews's chapter.

This failure of business communication journals to achieve prestigious tier 1 ranking is a significant constraint – and the consequences are readily apparent. By definition, our field's scholars should want to publish in journals such as the *Journal of Business Communication* and *Management Communications Quarterly*. Arguably, these are the field's leading journals. However, if publication in such journals does not advance the case for promotion, tenure or merit raises, then business communication staff must of necessity search elsewhere for more prestigious homes for their research.

It is also important to note, as a speculative aside, the probable collateral damage that occurs to the field's journals through the above-mentioned process. Stated simply, a vicious cycle ensues when our scholars are encouraged and rewarded for publications outside of our specialist journals. These actions cause the number and quality of articles sent to these journals to drop precipitously. This decline then results in further diminishment of the outlet's prestige. And as prestige declines further, the number of quality articles sent to the journals declines proportionately. One can easily see the ultimate outcome of this process.

A second result from this journal constraint also needs to be acknowledged. We earlier noted Graham's observation (2006a) that researchers in the multidisciplinary field of business communication have a variety of methodological skills. Locker (1998) earlier also observed this multiplicity of skills and warned of the danger of dismissing a researcher as inadequate when one who is skilled in one method is a novice in another. But the end consequence of this multiplicity of skills also needs to be acknowledged: the depth of our skills is often not suited to the discipline-based journals that appear in the tier 1 listings. In fact, as Wilkinson observed in 1984, and as Locker et al. demonstrate in 1996, our work more often involves discussing research areas, and summarising others' research projects and applying the findings of these projects to our own field than it does actually analysing a topic scientifically. While one can certainly defend these research acts as valued and worthwhile, they are not the type of work that appears in the traditionally pseudo-scientific tier 1 journals.

Constraint 5: The Lack of Doctoral Programmes in Business Communication

The Graduate Studies Committee of the American Business Communication Association, the predecessor of the Association for Business Communication, called in 1978 for the development of doctoral programmes in business communication. Twenty years later others followed suit by either hinting at the need for such a programme (Kogen 1989; Reinsch 1991; Shelby 1992; Shaw 1993; Suchan and Charles 2006) or directly calling for its development (Dulek 1993; Locker 1998).

An online search for North American doctoral programmes in business communication revealed the following programmes: University of Phoenix; Jones International University; Ashford University; Kaplan University; Golden Gate University Online; and Regis University. Others do exist, as we shall note shortly in the theory of opportunity analysis. However, the other programmes fall under the auspices of larger departments and thus are 'field specialisms' within a larger domain. Hence, these latter programmes meet the 'spirit' though probably not the 'letter' of the Graduate Studies Committee's call some thirty years ago.

From a theory of constraints perspective, this lack of PhD programmes is enormously important. Suchan and Charles (2006) note that this lack severely limits the research productivity of the field. The increased productivity that academic staff members gain through the assistance of doctoral students does not occur. Additionally, this failure to produce doctoral students negatively impacts on the field's overall research productivity in terms of both quantity and quality. Theory development, field research and methodological rigour are thus all adversely affected by the lack of doctoral programmes in business communication.

Theory of opportunity analysis

The theory of constraints analysis above demonstrates that the field of business communication in North America faces a host of problems and challenges. All is not well. The future is definitely in flux. But all is not lost. Let us take a look at the field from the 'other side' of the coin – from the perspective of a theory of opportunity. This second approach will help us to gain a different, more hopeful perspective on the field's future. This second perspective will show us some opportunities that we can pursue as we drive the field through its crossroads.

We mentioned earlier that Ardichvili et al. developed the theory of opportunity to understand better the ongoing development in the field of entrepreneurial studies. We also mentioned that Ardichvili et al. identified three key factors for opportunity development: personality traits, social networks and prior knowledge. An examination of the field of business communication from each of these opportunistic perspectives provides some important guideposts to overcoming the above-mentioned constraints.

Opportunity 1: personality traits

Ardichvili et al. list two essential personality traits for long-term entrepreneurial success: creativity and optimism. These traits apply not just to individuals at the micro-level; they are also equally applicable at the macro-level, such as academic disciplines. Even a cursory review of the field's journals demonstrates that creativity is alive, well and growing at the macro-level of North American business communication.

A review of the table of contents of any recent issue of the *Journal of Business Communication*, as well as *Management Communication Quarterly* or the *Journal of Business and Technical Communication*, reveals the breadth of scholarship as well as the creative bent within the field. Additionally, a content analysis of the author-supplied key words listed in the *Journal of Business Communication* shows that in one year, 2006, the journal covered more than fifty different topics. These topics ranged from business and business research to social constructionism and sense-making; from organisational change and culture to polychronicity and liminality; and from job satisfaction and persuasion to telematics and asynchronous communication. Research in business communication certainly demonstrates the quality of 'abundance' that Pink (2006) identifies as essential to creativity in the twenty-first century.

Opportunity 2: social networks

Ardichvili et al. characterise social networks as having weak ties, partnerships, an inner circle of connections and an action orientation. While some of these characteristics are distinctly entrepreneurial, they also provide an outline for possible disciplinary development within North American business communication.

More than a decade ago Reinsch (1996) chastised the field and called for more research output from its scholars. Specifically, Reinsch proposed the following alternative actions: '[B]usiness communication will not mature further as an academic field without a strong, consistent emphasis on research . . . What should business communication do? Stop looking in the window. Go to the library. Get to work' (p. 44). Ten years later, Suchan and Charles (2006) made suggestions similar to those of Reinsch. If we combine these 'calls for research' with the 'social networking' opportunities listed by Ardichvili et al., we may see that both sides provide a ready, though often overlooked dimension for business communication research. Stated simply, we should continue to do research in the field, but we should spread the outlets for that research beyond the narrow dimensions of our own journals. Hence, hypothetically, the more we publish in the mainstream journals of other disciplines, the more we network and gain additional status for our own field and journals.

We realise that the above opportunity observations seem exactly the opposite of those listed as constraints to the field's specialist journals within constraint 4. Hence, we realise that by pursuing these opportunities we jeopardise the quality of research appearing in our own journals. However, we agree with Reinsch's call for more research in the field. And we hope that if this call is heeded, then the field's scholars will produce adequate amounts of high-quality research for a variety of specialist journals.

Even a cursory glance reveals that the field's leading scholars have begun successfully to reach out in this direction. In the last ten to fifteen years a number of scholars closely associated with the field of business communication have published significant pieces in the premier journals of a number of different disciplines. Cross-referencing the membership list of the Association for Business Communication with acknowledged tier 1 journals reveals publications in the *Academy of Management Journal* (Reinsch and Beswick 1990), the *Academy of Management Review* (Yates and Orlikowski 1992), *Organization*

Science (Yates et al. 1999) and the *California Management Review* (Argenti 2004), along with numerous presentations at the Academy of Management annual meetings as well as the Modern Language Association's meetings. These publications, along with numerous others in the *Journal of Advertising Research* and *Business Horizons*, demonstrate that some of our field's leading scholars have broadened the field's reach and enhanced their own and the field's reputation as well. We are thus already actively extending our social networking reach.

There is another side of the networking theory, which we also need to be aware of and promote. Stated simply, we need to invite, encourage and promote business-communication-related research emanating from other fields to appear in our mainstream journals as well. This encouragement has already begun to take place, with professors in strategic management, accounting and finance publishing recent articles on signalling investors, information disclosure strategies and prospectus information in our mainstream journals. Publications on such topics will serve to enhance further the reputation of our field's journals while also forming vital, highly important links to other disciplines.

Opportunity 3: prior knowledge

The key criteria Ardchivili et al. list for prior knowledge consist of understanding markets, customer problems and ways to serve customers. While appropriate to entrepreneurship research, these dimensions of 'prior knowledge' transform readily into disciplinary criteria when discussing opportunities in North American business communication.

Linking closely with the aforementioned theory of constraints, we would respectfully contend that the prior knowledge opportunity that is readily apparent within North American business communication rests in the field's published research and in the development of much-needed doctoral programmes in the field. Additionally, we would add, these programmes must focus both on vertical knowledge in the field and on the multidisciplinary dimension of the field. This latter area could easily develop, we believe, as a special niche for business communication doctoral programmes.

The Association for Teachers of Technical Communication lists nineteen doctoral programmes on its website (Graham 2006a). Of these programmes, two specialise in rhetoric and professional communication (Iowa State University, New Mexico State University); three in rhetoric and technical discourse (East Carolina University, Michigan Technological University, Texas Tech University); one in rhetoric and composition (Purdue); two in professional writing (University of Memphis, University of Wisconsin at Milwaukee); one in professional communication (Utah State); and eight in various specialisms within communication (Ohio University, University of Denver, University of Kansas, University of Memphis, University of Southern Mississippi, University of South Florida, University of Texas at Austin, Washington State University). These programmes form the nucleus of what could become a vital knowledge base of business communication within the US section of North America.

A second knowledge base for business communication is developing more recently but quite strongly to the north in Canada. As in the USA, Canadian academic staff who teach professional communication – the predominant term in Canada, as opposed to business discourse or business communication – teach in a variety of disciplinary sites. Canadians who belong to the Association for Business Communication are found in communication departments, undergraduate writing programmemes, business schools, education departments and linguistic programmes.

Interestingly, from a knowledge base perspective, professional communication programmemes have developed only recently in Canada – mostly since 1995. Certain factors – a resistance to copying US writing programmes, the inclination to model themselves on British universities that generally do not have writing programmes, the low status that comes from teaching so-called 'service' courses, and university funding cuts – led to this slower initial development. Comprehensive universities, those that already have graduate programmes and research staff, have been the most resistant to developing professional communication courses. Consequently, the country does not have the number of doctoral programmes and the developed research agendas that the USA has had for two or three decades (Smith 2006).

At the same time, though, Canadian writing specialists see exciting opportunities in the future as communication programmes in business, law and engineering are being developed, as well as graduate programmes dedicated to communication pedagogy and research (Graves 1994; Smith 2006). For example, the School of Linguistics and Language Studies at Carleton University offers an MA degree. Housing such graduate programmes in linguistic departments will set Canadian programmes apart from those in the aforementioned rhetoric/English and communication departments in the USA. Moreover, as a bilingual country, Canada is well positioned to pursue research agendas in workplace diversity, multiculturalism and language policy.

Finally, it is important to note that the initial constraint that we listed, that relating to the interdisciplinary nature of the field, can also be seen as an extremely significant opportunity when viewed from the perspective of prior knowledge. Stated simply, our field's experts bring knowledge from a variety of different disciplines to the field; hence, they also bring an extremely diverse knowledge base. This base provides tremendous opportunities for the field, especially if we begin to view it from a multidisciplinary rather than an interdisciplinary perspective. Thus, instead of seeing our diversity of knowledge and methodologies as burdens (Dulek 1993; Graham and Thralls 1998; Locker 1994), we should applaud them as strengths. Stated differently, our field's future rests in letting business discourse become a multidisciplinary research epicentre. It must become an epicentre encompassing the knowledge of a multitude of disciplines along with the concurrent multitude of theories and methodologies brought by those disciplines.

This concept of multidisciplinarity has important differences from the interdisciplinary constraint listed earlier. Interdisciplinarity implies a series of intersecting diagrams with business communication buried quietly at the centre. Figure 35.1 shows this description visually. Multidisciplinarity involves business communication sitting at the centre of a diagram with other circles feeding but not in contact with it. Figure 35.2 shows this position.

Figure 35.2 posits business communication as a separate and distinct discipline fed by – but neither subordinate to nor buried within – a number of other disciplines. The surrounding disciplines contribute to the field, but do not overshadow it.

If accepted, this multidisciplinary perspective will demonstrate that business communication is the separate and distinct discipline that Locker and others have long called for. It will also show that business communication is fed by a number of aligning fields – all assisting in the discipline's development but not subordinating it to their own interests.

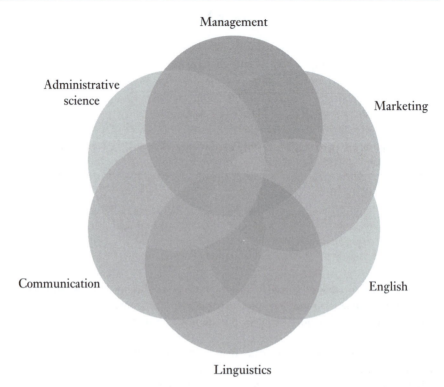

Figure 35.1

The distinct advantage of this visual model is that it shows that business communication 'stands alone' as a separate and distinct field. It is not lost in the hodge-podge of other disciplines that overlap and overreach in the interdisciplinary model.

It is important to mention that this concept of multidisciplinarity is a late addition to this chapter and was suggested by Francesca Bargiela in a review of an earlier draft. In her book *Business Discourse*, Bargiela and her co-authors, Nickerson and Planken, acknowledge 'the practical difficulties of achieving' multidisciplinarity (2007: 57). At the same time, they recognise that some subjects (e.g. gender studies in language) are inherently multidisciplinary and that anthropology, linguistics, social linguistics and social psychology are disciplines that can be used together for fruitful research in business discourse. The concept of multidisciplinarity, therefore, holds significant promise for the field's future and needs to be fleshed out in future, more theoretical pieces.

Conclusion

In the end, this analysis of North American business communication shows that while the field faces many obstacles and hurdles, there is hope and promise for the future. Perhaps, to return to the opening metaphor, the field needs to stop looking at itself as being at a crossroads, especially if we view a crossroads as a geographic place that others pass through

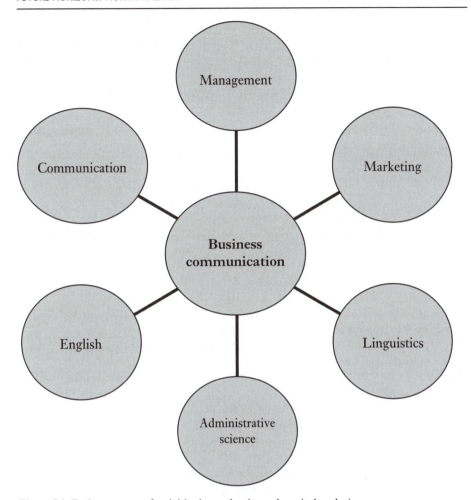

Figure 5.1 Basic sequence of activities in conducting a rhetorical analysis

to reach some other point. Instead, perhaps we need to begin to see the field as being an end point, a location to which others aspire to arrive. If we become such a location, we can overcome our constraints and take advantage of our opportunities. If we do that, our future will be far brighter than even our most ardent advocates have ever envisioned.

References

Ardichvili, A., R. Cardozo and S. Ray (2003) A theory of entrepreneurial opportunity identification and development. *Journal of Business Venturing*, 18: 105–23.

Argenti, P. A. (1996) Corporate communication as a discipline: Towards a definition. *Management Communication Quarterly*, 10: 73–97.

Argenti, P. A. (2004) Collaborating with activists: How Starbucks works with NGOs. *California Management Review*, 47: 91–116.

Bargiela-Chiappini, F. and C. Nickerson (2001) Partnership research: A response to Priscilla Rogers. *Journal of Business Communication*, 38: 248–51.

Bargiela-Chiappini, F., C. Nickerson and B. Planken (2007) *Business Discourse*. Basingstoke: Palgrave Macmillan.

Barton, E. (2001) Design in observational research on the discourse of medicine: Toward disciplined interdisciplinarity. *Journal of Business and Technical Communication*, 15: 309–32.

Beard, J. D. and D. L. Williams (1993) A professional profile of business communication educators and their research preferences: Survey results. *Journal of Business Communication*, 30: 269–95.

Bhave, M. (1994) A process model of entrepreneurial venture creation. *Journal of Business Venturing*, 9: 223–42.

Bluedorn, A. C., T. J. Kallaith and P. M. Lane (1999) Polychronicity and the inventory of polychronic values (IVP): The development of an instrument to measure a fundamental dimension of organisational culture. *Journal of Managerial Psychology*, 14: 205–30.

Daniel, C. A. (1983) Remembering our charter: Business communication at the crossroads. *Journal of Business Communication*, 20: 3–12.

Deming, W. E. (1982) *Out of the Crisis*. Cambridge, MA: MIT Press.

Douglas, G. H. and H. W. Hildbrandt (eds) (1985) *Studies in the History of Business Writing*. Champaign, IL: Association for Business Communication.

Du-Babcock, B. (2006) Teaching business communication: Past, present, and future. *Journal of Business Communication*, 43: 253–64.

DuBois, F. L. and D. Reeb (2000) Ranking the international business journals. *Journal of International Business Studies*, 31: 689–704.

Dulek, R. E. (1993) Models of development: Business schools and business communication. *Journal of Business Communication*, 30: 315–31.

Dulek, R. E. (2006) On networking, friends, research, respect, and diversity: The insights of Margaret Graham. *Journal of Business Communication*, 43: 278–82

Forman, J. and M. L. Markus (2005) Research on collaboration, business communication, and technology: Reflection on an interdisciplinary academic collaboration. *Journal of Business Communication*, 42: 78–102.

Gieselman, R. D. (1989) Business communication as an academic discipline. *Issues in Writing*, 2: 20–35.

Goldratt, E. M. and J. Cox (1986) *The Goal: A Process of Ongoing Improvement*. New York: North River Press.

Graham, M. B. (2006a) Disciplinary practice(s) in business communication, 1985 to *Journal of Business Communication*, 43: 268–77.

Graham, M. B. (2006b) Publishing in the ABC journals. Paper delivered at the Association for Business Communication International Convention, San Antonio, TX, 27 October.

Graham, M. B. and C. Thralls (1998) Connections and fissures: Discipline formation in business communication. *Journal of Business Communication*, 35: 7–13.

Graves, R. (1994) *Writing Instruction in Canadian Universities*. Winnipeg: Inkshed.

Hagge, J. (1986) Business communication, the orphaned discipline: A historical review of business communication teachers' perspectives of their field's place in the college curriculum. *Proceedings of the 51st ABC International Convention*: 168–77.

Jones, S. L. (2007) Evolution of corporate homepages: 1996 to 2006. *Journal of Business Communication*, 44: 236–57.

Kogen, M. (ed.) (1989) *Writing in the Business Professions*. Urbana, IL: National Council of Teachers of English and the Association for Business Communication.

Liebig, J. V. (1855) *Die Grundsa¨tze der agricultur-chemie mit Ru¨cksicht auf die in Englend angestellten Untersuchchungen*. Braunschweig: Friedrich Vieweg.

Locker, K. O. (1994) The challenge of interdisciplinary research. *Journal of Business Communication*, 31: 137–51.

Locker, K. O. (1998) The role of the Association for Business Communication in shaping business communication as an academic discipline. *Journal of Business Communication*, 35: 14–49.

Locker, K. O. (2003) Will professional communication be the death of business communication? *Business Communication Quarterly*, 66: 118–32.

Locker, K. O., S. L. Miller, M. Richardson, E. Tebeaux and J. Yates (1996) Studying the history of business communication. *Business Communication Quarterly*, 59: 109–27.

Lowry, P. B., A. Curtis and M. R. Lowry (2004) Building a taxonomy and nomenclature of collaborative writing to improve interdisciplinary research and practice. *Journal of Business Communication*, 4: 66–99.

Pink, D. H. (2006) *A Whole New Mind: Why Right-Brainers Will Rule the Future*. London: Cyan Books.

Reinsch, L. (1991) Editorial: Boundaries and banners. *Journal of Business Communication*, 28: 97–9.

Reinsch, N. L. (1996) Business communication: Present, past, and future. *Management Communications Quarterly*, 10: 27–49.

Reinsch, N. L. and R. W. Beswick (1990) Voice mail versus conventional channels: A cost minimization analysis of individuals' preferences. *Academy of Management Journal*, 33: 801–16.

Rentz, K. (1993) Editorial: Negotiating the field of business communication. *Journal of Business Communication*, 30: 233–40.

Rogers, P. S. (1996) Disciplinary distinction or responsibility? *Management Communication Quarterly*, 10: 112–23.

Rogers, P. S. (2001) Convergence and commonality: Challenging business communication research. *Journal of Business Communication*, 38: 14–23.

Russell, R. (1991) *Writing in the Academic Disciplines, 1870–1990*. Carbondale: Southern Illinois Press.

Saunders, A. G. (1926) *Effective Business English as Applied to Business Letters and Reports*. New York: Macmillan.

Shaw, G. (1993) The shape of our field: Business communication as a hybrid discipline. *Journal of Business Communication*, 30: 297–313.

Shelby, A. (1992) Business communication as strategy. *Journal of Education for Business*, 67: 279.

Shelby, A. (1993) Organisational, business, management, and corporate communication: An analysis of boundaries and relationships. *Journal of Business Communication*, 30: 241–67.

Shelby, A. (1996) A discipline organisation: Analysis and critique. *Management Communication Quarterly*, 10: 98–105.

Smeltzer, L. R. (1993) Emerging questions and research paradigms in business commu-
    nication research. *Journal of Business Communication*, 30: 181–98.
Smeltzer, L. R. and J. Suchan (1991) Guest editorial: Theory building and relevance.
    Journal of Business Communication, 28: 181–86.
Smith, T. S. (2006) Recent trends in undergraduate writing courses and programme
    in Canadian universities. In R. Graves and H. Graves (eds), *Writing Centres,
    Writing Seminars, Writing Culture: Writing Instruction in Anglo-Canadian Universities*.
    Winnipeg: Inkshed Press, pp. 319–70.
Stevenson, H. H., M. J. Roberts and H. I. Grousbeck (1985) *New Business Ventures and
    the Entrepreneur*. Homewood, IL: Irwin.
Suchan, J. and M. Charles (2006) Business communication research: Past, present, and
    future. *Journal of Business Communication*, 43: 389–97.
Venkataraman, S. (1997) The distinctive domain of entrepreneurship research: An edi-
    tor's perspective. In J. Katz and R. Brockhaus (eds), *Advances in Entrepreneurship, Firm
    Emergence, and Growth*. Greenwich, CT: JAI Press, vol. 3, pp. 119–38.
Vokurka, R. (1996) The relative importance of journals used in operations management
    research: A citation analysis. *Journal of Operations Management*, 14: 345–55.
Wardrope, W. T. (2001) 'Challenge' is a positive word: Embracing the interdisciplinary
    nature of business communication. *Journal of Business Communication*, 38: 242–7.
Wilkinson, C. W. (1984) ABWA and ABCA: The growth of an organization. *Business
    Communication Quarterly*, 47: 24–8.
Yates, J. and W. J. Orlikowski (1992) Genres of organisational communication: An
    approach to studying communication and media. *Academy of Management Review*, 17:
    299–326.
Yates, J., W. J. Orlikowski and K. Okamura (1999) Explicit and implicit structuring of
    genres in electronic communication: Reinforcement and change of social interaction.
    Organization Science, 10: 83–103.
Zivney, T. and W. Reichenstein (1994) The pecking order of finance journals. *Financial
    Practices and Education*, 4: 77–87.

36

Future horizons: Asia

Winnie Cheng

Introduction

This chapter outlines a brief review that was conducted of research studies in business communication and business discourse in recent years in Asian countries, including the People's Republic of China, Hong Kong, India, Indonesia, Japan, South Korea, Malaysia, the Philippines, Singapore, Taiwan, Thailand, Vietnam, Pakistan and Nepal. These studies vary in their goals and the nature of their inquiries; the range of theories, approaches and methodologies adopted; the various linguistic, paralinguistic, pragmatic and communicative features examined; the diversity of disciplinary perspectives taken; and the array of authentic business sites in which these studies are situated. These studies, in their unique and admirable ways, have made useful contributions to this field of research through their research results and recommendations. However, many studies, as can well be understood, have examined only one feature or phenomenon, be it register, genres, turn-taking, rhetorical style, discoursal structure, lexico-grammar, communication strategies, communicative competencies, politeness, or the description of a variety of business English. In addition, these current studies are primarily conducted by academia alone. A limitation is therefore that business communication research and business communication practices have been operating as two distinct and separate worlds.

Many of these studies thus pose the question: would the contribution to knowledge and the impact on the business world have been much greater if the business discourse and communication projects had formed alliances with the industries concerned from the outset? Would these studies of business discourse have been broader in scope and much more comprehensive if they had incorporated as many methodologies and had examined as many features and phenomena as possible? Motivated by these concerns, this chapter describes a possible model for the design, implementation and evaluation of interdisciplinary collaborative projects by academia and business practitioners, and then illustrates the potential benefits that could be reaped from this model, with examples of collaborative projects with land surveyors in a consultancy firm and practitioners in the financial services industry in Hong Kong.

Business discourse research in Asia

Business discourse and communication in Asia are developing, though they are not as developed as in other parts of the world. In China, for instance, there is research into the present role, status and usage of English under the influence of economic globalisation and China's accession to the WTO (Pang et al. 2002; Zhu 2003). In Hong Kong, which is characterised by biliteracy and trilingualism, a number of studies have been conducted to examine a range of business contexts and genres, and a variety of communication phenomena. Hyland (1988), for instance, examined the metadiscourse in CEOs' letters, and Du-Babcock (2006) the impact of culture and language use on topic management strategies and turn-taking behaviour. Others include the exploitation of linguistic resources in network marketing directors' messages to construct realities and identities (Kong 2001), the use of accounts as a politeness strategy in internal emails in a business firm in Hong Kong (Kong 2006), the impact of the new media on the discourse structure of online sales letters (Cheung 2006), the structure and language of tax computation letters written by accountants (Flowerdew and Wan 2006), and business and legal discourse (Bhatia 2005; Bhatia et al. 2004). Investigating the business sub-corpus of the Hong Kong Corpus of Spoken English, Cheng and Warren (2005a, 2005b, 2006) investigated the use of pragmatic speech acts of disagreement, giving an opinion and checking understanding, and the use of discourse intonation, and the discourse of check-out service encounters in a hotel (Cheng 2004). Cheng and Mok's (2006) study, examining the cultural preference for rhetorical patterns in business writing, has a dual focus on intercultural communication and business communication.

Examples of research in India include the discourse patterns of non-conflict situations and dispute settlement in Marwaris (Dhanania and Gopakumaran 2005), the use of upward-influencing language in a multinational fast-moving consumer goods company (Kaul and Brammer 2004), and the language strategies employed between Israeli and Indian businesspeople (Zaidman 2001). In Japan, research studies include communication style and skills of Japanese in English business communication (Kameda 2000, 2001), emerging English spoken and written business discourses in terms of linguistic and rhetorical features (Tanaka 2006), and persuasive strategies in business meetings (Emmett 2003). In South Korea, Shim (1999) examines 'codified Korean English', which differs from American English in morpho-syntactic, lexical and pragmatic uses. In Malaysia, a multiracial country (Malay, Chinese and Indian), Nair-Venugopal (2000) describes Malaysian English, the prevailing sociolect which captures the indigenous language use in context, in two business organisations. Many more studies are reported, for instance, in a double journal issue and a volume on *Asian Business Discourse(s)* (Bargiela-Chiappini 2005/2006; Bargiela-Chiappini and Gotti 2005) and a volume on *Intercultural and International Business Communication* (Palmer-Silveira et al. 2006).

The proposed model

As described, very few of the studies reviewed have evolved from systematically designed and developed, mutually benefiting and long-term collaborative, interdisciplinary and interinstitutional projects between academics and researchers in the universities on the one hand, and practitioners and practitioners-in-training in the real business world on the other. Elsewhere, in recent years, there has been an increase in collaborative alliances between practitioners and discourse and communication researchers in a range of disciplines and contexts. Examples of such collaborative alliances include organisational and professional communication in the fields of health-care, law and management (e.g. Candlin 2001; Sarangi 2000; Sarangi and Candlin 2003; Bhatia et al. 2003a, 2003b; Bhatia and Candlin 2003). Another example is provided by the publicly funded projects led by Vijay Bhatia and his team of co-researchers in law (arbitration and litigation) from more than fifteen countries working on the professional legal language (e.g. Bhatia 2005; Bhatia et al. 2004).

The discipline of discourse studies is premised on the central notion that the study of naturally occurring spoken and written interaction provides insights about the manifestations, enactments and reproduction of such phenomena as group relations, organisations, institutions, processes, routines and structures (van Dijk 1997: 32). The fundamental claim that text is both process and product has long been established (e.g. Halliday and Hasan 1989; Dixon and Bortolussi 2001; Geluykens 2003), and therefore the discourse analyst needs to be able to study both the process and product in the communication flow. However, in business communication, the nature of business discourse as product is very elusive. It is often difficult for the researcher to access business discourse, such as meetings, interviews, office talk, email messages, business letters and contracts, for reasons of confidentiality or simply reluctance on the part of professionals, practitioners or their organisations to allow outsiders in to scrutinise their activities. The nature of business discourse as process is even more elusive, as this requires even greater access to the business setting in which the discourse occurs. The result is that there is a real paucity of research based on naturally occurring business discourse data. This limitation has been pointed out by those who have sought to access such data in order to provide descriptions of business and professional discourses (St John 1996; Louhiala-Salminen 2002; Sarangi 2002; McCarthy and Handford 2004). This, then, is the case generally, and is particularly true for the linguistically complex and communicatively demanding world of Hong Kong Chinese practitioners, who typically operate using English as the lingua franca, interspersed with (usually) spoken Chinese. The spoken Chinese is mainly Cantonese, but increasingly Putonghua (the official language of the People's Republic of China) is used.

A research team based in the Research Centre for Professional Communication in English (RCPCE), The Hong Kong Polytechnic University, has set itself the ambitious long-term aim of constructing taxonomies of professional communicative competencies derived from the study of the four key industries in Hong Kong (i.e. financial services, trading and logistics, tourism, and professional and other producers' services). Examples of communicative competences or ability are van Ek's (1986: 35–65) model of communicative ability, comprising six competences: linguistic, sociolinguistic, discourse, strategic, sociocultural and social competence; and Douglas's (2000) notion of 'specific purpose language ability', made up of language knowledge, strategic competence and background knowledge. Bhatia's (2004: 144) notion of 'discursive competence', together with disciplinary knowledge and professional practice, defines 'professional expertise'.

This large-scale investigation into business and professional communication will begin with an examination of different companies and organisations based in Hong Kong in terms of their overt and covert statements about the importance of English-language and communication skills. The study will then proceed to determine what constitutes the communicative competencies of practitioners working in each of the key industries. After business- and industry-specific competencies have been determined, the team will then be in a position to identify and describe the attributes which are generally shared across, as well as specifically unique to, industries and businesses. The taxonomies thus derived will have practical implications for improving business communication education and practices.

The overall project has adopted three main research methods in the collection and analysis of data, namely the survey method, ethnography, and textual analysis (the corpus-driven approach to examining the phraseological patterns and meanings will be described in this chapter). The first method, i.e. the survey method, involves, for instance, interviewing practitioners in the workplaces about different aspects of communication and language use, as well as requesting them to log their communication activities on a daily basis for a week on a professional discourse checklist. The main advantage is that a lot of factual data can be collected within a short span of time.

The second research method, ethnography, involves observation and collection of information about the communicative activities in the workplace, and critical analysis of the communication flow as experienced by professionals drawn from the four key industries in Hong Kong. From the outset, issues of methodological design are important. Sarangi points out the importance for discourse researchers of studying not only 'how language mediates professional activities' but also 'what constitutes professional knowledge and practice beyond performance' (2002: 99). He raises three issues for researchers to consider when collecting and analysing professional discourse, namely accessing, problematising and interpreting professional discourse (pp. 100–3). 'Accessibility' refers to the ongoing problem for researchers of gaining access to business and professional data. In the case of this project, even when permission is granted by the practitioners and organisations for the research team to collect data, it is always made clear that the former retain the right to censor or delete any data collected at any time. With regard to the future use of the data, the practitioners and organisations are asked to give their permission to the research team for the data to be used for other academic research purposes. The second issue, 'salience/ problem identification', is the mutual identification of salient issues and problems, and the third, 'coding/interpretability/articulation', is the process by which the researcher, through collaborating with practitioners, gains insider knowledge in order to interpret the data better (Sarangi 2002). At the commencement of the project, the research team meet with individuals in the organisations to review further and agree upon the project aims. After the data have been collected, a series of follow-up meetings take place to enable the research team to better interpret the data. Once the findings are compiled, meetings take place again to discuss them with the practitioners to ensure that the analysis of the communication events and discourses is well informed from all perspectives. This approach to data analysis is based on tried and tested methods developed by interactional sociolinguists (e.g. Gumperz et al. 1979; Tannen 1984), and has been usefully employed in studies of intercultural communication (e.g. Pan et al. 2002).

The third method is textual analysis, whereby spoken and written discourses can be analysed linguistically, structurally, pragmatically, prosodically and semiotically to address a wide array of research questions in business discourse and communication. In the last two or three decades, corpora, corpus analytic tools and corpus evidence have been increasingly used in English-language teaching and learning (Sinclair 1987, 1991, 2004), but they are not as well developed in business discourses. Some recent studies include negotiating moves in Japanese business discourse (Yotsukura 2003), hotel check-out service encounters (Cheng 2004), discourse intonation in spoken business English (Warren 2004) and the genre of grant proposals (Connor and Upton 2004). Corpus-driven research emphasises that theoretical statements are a product of the evidence from the corpus (Tognini-Bonelli 2002: 75). In this project, adopting the corpus-driven approach to the analysis of business discourses involves, with the active participation and advice of practitioners, the collection of large representative corpora from each of the main industries in Hong Kong. Such an approach is primarily quantitative, but also permits the qualitative analysis of the texts contained in the corpora, although this is without the benefits of the detailed ethnographic data collected using the first approach. These corpora will enable the project team to analyse critically and describe the key words and phraseology of each key industry. They will permit researchers 'to observe repeated and parallel events over a wide range of different speakers and contexts' (McCarthy and Handford 2004: 187).

Care has to be taken in the design of each corpus, and here Sinclair's (2005) corpus design principles are useful, to enable the team to establish the technical key words and phraseology (terminology) of each key industry in Hong Kong, and to determine the distinctive usages. The distinctive patterns of word co-occurrences found in the texts of each key industry also have meanings that are specific to the field and different to general English usage. Those practitioners who fail to communicate using the conventional key words and phraseologies of their industry may be misunderstood and, as readers, practitioners may misunderstand the subtle shifts in meanings that result in particular choices (Gledhill 2000; Sinclair 2004; Kemppanen 2004).

In this proposed model of investigating business discourses, the three main research methods outlined above are deemed to be complementary in that each has the potential to provide both discourse and communication researchers and practitioners with insights denied to them by the others.

The following sections discuss examples of the kinds of findings that can be afforded both by detailed studies of the processes and products of discourse practitioners and by corpus-driven studies of patterns of language use.

Land surveying: analysis of the intertextuality of an external email

In business communication, the borderline between spoken and written modes of communication, as well as the complexities regarding the choice of communication channel, are usually difficult to define in practice, as the flow of discourses inevitably mixes one with the other when the practitioners go about their work, interacting with colleagues both within and outside of the organisation. Discourse as process and discourse as product are connected with the notion of 'intertextuality' (e.g. de Beaugrande 1980; de Beaugrande and Dressler 1981; Kristeva 1980; Devitt 1991; Fairclough 1992), which refers to the intertwining of textual and discoursal connections among texts within the discourse flow, making 'the utilisation of one text dependent upon knowledge of one or more previously encountered texts' (de Beaugrande and Dressler 1981: 10).

Using data collected during the shadowing of land surveyors in a civil engineering consultancy firm in Hong Kong, an example is given below of how it is possible to analyse the intertextuality of a text. The example is an external email from the main contractor to a subcontractor. The intertextual links are divided under two headings, intertextual link with prior texts (*shown in italics*) and intertextual link with project works (<u>underlined</u>), because it has been found that in the discourses of land surveyors engaged in construction project management, the 'project works' is the key discourse which is often being referred to. This 'project works' discourse consists of text, design drawings, tables and diagrams which constitute the definitive plan of the entire construction project, and it is constantly being revised and updated as the construction work progresses.

The external email has been anonymised (xxx stands for anonymised words or numbers) and is reproduced below in its entirety, unedited except for the addition of line numbers.

Example: Email (external)
1 From: xxx (contractor)
2 To: xxx (sub-contractor)
3 Subject: Determination of Setting Out of <u>Slope Boundary</u>
4 Gentlemen
5 *Further to my email dated 9 August 2005* and *the meeting amongst ourselves*
6 *yesterday morning* I have undertaken *a site inspection* of <u>xxx, xxx,</u>
7 <u>Retaining Wall H slopes (unreg and xxx)</u> and <u>Slope HA</u> this morning. I
8 provide the following advice.
9   i) Subject to the completion of *the minor outstanding works and defects the*
10   <u>slopes</u> can be considered to be acceptable.
11 ii) The <u>slope boundary</u> is generally coincident with <u>the maintenance</u>
12   <u>staircase</u>.
13   *As confirmed by the surveyors yesterday, the extent of excavation and*
14   *checking with the* <u>design requirement</u> *has been carried out during the*
15   *course of the works.*
16 iii) *With respect to the determination of the extent of* <u>those minor outstanding</u>
17   <u>works which still remain at the crest of the slopes</u> I would comment that
18   this is a very simple, routine construction matter that can be easily dealt
19   with by the site supervisory staff.
20 <u>The bulk excavation and filling works</u> have been completed last year. *Xxx*
21 *stated in yesterday's meeting that the issue is not related to quantities. Further to*
22 *my inspections this morning* I am none the wiser as to why my input at the
23 current stage of <u>the works</u> is considered necessary.
24 If you consider *my input* is still necessary please feel free to contact me.
25 Regards,
26 xxx (name)
27 xxx (post)

Table 36.1. Analysis of intertextuality of an external email

Intertextual link with prior texts	Intertextual link with project works
Further to my email dated 9 August (line 5) **[prior email]**	Slope Boundary (line 3)
the meeting amongst ourselves yesterday morning (lines 5–6) **[prior meeting]**	xxx, xxx, Retaining Wall H slopes (unreg and xxx) and Slope HA (line 7)
a site inspection (line 6) **[prior site inspection]**	the minor outstanding works and defects (line 9)
As confirmed by the surveyors yesterday, the extent of excavation and checking with the (lines 13–14) **[prior meeting]**	The slope boundary (line 11)
has been carried out during the course of the works (lines 14–15) **[prior site inspection]**	the maintenance staircase (lines 11–12)
With respect to the determination of the extent of (line 16) **[prior site inspection]**	design requirement (line 14)
Xxx stated in yesterday's meeting that the issue is not related to quantities(lines 20–21). **[prior meeting]** *Further to my inspections this morning* (lines 20–1) **[prior site inspection]**	those minor outstanding works which still remain at the crest of the slopes (lines 16–17)
my input (line 22) **[prior email] [prior meeting] [prior site inspection] [prospective discourse(s)]**	The bulk excavation and filling works (line 20)
	the works (line 23)

Table 36.1 shows a detailed breakdown of the intertextuality contained in the above external email. It illustrates the intertextuality common to many of the discourses collected from the construction consultancy firm. Barely a line is written without referring to prior or, less frequently, prospective discourses. The intertwining of prior, current and prospective discourses makes texts such as this one very complex and sophisticated discourses to write, and also to read. The ability to master intertextuality, both as a writer and as a reader, is a key element in the discursive competence (Bhatia 2004) of practitioners generally, and especially in professions such as land surveying, where many of the discourses have legal ramifications, which makes a mastery of intertextuality a high-stakes issue should legal recourse be sought by one of the parties.

Discourse flow

In Figure 36.1, the discourse flow of which the external email analysed above forms an integral part is presented as a flow diagram.

From the analysis of the intertextuality contained within this one external email, useful insights can be gained into the complex array of discourses that precede this one discourse, as well as prospective discourses. The external email explicitly mentions four prior discourses: a prior email, prior meeting, prior site inspection and the project works. This

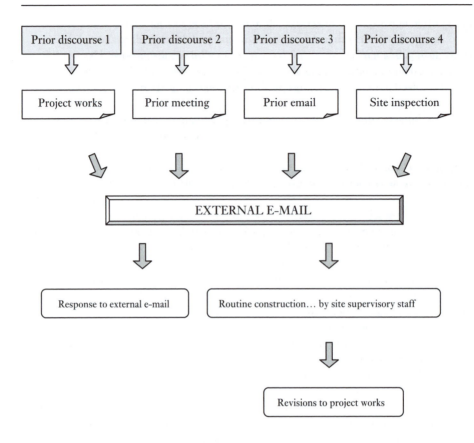

Figure 36.1 Example of a discourse flow

reveals the richness of the intertextuality found in discourse flows such as this. However, each of these four texts mentioned in the external email can be reasonably assumed to be part of separate, or overlapping, discourse flows. For example, the project works are constantly being revised as the construction work progresses, and these revisions are all based on exchange of discourses, both spoken and written.

Similarly, the site inspection conducted by the writer of the external email is a discourse in its own right, which appears to have its origins in the prior meeting, also mentioned in the external email, but will have then necessitated additional prior discourses to set up the site inspection and to generate prospective discourses (e.g. reports and emails, including the one examined here). This external email also generates future discourses both explicitly and implicitly. For example, there will almost certainly be a direct response to this external email from the receiver, which may or may not trigger the further input (i.e. 'my input', line 22) mentioned at the end of the external email. Also, the 'routine construction . . . dealt with by the site supervisory staff' (lines 18–19) mentioned in the external email will generate discourses of various kinds, including yet another round of revisions to the project works.

Hong Kong Corpus of Financial Services: specific words and specificity

One of the many advantages of collecting large representative specialised corpora, based on Sinclair's (2005) corpus design principles, is that it is possible to identify the key words (Scott 2006), termed the 'specific words' here, that are more frequently used in a particular industry than in general English. So far 6.7 million words have been collected from the financial services industry in Hong Kong (Hong Kong Financial Services Corpus, HKFSC), and so comparisons can be made between this specialised corpus and a 5-million-word general English corpus drawn from the 100-million-word British National Corpus (BNC) (henceforth BNC (5m)).

A corpus access software program, ConcGram©, created by Chris Greaves, senior project fellow at The Hong Kong Polytechnic University, is used to investigate this specialised financial services corpus. ConcGram enables the user to determine whether or not a word is specific to the corpus being examined, relative to the BNC (5m), or the 'specificity index', also called the 'weirdness index' (Ahmad 2005). The fairly simple formula (see below) is based on the proportional usage of a word in the specialised and general corpora, which reveals the asymmetry in the distribution of a word.

$$\text{Specificity index (term)} = \frac{f\,(\text{special}) \,/\, N\,(\text{special})}{f\,(\text{general}) \,/\, N\,(\text{general})}$$

If specificity index >1 then a specialist term;
If specificity index <1 then not a specialist term.

Table 36.2 lists only a small sample of some of the most specific words found in the HKFSC. It is interesting to find that none of these words is found in the BNC (5m). Specific words which are unique to the field of business being studied give the lexical profiles or 'aboutness' of texts (Sinclair 2005: 7). This suggests that the more specific a set of words in a discourse, the more unreadable the text is (by using, for example, the Flesch Reading Ease score as a measure of text readability) to readers who are outside of the specific field of business. Nevertheless, the text should be comprehensible to members of the discourse community in the field.

Collocates and phraseology

Determining the specificity of certain words can be useful for compiling business- and industry-specific glossaries and lexicons for practitioners, and for informing training materials for novice practitioners. However, as observed by corpus linguists (e.g. Sinclair 1996, 2004), speakers and writers select words in combination, and so it is the study of collocation, colligation and the resultant phraseology that is far more meaningful.

To illustrate briefly the usefulness of specialised corpora in uncovering patterns of language use, the top three lexical collocates of 'money' in both the HKFSC (586 instances of 'money': 0.017 per cent) and the BNC (5m) (3,024 instances: 0.06 per cent) have been examined. First, it is interesting to note that the word 'money' occurs almost four times more often in general English usage than in the financial services corpus. This suggests that 'money' has a low specificity index, which is perhaps contrary to our intuition. An

Table 36.2 Sample of specific words in the HKFSC

abitral	appraisers	calamity cardholder	creditworthy	encumbrance
allotting acquirer(ee)	assertion-based	collateralised	demutualisation	evidencing
amortise	assigner(ee)	comparables	derecognition	expiries
anti-money	benchmarked	consummation	disclosure-based	
appointer	brokerage	consolidations	dispensations	

examination of the collocates of 'money' shows that in the BNC (5m), the top three collocates are 'spend' (84 times), 'market' (46 times) and 'save' (27), while in the HKFSC they are 'client' (99), 'market' (63) and 'laundering' (58). This, in itself, demonstrates different patterns of use in the financial services industry and in general English use. What is also interesting is that when the HKFSC is searched for 'money' in combination with 'spend' and 'save', only one instance of 'money' + 'spend' is found, and no instances of 'money' + 'save'. Also, while in both corpora 'value' is a strong collocate of 'money', in the HKFSC, 22 of the 28 instances of 'money' + 'value' are part of the larger phrase 'the time value of money', which is not found in the BNC (5m) at all.

Given below are the first ten concordance lines for 'money' and its top three collocates in the HKFSC to illustrate further their distinctive patterns of use.

money + client

1   securities collateral, means the maximum amount of money which a **client** of an intermediary is permitted to borro
2   that cheque.Cap 571I s 10 Requirement to pay money other than **client** money out of segregated accounts A
3   571 sub. leg. I); or an account for holding **client** money which is separate from a licensed corporations own acco
4   quire interest accruing from the holding of the **client** money in such accounts to be dealt with and paid in the speci
5   written notice that-relates to an amount of **client** money of a licensed corporation referred to in that section;
6   t of money in a segregated account that is not **client** money of the licensed corporation shall, within one business
7   ith an authorized financial institution; and **client** money held by it in a segregated account with a recognized cl
8   ith section 4(1) of the Securities and Futures (**Client** Money) Rules (Cap 571 sub. leg. I); all other accounts hel
9   censed corporation shall not pay any amount of **client** money of the licensed corporation under subsection (1)(c) if-
10   ted entity of a licensed corporation that holds **client** money of the licensed corporation shall deal with amounts of

In the above concordance lines, 'client' and 'money' typically, but not always (see lines 1 and 2), form a contiguous lexical item. In the financial services industry, practitioners are often talking and writing about their client's money rather than their own. There are other collocates of this lexical item, such as 'holds', 'holding', 'held' and 'licensed corporation', which all help to indicate the semantic preference of this multiword unit in the financial services industry.

money + market

1   our treasury operations, we participate in inter-bank money **market** transactions and provide order execution service
2   treasury operations include, among others, inter-bank money **market** transactions, foreign exchange trading and gover
3   its but compressed those on Treasury investments and money **market** portfolios, leading to a 55.2 per cent drop in
4   credit card and remittance. Treasury mainly comprises money **market** placements and takings, investment in securities
5   llion on forward foreign exchange contracts linked to money **market** transactions, and the reduction in the income o
6   t our liquidity requirements are met. We generally use money **market** transactions, including inter-bank placement an
7   t, which will become due in July 2002; deposits and money **market** takings from customers and other banks accepted
8   and overdraft facilities. Treasury activities include money **market**, foreign exchange dealing and capital market act
9   lion on forward foreign exchange contracts linked to money **market** transactions and a change in classification of
10   are one of the leading participants in the inter-bank money **market** in Hong Kong. We maintain money market lines wit

This co-selection 'money' + 'market' seems to result in the invariant and contiguous 'money market', which is sometimes preceded by collocates 'inter-bank', 'foreign exchange contracts' and 'treasury' to the left, and with the collocates 'transactions' and 'takings' occurring to the right of the lexical item. Again, looking at the co-selections of co-occurring words can tell us a lot about patterns of usage.

money + laundering
1   section 5A of the Exchange Fund Ordinance (Cap 66); money laundering activities means activities intended to hav
2   dures in all areas of reputational risk, including money laundering deterrence, environmental impact, anti-cor
3   BOCHK, and is chaired by our chief executive. The anti-money laundering committee is responsible for managing our mo
4   sk exposure and ensuring implementation of proper anti-money laundering control procedures, and is chaired by our ch
5   markets of the world offer marvelous opportunities for money laundering across national borders or the manipulation
6   ons in 2003 and is in the process of drafting an anti-money laundering law, which we expect will have a significan
7   g subjects such as risk management procedures and anti-money laundering control procedures. SHARE OPTION
     SCHEME AND
8   sis points. In addition, the PBOC enacted several anti-money laundering rules and regulations in 2003 and is in the
9   also required to either establish an independent anti-money laundering department, or to designate a relevant depa
10   thermore, we provide specific training courses on anti-money laundering procedures to our front line employees in th

The concordance lines above show an invariant contiguous pairing of 'money' and 'laundering', which is often part of a larger phrase 'anti-money laundering' (in 39 of the 58 instances), and which is followed by collocates such as 'control procedures'. This again exemplifies the semantic preference of this lexical item in the financial services sector.

The examples so far show that the study of patterns of co-selection of words in a specialised corpus can be very useful in our attempts to describe the language used by practitioners. Such analyses can be detailed and can lead to a description of the invariant core, and its collocates, colligates, semantic preference and semantic prosody (Sinclair 1996, 1998).

Conclusions and implications

This chapter has made a brief but strong argument for the need to bridge the gap between business communication research and business communication practices. It has raised a theoretical as well as practical research agenda. What is worthy of our attention is whether or not, in what way, and to what extent these research studies have succeeded in making their way into the different levels of communication and language use in business settings, and to what extent these studies have impacted on business policies and practices in the respective organisations. As reported in this chapter, the few examples of findings produced by academic and business collaborative research have illustrated areas of useful investigations that have potential benefits and value for various interest groups and stakeholders, including the government, businesspeople, business organisations, specialists in English for Specific Purposes (ESP) and Languages for Specific Purposes (LSP), researchers and learners. In each of the examples, the findings have been discussed and disseminated through project meetings with the companies and through seminars for organisations and professional associations.

In recent years, research studies on business and professional communication around the world have varied with regard to their goals and nature; the range of theories and approaches that underpin the methodologies adopted; the various linguistic, paralinguistic,

pragmatic and communicative phenomena and features examined; the range of disciplinary perspectives taken; and the array of authentic contexts of communication. The next
stage of this interdisciplinary and collaborative project will be, by means of surveys, ethnographic methods and textual analysis, to collect more situated and qualitative data from
a greater number of organisations in a wide range of businesses, in order to describe more
fully both the processes and products of business communication. The findings so derived
would then be explored with respect to the practical implications for informing business
communicative practices, locally and internationally, as well as for curriculum design and
materials writing for ESP or LSP.

Acknowledgements

The work described in this chapter was substantially supported by a grant from the
Research Grants Council of the Hong Kong Special Administration Region (Project No.
PolyU 5480/06H).

References

Ahmad, K. (2005) Terminology in text. Paper delivered at the Tuscan Word Centre
    Workshop, Siena, June.
Bargiela-Chiappini, F. (ed.) (2005/2006) *Asian Business Discourse(s): Parts I and II.*
    Journal of Asian Pacific Communication (double special issue), 15(2) and 16(1).
Bargiela-Chiappini, F. and M. Gotti (eds) (2005) *Asian Business Discourse(s).* Bern: Peter
    Lang.
Bhatia, V. K. (2004) *Worlds of Written Discourse.* London and New York: Continuum.
Bhatia, V. K. (2005) Specificity and generality in legislative expression: Two sides of the
    coin. In V. K. Bhatia, M. Gotti, J. Engberg et al. (eds), *Vagueness in Normative Texts.*
    Bern: Peter Lang, pp. 337–56.
Bhatia, V. K. and C. N. Candlin (2003) Analysing arbitration laws across legal systems.
    Hermes: Journal of Language and Communication Studies, 32: 13–43.
Bhatia, V. K., C. N. Candlin, J. Engberg and A. Trosborg (eds) (2003a) *Multilingual and
    Multicultural Contexts of Legislation: An International Perspective.* Tubingen: Peter
    Lang.
Bhatia, V. K., C. N. Candlin and M. Gotti (eds) (2003b) *Arbitration in Europe: Legal
    Discourse in a Multilingual and Multicultural Context.* Bern: Peter Lang.
Bhatia, V. K., N. M. Langton and J. W. Y. Lung (2004) Legal discourse: Opportunities
    and threats for corpus linguistics. In U. Connor and T. Upton (eds), *Discourse in
    the Professions: Perspectives from Corpus Linguistics.* Amsterdam: John Benjamins,
    pp. 203–34.
Candlin, C. N. (2001) Medical discourse as professional and institutional action: Challenges
    to teaching and researching languages for special purposes. In M. Bax and J.-W. Zwart
    (eds) *Essays in Language, Language Education and the History of Linguistics in Honour of
    Arthur van Essen.* Berlin: Mouton de Gruyter, pp. 185–207.
Cheng, W. (2004) // → did you TOOK // ↗ from the miniBAR //: What is the practi-
    cal relevance of a corpus-driven language study to practitioners in Hong Kong's hotel

industry? In U. Connor and T. Upton (eds), *Discourse in the Professions: Perspectives from Corpus Linguistics*. Amsterdam: John Benjamins, pp. 141–66.

Cheng, W. and E. Mok (2006) Cultural preference for rhetorical patterns in business writing. *Hong Kong Linguist*, 26: 69–80.

Cheng, W. and M. Warren (2005a) // ↗ <u>CAN</u> i help you //: The use of rise and rise-fall tones in the Hong Kong Corpus of Spoken English. *International Journal of Corpus Linguistics*, 10(1): 85–107.

Cheng, W and M. Warren (2005b) // → well I have a <u>DI</u>fferent // ↘ <u>THIN</u>king you know //: A corpus-driven study of disagreement in Hong Kong business discourse. In F. Bargiela-Chiappini and M. Gotti (eds), *Asian Business Discourse(s)*. Bern: Peter Lang, pp. 241–70.

Cheng, W. and M. Warren (2006) I would say be very careful of . . .: Opine markers in an intercultural business corpus of spoken English. In J. Bamford and M. Bondi (eds), *Managing Interaction in Professional Discourse: Intercultural and Interdiscoursal Perspectives*. Rome: Officina Edizioni, pp. 46–58.

Cheung, M. (2006) Producing and communicating electronic sales messages in Hong Kong: Insights from a discourse study and from industry practitioners. Paper delivered at the 5th International Conference of the European Association of Languages for Specific Purposes, Zaragoza, 14–16 September.

Connor, U. and T. Upton (2004) The genre of grant proposals: A corpus linguistic analysis. In U. Connor and T. Upton (eds), *Discourse in the Professions: Perspectives from Corpus Linguistics*. Amsterdam: John Benjamins, pp. 235–56.

de Beaugrande, R. (1980) *Text, Discourse and Process*. London: Longman.

de Beaugrande, R.-A. and W. Dressler (1981) *Introduction to Text Linguistics*. London and New York: Longman.

Devitt, A. (1991) Intertextuality in tax accounting: Generic, referential, and functional. In C. Bazerman and J. Paradis (eds), *Textual Dynamics of the Professions: Historical and Contemporary Studies of Writing in Professional Communities*Madison: University of Wisconsin, pp. 336–57.

Dhanania, K. and S. Gopakumaran (2005) Marwari business discourse: An analysis. *Journal of Asian Pacific Communication*, 15(2): 287–312.

Dixon, P. and M. Bortolussi (2001) Text is not communication: A challenge to a common assumption. *Discourse Processes*, 31(1): 1–25.

Douglas, D. (2000) *Assessing Language for Specific Purposes*. Cambridge: Cambridge University Press.

Du-Babcock, B. (2006) An analysis of topic management strategies and turn-taking behavior in the Hong Kong bilingual environment: The impact of culture and language use. *Journal of Business Communication*, 43(1): 21–42.

Emmett, K. (2003) Persuasion strategies in Japanese business meetings. *Journal of Intercultural Studies*, 24(1): 65–79.

Fairclough, N. (1992) *Discourse and Social Change*. Cambridge: Polity.

Flowerdew, J. and A. Wan (2006) Genre analysis of tax computation letters: How and why tax accountants write the way they do. *English for Specific Purposes*, 25: 133–53.

Geluykens, R. (2003) *From Discourse Process to Grammatical Construction: On Left-Dislocation in English*. Amsterdam: John Benjamins.

Gledhill, C. (2000) The discourse function of collocation in research article introductions. *English for Specific Purposes*, 19(1): 115–35.

Gumperz, J., T. C. Jupp and C. Roberts (1979) *Crosstalk: A Study of Cross-Cultural Communication*. Southall: National Center for Industrial Language Training.

Halliday, M. and R. Hasan (1989) *Language, Context, and Text: Aspects of Language in a Social-Semiotic Perspective*. Oxford: Oxford University Press.

Hyland, K. (1998) Exploring corporate rhetoric: Metadiscourse in the CEO's letter. *Journal of Business Communication*, 35(2): 224–45.

Kameda, N. (2000) Communication competency of Japanese managers in Singapore. *Corporate Communications*, 5(4): 204–10.

Kameda, N. (2001) The implication of language style in business communication: Focus on English versus Japanese. *Corporate Communications*, 6(3): 144–9.

Kaul, A. and C. D. Brammer (2004) Face considerations in upward influencing in an Indian workplace. *Proceedings of the 69th Association for Business Communication Annual Convention*: 164–78.

Kemppanen, H. (2004) Keywords and ideology in translated history texts: A corpus-based analysis. *Across Languages and Cultures*, 5(1): 89–106.

Kong, K. C. C. (2001) Marketing of belief: Intertextual construction of network marketers' identities. *Discourse & Society*, 12(4): 473–503.

Kong, K. C. C. (2006) Accounts as a politeness strategy in the internal directive documents of a business firm in Hong Kong. *Text*, 18(1): 103–41.

Kristeva, J. (1980) *Desire in Language: A Semiotic Approach to Literature and Art*, ed. L. S. Roudiez, trans. T. Gora, A. Jardine and L. S. Roudiez. New York: Columbia University Press.

Louhiala-Salminen, L. (2002) The fly's perspective: Discourse in the daily routine of a business manager. *English for Specific Purposes*, 21: 211–31.

McCarthy, M. and M. Handford (2004) 'Invisible to us': A preliminary corpus-based study of spoken business English. In U. Connor and U. Thomas (eds), *Discourse in the Professions: Perspectives from Corpus Linguistics*. Amsterdam: John Benjamins, pp. 167–202.

Nair-Venugopal, S. (2000) English, identity and the Malaysian workplace. *World Englishes*, 19(2): 205–13.

Palmer-Silveira, J. C., M. F. Ruiz-Garrido and I. Fortanet-Gómez (eds) (2006) *Intercultural and International Business Communication*. Bern: Peter Lang.

Pan, Y., Scollon, S. Wong and R. Scollon (2002) *Professional Communication in International Settings*. Oxford: Blackwell.

Pang, J., X. Zhou and Z. Fu (2002) English for international trade: China enters WTO. *World Englishes*, 21(2): 201–16.

St John, M.-J. (1996) Business is booming: Business English in the 1990s. *English for Specific Purposes*, 15(1): 3–18.

Sarangi, S. (2000) Activity types, discourse types and interactional hybridity: The case of genetic counselling. In S. Sarangi and M. Coulthard (eds), *Discourse and Social Life*. London: Pearson, pp. 1–27.

Sarangi, S. (2002) Discourse practitioners as a community of interprofessional practice: Some insights from health communication research. In C. N. Candlin (ed.), *Research and Practice in Professional Discourse*. Hong Kong: City University of Hong Kong, pp. 95–133.

Sarangi, S. and C. N. Candlin (2003) Categorization and explanation of risk: A discourse analytical perspective. *Health, Risk & Society*, 5(2): 115–24.

Scott, M. (2006) *Textual Patterns: Key Words and Corpus Analysis in Language Education*. Amsterdam: John Benjamins.

Shim, R. J.-Y. (1999) Codified Korean English: process, characteristics and consequences. *World Englishes*, 18(2): 247–58.

Sinclair, J. McH. (1987) The nature of the evidence. In J. McH. Sinclair (ed.), *Looking Up: An Account of the COBUILD Project in Lexical Computing*. London: Collins, pp. 150–9.

Sinclair, J. McH. (1991) *Corpus Concordance Collocation*. Oxford: Oxford University Press.

Sinclair, J. McH. (1996) The search for units of meaning. *Textus*, 9(1): 75–106.

Sinclair, J. McH. (1998) The lexical item. In E. Weigand (ed.), *Contrastive Lexical Semantics*. Amsterdam: John Benjamins, pp. 1–24.

Sinclair, J. McH. (ed.) (2004) *How to Use Corpora in Language Teaching*. Amsterdam: John Benjamins.

Sinclair, J. McH. (2005) Corpus and text: Basic principles. In M. Wynne (ed.), *Developing Linguistic Corpora: A Guide to Good Practice*. Oxford: Oxbow Books, pp. 1–16. http://ahds.ac.uk/linguistic-corpora/. Accessed 10 April 2007.

Tanaka, H. (2006) Emerging English-speaking business discourses in Japan. *Journal of Asian Pacific Communication*, 16(1): 25–50.

Tannen, D. (1984) *Conversational Style: Analyzing Talk among Friends*. Norwood, NJ: Ablex.

Tognini-Bonelli, E. (2002) Functionally complete units of meaning across English and Italian: Towards a corpus-driven approach. In B. Altenberg and S. Granger (eds), *Lexis in Contrast: Corpus-based Approaches*. Amsterdam: John Benjamins, pp. 73–96.

van Dijk, T. (ed.) (1997) *Discourse as Social Interaction*. London: Sage.

van Ek, J. A. (1986) *Objectives for Foreign Language Learning. Vol. 1: Scope*. Strasbourg: Council of Europe.

Warren, M. (2004) // ↘ so what have YOU been WORking on REcently //: Compiling a specialized corpus of spoken business English. In U. Connor and T. Upton (eds), *Discourse in the Professions: Perspectives from Corpus Linguistics*. Amsterdam: John Benjamins, pp. 115–40.

Yotsukura, L. A. (2003) *Negotiating Moves: Problem Presentation and Resolution in Japanese Business Discourse*. Oxford: Elsevier.

Zaidman, N. (2001) Cultural codes and language strategies in business communication: Interactions between Israeli and Indian businesspeople. *Management Communication Quarterly*, 14(3): 408–41.

Zhu, H. (2003) Globalization and new ELT challenges in China. *English Today*, 76(19.4): 36–41.

Index